WOODWORKING WITH THE ROUTER

Professional Router Techniques and Jigs Any Woodworker Can Use

Bill Hylton and Fred Matlack

Illustrations by Frank Rohrbach

Photographs by Mitch Mandel

Rodale Press, Emmaus, Pennsylvania

Our Mission

We publish books that empower people's lives.

RODALE BOOKS

Executive Editor: Margaret Lydic Balitas
Managing Editor: Jeff Day
Copy Manager: Dolores Plikaitis
Copy Editor: Barbara Webb
Administrative Assistant: Susan Nickol
Office Manager: Karen Earl-Braymer
Art Director: Anita Patterson
Book Designer: Jerry O'Brien
Cover Designer: Frank Milloni
Photographer: Mitch Mandel
Illustrator: Frank Rohrbach

Library of Congress Cataloging-in-Publication Data

Hylton, Bill.
    Woodworking with the router : professional router techniques and jigs any woodworker can use / Bill Hylton and Fred Matlack ; illustrations by Frank Rohrbach ; photographs by Mitch Mandel.
        p.   cm.
    Includes index.
    ISBN 0–87596–577–6 hardcover
    1. Routers (Tools)   2. Woodwork.   3. Jigs and fixtures.
I. Matlack, Fred.   II. Title.
TT203.5.H95   1993
964' .083—dc20   93–4476
                                                        CIP

If you have any questions or comments concerning this book, please write to:
    Rodale Press
    Book Readers' Service
    33 East Minor Street
    Emmaus, PA 18098

Distributed in the book trade by St. Martin's Press

2 4 6 8 10 9 7 5 3 1 hardcover

CONTENTS

CONTENTS

CONTENTS

CONTENTS

INTRODUCTION

The router is woodworking's most versatile power tool. You can use it in just about every aspect of a job but assembly (it won't drive nails or screws). In the extreme, used creatively, it'll do almost any kind of cutting and shaping of wood. You can use it to prepare rough-cut lumber for a project, shape the pieces, cut the joinery, and embellish the finished assembly with decorative edge profiles. Though configured by manufacturers as a portable tool, one that you hold in your hands and pass over the work, it's just about the only portable tool that can sensibly be mounted and used as a stationary tool.

Not every woodworker has a router, but most do. An increasing number of them are aware of all the terrific things you can do with a router. A half-dozen or more books on router woodworking are available. Every woodworking magazine has articles about router woodworking. Tool catalogs are loaded with routers, bits, and all sorts of router jigs and fixtures. At every woodworking show, there's at least one person demonstrating novel router uses—and selling gizmos so you can make your router do the same jobs.

Fred and I want you to be more than aware. Get out there and try that router in new applications. You may discover that the old way isn't the best way.

This book will be your basic router woodworking manual. It tells how to do all sorts of woodworking operations using the router. There are jobs that can be done *only* with a router—edge treatments and template-guided work, to name two. Other jobs—cutting curves, most joinery work—can be done exceptionally well with a router, though there are other options. And finally, in some situations, the router wouldn't be your first-choice tool for the job—we're willing to concede that. But the router may be a reasonable alternative.

The "whys" lead to the "hows." How to do a job may be easier to assimilate if you grasp why it's being done a certain way. And knowing *why* may lead you to another way that's better for you—maybe better *period*. Which leads us to the next point.

In all these situations, there's always more than one way to do a given thing. Fred and I have tried pretty conscientiously to find more than one way to do every operation we talk about in this book (more than one router-oriented approach, that is). For example, a plunge router may make an operation simple. We explain how. But not everyone has a plunge router, so we explain how to do the job with a fixed-base router, too (if that's possible). And finally, you may want to try doing the very same operation on a router table, so how to do that is covered as well.

Though the opening chapter is on routers and is followed by one on bits, *Woodworking with the Router* isn't really a shopping guide. What we are trying to do is open your eyes to the variety of routers available and to features and configurations that you may not know about. Instead of telling you what jigs to buy, we show you what jigs to *make*. A jig may be as simple as an oversized baseplate, but it's never more complex than an adjustable trammel. Sure, you can open your wallet and buy a lot of these jigs, but why buy a jig if you can make it. (It's always seemed odd that folks who consider themselves to be woodworkers would buy items they can easily—and more economically—make themselves.)

Our projects include several different router tables, including one in which the router is mounted horizontally. It offers an "angle of attack" that makes some jobs easier to perform than they would be on a regular router table. To increase the value of any router table you make, we have a range of accessories—bit guards, fences, sleds (which are like your table saw's miter gauge), and a variety of hold-downs and guides. Most are surprisingly easy to make.

Is all this information original? Of course not. Cutting a dado is cutting a dado. Sometimes the best techniques are the tried-and-true ones.

What is original, you'll find, is the logical, thorough, in-depth presentation. For this to be a basic operating manual, it's got to cover those solid, traditional techniques, as well as the exciting, new derivations. Likewise, the information must be easy to find, complete, and clearly presented. It's got to be down-to-earth and practical. When you've got a question, when you can't remember an operation's exact sequence of steps, you want to be able to flip to the proper page without thumbing through the entire book. You need to be confident that the operation is covered, and that it's covered thoroughly and understandably, and that what's being presented isn't some speculation, however well-intentioned.

INTRODUCTION

A basic operating manual is exactly what we were trying to produce here, a systematic, thorough guidebook to router woodworking. So we've included an index and cross-references. Cutting laps is a lot like cutting tenons, for example, so you'll find cross-references from one chapter to another where such references are pertinent.

Whether we've invented a technique or not, we've tried it in the Rodale shop. Thanks to the cooperation and generosity of router and bit manufacturers, we've been able to prove out our techniques using a simply capital assortment of routers and bits. And we had a ready supply of criticism and advice, as well as an abundance of suggestions, from our woodworking colleagues here at Rodale. There's nothing in here that we aren't confident about, nothing that we haven't successfully done. What's here is not the sum total of what we tried, of course. We left out techniques that proved to be problematic, excessively involved, too specialized, or simply hazardous.

What you will find is the distillation: Bill and Fred's *most excellent* router techniques.

The Authorial Team

Bill Hylton has been writing and editing Rodale Press books for 20 years. He created Rodale's first woodworking title, *Build It Better Yourself,* as well as its most recent backyard building titles, *Projects for Outdoor Living* and *Outdoor Furniture.*

Fred Matlack has been building projects for Rodale's magazines and books for 12 years. He has designed and constructed hundreds of projects, ranging from solar food dryers to toys to antique reproductions.

Frank Rohrbach created *Woodworking with the Router*'s countless illustrations. A longtime draftsman, Frank illustrated *Jigs, Fixtures, and Setups, Outdoor Furniture,* and other books. He is a regular contributor to *American Woodworker* magazine.

Mitch Mandel took the photos in *Woodworking with the Router.* A Rodale photographer for more than 12 years, Mitch is an avid and accomplished woodworker. He is a contributing writer and photographer for *American Woodworker* magazine.

(Left to right) Bill, Fred, photographer Mitch Mandel, book designer Jerry O'Brien, and illustrator Frank Rohrbach.

ROUTERS

The basic router is extremely simple.

In general terms, it's a motor and several crucial controls. The motor can range up to about 3½ horsepower and can turn anywhere from 10,000 rpm up to around 30,000. A rotary cutter is fitted into the collet on the lower end of the router motor. It is direct drive in the purest form. But just to complicate things a bit, a huge variety of cutters is available. (See the chapter "Bits.") Being the business end of the machine, the cutters largely determine what you can do with the router.

There are four main parts to a router: the motor, the collet, the base, and the baseplate.

The motor is the type known as a universal motor, the same sort that's used in your other portable power tools. (Your table saw, jointer, and other stationary tools use a different kind of motor called an induction motor.) The power ratings of the motors used in routers range from ¾ horsepower up to about 3½ horsepower. The more power the motor has, the bigger the router is.

The collet is a simple but accurate chuck. Attached to the end of the motor armature, it holds the bit so the motor can make the bit spin. Designs vary, and some collets are intrinsically better than others. All collets, however, allow you to change bits.

The router base is what holds the motor, positioning it in relation to the work. It usually incorporates two handles so the operator can hold and control the machine. One of the most critical elements of the base is its depth-of-cut adjustment mechanism. There are two fundamental types of bases: the fixed base and the plunge base. The type of base your router has is pivotal to what your router does, how it handles, and what it costs.

The baseplate is a plastic sole on the bottom of the base. It serves as a bearing between the router and the work, enabling the router to slide smoothly across the work without marring it.

Let's take a closer look at each of these four parts.

THE MOTOR

Here's a curiosity. Mentally check over the power tools you have, and those you'd like to have. What is the measure of utility or capacity most commonly used with each tool? Does any, other than the router, depend upon its horsepower rating as the primary measure?

You talk of your table saw, circular saw, chop saw, or radial arm saw in terms of the blade diameter first. Drills? Chuck capacity for portables, measure from chuck to column for drill presses. Band saw? Depth of the throat. Planer or jointer? Length of the cutting knives. Sanders? Size of the sanding area or belt.

But with the router, it's the horsepower rating you mention first. You're going to find that's so throughout this book. (I know that because we've already written most of it). There are some other measures that might be meaningful—collet capacity, range of motor travel, baseplate diameter (or length and width for a rectilinear one), weight. But the power rating conveys the size of the bits it will drive, and suggests a size and weight.

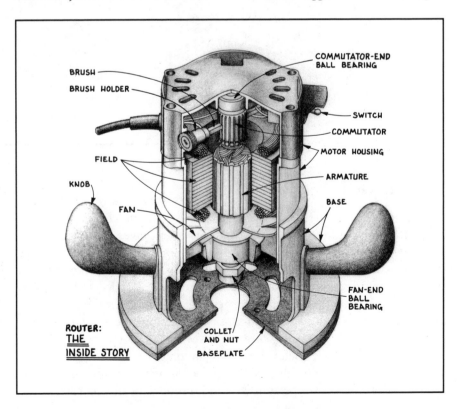

BRUSH
BRUSH HOLDER
FIELD
KNOB
FAN
COMMUTATOR-END BALL BEARING
SWITCH
COMMUTATOR
MOTOR HOUSING
ARMATURE
BASE
FAN-END BALL BEARING
COLLET AND NUT
BASEPLATE
ROUTER: THE INSIDE STORY

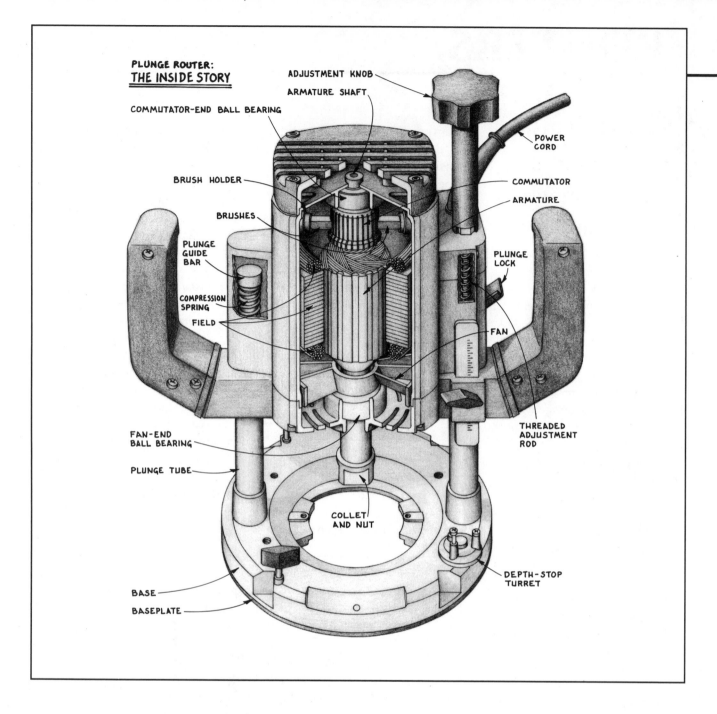

PLUNGE ROUTER:
THE INSIDE STORY

ADJUSTMENT KNOB
ARMATURE SHAFT
COMMUTATOR-END BALL BEARING
POWER CORD
BRUSH HOLDER
COMMUTATOR
ARMATURE
BRUSHES
PLUNGE GUIDE BAR
COMPRESSION SPRING
FIELD
PLUNGE LOCK
FAN
FAN-END BALL BEARING
THREADED ADJUSTMENT ROD
PLUNGE TUBE
COLLET AND NUT
DEPTH-STOP TURRET
BASE
BASEPLATE

Power Ratings

What may be more important than the horsepower rating, however, is the amperage rating. The amperage rating of each tool is assigned by Underwriters Laboratories (UL). It is the maximum amount of current the tool can draw in continuous use without overheating and, eventually, burning out. (Overheating is defined as raising its temperature more than 60° Celsius above ambient temperature.)

Horsepower ratings, on the other hand, are assigned by the manufacturers themselves, based on tests they've conducted. The horsepower rating may reflect a marketing plan as much as it reflects the design engineer's intent for the tool.

The rating procedure usually begins with the motor mounted on a dynamometer, which applies artificial loads as the motor runs. Speed and torque data are recorded as the

test ranges from a no-load state to the point at which the load simply stalls the motor. The data are charted as the horsepower curve, and that is generally reported in terms either of peak horsepower or of continuous horsepower. And, of course, there's a certain amount of data massaging involved—rounding up to the nearest quarter horse, for example.

Peak horsepower is the absolute maximum horsepower generated,

very probably when the motor is drawing two to four times the UL's amperage rating and consequently starting to overheat, stink, and smoke. (According to one manufacturer's documentation of its test of its 15-amp router, the motor was pulling 54 amps at the moment it squeezed out its 3 horsepower. That's an *incredible* draw, and translates into a lot of heat.)

Continuous horsepower is what the motor can produce during continuous, safe operation, meaning hours of operation when drawing no more than the UL's rated amperage.

The industry convention is to report peak horsepower on a universal motor, the type that drives a router, and continuous horsepower on an induction motor, the type used in stationary power tools. The universal (brush-type) motor is used primarily for intermittent, variable-speed operation. The induction (brushless) motor is used primarily for long-term, fixed-speed operation. These differences will help explain why a 1½-horsepower router is so much smaller than the 1½-horsepower motor on your table saw. The big table saw motor will deliver that power for hours on end, while the router motor will squeeze it out for about 30 seconds, then die.

Now let's go back to the amperage ratings. An amp is a reflection of power output, even though it is a measure of electrical input. The UL

is an independent testing agency, using uniform methods. Its ratings will be consistent from brand to brand and model to model. So if you want to compare the power output of one brand of router to another, compare their amperage ratings.

Here's an example of what you'll find:

- Black & Decker's model 3310, rated at 1½ hp, draws 8 amps.
- Bosch's model 1602, rated at 1½ hp, draws 9 amps.
- Ryobi's R-230 model, rated at 1½ hp, draws 9.5 amps.
- Porter-Cable's model 690, rated at 1½ hp, draws 10 amps.
- Bosch's 1604, rated at 1¾ hp, draws 10 amps.

You would *probably* be justified in concluding that the Porter-Cable unit is more powerful than the Black & Decker, even though their horsepower ratings are the same. And that the Bosch isn't any more powerful, though it's rated with an extra quarter horse. (However, horsepower differences between two routers of the same amperage rating *may* result from some design or efficiency advantage. The higher-horsepower router may have a slightly better cooling system—a fan that moves air faster, for example—that allows it to run somewhat longer at some mega-amperage draw than the other.)

An interesting sidelight on amperage ratings is that the biggest

General-purpose routers range in size and power from a small 1-horsepower model (left center) through 2-horsepower models to the 3-horsepower, 18-pound production behemoth (far left). Even plunge routers are available in a range of sizes: 1-horsepower (right center), 2-horsepower, and 3¼-horsepower (far right).

Both the router and the induction motor it rests on are rated at 1 horsepower. The relatively huge induction motor, which powers a dust collector, will run all day, continuously producing its rated horsepower. The much smaller universal motor runs at more than 5 times the speed of the large motor but can produce its rated horsepower for relatively brief spurts when under very heavy load.

routers may actually be slightly underrated. Though testing may demonstrate that the router could be rated at 17, 18, or even 20 amps, the maker rates it at 15 amps and puts a 15-amp cord and plug on it. Why? Because America is wired primarily with 15-amp receptacles (yes, even on 20-amp circuits, and yes, that meets the electrical code). A 20-amp plug won't fit into a 15-amp receptacle. Rather than put a 20-amp plug on a router and consequently limiting severely where it can be used, the manufacturer rates it at 15 amps.

Consider the router work you envision in terms of amps. An 8- to 10-amp router has power enough to drive any bits up to 2 inches in diameter. It will be adequate for trimming cuts—¼ inch at a pass. A larger bit or a heavier cut will require more amperage.

Consumer versus Professional

Beyond horsepower and amperage ratings, there's one other crucial matter to consider about a router motor, and that's whether it is what is called a consumer-grade unit or a professional-grade one.

Compared to their consumer counterparts, professional-grade routers are designed to be more powerful, last longer, and perform better under stress. The motor in this router, for example, must be able to handle sustained use and heavy loading, even overloading. So it is constructed differently than one in a consumer model. The differences begin with the materials and how they are used.

Copper and aluminum can both be used as electrical conductors. Of the two, copper is by far the more efficient. A motor with copper windings will provide more power than a similarly sized motor with aluminum windings. So without increasing the physical size of the motor, just by using copper, the tool engineer can design more power in. And because copper is more expensive and heavier, he designs in more cost and weight.

Want more power? It's in the windings. The greater the volume of windings, the more power the motor pours out. And the heavier it will be. Asked to test routers for their power output, an engineer I know suggested simply weighing them. "The heaviest one will probably be the most powerful," he explained. It's all in the windings.

Heat buildup is concomitant to hard, sustained use, but heat's a motor killer. The designer does anything he can to make the professional unit more heat-resistant. A high-grade, heat-resistant insulation is used on the wires. Then, after the armature and the commutator are wound, a heat-resistant resin is dripped into the windings. Capillary attraction pulls the resin into the coils, completely coating every strand and bonding all into a single unit. The resin provides additional benefits: It keeps dust from infiltrating the windings, and it keeps every strand in place, preventing shorts as the armature spins at 22,000 rpm.

A major source of heat in a motor is arcing, which occurs as the electricity passes from the brushes to the commutator. The commutator is made up of copper bars encircling the armature and connected to the windings. The brushes are pieces of carbon that convey electricity from the power source—your shop outlet—to the commutator. One brush passes the power into a commutator bar. The power flows through the bar into the windings, then into a bar opposite the first. From there, it passes into the second brush, completing the circuit.

To reduce the arcing, the number of commutator bars is increased, and the brushes are positioned more precisely. In addition, the armature is slung in ball bearings, rather than sleeve bearings. The ball bearings not only last longer, they reduce friction and, by virtually eliminating vibration and lateral movement between the commutator and the brushes, they further reduce arcing.

The final heat-reduction measure taken in a professional-grade motor involves the fan. Most consumer-grade routers have stamped-steel fans. They are cheap to make, but they are pretty frail. When a blade snaps off at 22,000 rpm, you can imagine what it does inside the motor housing.

The better router has a heavy cast-aluminum or high-tech plastic fan. It moves lots of air very efficiently and is unlikely to break.

Though all these features are concealed inside the motor housing, and you can't see them, they'll be clearly evident. There's something unmistakably substantial about a professional-quality router. Something tactile.

THE COLLET

The typical home-shop router weighs about 7 or 8 pounds. Its collet probably weighs less than an ounce. For that 7-pound router to function the way its maker intended, that teeny part has to be virtually perfect. The catalog of routing woes that originate in a worn or dirty collet is short but damning. And unfortunately, some collets seem to have trouble designed into them.

Speed Control

The router is a high-speed tool, as you surely know. The general rule is that the faster the cutter spins, the smoother it'll cut.

But when you switch to a large cutter, those high rotational speeds translate into some pretty impressive chip-launching stats. A 3-inch cutter spinning at 20,000 rpm is moving about 262 feet per second at the cutter tips. That's about the length of a football field in the time it takes to say, "Oops."

Moreover, with such large bits, the high speeds tend to burn the wood and dull the cutters. So for some applications, the router is too fast. What to do?

More and more routers are available with integral speed controls. The very best approach is to buy one of these routers. I believe every major brand of plunge router has at least one model with an electronic speed control. Porter-Cable makes its biggest fixed-base router with a speed control. You just stroke a little thumbwheel to turn down the rpm.

A second, and somewhat more risky, approach is to buy an after-market speed controller. Commonly, the controller is a "black box" with a power cord, a grounded outlet, an on-off switch, and a dial. Plug your router into the controller's outlet and the controller into your shop outlet. Switch on the controller, dial up the speed you want, and operate your router.

So what's the risk? If your black box is a true and proper speed controller, then the risk is probably minimal. The kind of speed controller incorporated in routers by their manufacturers is really a sophisticated switching system that reduces the motor's speed by literally switching it off and on very rapidly. Through a feedback loop, it continually monitors rpm and compensates for varying load conditions by keeping the switch open for additional milliseconds. The machine is much less likely to bog down. This kind of controller is available as a separate unit, for use with any fixed-speed universal motor.

But if your black box is a rheostat, which reduces the motor's speed by reducing the voltage flow, the risk is that your router will burn up.

Most routers with electronic speed control use a thumbwheel (left) to change speeds. To determine the speeds, you have to consult a chart in the router's manual to translate the thumbwheel's letter markings. The speed control on Porter-Cable's 518 production router, on the other hand, is a slide with distinct stops (top). The router's speed at each stop is clearly marked.

Here's why. An increase in amperage must accompany a drop in voltage where the power remains constant. In a universal motor (the kind used in most portable power tools, including the router), amps equal heat, and an increase in amperage will cause the tool to heat up dramatically. Unfortunately, the motor—and consequently its fan—is running slower, which reduces the air flow. Run the router too long, and it's toast.

A good speed controller is a sophisticated electronic device. You can buy an inexpensive controller, imported from Asia by MLCS and marketed explicitly to control router speeds, from a number of mail-order sources. According to the folks at MLCS, it operates in a manner similar to the controllers built into Makita and Elu routers. It will "heat up some," they report, but so long as you don't use it more than 15 or 20 minutes at a time, it should give you no trouble, and it should not harm your router.

Still, the best approach in my opinion—and Fred agrees, too—is to buy a router with electronic speed control. The controller will be fully compatible with the motor, and, at least during the warranty period, it will have the manufacturer's guarantee. You won't have an extra gizmo to drag around, an extra cord to get snarled. And perhaps best of all, you'll get "soft start."

Getting a router up to speed takes quite a bit of force. As Sir Isaac Newton might have put it, "When you hit the switch on your router, the handles want to turn backward just as much as the bit wants to turn forward." That power-on jerk is startling, particularly with the more powerful routers, but more than that, the sudden torque is hard on the router's bearings. Soft start tempers the startup by easing the motor up to speed over a period of a second or so. Though "a period of a second or so" sounds awfully short, there is a distinct difference between a soft start and what I guess you'd have to call a hard start.

COMMON COLLET DESIGNS

The router collet, like a drill's chuck, is designed to grip and release the round shank of a bit. Unlike a drill chuck, which has three fingers that grip the bit shank, the router collet makes full contact with the bit shank. The router collet has one huge design advantage over the drill chuck: It only has to accept and hold a shank of one of three specific diameters: ¼ inch, ⅜ inch, or ½ inch. The drill chuck has to accept a continuous range of sizes, from ⅛-inch diameter or less up to ½-inch diameter or more. A router-bit shank must be sized to the collet's inside diameter, give or take a couple thousandths of an inch.

But there are a couple of demands placed on the router collet that aren't placed on the drill chuck. One is high-speed operation. A drill press peaks at about 4,200 rpm. The typical ⅜-inch portable drill is flat out turning 1,800 rpm. Running the machine with a drill bit that isn't perfectly concentric isn't going to rattle your eye teeth loose at those speeds. But a router runs at 22,000 rpm or more, and a bit that's ever so slightly imbalanced, for any reason, will communicate that fact to you very vociferously.

Another demand is side loading. The drill press and its chuck are designed to cope with stresses coming from one direction only. But the router has to deal with those stresses in addition to others coming at it from all sides. The router's collet has to hold that bit firmly and evenly.

Here is how the job is done. The typical collet is a tapered cylinder with a precisely sized, perfectly round, perfectly concentric hole through the center. It has at least one slit through its wall, from top to bottom. It fits into a conical socket in the end of

the motor's armature. When the collet nut is turned onto threads on the armature, it forces the collet down into the socket. The slit is forced closed, which reduces the diameter of the collet's bore. If a bit of the proper shank size is in the bore, an even pressure is exerted on that shank, not just at three points, as with a drill chuck, but on the entire surface of the shank.

Naturally, the collet and its socket have to be kept clean and free of grit, sawdust, rust, and the like. The bit likewise must be clean. You can imagine, given tolerances like plus or minus a thousandth of an inch, that

grit or dirt carried into the collet along with the bit shank can prevent it from properly gripping the shank.

You can also imagine that, given how you tighten the collet nut, and given how the bit spins and the various forces twist and wrench at it as it cuts, these several parts can get pretty firmly wedged together. Firmly enough that they don't always automatically pop free of each other when the collet nut is loosened. Usually, whacking the collet nut with the wrench—it's in your hand, after all—will spring the collet free of the socket, and the bit free of the collet. (You shouldn't have to knock the bit free

You may not think of collet nut styles as having much importance until you try to change bits. The nut with just two flats (bottom right) can be addressed from only two directions, 180 degrees apart, by the wrench. The hex nut (top left) and the octagonal nut (top right) each offer many more positions, which can expedite bit changes greatly.

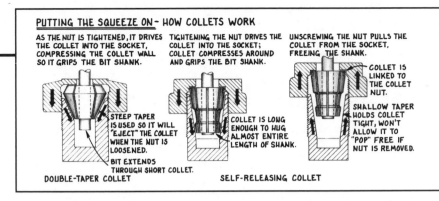

AS THE NUT IS TIGHTENED, IT DRIVES THE COLLET INTO THE SOCKET, COMPRESSING THE COLLET WALL SO IT GRIPS THE BIT SHANK.

TIGHTENING THE NUT DRIVES THE COLLET INTO THE SOCKET; COLLET COMPRESSES AROUND AND GRIPS THE BIT SHANK.

UNSCREWING THE NUT PULLS THE COLLET FROM THE SOCKET, FREEING THE SHANK.

STEEP TAPER IS USED SO IT WILL "EJECT" THE COLLET WHEN THE NUT IS LOOSENED.

BIT EXTENDS THROUGH SHORT COLLET.

DOUBLE-TAPER COLLET

COLLET IS LONG ENOUGH TO HUG ALMOST ENTIRE LENGTH OF SHANK.

SELF-RELEASING COLLET

COLLET IS LINKED TO THE COLLET NUT.

SHALLOW TAPER HOLDS COLLET TIGHT, WON'T ALLOW IT TO "POP" FREE IF NUT IS REMOVED.

To use a bit with a ¼-inch shank in some routers, you're expected to use a sleeve or bushing, because the router doesn't come with a ¼-inch collet. Fit the sleeve onto the bit shank, then slip the assembly into the ½-inch collet. It serves in a pinch, but if you use this setup too long or too often, you're bound to run into problems with bit slippage. If you do use a sleeve, be sure to line up the slit in the sleeve with the slit in the collet.

of the collet every time. If you do, you need to perform some maintenance. Polish up both the socket and the collet. If that doesn't clear up the problem, replace the collet.)

Just as all routers are not the same, all collets are not the same. A manufacturer aiming to produce a low-cost router will compromise on materials and design in the collet, just as it will in the motor and other aspects of the machine. And of course the buyer gets what he or she pays for.

The ideal collet is one that's sufficiently flexible to conform easily to the bit shank and long enough to grasp it along almost its entire length. In addition, the collet, if it's really ideal, will have some little design feature that will obviate the need to rap the collet nut to free the bit.

This ideal collet, sometimes called the self-releasing three-piece collet, is used on several routers currently on the market, including the Elu plunge routers, Ryobi's 600 series, all the Milwaukee routers, Freud's FT2000, the Makita 3612, and almost all Porter-Cable routers. The design particulars may differ slightly from brand to brand, but these features will stand out: It's long—anywhere from ¾ to 1¼ inches long; it's sufficiently flexible that squeezing it with your fingers has a visible effect; and it's very slender, tapering only 8 to 10 degrees. These three features allow the collet to grip the bit shank evenly and firmly.

That shallow taper is one of the key elements in making the collet

grip the bit so well. Once it gets pushed into the socket in the armature, it doesn't want to come out. So the ideal collet has one other vital feature: It is somehow connected to the collet nut. In most designs, there's a ring around the collet that fits tightly in a mating groove in the collet nut. As the collet nut is loosened, it literally pulls the collet from the socket. Even though the collet and nut are separate pieces, you can't pull them apart. (If you can, the parts are damaged or defective, and must be replaced.)

We had just such a collet let go of the collet nut in the midst of a bit change. I can testify to the iron grip that collet had on my bit. It wouldn't come out of the socket, and thus wouldn't let go of the bit. Fred eventually beat it free. (I wasn't a witness, and I don't *want* to know.) The collet itself was okay, and Fred determined that the cause of the problem was a mismatch between the retainer ring around the collet and the groove for it in the collet nut. The manufacturer confirmed that determination and replaced the entire assembly. Suffice it to say, then, that this collet design calls for precision machinework during manufacture.

A quite common collet style is called the three-piece or the double-taper, depending upon whom you talk to. It's a very diverse style, with variants ranging from the itty-bitty split ring used in laminate trimmers and other relatively low-horsepower, ¼-inch-shank-only routers, up to

the ounce-and-a-half behemoth— we're speaking in relative terms here—found until late 1992 in most Porter-Cable machines. This is the "typical collet" I described earlier: a tapered cylinder that is forced into a conical socket in the armature shaft by a collet nut. Squeezed by the socket, it in turn seizes the bit. The collet taper is pretty steep—20 to 35 degrees—and is intended to pop the collet up out of the socket when the nut is released. This isn't a totally elegant design solution, hence the occasional need for a rap with a collet wrench.

A collet style found in very low-end routers, the so-called consumer-grade models, is the split arbor. It's not really a collet, since *the socket in the armature* is the collet. The socket is a straight bore. The armature is tapered at the end and slit. When the collet nut is tightened down, it pinches on the taper, closing the slit and gripping the bit. This "collet" doesn't grip the bit evenly, firmly, or concentrically. Worse yet, when it wears, it can't be replaced without replacing the central stem of the motor.

A different design, better but still regarded by many experts on routers and other woodworking machinery as less than satisfactory, is the two-piece collet. It's found on some pretty upscale routers, including all the Hitachi models, one from Makita, and several from Ryobi. As you can see in the drawing, the collet and collet nut are integral, with the threads on the *inside* of the socket and the *outside* of the collet/collet nut—just the opposite of the usual arrangement. The collet piece usually has one slit through to the bore, and two partial slits.

The theory is that as the threads pull the collet down into the socket, it will be squeezed tightly to the bit shank. The theory might be sound, but the collet is bulky and stiff and doesn't willingly hug that bit shank. And maybe because the collet is so bulky and stiff, the routine tightening and loosening seems to wear the threads and, in time, to make the operation all the more difficult. It takes a lot of muscle to tighten, and even more to loosen. (If you are like me, this is the collet that rattles your confidence. You try to loosen it, and when it doesn't budge, you say to yourself, "Am I doing this in the right direction? Am I tightening it? Lemme think here . . .")

What struck me about this collet, the first time I used one, was how shallow it is. On most routers I've used, the bit body clunks against the collet nut before the shank end bottoms out. Not with this design.

THE BASE

With a router, you have some pretty impressive power at your fingertips and the ability to make it go or stop. To use this power effectively, you need to have a base to hold the motor in a controlled relationship to the work. There are two general types: fixed and plunge.

With a fixed base router you set the depth of cut and don't change it while the router is running. As long as you hold the base against the work, the motor will stay the same distance from the work, consequently controlling the depth of cut.

Almost all of the currently available fixed-base routers use the same simple clamping mechanism to hold the router motor securely, but with the possibility of vertical adjustment. The base is essentially a wide metal band with a slit in it. A bolt with a wing nut tightens this band around the motor housing, much like tightening a clamp on a hose. If you get the wing nut tight enough, the motor can't move. It can't turn inside the base. It can't shift up or down. But when the wing nut is loosened, the motor can be pulled right out of the base.

A key part of making vertical adjustments is maintaining the setting you have when you loosen the clamp wing nut. It's pretty doubtful that you want the weight of the motor to drop it as deep into the base as it can go each time you loosen the clamp. The other key to making vertical adjustments is being able to make incremental changes in the vertical position. Router makers have come up with four different approaches, as shown in the photos.

A significant drawback to all of these systems is sideplay. When you unclamp the base to raise or lower the motor, it also frees the motor to shift laterally. When you reclamp the base, the motor doesn't always return to its original position. It may shift a 64th this way or that. The axis of the motor is seldom precisely concentric to the baseplate. For most practical woodworking, this is not an insurmountable problem, though woodworkers who aspire to machine-shop precision have fits over it.

A plunge base, in contrast to the fixed base, allows you to alter the depth-of-cut setting on the fly. The router can be preset to a depth and used like a fixed base, yes. But what it can do that a fixed base can't is lower the spinning bit into the work in a controlled manner (and raise it again, too), allowing you to begin and end a cut in the middle of a workpiece. It allows you to make several incremental passes, each slightly deeper, and complete a cut without stopping to readjust the depth setting.

The plunge base consists of a round or square shoe and two hollow posts with springs inside. The router motor is mounted on the posts in such a way that it can slide up and down on them. The springs buoy the motor, keeping it up on the posts so the bit is clear of the work or the workbench. To plunge the router, you release a lock and conscientiously push down on the handles.

Every plunge-base router incorporates two separate depth-adjustment mechanisms. One might best be described as a router height stop. It serves on most routers to simply keep the router motor from popping up off the posts. The other is a depth-stop mechanism, which controls how far down the posts the router motor can be plunged.

On all plunge routers but the Ryobi 600 series routers and the Freud FT2000, the height stop setting is altered with wrenches. A stop nut or two hex nuts jammed against one another are turned up or down a threaded rod extending up from the router base. The router motor rides up the posts until it strikes the nuts. A number of accessory makers, Woodhaven among them (see "Sources" on page 337), sell adjusting knobs that replace the nuts and allow you to alter the setting with the twist of a wrist. (The Ryobi and Freud models cited are equipped with this knob.) What this mechanism allows you to do is methodically wind the router down the posts without the sideplay that besets fixed-base routers. To me, this is the ideal depth-setting approach for fixed router operations. It is the main reason I like using a plunge router in a router table.

The depth-stop mechanism varies from brand to brand and model to model. All seem to have bafflement designed into the rotating depth-stop turret, sliding depth-stop pole, and various depth-stop adjusting knobs. The first several times I used them, I discovered myself saying, "What? What?" to no one in particular.

The photos show what. The setup approach shown seems to work pretty consistently, regardless of the brand or model's peculiarities.

The goal in setting the depth stop is to establish a measured gap between the bottom of the depth-stop rod and a screw on the turret. The router then will plunge that distance, stopping when the stop rod contacts the screw. Every router has several positions on the turret. This feature can be handy when you have two cuts of different depths to

*In the **ring and spiral,** the motor casing is threaded and there's a metal or plastic ring turned onto it. The motor is lowered into the base, which is itself a simple sleeve, and the ring arrests its descent. Rotating the ring clockwise allows the motor to drop lower in the base; turning it counterclockwise raises the motor. The ring is segmented, and there's a pointer on the base; turning the ring one segment alters the vertical setting by some consistent, measurable fraction, usually $1/32$ inch. This system is used on all Milwaukee routers (shown), and some models made by Makita, Sears, Black & Decker, Ryobi, and Bosch.*

*The **helical spiral** approach is used exclusively on certain Bosch models. The top edge of the base is a ramp. A nub on the motor casing catches on this edge. Turn the motor counterclockwise and the nub rides up the ramp, raising the motor and bit. Turn the motor the other direction and it descends into the base, increasing the depth of cut.*

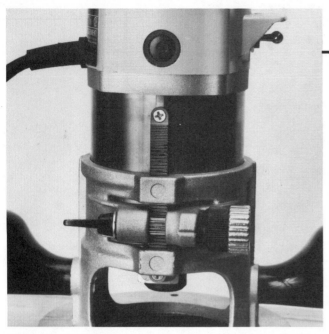

*One of the best mechanisms for changing the depth of cut quickly is the **rack and pinion**. Turning a knob on the base rotates a gear in a rack screwed to the motor housing, raising and lowering the motor. This is one system that doesn't clamp the motor in a split base. Rather, the wing nut cinches the pinion, preventing it from turning. The rack and pinion is used on selected Black & Decker routers, which are also sold with the Elu and DeWalt nameplates. Some Sears models also use a version of it.*

*Only Porter-Cable uses the **four-pin double-helix system**. The motor housing has four little pins sticking out of it, spaced 90 degrees apart. As the motor is turned, these pins ride up (or down, depending upon which direction the motor is turned) two helixes machined inside the router's split base. With this system, the depth-of-cut setting is held when the clamp is loosened, regardless of whether the router is right-side up or hung upside down in a router table.*

make from a single setup—mortises of two depths on a leg, for example. But it's pretty unlikely that in the middle of a cut you're actually going to retract the bit, turn the turret, and replunge the bit to get the incremental depth change. In practice, every router woodworker I know simply guesstimates the increments and uses the turret only for the final depth.

For the plunge router to live up to its potential, it has to have a secure but easy-to-release lock on the plunge action. Currently available models display at least three slightly different approaches. I've used all three, and the only problem I've experienced is in making the transition from one style to another. I experience a moment of indecision as I try to remember how to release the lock to plunge a little deeper.

Plunge routers have been aggressively marketed in recent years and seem to have all the advantages. However, there are distinct drawbacks to the plunge router. It is usually bulkier than a fixed-base router and decidedly top-heavy. In a lot of situations, it is more awkward to use.

In addition, the extra complexity and parts boost the cost of the plunge router. But there are special jobs that it can do like no other power tool.

THE BASEPLATE

The baseplate is the one part of the router you can tinker with and customize. And by doing just that, you can let yourself into whole new realms of router woodworking.

When you look at a new router, fresh from its carton, the baseplate is usually a piece of black phenolic plastic that matches the shape of

Depth-setting gauges are the key to fast, consistent setups. While such gauges can be made by carefully planing wood scraps to different thicknesses, the selection shown were cut from different-thickness scraps of acrylic plastic. To use a gauge to set the depth stop, bottom the bit against the workbench (just release the plunge lock and push the router down until the bit *touches the bench surface). Rest the gauge on the appropriate stop on the turret, and drop the depth rod onto the gauge (left). Lock the rod's position, and you are ready to rout. As you can see, when the router is plunged to the maximum the stop will allow, the bit projection matches the thickness of the gauge (right).*

the router's base. Three or four screws attach it to the router base. The baseplate always has a hole for the bit. On the typical fixed-base router, the hole is sized for template guide bushings, about 1¼ inches in diameter. On plunge-base routers, the opening is considerably larger.

Now in addition to greasing the router's slide across the work, the baseplate provides some bearing surface. Those plunge routers with their huge bit openings get very tippy when balanced on a narrow edge or when negotiating a corner at the end of a board.

A fair number of dedicated router woodworkers almost never use the baseplates fitted to their routers by the manufacturer. At the very least, they replace it with a clear acrylic or polycarbonate duplicate, on the theory that they can better see what the bit is doing. Or they make an assortment of special-use baseplates. Throughout this book, you'll find

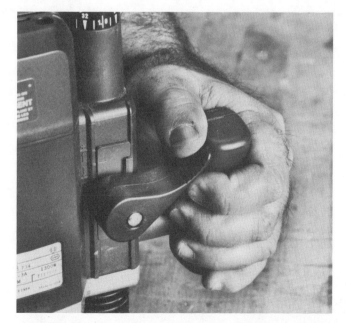

Most plunge routers have a lever-controlled plunge lock, located within reach of the handles. Most common—used on all Makita, Ryobi, and Hitachi plungers—is the manual lever-action lock. The router is "sprung" unless the lock lever is pressed down firmly, locking the router's position. A definite effort is involved; you know you are locked or unlocking by the resistance. Easiest to use is the self-locking lever, which functions like a dead-man's brake. The mechanism is locked until you depress the lever, and as soon as you release the spring-loaded lever, it relocks the mechanism. This style is used on all Porter-Cable and Bosch models, as well as the big Elus.

Here are three typical baseplates. Two are stock designs, one a custom-made replacement. Plunge routers (right) usually have a donut-style baseplate—one with a large center hole for the bit. Baseplates on fixed-base routers (center) tend toward a Swiss cheese style—lots of small viewing ports. The teardrop-shaped custom baseplate (left) offers expanded bearing surface and enhanced visibility.

plans and directions for making a lot of these. The chapter "Custom Baseplates" delves into appropriate materials and baseplate-making techniques.

Whatever you do, don't toss that factory-supplied baseplate. That's your pattern for making many custom baseplates and, at the least, for locating the mounting-screw holes in them. It may also be your mounting for guide bushings, should you ever want to try template-guided work. The first router I bought had a baseplate with its bit opening scaled to take standard guide bushings. Not realizing the reason for the smallish bit opening, I reamed it out to accommodate a large-diameter profile bit. I would have been much better off to preserve that factory baseplate and make an acrylic duplicate to open up for that big bit.

THE ASSEMBLED PACKAGE

Your first reaction to any router is probably not based on any of its four main parts. You look at the handles, judge the size and the router's stance. You pick it up, heft it, think about how comfortable the handles are. You look for the switch: Can you reach it without letting go of a handle?

It's only *after* you've made this largely tactile evaluation that you look for the plunge lock or consider the vertical adjuster. You may never look at the collet or try to find out how well the motor is constructed.

My initial response to a router is based on the material used for the base and housing. Most professional-grade routers have a fair amount of metal in them. The base is always

metal, usually an aluminum casting. The motor housing may be metal or plastic, or a combination. If plastic is used, it's usually a super-tough, high-tech material, chosen by the manufacturer not because it's less expensive than metal but because it performs better than metal. It definitely provides better electrical and heat insulation. Some plastics are stronger, more resistant to breakage. Corrosion-proof. A plastic may be lighter.

But there is a plastic that says, "Cheap!" It's used in consumer-grade routers, and it's the first thing about one of these routers that catches your attention. I don't know what it is about the stuff, but I know it when I see it. And so do you. In these cheapo routers, there's too much of it, and it seems to be inappropriate for some of the elements.

The result usually is an extraordinarily light router.

That light weight can signal more than that the router is cased in plastic. It's also, to me, signaling something important about the internals. A motor made with aluminum windings, rather than copper, will be lightweight.

Weight in a router is not bad.

Seldom do you really carry a router. When it's in use—motor running, bit cutting—it's resting on the work, and you are merely guiding it, not supporting its full weight. In fact, weight provides some stability.

So you pick up the router to evaluate its heft, and you have in your hands two of the most crucial controls on the router: the handles.

The handles give you control of the router. If you are uncomfortable with the handles, are you going to be comfortable with the router? The problem, of course, is that although lots of different styles are available, the style you prefer may not be available on the router you prefer.

Every router has two handles, nearly always spaced 180 degrees

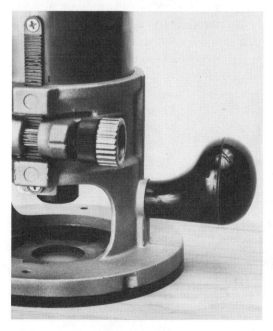

Routers typically have two handles, but many styles are used. Vertical (top left), pistol grip (top right), and D-ring (lower right) handles provide the easiest, surest grip because you can get your entire hand comfortably around them, putting your opposable thumb to optimum use. Such handles are common on high-horsepower routers. The traditional knob (lower left) is common on small and mid-sized fixed-base routers.

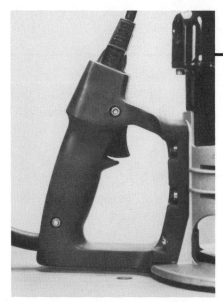

The D-handle configuration, available on some Bosch and Porter-Cable routers, has several practical benefits. The handle is easy to grip firmly and gives you good directional control, even with one hand. The on/off trigger is under your index finger—as with a circular saw or power drill or belt sander—which allows you to switch the motor on and off without lessening your hold on the router. Not to be overlooked is the fact that you can unplug the motor at the switch, making it easy to disconnect the power every time you change bits. The D-handle is supplemented by a knob on the opposite side of the base.

apart. In most cases, they are twins—two knobs, two hand-grips, two hand-sized rings. A few fixed-base models have one D-handle (with a trigger switch) and a knob, making the router "handle" more the way a circular saw or belt sander does. The bigger and heavier the router is, the less satisfactory the ball-type knob is. That's why you won't find a 2-horse-power or larger router with knobs; you get a better grip on the machine with the ring-style or grip-style handles.

On fixed-base routers, the handles are low on the base, in keeping with the generally low center of gravity. On plunge routers, the handles are a part of the motor assembly, positioning them fairly high. On a fixed-base machine, the handles allow you to pick the router up and carry it around, as well as guide the router through a cut. On a plunge router, the handles serve these purposes, but they are also your means for plunging the machine.

The next thing you may look for is the switch, which turns the motor on and off.

On some routers, you'll find it conveniently located under one of your fingers when you're gripping the handles. If it's there, it'll be a trigger, like on a power drill. Squeeze it and the router motor runs. Relax and the motor stops. Is this a dangerous arrangement? Are you likely to hit the switch inadvertently? I've not found it so. I'm partial to D-handled routers, which have trigger switches. I like the arrangement in part because of the trigger. I don't have to relinquish any control to stop the motor. I don't have to run the motor any longer than necessary to make the cut. Nevertheless, some folks don't like triggers, because then they have to worry about unintended router acceleration.

The one drawback to the handle-mounted trigger is found on a few older models. The connection between the motor and the switch is an exposed wire. The wire can hinder your ability to pull the motor from the base. Worse, it is what Fred calls "a failure opportunity." You can catch it on a clamp handle or something and rip it out.

The more common switch set-ups are toggles and slides. As a general rule, fixed-base routers have a toggle on the top of the motor, plunge routers a slide on the side. There are exceptions, of course. With a toggle mounted atop the motor, you *have* to release one handle to hit the switch. What's worse, a lot of these routers have a vertical-adjustment setup that turns the motor, so the toggle's not always where you think it's going to be. It might be at your right hand. Or your left. You end up fumbling at some pretty inopportune times. The slide is intended to be within reach of a thumb, so you can turn the router on and off without taking your hands off the handles. Woodworkers with small thumbs may find the slide too far a reach.

A number of qualities are overlooked all too often in the selection

Elu offers a gripping compromise on its small plunge router. As you can see, it has one pistol grip handle and one knob. The knob doubles as the plunge lock; twist your wrist to unlock and lock it. The handle gives you pretty firm one-handed control of the machine when you carry it from job to job, switch it on, or adjust the speed. For guiding a cut, use both hands.

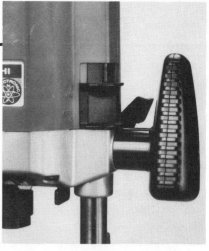

The handle-mounted trigger is great for controlling the motor's operation—you don't have to release your grip to turn it on or off, nor does the router have to run longer than absolutely necessary. But a trigger lock can be used to keep the motor running when your finger's not on the switch, if that's what you want.

Unless you have grotesquely long fingers, a toggle on the motor forces you to release one handle to switch on the router. The trick for the operator is dealing with the motor's startup kickback when holding the machine with one hand.

A slide or toggle that can be reached with a thumb or finger while maintaining a firm, two-handed grip on the router is a reasonable compromise. Most of the high-powered plunge routers have this arrangement.

process. You select a router based on power, style, apparent ease of use, and especially price. And you overlook things like how easy it is to see and change the bit.

In addition to keeping the motor square to the work and providing vertical adjustability, a good router base has to let you see the bit. It's inevitable, given the conflicting demands, that visibility from some angles will be obstructed. The wider and taller the viewing ports, the better. A plunge router, by virtue of its twin-post motor mounting, should provide the least obstructed view.

How easy it is to change bits also depends upon the router design. Many router users like to separate the motor from the base to change bits. With the motor resting on the workbench, you have unimpeded access to the collet. Obviously, you can't do this with a plunge router, and even some fixed-base routers are impossible, as a practical matter, to separate.

To me, the best routers in this regard are those with a flat-topped motor and a cord that comes out the

side. You can upend the router, rest it on its flat head, and use both hands to change the bit. But relatively few brands actually facilitate this. The Bosch 1600 series routers, for example, have flat-topped motors, but their cords are in the wrong place, so you can't really set these routers on end.

The alternative, of course, is to rest the router on its side, and work within the confines of the base.

Typically, two wrenches are needed to change a bit. One fits on-

to flats machined in the arbor, so you can prevent it from turning. The other fits on the collet nut. (In some designs, the arbor and the collet nut are different sizes; in others, both are the same.) Ideally, you can position the wrenches on the arbor and nut so the handles are just slightly offset from one another. You can grasp both in one hand, and a squeeze will bring the handles together, loosening the collet nut. Reposition them, and a similar squeeze will tighten the collet nut.

If you prefer to pull the router motor from its base to change bits, you want it to be easy to do. With fixed-base routers, this is usually easy to do. Occasionally, something like a cable running from the motor to a handle-mounted switch makes pulling the motor a lost cause.

Laminate Trimmers

A laminate trimmer is an extra-small router designed especially for routing plastic laminates. The small-diameter base has no handles. To hold the trimmer, you grip the motor barrel, which is about 3 inches in diameter.

The reduced size allows the trimmer to be used effectively in tight quarters. It can be balanced on a narrow edge more easily than a full-sized router. And because you can hold it in one hand, it's easy to maneuver.

Although it is ostensibly a tool for laminate work, it can be an extremely handy router for all sorts of woodworking. Any job requiring compactness and maneuverability is a job for a laminate trimmer.

Fred says that, were he to be tooling up his own home shop for the first time, a laminate trimmer is the router he'd buy second, *after* a 1½-horse fixed-base router and *before* any sort of plunge router.

One caveat: The trimmer is really just that. With a rating of ¾ horsepower or less, the trimmer is not able to drive big bits. It's designed to cut through ¹⁄₁₆-inch-thick layers of plastic laminate, not plowing deep or wide grooves or putting a ⅜-inch roundover on oak or maple in a single pass. I've used a trimmer with a slot cutter to make splined miter joints, but Fred believes a slot cutter is too big for a lam trimmer.

The danger is not to the bearings but to the motor itself. If it starts to bog down, the motor is under the kind of load that will pretty quickly overheat it. That'll burn the commutator and destroy the motor.

Light weight and one-handed maneuverability make the laminate trimmer an ideal general-purpose router.

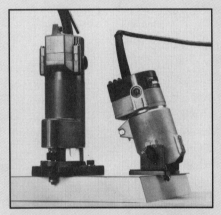

The offset-base laminate trimmer (left) has a belt-driven collet mounted at a corner of the base, not directly on the motor. It's designed to allow a cabinet installer to trim backsplashes (including inside corners) and to scribe-rout a countertop to a wall. The design puts the machine's weight squarely on the workpiece, not directly above the edge. No more tipping. The tilt-base model (right) allows you to set the motor—and thus the bit—at an angle to the work surface. While it's designed for trimming odd-angled edges and corners, the creative woodworker will find it has all sorts of other uses. And it functions perfectly well when it's bolt upright, too.

Not all collet designs facilitate this approach, however. Some collet nuts have only two flats, limiting wrench positions. You fumble with the wrenches, trying to find the arrangement that will give you the leverage you need. Just extra vexation.

A built-in arbor lock seems to be found mostly on plunge routers, though Sears has used it on some fixed-base models for a couple of decades. Press a button (and hold it, of course) to lock the arbor, then use a single wrench to loosen or tighten the collet nut. Try changing bits in a router with this feature before deciding whether or not you have to have it. It still takes two hands to loosen the collet. Because you don't have a second wrench to work against, you have to put more arm in the action. And if the nut cracks free—rather than gently giving—that wrench can really ding a plunge rod.

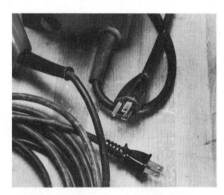

The cord can convey something about the router. On a quality tool, the cord is heavier and better insulated. There's a reinforcement, as on both of these machines, where the cord enters the motor housing, so the insulation won't crack and break at this heavy wear point. The cord on a Milwaukee router (top) is distinctive in its girth, while that on Makita's D-handled model is distinctive in its length—17 feet.

BITS

In woodworking with a router, there are three essential components to success. One is the router itself. Another is the woodworker—you. The last is the bit. A savvy woodworker using good bits can do a lot with a lousy router. But the best woodworker with the greatest router will be stymied by a dull, poorly balanced bit.

So the bit is easily the most important part of the whole routing operation. The bit is doing the cutting. The router only powers the bit.

The thing about woodworking with a router is that the more bits you have, the more different jobs you can do with the basic machine. That's not really true of other woodworking machines.

The table saw—vital as it is to the woodworker—is limited to sawing, dadoing and grooving with a dado set, and maybe forming moldings with a molding cutter. I've got a combination blade in my table saw, and I can't *remember* the last time I changed it. I could buy a rip blade, a crosscut blade, or a plywood blade, and they'd each produce a somewhat better finish. But each is really doing the same job as the others. Buying more blades doesn't make it a more versatile machine.

Okay, the drill press. The machine is useless without a collection of bits, but beyond boring holes, what does it do? Mortising with a hollow-chisel mortising attachment, an accessory that's time-consuming to install and remove. As with the table saw, buying different kinds of bits—twist-drill bits, brad-point bits, Forstner bits, hole saws—refines its ability to bore holes, but more bits don't expand its repertoire.

But the router's capabilities expand as you add bits. I recently saw a videotape showing a woodworker making a little tabletop cabinet using a router almost exclusively. He used the router to rip and crosscut the stock, to plane and joint it, to cut all the joinery. It's posturing, yes, but it's also demonstrating a versatility that no other woodshop power tool has. And without the bits, the router wouldn't have any use whatsoever.

YOUR NEED TO KNOW

What do you *need* to know about bits?

- What's available
- Something about buying them
- How to use them
- How to care for them

You should know that there are zillions of them out there, made in the United States and Canada, in Italy and Israel, in Asia. They're sold in hardware stores and building centers throughout the land. Tool dealers sell them. You can buy them through mail-order catalogs.

The lion's share of bits made and sold these days are carbide-tipped, because they work the best in the widest range of routing circumstances. Carbide is an extremely hard material, close to the hardness of diamonds. It's relatively insensitive to heat, so it won't lose its temper when the pressure to perform mounts. The main weakness of carbide is brittleness: It chips easily. It's also pretty expensive.

Hence the carbide-tipped bit. The shank and body of most bits are machined from steel, then slips of carbide—the cutting edges—are brazed to the bit.

The cost and quality of router bits range widely. A particular profile made by one manufacturer may cost two or three times that made by

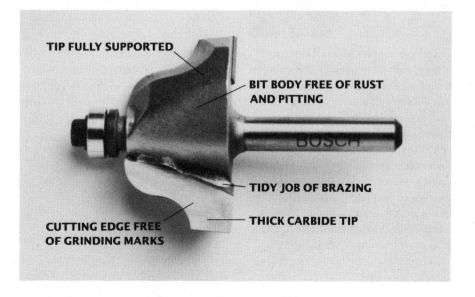

TIP FULLY SUPPORTED

BIT BODY FREE OF RUST AND PITTING

TIDY JOB OF BRAZING

THICK CARBIDE TIP

CUTTING EDGE FREE OF GRINDING MARKS

another. The cost difference may stem from where the bits are made (the United States versus the Far East, for example) and how they're marketed. It may stem from *how* they're made. So when purchasing a bit, look for visible signs of quality: the thickness of the carbide, how evenly it is brazed to the bit body, and the smoothness of the cutting edge. These aren't necessarily the most important aspects of bit quality, but they are things you can see. If they're poor, the likelihood is that the invisible aspects will also be poor.

The carbide's thickness suggests the ultimate life span of the bit. A skinny strip of carbide will disappear after a couple of sharpenings. (Whether or not you ever will have it

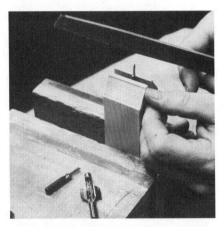

The cheapest bits around are made of steel that's stamped into bit shape, rolled to configuration, then hardened. The bits aren't meant for long-term routing or a depth of cut greater than 1/8 inch. Fred has a small selection that he uses when he wants to create a special profile for a small, one-of-a-kind job. The steel is soft enough to be shaped with a file or grind wheel. Fred picks the bit with the profile closest to what he wants, files or grinds and sharpens it, then makes the cut. The bits keep getting smaller and smaller.

resharpened is immaterial.) A fat carbide tip indicates the maker expects it to last a good many years, even if you are a pro and will have the bit resharpened a half-dozen times.

A corollary to thickness is support. The carbide tip should be supported along its full length. It's brittle, remember, and if it isn't fully supported, and especially if it's not too thick, the carbide may break. That could be dangerous! The steel behind the tip shouldn't be visibly pitted.

The quality of the brazing job is an indication of the skill of the workers who made the bit. If it looks sloppy, it probably was not made well. That's not a good sign.

Finally, check the quality of the edge ground onto the carbide. You may want serrations on a knife edge, but a router bit doesn't cut wood the way a knife slices bread or cheese. If you can see grinding marks, the edge has been ground only roughly. If the bit's cutting edges look under magnification like a serrated knife, pass it by. That bit will leave a serrated finish. Better bits will appear and feel smooth.

Of the quality aspects you *can't* see, the most critical are the roundness of the shank and the overall balance of the bit. You can't tell about the bit's balance until you use it. *Then you'll know!* If the bit's shank isn't perfectly rounded, or if the bit isn't perfectly balanced, it will vibrate. When you cut with it, it'll chatter. Vibration is hard on the router and the bit and the cut.

Somewhat less important than bit balance, though still critically important, is the quality of the carbide that makes up the tip. The carbide used for router bits usually is graded on a four-level hardness scale:

C1 to C4. To relate this to a more universal hardness scale—the Rockwell c scale (abbreviated Rc)—C1 carbide is approximately Rc89, while C4 carbide is Rc94. To put *this* in perspective, figure that a good woodworking chisel's edge will be between Rc58 and Rc62, while a diamond is Rc100. A few manufacturers specify in their catalogs the grade of carbide they use. This can be a little disingenuous, since even the hardest carbide can be poorly made, with hidden voids and weak spots. But knowing that the bit you're about to buy is made of C3 or C4 carbide is useful. C1 carbide is the softest and most brittle. Soft carbide dulls more quickly, and more of it must be ground away to renew the edge, so it simply won't last as long. In the absence of specifics, you have to rely on a manufacturer's reputation.

BIT LINGO

To start, it's useful to know the lingo. Here are some definitions and discussion, starting with the names of any bit's components.

Solid bit: A bit machined out of a single piece of tool steel. In some cases, a ball-bearing pilot is screwed to it. Also called one-piece bits, solid bits usually are machined to closer tolerances than assembled bits.

Assembled bit: A bit made up of several pieces. The arbor usually accommodates interchangeable cutters and pilots. Slot cutters typically are assembled bits.

Pilot: A bit's built-in steering mechanism. A noncutting portion of the bit, it is either a turned steel pin that's an integral part of the bit or a ball bearing attached to the bit. The pilot rubs on the edge of the workpiece, limiting the cut and guid-

Carbide-Free Bits

Yes, Johnny, there are bits that don't have any carbide in them. Used to be the only kind you could get. High-speed steel (HSS), they called 'em. We don't use them much anymore, but they're still out there. You see them in hardware stores and at building centers all across the country, though they're seldom advertised in woodworking periodicals.

You don't see HSS bits much anymore because they simply aren't as durable and maintenance-free as the carbide and carbide-tipped tools. The one advantage HSS bits have is cost: A HSS bit is generally about one-quarter the cost of a carbide-tipped bit of the same profile. I would say "comparable carbide-tipped bit," but the fact is, the two bits just don't compare.

HSS is relatively easy to machine, so bits made from it are inexpensive. It can be honed razor-sharp, much sharper than carbide, in fact, but it dulls quickly. Though good for routing softwood, it dulls pretty quickly if used more than occasionally on hardwood. And routing man-made materials like plywood and particleboard can burn out a HSS bit in a half-dozen passes.

A couple of manufacturers coat the cutting edges of their HSS bits with a gold-colored titanium alloy to make them more durable. Titanium-coated HSS bits stay sharp longer than the uncoated variety, but they still won't hold up long in hardwoods. Consequently, you've got to hone the cutting edges routinely.

Some will argue that a HSS bit is a reasonable choice in two situations: when you're working with softwoods, or when you need a profile that'll get limited use. Neither situation says "Buy high-speed steel" to me.

The softwood scenario overlooks the destructive properties of the pitch and resins that are so abundant in the most common softwood, pine. Heat is a natural part of cutting wood with a bit spinning at 22,000 rpm, but HSS bears up to heat less well than carbide.

The hotter the bit gets, the faster it loses its edge sharpness. The duller it gets, the hotter it gets. Accumulations of pitch and resins add substantially to heat buildup.

Now look at the second scenario. Only the most commonplace profiles are made in HSS: round-overs, coves, an ogee or two, maybe a Roman ogee. In each of these categories, you'll find a wider variety of sizes in the carbide-tipped form than in the HSS form. And you will find a broader array of categories in carbide-tipped forms: classical coves, cove-and-beads, edge-beading, flutes, full- and half-radius bull-nose, multiform molding cutters, and many others. Want that bit with a ½-inch shank? You are unlikely to find it in HSS.

Nevertheless, the cost difference can make your head swim. A HSS bit may cost only a quarter of what its manufacturer charges for a carbide-tipped bit of the same profile. Go ahead, think about it. Five bucks for HSS versus 20 bucks for carbide-tipped. Or $8 versus $30. Or $10 versus $35. The carbide-tipped bit has to last three to four times longer than a HSS bit to eliminate these price disparities. The claim most frequently bandied about is that

a carbide-tipped bit will last 20 times longer between sharpenings than a HSS bit.

See the value of the carbide-tipped bit? Three or four times the cost, but 20 times the life span. Good economics.

Here's how I look at it: If the opportunity to sharpen cutting tools is what draws you to woodworking, buy HSS and sharpen away. Me? I stick strictly with carbide-tipped tooling. If any of my bits ever do need sharpening—and so far they have not—I'll take them to an experienced tradesman and have him do it.

Two of the shortcomings of HSS bits are visible here. One is the delicate cutting edge. The dark blobs at the cutting edge of the rabbeting bit and the overall darkness of the straight bit are result of routing plywood. The glue used in composite materials and plywood is much more abrasive than wood and quickly damages a HSS cutting edge, as you can see. The second shortcoming is the integral pilot. It rotates at the same speed as the bit, heating up quickly. At best, it merely burnishes the stock's edge, and at worst, it burns it.

ing the path of the bit. The cut width of a piloted bit is half the difference between the bit's diameter and the pilot's diameter.

Arbor: The shaft of an assembled bit. The typical arbor consists of a shank, which fits into the router's collet, and a spindle, threaded at the end. The cutter fits onto the spindle and is secured by a nut.

Dust shield: A washerlike disk, sometimes called a slinger, that fits between the pilot bearing and the cutter. It deflects chips and dust coming off the cutter, helping to prolong the life of the bearing. Not every bearing-piloted bit has a dust shield.

Interchangeable cutter: A steel body with carbide cutting edges brazed to it that fits onto an arbor, thus forming a bit. In some interchangeable-cutter bit systems, a given cutter will fit both a ¼-inch-shank arbor and a ½-inch-shank arbor. Often, a cutter can be used with or without a pilot, depending upon the arbor used. (See "Interchangeable Cutter Systems" on page 24 for more information.)

Shank: The part of the bit inserted into the router collet. The majority of router bits have either ¼-inch or ½-inch shanks. Some manufacturers make bits with ⅜-inch shanks.

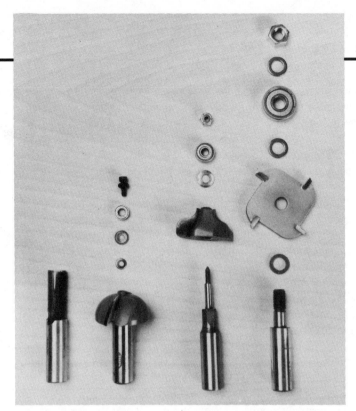

Bits are either solid or assembled. The straight bit (left) is the quintessential solid bit, but the cove bit next to it is also a solid bit, even though the pilot bearing can be removed. The assembled bit is an alternative, made up of an arbor and a removable cutter. The slot cutter (right) is the most common assembled bit.

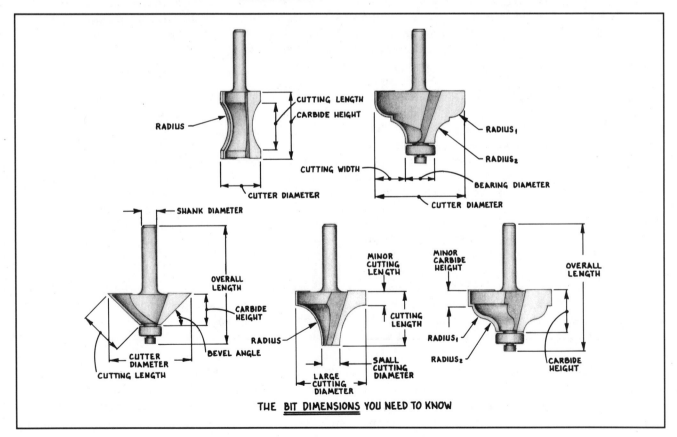

THE **BIT DIMENSIONS** YOU NEED TO KNOW

High-speed steel (HSS): The most common tool steel used to make woodworking cutters.

Carbide: An alloy formed of powdered tungsten-carbon particles fused together with a cobalt binder under extreme heat and pressure. It is one of the hardest synthetic substances. Though it is harder than steel and more heat-resistant than steel, it is also brittle and breaks much more easily than steel.

Carbide tip: A cutting edge, made from carbide, that is brazed to the router bit's steel body. This type of bit construction puts carbide where it does the most good.

Solid-carbide bit: A bit made completely of carbide. The size or design of some bits—spirals and small-diameter straights—precludes their being constructed of steel with carbide tips. Because carbide is so costly, these bits are expensive. And because carbide is so brittle, these bits are seldom guaranteed against breakage.

Titanium nitride: A surface coating applied to both HSS and carbide-tipped bits by some manufacturers as an extra-cost option. Applied to HSS, the gold-colored coating increases the surface hardness and supposedly provides "extra lubricity" to the bits. Applied to carbide-tipped bits, the coating is said to allow a sharper edge to be ground on the carbide.

Teflon: A surface coating applied to the bit body by at least one manufacturer, CMT. The slippery substance has been used on some saw blades for years, but it is best known as the operative coating on nonstick cooking pans. On a router bit, the Teflon is supposed to help the bit shed pitch and other residues and—arguably—to aid in chip clearance.

When you look at a bit catalog, you see a variety of dimensions listed. Some are helpful, some not. Some pertinent (and irrelevant) measures are explained below, to help you know what you're about to buy.

Cutting diameter: The largest diameter the bit cuts, which isn't always the bit's largest diameter (a ¼-inch straight with a ½-inch shank, for example). This dimension is most pertinent when used with straight bits and groove-forming bits. With some plunge-cutting profiles, it's useful to know both small and large cutting diameters. With an edge-forming bit, you must know the outside diameter of the pilot to calculate the cutting width from the cutting diameter.

Cutting length: The length of the cutting edge. This is usually a measurement parallel to the bit axis, telling you how deep into the wood the bit can cut at full extension. But sometimes it refers to the longest dimension of the cutting edge. If the edge is at an angle to the bit axis, knowing how long it is doesn't give you much of a clue as to how deep it cuts.

Carbide height: The vertical height of the carbide tip, a measurement that parallels the bit axis. This usually indicates how deep the bit will cut. With some profiles, an additional measurement—the minor carbide height—is provided so you know how deep a fillet or step the bit is able to cut.

Shank diameter: The largest diameter of the shank. The inside diameter of the router's collet must match this dimension.

Overall length: The total length of a router bit, from top to bottom.

Radius: Half the diameter. In bit lingo, this usually indicates the size of an arc in the profile formed by the bit. A ⅜-inch-radius round-over bit, for example, cuts a quarter-round profile with a radius of ⅜ inch. A cove-and-bead bit may have the same radius for both cove and bead. If the radii of cove and bead are different, they'll usually be labeled R_1 and R_2.

Bevel angle: The angle formed between the cutting edge and a line perpendicular to the shank axis. This is most pertinent in chamfer and V-groove bits.

The cutting properties of a bit depend upon a lot of angles. Hook angles, radial clearance angles, penetration angles. Even the cutting edges involve angles. And what the tool engineer designing a bit is angling for is a felicitous compromise. Incorporating a high hook angle so the bit cuts fast, for example, compromises the durability of the cutting edge. Adjusting this angle to strengthen the bit, on the other hand, compromises the cutting speed.

No bit catalog mentions this arcana of the tool engineer's work in more than general terms. You accept the choices he or she has made, without knowing what alternatives were considered. The catalog will razzle you with some tech talk, in the hope that you'll be dazzled enough to buy. But you won't get a choice of hook angles or radial clearances.

Will knowing what these terms refer to be of any practical value to you? Probably not. But you should know about flute designs, and about when to use what design.

Hook (or rake) angle: The degree to which the cutting edge "leans into the cut." It is the angle (or "hook") between the tip of the cutting edge and a straight line passing through, and perpendicular to, the bit axis. The hook angle affects feed

rate and bit control. High hook angles are easier to feed fast and give better chip clearance, but low ones are stronger.

Clearance (or relief): The space between the surface of the cut and the bit body. The greater the clearance, the faster the bit can be fed. Reduce clearance and you reduce the rate at which the bit can be fed. This is the principle behind the so-called safety or anti-kickback bit design. (See "Bit Drawer" on page 29.)

Penetration clearance: The angle formed between the cutting tool edge and a line perpendicular to the shank axis. This angle allows gradual penetration of the bit into the workpiece.

Web diameter: The thickness of the bit's ground steel body.

Flute: The opening in front of the bit's cutting edge. It provides clearance for the wood chips. Bits may have one or more flutes, and they may be straight, angular, or spiral. Flutes are also referred to as chip pockets or gullets.

Single-flute bit: A bit with a single cutting edge. A single-flute bit allows a higher feed rate but makes a cut with a rougher finish. It is always a straight bit, never a profile cutter, and seldom exceeds ⅝ inch in diameter.

The distinction between straight flutes and shear flutes is subtle but important. The cutting edges of the straight-flute bits (the bit on the left in each pair) hit the wood straight on, in a chopping action that requires brute power. The cutting edges of the shear-flute bits (on the right in each pair) slice into the wood, an action that yields a finer finish yet demands less power. While we tend to think of straight versus shear in terms of straight bits, good-quality profile cutters often have shear flutes, as you can see. (The straight bit is a downshear; the rabbet and cove bits are upshears.)

Double-flute bit: A bit with two cutting edges, 180 degrees apart. Because it cuts twice in each revolution, a double-flute bit can't be fed as fast as a single-flute bit. But those two cuts yield a smoother finish.

Triple-flute bit: A bit with three cutting edges, spaced 120 degrees apart. Used primarily on laminate trimming bits, three cutting edges provide an extremely smooth finish on plastic laminates, which tend to chip easily.

Straight flute: A cutting edge parallel to the bit axis. This is THE basic bit geometry.

Shear flute: A cutting edge that is slightly angled in relation to the bit axis. Much like hand planing at a slight angle, shear-angled bits slice the wood rather than chop at it. The results mimic hand planing at an angle, too. Because of the angle, it takes less effort (you can get by with less horsepower), yet it yields a better finish. More and more manufacturers are designing bits other than straights with shear flutes.

Spiral flute: This cutting edge resembles a twist-drill bit. It takes the shearing action a step or two further, combining it with chip augering. The spiral-flute bit is usually recommended for mortising and other deep-cutting work, where chip removal is a problem. The quality of the cut is improved, but the cutting action is slowed. Because of the twist-

The double flute configuration (top left) is the most common by far. All profile cutters—ogees, round-overs, coves, chamfers, and the like—have two flutes, and so do most straight bits. Some straight bits, usually small-diameter ones, have but a single flute (center), while others, called stagger-tooth bits, have two flutes but only half-height cutting edges. The latter style (right) shows the compromises designed into it much more baldly than do the other bits. Each cutting edge extends only half the length of the full cut, so the bit cuts fast and clears chips, just like a single-flute bit. But two cutting edges give a better finish than a single cutting edge (even if they are only half-length). In addition, the Paso Robles bit shown has one upcut edge and one downcut edge, a compromise intended to yield fuzz-free edges on both surfaces of through cuts.

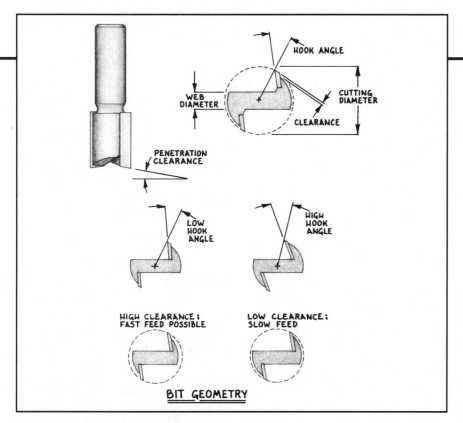

HOOK ANGLE

WEB DIAMETER

CUTTING DIAMETER

CLEARANCE

PENETRATION CLEARANCE

LOW HOOK ANGLE

HIGH HOOK ANGLE

HIGH CLEARANCE; FAST FEED POSSIBLE

LOW CLEARANCE; SLOW FEED

BIT GEOMETRY

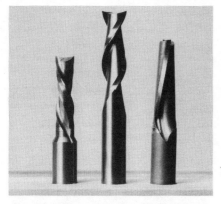

The spiral bit takes the shear action to its logical extreme. The downcut spiral (left)—its cutting edge descends in a counterclockwise twist—shears the wood fibers downward, giving the cut a cleaner edge, but it doesn't clear chips from the cut very well unless it is a through cut. The upcut spiral (center) —its cutting edge descends from the tip in a clockwise twist—will lift chips from the cut, but also the wood fibers from the edge of the cut. Both these bits are solid carbide. On the right is a carbide-tipped (upcut) spiral. Its spiral is less aggressive, but its steel body is considerably stronger than a solid carbide one.

ing edge, spirals are either solid HSS or solid carbide.

Downcut: A shear or spiral flute that slices downward as the bit rotates. The downward slicing action leaves a clean, generally fuzz-free edge on the cut. One disadvantage to it is that it tends to drive the router and the workpiece apart, so a secure grip or the use of hold-downs is important. Another disadvantage is that it doesn't clear chips from the cut quickly. On a through cut, however, it moves the chips away from the router (and onto the floor). You can identify a downcut shear or spiral by looking down on the bit's tip. If the flutes descend in a counterclockwise spiral, the bit is a downcut one.

Upcut: A shear or spiral flute that slices upward as the bit rotates. The upcut bit is favored for deep grooves and mortising, where the upward spiral helps clear chips from the cut. It also augers the bit into the workpiece, thus pulling work and router together. A disadvantage is that the upward slice tends to lift

the wood fibers at the edge of the cut. You can identify an upcut shear or spiral by looking down on the bit's tip. If the flutes descend in a clockwise spiral, the bit is an upcut one.

Stagger-tooth bit: A double-flute bit on which the cutting edges do not extend the complete length of the flute. Instead, the overall cutting length is split between the two flutes. Intended for cutting dense or abrasive man-made materials and panel goods, these bits combine the speed and chip clearance of single-flute bits with a better-quality finish. The finish is improved because the design balances the bit's weight and the cutting forces to reduce deflection and thus vibration. The bit movement is less erratic; its cut thus is smoother.

JUST STARTING ?

So many different bits! There are so many bits to choose from that whittling the possibilities down to the affordable and versatile few—the ones you need to start a router bit collection—can be overwhelming.

I started by buying a "set" of high-speed steel bits at the same time I bought my first router. I remember peeling the waxy coating off several of the new bits and trying them one at a time. And I remember musing about what I'd *ever* do with one or two of them. But pretty quickly the four that got the most use were replaced with carbide-tipped bits: ½-inch and ¾-inch straight bits, a ¼-inch round-over bit, and a ⅜-inch rabbeting bit. Later the Roman ogee bit was replaced. Then I branched out. (I still have the old HSS set, and a couple of the bits still have the waxy coating on them.)

You have to ask yourself, "What

Interchangeable Cutter Systems

An economical way to expand your bit collection is to buy from a manufacturer offering interchangeable cutters. The bits are assembled, meaning that the cutter is a separate piece from the arbor. You can buy a complete bit, but you can also buy just the cutters and use them interchangeably on a single arbor.

You save roughly $7 per profile by buying the cutter but not the arbor. Doesn't *seem* like a lot of money, but think of it this way: "Buy three and get the fourth *free!*" (Jeez, I could be a marketing consultant!)

In the system offered by Paso Robles Carbide (marketed under the Ocemco name), you can buy ¼-inch- and ½-inch-shank arbors with and without pilots. All the profile cutters—rabbet cutters, coves, ogees, round-overs, and others—can be purchased separately. Budget considerations aside, this can be a marvelously flexible system. You can use a cutter on a ¼-inch shank with a pilot in your 1-horsepower router, then switch it onto a ½-inch shank without a pilot to use in a 3-horsepower table-mounted router.

Paso Robles doesn't have the most extensive catalog, but it does have some unique cutters. Chamfer cutters are available with 25-, 30-, 45-, 60-, and 67-degree bevels. Rabbet cutters range in four steps from ⅛ inch to ½ inch; switching pilot bearings both expands that range and provides additional steps. The ogee profiles range not only in radii of the profiles, which is typical of other lines, but also in the proportions. (Look for Paso Robles in "Sources" on page 337.)

The other interchangeable cutter lines that I know of are more limited.

The Byrom line, for example, includes a small assortment of interchangeable cutters—two round-overs that can also bead, a Roman ogee, a chamfer, a cove, a rabbet, and two laminate trimmers. A ¼-inch-shank arbor, which comes with two different pilot bearings, is available.

The two beefs I've heard regarding interchangeable cutter systems are that "keeping track of all these small parts" is a hassle and that the pilots have come loose in use. Both are bogus to me. Keeping track of two or three arbors and a dozen cutters is no more taxing than keeping track of a dozen separate bits. If you lose cutters, you probably lose your router's second collet, the extra bearings for your rabbeting bit, maybe your drill bits, and any other small tools you have in your shop. With an interchangeable cutter system, all you have to do is set up your bit storage with spindles for the cutters, instead of holes for bit shanks.

As for pilots coming loose, I would

The hub of the interchangeable cutter system is the arbor. Paso Robles makes arbors in ¼-inch and ½-inch shank configurations, with and without pilots, all of which accept the same cutters. To keep it from spinning on the arbor, the Paso Robles cutter has a hex recess. It fits over a matching hex formed on the shank of the arbor. A stop nut with a nylon insert secures the cutter and pilot on the arbor's spindle. The nylon insert resists the rotational forces that would loosen a regular nut. To free the cutter from the arbor, you usually have to rap the end of the spindle onto the workbench (after removing the nut and bearing, of course).

think the potential for this exists with every bit that has a detachable pilot— and that's *every bit with a bearing as a pilot.* This is all a matter of router and bit maintenance. You have to tighten the collet properly, and you have to keep after nuts or screws on your bits.

did I buy this router for? What jobs will I do with it?" You have to buy the bits that will do those jobs. If you're asking my opinion on what you should start with, I'd recommend as a minimum the first four bits I bought in carbide:

- ½-inch straight bit
- ¾-inch straight bit
- ¼-inch round-over bit
- ⅜-inch rabbet bit

In writing this, I nosed around in back issues of magazines, a couple of books, and a half-dozen bit catalogs. There's considerable accord on what to start with. Two bits were on *everyone's* list: the ⅜-inch rabbeting bit and the ¼-inch straight bit (well, this wasn't on *my* list, was it?). Straights and round-over bits were on all lists, though not everyone agreed on the sizes to buy.

Round-over bits? Choose from ¼ inch, ⅜ inch, and ½ inch.

Straights? Select ¼ inch, ⅜ inch, ½ inch, and ¾ inch.

Beyond these, recommendations included a chamfer bit, a ½-inch dovetail, a ¼-inch Roman ogee, and a flush-trimmer. I wouldn't dispute the value of any of these bits. If yours is a bare-bones start-up in router woodworking, if your budget restricts you to the router and three or four individual bits, any of these choices would be good.

But if you can manage it, try to match your dollar investment in a router with a dollar investment in bits. Put $150 into a router and $150 into bits.

Very often, a woodworker new to router use will do what I did—spring for a "set." Nearly every bit source has a few sets. A dozen or 15 different bits in a nice box or case, at a price somewhat below the aggregate cost of the individual bits. Good way to get started.

▶ Shank Size

The majority of router bits made today have either ¼-inch or ½-inch shanks. Which size should you buy?

Look at the photo comparing the two shank sizes. Though the bits cut the same profile, they look dramatically different, simply because one has a ½-inch shank and the other a ¼-inch shank. The choice is obvious, isn't it? The ½-inch shank is bigger and thus stronger and thus better resists bending or breaking. While vibration in a long bit or large-diameter bit is usually amplified, the extra heft of the ½-inch shank will eliminate most vibration for a steady, smooth cut. If you shop around—drag out those catalogs!—you'll find that ½-inch-shank bits cost the same or only a little more than those with thinner shanks. You'll find, too, that the larger profiles

and all the big joinery and specialty bits are available only in the ½-inch-shank configuration. (You may also discover that a few manufacturers have ⅜-inch-shank bits. But the variety is limited, and there doesn't seem to be any sound reason to invest in them.)

Nevertheless, there may be two good reasons for buying ¼-inch-shank bits. One, your only router won't accept a ½-inch collet. Two, the bit is available only in the ¼-inch shank.

The questions for woodworkers who own ¼-inch-collet routers are: Do I continue to buy ¼-inch-shank bits? Or do I first upgrade to a ½-inch-collet router? Only your work can provide the answer.

But consider this: As you ask more of your router, you undoubtedly will seek out larger bits. A 2-inch-diameter cutter on a ¼-inch shank is pushing it. And a 1-horsepower router (probably the maximum produced by a ¼-inch-collet-only machine) driving a 2-inch-diameter bit is stressed to the max. Purchasing a higher-horsepower router—it'll come with both ½-inch and ¼-inch collets—will let you use all your ¼-inch bits, but it'll also broaden your woodworking opportunities by letting you use ½-inch-shank bits, too.

What you usually discover, as I did with my first set, is that these "starter" sets invariably include a couple of bits you seldom—if ever—use. That can put you off.

Naturally, the tendency is to dwell on that "if ever." Money spent on a bit *never* used is money wasted, of course.

But dwell instead on that "seldom." There are lots of bits in those catalogs that are *seldom* used. And in the collections of longtime router woodworkers, there are lots of "seldom-used" bits. But when one of those bits is needed, even if only for a single job, and no other bit can be substituted, then that bit becomes essential. Seldom used, but nonetheless essential. What I'm saying is: Don't let someone's gibe about "seldom-used bits" spook you. If the set's a good buy, a really good price, go for it!

An angle sometimes overlooked is that you don't realize how useful a particular bit is until you have it. In its absence, you work around certain joints or procedures. Then one day you spring for it. Suddenly you're discovering timesaving routines, you're trying more sophisticated joinery, joinery you had avoided as too difficult. And it's all *easy!*

Don't overlook specialty sets. Freud and Amana have sets of straight bits. The straight is the most basic bit, and if you are starting out, what better way is there to get a range of sizes? Others have sets of edge-forming bits: two or three round-overs, a Roman ogee, coves, a rabbet, and so forth. Eagle America packages five sizes of the same profile as a set—five coves or five round-overs, for example.

After you've got the basics, whether you bought a set or built up a basic collection bit by bit, expand your collection job by job.

USING BITS

There is a little more to using a router bit than slipping it into the router collet and cinching the collet nut down. You've got to match the

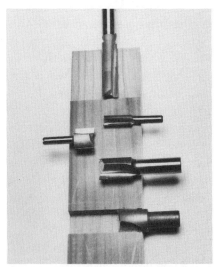

Using a bit with a cutting edge that's overly long for the job can lead to a broken bit. A 2-inch-long straight may be just right for tenoning, but it's way too long for a ³⁄₈-inch-deep groove. Most of us have a limited selection and use a midlength cutter—³⁄₄ to 1 inch long—for both jobs.

bit to the cut and the router. You've got to balance the bit speed with the feed rate. Here are some tips for using your bits to their best advantage.

Bit selection. Always use the bit with the shortest cutting edge that will do the job. The longer the bit, the greater the chance of its breaking. This is because excessive length amplifies vibration and deflection, which manufacturers cite as the leading causes of tool breakage. If you are cutting a ³⁄₈-inch-deep dado, use your dado bit with the ⁵⁄₈-inch-long cutting edges, rather than your straight bit with the 1½-inch-long cutting edges.

Always use the bit with the largest-diameter shank you can. (See "Shank Size" on page 25 for the rationale.)

Pilots. Each time you fit a bearing-piloted bit in your router, give the bearing a flick to ensure that it spins freely and that its rim is smooth and clean. A frozen bearing is the prime cause of tracks and scorch marks on the edge of a workpiece, but perhaps surprisingly, it isn't the only cause.

The purpose of the pilot is to guide the cut and to control its width. In the days when HSS was what all bits were made from, pilots were turned steel pins. You needed a light touch to avoid burn marks left by a pilot spinning at the same speed as the cutter. Nowadays, you need a heavier hand to avoid those burn marks. The bearing is supposed to roll along the workpiece edge at the feed rate, while the bit spins inside it at the router's speed. But if you don't put enough pressure on that bearing, it can spin along with the bit and really stink up the edge, if you know what I mean. (On the other hand, press that bearing too

The bearing really does have impact on the cut, and a dirty one like this—okay, okay, we exaggerate—causes an uneven finish. Instead of rolling evenly along the workpiece edge, it thumps along like a grocery cart with a gob of gum on one wheel. Even a tiny scablike pitch deposit can impact the cut enough to detract from its final feel and appearance. But even a clean bearing can damage the work, as the top workpiece shows, if it is frozen or pressed too hard against the wood during the cut.

hard against a softwood, and you crush the wood fibers, leaving a different sort of track along the edge.)

Dirt or grit stuck on the bearing's rim can cause a wavy or choppy cut. The dirty pilot acts like a kind of cam, lifting the cutting edge infinitesimally away from the work each time the dirt speck hits the guiding edge. (The same unsatisfactory finish can be achieved by running a clean pilot along a dirty, chipped work edge, by the way.)

That integral pilot on the HSS bit has one big advantage over the typical pilot bearing—its small diameter. That allows you to cut deeper into a corner than a ½-inch or ³⁄₈-inch ball-bearing pilot.

On the whole, though, the integral pilot is inflexible. Its size is what it is. But a bearing can be changed, thus altering the width of the cut

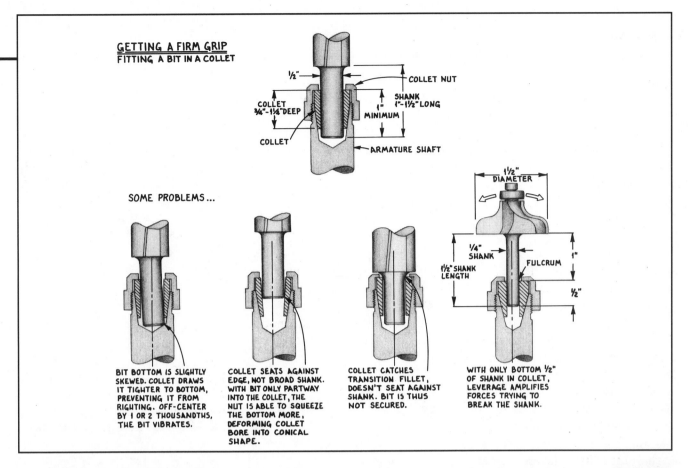

GETTING A FIRM GRIP
FITTING A BIT IN A COLLET

COLLET NUT

½"

SHANK 1"-1½" LONG

COLLET ¾"-1¼" DEEP

1" MINIMUM

COLLET

ARMATURE SHAFT

1½" DIAMETER

¼" SHANK

FULCRUM

½" SHANK LENGTH

1"

½"

SOME PROBLEMS...

BIT BOTTOM IS SLIGHTLY SKEWED. COLLET DRAWS IT TIGHTER TO BOTTOM, PREVENTING IT FROM RIGHTING. OFF-CENTER BY 1 OR 2 THOUSANDTHS, THE BIT VIBRATES.

COLLET SEATS AGAINST EDGE, NOT BROAD SHANK. WITH BIT ONLY PARTWAY INTO THE COLLET, THE NUT IS ABLE TO SQUEEZE THE BOTTOM MORE, DEFORMING COLLET BORE INTO CONICAL SHAPE.

COLLET CATCHES TRANSITION FILLET, DOESN'T SEAT AGAINST SHANK. BIT IS THUS NOT SECURED.

WITH ONLY BOTTOM ½" OF SHANK IN COLLET, LEVERAGE AMPLIFIES FORCES TRYING TO BREAK THE SHANK.

A side benefit of having a bearing as a pilot is that it can be removed. A different-sized bearing can replace it. This will affect the width of cut. The bigger the bearing, the more shallow the cut, as these samples show. All were cut with the same bit and different bearings.

to yield different profiles from the same bit.

The collet. Always use the correct collet for your router, and avoid using sleeves or bushings to make a ¼-inch-shank bit fit in a ½-inch collet.

These reducers add to vibration and runout, and they generally don't hold the bit as well as a collet alone. (A number of router manufacturers don't make separate ¼-inch collets for their ½-inch-collet machines, and if you've got one of them, using a bushing is unavoidable.)

Using a collet that's in good condition is essential. A worn, scored, or out-of-round collet doesn't hold the bit tightly, which increases runout and vibration. Don't assume that a new collet is perfectly round or even the correct diameter. Check the shank each time you remove a bit from the collet. Dark marks or grooves in it usually indicate slippage. Either you didn't tighten the collet nut sufficiently or the collet is worn and should be replaced.

Always insert the shank as far into the collet as it will go, then back it out slightly (approximately ¹⁄₁₆ inch). The reason for doing this is to ensure that the collet alone is securing the

A quick scan of our bit drawers suggests that the typical bit's shank is 1 to 1¼ inches long. If that shank is a half-incher like the core-box shown at left, its entire length needs to be in the collet. If it's a quarter-incher like the cove bit, you can extend the bit's reach a little, as shown. Most manufacturers will provide extra shank length when it seems clear it will be needed. The dovetail and ogee bits shown are likely to be used with template guides, so the extra shank length is there.

bit, and that the shank is centered in the collet. If you bottom the bit, and leave it bottomed when you tighten the collet nut, the bit can be off-center by a thousandth or two. That's enough to cause pretty severe vibration.

How deep the bit shank must be inserted in the collet is not something all bit manufacturers agree on. Most urge you to avoid cheating the bit out of the collet to extend its reach. It is a tempting idea. You need to cut jjuuussst a little deeper, so you back the bit out of the collet an extra ¼ inch or an extra ½ inch. The maker of Byrom bits says the minimum insertion is twice the shank diameter. As a practical matter, you don't always have a lot more length than that on ½-inch-shank cutters. But having a hefty cutter on a ¼-inch shank inserted only ½ inch into the collet seems excessively venturesome to me. Bear in mind that Byrom also recommends the ½-inch shank for any bit over ½ inch in diameter.

Feed rate. The rate at which the router is fed along the work (or the work is fed across a router table) is very important to the overall quality of the cut and to the longevity of the bit. You should feel a constant, even pressure when the work meets the cutter. Feed rate ultimately depends on the type of material being cut, the amount of material being removed, and the type of bit being used.

The most common feed rate mistake is excessive restraint. And feeding too slowly is a quick way to ruin a bit. Letting the bit "dwell" in the cut will lead to a burned cut, caused by the bit heating up, which in turn reduces the bit's life immensely. Remember, heat can ruin a sharp tool. So keep the router (or the work) moving.

If you are concerned about bogging the router down, make several light passes to complete the cut instead of trying to hog away too much material in one pass. This is especially true if you are using a large-diameter bit. This will reduce the stress on the bit and will generally be a safer practice.

Router speed. The speed at which the bit turns can be important. The typical router runs at somewhere between 20,000 and 24,000 rpm, depending upon the brand and model. Router bits are designed to cut at

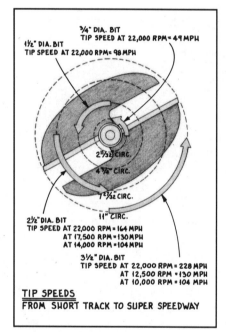

TIP SPEEDS
FROM SHORT TRACK TO SUPER SPEEDWAY

Each point along the cutting edge of a 3½-inch-diameter bit is traveling a different distance in each rotation of the bit. The farther out from the centerpoint you go, the faster the point must move. The critical point is the very tip. At 22,000 rpm, the tip of a ¾-inch bit is moving 49 mph, while the tip of the 3½-inch bit is moving 228 mph. A tip speed of 130 mph is probably the maximum you should run to achieve optimum cutting performance with appropriate safety.

Dwell burns are a common woe in router woodworking. Feeding the router too slowly or at an erratic pace is a common cause. A dull bit will burn the wood, regardless of the feed rate. And, unfortunately, some species of wood—maple, for example—burn more easily than others.

this operating speed. If you were to run the typical router bit at a reduced speed, say 10,000 to 12,000 rpm, you might be surprised at how poor a job it does. The finish of the cut probably will be rough and choppy.

This is true of *most* bits. But as the diameter of the bit increases, the router's high operating speed becomes a problem. The cutter is too darn big to be revolving at 22,000 rpm. While there's little dispute that large-diameter bits—for example, 3- to 3½-inch-diameter panel raisers—should be spun at about 12,000 to 14,000 rpm, opinions vary as to the the appropriate speeds for other sizes of bits.

One bit source recommends operating any bit larger in diameter than ½ inch at no more than 17,000 rpm, and cutting that speed to no more than 14,000 rpm when the diameter exceeds 1 inch. More commonly, you're advised to slow down the bit when its diameter hits 2 inches.

What's working here is a confusion between safe operating speed and an appropriate balance between bit speed and feed rate. We slow down big bits simply because they're unsafe at "full router speed." But we often slow down midsized bits so a workable balance can be struck between bit rpm and feed rate. As I mentioned before, a feed rate that's too slow is common. The bit moves too slowly through the cut, the heat builds up, the wood scorches.

The prevalence of plunging operations fuels this problem. Say you have a short slot to cut. Each time you want to plunge the bit deeper, you tend to pause, allowing the spinning bit to dwell in the cut. You can just smell the wood scorching. The cut is short, and each change in direction brings another slowing of the feed rate, another pause. One way to moderate the problem is to slow down the bit's revs—even when the cutter is relatively small in diameter.

BIT DRAWER

Is one bit safer to use than another? Some bit manufacturers would like you to believe so. CMT and Freud promote their bits as having "anti-kickback" designs, and Byrom, perhaps more blatantly, has marketed selected bits as "Safety Bits." By the time you read this, Eagle America will have switched its line to anti-kickback designs.

The concept comes from the European Community. A number of years ago, the *Holzberufsgenossenschaft*, the German woodworking safety commission, came up with a bit design that limits the size of chip that a cutting edge can remove.

The difference between a "non-safety" bit and a "safety" bit is most obvious in large-diameter edge-forming cutters, such as cove, chamfer, ogee, and round-over bits. Basically, the bit body is bulkier, with a very pronounced yet confined pocket just in front of each cutting edge. The design key, however, is not that pocket but the fact that the radius of the bit body is just 1/32 inch smaller than the radius of the cutting edge. The design makes it almost impossible for the bit to aggressively pull the router into the work, and it puts a governor on the rate at which you can feed the router.

Safety bits (bottom) have more body than non-safety bits (top) of the same profile. The extra body limits the size of the chip that can be removed.

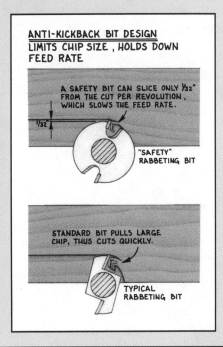

ANTI-KICKBACK BIT DESIGN
LIMITS CHIP SIZE, HOLDS DOWN
FEED RATE

A SAFETY BIT CAN SLICE ONLY 1/32"
FROM THE CUT PER REVOLUTION,
WHICH SLOWS THE FEED RATE.

1/32

"SAFETY"
RABBETING BIT

STANDARD BIT PULLS LARGE
CHIP, THUS CUTS QUICKLY.

TYPICAL
RABBETING BIT

The three manufacturers promoting the safety aspect of their bit designs have strong European connections. To sell in Germany, one of the world's healthiest markets, their bits have to meet the safety-design standards. Both CMT and Freud bits are manufactured in Italy and sold around the world. Ohio-based Byrom sells its American-made bits internationally. (Bosch, a German-based router and bit maker, naturally has chip-limiting bits available, but at this writing it isn't pushing them in the U.S. market.)

Okay, okay. So is the safety element truth or hype?

Truth, I'd say. It's subjective, of course, and it's based on work with CMT bits (the Freud bits we have predate their changeover to anti-kickback designs), but I find the CMT bits to be among the least "grabby" I've ever used. Though climb cuts aren't recommended, there are times when a climb cut is what you make—when routing stock that's prone to tear out, for example. With an anti-kickback bit, a climb cut seems less of a thrill. I think that's a recommendation.

Check "Sources" on page 337 for where to find CMT, Freud, Eagle America, and Byrom bits. Give the suppliers a call; get their catalogs. Their bits aren't the cheapest you can buy, but they just may be the safest.

Bill's Bit Case

As your bit collection swells, one of the stickiest problems is being able to identify which bit is which. Say you spring for that $^{23}/_{32}$-inch straight. Will you be able to tell it from your $^3/_4$-inch straight?

I don't consider myself to be particularly anal, but I did fret about getting the $^7/_{32}$-inch straight mixed up with the $^1/_4$-inch straight, the $^3/_{16}$-inch beading bit confused with the $^1/_4$-inch round-over bit. Would I remember which size of Roman ogee I had? I wanted to be able to *label* my bits as well as protect them.

My solution was the bit case shown here. The idea is to display both the bit and the label in a reasonably space-efficient way. I fit a bit in a hole in one of the bit-holder strips. Then I write a label on a strip cut from an index card, bend the label over a bit shank to give it a little bow, then fit it into the label slot. As long as each bit is returned to its spot after every use, there's no reason they should get mixed up.

The key element—the bit-holder strip—is a nominal 2 × 2, with $^1/_2$-inch-diameter holes drilled in one face and a shallow dovetail slot routed in the adjoining face. The back of the bit-holder strip is beveled at $22^1/_2$ degrees. Six of these bit-holder strips are screwed to a $^1/_4$-inch plywood base. You could screw the unit to the shop wall, but I made a case for it. I designed the basic case as a drawer (so that someday I can put it in a roll-around tool cabinet). Because I needed to carry the case of bits around—from home shop to editors' shop to office—while working on this book, I made three

sides of the drawer/case $^1/_2$ inch higher than the fourth. In this "extra" stock, I routed a $^1/_4$-inch-wide groove and fitted the unit with a sliding plywood cover. A handle makes the case easy to carry. Whether the case is standing on end like a cabinet or resting flat like a drawer, the bits are easy to view and identify. (Several people suggested that I use Plexiglas for the cover, so the bits are always on view. I didn't do it, but you might want to.)

As I mentioned, all the bit holes are $^1/_2$ inch. To accommodate $^1/_4$-inch-shank bits, I made reducers from $^1/_2$-inch dowel. This lets me intermix the bits, without having to do a lot of preplanning. I also made a few spindles for bearings, interchangeable cutters, and shims that accompany several cutter assemblies in our collection. The spindles are $^3/_{16}$-inch dowel glued into a $^1/_2$-inch dowel.

My bit case design provides orderly storage for router bits. The strips that hold the bits are attached to a false back (or bottom). With this holder assembly oriented one way, the case can be attached to a wall, stood on end as shown, or carried by the handle. If you turn the holder assembly around, the case becomes a drawer, with the handle functioning as a pull. Either way, you can easily see each bit and its label.

The bit holders themselves are easy to make. I used redwood, pine, poplar, and even some cherry. The redwood was the least satisfactory; I couldn't bore the holes clean enough to accept the $^1/_2$-inch shanks or the reducers. In harder woods, even the pine, the holes were perfectly satisfactory. I drilled the holes with a $^1/_2$-inch Forstner bit, making them about $^7/_8$ inch deep, spacing them about $1^1/_2$ inches apart.

BIT CARE

Keeping your bits in good condition starts with appropriate storage. The last thing you want is to have them scattered around the shop or tossed in a drawer. Loose in a drawer, they clatter into one another each time you pull it open. The sound of bits clinking together is also the sound of carbide chipping. A chipped cutter produces a "damaged" profile—like an irregular bead where it doesn't

belong. Sometimes a skilled sharpener can remove the nick. But that chip can also be the surface indication of a network of internal fractures; that carbide tip can be just waiting to fragment. (And you thought *splinters* were unappealing!)

It's important, then, to store bits in a way that prevents them from hitting one another. Fred built some drawers that hold a lot of bits and included them in the router table

and cabinet he built for *American Woodworker* magazine. (See the chapter "Cabinet Router Table.") A more elaborate setup that I like is shown in "Bill's Bit Case" above. Either approach will preserve your bits.

Whatever storage method you adopt should not be *dead* storage. Assuming your bits are being used, they'll get dirty, collecting deposits of pitch and resin. After all, tremendous heat builds up in a bit as it

Then I routed the dovetail slots, using a ½-inch dovetail bit set about ⅛ inch high and making two passes to get the slot about ⅜ inch wide. To bevel the strips, I set the gap between the table saw blade and fence to the width of the strips, then tilted the blade to 22½ degrees.

The case is made like a drawer. It's assembled with box joints, cut as explained in the chapter "Box Joint." The plywood bottom floats in a groove.

All the holes for bits are ½ inch. You can see the sleeves for ¼-inch-shank bits made from ½-inch dowels, as well as the spindled sleeves that hold interchangeable cutters, extra bearings, and the like. Each bit can be labeled with whatever information you think pertinent.

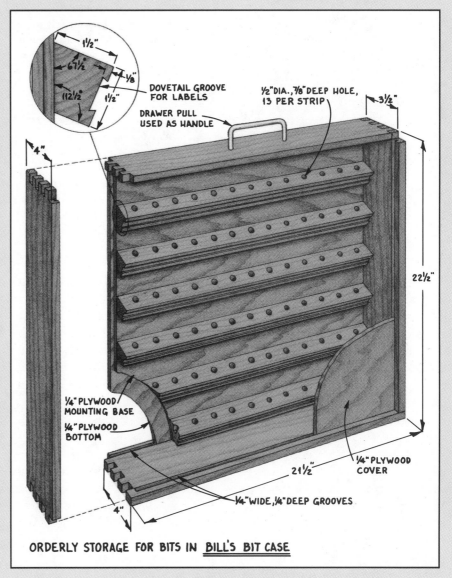

ORDERLY STORAGE FOR BITS IN <u>BILL'S BIT CASE</u>

spins at 22,000 rpm. The heat transfers to the wood, cooking the oil from it—especially from gummy woods. The oil fuses onto the bit. (Pine, incidentally, is one of the worst woods in this regard—even though you might think it's easy to cut. Working a dry hardwood, such as oak, creates far less resin buildup. But even with hardwoods, pitch and resin can and do build up.)

Now one of the worst things

you can do is to leave that buildup on the bit. When you use the bit, its cutting action is impeded. If you pause or even slow the feed rate, the cut can burn. That turns up the heat. Even a tough carbide bit can feel this kind of stress!

To remove the pitch from a router bit, remove the pilot bearing (if it has one), then soak the bit in one of several solvents. Lacquer thinner works fine. If you have gum and pitch re-

mover, that will work. And oven cleaner, which you may have in the kitchen, works great. Give the solvent a moment or two to work, then wipe off the bit with fine (#0000) steel wool. Polish the shaft with a piece of steel wool or a 3M Scotch-Brite pad. (This polishing will not affect the diameter of the shaft—HSS and other tool materials are a lot harder than steel wool and Scotch-Brite.)

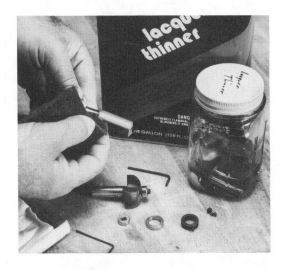

Cleaning a bit is largely a matter of softening the gunk that builds up, then rubbing it off. While special pitch solvents are sold, ordinary lacquer thinner works well. Because the thinner is very volatile—more so than gasoline—you should soak the bits, stripped of any bearings, in a closed container. An abrasive pad, like Scotch-Brite, can get the stubborn dirt and tarnish off.

Ball bearings are usually packed with a special grease, and though they are supposed to be sealed, solvents can seep in and break down the grease. This is why you should remove the bearing before solvent-cleaning a bit. Use an air gun to blow dust or dirt off the bearing. Frozen bearings—those that don't spin freely—should be tossed, as should those that are loose. A new bearing is a lot less dear than time wasted on sanding away burn marks. Worn or damaged hardware—the nuts, screws, and/or washers used to assemble the bit or mount the pilot—should be replaced, too.

If you feel the need to lube the bearing—it's sealed, remember—use a dry lubricant like Dry Cote.

Check the shank after each use. If there are any burrs or galling (rough spots) on the shank, sand them smooth with emery cloth. Then immediately check the collet carefully for dust or wear. Burrs and galling are a sure sign that the bit slipped while you were cutting. If the collet is bad, every bit you use can be damaged. And you know now how these things go: The collet damages the shank, then the shank damage exacerbates the collet damage. The old downward spiral. Replace that collet!

Most manufacturers suggest lightly coating the bit with machine oil to prevent rust. Most new bits, in fact, are so coated. Wipe off the oil before using the bit, of course. Oil left on the bit can stain the wood, as well as attract sawdust and turn it into paste.

Should you hone your bits between uses? We keep saying that carbide tools can be resharpened many times. Diamond hones are sold in many of the tool catalogs. And many woodworkers have residual bit-honing skills left from the HSS bit days.

Most manufacturers advise against it. "Always have your cutting tools resharpened by a reputable grinding firm only," warns Amana's catalog. "Do not attempt to sharpen your own router bits by means of files, whetstones, etc." When the bit starts getting dull—when it resists, when it burns the wood—take it to a professional shop to have it sharpened. You'll be charged somewhere around $5 to $8 to sharpen a carbide-tipped bit, but the job will be done right. Bits coming off a 400-grit diamond wheel are extremely

See Also . . .

"Dadoing and Grooving" on page 225 for various dado- and groove-cutting bits.

"Decorative Treatments" on page 115 for bits that produce coves, ogees, beads, and other profiles used for furniture, architectural molding, picture frame stock, and similar work.

"Edge Joints" on page 252 for joinery bits like tongue-and-groove sets, finger-joint cutters, and glue-joint bits.

"Template-Guided Work" on page 139 for pattern bits.

"Bit Drawer" on page 210 for panel-raising bits, both horizontal and vertical.

"Bit Drawer" on page 202 for rail-and-stile cutters.

sharp. (You might even get a new bit. It can happen! We took a dull Freud bit to our local sharpener, who happens to be a Freud dealer. He said first that sharpening the bit would void the warranty. Then he explained that the bit was dull because it was defective, and he replaced it. No charge.)

If you are determined, however, you can probably touch up a carbide bit with a diamond-impegnated sharpening stone. Rub the cutting surfaces of the flutes back and forth a few times along the corner of the stone. Count the strokes, sharpening each flute an equal amount. This will keep the bit balanced. Sharpen only the inside (flat) surfaces of the flutes. Leave the outside (curved) surfaces alone. If you try to sharpen these, you might change the diameter or the profile of the bit.

ROUTER 101

What are you going to do with your router?

It's a versatile machine and can be used in a vast assortment of woodworking operations.

Easiest to tackle first are edge treatments, such as rounding, molding, chamfering, or beading. These depend upon the pilot on the bit to guide the cut. The only adjustment is to set the depth of cut. While most such treatments are decorative, some are practical joinery cuts. The rabbet is cut with a piloted bit. And special bits are available to shape the edges of boards especially for edge-to-edge joinery.

A different range of operations produces grooves. The bits for these cuts have no pilots, so the router must be guided with an edge guide or along a fence. These operations produce dadoes and grooves, laps, sliding dovetails, and mortises and tenons.

Eventually, you'll try template work, which will allow you to produce dozens and dozens of exact duplicates. You make a template, clamp or temporarily bond it to the workpiece, then guide the router along its edge, cutting the work. What bears against the template is a guide bushing, an accessory you install in the baseplate's bit opening. The bushing surrounds the bit with a projecting flange, which references the edge of the template. An alternative to the guide bushing is a pattern bit, which has a bearing on the shank. With a pattern bit, the bearing references the template.

You may try cutting curves and circles. Or surfacing wood. The possibilities are endless.

But before you plunge into router woodworking, there are some basics you should know that will make your endeavors safer, easier, and altogether more satisfying.

SETTING UP

To avoid problems, you should be as methodical as you can in setting up a cut. The more precise you expect a cut to be, the more precise you have to be in setting up. You have a bit to chuck in the router. In every case, you have a vertical adjustment to make to the router. In some cases, you also have a horizontal adjustment to make. The workpiece has to be secured. All of these preparations offer opportunities for something to go wrong. The trick in routing—as in all woodworking—is to get the setup right. If not the first time, at least before you actually cut wood.

Let's take each setup step in order, anticipate the problems, and find ways to avoid each of them.

Chucking the Bit

Read over the section on using bits in the chapter "Bits." There you'll find detailed suggestions on checking over the bit and, if it has one, its pilot. You need to match the cutter to the cut as well as possible. You will get best results if the bit is sharp, the pilot bearing clean and free-spinning, and the shank clean and smooth—no scoring, no rust.

If the bit is damaged, try to fix it before using it. Replace that sticking or frozen pilot bearing. Have it sharp-ened if it is dull. Try to remove any scoring from the shank. Some experts advise really *polishing* bit shanks, so they are shiny, not just clean. If the bit is really spoiled goods—chipped carbide, shank scored beyond repair—chuck it. Meaning throw it away.

Look over the collet, too. Like the bit shank, it should be clean and smooth. No rust, no galls, no deformities. Inspect the collet socket and the collet nut, too.

How easy it is to actually "chuck" the bit into the router depends a lot upon the router design, as explained in the chapter "Routers." A lot of router users like to separate the motor from the base to change bits. Obviously, you can't do this with a plunge router, and even some fixed-base routers are impossible, as a practical matter, to separate. You often have to simply rest the router on its side and then work within the confines of the base.

Bits are easier to slip in and out of the collet if their shanks are clean and polished to a shine. Use an ordinary abrasive kitchen pad to shine up a bit shank after each use. Keeping after it is the best way to prevent rust and tarnish from forming.

With the motor removed from the base, you can use the workbench to help you loosen a jammed collet nut. Brace the wrench on the spindle against the bench top, and put your weight on the wrench on the collet nut. Just don't get your fingers between the wrenches.

You shouldn't have to be an arm-wrestling champ to tighten the collet. Tight enough is the one-handed squeeze, with the wrenches fitted on their respective parts of the collet so that you can grasp both in one hand.

Loss of Depth Setting

Ever had this problem? You chuck a bit in the collet, very carefully tighten it, set the depth of cut, and go to work. When you're done, *then* you discover that the cut ended up being deeper than you planned. What a headache!

There are a half-dozen things to check.

The first is the position of the bit in the collet. You can check for slippage by putting an alignment mark on both the bit and the collet with a marker. Make a test cut. It should be clear whether the bit has moved. Another sign of slippage is scarring on a previously smooth bit shank.

If the bit worked its way out of

the collet, then you need to inspect the collet and the bit for obvious damage. Is the collet galled or deformed? Is the bit's shank scored or nicked? If the damage existed when you installed the bit for the cut, it could have prevented the collet from really holding the bit.

Did you use a reducer? This is a split bushing you slide on a ¼-inch shank to make it fit in a ½-inch collet. It's not a good way to accommodate small-diameter shanks in large-diameter collets. Some router manufacturers provide such a reducer to avoid the expense of designing, making, and supplying two complete collets.

Think about how you tightened the collet. Was the bit bottomed? You need to back it out of the collet about ¹⁄₁₆ inch before cinching down

This bit has obviously been "spun" a few times. For some reason—it's hard to determine exactly why—the bit wasn't held tightly enough by the collet. The throes of cutting caused enough resistance to slow its rotation speed below that of the router motor, and the collet spinning around the shank caused this scoring. The scoring can probably be removed with some emery cloth, but it just might make the shank too under-sized to use.

the collet nut. Vibration might have caused the slippage if you didn't do this. Or the collet might have caught the transition fillet between the bit's body and its shank in the collet, preventing it from getting a full grip on the shank.

If it is clear the bit moved, but you can't pinpoint a reason, have the bit's shank measured with a micrometer. If it is undersized by more than 2 or 3 thousandths, or if it tapers, that is probably the problem. The only solution is to replace the bit (or, if it is an assembled bit, the arbor).

On the other hand, if the bit didn't move, if it is still just as you installed it, then the loss of depth setting probably lies in the router's base. In a fixed-base router, the base is the means for adjusting and holding a depth-of-cut setting.

The most obvious cause of a loss of depth setting is that you did not tighten the base clamp sufficiently. Though it may seem tight, rough handling and the motor's starting jerk may shift the motor slightly in the base. A poorly designed clamp

▶ TRY THIS!

Here's an easy fix. Go to an auto-parts store and buy a handful of ¼-inch or ½-inch O-rings. Take a bit along to test the fit, so you get the right size. Roll an O-ring onto the shank of each bit you have. Roll it right up almost to the cutter. Leave it there. Whenever you chuck the bit, the O-ring will keep the shank from dropping too far into the collet. It won't be in contact with the armature shaft, and the collet will squeeze the full shank, not just the fillet.

A shank that's undersized more than 3 thousandths is probably too small to be gripped securely by a collet. If you have trouble with a particular bit, measure its shank with a micrometer or a dial caliper, as shown here. This bit is 1 thousandth under a half-inch in diameter.

causes this at least as often as operator neglect does. Most designs use a wing nut to secure the base. Despite the nut's slightly elongated wings, it can be difficult to tighten because you simply can't get a good enough hold on it.

I don't know what the solution to this is. Maybe you can replace the wing nut with a plastic knob of the proper thread. Fred suggests adding an extra washer under the wing nut and putting a drop of oil on the threads from time to time. You might just replace the wing nut with a hex nut and tighten it with a wrench.

Base-to-Motor Squareness

Another flaw that sometimes undercuts the precision of the router is a base that isn't perfectly square to the axis of the bit. It is a problem with both fixed-base and plunge routers. With edge-forming cuts it is seldom a discernible problem, and even with shallow grooving cuts it is of little practical consequence. But on a deep cut, it can be annoying if precision is your goal. You cut a

mortise and tenon, and the assembled pieces won't lie flat.

How do you check your router? First check your collet for runout, as explained in "Router Maintenance" on page 43. To do this, you use a drill rod that is the correct size to tighten in the collet. After checking to ensure there's no appreciable runout, set a square against the router base and line up the blade with the rod.

The problem usually isn't with the base itself. The base is usually an aluminum casting. It's strong and rigid, and the bottom is flat. With some fixed-base routers, the base simply doesn't hold the motor square, and there doesn't seem to be a remedy. You need to be able to adjust the motor vertically to use the machine, so any shimming you do will last only until the next time you adjust the vertical height.

Try replacing the base. Get a new base, but before you actually buy it, see if it will solve the problem. If the new base won't solve the problem, there's no sense in buying

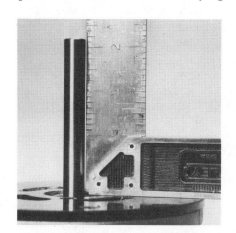

Your router's base must be square to the axis of the bit if you expect to make precise cuts. To check this, fit a drill rod in the collet and hold a square against the base beside the rod. This one looks pretty good.

it. If the problem is truly severe, you may have to replace the whole router.

With a plunge router, the problem is in the plunging mechanism. The rods may not be perpendicular to the base. Or, more likely, there's too much slop between the rods and the bores for them in the motor housing. A technician *may* be able to back out this slop, but I doubt it. Replacing the bearings that run on the rods may solve the problem. This is something you really should check either before you actually purchase the router or immediately after you buy it, so you can return it if there's a problem.

Setting an Edge Guide

In some router operations, you need to use an edge guide. An edge guide may or may not be supplied with your router. Plunge routers of European and Asian origin seem to have pretty good edge guides as standard equipment. The American manufacturers have a need, for some reason, to charge extra for the edge guide, but what they supply isn't usually very good.

The edge guide is a sort of shoe that attaches to the router base. It hangs just below the base, and it can be adjusted from a position surrounding the bit to one about 8 to 10 inches away. The guide slides along the edge of the work and ensures that the router's cut is parallel to it.

The guides that are supplied with Elu, Bosch, Hitachi, and Ryobi plunge routers—these are ones I've used—are dandy. You make coarse adjustments by sliding the mounting rods back and forth in relation to the base. Then you make fine adjustments with a vernier screw, which moves the guide itself in and out along the rods. These guides have fairly large plastic knobs, rather than wing nuts, to lock the rods and the guide in position. They are easy to adjust quite precisely, and they stay in position.

Most of the extra-cost guides I've tried are pretty dismal: The guide itself—the shoe—has a short contact surface, so it doesn't slide well along the work's edge. It lacks any sort of fine adjustment. The locking system uses thumbscrews, which aren't particularly secure. Usually, the guide mounts on two rods. Each rod is "locked" in a hole in the router base with a setscrew. Then the guide itself is secured on the rods with setscrews. What happens with these babies is that the router vibration shimmies the so-called setscrews loose, and as you rout, the guide slips out the mounting rods. Instead of a straight cut, you get an arc. Yet another router-induced headache.

My advice? If a guide comes with your router, try it out, evaluate how well it works, and if you're satisfied, use it. The two essentials are that

the guide must slide easily and that the setscrews must really set. If the guide fails on these points, toss it. If you have to pay extra, just make your own. The chapter "Dadoing and Grooving" has plans for a good guide you can make yourself. And in the chapter "Sliding Dovetail Joint," you'll find a plan for making a fixture with two edge guides, so you can trap the workpiece between them.

Holding the Workpiece

A final and vital part of setting up for a cut is anchoring the workpiece. You don't want the work to shift or slide away from you as you feed the router. Not only can it screw up your cut and ruin the work, it can put you at risk.

There are so many different variables that it's impossible to tell you how to clamp your work. In many situations, you simply have to clamp the work to a bench. Sometimes the clamps that secure a fence to the work can also secure the work.

Hand-held routing is full of these challenges: Holding the stock so you can move the router on it without

having the router tip and wobble, without hitting clamps, without having to move the clamps three times in the course of a single pass, and so forth. To me, the challenge is finding a way to secure the work that allows me to complete a cut in one operation. I just hate to unclamp, shift the work, and then reclamp it just to complete a single cut.

Here are some examples of measures you might take.

• To slot a narrow workpiece, you may need to wedge it somehow between two wider boards that will provide additional bearing for the router.

• To rout an edge treatment on a circular or oval blank, you may try "dogging" it—pinching the work between a bench dog and the vise's dog—on a narrow workbench, so the maximum amount of edge is overhanging the bench. After routing as much of the edge as possible, one shift of the workpiece exposes the remaining uncut edge.

• Small workpieces can be set on a router pad, which is somewhat like a very stiff carpet pad or the pad used with a computer's mouse. The router pad has enough "bite" to keep the workpiece from shifting as you rout.

• Sheets of sandpaper glued back-to-back can be slipped between a workpiece and the workbench to keep the work from sliding around. This is an effective way to keep a

This edge guide, an accessory for Bosch's newest plunge routers, has all the features you should look for in a guide. The plastic wing nuts that seat against the mounting rods are easy on the hands and vibration-proof. Loosening the wing nuts on the guide allows you to dial in the exact setting you need with the fine-adjustment knob. It's easy to set precisely, and it won't work loose during use.

A router pad provides traction between a workpiece and a work surface, keeping the work from sliding around, even when you maneuver a working router across it. This makes it a lot easier to rout the edges of small workpieces that are tough to clamp. The rubbery pad can be folded and cut with scissors (or the router bit or even the screw that secures the pilot bearing).

panel in place while you make a trammel-guided cut, for example.

• A clamp that secures a T-square to a workpiece can also secure the workpiece to the bench. It's a double-duty clamp.

• Hot-melt glue has enough strength to bond a template to a workpiece, or a workpiece to a bench. Yet it is too weak to resist a sharp mallet blow or a little prying with a chisel.

• A shop-made fixture with toggle clamps can expedite repetitive routing by making it easy to switch workpieces. Clamp or dog the fixture to a bench, then switch work by flipping the toggles open and closed.

WORK LOADS

Like every other power tool in your shop, the router does have limits. You do have to use some common sense in making a cut.

Just because your bit has a 1-inch-long cutting edge doesn't mean the router will make a 1-inch-deep cut in a single pass. Try it. Your router will probably tell you it's overloaded. It will start to bog down, losing speed sharply. If you persist, it will probably stall completely, maybe trip the circuit breaker, maybe burn up.

The conventional wisdom is that the router is a trimming machine. If you have a heavy cut to make, nibble at it: Make a sequence of light cuts. If you can make a rough cut on a table saw or band saw and remove a lot of the waste that way, do it.

The conventional rule of thumb is to cut about ¼ inch deep at each pass. This is safe and reasonable.

But as you get more experience in router work, you probably will come to view that rule of thumb as a little wimpy in many situations. If you are using a sharp ½-inch-shank bit, even a 1½-horsepower router can hog away more than ¼ inch of material. You have to listen to the router. Is it running free or starting to bog down? Is the bit whizzing through the wood, or is it chattering? Do you have to feed so slowly that the wood burns?

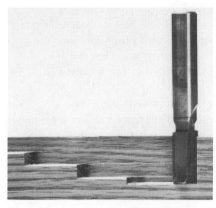

A plunge router's depth-stop system allows you to make a full-depth cut in several passes, each cutting progressively deeper. Using the turret stop allows you to control exactly how deep each pass cuts.

▶ Problem Solver

One of the most important things you can do to improve the accuracy of your router woodworking is to mill the working stock properly. The router is capable of incredible accuracy and precision, but it's usually dependent upon the surfaces and edges of the workpiece for guidance.

In hand-held operations, the router slides across the surface of the work. If the workpiece is bowed or twisted, if its surface is rough or rippled, the router won't be able to even them out. The cut may be of uneven depth; it may be choppy. When you're using a piloted bit, the pilot will telegraph any imperfections in the edge very visibly into the cut.

Make sure the stock is smooth, flat, and square.

A nick in the edge of the work is magnified by a piloted bit. If you bump the edge of a workpiece against a saw table or the like, plane the nick out before routing a profile.

The point of the rule is to get a good-quality cut without overtaxing the router and the bit. So consider the power of the router, the configuration of the bit, and even the hardness of the stock. Hard maple? Lighten up. Pine? Hog away. A ¼-inch straight bit? Take it easy, even if it's on a ½-inch shank.

Safety

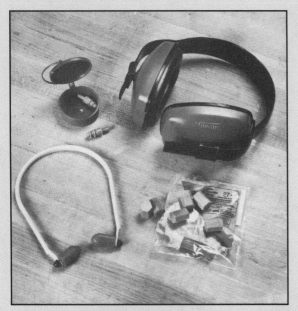

Three general types of hearing protectors are available.

Canal caps (lower left) are soft pads (usually foam) attached to a headband. The pads are supposed to cover the ear canal opening and seal it off. The headband is intended to keep the pads in place. If you put them on just right, they work fine, but they're tricky to put on correctly, and they are dislodged relatively easily.

Muffs (top right) generally work better than any other protectors. Their large pads cover the entire outer ear, sealing against the surrounding bone. The obvious drawback is that they're bulky. With protracted use, they squash the ears, and they make you sweat. So you end up putting them on and taking them off, putting them on and taking them off.

Ear plugs (top left) are designed for protracted use. You insert them in the ear canals and leave them there for the duration of your work session. There are many types—foam, wax, and rubber, air-cushioned plugs, and custom earmolds. Among the best ear plugs are those made of foam (lower right). Though labeled disposable, foam plugs are washable and can be reused.

Prominently displayed on the packaging is the Noise Reduction Rating, reflecting the number of decibels the protector will cut from a noise. The higher the number, the better the protection. As you make a selection, try to balance NRR with comfort and convenience. After all, the best NRR does you no good if you don't wear the protectors. If they aren't comfortable and convenient, you probably won't wear them.

For the best protection, insert foam ear plugs when you enter the shop, then put on muffs each time you use a power tool like the router.

A router is an intimidating tool. Oh, it's just a little package, but when you switch it on, it gives that startling jerk. And it runs roughly six times faster than your power saw or your drill. If you simply wobble it a little in the air as it runs, you can feel the dynamic power.

More than anything, it is the noise it makes that gets you. Not only is the usual router loud, but the shriek has a frantic urgency about it. The router just plain *sounds* dangerous. Nevertheless, the *gruesome* router injury is atypical. It's the long-term, debilitating injuries that are the router's primary threats.

The router's noise is a threat. Most people know that extended exposure to loud noise not only can, but will, cause impaired hearing. Of two sounds of equal intensity, the higher-frequency sound is more likely to cause hearing damage. So a router cutting at high speed, emitting its characteristic high-pitched whine, produces exactly the sort of sound that damages hearing.

Be smart. Wear your hearing protection.

The dust and chips a router spews are threats. Because of the barrage of particles the router produces, it's almost impossible to effectively use one without eye protection.

The dust that accompanies the chips is another ubiquitous hazard. The router can produce some pretty small particles that hang in the air for a long time. The routing action works like a seed spreader to scatter the stuff, and this makes it really difficult to accomplish any kind of source dust collection.

The only real protection available to us is to wear some kind of dust mask.

Safety is more than simply wearing goggles. It's working thoughtfully and staying alert. It's keeping tools in good repair and using the correct tool for each job. It's routinely cleaning up after yourself. It's having a helper around when you need extra hands, and not having distractions when you need to concentrate.

Here are some general safety guidelines:

• Be ready mentally for the work. Don't drag yourself into the shop if you are tired, irritable, distracted, or preoccupied.

• Dress the part. Leave the loose, showy jewelry on the dresser. Wear fairly close-fitting clothes, and roll up your sleeves. Don't underestimate the value of wearing comfortable clothes and shoes. Do wear goggles and ear muffs or plugs when appropriate. Use a dust mask when appropriate.

• Maintain a well-ordered workplace. Get yourself a big waste barrel, use it, and empty it regularly. Heavily engaged, the router generates mounds of chips. Sweep up as you work, picking up and tossing scraps. Keep tools and materials stored neatly, accessibly, and out of the way. Give yourself enough room to work.

• Know your tools. Read tool manuals and books, or take a course to learn how to adjust, maintain, and operate power tools correctly and safely. Take time to set up for a task, using firm work supports and whatever clamps, jigs, guides, or guards are necessary and appropriate.

• Plan your work. Sketch the project and note its dimensions and parts. Beyond that, visualize the tasks so you can control each operation. Don't stretch so far, in making a cut, that you lose your grip on and control of the router.

• Focus on the job at hand. A helper isn't helping if he or she distracts you. You need to concentrate.

Finally, don't be a cheapskate about safety. If you're willing to spend $200 for a router and hundreds more for bits, invest in top-quality eye and hearing protection. It shouldn't cost you more than $50 for goggles *and* a face shield, for muffs *and* some ear plugs, *and* a supply of nuisance-dust masks.

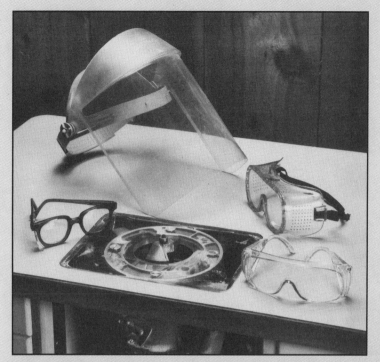

Eye protection is available for everyone. People who wear prescription glasses will find as many options as those who don't.

Safety glasses have two forms these days: the traditional spectacles with side shields (lower left), which can be fitted with prescription lenses, and the wraparound glasses (lower right), which will fit over prescription glasses. Both forms are made of impact-resistant, shatterproof plastic and are light and comfortable.

Goggles (top right) have a soft, usually vented, body and an impact-resistant and shatterproof polycarbonate lens. Their advantage over safety glasses is that they seat tightly against the face, sealing off the area around the eyes. (A lot of safety glasses leave gaps, notably between the rims and eyebrows.) They can be worn over prescription glasses. Goggles tend to fog up, though most makers offer models that are not supposed to.

Face shields (top left) protect the entire face, not just the eyes. Most models feature a curved, clear-plastic barrier to shield the face from ear to ear and from eyebrows to chin. This shield is attached to an opaque shell that protects the forehead, and the unit is attached to a headband.

When shopping for eye protection, look for a marking "Z87.1," the identifier for the eye protection requirements established by the American National Standards Institute (ANSI). If the eye protection is marked ANSI Z87.1 or just Z87.1, it is the manufacturer's guarantee that the protector conforms to the government standard and is suitable for use in the commercial or industrial workplace. The differences between eye wear that meets the standard and eye wear that doesn't is not obvious. Price differences will be minimal. Look for the ANSI marking.

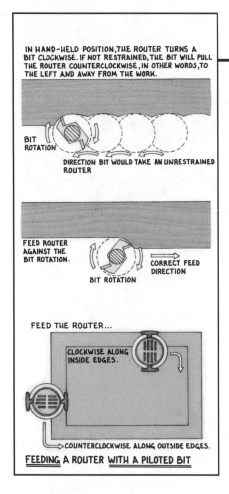

IN HAND-HELD POSITION, THE ROUTER TURNS A BIT CLOCKWISE. IF NOT RESTRAINED, THE BIT WILL PULL THE ROUTER COUNTERCLOCKWISE, IN OTHER WORDS, TO THE LEFT AND AWAY FROM THE WORK.

BIT ROTATION

DIRECTION BIT WOULD TAKE AN UNRESTRAINED ROUTER

FEED ROUTER AGAINST THE BIT ROTATION.

BIT ROTATION

CORRECT FEED DIRECTION

FEED THE ROUTER...

CLOCKWISE ALONG INSIDE EDGES.

COUNTERCLOCKWISE ALONG OUTSIDE EDGES.

FEEDING A ROUTER WITH A PILOTED BIT

FEED DIRECTION

All commercially available routers turn the same way, even in the Southern Hemisphere. If you hold the router with the bit down, in standard hand-held operating orientation, the bit will turn clockwise. This allows bit manufacturers to make all of their wares to cut the same direction, but it also allows us to make some rules about how to use the router safely and effectively.

A fair percentage of the work done by routers is edge work with a piloted cutter. That means that the cutter has a small end projecting down past the cutting edges. This projection rubs the edge of the workpiece and guides the cutter. Most piloted cutters have a ball-bearing tip to prevent undue friction and

burning of the wood. To be sure you feed the proper direction, the cardinal rule of router feeding for edge work is:

MOVE THE ROUTER OPPOSITE THE WAY IT WOULD GO IF YOU LET IT.

Confused? Here's a translation. Think of the router bit as a tire. Imagine that as you touch the spinning bit/tire to the edge of the workpiece, it smokes like a dragster and takes off along the edge of the work, with you along for the ride. That's the direction the router would go if you let it. But don't let it. Feed it the opposite way.

The main reasons you feed the router the opposite way are safety and control. You're dealing with a lot of power and speed, and they don't automatically take a break every time your human concentration does. If you feed the contrary way we suggest, you'll notice that when you slip, lose concentration, or get a little off balance, the router will minutely back up into an area that has already been cut. This allows the cutter to spin freely while you regain your balance and poise.

If you feed in the direction the router wants to go, which is called climb cutting, you'll probably do okay for a while. But sooner or later you'll relax a bit, and then what happens? The bit will climb right out of the cut—See! A climb cut—assume the character of a tire, and take you for that dragster ride. Usually not life-threatening, but certainly not dignified.

Of course, this is effective only so long as you're doing edge work with a piloted bit or with a fence, either of which prevents the cutter from "forging inland." With an un-

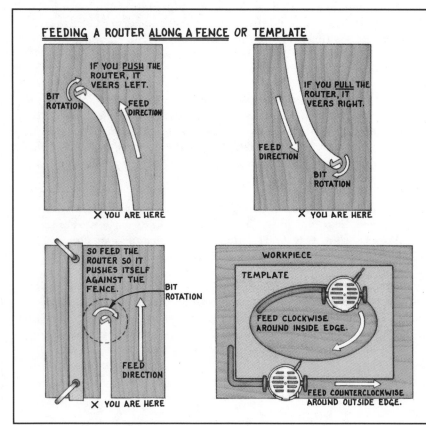

FEEDING A ROUTER ALONG A FENCE OR TEMPLATE

IF YOU PUSH THE ROUTER, IT VEERS LEFT.

BIT ROTATION

FEED DIRECTION

X YOU ARE HERE

IF YOU PULL THE ROUTER, IT VEERS RIGHT.

FEED DIRECTION

BIT ROTATION

X YOU ARE HERE

SO FEED THE ROUTER SO IT PUSHES ITSELF AGAINST THE FENCE.

BIT ROTATION

FEED DIRECTION

X YOU ARE HERE

WORKPIECE

TEMPLATE

FEED CLOCKWISE AROUND INSIDE EDGE.

FEED COUNTERCLOCKWISE AROUND OUTSIDE EDGE.

piloted cutter, you'll very quickly notice that as you push the router away from you, the rotation of the cutter will drag the router to your left. As you pull it toward you, it will claw its way to your right.

You can use that tendency to your advantage. Most router work, whether on edges or out in the middle of the stock, calls for straight lines or smooth curves rather than the jerky, jagged edges you'd get freehand. That means that most router work is done with either piloted cutters or some type of fence or template. In any of those cases this rule will apply:

FEED THE ROUTER SO THE CUTTER ROTATION PUSHES THE ROUTER AGAINST THE GUIDE.

From this rule come all of the more specific ones that say things such as "When you push the router the fence must be on the left; when you pull, the fence must be on the right," or "When you rout around the outside of a frame, go counterclockwise; when you rout around the inside of a frame, go clockwise." It's a lot easier to remember only one.

Splintering

Here's another dilemma: splinters. Anytime you rout across a board's end grain, you're going to get some degree of splintering as you exit at the corner. If you're routing all around a piece—say, something like a plaque—you can rout the ends first, letting the corners blow away. Then rout the long-grained sides, which will, in most cases, clean up the blown-out corners.

If you're not routing the long-grained sides—let's say you're cutting shelf dadoes in a cabinet side—you can't get away with the previous

ELIMINATE END-GRAIN TEAR-OUT
THREE OPTIONS

PROPER FEED DIRECTION

ONE: CUT END GRAIN AND LET CORNERS TEAR OUT.

PROPER FEED DIRECTION

LONG-GRAIN CUT WILL REMOVE TORN-OUT AREA.

PROPER FEED DIRECTION

TWO: BACK UP END GRAIN WITH SCRAP.

THREE: FEED IN PROPER DIRECTION ALMOST TO CORNER, STOP, AND CLIMB-CUT IN FROM CORNER.

CLIMB CUT

PROPER FEED DIRECTION

strategy. Here you need to clamp pieces of scrap stock to the edges where your cuts will exit. Cut right into the scrap, and let it support the good edges of the project to prevent blowout.

There's another splintering problem that's fairly common. It's one that takes a little more imagination to remedy. Sometimes, when you're routing along the edge of a board, the cutter will pull out a splinter from the area ahead of the cut. That's

always annoying, but it becomes a real problem when the grain "runs in" so that the split extends into the area that isn't supposed to be cut.

Let's take a quick look at what's really making the splinters. As the cutter arcs through the wood, it starts to cut nearly parallel with the grain. As it nears the edge of the stock, it is cutting almost perpendicular to it. This is the most difficult direction for the cutting action, as well as the weakest situation for the wood to

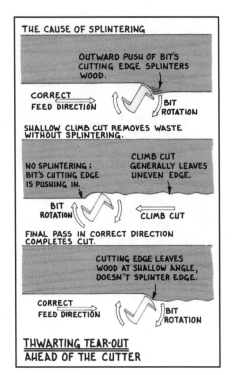

THE CAUSE OF SPLINTERING

OUTWARD PUSH OF BIT'S CUTTING EDGE SPLINTERS WOOD.

CORRECT FEED DIRECTION

BIT ROTATION

SHALLOW CLIMB CUT REMOVES WASTE WITHOUT SPLINTERING.

NO SPLINTERING; BIT'S CUTTING EDGE IS PUSHING IN.

CLIMB CUT GENERALLY LEAVES UNEVEN EDGE.

BIT ROTATION

CLIMB CUT

FINAL PASS IN CORRECT DIRECTION COMPLETES CUT.

CUTTING EDGE LEAVES WOOD AT SHALLOW ANGLE, DOESN'T SPLINTER EDGE.

CORRECT FEED DIRECTION

BIT ROTATION

THWARTING TEAR-OUT AHEAD OF THE CUTTER

resist splitting. The cutter passes a point where it takes less force to split the wood than to cut through it.

So what can we change to prevent splitting? Either make the bit cut better or make the wood stronger! Don't laugh; we can do both. Obviously, a sharp bit will cut more easily than a dull one. In many cases a shearing or spiral bit will cut more easily than a straight one. And anything you can do to "back up" the wood will help it to stay together.

Many router experts suggest that you take a light pass in the wrong direction—make a climb cut—to eliminate some of the outside wood where the angle of attack is too abrupt.

JIGS AND FIXTURES

In every chapter of this book, we try to answer that key woodworking question: "How do I get the job done with the router I have in my shop?"

And in every chapter, the answers involve jigs and fixtures that *you can make yourself*. In a few cases, you can *buy* a jig that does much the same thing. But why would you buy a commercial jig when you can realize two satisfactions by making it yourself? First, there's the joy of having successfully built it. Then there's the joy of having saved a lot of money.

When the jig is completed, your payoff is that it helps you do better woodworking and thus improves your skill level and your—yes—*satisfaction.*

I should point out that the difference between a jig and a fixture is purely technical. A *fixture* is something that "fixes" the work, holding it securely so the router can be moved over it. A vise is a fixture. A *jig* puts the work or the router through controlled movements (think of the dance known as the jig). It guides the cut, by guiding either the work or the router. A trammel is a jig. (A jig can have fixtures on it: A sled for the router table is a jig, and the toggle clamp on it is a fixture.)

One of the things that make woodworking so interesting is that there are usually several ways to accomplish the same task. For example, if you page through the chapter "Dadoing and Grooving," you'll find several different jigs and fixtures that'll enable you to cut accurate, consistent dadoes. There are several different fences (jigs) to use if you have a bit of the correct size for the dado you want to cut. There's one jig—the double-bar dadoing guide—to use if you want to cut, say, a ⅝-inch-wide dado with a ½-inch bit. And there's another—the fractionating baseplate—to use in conjunction with a fence to cut that same dado with that same bit.

There are some jigs and fixtures you'll build without a specific task in mind. Maybe you'll build a router table, knowing it will expand your router woodworking horizons, yet without knowing just how far in all directions those new horizons will stretch. If you are like me, you'll quickly take to wondering why you waited so long to get it built.

In making the jigs and fixtures in this book, keep in mind that jig making can be very creative and spontaneous. Solving problems is definitely an eclectic process. Most of the router jigs and fixtures in this book came into being because some woodworker faced a problem and found a way to solve it. He shared his solution with others, some of whom adopted his solution, but more of whom adapted it.

That's the evolutionary part of woodworking! You confront problems and struggle to find solutions. The more you read—in magazines, in books like this one—the better prepared you are to solve those woodworking problems. You've seen similar problems solved, you know the parameters of your particular problem, then one day, Pow!—it hits you. An adaptation is what you need.

In this book, you'll find detailed plans for making and specific instructions for using every router jig and fixture presented. If the jig suits your needs exactly, follow the directions exactly. However, if after reading about the jig or fixture you say to yourself, "This jig would work better for me if I . . . ," make it your own way! We've given you an idea and goaded you into creating your own design that'll solve your particular problem.

ROUTER MAINTENANCE

The most basic maintenance action you can take is to keep your router clean. It's a really simple thing, and we so often neglect to just dust the chips off. Use a dust brush or a dry cloth. That's all it takes.

Do you need to vacuum the motor? Or, as some experts suggest, blow compressed air through the vents in the motor housing?

I don't think either is vital. If you have the equipment, go ahead. I merely clean off the dust at the end of a session so the vents aren't blocked at the beginning of the next session, and so the fan doesn't suck a great charge of dust in when it's first started up. Routing puts a lot of dirt in the air, unfortunately, and when the machine is shut down, the dust settles. I don't think it settles inside the motor housing; it needs the fan's active help to get in there. If the machine can breathe dust and chips when it's operating, then it'll sur-

vive the little dust left inside when the fan stops.

Oh, compressed air is really great, don't get me wrong. But outside of commercial shops, how many of us have air compressors? I sure don't. I don't even have one on my wish list.

The router most at risk from dust is the one hanging under a table, especially in an enclosed cabinet. This is the router that doesn't get dusted off after every use. It does get dumped on whenever you run a dust brush across the tabletop; dirt almost always drops through the bit opening, settling into the collet and onto the motor. Presumably, this dust gets blown into the air the instant the router is turned on, since air flow is always from the brush end of the motor to the collet end. But if the router's enclosed, the cabinet can literally fill with chips and dust and smother the motor. That's one of the reasons why Fred never encloses a table-mounted router. (See the chapter "Router Table Design.")

A router hanging under a table gets neglected more often than not. You can circumvent a lot of router and collet problems by lifting the router out of the table, dusting it, and vacuuming the dust out of the collet every time you clean off the table.

Dusting off the machine provides an opportunity to check it over. Is the cord okay? Anything loose that should be tight? Any cracks? Is pitch streaked on the baseplate? If you pull the bit after each session, it's an opportunity to clean and check the collet, and maybe pull at the arbor to check the router bearings as well. These things get overlooked when you're concentrating on the

▶ Dust Collection

Don't be passive about woodworking dust. You can attack it two ways—by trying to capture as much of it as possible before it gets into the air, and by filtering the air you breathe through an appropriate mask.

Dust collection is problematic at best. A number of router manufacturers (notably Elu and Bosch) sell dust-collection accessories for their machines. Connected to a shop vac, these accessories do a pretty good job of capturing the chips and dust kicked up by the router during hand-held opera-

tions. The range of bits you can use in conjunction with them is somewhat limited, as is the range of operations. And not only do you have a power cord to deal with, you also have a vacuum hose to manage and a shop vac to keep at hand (but not underfoot).

If you are doing a protracted operation, it's prudent to combine the use of a collector with the wearing of a dust mask. Your nose is a pretty good dust collector, but if you overload it, which is easy to do, the dust will go straight to your lungs.

Elu's dust collection system has a clear plastic shroud around the bit, with a connection for a long, flexible hose. You connect the hose to your shop vac, and that provides the necessary suction and dust collection point. It works surprisingly well.

Rout a stack of pine boards, and you'll have a baseplate streaked with pitch. Clean off the pitch, and wax the baseplate at the same time, by applying paste wax with a plastic abrasive pad. The pad will loosen and carry away the grit and dirt. Then polish off the waxy residue with a dry cloth to keep the router sliding smoothly on subsequent jobs.

Particularly if it's used in a router table, a plunge router's plunging mechanism periodically needs to be disassembled, cleared of sawdust, cleaned, and lightly oiled. Blow out the bores in the motor housing, clean the springs, and burnish the rods with a Teflon-safe abrasive pad (if it won't scratch Teflon, the pad won't scratch the rods either). Lube the rods with a light machine oil, wiping it on with a soft cloth. Then reassemble the router.

bit and the setting you need for the next cut. But at the end of the job, you need to make sure the tool will be ready to use the next time you need it.

Don't you just hate it when you're all fired up about some woodworking, and you pull out a tool and discover you've got to tinker with it for 10 or 20 minutes, just to get it ready to use?

Bearings

We've probably all read articles by folks who seem to be bragging about how fast they wore out their router's bearings, as if that validates their seriousness as woodworkers. Don't let such stuff spook you. Unless you are in a commercial situation, where the router is running constantly, day in and day out, or unless you abuse the router by running out-of-balance bits persistently, its bearings are going to last a good long time.

This is true even though the router, spinning at 22,000 rpm, is harder on bearings than any other power tool.

Curiously, the bearings in a router wear most quickly when they are *not* under load. The device and its bearings are designed to run true when under load, which is what the engineer designs for, figuring that 99 percent of the time that the router's running it's under load. And mostly that's a safe assumption. You switch on the motor, make your cut, then switch it off. You seldom stand around with the motor just running . . . unless you have the machine mounted under a table. Then, instead of killing the power between cuts, you let it run. You aren't unclamping and clamping workpieces between cuts, you're merely setting one aside and

reaching for the next. And the router is wailing away the whole time. This is called "run on." Hard on the bearings. Don't let your router run on. Use a foot switch with your table-mounted router.

Worn bearings generate heat. The router should never be too hot to handle. If it is, failing bearings may be the cause. Worn bearings sometimes make popping or cracking noises. Slowly turn the arbor with your fingers. Hear anything? Or feel anything? A spot on every rotation where the arbor drags or slows down can be signaling a bad bearing. Try wiggling the arbor from side to side. Pull on it. See if it seems loose. Any play or looseness, any of what engineers call slop, tells you to have the bearings replaced.

Collet

The most troublesome part of the router—the collet—needs to be checked frequently. Remember that the collet is the connection between the power source and the cutter. If it isn't in perfect condition, a number of bad things can happen.

The usual collet ills stem from dirt and pitch. You inadvertently get some chips in the collet. Maybe it rusts a little or gets pitted. These little things can lead to slippage. If the slippage is egregious, both the bit and the collet can suffer galling, which is the damage that results when two unlubricated metal parts rub against one another.

Keep the collet clean and polished. If it gets pitch on it, use the appropriate solvent to remove it (even oven cleaner will work). (One note of caution: If you use a solvent, like lacquer thinner, that removes oils from the metal, you should follow up with a little WD-40 to prevent rusting. Blow or wipe off the excess.) Scour the outside regularly with fine steel wool or an abrasive kitchen pad. Brush the bore with a fine-bristled brass brush. What you want to do is prevent rust from attacking the collet. Rust is very hard to remove without affecting the size of the collet and without leaving a gritty residue that itself can contribute to bit slippage.

Even if you do give the collet this routine care, it can be damaged. It will wear out. Perhaps one of your bits has an undersized shank. It slips regardless of how you tighten the collet nut. Galling results. Maybe you've let a bit get too dull, and the clash between the router's power and the bit's resistance is too much for the collet. Slippage. Galling.

If the bit creeps out of the collet, regardless of how tight you jam the

While it's important to clean the collet and socket regularly, you don't want to use a cleaner that will abrade the surfaces. Repeated cleanings could conceivably alter the dimensions of the collet—remember that tolerances are measured in thousandths of an inch. Use a Teflon-safe abrasive kitchen pad to burnish the collet, its nut, and the arbor socket.

collet nut, one way or another you've got a collet problem. When the bit creeps out, it's undoubtedly cutting deeper than you intended and is possibly ruining your work. Obviously, that's bad.

If the bit develops rings around the shank, you know the bit is slipping—meaning it's spinning more slowly than the motor. In the worst of cases, the bit stops completely when it contacts the work. You can be pretty sure that either you didn't tighten the collet—it's possible!—or the collet is worn. If the rings are deep enough and extensive enough, the bit can be unusable.

If the bit bends or breaks, it is not unlikely that a worn collet contributed to its demise. Maybe it let the bit wobble. Maybe it let the bit shank creep out. It probably did both: The more it wobbled, the more it crept; the more it crept, the more it wobbled. Pretty quickly the bit's leverage overcomes the shank's strength.

I've never wrestled with a router that's spinning a bent-shank bit. My colleague Jeff Day, who has, tells me it's like wrestling with a vicious animal. You know you are barely in control. It's giving you the shaking of your life, and you know that if you relax for just a millisecond, it's going to bite you. Severely. So you do a weird bob and weave around the shop, trying to kick the plug out of the outlet to kill the motor, knowing that if you relax your grip enough to get to the switch, you'll lose control completely.

And very probably, the villain in this act is that one-ounce bit of metal: the collet. (The scene, by the way, is a pretty convincing testimonial for trigger and foot switches.)

Ordinary wear produces a condition known to machine tool tech-

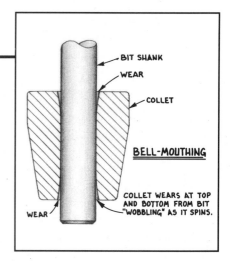

BIT SHANK
WEAR
COLLET

BELL-MOUTHING

COLLET WEARS AT TOP AND BOTTOM FROM BIT "WOBBLING" AS IT SPINS.

WEAR

nicians as "bell-mouthing." The ends of the collet bore get larger than the center portion. It's the sort of thing that happens when you try to pull a partially driven nail with your fingers. You wiggle it back and forth, trying to work it loose, and at the surface of the wood, the nail hole gets distorted and enlarged. Well, centrifugal force does the same thing to the bit that you did to the nail. It tries to pull it away from the axis of the arbor. When the bell-mouthing gets pronounced, the bit spins in an axis that's not concentric to the axis of the arbor. The measured difference between the two axes is known as runout.

A good way to monitor collet wear is to periodically check the runout. A machine tool technician will use a dial indicator to measure runout, but you can do it with a length of drill rod and a feeler gauge. (If you can't find a drill rod, you can buy a "Know Bit" from Woodhaven, listed in "Sources" on page 337. A feeler gauge you can buy at an auto-parts store.) Tighten the drill rod in the collet, and set the collet about 1 inch from the baseplate. Clamp a straight stick of wood or acrylic to the baseplate, tight against the side of the drill rod. Turn the router's arbor by hand; the rod should turn without separating from the stick. If a gap does open between the rod and the stick, measure the distance between them by gingerly fitting different feeler-gauge blades in the maximum gap. If you measure a gap of 0.005 inch or greater (technically, the runout is half this measurement), your router has too much runout.

Replacing the collet will probably correct the runout. But tug on the arbor a little to make sure the bearings aren't causing the problem. Then replace the collet and check the runout again. If the problem isn't solved, take the machine to a service technician for evaluation.

A very accurate reading of runout can be obtained with a dial indicator. While the magnetic base won't stick to a plastic baseplate, it can be clamped. Note that the router motor is backed down enough that the collet is an inch or so below the mounting plate surface. The indicator's contact point is against the drill rod, though it ought to be closer to the plate for a practical reading.

A usable runout measurement can be taken using inexpensive feeler gauges. We used a short piece of square aluminum tubing as the straightedge, clamping one end of it to the router with a spring clamp. You measure the runout by trial and error, fitting the gauges into any gap that opens between drill rod and straightedge when you rotate the rod very slowly.

Okay, it looks goofy. But the best way to assess the condition of the collet socket in the router's arbor is to feel it with your little finger. You'll be able to feel galls and the roughness of rust and tarnish more easily than you'll be able to see them.

Keeping Your Perspective

A critical element of router maintenance is maintaining your perspective. In several places, I've emphasized the worst problems. You need to understand that bits do occasionally break, do occasionally bend. Bearings do wear out. But the chances that you are going to have problems from the get-go are really slim.

Remember that a router is basically a pretty simple machine. There aren't a whole lot of things to go wrong. A quality router will last a long, long time.

CUSTOM BASEPLATES

The router's baseplate is smooth and slippery

so it can function as the bearing between the router's base and the workpiece. Made of a phenolic plastic, the baseplate is usually about ¼ inch thick, follows the contour of the base itself, has a hole for the bit and perhaps a viewing port or two, and is attached to the base with three or four screws. Almost invariably, it's the first part of the router you tinker with.

Custom router baseplates don't have to be fancy. Some are made as one-use throwaway items, such as when you want to attach a special fence or stop to the router without damaging the factory baseplate. Even more are built to be used again and again—a flush-trimming base, for example, or one with an edge guide. Some router woodworkers replace the factory base completely, never using it at all (except as a template for making custom baseplates).

To break the ice, simply unscrew the factory baseplate, set the screws aside, and remove the baseplate. Cut a square of plywood for a new, larger base. Use the factory baseplate as a template to lay out mounting holes in the custom baseplate. Drill and countersink (or counterbore) the holes, and cut a hole for the bit you want to use. Attach the new baseplate to the router and you're in business.

Once you've made a custom baseplate or two, you'll easily advance into the construction of all manner of router jigs and fixtures. You'll use the same materials and

employ the same skills in building the jigs and fixtures as you did in making the custom baseplates, and you'll expand the range of your router woodworking.

BASEPLATE MATERIALS

Router bases can be made from a variety of materials, all of which have advantages and disadvantages. While some of the materials cited below don't make good baseplates per se, they do make first-rate accessories.

Plywood is a good choice for quick bases. Birch plywood is fairly smooth and can be sanded, sealed, and waxed to provide a smooth-sliding baseplate. Plywood's worst problem is that the edges tend to get splintery and lose their accuracy. And, of course, ¼-inch plywood can have an annoying amount of flex in some applications. Sometimes you can use thicker plywood to gain rigidity, but you limit the depth of cut by raising the router away from the work.

Tempered hardboard is another good choice for a quickie. It is quite uniform with no voids or splinters,

ACRYLIC PLASTIC
POLYCARBONATE
PLASTIC LAMINATE

½" PLYWOOD
HARDBOARD
¼" PLYWOOD
⅜" PLYWOOD

Here are materials suitable for making custom baseplates. When choosing a material to use for a specific baseplate, think about how often you'll use it, what your appearance expectations are, and what you have on hand. Match the material to the job. Use scraps for single-use projects.

Upgrading the Mounting Screws

Some router manufacturers seem to cut corners on baseplate attachment. For example, they'll use slender little screws. They'll only use three. They'll use roundhead or panhead screws, and mold counterbores in the baseplate so the screwheads will be recessed, and thus kept from marring the work.

If your router is like this, try to find flathead screws of the same thread to replace the factory-supplied screws. And look into using screws of slightly greater length, too.

Here's the rationale.

Those factory-supplied screws are okay for attaching the factory-supplied baseplate. And they do allow some side-to-side adjustment of the baseplate. But when you switch to a baseplate with greater surface area or to one that will support the weight of the router, you're putting more stress on the fastening points. Counterboring weakens your baseplate right where it needs its maximum strength. Countersinking doesn't.

In addition, if you switch to a baseplate thicker than the one supplied by the factory, the stock screws may come up short. You need to be sure several of the screw's threads will engage those in the router base, especially if the router's going to hang from the baseplate, as in a router table. Go to a longer screw if necessary.

Finally, if the screws seem too frail, get out the drill and the tap. Bore out the holes in the base for larger-diameter screws, then thread the holes with the appropriate tap.

Here's one of the perils of making your own baseplates. I made a wide baseplate for our Porter-Cable plunger. Using the stock panhead/roundhead screws prompted me to counterbore the plywood too deeply, and the screws pulled through the plywood.

My old Black & Decker router is a swell little machine, but the screws used to attach the factory-supplied baseplate were too short to use with any baseplate thicker than 3/16 inch. Worse yet, the holes for the screws in the router base were unbelievably shallow; I couldn't just use longer screws, because they'd hit bottom before they'd cinch down the baseplate. With a little goading from Fred, I drilled the holes through the base, then retapped them. Now one set of screws can be used both for the relatively thin factory baseplate and for custom jobs as thick as 1/2 inch.

but you may have to apply several coats of sealer to prevent the edges from getting fuzzy. There are several grades of hardboard available, and for this purpose, the harder the better. Quarter-inch hardboard is suitable for many custom baseplates, though it may be a bit limber for some applications.

Some of the better grades of composites—chipboards, flakeboards—will work well for bases, particularly if you happen to have a bit of the fine-textured, applied-surface stuff known as signboard or medium-density fiberboard (MDF). The hitch with these latter materials is that you probably won't be able to find any less than 1/2 inch thick.

Plastic laminate is a great material to use in making custom baseplates because it wears well, slides easily on wood, and is easily machinable. By itself, of course, it can't be a baseplate; you have to back it up with plywood or some other material to make it structural. For a low-cost, durable baseplate that you'll be using again and again, it's worth the bother to cement plastic laminate to a 1/4-inch plywood base element. If you know anyone who does any counter or cabinet work, you can easily obtain router base-sized scraps of the material.

Acrylic and polycarbonate, two common plastics, are very popular for custom baseplates.

Acrylic may be more familiar to you as Plexiglas, the brand manufactured by Rohm and Haas, or as Lucite, the brand made by DuPont. There are other brands, as well as generics. This name game is true also of polycarbonate: You may have heard of General Electric's Lexan, or Rohm and Haas's Tuffak, without knowing both were brands of poly-

TRY THIS!

If you have to switch over to a custom baseplate for a quick operation, you can save yourself a little time if you attach the baseplate to the router with double-sided carpet tape. Cut three little pieces, and stick them on whatever baseplate is already screwed to the router. Peel the waxy protective paper from the tape's second side and press the baseplate you need to use in place. After the operation is completed, pull off the baseplate and peel off the tape.

carbonate, and without knowing that you could buy a "generic" polycarb and save a little money.

Both acrylic and polycarbonate plastics are pretty commonly available. They're stocked in sheets in a range of thicknesses, lengths, and widths, but you can usually buy odds and ends that are perfectly suited for baseplates. Best thicknesses: 1/4 inch and 3/8 inch.

The practical difference between the two types of plastic? The acrylic is crystal-clear, rigid, and quite strong, and as such is well regarded as a less fragile glass substitute. Nevertheless, it is possible to break. Polycarbonate, conversely, is very hard to break (it's the stuff safety glasses are made of), but it is less rigid than acrylic. Under stress, polycarb will tend to give, and the stress of supporting an 18-pound router can produce measurable sag. So make durable, unbreakable baseplates for hand-held routing from polycarb, and router-table mounting plates from acrylic.

Both materials are quite easily worked with carbide-tipped woodworking tools. These plastics are popular primarily because they are

available in clear sheets. Ostensibly, a baseplate made of either affords a nearly unobstructed view of the work at hand. But both plastics scratch easily, so after being used a while, baseplates made from them become webbed with scratches and thus fairly opaque.

Phenolic plastic is gaining popularity for custom baseplates. It's the material that the factory baseplates have been made of for years. Phenolic sheet is a hard, dense material made by applying heat and pressure to layers of paper or cloth impregnated with synthetic resin. The layers can be made of cellulose paper or cotton, synthetic fabric, or glass fabric. Under the heat and pressure, a chemical reaction—polymerization—transforms the layers into an industrial laminated plastic.

Phenolic wears and slides extremely well, it's heat resistant, and depending on a particular phenolic's composition, it can be very rigid and strong. It machines well and doesn't tend to melt and stick like the other plastics. Typically, phenolic plastic is brown or black.

The range of grades is bewildering, and it's difficult to know whether a particular piece will be suitable for your purpose. Try NEMA XX, the lowest grade. The cost of 1/4-inch phenolic in this grade is comparable to the cost of 3/8-inch acrylic, and so is the strength.

The problem with phenolics is availability. The plastics dealer who sells you scraps of acrylic and polycarb is unlikely to have scraps of phenolic around. Few of the wholesale-retail dealers even stock phenolics.

There are, however, a few mail-order tool companies offering small pieces of phenolic material for custom baseplate use.

Polyethylene is a lubricious white plastic that can be used to make accessories for baseplates and router tables. Because it is pretty soft and very limber, it isn't a great material for a baseplate. But for add-on guide strips, it's great. Credit that primarily to its inherent slipperiness. It's easily worked with woodworking cutters.

HOW TO WORK PLASTIC

Plastic has some worthy uses in woodworking, especially in making strong, practical baseplates, naturally slick router-table sleds, and virtually bulletproof router-table bit guards.

The plastics we are talking about here are easily worked with typical woodworking tools—saws, drills, sanders. And, yes, routers.

Acrylics and polycarbonates are easily scratched. For this reason, most of these plastics are covered on both sides with protective masking paper. Leave the paper on while you work. Do your layouts with a pencil on the masking paper. After you've cut it, bored the holes, and sanded the edges, peel the paper off.

Cutting

Almost any rigid plastic, from a laminate to an acrylic to a phenolic, can be cut on your table saw with a carbide-tipped combination blade. The band saw, fitted with a metal-cutting blade, cuts plastics well, especially curves. Of the portable power saws, the saber saw is the most versatile, since it will handle a range of cuts, from bevels to curves. It's especially good for cutting tight-radius curves. And don't forget the router.

With the appropriate bit (see "Bit Drawer" below), you can cut out your plastic baseplate, as well as plunge-bore a throat for the bit and slots for adjusting hardware. Equipped with either a pattern bit or a flush-trimming bit, your router will produce as many duplicate baseplates as you want from a pattern.

Acrylics and polycarbonates are thermoplastics, which means they are sensitive to heat. Generate too much heat in working them, and they'll gum up that work. So when cutting, back the blade out of the cut as soon as it starts to bind. The length of the band saw blade keeps it cool, so this is less of a problem with the band saw. (In addition, the band saw blade clears chips well, producing a very smooth cut.)

Use a flush-trimming bit to duplicate a router baseplate in clear acrylic. Bond the factory baseplate to the acrylic blank using carpet tape. Cut away most of the waste on the band saw or with a saber saw, then use the flush-trimming bit to trim the edge to match the factory baseplate.

Drilling and Counterboring

Drilling holes in plastic is more problematic than cutting it because of its incompressibility, brittleness, and/or low softening temperature. The usual advice is to use a high-speed twist bit that's been reground slightly to keep it from splitting or cracking the plastic. The idea is to change the cutting edges from an acute angle to a right, or even an obtuse, angle. What usually happens with an unaltered bit is that it augers into the plastic like a screw, rather than boring a hole. Chuck the customized bit in a variable-speed drill.

Clamp the plastic to a bench top or in a vise. Back it up with a clean board, and protect it from clamp or vise jaws with another wood scrap. Feed the bit into the work slowly and steadily; the drill's speed should be 500 to 1,000 rpm. If the hole is deep and the material a thermoplastic, back the bit out often to clear the chips. Don't stop the bit in the hole; it may get stuck there. As the tip nears the breakthrough point, slow the bit even more.

All this advice notwithstanding, I've found that standard brad-point

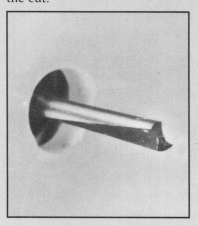
TRY THIS!

You can make a custom baseplate that'll accommodate standard template guide bushings. To bore the rabbeted bit opening, use two Forstner bits.

To ensure that the opening is concentric to the bit axis, mount the blank on the router and use a V-groove bit to just mark the center of the opening. Remove the baseplate from the router. On the drill press, first bore through the plate at the centerpoint with a ⅛-inch drill bit. Switch to a 1⅜-inch Forstner bit, and with an in-and-out action, drill the counterbore. The bit's center spur should locate the hole using the ⅛-inch center hole. Be sure you don't bore all the way through the plate, but do bore deep enough that the bushing's flange will be flush with or below the surface. Complete the hole with a 1¼-inch Forstner bit. Again, to bore the hole, feed the bit hard for a second, then back it completely out of the work. Feed again briefly, then back out. Repeat this in-and-out action until the bit completely penetrates the plastic.

bits and even Forstner bits work just fine. Drill the hole with an in-and-out action, so things have a chance to keep cool—cool enough, anyway, to prevent the plastic from melting. A standard countersink similarly works just fine for countersinking mounting holes.

Be particularly careful when drilling large holes, since this operation can create enough heat to soften the plastic and make it stick to the bit. If possible, use a good sharp hole saw at slow speed to cut the center hole in your custom bases. Or try drilling a small hole, then enlarging it with a router and bit. If you have a template with the proper-sized hole—the factory baseplate, for example—attach it to your plastic with double-sided carpet tape. Drill a starter hole, then use your router with a flush-trimming bit or a pattern bit to enlarge the hole. Either bit's bearing rides the template, while its cutting edge makes the cut.

Bending Acrylics

The acrylics—and thermoplastics in general—have the useful property of becoming pliable when heated. This means you can easily bend them into new shapes. The working temperatures range from 250° to 300° F, which is within the realm of your kitchen's range and your shop's heat gun. (While this bit of know-how may not be useful in making baseplates, it may be handy in making router-table accessories and other jigs and fixtures.)

The general procedure is to heat the plastic, then form it quickly, before it cools. Because it has "memory," the acrylic has to be bent a little beyond any angle you want—say, 5 degrees beyond it—and allowed to come back to the finished angle. There you hold or clamp it for a few minutes until the plastic has cooled and recaptured its rigidity. Make a mold for the plastic, by all means, even if it is merely a wood block over which you bend and clamp the warm and pliant plastic.

Bear in mind that your acrylic will have rounded edges where you bend it. Thus, if you do use a wood block as a form, bevel its edges to accommodate this characteristic of the plastic. If a sharp interior corner is essential, you can achieve it by routing a V-groove along the axis of the bend before the acrylic is heated; the groove's depth should be half the thickness of the plastic. When bent, the groove will form a sharp inside corner.

The procedure isn't totally trouble-free, of course. Both underheating and overheating cause problems. If the plastic is bent before reaching the proper temperature, small cracks, called crazing, may appear. On the other hand, if the plastic is left too long in the heat, it will bubble and scorch, yielding an uneven, rippled shape. In either case, the bends will be weakened.

To make a single bend, you can probably heat the plastic satisfactorily with a heat gun. Otherwise, heat it in an oven preheated to 300° F. Lay the plastic—with the masking paper removed, of course—on a clean, flat cookie sheet and put it in the oven, leaving the door slightly ajar. A ¼-inch-thick piece of acrylic should "bake" about 10 minutes.

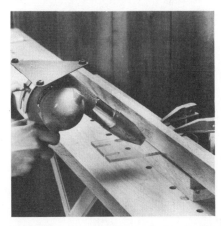 

Here's how we bent one of our acrylic bit guards. The acrylic is clamped between two wood blocks and heated with a heat gun. Play the blast of hot air back and forth along the area you will bend; in this case, you need two bends, which are close enough together that you can do both at once. As the plastic becomes flexible, use a third wood block—don't burn your hands on the plastic—to bend the plastic down and into. Clamp the block until the plastic cools.

▶ Sources for Plastics and Hardware

You can buy most plastics over the counter. The retailer often will cut a piece to the size you want, rather than insisting that you buy a stock sheet. And because he cuts to order, he'll likely have an assortment of odd-sized scraps you can pick through and buy cheaply.

What retailer do you go to? Look in the yellow pages under "Plastics." Most regions will have a choice of suppliers, maybe even one near *you.*

If you'd prefer to shop by mail, page through your woodworking tool catalogs. Most diversified tool catalogs list acrylic and polycarbonate—usually in foot-square pieces—specifically for custom router bases. A few have pieces of phenolic plastic drilled and slotted for mounting specific routers in a table. And at least one—Trendlines—sells foot-square pieces of phenolic for you to turn into your own custom baseplates.

Clearing the Throat

Factory baseplates have a throat opening sized to accommodate a template guide bushing. When you want to use a template guide, it's just the right size. But in many other situations, it can be just the wrong size.

If you are working on a narrow workpiece, this opening is big enough that it can make it difficult to support the router, especially at a corner or the end of the piece. The danger is that as the end or corner passes underneath the throat, the router might tip,

causing the bit to gouge the work. In this situation, you want the throat to closely match the diameter of the bit you're using.

On the other hand, a big bit may not fit through the guide bushing–sized throat. Here you want a BIG opening.

With your own selection of baseplates, you can tailor your equipment to the job. Make one baseplate with a ¾-inch throat and another with a 2- to 2½-inch throat. Keep the factory baseplate for template-guided work.

Joining Plastics

Plastic can be joined to plastic or to wood or to metal. Use common mechanical fasteners like bolts and screws. Or use glue. Though both approaches are familiar to every woodworker, there are some novel twists in how these apply to plastics.

Take the fastener approach first. Here are a few twists:

• Use wood screws in acrylics and polycarbonates. Clamp the assembly together and drill a pilot hole, making it slightly smaller than the screw's outside diameter, and as deep as the screw is long. With a propane torch, heat the screw till it's deep blue. *Push* it into the pilot hole. The plastic will melt and conform to the

screw's shape. When the screw is cool, remove it with a screwdriver, and replace it with a new screw.

• Cut threads in acrylic or polycarbonate with a tap. You then can turn a machine screw directly into the plastic, eliminating the need for a nut. Drill a pilot hole of a diameter halfway between the inside and outside diameters of the fastener's threads.

• Use self-tapping screws designed for use in metal. When turned into a pilot hole, a self-tapping screw will cut its own threads. (Repeatedly screwing and unscrewing this fastener destroys the threads, however, so use it only where assembly is a once-and-done proposition.)

You can, of course, just use machine screws with nuts or bolts with nuts. Easy and familiar and practical and effective. Connect, for example, two pieces of plastic, a piece of plastic and a block of wood, or a plastic bit and a metal part. Use washers for best results.

When it comes to *bonding* plastic to plastic, wood, or metal, forget the familiar glues. They probably won't be satisfactory. Instead, you need epoxies and special cements and solvents. Check the table below. To glue the plastic listed in the left column to various materials, use the bonding agent listed in the appropriate adjacent column.

Although you may never have

plastic . . .	to itself	to other plastic	to wood	to metal
Acrylic	Solvent Acrylic cement	Acrylic cement	Acrylic cement	Contact cement
Polycarbonate	Solvent Polycarb cement	Synthetic rubber adhesive	Epoxy	Epoxy
Phenolics	Epoxy	Epoxy	Contact cement	Epoxy Synthetic rubber adhesive

To tap threads in a piece of plastic, you must first drill the hole to be tapped. Most taps are labeled with their size along with the size of the drill bit used to bore the pilot hole. Fit the tap in the tap wrench. Dip the tap in soapy water and, working clockwise, slowly twist it into the hole. Back it out of the hole periodically to clear it of plastic chips.

used contact cement or epoxy, you certainly have heard of them. Less familiar, perhaps, is synthetic rubber adhesive, which refers to the range of caulklike adhesives stocked by every hardware store and building center. (Silicone-based adhesives work here, too.) Solvent and acrylic cement are probably new to you;

Fence-Rider Baseplate

Simple to make, this baseplate has a long, straight edge that rides any fence you clamp to your workpiece, hence its name. The fence-rider has three benefits.

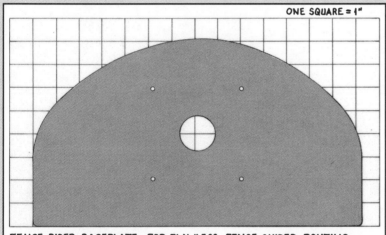

ONE SQUARE = 1"

FENCE-RIDER BASEPLATE FOR FLAWLESS, FENCE-GUIDED ROUTING

For routing along a straightedge, the fence-rider baseplate can't be beat. The baseplate design makes setup a snap and your cuts arrow-straight. The laminate-clad plywood we used is slick-sliding, too.

First—and most obvious—it provides a long bearing surface to ride along any fence you clamp to a workpiece; you won't get a gouge or snipe at the beginning or end of a cut, where the round factory baseplate might lose contact with a short fence. Your cuts will be straight, too: The baseplate won't telegraph every dip and dent in your fence.

Second, it's dimensioned so the measurement from the bearing edge to the center of the collet is an easy-to-remember 4 inches. (Not something like 2$\frac{5}{16}$ inches, the measurement on one router I've used.)

Third, the cuts you make will be consistently placed from the bearing edge. On many "stock" routers, the baseplate isn't concentric to the collet. If you twist the router a little as you slide it along the fence, the position of the cut swerves, giving you an uneven cut. The fence-rider's long bearing edge eliminates this maddening router foible.

The baseplate is an elementary project. Copy the layout from the drawing, duplicating it on your choice of materials. Cut it out. Using the factory baseplate as a template, mark the locations of the mounting-screw holes. Drill and countersink the holes,

then attach the baseplate to the router. Cut a ¼-inch-diameter bit hole by switching on the router and advancing the depth of cut to plunge the bit through the baseplate. Measure 4 inches from the center of this hole to the fence-riding edge of the baseplate. Mark it. Remove the baseplate from the router and trim the edge. Finally, enlarge the bit hole.

The baseplate shown we made from ¼-inch plywood. It's covered on both sides with plastic laminate, which makes it smooth-sliding. The laminate, incidentally, reinforces the plywood enough to permit the use of the "stock" panhead mounting screws, sunk in counterbores.

both are sold by the same retailer who sells the plastic.

Of the latter two bonding agents, solvent *sounds* easier to use, but for router jigs-and-fixtures work, the acrylic cement may work better.

The solvents used effectively weld the plastics together. The parts to be joined are assembled, then the solvent—usually methylene dichloride—is applied along the seams with

Solvent is a good way to bond two pieces of acrylic. The joint should be tightly fitted. Clamp the two parts together, as shown, and apply the solvent along the seam. Solvent is packaged in a plastic squeeze bottle with a handy syringe-type applicator top that makes this easy to do.

Offset Baseplate

So many router operations involve shaping an edge. You perch the machine on the work, but more than half of it is unsupported. Okay, maybe you keep the handles aligned with the edge of the cut. But as often as not, you've got one handle over the work, the other out there in "unsupported" territory. It's a balancing act.

So is it any wonder you occasionally bobble, tipping the router and sniping the edge?

An offset baseplate like this can help you prevent those bobbles. Its oblong shape changes a router's balance. It has a hefty knob at its farthest reach, so you can outleverage the bobble.

The baseplate is a fairly simple project. Copy the layout from the drawing, duplicating it on your choice of materials. (We used a piece of ⅜-inch polycarbonate.) Cut it out. Using the factory baseplate as a template, mark the locations of the mounting-screw holes and the bit orifice. Drill and countersink the holes. Cut the bit hole.

Install the knob next. We used a cherry knob that Fred turned. The knob is patterned—roughly, anyway—after the one on a Stanley plane. Install a threaded insert in your blank, then use it to mount the blank on the lathe. After turning and finishing the knob, drive a flathead machine screw through the baseplate into the threaded insert.

Not a turner? Page through some hardware catalogs. Reid Tool Supply Co., 2265 Black Creek Road, Muskegon, MI 49444 (800-253-0421), sells a 1⅞-inch-diameter black plastic knob (part #DK-320) that looks perfect. Mount the knob, then mount the baseplate on your router.

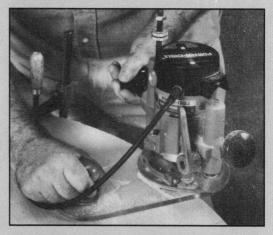

An offset baseplate is easily made and eminently useful for edge-routing. Hold down on the offset knob to keep the router from tipping, and push or pull the router along the edge with one of its knobs.

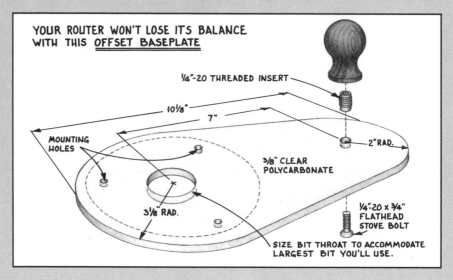

YOUR ROUTER WON'T LOSE ITS BALANCE WITH THIS **OFFSET BASEPLATE**

¼"-20 THREADED INSERT

10⅛"

7"

MOUNTING HOLES

2" RAD.

⅜" CLEAR POLYCARBONATE

3⅛" RAD.

¼"-20 x ¾" FLATHEAD STOVE BOLT

SIZE BIT THROAT TO ACCOMMODATE LARGEST BIT YOU'LL USE.

a brush or syringe. So long as the joint is perfectly matched, capillary action pulls the solvent into the joint. There it softens the plastics, allowing them to intermingle and, as the solvent evaporates, to fuse. If the joint is not perfectly fitted, the solvent will be pulled in only here and there, and the bond will be spotty.

You can circumvent this somewhat by soaking one part in a shallow puddle of the solvent, then pressing it to the other part. Still, when using the solvent, it's best to have tight-fitting joints.

The acrylic cement, on the other hand, works best in gappy joints. Two constituents, a resin and a hardener, are mixed, and the resulting syruplike cement is applied with a syringe. Usually, it will form a reinforcing fillet along the seam.

Polishing the Edges

If you are as meticulous about finishing your jigs and fixtures as you are about finishing your woodworking projects, you may want to smooth and polish the cut edges of your plastic baseplate. It's a several-step process, and if you're like us, you'll probably compromise by scraping the rough spots and beveling the edges just enough to eliminate their sharpness.

Uncompromising? Then scrape and file the edges to remove rough edges and tool marks. Sand those edges next to remove the scars of scraping and filing. And finally, buff

▶ *TRY THIS!*

Edges can be "flame polished" quickly and easily. Use your propane torch. Just pass the edge of the plastic through the flame. When you do it just right, the heat melts the plastic enough to smooth out the roughness and add a sheen. It's like an ice cube that's just started to melt.

Don't let the flame dwell on one spot. The melting progresses to the bubbling, warping, gooey-mess stage in the blink of an eye. Sweep the flame over the edge. Examine the result. Sweep again, and examine. Keep it up until you have the edge appearance you want.

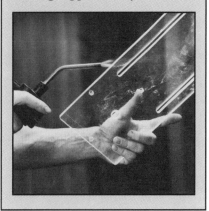

and polish the edges to bring them to a high gloss.

For the first step, use a regular cabinet scraper. Clamp the plastic between wooden cauls in a vise. Position the scraper across the plastic's edge, tilting it back toward you at an angle of about 60 degrees. Pull the scraper toward you; never push it away. Use moderate pressure and long strokes to avoid creating depressions in the piece. Use a file to smooth interior cutouts where a scraper won't fit. Smooth-cut rasps and bastard-cut mill files are best. Rub chalk over the file to keep it from sticking.

Sanding is next. Abrasive papers for plastics are available in hardware stores. Because the heat of sanding can soften most thermoplastics, you should wet sand the plastic. Wet the sandpaper and the work at the outset, and rinse them at regular intervals as you work. Repeat the process with progressively finer grades of paper. Using a power sander is okay, so long as you keep either the sander or the plastic in constant motion, avoid extreme pressure, and frequently wet the surface being sanded.

Like sanding, buffing can be done either by hand or mechanically. Use a buffing compound, selecting one used for metal. Apply the compound to the buffer, then buff the plastic with it. Next, wash the plastic with soap and water to remove the abrasive buffing compound, and finally, polish your baseplate with paste wax.

See Also . . .

Page 250 for a baseplate with an adjustable fence for rabbeting and grooving.

Page 185 for an edge band-trimming baseplate.

Page 197 for an extra-wide baseplate for surfacing.

Page 230 for a baseplate that allows you to widen any straight bit's fence-guided cut by 1/16 to 3/16 inch.

ROUTER TABLE DESIGN

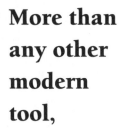

More than any other modern tool, the router has changed the way we work wood. Its ability to be an all-purpose cutter, groover, molder, and shaper has encouraged a revolution of creative ways to use a router in home shops and small production shops. When you mount a router upside down in a stationary table, it works like a small shaper, but it's more versatile than that: Now you can bring the work to the router. Good ideas get around. As the use of router tables has expanded, manufacturers have responded by offering larger, more powerful routers and a greater variety of bits, many intended for router table use exclusively.

The reasons to hang your router under a table are many. To begin with, the table holds the router securely, leaving both your hands free to manipulate the work. This is particularly advantageous when the workpieces are small or odd-shaped things that would be difficult to clamp. Furthermore, the table upends the router, exposing the bit, so on through cuts or edge work, you can see what the bit is doing to the wood.

The table provides a surface larger than the router base to support and reference your work. It's a surface you can clamp things to, or screw things to, giving you an extensive options list—fences, stops, hold-downs, and commercial or homemade jigs.

DESIGN ALTERNATIVES

To realize its full potential, a router table should be carefully designed. You can make a router table as simple or as complex as you want.

Most of the Build-Your-Router-Table plans you'll see are for full-blown (even overblown) "industrial models" that do everything and have options for even more. But don't feel that you have to have a 24-inch by 36-inch Formica top mounted on

a million-dollar cabinet. For some woodworkers, a piece of plywood clamped over a couple of sawhorses is all that's needed. Cut a hole in the center and hang the router in it. Consider the *other* possibilities shown in the photos below.

When you first think about a router table, think about what you are going to rout on it and about what router you are going to use. Ask yourself where you are going to put it. (Do you have a spacious shop, or only a tight corner?) The answer to this—along with your thoughts on what work you'll be doing and what router you'll be using to do it—may help you determine how big the tabletop will be. A foot square? One foot by 2 feet? Two feet by 3 feet?

And how will that tabletop be supported? Short pedestal legs to clamp to a bench top? A small plywood box for bench-top use? Trestle legs of some sort, or a leg-and-apron structure? How about a full cabinet, with storage for bits and accessories?

Router Placement

While we're at this stage of the design, here are two recommendations for you to consider.

1. Offset the router toward the front of the tabletop.

2. Don't completely enclose the router in a cabinet.

Offsetting the router does several things. First, it makes the router table more comfortable to use, by locating the center of the action—the router bit—close to you. You don't have to bend and reach. For most operations, you need support on the left and right, not between

Need to conserve space in a small shop? Hang a router from your table saw's extension wing. This homemade table extends the saw's capacity to accommodate full-sized sheet goods, and it doubles as a router table. The rip fence can double as a router table fence.

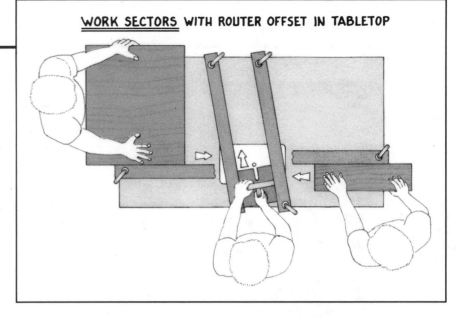

the bit and the table's edge. For those occasional operations that do need broad support between bit and edge, address the table from the back.

Keeping the router close to one edge also allows you to use a sled rather than a miter gauge. (See the chapter "Router Table Accessories.") A sled does the same work as a miter gauge, but it rides against the table's edge rather than requiring a slot in the table. Slots are a nuisance: They gather dirt, they catch your work and cause mistakes, and they usually cause your table to warp.

With the router offset, you can run a support under the center of the table to ensure that it stays straight.

Finally, if the router is close to the front edge, it is accessible. It's easier to adjust. You can even change

bits without taking the router out of the table, a really handy feature. Even if you use a drop-in mounting plate, even if you routinely pop the machine up out of the table to change bits, there will be times when you'll want to adjust the router without moving it. For example, you want to hog out

a groove with a straight bit, then switch to a dovetail cutter for a final pass. If you leave your fence set up, you know that the final pass will center up on the groove cut by the first pass. But nine times out of ten, the fence is across the mounting plate. If you're going to save your setup, the router has to be accessible.

But there's another aspect to accessibility—openness. If the router's behind doors, it isn't particularly accessible. That's one of the reasons Fred and I recommend that you *not* completely enclose your router in a cabinet.

The second reason has to do with the router's longevity. Your router needs some breathing room. An electric motor, especially one under load, generates heat. And routing generates chips and dust. Your best efforts at bit-side dust collection notwithstanding, chips and dust are going to funnel out of the cut and cascade down over your router. Enclosing the router—concealing it behind doors, for example—will keep all the dust and heat in. In that constricted area, it will have to recirculate the same air over and over. The router's fan will suck the heat and dirt through the motor. Clearly, this is bad.

If you're cramped for space, try hinging a work surface to the wall. Swing-out braces or legs (or drop-down legs) support the tabletop when it's in use, and they fold or collapse out of the way when the table drops (or is raised) against the wall. This configuration limits some operations, but it saves a lot of space and can be better than no table at all.

If you're into doing a lot of small, detailed work, try building a bench-top model. This configuration is well suited for small-scale work, because you don't have to bend over to see what you're doing.

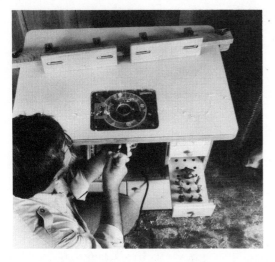

With the router offset toward the front of the router table, it's easy to change bits without removing the router. You can sight through the clear baseplate to see the collet nut, and the wrenches are long enough to clear the edge of the tabletop.

Don't take these recommendations as arguments against mounting your router tabletop on a cabinet. That's not what they are. Build a cabinet, by all means, including bit and accessory storage. But somehow create an open area for the router, so it is accessible and well ventilated. See the chapter "Cabinet Router Table" for an example.

MATERIALS AND CONSTRUCTION

It's interesting how router table design and construction has evolved. If you were following woodworking periodicals 10 or 15 years ago, you saw plans for smallish bench-top units: maybe a three-sided plywood box with a ¾-inch plywood tabletop, or something with short legs. Often, the router was hung directly from the tabletop—you'd rout a recess in the plywood and hang your machine from the ¼ or ⅜ inch of material left. Or you'd cut a hole in the plywood, then hang the router from a piece of hardboard with which you covered the entire tabletop. (A tempered hardboard surface would be slicker than plain plywood.)

Then a crafty woodworker modified a sink cutout, purchased cheaply at the local lumberyard, and captured the slickness and durability of plastic laminate for the router tabletop. With this sort of tabletop, a mounting plate was needed. Usually, it was an aluminum plate.

More recently, woodworkers have been applying plastic laminate to both sides of a plywood, particleboard, or medium-density fiberboard (MDF) substrate, then cutting a hole in it and suspending the router from a mounting plate of acrylic, polycarbonate, or even phenolic plastic.

The older approaches are generally regarded, these days, as deficient. But remember that a decade ago, the typical router was a 1- to 1¾-horsepower model that weighed 6 to 8 pounds. Three-horse, 18-pound behemoths weren't common. A lot of those old tables were built, and many are still in use.

Consider the criteria for a good router tabletop. (This is the most important part of the router table, after all.) It must be flat, strong, and stable, must both withstand and dampen vibration, must have a hard, tough, slick surface. It must also be made of fairly commonplace materials, ones that can be purchased in small towns across America and that can be worked in the typical home woodworking shop.

MDF is a good core material. It is dense, made up of very fine particles, and very stable. But it isn't as readily available as plain fir plywood. If you have access to it, if you like it, then use it. But laminate *both* sides to maintain its flatness.

Particleboard is probably okay as a core for your tabletop. While some routerheads recommend particleboard for this use, others contend that it disintegrates from the vibrations of a router. My guess is that a behemoth router and a cheap particleboard make a poor partnership. For an occasional-use table equipped with a midsized router, particleboard is probably okay. For a heavily used table with a big router, go to plywood. As you may know, particleboard is a sheet product composed primarily of sawdust and glue. It has no grain structure, so it lacks

The first router table Fred made for the Rodale shop—built about 12 years ago and still in regular use—has an aluminum mounting plate. Over the years, having been used with a half-dozen different routers, it's acquired enough perforations to be called the Holey Router Table.

Plywood can be edged several ways. You can carefully square the top before applying the laminate, then laminate the edges as well as the faces (center). You can apply the laminate, then glue on ½- to 1-inch-thick edge banding cut from maple, oak, or other durable hardwood (top). Or you can edge-band the plywood and run the laminate out to the edge of this assembled core (bottom), which is how we handled the tabletop in the router-table project "Cabinet Router Table."

plywood's strength. It's made in a variety of grades for a variety of purposes, but it surely is the most common substrate for laminate-covered kitchen counters. Thus, the sink cutouts I mentioned are likely to be particleboard.

As far as I can tell, the big motivation to use a sink cutout for something like a router tabletop is that it's already laminated. Oh, and it's cheap. The hitch is that your tabletop should be laminated on both sides if it is to maintain its flatness throughout the seasons. The low price and the labor saving thus may be illusions. You buy the cutout, but you still need laminate and contact cement. You laminate the second side, but you still have a less-than-ideal tabletop because it's particleboard inside.

Plywood, in my book (*this* book), is the ideal substrate. Because its individual veneers have grain direction and strength, and because these veneers crisscross in layers, plywood has great strength that the other sheet goods don't. The big shortcoming of plywood is that it isn't always perfectly flat. You can compensate for this, however, if you glue up a substrate from two pieces of the plywood. You will probably do this, since in most instances you'll want a tabletop at least 1 inch thick.

CONSTRUCTING THE IDEAL TOP

The ideal tabletop has a 1- to 1½-inch-thick plywood core with plastic laminate on both sides. The dimensions of it, other than the thickness, are pretty much irrelevant. It can be small enough (say, 14 inches by 24 inches) to use for a bench-top router table, or large enough (say, 48 inches by 30 inches) to serve also as a table saw outfeed (or as a multirouter workstation). The materials used and the method of construction remain the same.

1. Cut two pieces of plywood to size. Standard fir plywood is fine, but choose the sheet carefully. The crowned face of each piece—regardless of its quality—must be oriented to the inside when you glue them together; this is how you create a flat, balanced top. Since either could end up as the work surface, both faces of each piece should be as smooth and defect-free as possible.

2. After assessing the pieces for crowning and face quality, spread yellow glue on what you've selected as the mating faces. Using a brush, roller, or makeshift trowel, put on a thin but thorough coating, avoiding dry spots. When both surfaces are ready, lay one carefully atop the other.

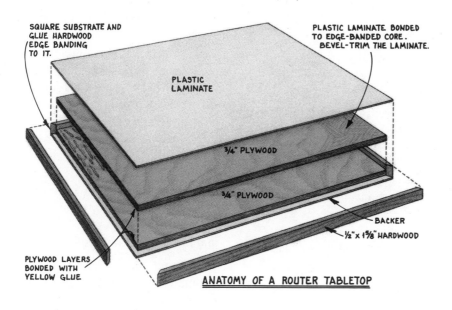

SQUARE SUBSTRATE AND GLUE HARDWOOD EDGE BANDING TO IT.

PLASTIC LAMINATE BONDED TO EDGE-BANDED CORE. BEVEL-TRIM THE LAMINATE.

PLASTIC LAMINATE

3/4" PLYWOOD

3/4" PLYWOOD

PLYWOOD LAYERS BONDED WITH YELLOW GLUE

BACKER
½" x 1⅝" HARDWOOD

ANATOMY OF A ROUTER TABLETOP

Keeping That Top FLAT

How many times have you experienced this at the lumberyard?

You pull the top sheet from the stack of plywood. The exposed face has picked up moisture from the open air, while the other face, having been virtually sealed against the sheet beneath it, has stayed drier. Is this sheet flat? Though we think of sheet goods as being *flat*, we all know from experience that they aren't. One face gets damp, the other stays dry: The sheet cups.

If you apply laminate to one side of plywood or particleboard or even medium-density fiberboard (MDF), you are setting it up for a warp. The laminated side will stay dry, but the unlaminated side can pick up moisture. The panel is out of balance. The damper side will expand, and the panel will cup. In context, your router will be in a subtle saucer.

You want a FLAT tabletop. So...

• Laminate both faces to create a balanced panel that will stay flat.

• Seal the edges as well. If you apply hardwood edge banding, seal it with a couple of coats of finish.

• Paint or otherwise seal the edges of the mounting plate opening.

• Forget the miter gauge slot in the tabletop. It's unnecessary (see the chapter "Router Table Accessories"), and it breeches the seal.

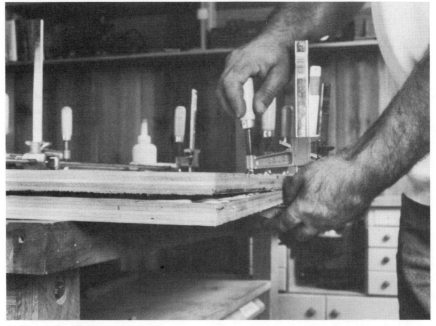

If one or both plywood panels for your tabletop are bowed, don't worry. Orient them with the crowns in. As you apply the clamps along one edge during glue-up, the others will tend to open up. Eventually, the clamps will close the gaps, and the bowing will spread the pressure across the entire surface. The glue bond will be that much better overall, and the bowing of one sheet will counteract that of the other, leaving you with a flat tabletop core.

Slide one against the other, moving them slightly back and forth. Align the edges. Apply clamps around the edges, letting the core cure overnight with the clamps in place.

3. Prepare your edge-banding stock. As previously noted, it should be made of a hard, straight-grained hardwood like maple, ash, oak, or birch. It should be wide enough to stand slightly proud of the plywood core on both sides, and about ¾ inch thick. Make it about 1⅛ inches wide for a 1-inch-thick core, 1⅝ inches for a 1½-inch core. After it's applied, you'll use a router and flush-trimming bit to—what else?—trim it flush with the plywood on both sides.

4. Unclamp the core, and square it up on the table saw. Cut the edge banding to fit, mitering it at the corners. Glue it in place. After the glue dries, trim the banding flush.

5. Now you are ready for the plastic laminate. Cut the two pieces required to make a balanced, stable, warp-resistant top about a half to a full inch larger than the edge-banded core. Because of the irreversible nature of the bonding process, and because you will trim the edges of the laminate after installation anyway, it's best to cut the pieces with extra length and width.

You can saw laminate with carbide-tipped blades, cut it with carbide router bits, or score and break it. For the last type of process, use a special scoring tool, which you can buy for $3 to $5. Laminate will chip out quite easily as it's sawed, and the chips are hard and sharp. Wear those safety goggles!

6. Contact cement is what bonds the laminate to the substrate. It's a sophisticated rubber cement that you spread on the mating pieces and leave to dry. When you touch the dried cement on the laminate to the dried cement on the substrate, they stick. Immediately. Therefore, the laminate must be accurately aligned before it can be allowed to touch the substrate. A typical approach is to lay dowel rods or sticker strips across the substrate, and then set the laminate on them. Beginning either in the middle or at one end, you pull the spacers out one at a time and press the laminate to the substrate.

Repeat the process to apply the laminate to the other side.

7. Complete the top by trimming the laminate, slightly beveling the edge of the laminate and the hardwood

A Router Mini-Table

Here's how simple a router table can be. Three pieces of plywood, a foot-square piece of acrylic, and less than a dozen screws.

It isn't big, but it's perfect for small work. And it supports a full-sized router, colleted for ½-inch-shank bits. The back has an extension that you trap in a vise to secure the table, while the sides rest on the workbench. This puts the work surface about 15 inches above workbench height, a good placement for small or close work.

Here's an ideal table for routing small pieces. It stands on the workbench, so it is higher than the usual router table. Because it has a tail that clamps in the bench's vise, it is quick to set up and very steady.

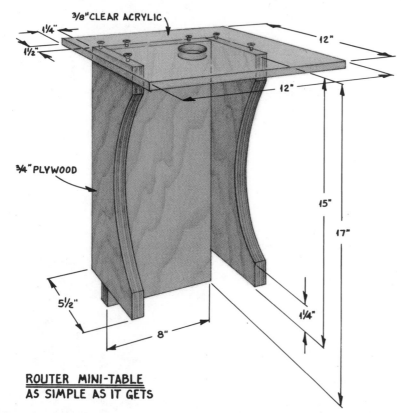

ROUTER MINI-TABLE
AS SIMPLE AS IT GETS

CUTTING LIST

Piece	Number	Thickness	Width	Length	Material
Sides	2	¾"	5½"	15"	Fir plywood
Back	1	¾"	8"	17"	Fir plywood
Top	1	⅜"	12"	12"	Clear acrylic

Hardware
6 pcs. #6 × 2" drywall screws
3 pcs. #6 × ¾" flathead wood screws

1. Cut the plywood parts to the sizes specified in the Cutting List. Lay out and cut the arcs in the side pieces. Mark points 1¼ inches from the top and bottom edges. Flex a steel ruler, a scrap of plastic laminate, or a strip of thin stock and position it between the two marks so it connects them, form-ing the arc. Have a helper trace along the bow on the plywood. Then cut with a saber saw or on the band saw.

2. Assemble the sides and back with glue and drywall screws. The assembly should be flush around the top edge.

3. Cut the acrylic to size, then position it atop the plywood assembly. Mark the locations of the three attachment screws. Set the stock baseplate from your router on the acrylic and transfer the locations of the mounting-screw holes. Carefully drill and countersink these holes.

4. Attach the top to the base with flathead screws. Attach the router base to the top's underside, and install the motor. Set up the mini-router table, with the back extension trapped in the workbench vise. Chuck a straight bit in the collet, turn on the motor, and slowly advance the depth setting as the bit cuts a hole for itself in the acrylic top. (If you plan to use bits larger than a ¾-inch straight bit in the little table, you can use a circle template to cut a large hole.)

TRY THIS!

You can save some money if you cement "backer" to the bottom side of the tabletop. Backer is laminate without the color layer, and it is designed specifically for sealing the bottoms of counters and other laminated surfaces. Backer is kraft-paper brown and only half the thickness of regular laminate, but it nonetheless has the same moisture-resistant qualities, works the same way, and is bonded with the same contact cement.

An advantage backer has over laminate is that it isn't as slippery, so clamps can get a better purchase on it. Thus, a clamped-down fence is somewhat more likely to stay put if the the tabletop's underside is backer rather than laminate.

edge banding. Use a bevel-trimmer in your router. Set the depth of cut to about 1/8 inch, which is about twice the thickness of the laminate. With the router on the laminate surface and the bit's pilot riding the edge banding, rout around the tabletop. Turn the top over and trim the other side's laminate.

Two substantial steps in the project remain: supporting the tabletop, and hanging the router from it. Accessorizing it is the subject of another chapter, "Router Table Accessories."

BENEATH THE TABLETOP

This will be short. We've already articulated a few ideas for router table underpinnings, ranging from sawhorses to cabinets. In the following chapter, "Cabinet Router Table," you'll see one approach: A

cabinet with drawers for bits and collets and a large compartment for routers and accessories supports the table. Another option is to use open legs to support the table.

What's important as you design and build the support structure for your router table is that you keep the router accessible and well ventilated. Make the table a comfortable working height. Make the structure sturdy and well triangulated.

MOUNTING THE ROUTER

The plate from which the router hangs in the router table is a critical component. A decade ago, as I mentioned, the router was often attached directly to the tabletop. Now the conventional practice is to attach the router to a separate, easily removed mounting plate. It's essentially a custom baseplate.

A hole is cut in the tabletop, then rabbeted. A precisely fitted plastic plate drops into the hole, resting on the rabbet. If done correctly, the plate is flush with the tabletop. The weight of the router keeps the plate in position. A proper fit means there's no sideplay, so the plate doesn't

Bit Storage

In, on, or near your router table is a logical place to store your bits, accessories, and other routers. If you build a permanent router table, be sure to include the storage space you'll need. Avoid the common tendency to throw your bits into a box or drawer. Not only are they hard to keep track of that way but they're also hard to keep clean, sharp, and undamaged. Even carbide edges will quickly be destroyed if they knock together.

Make a drawer, a box, or just a block of wood and drill 9/32-inch (for 1/4-inch shanks) and/or 17/32-inch (for 1/2-inch shanks) holes about 3/4 inch deep. Insert the bit shanks. The bits will be held both securely (so their cutting edges don't bang together) and openly (so you can easily see what you have).

A more elaborate bit storage case is presented in the chapter "Bits."

By leaving the plate (relatively) loose and easy to remove, woodworkers who prefer to can lift the router up out of the table and set it on its side to change bits. Ideally, the throat is tight around the bit, so you can't hook a finger in there and tug on the plate to lift it. Thus, you've usually got to push the router up out of its berth. (Keep it accessible!) Even if you leave the router in place when you change bits, it's nice to be able to remove it easily (especially if it is also your machine for hand-held operations).

shimmy around in the hole. Obviously, that would be a dangerous dance.

Are you a worrier? Has your plate come loose? Drill and countersink a couple of holes through it into the rabbet and drive flathead screws in place to secure it.

Now you can buy a mounting plate. Or you can make your own. Once a favorite, aluminum is seldom used anymore because it sometimes discolors wood that's pushed across it. Why risk that when other materials are readily available. Today, the usual materials are plastic: acrylic, polycarbonate, and phenolic. In three nutshells:

• **Polycarbonate** is easy to work with woodworking tools and is readily available at plastics stores and through mail-order woodworking suppliers. Virtually unbreakable, it is a tad flexible—it gives rather than shatters—and may sag under the weight of a behemoth router. *Third choice.*

• **Acrylic** also is easy to work with woodworking tools and is readily available at plastics stores and through mail-order woodworking suppliers. It isn't as unbreakable as polycarbonate, but it is more rigid. A ³⁄₈-inch-thick piece will support a screaming 18-pounder without sagging. *Second choice.*

• **Phenolic** is easy to work with woodworking tools, but it is difficult to find; a few mail-order woodworking suppliers carry pieces. It is very strong, very rigid. A ¼-inch-thick piece of the right grade will support that 18-pounder. *First choice.*

Commercial mounting plates have one of two configurations. The first is the so-called universal plate; it has a bit throat that's sized—and rabbeted—for standard template guides, and either a welter of mounting screw holes or a pattern of slots for the mounting screws. The second configuration is the blank plate, which has a bit throat, again sized

Dust Collection

Routers make dirt. Most router cuts create handfuls of chips and lungfuls of fine dust. When you mount the router in a table, you change the distribution of the dirt, but you can't diminish it. For some reason, though, we get the idea we can trap or capture the dirt when the router is table-mounted.

Well, it ain't entirely so.

When Fred built the cabinet router table, he made a couple of dust pickups (see the chapter "Router Table Accessories"), one a stand-alone, the other an add-on for the fence. Both served as pickups for a typical shop vac (long on loud, shrill noise, short on actual suction). Use of them since has demonstrated several things:

• Most of the dirt goes straight to the floor (or into the router compartment). This is inescapable, a function of bit design. Bits are designed first to cut, then to excavate the waste from the cut. This means that when chucked in a table-mounted router, the bit pulls the waste out of the cut and blows it down over the router. A pickup mounted on the table surface isn't going to capture this dirt.

Even with a shop vac sucking through a fence-mounted dust pickup, a lot of dust and chips gets tossed onto your trousers and shoes.

• An open-legged design—a router table that's really a table, in other words—doesn't provide a means for capturing any of the dirt blown below the table. (When you're done, you capture it with a broom.) A compartment in which the router hangs *will* capture this dirt. An open compartment will hold the chips until they spill onto the floor. An enclosed one will hold the chips until they smother the router.

• A surface-mounted pickup works most effectively if it is *on* the surface. A pickup on top of a fence—even if on-

ly an inch up from the table surface—will miss dirt blowing across the table.

The upshot is that to capture a router table's dirt production, you've got to have a two-level system. The bulk of the chips you collect from beneath the table, ideally via a 4-inch duct from a real dust collector (as opposed to a shop vac). A spacious compartment around the router will serve as a pickup for the system, and if the suction is there, it will be effective even if the compartment is open to the front. The system's secondary level is a pickup on the table surface.

What Router to Use?

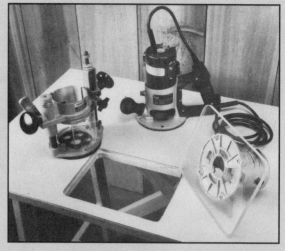

The easy, economical, sensible answer is: Use what you've got. You already have it, so you don't have to spend any money for it. Your bits fit it. You probably know its foibles.

Here are several alternative answers. Pick the one that works for you.

• Get a midsized Bosch, Elu, Porter-Cable, or other manufacturer's fixed-base router with a 3½-inch-diameter motor. Buy an extra base for it. Buy Porter-Cable's plunge base, too. Mount the extra fixed base on the router table's mounting plate and leave it there. Switch the motor from fixed base to plunge base to table-mounted base as the job demands. One router, three very different applications. All at a considerable savings.

• Use a fixed-base router. It is by design more rigid than a comparable plunge router. When powering a heavy and/or large-diameter bit, this rigidity will reduce flexing and consequent bit chattering.

• Use a plunge router because, contrary to what you might think, it's easier to adjust its depth of cut. Just be sure to kit it out with a micro-adjusting handle. This gizmo turns the plunger into a fixed-base machine, but one with a very precision adjusting mechanism.

• Use the biggest horse you can afford. It will run all day long, doing the small jobs as well as the big ones. A small or midsized router may run just as long, but it won't handle the big jobs as easily as it does the small and midsized ones. In other words, a BIG router gives across-the-board capability. Nothing else does.

• Don't use more router for the job than you need. A BIG router sucks a lot of juice, regardless of the job it's doing. It costs more to buy; ergo, it's going to cost more to repair. With a midsized router—it's easy on the pocketbook, easy on energy—you can even raise panels if you select the right bit and setup. (See "Making Panels" on page 206 for proof.)

• Equip every router you own with a mounting plate sized for your router table. When doing hand-held operations, you work with an oversized baseplate. And any router will drop into your table.

Thoroughly annoyed by these conflicting answers? Please don't be. All have truth in them. But the initial question is one that begets questions. What work are you going to do? Just general woodworking? Or do you have a special project lined up? What router do you already have? What router do you want to buy? Or would you rather not buy a router for this? Only you know what's in your mind. Maybe the router table is an excuse to buy some dream router. Maybe it's an excuse to add to a collection. Maybe your rallying cry is: "More power!" Maybe you are on a tight budget.

Ask *yourself* the question, and you'll find yourself the answer that's correct for you.

The $20 micro-adjusting rod turns a plunge router into a fixed-base router. The rod makes minute adjustments to depth of cut easier to accomplish than with any existing fixed-base machine; for router-table use, this is great! The threaded rod links the motor to the base. As you "tighten" the rod, it screws the motor slowly and evenly toward the base. If a full turn of the rod raises the bit ¹⁄₆₄ inch, imagine what a half-turn or quarter turn will do.

If cost is a sticking point, you can get the effect of having three routers when you only have one. Porter-Cable makes a plunge base that accommodates most any 3½-inch-diameter router motor, regardless of make. Buy this base for hand-held plunge-routing operations, plus an extra (fixed) base to dedicate to your router table. Your midsized, hand-held, fixed-base router thus can be "three routers." The cost of one router with two extra bases is about $150 less than that of three comparable routers.

and rabbeted for template guides, but without any mounting holes. These you lay out and drill yourself. (Both configurations will have a hole for a starting pin.)

If you can make a custom baseplate, there's no reason you can't make a mounting plate. More information about the materials and about techniques for working them is in the chapter "Custom Baseplates."

Installing the Mounting Plate

Whether you buy the plate or make it, you should have it in hand before cutting the tabletop opening for it. There's no question that the mounting plate must fit properly in the tabletop.

It's got to be dead *flush* with the tabletop surface, so work doesn't get hung up. If the plate is high or low, there's an edge somewhere to catch and stop work being fed across it. If the plate is loose in the opening, the gap between plate and tabletop fills with dust and chips, hindering the smooth movement of the work, perhaps throwing off setups. Moreover, a loose plate can shift position when the router is switched on, again throwing off a precise setup. If the

fit is too tight, you may not even get the plate into the opening. If you do, the plate may be distorted.

So the real question is: How do I achieve that just-right fit?

The answer: Use a router and a ⅜-inch straight bit to make the critical first cut, guiding it with a template derived from the mounting plate. Make the framelike template from ¼-inch plywood or hardboard, and use it to guide the router base.

1. To start, place the mounting plate on the template stock and trace around it with a sharp pencil. If the plate has rounded corners, as some commercial plates do, use a draftsman's circle template to locate the centerpoint of each corner's radius.

2. The next step is to bump up the template outline to account for the base of the router you'll use to cut the top. Draw lines on the template stock parallel to those traced from the mounting plate. The distance away from the plate tracing that you position these new lines is the difference between the bit's radius and the baseplate's radius, as shown in the drawing below. If the corners are rounded, use a compass to scribe them, pivoting on the corner centerpoints.

3. With a saber saw, cut out the template. While you want to avoid a cut that wanders, little ripples and rough saw marks shouldn't transfer to the router cut (though they would if you were referencing a template guide against the template rather than the router baseplate).

4. Test the template. Use a piece of plywood the size of the template. Position the template on the test panel and clamp it. Use the router and a ⅜-inch straight bit to cut a groove. Lay the mounting plate over the test cut; its outside edge should just line up with the outside edge of the groove. If the test cut demonstrates that the template is too big or too small, repeat the whole process to make and test a new template.

▶ Not in My Router Table!

Not every router is well suited for use in a router table. Some examples:

• A trigger switch poses a challenge: How do you keep the blamed thing running without holding the trigger?

• Some routers—older Bosch models, for example—have gravity-dependent depth-adjustment mechanisms; loosen the set clamp and you can pop the motor right out of its base. With the machine hung upside down, this is trouble. Loosen the clamp to alter the depth of cut and the motor falls right out. Surprise!

• A lot of Sears routers have exposed fans that collect debris. The debris naturally can damage the fan and, consequently, the motor.

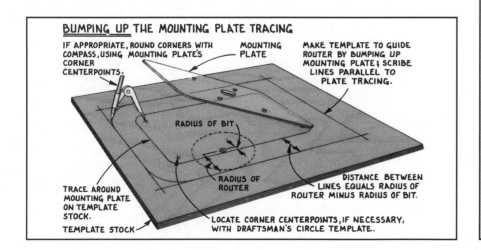

BUMPING UP THE MOUNTING PLATE TRACING

IF APPROPRIATE, ROUND CORNERS WITH COMPASS, USING MOUNTING PLATE'S CORNER CENTERPOINTS.

MOUNTING PLATE

MAKE TEMPLATE TO GUIDE ROUTER BY BUMPING UP MOUNTING PLATE; SCRIBE LINES PARALLEL TO PLATE TRACING.

RADIUS OF BIT

RADIUS OF ROUTER

DISTANCE BETWEEN LINES EQUALS RADIUS OF ROUTER MINUS RADIUS OF BIT.

TRACE AROUND MOUNTING PLATE ON TEMPLATE STOCK.

TEMPLATE STOCK

LOCATE CORNER CENTERPOINTS, IF NECESSARY, WITH DRAFTSMAN'S CIRCLE TEMPLATE.

Electrifying!

Put some power in that router table. Yes, a Killer Router is nice, but unless it's cordless, it needs some 110.

You can tack the end of an extension cord to the bottom of the tabletop. Plug in the router, and use the switch the manufacturer gave it. Not elegant, but direct. Until you get your fill of fumbling under the table for the switch.

Then you'll think about electrifying your router table.

The advantages are several. You can position an outlet next to the router, making it convenient to unplug when changing bits. (The main reason woodworkers fail to take this simple safety step is that it's inconvenient.) You can position an on-off switch where it's easy to find. (This is especially appealing when you need to kill the router *fast*.) You can add an outlet for something like a dust collector or a shop vac, making it switch-controlled: When the router goes on, so does the dust collector. (This works if your router has the "soft-start" feature, or if both router and dust collector are relatively low-amperage. But two high-amperage motors—say, a 14-amp router and a 12-amp dust collector—kicking on at the same instant can overload a 20-amp circuit, tripping the circuit breaker.)

To start, get some electrical supplies. You'll need a couple of receptacle boxes, a 20-amp duplex receptacle, a 20-amp single-pole switch, a few feet of type NM cable (12/2 with ground), a few wire nuts, a receptacle plate, a switch plate, a length of type SJT appliance cable (again, 12/2 with ground), and a ground plug rated at 20 amps.

Begin by attaching the receptacle boxes to the router table. Place the "outlet" box close to the router, and the "switch" box where you can find it without fumbling, without looking. Run the type NM cable from one box to the other. Install the plug on one end of the appliance cable, and insert the other end into the switch box. Wire the switch following the wiring diagram, and install the switch plate. Likewise, wire the receptacle and install the receptacle plate.

Plug everything in, and you're ready to go.

A switched outlet strip can be screwed to the underside of the tabletop or to a leg. Such strips often have two or three outlets controlled by a switch, plus one or two that are always hot. Plug the router and dust collector into the switched outlets, and plug a worklight into the unswitched outlet.

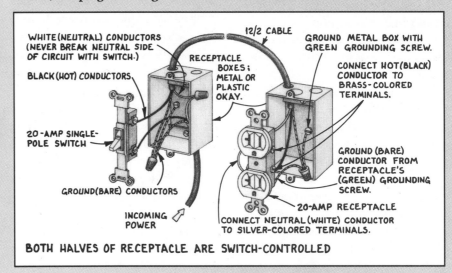

WHITE (NEUTRAL) CONDUCTORS (NEVER BREAK NEUTRAL SIDE OF CIRCUIT WITH SWITCH.)

BLACK (HOT) CONDUCTORS

20-AMP SINGLE-POLE SWITCH

GROUND (BARE) CONDUCTORS

INCOMING POWER

12/2 CABLE

RECEPTACLE BOXES; METAL OR PLASTIC OKAY.

GROUND METAL BOX WITH GREEN GROUNDING SCREW.

CONNECT HOT (BLACK) CONDUCTOR TO BRASS-COLORED TERMINALS.

GROUND (BARE) CONDUCTOR FROM RECEPTACLE'S (GREEN) GROUNDING SCREW.

20-AMP RECEPTACLE

CONNECT NEUTRAL (WHITE) CONDUCTOR TO SILVER-COLORED TERMINALS.

BOTH HALVES OF RECEPTACLE ARE SWITCH-CONTROLLED

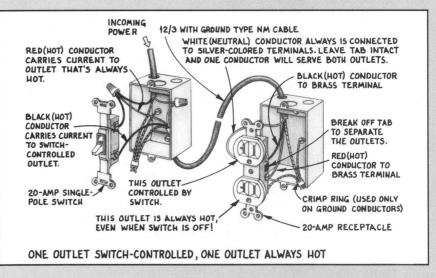

INCOMING POWER

RED (HOT) CONDUCTOR CARRIES CURRENT TO OUTLET THAT'S ALWAYS HOT.

BLACK (HOT) CONDUCTOR CARRIES CURRENT TO SWITCH-CONTROLLED OUTLET.

20-AMP SINGLE-POLE SWITCH

THIS OUTLET CONTROLLED BY SWITCH.

THIS OUTLET IS ALWAYS HOT, EVEN WHEN SWITCH IS OFF!

12/3 WITH GROUND TYPE NM CABLE

WHITE (NEUTRAL) CONDUCTOR ALWAYS IS CONNECTED TO SILVER-COLORED TERMINALS. LEAVE TAB INTACT AND ONE CONDUCTOR WILL SERVE BOTH OUTLETS.

BLACK (HOT) CONDUCTOR TO BRASS TERMINAL

BREAK OFF TAB TO SEPARATE THE OUTLETS.

RED (HOT) CONDUCTOR TO BRASS TERMINAL

CRIMP RING (USED ONLY ON GROUND CONDUCTORS)

20-AMP RECEPTACLE

ONE OUTLET SWITCH-CONTROLLED, ONE OUTLET ALWAYS HOT

Because the groove becomes the rabbet into which the mounting plate sets, it is vital that the depth of the groove perfectly match the plate thickness. To ensure this, use the plate to set the router's depth of cut.

Cutting the groove for the mounting plate isn't too big a job for a laminate trimmer. In fact, the trimmer's smaller baseplate minimizes the size of template needed to guide the cut.

5. If the test demonstrates the template is sized correctly, position it on the tabletop, clamp it securely, and use the router to groove the tabletop. After the waste is cut out, the groove becomes the rabbet into which the mounting plate is set.

6. Cut out the waste, completing the opening. Use a saber saw, and guide it along the inner edge of the groove. To start the cut, drill a pilot hole for the saber saw blade. When you are done, the plate should just fit. After all, you've tested it.

Router Mounting

Make sure you have reasonably beefy screws holding the router to the mounting plate. Many older routers had only three #8-32 screws holding the baseplate on. That was fine for the use intended, but when you hang the router from the plate, you're better off to either tap those holes out to a bigger size or drill and tap new holes in your base. The Porter-Cable we use has four 5/16-inch-18 screws holding it to the plate.

By all means, use flathead screws and countersink them so that they are just barely recessed. (Recessing too much not only weakens the plate, it creates a collection point for chips that will invariably catch your work and ruin your cut, if not your fingers.) Flatheads give the best load-spreading grip and are least likely to crack the plate and pull through. Don't use roundhead screws; they require a flat-bottomed counterbore that can seriously compromise the strength of the plate. The counterbores collect a lot of chips, too.

The situation most likely to test the strength of the plate and mountings is when you make a mistake in feed direction. A 3-horsepower router sucking a 3/4-inch piece of oak into a 1/2-inch space between the cutter and the fence can create an amazing amount of pressure. If your router is securely mounted, the fence should give enough to allow the stock to be plucked from your fingers and thrown across the shop. If the router mounts give first, you could end up with an angry router coming out from under the table after you.

CABINET ROUTER TABLE

This router table will handle most any job.

It was designed and built by Fred Matlack at the behest of *American Woodworker* magazine. The goal was to incorporate features that make routing easier and safer, while keeping the design as simple as possible. (The niftiest feature isn't worth much if it's too complicated or cumbersome to use.) So the complete project has features like an adjustable fence, dust collection, an easy-to-reach switch, and convenient storage for bits, accessories, and even a router or two. The router table looks pretty good, too.

The heart of this router table is a *big* router. Fred chose Porter-Cable's Speedmatic, a 3¼-horsepower fixed-base production router. Although plunge routers are a popular choice for router tables, he decided against using one. Compared to a fixed-base production router, a plunge router has more mechanical play in its structure. Most of the time this wouldn't be a concern. But when powering a big 2- or 3-inch-diameter panel-raising bit, for example, the extra rigidity of a fixed-base router will help eliminate any flexing of the machine and chattering of the bit from the huge forces involved. And the Speedmatic's built-in variable-speed control allows users to slow down those huge bits.

A key design element is the router's position near the front edge of the top. Fred positioned it there for a number of reasons.

- It's easier to reach the router for adjustments or to push it out of the top.
- It's easier to control the work when pushing it past the bit.
- The offset position leaves a lot of room in back of the fence to place an indexing jig (like the Incra Jig).
- The wide rear portion of the top is easily used if you need to work on a wide piece of wood; simply turn the fence around and stand "behind" the router table.

The tabletop is constructed like a sturdy counter; the oak-edged, two-layer plywood core is covered on both sides with durable, smooth, plastic laminate. Fred made the top wide enough to support fairly large

Here's a router table with frills—a split fence with integral clamps, lots of storage, a conveniently placed switch to control both the router and dust collector. Without question, this is one of our shop's workhorses.

More bits than you can afford will fit in the seven bit drawers. And they couldn't be more close-at-hand, either. Beneath the router compartment is a commodious storage area for jigs and fixtures, and for a spare router, too.

pieces of wood. To facilitate clamping, it overhangs the cabinet by 3 inches on the sides and by 1½ inches in the front and back. To eliminate accidental goring, Fred rounded off the corners of the top.

The big router hangs from a rectangular baseplate of ⅜-inch clear acrylic that fits in a rabbeted cutout in the top. With the router mounted this way, it's easy to pop it out to change bits. Although he was prepared to make a mounting plate, Fred instead used a commercial one made and sold by Woodhaven. (See "Sources" on page 337.)

Fred built the cabinet of the router table big enough to provide a solid base for the top and roomy enough for lots of storage. The compartment housing the router is open to the front. A door on it would limit access to the router for those adjustments that always have to be made. And it would restrict the air circulation that's so important to router cooling. The cabinet has a stack of drawers on each side of the router compartment to hold bits and accessories. Double doors with self-closing hinges close in the large bottom storage space.

After considerable use, Fred added a 4-inch dust collection port to the router compartment, since it proved to be the principal collection spot for chips. Behind the opening in the compartment back is a standard sheet-metal T-fitting. The inlet end was formed into an oval shape and butted against the port. A hose from a dust collector was coupled to the outlet end. The T was fitted with a reduction cap so the shop-vac hose coming off the surface pickup could be plugged into the system. The router compartment port has a movable gate made of clear acrylic. The dust

Fred demonstrates just how comfortable it is to use the cabinet router table. He doesn't have to stretch in the least to feed the work into the bit.

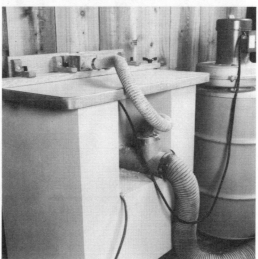

A serious router and cutter generate enough chips and dust to warrant a no-nonsense dust collection system. A pickup on the fence captures some dust from the table surface, but the bulk of it is drawn from the router compartment through the 4-inch hose.

collector itself is plugged into the switched outlet, so it comes on when the router does.

Birch plywood, joined with dado, rabbet, and butt joints, was used for the cabinet construction. An oak face frame, a recessed plinth on the bottom, and an inlaid ¼-inch plywood back complete the cabinet. Fred finished the router table with a coat of primer and a top coat of semi-gloss acrylic enamel paint.

CONSTRUCTION

1. Cut the plywood case parts. Start by cutting out the plywood parts. All the parts listed as being birch plywood can be cut from a single sheet. Fred used good-quality

cabinet-grade birch plywood because it takes paint well. Since they aren't exposed, the two case tops can be cut from less-expensive fir plywood. (Later, you can cut the tabletop core pieces and the drawer bottoms from this plywood.) Cut the drawer runners from ½-inch fir plywood. Finally, cut the back from a sheet of ¼-inch lauan plywood.

The sides are rabbeted for the case tops (as are the divider panels) and are dadoed for the middle and bottom panels. The sides are also rabbeted—⅜ inch by ¼ inch—for the back panel. Cut the rabbets and dadoes, then glue and nail the drawer runners in place on the sides. (Note that the top-right drawer position has a false front where the on/off switch will be mounted, so it isn't

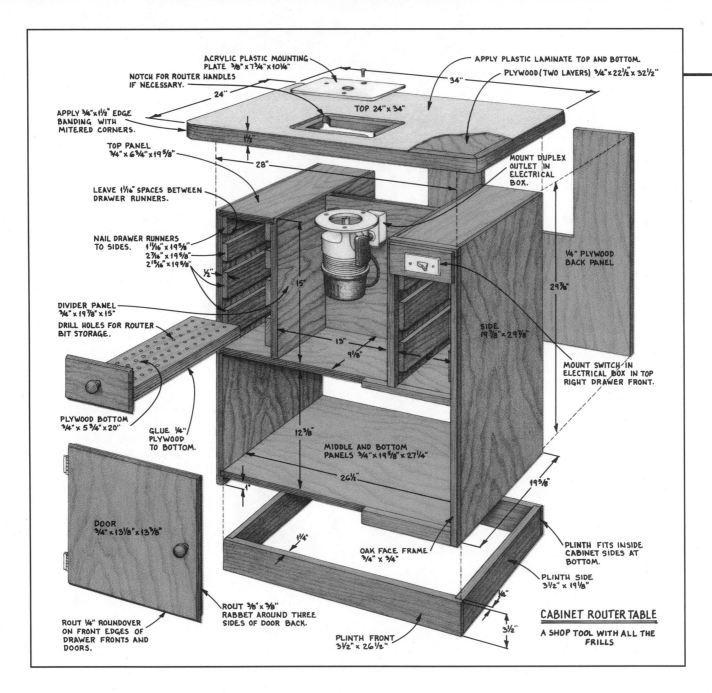

APPLY 3/4"x1/2" EDGE
BANDING WITH
MITERED CORNERS.

ACRYLIC PLASTIC MOUNTING
PLATE 3/8" x 7 3/4" x 10 1/4"

NOTCH FOR ROUTER HANDLES
IF NECESSARY.

24"

TOP 24" x 34"

APPLY PLASTIC LAMINATE TOP AND BOTTOM.
PLYWOOD (TWO LAYERS) 3/4" x 22 1/2" x 32 1/2"

34"

1 1/2"

28"

MOUNT DUPLEX
OUTLET IN
ELECTRICAL
BOX.

TOP PANEL
3/4" x 6 3/4" x 19 5/8"

LEAVE 1 1/16" SPACES BETWEEN
DRAWER RUNNERS.

NAIL DRAWER RUNNERS
TO SIDES.   1 1/16" x 19 5/8"
2 7/16" x 19 5/8"
2 15/16" x 19 5/8"

1/2"

15"

1/4" PLYWOOD
BACK PANEL

29 7/8"

SIDE
19 7/8" x 29 7/8"

DIVIDER PANEL
3/4" x 19 7/8" x 15"

DRILL HOLES FOR ROUTER
BIT STORAGE.

13"

9 1/8"

MOUNT SWITCH IN
ELECTRICAL BOX IN TOP
RIGHT DRAWER FRONT.

PLYWOOD BOTTOM
3/4" x 5 3/4" x 20"

GLUE 1/4"
PLYWOOD
TO BOTTOM.

12 3/8"

MIDDLE AND BOTTOM
PANELS 3/4" x 19 5/8" x 27 1/4"

26 1/2"

19 5/8"

DOOR
3/4" x 13 7/8" x 13 7/8"

1"

1/4"

OAK FACE FRAME
3/4" x 3/4"

PLINTH FITS INSIDE
CABINET SIDES AT
BOTTOM.

PLINTH SIDE
3 1/2" x 19 1/8"

ROUT 1/4" ROUNDOVER
ON FRONT EDGES OF
DRAWER FRONTS AND
DOORS.

ROUT 3/8" x 3/8"
RABBET AROUND THREE
SIDES OF DOOR BACK.

PLINTH FRONT
3 1/2" x 26 1/2"

1/4"

3 1/2"

CABINET ROUTER TABLE

A SHOP TOOL WITH ALL THE
FRILLS

necessary to attach runners for a top drawer there.)

The divider panels, too, are rabbeted for the back. After cutting the rabbets, attach the runners to the rabbeted face.

A port for the dust collector must be cut in the lower left corner of the router compartment back. The opening is roughly oval, about 3½ inches high and 4½ inches long.

The middle panel must be trimmed and rabbeted for the back. First, cut a ⅜-inch-wide by ¼-inch-

deep rabbet along the entire back edge. Then measure 6¾ inches in from each side, and mark these two spots. With a piloted flush-trimming bit, trim away the lip forming the rabbet, beginning at the ends of the panel and stopping at the two points just marked. The bit's pilot should ride on the bottom of the rabbet as you trim.

2. Assemble the case. Begin assembly by gluing and nailing the sides to the bottom and middle

panels. The edges of these parts should be flush in the front. Use 6d finish nails. Next, glue and nail the two divider panels to the router compartment back. Glue and nail this unit to the middle panel, then fit the two small case tops into the rabbets cut for them. Again, the case tops' front edges should be flush with the case's front edges. Cut out the ¼-inch plywood back to fit in the rabbets cut for it (leaving the space behind the router compartment open).

3. Make the cabinet's face frame.

Make a face frame for the front of the cabinet by cutting ¾-inch by ¾-inch oak strips to fit. Glue and nail them in place on the front edges of the cabinet parts. Make the bottom strip 1¾ inches wide to cover part of the plinth. The oak strips are simply butted together. Chamfer the edges of the oak strips slightly with a chamfer bit.

4. Build and install the plinth.

Cut out the four pieces for the plinth, and rabbet the ends of the front and back ones. Assemble the plinth with glue and nails, then attach it to the bottom of the cabinet.

5. Make and hang the doors.

The two doors that close in the storage compartment are simple lipped doors. Cut them from the remaining birch plywood. Cut a ⅜-inch by ⅜-inch rabbet along the top and bottom and outer edges of each. Don't rabbet the inner edge. Radius all four edges of the doors with a ⅜-inch round-over bit. Hang the doors on self-closing offset hinges. Install the wooden knobs.

6. Build the drawers.

The drawers are simply flat pieces of plywood drilled with holes for bit storage and fitted with a lipped birch-plywood front. To make the drawer bottoms, cut pieces of ¾-inch and ¼-inch plywood to the length and width specified in the Cutting List.

Before you drill the holes in the drawer bottoms, inventory your collection of bits and small router accessories. Plan how you want to store them, and give yourself space for expansion. Drill $\frac{9}{32}$-inch holes for the ¼-inch-shank bits and $\frac{17}{32}$-inch holes for the ½-inch-shank bits. Bore the holes all the way through the ¾-inch plywood. Then glue on a

CUTTING LIST

Piece	Number	Thickness	Width	Length	Material
Top core pieces	2	¾"	22½"	32½"	AC plywood
Edge banding	2	¾"	1½"	24"	4/4 oak
Edge banding	2	¾"	1½"	34"	4/4 oak
Sides	2	¾"	19⅞"	29⅞"	Birch plywood
Middle panel	1	¾"	19⅞"	27¼"	Birch plywood
Bottom panel	1	¾"	19⅝"	27¼"	Birch plywood
Divider panels	2	¾"	19⅞"	15"	Birch plywood
Router compartment back	1	¾"	13"	15"	Birch plywood
Top panels	2	¾"	6¾"	19⅝"	AC plywood
Drawer runners	2	½"	1¹¹⁄₁₆"	19⅝"	AC plywood
Drawer runners	4	½"	2⁷⁄₁₆"	19⅝"	AC plywood
Drawer runners	8	½"	2¹⁵⁄₁₆"	19⅝"	AC plywood
Back panel	1	¼"	27¼"	29⅞"	Lauan plywood
Face frame rail	1	¾"	¾"	26½"	4/4 oak
Face frame bottom rail	1	¾"	1¾"	26½"	4/4 oak
Face frame rails	2	¾"	¾"	7½"	4/4 oak
Face frame stiles	2	¾"	¾"	29⅛"	4/4 oak
Face frame stiles	2	¾"	¾"	14¼"	4/4 oak
Plinth front and back	2	1½"	3½"	26½"	Fir
Plinth sides	2	1½"	3½"	19⅛"	Fir
Doors	2	¾"	13⅛"	13⅜"	Birch plywood
Drawer fronts	4	¾"	6⁷⁄₁₆"	3½"	Birch plywood
Drawer fronts	4	¾"	6⁷⁄₁₆"	4"	Birch plywood
Drawer bottoms	7	¾"	5¾"	20"	AC plywood
Drawer bottoms	7	¼"	5¾"	20"	Lauan plywood

Hardware

2 pcs. 24" × 34" plastic laminate
1 pc. ⅜" × 7¾" × 10¼" clear acrylic
1 pc. ¼" × 4" × 5" clear acrylic
1 pc. 4" sheet metal T-fitting
6d finish nails, as needed
4 pcs. 2" drywall screws
1 pc. #8 × ½" panhead screw
4 pcs. ⅜" self-closing offset hinges
9 pcs. 1" dia. wooden knobs, with screws
contact cement
yellow glue
2 steel receptacle boxes
1 pc. 20-amp duplex receptacle
1 pc. 20-amp single-pole switch
1 steel receptacle plate
1 switch plate
5' electric cable, 12/2 with ground
1 pc. 3-prong plug
10'-20' electric cord, 12/2 with ground

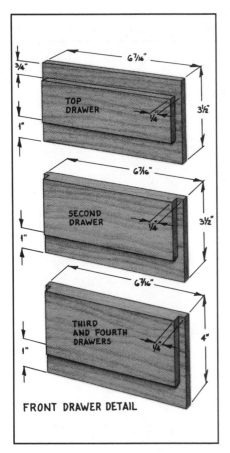

FRONT DRAWER DETAIL

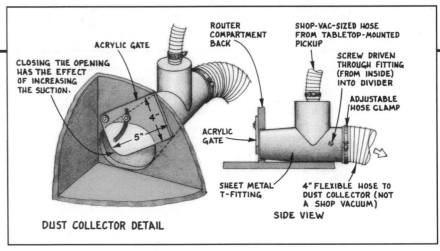

DUST COLLECTOR DETAIL

SIDE VIEW

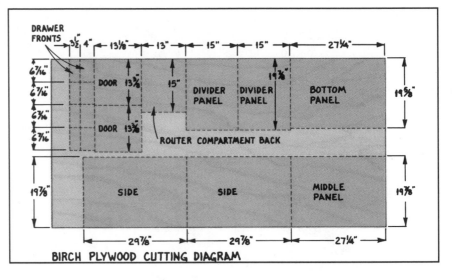

BIRCH PLYWOOD CUTTING DIAGRAM

piece of ¼-inch plywood to act as a stop.

Finally, cut out the drawer fronts, rabbet their back sides to form a lipped edge (see *Front Drawer Detail*), and fasten them to the bottoms.

Install the knobs. You can modify one or more drawers by installing sides so the drawers can hold router accessories.

You should have one drawer front left. This is the mounting front for the on-off switch. After rounding-over the edges and rabbeting the top and sides, cut an opening for a standard steel receptacle box. Then glue and nail the front in place.

7. Finish the router cabinet.

Before moving on to the router tabletop, finish the cabinet. Fred varnished the oak face frame and the wooden drawer and door knobs. He painted the remaining surfaces with a latex primer, then applied a finish coat of semi-gloss acrylic latex enamel, black on the plinth, beige elsewhere.

After the paint dries, install the T-fitting for the dust collector. The end of the fitting that butts against the compartment back can be deformed into an oval shape. Butt the fitting in place, its side against the left divider panel. At the very back, drill a pilot hole through the fitting's side into the left divider panel. One panhead screw will hold it.

Make a reducer for the T-fitting's top inlet from a scrap of wood. Cut a hole in the center for a shop-vac hose. Install it in the appropriate opening. Attach the 4-inch flexible hose from the dust collector to the fitting with an adjustable hose clamp.

Finally, make an adjustable gate, as shown in the *Dust Collector Detail*, and attach it to the router compartment back.

8. Make the tabletop. To make the top, cut two pieces of ¾-inch plywood to size and glue them together to make the required 1½-inch thickness.

While the glue dries, plane, joint, and cut the ¾-inch by 1½-inch oak required for the edge banding. After the clamps are off the core, fit the edge banding to the core one piece at a time. Miter the ends, then glue on the edge banding.

To prevent painful goring, round off the corners of the tabletop. Lay out the 1¼-inch radii and cut off each corner with a saber saw. Sand away the saw marks.

The top should be laminated on both sides with the same-density material to keep it flat and stable. Use contact cement to bond the plastic laminate to the core. Don't worry too much about squaring up the laminate; just make sure it overhangs the top on all sides. To trim the laminate flush with the edge banding, use a carbide-tipped flush-trimming bit. Set the depth of cut to about ¼ inch. Starting at an edge, run the bit into the laminate until the pilot contacts the edge banding. The pilot then will guide your cut around the perimeter of the tabletop.

Attach the top to the cabinet with four 2-inch drywall screws. Be sure to drill pilot holes first.

9. Make the router mounting plate. Unless you are using a purchased mounting plate, which is what Fred did, now is the time to make your mounting plate. The dimensions of the plate are of minor significance—provided it will fit the router and support it. You'll be us-

ing the plate itself as a guide in cutting the hole for it in the tabletop.

The plate Fred purchased from Woodhaven is ⅜-inch-thick clear acrylic. Measuring 7¾ inches by 10¼ inches, it is barely large enough to accommodate the big router hanging from it. To get everything to fit, Fred oriented the router with its two big D-handles diagonally on the plate.

See the chapters "Router Table Design" and "Custom Baseplates" for more details on materials choices, design considerations, and fabrication techniques.

10. Cut out the tabletop for the mounting plate. The router is hung in the router table more than mounted. It is attached to the mounting plate, which drops into a rabbeted opening cut in the tabletop. The weight of the router keeps it in place. The real trick is to cut an opening that is just the right size. The details of how to do this are found in the chapter "Router Table Design."

In brief, you use the mounting plate to lay out a framelike template. After the template has been cut and tested, you clamp it to the tabletop. Then cut a groove that's as deep as the plate is thick, guiding the router against the template. This groove forms the rabbet when the waste is cut away with a saber saw. Cut along the inside edge of the groove and remove the waste, and the opening is ready for the mounting plate.

11. Install the router. Before you drill holes in the mounting plate for the router's mounting screws,

check the fit of the router and its orientation in the router compartment. Even with the router oriented diagonally on the mounting plate, Fred had to notch into the rabbet in the tabletop opening to provide clearance for its handles. Having assured yourself the router will fit the plate and the opening, make sure the router's clamping mechanism will be easy to reach.

Having checked these points, use the router's original baseplate as a pattern to mark the mounting-screw hole locations. Drill and countersink the mounting holes, and mount the router on the baseplate.

12. Wire the router table. Fred provided an auxiliary on/off switch for the router by mounting an electrical outlet box (available at any hardware store) in the top-right (false) drawer front. You should already have cut an opening in the drawer front, so mount the receptacle box in it. Mount a second box in the router compartment. A 20-amp household electrical switch goes in the first box, a 20-amp duplex receptacle in the second. Run a power cord with a plug to the switch, then to the outlet. The switch controls the power to the outlet. You plug the router into the outlet, and leave it switched on. Thus the switch, just below the front edge of the tabletop, turns the router on and off. This scheme and an alternative are detailed in the wiring diagrams in the chapter "Router Table Design."

If you plug your shop vac or dust collector into the outlet, it too will go on when you switch on the router.

HORIZONTAL ROUTER TABLE

Brought to life as a mortising machine,

this router table does a whole lot more than mortising. The router is mounted horizontally, so the bit's axis is parallel to the table surface. It's perfect for *any* operation that, performed on an ordinary router table, would require you to balance the workpiece on edge, including:

• Mortising, for one
• Cutting tenons, too
• Cutting dovetail pins for sliding dovetails
• Grooving the edges of straight, flat boards
• Raising panels with a vertical bit
• Cutting wide rabbets
• Routing architectural molding with tall face-molding bits

I've seen plans for a number of these tables, all of which seem to share the same basic layout, and all of which seem to work. But all have some drawbacks that I perceived and wanted to sidestep.

One design, for example, has the router on a plate, and the plate bolted in turn to the mounting board. The bit has to extend through about an inch of mounting material before it can do any productive cutting. Another design has the mounting board extending like a skirt, below the base. The way you have to orient and clamp it—with that skirt off the workbench edge—limits your access to the worktable. And none of the designs I saw had any fine-adjustment capability. Just the opposite, in fact.

Loosen the set-bolts, and the weight of the router drops the mounting board onto its stops. The setting you had is gone, just like that.

The plan Fred and I came up with does share the basic layout of other designs, though the base unit is a bit taller. The mounting board does not extend below the base, so we can easily clamp the unit at the edge of the workbench and stand directly opposite the router bit, if that's what the operation requires. We covered both the tabletop and the mounting board with plastic laminate to keep them flat and to provide smooth sliding for the workpieces. At the same time, we eliminated the miter-gauge groove that most woodworkers unnecessarily inflict on such constructions.

We imported the mounting plate system from the router tables in our shop. The horizontal table uses the same 3/8-inch acrylic mounting plate as our regular router tables, but we bolted it into the horizontal table. This means we can pop a router out of the router table and pretty quickly bolt it into the horizontal table. (If you decide it's easier to make two plates, and unscrew and rescrew the router's baseplate mounting screws to switch your router from table to table, do it.) The plate has to be bolted to the mounting board, obviously, so that the router is held securely in the required, gravity-defying, horizontal position.

Perhaps the biggest single design improvement is the fine-adjustment system. Loosen the set-knobs. Don't worry! You won't lose the setting you have. Turn either adjustment knob—they're on the threaded rods projecting from the mounting board's top edge—and the board pivots in a controlled, progressive fashion. Slick!

The horizontal router table can be clamped right at the edge of your regular router table or at the end of a workbench. That way you can work easily from the front or either side. And the tallish base puts the work surface at a comfortable height, too.

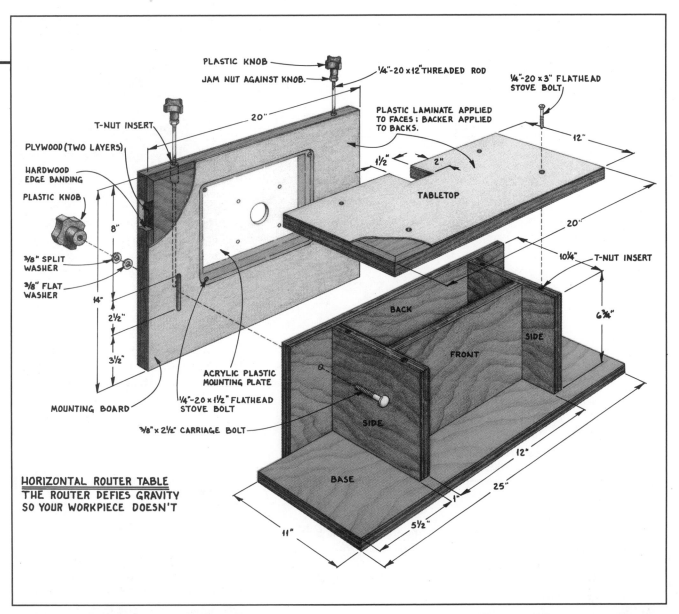

PLASTIC KNOB

JAM NUT AGAINST KNOB.

¼"-20 x 12" THREADED ROD

¼"-20 x 3" FLATHEAD STOVE BOLT

T-NUT INSERT

PLYWOOD (TWO LAYERS)

HARDWOOD EDGE BANDING

PLASTIC KNOB

20"

PLASTIC LAMINATE APPLIED TO FACES; BACKER APPLIED TO BACKS.

1½"

2"

12"

TABLETOP

⅜" SPLIT WASHER

⅜" FLAT WASHER

8"

20"

10¼"

T-NUT INSERT

14"

6¾"

BACK

SIDE

2½"

FRONT

3½"

ACRYLIC PLASTIC MOUNTING PLATE

MOUNTING BOARD

¼"-20 x 1½" FLATHEAD STOVE BOLT

SIDE

⅜" x 2½" CARRIAGE BOLT

12"

BASE

25"

11"

5½"

1"

HORIZONTAL ROUTER TABLE
THE ROUTER DEFIES GRAVITY
SO YOUR WORKPIECE DOESN'T

The mechanical side of the table is visible here. The large plastic knobs below the router cinch the mounting board tight to the table. Loosen them and turn one or both height adjusters to alter the distance between the bit and the tabletop. The plunge router we use has an add-on micro-adjusting knob to simplify bit extension changes.

Catch a sled against the front edge of the tabletop, and you have a miter gauge to guide and back up the workpiece. You don't need a slot, which would just catch dust and chips and compromise the tabletop's flatness.

CUTTING LIST

Piece	Number	Thickness	Width	Length	Material
Base	1	¾"	11"	25"	Plywood
Back	1	¾"	7½"	20"	Plywood
Front	1	¾"	7"	12"	Plywood
Side pieces	4	½"	7"	10¼"	Plywood
Tabletop pieces	2	½"	11"	19"	Plywood
Mounting board pieces	2	½"	13"	19"	Plywood
Edge banding*	1	½"	1⅛"	144"	Hardwood
T-nut inserts	6	¾" dia.		2"	Dowel

Hardware

2 pcs. plastic laminate, each approximately 24" × 16"

2 pcs. plastic laminate backer board, each approximately 24" × 16"

1 pc. ⅜" × 7¾" × 10¼" clear acrylic

6 pcs. ¼"-20 T-nuts

2 pcs. ¼"-20 hex nuts

4 pcs. ¼"-20 wing nuts

2 pcs. ¼"-20 × 12" threaded rods

6 pcs. ¼" I.D. flat washers

4 pcs. ¼"-20 × 3" flathead stove bolts

4 pcs. ¼"-20 × 1½" flathead stove bolts

2 pcs. ⅜" × 2½" carriage bolts

2 pcs. ⅜" I.D. flat washers

2 pcs. ⅜" I.D. split washers

2 pcs. 1¾" dia. plastic knobs, with ¼"-20 blind insert. Available from Reid Tool Supply Co., 2265 Black Creek Road, Muskegon, MI 49444 (800-253-0421). Part #DK-59

2 pcs. 2½" dia. plastic knobs, with ⅜"-16 blind insert. Available from Reid Tool Supply Co. Part #DK-530

*Cut as required to edge-band tabletop and mounting board.

Dadoing the mounting board layers before glue-up creates a channel for the adjustment rods. Unless you have a 5/16-inch straight bit, the easiest way to cut these dadoes is to use a 1/4-inch straight and to guide a router fitted with a fractionating baseplate along a fence clamped to the work. (See "Fractionating Baseplate" on page 230 for details on making this baseplate.) Make one pass to cut the 1/4-inch-wide dado, then turn the router and make a pass to widen the dado to 5/16 inch.

CONSTRUCTION

1. Cut the plywood parts.
All of the table's wooden parts, except the edge banding and the dowels for the T-nut inserts, are plywood. I used cabinet-grade birch plywood throughout. Just run down the Cutting List, cutting the parts to the sizes specified.

I have found it useful to make the parts that will be layered together a little oversized, so I can square and smooth the edges—and square the resulting blanks in the process—on the table saw. The sizes specified are the finished sizes.

2. Glue up the sides, tabletop, and mounting board.
These parts are a full inch thick. Rather than special-order a sheet of 1-inch plywood, I face-glued pieces of ½-inch plywood to make these parts. Ordinary yellow glue is all it takes.

Before gluing the mounting board layers together, dado the pieces to create channels for the adjusting rods. Use a ¼-inch straight bit, and cut no more than 3/16 inch deep, 1¾ inches in from each end of both pieces. (If you're working with oversized pieces,

bear in mind that the dadoes need to be 1¾ inches from the trimmed ends.) When you glue up the pieces, the dadoes should be on the inside and should line up, forming two channels from the top edge through to the bottom edge. Mark the locations of these channels on the faces of the glued-up blank.

3. Assemble the base unit.
The base unit's joinery is pretty simple. The sides and front fit into shallow dadoes in the base—only ¼ inch deep—and the front is trapped between the sides, which are locked in shallow dadoes. The back merely butts against the base and sides, and is fastened with glue and several drywall screws.

4. Complete the blanks for the tabletop and mounting board.
After the glue is dry and the clamps are off, square up these two parts on the table saw. Lay out and cut the bit notch in the tabletop.

Glue the edge banding in place next. I used maple, but you can use oak or any other hardwood. Prepare about 12 feet of ½-inch by 1⅛-inch stock. Cut the banding to fit, mitering the corners. Glue it to the edges with the excess width roughly split between the faces; you want to be able to trim the banding flush with the faces on both sides.

Use a flush-trimming bit to finish the edge banding. The only area you can't reach with the bit is the bit notch in the tabletop. I did this area with a plane, but you could also screw the flush-trimming base to the laminate trimmer and do this little area with a straight bit. (See "Flush-Trimming Baseplate" on page 187 for plans for this baseplate.)

Before you cover them with laminate, transfer the marks locating the kerfs in the mounting board to the edge.

Now cement the plastic laminate and backer to the two blanks. Cut the laminate oversized so when it is cemented in place, you have excess all around to trim off. (See the chapters "Working Laminates" and "Router Table Design" for additional details on applying plastic laminate.) In one operation, trim the excess laminate away and finish the blanks by routing a slight chamfer around the edges with a 45-degree chamfer bit.

5. Make the T-nut inserts.
To attach the tabletop to the base unit and to mount the adjusters, I made "threaded inserts" using T-nuts and ¾-inch dowel. Real threaded inserts don't always work in the edges of plywood; they often force out the sides, creating lumps on the faces. Drill a ⁵⁄₁₆-inch hole through a 2-inch length of dowel. With a backsaw or

on the band saw, kerf one end of the dowel so it won't split when you drive the T-nut into place.

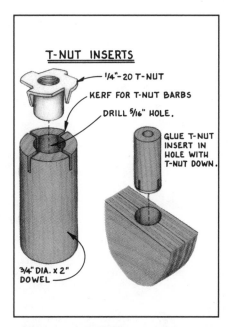

To drill the dowels to make T-nut inserts, you need to devise a method of holding the dowels. Clamp a scrap board to the drill press table with its edge under the center of the chuck. Use a ¾-inch Forstner bit to drill a half-hole through it. Now attach a second scrap to the drill press with a single screw, so you can swing it against the first board. Drop a dowel into the half-hole, and pinch it tightly with the swing arm, as shown. With a ⁵⁄₁₆-inch bit, drill the hole through the dowel.

6. Install the tabletop.
The tabletop is attached to the base unit with four flathead stove bolts threaded into T-nut inserts.

First, set the tabletop in place. On the edge of the top, mark the approximate center of each side, so you can drill the required holes into the center of the 1-inch-thick sides. Use a try square and pencil to extend the mark across the table, then mark the hole locations, as indicated in *T-Nut Inserts*.

Take the unit to the drill press, and drill a ¼-inch hole completely through the tabletop and into the base unit at each of the four spots. Switch to a countersink, and countersink each hole in the tabletop deep enough that the bolt heads will be just below the surface.

Remove the tabletop from the base. Chuck a ¾-inch Forstner bit in the drill press. Using the holes left by the ¼-inch bit as the centerpoints, drill four 2-inch-deep holes for the T-nut inserts. To allow the bolt shank to extend through the T-nut, drill the ¼-inch hole a little deeper than the bottom of the ¾-inch hole at each spot.

Spread glue on each T-nut insert, and put one in each hole. Be sure the T-nut is on the bottom of the insert. Don't be too generous with the glue; you don't want it to well up through the T-nut and clog the threads. When the glue is dry, sand the insert tops flush.

Set the top back in place and drive a bolt through each hole, fastening the top.

7. Install the mounting plate.
Lay the acrylic mounting plate on the mounting board, align it, then trace around it. Use a ¾-inch straight bit to cut a groove around the inside

Horizontal Savvy

A 3-horsepower router isn't necessary in the horizontal router table. You'll probably find, as I did, that you don't use those huge bits—panel raisers, for example—that need lots of power to drive. A medium-sized router is more than adequate.

With the router's orientation changed, the methods for adjusting your cut change, too. "Bit height" becomes a confusing term. Does it refer to the adjustment made on the router, as it does when working at a regular router table? Or does it refer to the height of the bit in relation to the plane of the tabletop?

To eliminate the confusion, let me define a couple of terms as I use them in talking about the horizontal router table. When I talk about *bit extension,* I'm referring to the adjustment you make on the router itself, and to how far out from the mounting board the bit extends. When talking about the horizontal router table, I use *bit height* to refer to the height of the bit in relation to the plane of the tabletop.

When you begin to rout, you have to deal with feed direction. It's different: You feed from left to right. But let's not get ahead of ourselves. Do the adjustments first.

Bit extension adjustment. Easy to do. The tabletop is a foot closer to your eyes than the regular router table.

The router is at the same level, and it's hanging out in the open, readily visible and accessible. No stooping is necessary to see what you're doing. Moreover, you don't have to worry about losing the router's bit height setting when you loosen the clamp securing the motor in its base. You aren't fighting gravity in this adjustment.

Hold a rule next to the bit and move the router.

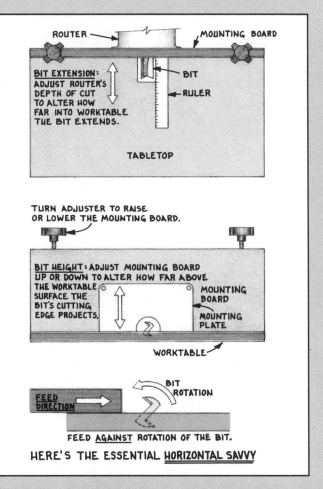

HERE'S THE ESSENTIAL <u>HORIZONTAL SAVVY</u>

Bit height adjustment. The mounting board's fine-adjustment system works great. Because of the swing-action of this adjusting system, the effect of one adjuster's movement is halved at the bit. In other words, if I raise the board a full inch at one adjustment, the bit will rise only ½ inch. To raise the bit a full inch, I have to either raise *both sides* 1 inch or one side *2 inches.*

To get a coarse setting, I just loosen both locking knobs and lift one side of the mounting board. When the setting *looks* right, I tighten the knobs, then spin the adjusters down to the bolt. To refine that setting, I loosen the locking knobs again, then turn one adjuster to raise or lower the bit.

If you are methodical, you can mark the knobs so you can track your mounting board movements by counting turns. The adjusting

rods's pitch of 20 threads per inch means that 20 complete turns of an adjuster will raise that adjuster's side of the mounting board 1 inch. As I pointed out, this raises the bit only ½ inch.

Feed direction. As I said, it is from left to right, unlike on a regular router table. This is because you're using what would be, on a regular router table, the back of the bit.

It's easy to figure out. Look at the bit as it extends into the tabletop bit opening. Look at the cutting edge. Does it remind you of the cutters on a jointer, the way they are pitched into the cut? It does to me. I look at that router bit and I just can see it's going to spin toward the left. Counterclockwise.

And because one always feeds *against* the cutter rotation, I know I'm going to feed the stock from left to right.

of the traced outline. The bottom of this groove is the surface against which the plate will mount, so set the bit height using the plate itself as a guide.

I set up a T-square to guide the router as it grooved each side of the area. Our plate has rounded corners, and I routed the corners to the outline freehand.

With the groove completed, drill a small starting hole and use a saber saw to saw out the router hole. Cut around the inner wall of the groove, so the bottom remains to support the plate.

Set the mounting plate in the hole, checking that it is flush with the face of the mounting board. At each corner, drill (then countersink) a ¼-inch hole through the acrylic and the mounting board. The plate is bolted to the board with a stove bolt in each hole. Using wing nuts on the bolts makes it relatively easy to remove the plate.

8. Make the adjusting system.
The mounting board is attached to the base unit by two ⅜-inch carriage bolts. Slots in the mounting board allow it to be moved up and down, then cinched in position by tightening the knobs on the bolts. The adjusters penetrate the board from the top edge, extending to and seating on the bolts. In effect, the adjusters push against the bolts to raise the mounting board.

Drill the bolt holes first. The slots have to be cut along the line of the dadoes cut in Step 2, so use a square and a pencil to carry the kerf indication across the back of the mounting board. Set the mounting board in place, with its bottom edge resting on the workbench. Clamp it to the base unit. Measure and mark

the bolt hole locations, which will be the top of the adjustment slot. Drill the hole through the mounting board and the base unit's back.

Unclamp the mounting board and use a router and a ½-inch straight bit to cut 2-inch-long adjustment slots. They extend down from the bolt holes and are centered on the line. The ½-inch slot width in conjunction with ⅜-inch bolts provides enough play to permit easy adjustments.

Now you must bore the holes for the T-nut inserts. Bolt the mounting board to the base unit. Set the unit on the drill press table, and using the ¾-inch Forstner bit, drill 2-inch-deep holes for the two T-nut inserts. These holes should be cen-

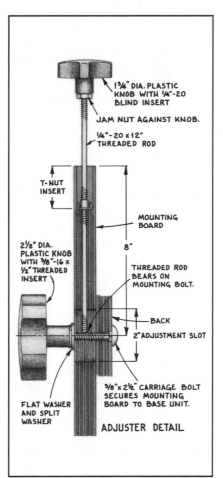

1¾" DIA. PLASTIC KNOB WITH ¼"-20 BLIND INSERT

JAM NUT AGAINST KNOB.

¼"-20 x 12" THREADED ROD

T-NUT INSERT

MOUNTING BOARD

2½" DIA. PLASTIC KNOB WITH ⅜"-16 x ½" THREADED INSERT

8"

THREADED ROD BEARS ON MOUNTING BOLT.

BACK

2" ADJUSTMENT SLOT

⅜" x 2½" CARRIAGE BOLT SECURES MOUNTING BOARD TO BASE UNIT.

FLAT WASHER AND SPLIT WASHER

ADJUSTER DETAIL

Safety First!

A bit guard is just as necessary on this router table as it is on others.

The L-shaped guard shown is much like the one used on the L-shaped router table fence, detailed in the next chapter, "Router Table Accessories." It is secured by a couple of plastic knobs (available from Reid Tool Supply Co., part #DK-44; see "Sources" on page 337) with studs that turn into threaded holes in the mounting plate. The slotted extension is a couple of inches longer than the guard made for the fence, and we didn't cut the slots through the edge. This way, the guard won't fall off completely when the mounting knobs are loosened.

tered across the thickness of the board at the kerf mark.

Glue an insert into each. Thread the adjuster rod through the T-nut and on down to the bolt. Turn a hex nut on each adjuster rod, then turn on the knob. After the knob seats, spin the nut up against the knob and jam it tight with a wrench; that will keep the knob from unthreading from the rod when you make adjustments.

Install the router, and you are ready to do some real work!

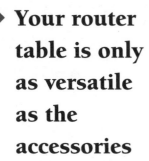

Your router table is only as versatile as the accessories

you have for it. In this chapter, you'll find a basic selection, to which you can add a dozen more by simply paging through the rest of the book. All of the accessories here are scaled to the cabinet table, which is the most used of the several in the Rodale shop.

Altering the dimensions to suit *your* router table should be easy.

The basic list of accessories isn't long: a fence, a bit guard, a push sled, a dust pickup. To these we've added an overarm guide pin, which turns your router table into a pin router.

STARTING PIN

With a hand-held router, a piloted bit is used without a guide or fence. Some woodworkers do the same on a router table. This is usually okay.

But once in a while, at the start of a cut, the cutter will catch the wood and rip it out of your grasp. For the pilot to control things, it has to contact the wood. But because the cutter is larger than the pilot, it engages the wood first. If the circumstances are just a wee bit wrong, the cutter can flick the workpiece aside before it touches the pilot. The workpiece gets a gouge, you get a surprise, and usually, that's the end of it. But you can get injured if your fingers get into the bit.

A starting pin is the best way to avoid this. Always use one with a piloted bit (unless you are using a fence). A starting pin is a fixed shaft or edge against which you brace the work as you "lever" it into the bit. It controls things until the stock gets to the pilot. The most common manifestation of the starting pin is a wooden peg or metal or plastic pin projecting from the mounting plate 1½ to 4 inches from the bit.

A commercial mounting plate will come with a starting pin. A shop-made plate needs a shop-made pin. To make one, simply rout a ⅜- to ½-inch tenon on a length of dowel (see "Routing Tenons" on page 281), then cut the dowel so you have a pin about 1 to 1½ inches long.

STAND-ALONE BIT GUARDS

Guard your hands from the bit when working at the router table. While this may seem difficult to do if you're working with a piloted bit and the starting pin, it's not. The usual approach is to hold a scrap-sized shield of acrylic or polycarbonate just above the bit. The shield deflects chips arcing up off the bit and serves as a physical deflector for your fingers, while nonetheless allowing the workpiece access to the bit.

Shown on the next few pages are some stand-alone guards you can make. Two are simple affairs that you secure to the mounting plate with studded knobs. A third clamps to the tabletop. The last is a more elaborate construction—it serves simultaneously as a dust pickup, starting pin, and bit guard—that you connect to the mounting plate *and* clamp to the tabletop.

Tips on working with acrylic and polycarbonate can be found in the chapter "Custom Baseplates." It is easy to do using your woodworking tools.

Bent Acrylic Bit Guard

This guard is a strip of clear acrylic that's bent into an angular sort of S-shape. To attach it to the router table, you need first to drill and tap two holes in the mounting plate. The positions of the holes correspond to the positions of two slots cut in the guard. Hold the guard over the holes, then turn plastic thumbscrews into them, cinching the guard in place. The slots provide about an inch of fore-and-aft adjustment.

The guard has a coverage area 4 inches in diameter. It is high enough to clear a 1½-inch-thick workpiece, but its height is fixed. If you want the guard down closer to a ¾-inch or a 1-inch workpiece, then you need to make a separate guard that's less tall than the one shown on the opposite page.

The trick here is bending the acrylic. Basic information on heating and bending acrylic, as well as cutting and drilling it, is found in the chapter "Custom Baseplates." There aren't enough parts to merit a Cutting List, so here's a list of what you need:

- One 4-inch by 8-inch piece of ¼-inch clear acrylic
- Two thumbscrews with hex nuts

1. Begin with the piece of clear acrylic. Lay out the guard on the paper masking, as shown in *Bent Acrylic Bit Guard.*

Simple though it is, this one-piece acrylic guard shields the bit effectively. There's room for a typical workpiece to pass underneath it.

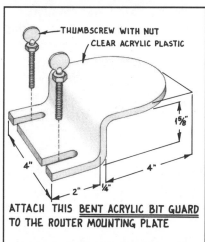

THUMBSCREW WITH NUT
CLEAR ACRYLIC PLASTIC

1⅝"

4"   4"

2"   ¼"

ATTACH THIS BENT ACRYLIC BIT GUARD TO THE ROUTER MOUNTING PLATE

Safety First!

Using the router table without a bit guard is asking for injury. As with other power woodworking tools, a momentary lapse—a one-time happening—can cause an eon of misery and grief. Spinning at 22,000 rpm, a carbide bit will cut flesh faster than it will rock maple.

Hang a bit guard on your fence. As you will see elsewhere in this chapter, there are ways of equipping every fence with a bit guard. If you are doing work with a piloted bit, equip your router table with a bit guard as well as the starting pin.

2. With the masking still in place, cut the rounded edge of the guard using a saber saw or band saw. With a ¼-inch straight bit in a table-mounted router, cut the two mounting slots. Guide the acrylic workpiece along the router table fence.

3. Select a scrap of wood to use as a bending mold. Radius one edge with a ⅜-inch round-over bit. This is the edge you will use to form the guard's two bends.

4. Strip the masking from the acrylic. Mark the locations of the two bends. Cut a scrap block as thick as the guard offset is high. Set the guard on it, aligning the guard's top bend line with the block's edge. Set a second

scrap atop the guard and clamp the stack. With a heat gun, heat the acrylic. When the plastic is limber, bend it down. The bench top will force the second bend at just the right spot. Set another scrap block on the slotted extension, and clamp it until it cools and hardens. (This operation is shown in photos in the chapter "Custom Baseplates.")

5. For a finished appearance, sand and polish the edges of the acrylic. Or simply "flame polish" the edges.

6. Drill and tap two holes in the mounting plate for the thumbscrews. Use the drill bit and tap that are appropriate for the size and thread of the thumbscrews you are using. Turn a hex nut onto each screw to provide a shoulder to seat against the guard.

Adjustable Acrylic Bit Guard

This bit guard is very similar to the bent shield. But this one is height-adjustable, and making it doesn't involve bending the acrylic. For the latter reason, you could, if you wanted, make this using polycarbonate, which is tougher than acrylic. (Polycarb

shares many of acrylic's working characteristics, but it doesn't respond well to heating and thus isn't easy to bend.)

The adjustable shield is composed of a plastic baseplate, a plastic guard, and several wooden spacers. Two thumbscrews secure the unit to the mounting plate, while a stove bolt and wing nut secure the guard to the spacers. By varying the spacers used, you can adjust the gap beneath the guard from ¾ inch up to 2 inches.

Basic information on working acrylic is found in the chapter "Custom Baseplates." There aren't enough parts to merit a Cutting List, so here's a list of what you need:

• One 4-inch by 4¾-inch piece of ¼-inch clear acrylic
• One 4-inch by 3-inch piece of ¼-inch acrylic
• Two ½-inch by ¾-inch by 4-inch hardwood blocks
• Three ¼-inch by ¾-inch by 4-inch hardwood blocks
• One scrap of ⅛-inch dowel
• One 3-inch-long ¼-inch flathead stove bolt
• One ¼-inch T-nut
• One ¼-inch wing nut
• Two thumbscrews with nuts

1. Without stripping off the paper masking, lay out the larger piece of acrylic—the guard—as shown in *Adjustable Bit Guard*. Cut the curved edge with a saber saw or on the band saw, then bore the three holes. For a finished appearance, sand and polish the edges of the guard.

2. With a ¼-inch straight bit in a table-mounted router, cut the two mounting slots in the smaller piece of acrylic. Guide the workpiece along the router table fence. For a finished appearance, sand and polish the edges of the base.

3. Stack the hardwood blocks, and clamp or tape them together. Using the guard as a pattern, lay out the

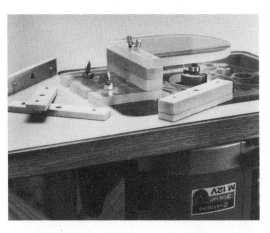

This guard has a set of spacers that allow you to raise the guard to accommodate an especially thick workpiece. But when working an especially thin piece, you can lower the guard to keep it close to the work's surface.

locations of the two ⅛-inch-diameter alignment pin holes and the ¼-inch-diameter mounting hole. Drill the holes. The mounting hole in *one* of the ½-inch blocks must be bored out to accommodate the T-nut.

4. Using a thin block as a pattern, transfer the hole locations to the acrylic base. Drill and countersink the hole for the bolt; the side of the base with the countersink is the bottom. Drill the holes for the alignment pins. These holes can be stopped; they don't need to penetrate the base, but they do need to be in the top face.

5. Glue bits of the ⅛-inch dowel in the alignment pin holes, as shown in the *Alignment Pin Detail*. The idea is to have holes in the bottom surfaces of the blocks and corresponding pins protruding from the tops. The exception is the block that gets the T-nut; it has pins protruding top and bottom. It's easiest to fit the pins if you use fairly long bits of dowel, then trim them to nubs after the glue dries.

6. Drive the T-nut into the hardwood block bored out for it. With the stove bolt, fasten that block to the base. Stack the other spacer blocks on the bolt, add the guard, and turn the wing nut onto the bolt, fastening the assembly together.

7. Drill and tap two holes in the mounting plate for the plastic thumbscrews. Use the drill bit and tap that are appropriate for the size and thread of the thumbscrews you are using.

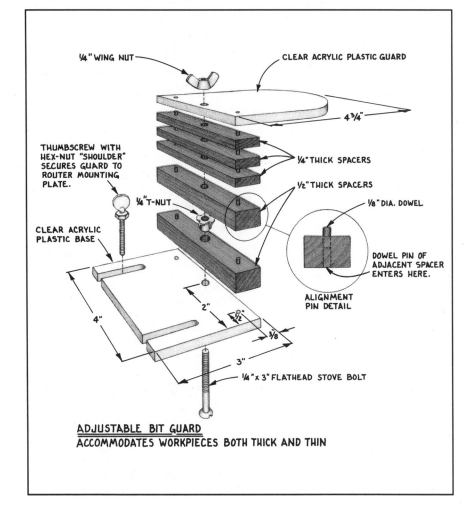

¼" WING NUT

CLEAR ACRYLIC PLASTIC GUARD

THUMBSCREW WITH HEX-NUT "SHOULDER" SECURES GUARD TO ROUTER MOUNTING PLATE.

4 ¾"

¼" THICK SPACERS

½" THICK SPACERS

⅛" DIA. DOWEL

¼" T-NUT

CLEAR ACRYLIC PLASTIC BASE

DOWEL PIN OF ADJACENT SPACER ENTERS HERE.

ALIGNMENT PIN DETAIL

2"

4"

½"

⅜"

3"

¼" x 3" FLATHEAD STOVE BOLT

ADJUSTABLE BIT GUARD
ACCOMMODATES WORKPIECES BOTH THICK AND THIN

Clamp-On Acrylic Bit Guard

As a variation on the adjustable bit guard, here is an adjustable guard that clamps to the router table. This arrangement offers more flexibility in positioning the guard. If you need to work on the broad part of the table, or from the side, you can shift the guard to accommodate the work.

The guard itself can be acrylic or polycarbonate, but it should be clear, of course, so you can see what you're doing. The base, instead of being plastic, is a 2-foot strip of hardwood. The same hardwood spacer blocks are used to set the height of the guard, and the assembly is fastened together with a stove bolt and wing nut. By varying the spacers used, you can adjust the gap beneath the guard from ¾ inch up to 2 inches.

Basic information on working acrylic is found in the chapter "Custom Baseplates." There aren't enough parts to merit a Cutting List, so here's a list of what you need:

- One 4-inch by 4¾-inch piece of ¼-inch clear acrylic
- One ½-inch by ¾-inch by 4-inch hardwood block

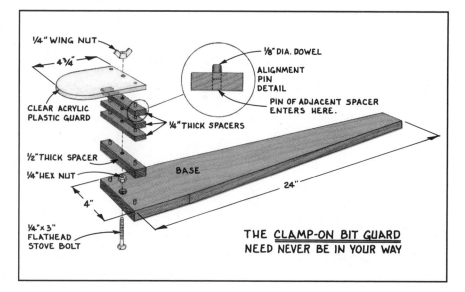

THE **CLAMP-ON BIT GUARD** NEED NEVER BE IN YOUR WAY

- Three ¼-inch by ¾-inch by 4-inch hardwood blocks
- One ¾-inch by 4-inch by 24-inch hardwood strip
- One scrap of ⅛-inch dowel
- One 3-inch-long ¼-inch flathead stove bolt and hex nut
- One ¼-inch wing nut

1. Without stripping off the paper masking, lay out the larger piece of acrylic—the guard—as shown in *Clamp-On Bit Guard*. Cut the curved edge with a saber saw or on the band saw, then bore the mounting hole and the two alignment pin holes. For a finished appearance, sand and polish the edges of the guard. Remove the paper masking.

2. Stack the spacer blocks, and clamp them to one end of the base. Using the guard as a pattern, lay out the locations of the two ⅛-inch-diameter alignment pin holes and the ¼-inch-diameter mounting hole. Drill the holes. The mounting hole in the base must be countersunk for the stove bolt on one side and counterbored for a nut on the other.

3. Glue bits of the ⅛-inch dowel in the alignment pin holes in the spacers and the base, as shown in the *Alignment Pin Detail*. The idea is to have holes in the bottom surfaces of the blocks and corresponding pins protruding from the tops. It easiest to do this if you use fairly long bits of dowel, then trim them to nubs after the glue dries.

4. Slip the stove bolt into the base and secure it with the nut. Stack the other spacer blocks on the bolt, add the guard, and turn the wing nut onto the bolt, fastening the assembly together.

This guard combines height adjustability with positioning flexibility. You can clamp the guard in whatever position will shield the bit without interfering with your movements or those of the workpiece.

Three-in-One Guard

More than a bit guard, this accessory is a starting pin/dust pickup/bit guard. It's designed to be placed almost anywhere on the top of the table, independent of a fence. It has a long extension arm that allows it to be clamped anywhere around the top's edge. When routing against a piloted bit without the fence, you can put this pickup where it can collect the stream of chips coming off the bit. What's more, this dust pickup has a rounded right-front edge that, like a starting pin, supports the work.

To use it, you fit the carriage bolt that extends through the pivot side into the starting pin hole in the mounting plate. Clamp the pivot side extension to the edge of the table, and plug in the hose from your shop vac.

1. Cut out the pieces for the dust pickup, and glue and screw them together, as shown in *Three-in-One Guard*.

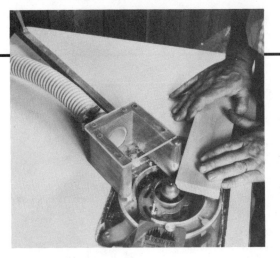

Although its clear acrylic top doesn't cantilever over the bit, this guard shields the bit quite effectively. And with a shop vac pulling the chips and dust off the tabletop, it improves on the chip deflection capacity of other guard designs.

2. Screw the clear acrylic top on the pickup.

3. Measure the diameter of your shop vac hose, and drill a hole that size in a scrap. Test the fit of the hose, and adjust the size of the hole as ne-cessary to get an easy press fit. When you've got the size right, drill a hole that size in the back of the pickup.

4. If necessary, drill an extra hole in the router table's mounting plate for the pickup's carriage bolt.

CUTTING LIST					
Piece	Number	Thickness	Width	Length	Material
Pivot side	1	¾"	3"	24½"	4/4 oak
Side	1	¾"	3"	3¾"	4/4 oak
Back	1	¾"	3"	3⅝"	4/4 oak

Hardware
1 pc. ¼" × 4½" × 4⅜" clear acrylic
6 pcs. ¾" × #6 flathead wood screws
1 pc. ¼" × 3½" carriage bolt

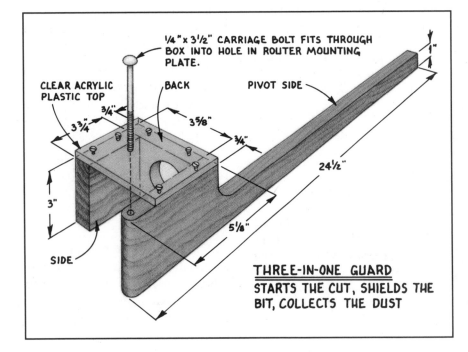

¼"x 3½" CARRIAGE BOLT FITS THROUGH BOX INTO HOLE IN ROUTER MOUNTING PLATE.

CLEAR ACRYLIC PLASTIC TOP

BACK

PIVOT SIDE

¾"

3¾"

3⅝"

¾"

24½"

1"

3"

5⅛"

SIDE

THREE-IN-ONE GUARD
STARTS THE CUT, SHIELDS THE BIT, COLLECTS THE DUST

FENCE

A router table without a fence is like a table saw without one. You can do some work, but not a whole lot. Just as the router table is shop-built, so too is the fence. We've got three fences here, each a little more sophisticated than the last. In addition to these three, there are a few others scattered throughout the book. Like the jointing fence in the chapter "Edge Joints," these tend to be designed for one specific operation and nothing more, so we present them in conjunction with the appropriate operation.

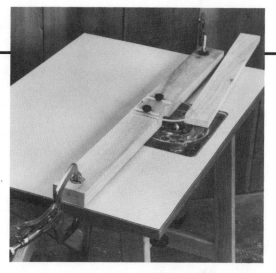

The Basic Fence

The foremost fence you'll use is also the most simple. It's a straight, knot-free, hardwood board.

A lot of router wonks perceive such fences as disposable. It's akin to the fence they clamp to work for a hand-held router operation. Rather than set a fence board aside, they clamp whatever straight piece is at hand to the tabletop. When the operation is done, the "fence" goes back onto the wood rack or into the scrap bin.

I personally have a "keeper" fence of this sort: I have a hook driven into one end so I can hang it beside the router table when I'm not using it. And it's been worked a bit, so it *is* something more than a "board."

The principal requirement is that the fence be perfectly straight, flat, and square—and so it won't warp, straight-grained. It ought to be just a little longer than your table is wide, but other than that, the dimensions are up to you. Make it of 5/4 or 8/4 stock, and rip it 3 or 4 inches wide. Choose a hard wood, one that will withstand the kind of rubbing and squeezing and impacts that a fence has to endure.

My fence is doubled-edged. One edge has been chamfered. This is a common practice; the idea is to give sawdust a place to go, so it doesn't collect at the fence and keep the

This one-board fence is obviously a keeper. It's notched so it can house the bit, it's chamfered so dust doesn't keep the work from accurately referencing the fence, and it has an adjustable guard.

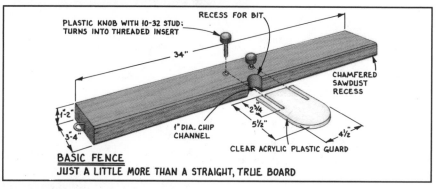

BASIC FENCE
JUST A LITTLE MORE THAN A STRAIGHT, TRUE BOARD

workpiece from seating squarely against it. But because the chamfer can catch really thin stock—like a piece of plastic laminate I might be cutting—I didn't chamfer the second edge. I just turn the fence around for such operations.

The next thing I did was to rout a channel across each edge for the bit. The fence fits right up around most bits, and it will do so regard-

Clamps are the most straightforward way to secure a fence to the router table. So-called quick clamps get a lot of use in the Rodale shop, but some woodworkers, complaining that they vibrate loose too easily, won't use them. C-clamps are more secure in this regard, but I like the ease of application of Vise-Grip C-clamps. Once set to the thickness of the material being clamped, these plierlike clamps lock in place with the squeeze of one hand. You can hold the fence with one hand and snap the clamp in place with the other.

less of which edge is used as the reference face. A similar channel across the bottom face is for router chips to blow through. All these channels were routed with a 1-inch-diameter roundnose (or core-box) bit.

Finally, I installed a couple of threaded inserts in the top face of the fence so that I can attach a flat, clear plastic bit guard to the fence with plastic thumbscrews.

L-Shaped Fence

The improvement this fence offers over the basic fence, above, is support. The fence is reversible: You can rest the 4-inch-wide face on the tabletop and have a 3-inch-high support, or you can get a 4-inch-high support by resting the 3-inch-wide face on the tabletop. Either way, the fence provides better support for work that has to be presented to the bit on edge or on end, rather than flat on the table. Like the basic fence, it is designed to be clamped to the router table.

It is only a little more difficult to make than the basic fence. Its two boards have to be glued together. The other basic-fence embellishments—the chip channel, for example, or the dust chamfer—can be added to this fence or not, as you see fit.

As with any router table fence, this one should be equipped with a guard. We bent a scrap of acrylic into an L-shape—to match the fence—and secured it to the fence with studded knobs turned into threaded inserts. There are inserts, of course, in both faces.

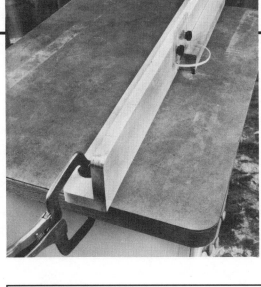

This L-shaped fence offers more vertical support than a basic one-board fence. Because it is unfettered by built-on clamps, it can be flip-flopped to present either a 3-inch-high face or a 4-inch-high face to the work.

CUTTING LIST					
Piece	Number	Thickness	Width	Length	Material
Fence base	1	1"	3"	34"	Hardwood
Fence back	1	1"	3"	34"	Hardwood

Hardware
1 pc. ¼" × 6" × 7" clear acrylic
4 pcs. 8-32 threaded inserts
2 pcs. 8-32 × ½" studded knobs

1. Joint and plane stock for the fence and fence back to the dimensions specified by the Cutting List. The exact width and thickness of these pieces is not important. It is important that they be jointed and planed perfectly square and straight.

2. Cut the fence and fence back to the lengths specified by the Cutting List.

3. With a belt sander, round off the top corners of the fence, as shown in *L-Shaped Fence*.

4. Glue and clamp the two fence parts together.

5. With the masking still in place, cut the shape of the bit guard from the clear acrylic using a saber saw or band saw. With a ¼-inch straight bit in a table-mounted router, cut the two mounting slots. Guide the acrylic workpiece along a fence.

6. Select a scrap of wood to use as a bending mold. Radius one edge with a ⅜-inch round-over bit. This is the edge you will use to form the guard's two bends.

7. Strip the masking from the acrylic. Mark the location of the bend. With a heat gun, heat just a band of the

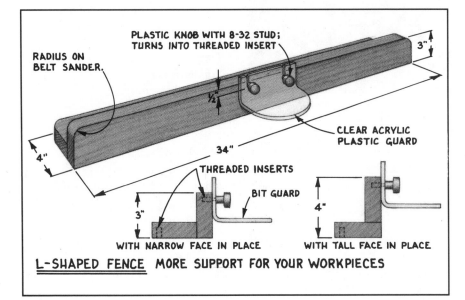

RADIUS ON BELT SANDER.
PLASTIC KNOB WITH 8-32 STUD; TURNS INTO THREADED INSERT
3"
½"
CLEAR ACRYLIC PLASTIC GUARD
34"
4"
THREADED INSERTS
BIT GUARD
3"
WITH NARROW FACE IN PLACE
4"
WITH TALL FACE IN PLACE

L-SHAPED FENCE MORE SUPPORT FOR YOUR WORKPIECES

You can't build a router table and a lot of accessories for it without also making a set of stop blocks. Yeah, sure, you can fetch stop blocks out of the scrap bin anytime. But these, as you can see, are custom-tailored to fit over the L-shaped fence. The stop block itself is long enough to reach all the way to the router tabletop, while the shorter cinch block carries the means for securing the assembly to the fence. To make them, you need some hardwood scraps, a couple of T-nuts or threaded inserts, two carriage bolts with nuts, and two wing nuts. The dimensions are shown in *Stop Blocks*. Construction is evident. One important tip: Be sure you turn the carriage bolts into the T-nuts *before* you glue the pieces together.

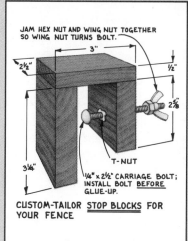

JAM HEX NUT AND WING NUT TOGETHER SO WING NUT TURNS BOLT.

3"

2½"

½"

2⅝"

T-NUT

3¼"

¼" x 2½" CARRIAGE BOLT; INSTALL BOLT BEFORE GLUE-UP.

CUSTOM-TAILOR STOP BLOCKS FOR YOUR FENCE

acrylic where the bend will be. When the plastic is limber, bend it a little beyond the right angle that's desired, then lay it over the mold, bringing it back to a right angle. Hold or clamp it until it cools and hardens.

8. For a finished appearance, sand and polish the edges of the guard.

9. Remove the clamps from the fence, and scrape off any dried glue. Next, true the fence on the jointer. Take a light cut from the bottom, then, holding the bottom firmly to the jointer fence, take however many cuts are required to make the fence face absolutely square to the fence bottom.

10. Using the bit guard as a template, mark the locations for the threaded inserts on both the 3-inch-wide and 4-inch-wide faces. Drill holes in the fence, then drive the inserts. Be sure you set them well below the wood surface, so they don't catch or scratch your work when you use the fence without the guard. Attach the guard to the fence.

SPLIT FENCE

The fence is perhaps the trickiest part of a router table to design. The most straightforward design, without doubt, is a stout board, straight and flat, that is clamped to the tabletop. It can be oriented any which way across the tabletop, and secured with whatever clamps are available—quick-clamps, C-clamps, even hand screws.

In some designs, the fence is secured with bolts that pass through holes or slots routed in the tabletop. Such slots gather dirt, though, and a fence like that can only move more or less parallel to the edge of the top. But with such a fence, you don't have to scour the shop for clamps every time you need to use the router table with a fence.

Our fence here combines advantages: It is strong and straight, yet its design is flexible enough that you can skew the fence at an angle across the top if need be. Best of all, it has integral clamps cinched by big, plastic wing nuts—easy on the hands.

The main fence can be used the way it is, though it's not high enough to support wide pieces on edge. To give the fence more versatility, we mounted two adjustable auxiliary fences to the main fence. The auxiliaries are bolted to slotted wooden angle brackets, which in turn are bolted to the main fence. You can

Versatility is the hallmark of the split fence. One of many possibilities: Shift the outfeed half of the fence so it can serve as a stop.

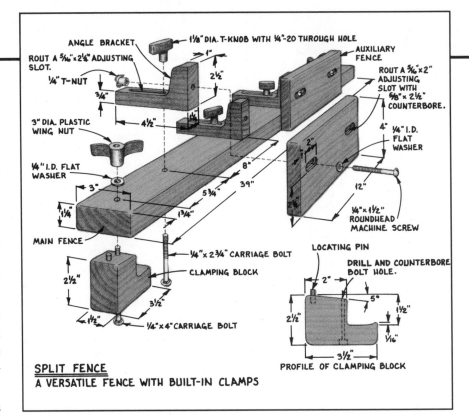

SPLIT FENCE
A VERSATILE FENCE WITH BUILT-IN CLAMPS

move the auxiliary fences closer together or farther apart to adjust the width of the opening between them at the router bit. You can also move either auxiliary fence forward toward the front edge of the table.

1. To begin, cut out a piece for the main fence from 6/4 stock, as specified by the Cutting List. We used oak for the fence parts, but hard maple or some other stable hardwood would work as well.

2. Cut out the various parts of the fence and shape them, as shown in *Split Fence*. Radius the edges of the fence parts with a ³⁄₁₆-inch round-over bit.

3. Drill the holes and counterbores for the threaded carriage bolts and T-nuts, as shown in the drawing.

The integral clamps are among the best features of the split fence. You can hold your rule in one hand and loosen and tighten the fence with the other. A long carriage bolt fitted with a large plastic wing nut secures the clamping block to the fence, while the small screw projecting from the block catches in a stopped hole in the fence to keep the clamping block from twisting.

CUTTING LIST

Piece	Number	Thickness	Width	Length	Material
Main fence	1	1¼"	3"	39"	6/4 oak
Auxiliary fences	2	¾"	4"	12"	4/4 oak
Angle brackets	2	1¼"	2½"	4½"	6/4 oak
Clamping blocks	2	1½"	2½"	3½"	8/4 oak

Hardware

2 pcs. ¼" × 4" carriage bolts (for clamping blocks)
4 pcs. ¼" × 1½" roundhead machine screws (for auxiliary fences)
4 pcs. ¼" × 2¾" carriage bolts (for angle brackets)
2 pcs. ¾" #6 panhead screws
6 pcs. ¼" I.D. flat washers
4 pcs. ¼" T-nuts
4 pcs. 1⅛" diameter plastic T-knobs, with ¼"-20 through hole. Available from Woodhaven, 5323 West Kimberly, Davenport, IA 52806. Part #554.
2 pcs. 3" diameter plastic wing nuts, with ¼"-20 through hole. Available from Woodhaven. Part #556.

At each end of the main fence and in each clamp block, drill a small hole for the locating pin. These pins—they're really panhead screws —prevent the clamping blocks from twisting when you tighten down the fence. The holes in the fence should provide loose fits for them. Drive a screw into the top of each clamping block.

4. Cut the adjusting slots in the angle brackets and the auxiliary fences. Assuming you've already made your router table, use a straight bit in your table-mounted router to cut these slots.

5. After applying a clear finish to the wooden fence parts, assemble the unit and clamp it to the router table.

Problem Solver

Holding the work on the router table, and simultaneously feeding it into the bit, is fraught with difficulties. Especially if the piece is outsized, it's easy for it to drift away from the fence, tip up off the bit, or chatter and shake.

Three shop-made hold-downs can solve a lot of these problems. They'll keep the work tight against the table and firmly against the fence. Use them individually or in pairs. Make a couple of the featherboards (sometimes called fingerboards) and the springboards.

Plesiosaur is what Fred calls this hold-down. Like a dinosaur, it cranes its long neck over the fence and presses its outsized head against the work, pinning it against the router table. The brains are in the tail end; a wedge cut from the base lets you adjust the head position. With the wedge removed, the head is suspended about 2⅝ inches above the tabletop; with it driven completely into place, the head rests against the tabletop. What you do is adjust the wedge so the head is a tad below the top surface of the workpiece. Apply a clamp, holding both the hold-down and the wedge. Push the workpiece under the head, which will hold it tightly against the tabletop.

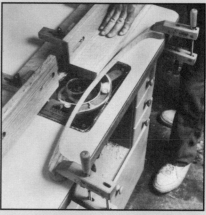

The springboard is a bowlike affair with clamp pads at each end. Cut it from a strip of springy wood like oak or ash. To use it, clamp one end to either the fence or the tabletop—depending upon whether it is to hold down or in. Flex the other end to create pressure against the work, then clamp the other end.

Featherboards are pretty common-place and can be used throughout the shop. This one is a little different, in that it has clamping pads beside the fingers as well as behind them. It's short enough for you to clamp it to the front of any router table—as well as to the fence.

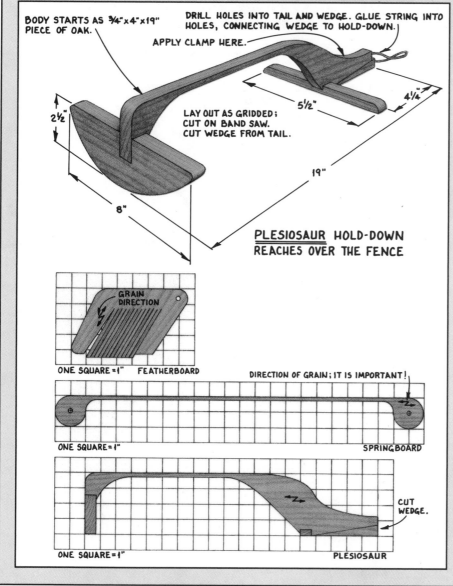

BODY STARTS AS ¾"×4"×19" PIECE OF OAK.

DRILL HOLES INTO TAIL AND WEDGE. GLUE STRING INTO HOLES, CONNECTING WEDGE TO HOLD-DOWN.

APPLY CLAMP HERE.

LAY OUT AS GRIDDED; CUT ON BAND SAW. CUT WEDGE FROM TAIL.

2½"

5½"

4¼"

19"

8"

PLESIOSAUR HOLD-DOWN REACHES OVER THE FENCE

GRAIN DIRECTION

ONE SQUARE = 1"   FEATHERBOARD

DIRECTION OF GRAIN; IT IS IMPORTANT!

ONE SQUARE = 1"   SPRINGBOARD

ONE SQUARE = 1"

CUT WEDGE.

PLESIOSAUR

Fence-Mounted Dust Pickup

This pickup is a simple, open-sided wooden box covered with clear plastic. It's designed to be used with the split fence. It sits atop the main fence between the auxiliary fences. The box has a large hole in the back to accept a standard-sized shop-vac hose.

1. Cut out the pieces for the dust pickup, and glue and screw them together, as shown in *Fence-Mounted Dust Pickup.*

2. Screw the clear acrylic top onto the pickup.

3. Measure the diameter of your shop-vac hose, and drill a hole that size in a scrap. Test the fit of the hose and adjust the size of the hole as necessary to get an easy press fit. When you've got the size right, drill a hole that size in the back of the pickup.

4. Glue the mounting block to the side, as shown. Attach it to the slot in the auxiliary fence with a round-head machine screw and a T-nut.

SLED

The sled combines the roles of miter gauge, push block, and chip breaker. We use it when doing end-grain cuts. Because it hooks over the table edge, it doesn't need to be used with the fence, nor does it require a slot.

When the sled is serving as a chip breaker, the bit cuts through the work and into the sled itself. It gets chewed up in this kind of use, so the sled is, in a strong sense, a consumable. It's easy to make another, so you can make special sleds for different cuts. The sled shown has been used exclusively for cope-and-stick

You shouldn't have to forgo the benefits of a surface-mounted dust pickup just because you are using a fence. This dust pickup is attached to the fence.

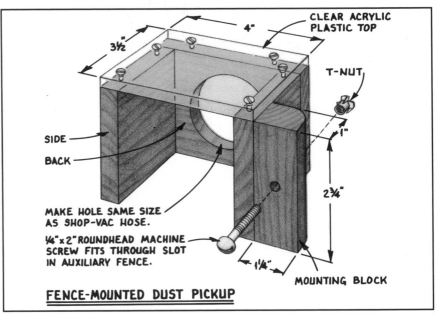

FENCE-MOUNTED DUST PICKUP

CUTTING LIST

Piece	Number	Thickness	Width	Length	Material
Sides	2	½"	2¾"	3"	4/4 oak
Back	1	½"	2¾"	4"	4/4 oak
Mounting block	1	1"	1¼"	2¾"	5/4 oak
Top	1	¼"	3½"	4"	Clear acrylic

Hardware

6 pcs. #6 × ¾" flathead wood screws
1 pc. ¼" × 2" roundhead machine screw
1 pc. ¼" I.D. flat washer
1 pc. ¼" T-nut

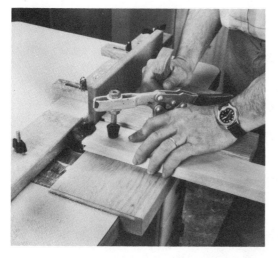

You can have a miter gauge for your router table without having a tabletop slot to guide it. A fence attached to a bottom of the sled slides along the tabletop edge and maintains the sled's position vis-à-vis the bit. It's just what you need for the cope-and-stick work being done here, as well as for many other router table operations.

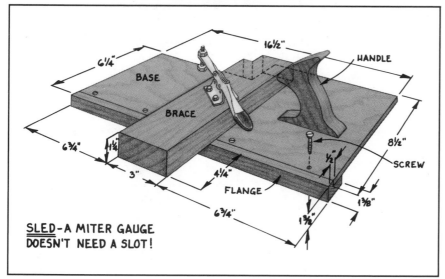

BASE
BRACE
FLANGE
HANDLE
SCREW
6¼"
16½"
6¾"
6¾"
3"
4¼"
1½"
½"
8½"
1⅜"
1½"

SLED - A MITER GAUGE DOESN'T NEED A SLOT!

CUTTING LIST

Piece	Number	Thickness	Width	Length	Material
Base	1	½"	8"	16½"	Fir plywood
Flange	1	1⅜"	1⅜"	16½"	8/4 oak
Brace	1	1¼"	3"	11"	6/4 oak
Handle	1	1"	4½"	4½"	5/4 oak

Hardware
6 pcs. #6 × 1" drywall screws
1 quick-release toggle clamp

work, and it was made of scrap-bin materials.

The toggle clamp is a practical feature. It keeps your work firmly in place, freeing both hands to guide the sled. Its position is designed to keep the end of the work from bowing up away from the bit, which could give you an irregular cut.

For cope-and-stick work, the clamp is almost essential. The reason? In action, the bit is self-feeding, and though you are moving the work counter to the bit's rotation, it will pull the work into itself. The cut that starts square may end up slightly angled, and the matched joints you cut may not fit tightly. Although you may not believe this, that toggle clamp can pinch the work a lot tighter than you can with your hand.

1. Cut the parts to the sizes specified by the Cutting List. The parts need to be flat and square. Cut the handle to shape on the band saw or with a saber saw. The exact shape is less important than its fit in your hand; achieve the latter.

2. Cut a rabbet for the base in the flange, then glue and screw the two parts together.

3. Glue and screw the brace in place. Be sure it is at right angles to the edge of the flange. Keep the screws back from the edge where the bit might hit them.

4. Screw the toggle clamp to the brace.

5. Glue and screw the handle to the sled.

PIN ROUTER ARM

The pin is another guide device used in router woodworking. It is positioned in the same axis as the bit, either above the bit in the case of a table-mounted router or beneath it in the case of an (expensive) over-arm router. As the work—or more often a template attached to the work—rubs against the pin, it controls where the bit cuts. (Tips on using the pin router arm can be found in the chapters "Template-Guided Work" and "Rabbeting.")

This accessory holds a pin directly

Feel you just *have* to have a miter gauge slot in your router table? You can have the slot and maintain the integrity of your laminated tabletop by screwing a rabbeted hardwood strip to the front edge of your tabletop.

Joint, plane, and rip a strip of oak, maple, ash, or similar *hard* wood to a 1½-inch-square girth. Crosscut a piece as long as your router tabletop. Cut a ⅜-inch-wide by ¾-inch-deep rabbet along its full length; make three or four passes to achieve the full depth.

You want to attach the strip to the front edge of the tabletop so that it forms a ¾-inch-wide groove. The top of the strip must be flush with the tabletop. Clamp the strip in place and drill holes for an appropriate number of mounting screws.

• If the installation is to be permanent, countersink and counterbore the holes. Glue and screw the strip in place, then conceal the screwheads with wood plugs. Trim the plugs flush, sand, and apply a finish.

• If the strip is to be removable, drill and countersink pilot holes for flathead machine screws. Drill holes of the appropriate size in the tabletop edge, then install threaded inserts. Sand and finish the strip, then screw it in place.

Though the slot is at the very edge of the table, it is within 6 inches of the bit if you've offset your router in the tabletop. Adapt the sled with a guide strip sized to fit the slot. Make other router table accessories that use the slot as a guide.

A pin routing arm is generally used for template work, but you can also use it for cutting deep rabbets, as here. See the chapter "Template-Guided Work" for additional information on using the pin router arm.

above the bit of the cabinet router table. The crossbar rests on the tabletop with the flange against the back edge. When aligned between marks made on the tabletop during the arm's construction, the pin is concentric with the bit. You use clamps to secure the arm.

If the workpiece is thick and you need to raise the pin, unclamp the arm and slip a spacer or two under the crossbar. Then reclamp the arm.

1. Select straight-grained, defect-free stock. Plane, rip, joint, and crosscut the parts to the sizes specified by the Cutting List.

2. On the band saw, round off one end of the arm, as shown in *Pin Router Arm.* Clamp the arm to the elevator block, and lay out the bevel that blends the two parts, as shown. Also, mark the block's position on the arm. Unclamp the parts, and cut the bevels.

3. Glue the flange to the back edge of the crossbar. When the glue is dry, set the block in position and mark that position on the crossbar. With a router and a ¼-inch round-over bit, radius all the edges that will

be exposed on the assembled unit. Then glue the elevator block and the arm to the crossbar.

4. Set the arm on the router table with the arm centered—as closely as possible—above the router collet. Clamp it. Mark the router table's edge banding on each end of the crossbar, so you can quickly and reliably align the arm unit on the router table whenever you need to use it. For the sake of permanence, you may want to chisel marks into wooden banding, if your table has it.

5. To mark the hole for the pin, you need to chuck the longest ¼-inch straight bit you have in the router, backing it as far out of the collet as possible. No, you aren't actually going to run the router. Elevate the router until the bit contacts the arm. If you spin the collet by hand, the bit should mark the arm. When the arm is well marked, remove it from the router table and bore a ¼-inch-diameter hole through it on the drill press.

6. Several pins were made for the pin router arm. All use ¼-inch bolts. The "standard" pin is a ¼-inch bolt with the head sawed off. A wing nut holds it in place. The smooth shank between the head (now missing) and the threads is the rub surface. Larger-diameter pins can be made by centerboring 1¼-inch pieces of oak dowel of the desired diameter. The most accurate way to centerbore the dowel is on a lathe. Bore a ¼-inch-diameter hole clean through the dowel, then make a ⅜-inch-diameter counterbore about ½ inch deep. Use a cap bolt, which has a round head with a socket it in for an allen wrench. Pull the bolt into the dowel and sink the head in the counterbore.

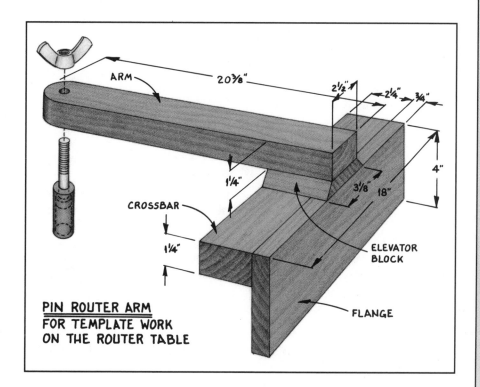

**PIN ROUTER ARM
FOR TEMPLATE WORK
ON THE ROUTER TABLE**

CUTTING LIST

Piece	Number	Thickness	Width	Length	Material
Arm	1	1¼"	2½"	20⅜"	6/4 oak
Elevator block	1	¾"	3"	3⅛"	4/4 oak
Crossbar	1	1¼"	2¼"	18"	6/4 oak
Flange	1	¾"	4"	18"	4/4 oak

Hardware

1 pc. ¼" × 2½" cap bolt
1 pc. ¼" wing nut

TRY THIS!

The router table provides a perfect place to mount a couple of other portable power tools. The impact for them is the same as it is for the router. You manipulate the work rather than the tool, and you see what's going on.

All you need is a couple of extra mounting plates.

One tool that comes to mind for this treatment is the saber saw. Screw a mounting plate to a saber saw's shoe. The blade juts through a hole in the plate. Drop the plate into the opening in the router tabletop, and you've got a kind of scroll saw.

You can turn a portable power drill into a stationary drum sander —a small one to be sure—with a mounting plate, a Port-A-Lign drill guide, and a sanding drum scaled to the drill. Attach the guide to the mounting plate, positioning it so the chuck will be just below the bit throat in the plate. Install the drill on the guide, fit the drum in the chuck, and go to work.

Acrylic is sufficiently cheap that you can make the extra mounting plates and keep them handy for those jobs when you want to table-mount these other tools.

ROUTER TABLE SAVVY

It's one thing to design and build a good router table, another matter entirely to use it effectively—and safely.

The very best way to learn is to watch a savvy hand at work. The next best is to read up—starting here, of course!—and to experiment. Do some cuts with a piloted bit and the starting pin. Work with the fence. Pay close attention to feed direction.

You'll learn the tricks, starting with changing bits, and progressing through setting the bit height and positioning the fence. You'll learn the safe ways—and safe directions—to move the workpiece.

CHANGING BITS

Changing bits always seems harder than it should be. Hanging the router under a table increases the aggravation.

Two common approaches come to mind. The "best method" will ofttimes change with the situation. I suggest that you try them both and use the one that better suits the moment. Regardless of the method, unplug the router first.

SETTING THE BIT HEIGHT

After the bit is firmly chucked in the collet, you need to set the height. This isn't a difficult task by any means, but a couple of tricks can make the job easier and the result more accurate.

First of all, use a steel ruler rather than a tape measure. The hook riveted to the tape makes the first inch of the tape virtually unusable for measuring purposes. Of course, the first inch is the most important in setting the bit height.

A practical measuring device is a 6-inch steel rule, which you can usually buy at an art-and-drafting supplies store. A lot of woodworkers keep a combination square at the router table and use it to set both the bit height and the fence. These squares have a variety of graduations on the rule, one of which is certain to suit your purpose. A 6-inch square is ideal to use with the router table, in my estimation.

To set the bit's height accurately, you need to get your line of sight even with the bit. Stand the rule right next to it. It helps immeasurably to have the bit opening in the mounting plate closely matched to the bit diameter. A ½-inch dovetail bit jutting through a 2-inch opening isn't one your rule can cozy up to. (This isn't a particularly safe operating situation, either.) Using the combination square is your best bet here.

You can make an alternative

Work with the motor in "table position." Back the motor down enough to get at the collet nut, and work the wrenches in the gaps between the base's buttresses or the plunge rods. Lift the bits in and out through the bit throat in the baseplate. If the mounting plate is clear, it's easy to see where your wrenches are and what you're doing.

Lift the router, mounting plate and all, out of the table. Lay it on the table and change the bit. (This router has an arbor lock, so only one wrench is needed.) If your mounting plate is screwed down, or if the router is attached directly to the table, you can't try this one.

Need three hands to change bits? When you do this with the router in "table position," it often seems that way, especially if you want to avoid bottoming the bit (that is, letting the bit rest against the collet bottom). And all bit makers entreat you to avoid bottoming the bit. (See the chapter "Bits" for the reasons why.)

Here's a trick to try.

Fit an O-ring—buy 'em at an auto-parts store—on the shank of each bit you have. The rubber ring will catch on the collet and limit the shank's penetration into it. In most cases, you'll position the ring to keep the bit from bottoming. On short-shanked bits, this will be near the cutter.

approach possible by making a simple adjustable depth gauge. Join two scraps of wood with a sliding dovetail joint, and apply a short length of adhesive-backed measuring tape to one of them. Instead of trying to carry a graduation by eye from your rule to the bit, you can rest one segment of this gauge atop the bit and easily read the graduation next to it. See *Adjustable Depth Gauge* for dimensions and construction details.

There's one critical element of bit height adjustment we haven't mentioned yet. That's the router's adjustment mechanism.

To me, the most accurate, controllable bit height adjustment is offered by plunge routers equipped with a so-called micro-adjusting knob. This is a sort of "manual override" of the machine's plunging action. As you rotate the knob, the router is forced steadily down the plunge rods (or allowed to steadily slide up the rods). Because the knob is turning a nut on a threaded rod to cause the movement, you should be able to convert the rod's threads-per-inch into a ratio of bit height movement. For example, if the rod has 20 threads per inch, turning the knob five times should raise or lower the bit 1/4 inch.

Some plunge routers have a micro-adjusting knob as standard equipment, but you can buy one for those that don't. Check with Woodhaven and Eagle America (see "Sources" on page 337).

Not only is the vertical movement thus controllable, the plunge router's structure prevents the bit

A good steel rule is ideal for setting bit height. This one has the first inch graduated in 32nds. Machinist's rules often are graduated to 64ths, which is too fine for my bifocaled eyes. For my router work, 32nds is usually sufficient.

Where the bit opening is not closely matched to the bit diameter, a combination square is the best for setting bit height. You can stand it next to the bit, then use both hands to adjust the router.

Using this shop-made depth gauge eliminates bending and squinting. Set the height you want, then set the gauge over the bit. Crank the bit up until it touches the end of the slide. With a piloted bit, you simply have to be sure that the slide is positioned clear of the pilot and that it is touched only by the cutting edge.

Sideplay in the depth-of-cut mechanisms of some fixed-base routers can lead to less-than-perfect finished cuts. Eliminate this problem by using a spacer to lift the workpiece for the first pass. The spacer should extend the full width of the tabletop, but it need be only wide enough to cover the area between the fence and the table's front edge.

TRY THIS!

Have trouble keeping track of the number of times you've turned that micro-adjusting knob? Dab a spot of bright-colored paint on the knob. Each time the paint-spot passes a matching mark on the router is a full turn.

from shifting from side to side as you raise it.

Few fixed-base routers can offer this kind of fine adjustment. Several different adjustment systems are used by the makers of fixed-base routers (they are discussed in some detail in the chapter "Routers"), but all involve a knob or wing nut that cinches the base tightly around the motor to hold the setting. In a router table setup, loosening the wing nut on some brands and models sacrifices the setting you have, because it frees the motor to drop. And with the motor loose, you fight gravity to find a specific setting. In addition, almost all the systems allow sideplay, so the bit's position in relation to the fence can shift when the bit height is altered.

The response to the latter problem is circumvention: Don't set the fence until you've set the bit height. It's in raising the bit for a second pass that the sideplay becomes a real irritant. In deepening a groove, for example, you can end up with a stepped groove that's the correct width at the bottom but too wide at the surface. To circumvent this problem, set the bit for the final depth of cut right at the start, and make the initial pass with an auxiliary top in place, so that the workpiece is raised. Remove the auxiliary top for the second pass, lowering the workpiece.

Figure

2" LONG PIECE OF ADHESIVE-BACKED MEASURING TAPE; POSITION TAPE SO POINTER INDICATES "0" WHEN SLIDE IS BOTTOMED.

1/4" x 1" THUMBSCREW

POINTER CUT FROM SCRAP METAL; SECURE WITH #4 x 1/2" PANHEAD SCREW.

1/2" x 1" x 6" HARDWOOD SLIDE

6"

5/16" DIA. THROUGH HOLE

3/4" DIA. COUNTERBORE FOR T-NUT

1" DIA. COUNTERBORE FOR KNOCKOUT

GRAIN DIRECTION

2" RAD.

4"

1/2" RAD.

1/4" T-NUT

2"

ELECTRICAL BOX KNOCKOUT OR NICKEL KEEPS THUMBSCREW FROM DIGGING INTO SLIDE.

1"

2"

8"

MAKE YOUR OWN ADJUSTABLE DEPTH GAUGE

Choking Up on the Bit

This is safety as much as savvy. You should have the bit opening in the mounting plate closed down around the bit just as closely as possible. This prevents the workpiece from dipping into the bit opening, snagging the edge, maybe stalling the cut.

If you've opened up the bit hole to accommodate a 3-inch (or larger) panel-raising bit, don't then fit a ½-inch dovetail bit or ¼-inch straight bit in the router and expect to rout a groove without hazard or hang-up.

What you can do, when you need to close down that throat, is drop the router down so the bit's below the table. Then lay a piece of Masonite over the tabletop. Stick it in place with double-sided carpet tape—say, just a piece at each corner. The fence will help hold it, too. Turn on the router and run your bit up through the Masonite. The bit hole will perfectly match the bit. You can set this auxiliary top aside and use it again and again, every time you use that bit. Just center it by fitting it over the bit, stick it down, set the fence, and rout your work.

An alternative is to make a set of reducing rings from the same material used for the mounting plate. We made such a set from ⅜-inch clear acrylic. The basic bit opening in the mounting plate is 3½ inches in diameter, large enough to accommodate the largest panel-raiser in our collection. It has a ⅛-inch-wide by 3/16-inch-deep rabbet around it. The reducers are 3¾ inches in diameter and are similarly rabbeted, so the reducer fits into the bit opening and rests flush. The bit openings in the reducers can be matched to different commonly used bit sizes—¼ inch, ½ inch, ¾ inch, 1 inch, and so on. We've got one that's

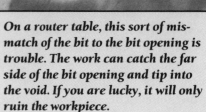

On a router table, this sort of mismatch of the bit to the bit opening is trouble. The work can catch the far side of the bit opening and tip into the void. If you are lucky, it will only ruin the workpiece.

bored out and rabbeted for template guides.

We cut the mounting plate's bit opening with a plastic-cutting bit in a trammel-equipped laminate trimmer. The centerpoint was established by mounting the router on the plate and marking the plate using a V-groove bit. After the hole was routed, cutting the rabbet with a rabbeting bit was simple.

A reducer pattern was also cut with the trammel. I deliberately made the pattern a bit oversized to start, and I

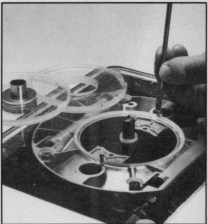

carefully trimmed it until it fit tightly in the plate's opening. Then I used the pattern to knock out duplicates using a flushing-trimming bit. I found it useful to transfer the reducer pattern's centerpoint to each duplicate by drilling through the pattern into the dupe with a ⅛-inch drill bit.

A set of reducers, cut from the same material as the mounting plate, keeps the bit opening matched to the bit being used. To keep the router's vibrations from popping the reducers out of place, use a couple of 10-32 flathead machine screws to secure them. Drill and tap holes for the screws in the mounting plate, positioning them in the seam between the mounting plate and the reducer. On the router table, rout tiny chamfers for the screw heads into the reducers.

CONTROLLING THE WORKPIECE

Freehand routing on the router table may occasionally be appropriate—though I can't think of a good example of such an occasion just now. In every operation that may come to mind, you use either a starting pin or a fence, even a sled, a template guide, or an overhead pin, to help you guide and control the workpiece.

Small as it may seem, a router bit does generate a lot of force. As the size of the bit increases, of course, the force gets greater. The "gotcha"

in routing lies in the multiplicity of bits in most collections. You probably use relatively small straights and round-over bits most, and you get accustomed to how they act. Then you cinch a large-diameter bit—a lock-miter bit or a panel-raiser—in the collet, approach it the way you would your typical cove bit, and *Gotcha!*

This is where the chip-limiting design of some bits is of greatest value. It minimizes their grabby nature.

An absolute essential here is having internalized feed direction savvy. Sure, sure. For a lot of work, the direction in which you feed the work doesn't come up until your fence is set. But feed direction savvy can be important in positioning the fence so the work has adequate support throughout a cut, or so the fence isn't in your way. One of the biggest factors in controlling the workpiece during a cut is getting the bit's energy working in your favor. Equally important is knowing when that energy can't be harnessed and thus being able to take appropriate measures—setting hold-downs, for example.

Feed Direction

Stop and think before each operation you perform: Which way do I feed the workpiece?

Almost invariably, you want to push the work *against* the rotation of the cutter. You want the bit to be pushing the work back, whether you are pushing it side to side or away from you. (If you are pulling the work, you want the bit to be pulling back.) An ancillary result of feeding against the bit rotation is that the force generated by the rotation helps drive the work against whatever guide you are using—the pilot bearing or the fence.

Feeding the work *with* the cutter's rotation gives it the opportunity to take control of the situation. It'll *help* you move that work. Spinning at 22,000 rpm, it's going to hurry things along, even if it has to pull

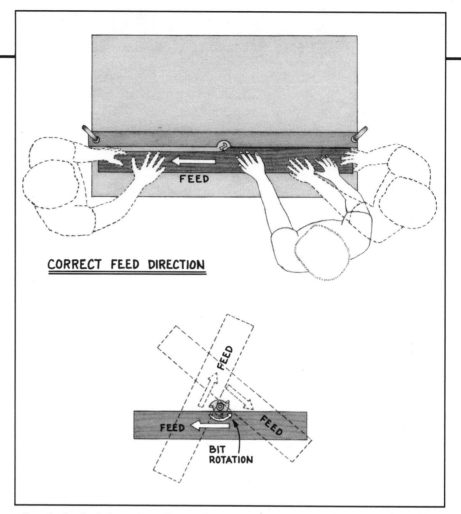

CORRECT FEED DIRECTION

Though the feed direction along a fence is always the same—from the right side of the bit to the left—your perception of it may change, depending upon where you stand. If you stand in front of the table, the feed is right to left. If you stand on the right side of the table, it may appear that you push the stock away from you along the fence. And if you stand on the left side, it may appear that you pull the stock toward you. But it's all the same direction.

When working with a piloted bit and no fence, the pilot is the point of demarcation. The bit rotates counterclockwise around the pilot. The feed direction rotates clockwise around the pilot.

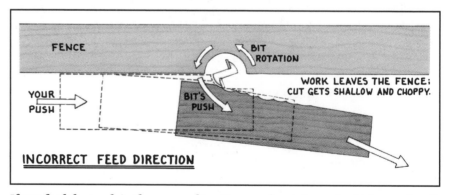

INCORRECT FEED DIRECTION

If you feed the work in the wrong direction, as shown here, the bit's rotational forces can shoot the work away from you. When it does, the cut goes away too, because the bit pushes it away from the fence.

FEED DIRECTION FOR <u>WIDENING A GROOVE</u>

BAD

BIT'S PUSH

BIT ROTATION

YOUR PUSH

CUTTING ON FENCE SIDE OF GROOVE: FEEDING RIGHT TO LEFT IS A CLIMB CUT.

OK

YOUR PUSH

BIT'S PUSH

BIT ROTATION

FEATHERBOARDS

CUTTING ON FENCE SIDE OF GROOVE: FEEDING LEFT TO RIGHT; NOT A CLIMB CUT, BUT BIT PUSHES WORK AWAY FROM FENCE.

BEST

BIT ROTATION

BIT'S PUSH

YOUR PUSH

CUTTING ON SIDE OF GROOVE <u>AWAY</u> FROM FENCE: FEED RIGHT TO LEFT; NOT A CLIMB CUT, AND BIT PUSHES WORK AGAINST FENCE.

the work right out of your hands to do it. Believe me: You don't want this.

There's an ancillary result here, too. Feeding with the bit rotation allows the cutter's force to throw the work *away* from your guide. This isn't a real problem with an edge cut, but it's an unmitigated disaster if you're cutting a groove.

Look at the bit. Even if you can't remember that the router—hanging upside down in a router table—will turn the bit counterclockwise, looking at the bit should clarify which direction it's going to spin. That, coupled with the stipulation that you feed the work *against* the cutter's rotation, should tell you which way to feed the work, regardless of where you stand and regardless of whether you are pushing the stock away from you, pulling it into you, or shoving it from one side to the other.

But let me put it another way: *Feed from right to left across the cutter in most router operations.*

Piloted work feeds that way as long as you keep the stock between you and the cutter. If the cutter is between you and the work, the feed direction is left to right.

Fence-guided work feeds the same way if you're routing an edge—the edge against the fence. The work is between you and the cutter; you feed it from your right to your left. (Don't ever set the fence one board's width away from the bit, and then feed the board along the fence, routing the exposed edge. This traps the work between the bit and the fence, something savvy router-table woodworkers NEVER do.)

The right-to-left feed applies where you are plowing a groove the full width of the cutter. *It may not apply* where you are using only part

of the bit's cutting width. Here's one of the exceptions:

You are cutting a groove in two passes—forming a ¾-inch-wide groove with a ½-inch straight bit. The first pass is made right to left. But if, in the second pass, the bit is cutting on the side of the groove away from you and toward the fence, you must feed from left to right. (See the drawing at left.) This cut is a bit tricky because the rotation of the cutter will be trying to pull the stock away from the fence as you feed, so set up fingerboards to hold the stock against the fence, both before it contacts the cutter and after.

In this situation, you are probably better off to make the first cut in the usual way, then back the fence away from the bit. Thus, on the second cut, the bit will be working the side of the cut closest to you (rather than to the fence). And you still feed right to left.

USING A STARTING PIN

Because with a hand-held router a piloted bit usually is used without any other sort of guide, woodworkers sometimes do the same with a table-mounted router. Usually, no harm results; the workpiece has enough mass, and you're holding it tightly enough that the operation is successfully completed.

But once in a while—and it has to happen only once for you to experience a lifetime of regret—the cutter will catch the wood and rip the workpiece out of your grasp. It happens at the very start of a cut.

Here's why: With most piloted bits, the cutter is larger than the pilot. It therefore engages the wood

first. For the pilot to control things, it has to contact the wood, and it can do that only if the cutter bites into the wood deeply enough to draw it against the pilot. If the combination of circumstances is just right, the cutter can, instead, flick the workpiece aside. You're *never* ready for this—that's why it's a surprise. You're pushing the wood into the bit, and when the wood *suddenly* exits right, it isn't unusual for your hands to keep moving . . . right into the cutter.

The best way to avoid this accident is to always use a starting pin with a piloted bit (unless you are using a fence). It controls things until the stock gets to the pilot. A starting pin is a fulcrum for the work; you brace the work first against the non-moving pin, then "lever" it into the bit. The pin is nonmoving, so you can securely brace the work against it. Moreover, the pin gives you leverage, multiplying the strength of your hold on the wood and dampening the cutter's energy. (If you are working without a starting pin, then the spinning pilot is your fulcrum.) The most common manifestation of the starting pin is a wooden peg or metal or plastic pin projecting from the mounting plate 2 to 4 inches from the bit.

A starting pin is the fulcrum for starting a cut with a piloted bit. Brace the work against the stationary pin, then pivot it until it contacts the bit. Even if the cutter grabs the work, the pin's position prevents it from shooting it to the right, or worse, snatching it from your grasp.

The starting pin is called a *starting* pin because it helps at the beginning of a cut. Once the cutter is engaged and the work is in firm contact with the pilot, the pin is superfluous. It won't hurt to keep the work against it throughout as much of the cut as possible; but you can't always keep the work against both the pin and the cutter. You'll probably find that if you concentrate on keeping the work against the pin throughout the cut, you'll

A starting pin doesn't have to be a "pin." This triangular scrap, clamped to the router table, is as good a fulcrum as a more elaborate, hand-crafted accessory. It is particularly easy, with this approach, to vary the distance between the "pin" and the bit.

occasionally let it get away from the pilot.

An alternative to the starting pin, useful only when you're routing all around a workpiece, is to sweep in on a long-grained side, rather than starting at a corner.

FIXING THE FENCE

The fence is easily the most frequently used router-table guidance system. You use it to direct the movement of the workpiece to the bit. You use it to position the cut, and sometimes to control how deep the cut is or what its profile will be.

The fence itself can be a straight, flat board, a sophisticated, multipart construction, or something in between. (See the chapter "Router Table Accessories" for fence designs.) It's not unlikely that the more you use your router table, the more special-purpose fences you'll end up with.

Typically, the fence is clamped in place, though Fred's split fence has integral clamps that are secured with easy-on-the-fingers plastic wing nuts. You can use whatever clamps are available, except Quick-Grip clamps. The Quick-Grip clamps are easy to apply, but even when tightened to the maximum, their rubbery jaws don't get enough purchase to keep the fence in position. Hand screws work well so long as you get the jaws parallel and firmly set; otherwise the router's vibrations can shake them loose. Small bar clamps are used a lot in our shop. Though I'm not aware of such problems firsthand, I have read that some woodworkers have trouble with them shaking loose. C-clamps are probably the most sure, but also the most vexing to tighten and untighten. I personally like Vise-Grip C-clamps, which can be set and released with one hand.

Positioning the fence is a key step in setting up. The main concept to remember here is that you only have to establish the distance between the bit and the fence. With a router table, unlike a table saw, you don't have to worry about whether your fence is or isn't parallel with the cutter.

The usual fence-setting procedure is to place the fence on the tabletop, quickly get a rough setting, and clamp one end. Then you refine the setting by shifting the free end by the necessary fractions of an inch as you measure the gap between bit and fence. Then you clamp the second end of the fence.

Ideally, you measure between fence and bit with a square of some sort, and you measure from the fence to either the cutting edges or the axis of the bit. While the fence doesn't have to be square to an edge or parallel to an edge, the line you measure between bit and fence must be perpendicular to the fence. If you set the head of a square against the fence's face, the blade will jut away from it at a right angle. Slide the blade up to the bit and measure.

Again, to get a really accurate setting, you need to measure from the axis of the bit or from the cutting edges. Rotate the bit a little with your hand to align the cutting edges, and get the rule as close as possible to the appropriate edge. Pinpointing the axis? Good luck! It's tough to estimate accurately where the exact center of the bit is.

One important bit of savvy is that when you move only one end of the fence, the amount the cut moves is one-half the distance you move

To set the fence with a combination square, you first need to slide the head to the end of the rule. Set the head against the fence with the rule crossing above the bit, as shown here. You can establish the fence position from the near or far cutting edge or the (presumed) bit axis.

The shop-made depth gauge used to set the bit height can be a big help in setting the fence, too. Determine the distance from fence to the edge of the cut farthest from it. Set the gauge to that measurement. Butt the gauge slide against the bit's cutting edge, as shown, and bring the fence up against the base.

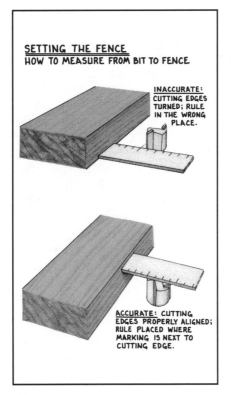

SETTING THE FENCE
HOW TO MEASURE FROM BIT TO FENCE.

INACCURATE:
CUTTING EDGES TURNED; RULE IN THE WRONG PLACE.

ACCURATE: CUTTING EDGES PROPERLY ALIGNED; RULE PLACED WHERE MARKING IS NEXT TO CUTTING EDGE.

A test cut will tell you all about the fence setting; the proof is in the cut, so to speak. To adjust the fence a small amount, scribe a pencil line along the fence—where the fence will be moving away from it—and measure with your rule from that line to the fence. Just remember that the distance you move one end of the fence will be halved at the bit.

the fence. I'm not talking here about a change where you move the fence while you're monitoring the change at the bit with a rule. I'm talking about measuring a sample cut and determining that you want to adjust the cut 1/8 inch. To get that 1/8-inch adjustment, you can pencil a line

along the fence at one end, then move the fence 1/4 inch away from the line. Obviously, you don't want to put the line where the movement will cover it. (And on a laminate-covered tabletop, you can erase the line completely when the job's done.)

After you've done it a zillion

times, you fall into a comfortable routine. You're even a little cavalier about it. You just eyeball the initial setting, then adjust it through a test cut or two.

As often as not, you use the fence with a piloted bit. Why? It provides excellent support for the workpiece, especially if the angle of

attack you've chosen requires you to perch it on edge. It gives you better control of the work. It conceals the segment of the bit that isn't cutting the work, protecting you from it.

An ancillary benefit is that you can reduce the bite without switching pilot bearings. Through judicious setting of bit height and fence position, for example, you can use an ogee bit to cut a cove. Or use a beading bit to round-over an edge. Or . . . well, be creative. Experiment.

Where a segment of the bit is to be buried in the fence, the fence,

perhaps obviously, has to be hogged out to accommodate the bit. This is how fences get "used up." Using a small bit in a fence cutout sized to accommodate a big bit can lead to the same problems you face in using that small bit in a mounting plate with a big bit opening. The work can dip into the cutout, and its end can catch on the cutout edge, stalling its movement along the fence. So for most jobs, use a fence with a modest bit cutout. When the time comes to use massive joinery or panel-raising bits, make a second fence with a larger cutout.

To set the fence for use with a piloted bit, clamp one end and swing it up to the bit, housing it enough that the pilot is "inside" the fence. Set the edge of a steel rule against the fence so it bridges the cutout, and shift the fence so the pilot just touches the rule, as shown here.

TRY THIS!

Here's how to fine-tune a fence setting. *Fine-tune?* you're asking. I use a little steel rule to measure from bit to fence. What's to fine-tune?

Well, how about a sliding dovetail setup.

You've cut the groove, and you're closing in on the fence setting to cut the pin. The test cut yields a pin that's just a little tight. You need to move the fence a little more. Just enough to take a shaving off the pin. Any more than that and the tail will be too small and will rattle in the slot. Your steel rule, Bunkie, is going to keep you going back and forth, back and forth; you may never get it quite right.

You need *fine-tuning*.

To take off that shaving, your fence adjustment has got to be paper-thin. The trick is to control the fence movement. What you do is this: You put a shim between the fence and a stop block you clamp to the router table. Then you unclamp the fence, remove the shim, and set the fence against the stop block. Reclamp the fence. You've moved it the thickness of the shim.

This trick works going either way. You "open up" the fence setting by putting the shim in when you set the block. But you could also set the block right against the fence, then close the fence by putting in the shim to move the fence away from the block.

To fine-tune a fence setting, clamp a scrap block at the fence with a shim of some sort between it and the fence. Loosen the fence, pull the shim, slide the fence tight to the stop, and reclamp it. The impact at the bit will be one-half the thickness of the shim. Use a piece of laminate if you want to move the fence 1/16 inch. For less movement, use a scrap of sandpaper (as here), an index card or two, or a thickness or two of paper.

SPECIAL-DUTY CONTROLS

Pilot bearings, starting pins, and fences are the primary means for controlling the cut and the movement of the work. But there are other measures you can take to further control risk—both to yourself and to your work.

The design of the typical router table, with its flat-bottomed tabletop and its open construction, eases the use of extra hold-downs and hold-ins and even trap fences. All of these you can make yourself. (See the chapter "Router Table Accessories" for an assortment of these safety devices.)

The featherboard—often called a fingerboard—is probably most familiar, since it's used on the table saw, the jointer, and some other stationary tools as well. The featherboard is easy to make. A couple of clamps secure it to the table so it can exert its steady, untiring pressure on the work. Properly positioned and adjusted, featherboards keep the work erect and tight to the fence—and the bit—and free you to simply push the work along the fence. (This is a godsend when routing long stock.) Their angled fingers flex to allow the work to advance, but they jam against the work should you try to pull it back toward you. And the bit can't kick it back, either.

Trap fences can guide a jointing-cutting jig like a box-joint cutter or a slotter for dovetail keys, as you can discover in the appropriate chapters. The idea in a trap-fence setup is to create a channel for the workpiece's movement. There's a fence on each side, so the work can only slide forward or back. With a special-purpose sled (like a box-joint jig), the trap

Occasionally, as when raising a panel with a vertical panel-raising bit, an extra "trap" fence can help you. The trap fence is simply a straight board clamped to the table-top parallel to the regular fence. It keeps the bottom of the workpiece from sliding away from the fence—and the bit. It takes surprisingly little pressure to keep the work against the vertical fence.

fences are usually a couple of strips of material no thicker than the jig's base. This means the work can extend beyond the jig on either side and can be moved without restriction. The same principle can be applied to keep the bottom edge of a tall workpiece from skidding away from the fence, especially a canted fence.

A template guide bushing can be a woodworker's helper, too. As you can discover in the chapter "Template-Guided Work," this little metal gizmo, used in conjunction with a template, can exercise a *lot* of control over the router and bit. And it can be used in conjunction with some special jigs to direct and control some unusual joint-cutting operations, too.

The details of making and using these special jigs and fixtures are laid out in the pages that follow. As each operation is explained, all the savvy peculiar to it is presented.

Making Stopped Cuts

If you are doing through cuts, preparation is largely limited to setting the depth of cut and the fence. Stopped cuts, however, take a little more setting up. To know where to begin and end a stopped cut, you first need to mark the tangents of the bit on a piece of tape stuck either on the fence or on the mounting plate or tabletop. Where you put the marks depends upon where they'll be visible when you are making the cut.

To make the marks, set a square against the fence, with the blade just touching the bit's cutting edge. Don't clunk the metal square into the carbide; do this gingerly. Scribe along the blade on the tape. Now shift the square to the other side of the bit and mark that side. Remember that you want to capture the full cutting diameter of the bit, so you have to catch the cutting edge, not the bit body. If you are using a single-flute bit, this means you must mark one side, then rotate the bit 180 degrees to mark the other.

Naturally, you need to mark each workpiece, too, indicating where the cut is to begin and end.

Since the proper feed direction is right to left, line up the mark for the beginning of the cut with the mark that's to the *left* of the bit. Plunge the stock onto the bit, beginning the cut. (Depending on the cut, this plunging action can either lower the work onto the top of a plunge-cutting bit or slide it across the tabletop against the edge of an edge-forming bit.) Feed the work to the left. As the end-of-cut mark on the stock comes up to the mark at the *right* of the bit, carefully lift or pull the end of the workpiece off the bit.

Carbide is hard, but it's brittle too, and I get nervous about knocking the bit's cutting edges with a steel rule. A square of wood is therefore a good substitute for a rule when marking the bit tangents in preparation for making a stopped cut.

Stop blocks are time savers when you have a large number of identical pieces to work. The easiest way to set stops accurately is to use an already-cut workpiece. With the router switched off, set the cut piece on the bit, at the beginning of the cut (we've ripped the workpiece shown here so you can see the bit in the cut). Set and clamp a stop at the back. Slide the piece to the end of the cut. Set a stop against its front end, as shown here, and clamp it to the fence. Now you can cut the remaining work and have all cuts turn out the same.

I've emphasized which mark on the router table is correct for starting and which is correct for ending. If you mix up the marks, you will have a cut that's two bit-diameters longer than you want.

If you have a stack of parts to rout, set a couple of stop blocks on the fence, so you don't have to eyeball the marks so carefully. Small hand screws make good stops. You can use little scraps and any sort of clamp, but the hand screws are pretty direct. The clamp *is* the block.

To set the blocks, you can measure toward the right from the left side of the bit to set the starting block, and toward the left from the right of the bit to set the stop block. But it's easier to cut the first piece from mark to mark—eyeballing it, in other words—and then to use that workpiece to set the blocks. With the router switched off, set the already-cut workpiece on the bit, just as it was when you started the cut. Set the starting block gently against its trailing end and clamp the block to the fence. Advance the workpiece to the end-of-cut position. Place the stop block against the leading end of the workpiece, and clamp that block to the fence.

To cut your stopped groove now, you just have to set the piece against the starting block, drop it on the cutter, feed it till it hits the stop block, then tip it up off the bit (or swing it away from the fence and the bit). While stops usually make these kinds of cuts more sure—they take the error out of the operation—you do have to take enough care to get the stops set right. For myself, if I'm only doing a couple of the cuts, I just eyeball it.

Small Work

Small work presents another challenge to the operator. First, you'll realize that after you've used your router table for a variety of jobs, the hole in the middle will be fairly large. The options that allow you to work small items without having them fall through the hole around the bit are presented in "Choking Up on the Bit" on page 97.

The next thing you'll realize is that routing really small pieces can put your fingers in dangerous proximity to the cutter. Even if you're "brave" (read "foolhardy") enough to go ahead and run the job, you'll find that your fingers get very stiff in a hurry due to the tension. They tend to get numb from the vibration, too. (Little pieces don't have enough mass to sit still.)

If the pieces are fairly rectilinear, you may be able to hold them very

Safety First!

An oft-overlooked router-table safety device is the toggle clamp. Many of the sleds we show in this book—the sled for coping cuts shown in the chapter "Frame and Panel Construction," for example, or the sleds for mortising and tenoning shown in the chapter "Mortise-and-Tenon Joints"—are equipped with toggle clamps.

These clamps are not just for looks. If you are doing cope cuts, for example, you need to clamp the workpiece! The reason is that the rotation of the cutter will pull it in. If you allow that to happen, your router will act like a tree trimmer's chipper for a split second. Then something will probably break and go flying across the room. I don't want to be there when it happens, and neither do you.

Now, you may have strong fingers, and they may be strong enough to clench the workpiece sufficiently tight to prevent this disaster. But a toggle clamp is a strong, untiring device that's superior to fingers for the job. And unlike screw-action clamps of various kinds, toggle clamps are NOT inconvenient or time-consuming to use.

Toggle clamps are available in an intoxicating variety of styles and sizes. The style shown here—in two sizes—is well suited to use on a sled. I like the T-handle because it doubles as a sled handle: As you push the clamp handle to advance the sled, you are also pressing the clamp closed.

Several spindles and spindle accessories are shown in the photo. I'd recommend that you replace the standard spindle with a slightly longer one and that you ditch the hex nuts used to adjust and lock the spindle. Use a check nut and a wing nut instead. The extra spindle length allows you to accommodate a greater range of workpiece thicknesses. The check nut–wing nut combination allows you to make adjustments without using wrenches.

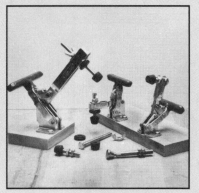

Is a Table-Mounted Router a Shaper?

In a word, no.

A more gracious answer would be: sort of. Broadly, the two rigs do the same jobs. But when you become specific, the capabilities diverge.

A true shaper is a stationary tool. It isn't as versatile as a router: You can't run it over the work, you can't make plunge or piercing cuts. But it's got mass and power. In the woodworking shop, a quarter-ton stationary machine has it all over a 15-pounder. Moreover, the practical power of a 3-horsepower shaper far exceeds that of a 3-horsepower router. The shaper has an induction motor, which generates a lot more torque than a router's universal motor (and a lot more kickback, too). On the shaper, you can combine cutters, stacking two or three on the spindle. A strip of molding, even a complex one, can be produced in a single pass. You can hog away substantial amounts of waste in a single pass.

The shaper simply accomplishes a lot more work in less time than a router table setup.

Consider the varieties of shapers. Just as routers are available in a range of grades and power ratings, shapers are available in a range of models. A table-mounted router is fairly equivalent to the low-end shaper, the so-called bench router/shaper. (Because woodworkers seem to be familiar with the different models of table saw, let me relate the different shaper models to table saw models.)

At the top end, for a grand and a half, you can get a 3- to 5-horsepower, 500-pound behemoth, the rough equivalent of a Unisaw. Its cast-iron tabletop and drivetrain are mounted on an enclosed cabinet. It has two speeds, runs in forward and reverse, and takes ½-inch, ¾-inch, and 1-inch spindles.

The midrange shaper, roughly equivalent to a so-called contractor's table saw, has a somewhat smaller cast-iron tabletop and a less sophisticated fence, mounted on an open-legged, sheet-metal stand. The unit weighs about 180 pounds. The motor has 1½ horsepower and drives either ½-inch or ¾-inch spindles at two speeds, in forward and reverse. Should cost you about $700.

A benchtop router/shaper is at the low end, like a benchtop motorized table saw. To make it as inexpensive as possible, a lot of the shaper qualities are designed out. Often, the tabletop is cast aluminum; it's flat and true and durable, but it's also lightweight. The fence is more simple, less precise. The motor is down to 1 horsepower or less. Only a ½-inch spindle will fit, and though it may have forward and reverse, it probably has only one speed. It weighs from 30 to 50 pounds. Depending on the brand, it costs between $200 and $500.

This is the unit that most closely resembles the router table. In fact, in a few instances it *is* a router table, one to which some marketing wizard has added the term shaper (hence the shaper/router table designation).

A true shaper is a cast-iron-and-steel shop behemoth, as you can see. Though it has much in common with a router table, it's clearly designed and built for high-volume production. Everything about it is bigger and stronger—and more costly—than a router table. Shaper cutters are steel-and-carbide donuts that fit over the shaper's spindle, typically a ¾- or 1-inch steel shaft. Several cutters can be stacked on the spindle at once so you can form complex profiles in a single pass. Because the spindle rotation can be reversed, the cutters can be installed on the spindle right-side up or upside down. And because the spindle is so thick and the operating speed is less than half that of the router, cutters that are considerably larger than the biggest panel-raising router bit can be used.

If what you need is a machine to create miles of different moldings—complex moldings—and to do it quickly and efficiently, get a shaper. If you think you need a low-end shaper, use your router.

You have to be creative to be safe. Here's a setup for routing small parts that you might be able to adapt to your own routing problem. Pinch the workpiece in the jaws of a small hand screw. With the end of the work against the tabletop, the hand screw should be flat against the fence's top edge. Then slide the work along the fence, as shown.

Here's a way to grasp a small workpiece for routing: Use a hand screw instead of your hand. The hand screw is big enough to hold and provides some mass to the piece being routed. To hold the workpiece while attaching the hand screw, Fred propped it on the fence in the background.

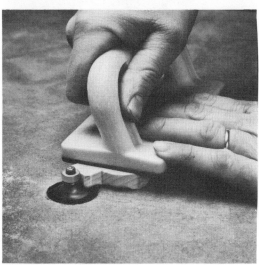

For some cuts, a small part can be "troweled" by the bit. The trowel-like pusher shown is made of plastic and has a rubber pad—the same material as the router pad mentioned in the chapter "Router 101"—bonded to the sole. The rubber sole grips the work remarkably well, allowing you to slide it around on the tabletop and feed it by the bit confidently.

nicely with a wooden hand screw. Lay the hand screw on the table with the piece between the jaws, and tighten them. That will keep the work flat on the tabletop, while allowing you to accomplish certain operations. Of course, you'll have to unclamp and reclamp every time you want to turn the work.

Another option is to use a rubber or stiff-foam handle. A grout trowel or a foam-bottomed stock pusher will work very well for this because they have the ability to grip the part well enough to slide it around the cutter while absorbing the vibration. Your fingers will thank you.

End Grain

Routing end-grain stock can give you a real kick, particularly when it's too narrow to guide against a fence. The preferable option if you have a lot to do—say, coping pieces for a bunch of windows—is to build a sled. (See "Sled" on page 90 for details on making one of these accessories.)

There's a much simpler approach for a small job that's not worth the bother of building a sled. Let's say you have a piece that is just wide enough to bridge the gap in the fence but not enough to stay square while you cut. In this case you can simply back it up with a scrap of plywood that has a good square corner. Run one side of the scrap against the fence and grip the stock across the front as you push it past the cutter.

Can you safely work ends with a piloted cutter? You bet! And quickly, too, once you get the hang of it. With a piloted cutter, there's still a tendency to pull into the cutter at the very beginning of the cut, before the corner of the stock reaches the bearing. To prevent this, either you can set the fence to support one corner until the other reaches the bearing or you can use a starting pin the same way.

Another way that is quicker and looks really salty (if you're trying to impress the crowd) is to grip the stock with your right hand so you can butt the second segment of your index finger against the front edge of the table. Using that finger as a stop, pivot the work into the cutter until the corner contacts the pilot. At that point you can relax your right hand a bit and feed the stock on through with your left.

Use that index finger again as the stock exits the cut. Here the stock will again lose contact with the pilot, but the cutter will be pushing toward you rather than trying to grab the stock. Slow your rate of feed as you exit to lessen the tendency to split off the trailing edge. Don't be surprised to see a few splin-

It is possible to freehand a cut across the end of a workpiece. If you hold the piece so your fingers catch against the edge of the tabletop, as Fred is doing here, the bit can't pull the work. Be sure your grip is firm, and position your hand so that as the end of the work is at the pilot, your fingers are against the tabletop edge. Once the work contacts the pilot, it controls the cut, but maintain your grip throughout the cut.

ters no matter how slowly you exit. If at all possible, rout the ends of these pieces before you do the edges. That way you'll remove the splintery corners.

If you can't do the ends first, you're better off to go back to the sled. Make up a backer that fits tightly against the back edge of the stock, and screw that to the sled. Then clamp the stock against it so the backer supports the stock where the cutter exits. You should be able to reduce splintering to the sandable range.

ROUTER BENCH

Clamping options at a comfortable working height

is what this bench provides. It is narrow, long, and tall. I made it to facilitate working with a hand-held router, and I'm really happy with it.

Think about your workbench. It's probably about fingertip or waist height—roughly 30 to 36 inches high—and about 24 inches wide. Maybe it has shelves or bins or drawers underneath. A couple of vises: one on the end, one along the front. The benches in the Rodale shop are like this, as is the one in my home shop.

Problems for router woodworking: The cabinet or framework supporting the bench top limits clamping locations. The proportions of the bench top force you to clamp and reclamp and re-reclamp to complete relatively simple edge-forming operations. To closely observe the workings of the bit, you have to bend or stoop—an unnatural working stance. And the bench isn't particularly portable.

The router bench addresses all these problems and, for me, solves them.

• There's no cabinet or massive framework underneath to get in the way of clamps.

• The long, narrow proportion of the top lets me clamp work to the bench in ways that yield maximum access for my routers. I usually can machine three edges, for example, without having to reposition the work. I can clamp a piece against the bench-

top edge, allowing me to use the bench top as a bearing surface for the router base.

• The vise on one end of the bench, along with the rank of bench-dog holes running down the center of the bench top, expands the work-holding versatility of the bench. In a lot of cases, I don't have to fumble with clamps at all: I can clamp work in the vise, and I can pinch work between the vise and a dog.

• Because the bench is elbow height, I can control my router better, and I can see what's happening without bending uncomfortably.

• And, finally, I designed and constructed the bench as a knockdown piece. With a screwdriver and an adjustable wrench, I can quickly disassemble it into five components—bench top, two leg units, and two cross-braces—for efficient storage or for transport.

The inspiration for this bench was a bench produced by Pat Warner, a West Coast router wonk. Warner's has slightly different dimensions and considerably different construction. For more information about his bench, contact him at 1427 Kenora Street, Escondido, CA 92027.

It's tall. It's skinny. But don't let its looks deceive you. This router bench is really handy for all sorts of hand-held router operations. And other woodworking tasks as well.

Perching a router on the edge of a workpiece is always precarious. But the narrow top of the router bench allows you to easily clamp such work to its edge. Then the router can bear on the bench top.

The router bench's three-point bench-dog system—two on the vise, one on the bench top—makes securing odd-shaped workpieces a cinch. We'll only have to shift this oval tabletop once in order to rout the entire edge. And that shift is as easy as opening and closing the vise. No clamps to take off and put back on.

1. Gather the materials, and cut the parts. To get a flat, stable top, I laminated two pieces of birch plywood and banded its edges with thick oak. The top is pretty monolithic. It isn't anchored to a heavy frame that will help it to hold its shape, so a material that's smooth, flat, and stable is essential. Plywood is that material. The oak edge banding provides protection for the edges and corners.

For the legs, feet, and cross-

▶ Scaling Your Bench

At nearly 4 feet high, this bench may be a little too tall for the average woodworker. I made the bench for myself, making it a working height comfortable for me. At 6 feet 2, I'm probably taller than the average woodworker.

For me, doing a lot of router work at a typical workbench is a pain in the ne . . . , eh, back. I've got to hunch over to see the cut (left), and it simply isn't a comfortable stance. But with the work clamped to my router bench (right), I can stand with my back straight yet still see the action.

Moreover, having your work surface at elbow height improves your view of what you're doing. As compared to work done at standard workbench height, this work is a foot or more closer to your eyes. Widen your stance and flex your knees, and you can just about sight along the bench top. You have an even better view of what the router and its bit are doing.

My theory is that elbow height is about right for router woodworking. Hold the router at about chest height. You've got your elbows bent, wrists and forearms roughly parallel to the ground. This is a good control position. You aren't stoop-shouldered or bent at the waist. You can push the router

2 feet or more away from your body without having to bend at the waist. When you bend at the waist, your center of gravity shifts, and you have to work just a little harder to maintain your balance. This little extra height for router operations can lessen fatigue and increase control.

What I did, then, when planning the bench, was measure myself from foot to elbow. I used that figure—47 inches—as the finished height of my bench. I'd recommend you do the same.

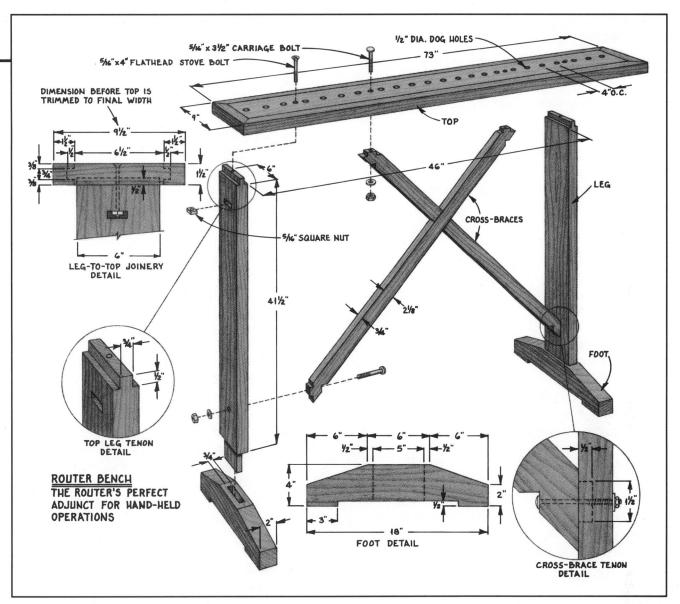

5/16" x 4" FLATHEAD STOVE BOLT

5/16" x 3½" CARRIAGE BOLT

½" DIA. DOG HOLES

73"

4" O.C.

TOP

9"

DIMENSION BEFORE TOP IS
TRIMMED TO FINAL WIDTH

9½"

6½"

1½"

3/8"
3/4"
3/8"

½"

6"

LEG-TO-TOP JOINERY DETAIL

6"

5/16" SQUARE NUT

46"

CROSS-BRACES

LEG

41½"

2⅛"

3/4"

3/4"

½"

TOP LEG TENON DETAIL

FOOT

ROUTER BENCH
**THE ROUTER'S PERFECT
ADJUNCT FOR HAND-HELD
OPERATIONS**

3/4"

2"

6" **6"** **6"**
½" **5"** **½"**

4"

½"

2"

½"

1½"

3"

18"

FOOT DETAIL

CROSS-BRACE TENON DETAIL

CUTTING LIST

Piece	Number	Thickness	Width	Length	Material
Top core pieces	2	¾"	8"	72"	Birch plywood
Edge banding	2	1⅝"	1½"	73"	8/4 oak
Edge banding	2	1⅝"	1½"	9"	8/4 oak
Legs	2	1¼"	6"	45½"	6/4 oak
Feet	4	1¼"	4"	18"	6/4 oak
Cross-braces	2	1¼"	2⅛"	52½"	6/4 oak
Vise spacers	2	½"	5"	7"	Plywood
Vise cauls	2	1¼"	3"	9"	6/4 oak

Hardware

8 pcs. 5/16" × 3½" carriage bolts with washers and nuts
2 pcs. 5/16" × 4" stove bolts with square nuts
3 pcs. ½" × 2" hex-head bolts
2 pcs. #8 × 2" flathead wood screws
2 pcs. #8 × 1¼" flathead wood screws
1 Record V175 vise

braces, I used oak. It's heavy and hard, good for a bench that will be used hard in the shop. While attractiveness is appealing, so is economy. I used an economy grade of oak—"skid grade," Fred calls it. The knots and defects in the legs don't enhance the appearance of the bench, but they aren't serious enough to erode the bench's strength.

Choose the materials you want to use, then cut the parts to the sizes specified by the Cutting List. Here are some possible exceptions:

• It's a good idea to cut the two elements of the top core and the edge bands a bit oversized and trim them to fit during assembly.

- You may want to allow extra length in the legs, which can be trimmed away after the bottom tenon is cut. (See Step 5 on the opposite page.)
- If you are altering the height of the bench, adjust the lengths of the legs and the cross-braces.

2. Make the bench top.
Begin by gluing the two plywood core elements face-to-face. Use regular carpenter's glue, and clamp the lamination with hand screws, C-clamps, and/or quick clamps. If your plywood has any bow to it, glue the crowned faces together to cancel out the bow.

While the glue sets, prepare the edge banding. Assuming the stock is surfaced, plow a ¾-inch-wide by ½-inch-deep groove in each piece. (See the chapter "Dadoing and Grooving" for details on this procedure.) Be sure you cut the groove in the broader face.

After the clamps are off the core, run it through the table saw to square the long edges, reducing the width to about 7½ inches. With the crosscut saw of your choice, do the same for the ends. Form the tongue that fits into the groove in the edge banding by cutting a ½-inch-wide by ⅜-inch-deep rabbet around the top and bottom edges. (See the chapter "Rabbeting" for details on this procedure.) It's a good idea to test cut a short section of the core and fit a grooved scrap of the banding in place, to ensure that you get a good mechanical fit.

Fit the edge banding in place, piece by piece, marking and cutting it to fit. The corners, of course, are mitered. Glue and clamp the banding to the core.

Because the top core is 1½ inches thick, and the banding is 1⅜ inches thick, you have to trim the banding flush to the core surface. I fitted a laminate trimmer with a custom flush-trimming base, chucked a ½-inch straight bit in the collet, and trimmed the banding on both the top and bottom surfaces. (See the chapter "Surfacing with the Router" for more details.)

Finally, I ripped and crosscut the bench top one last time to true the edges. I took about ¼ inch off each edge, bringing the bench top to its final 9-inch by 73-inch dimensions.

3. Make the feet.
Each foot is formed by face-gluing two pieces of oak together. Before the glue-up, cut a 5-inch-wide by ⅜-inch-deep recess (or lap) across the center of each piece. When the parts are face-glued, these laps will form the through mortises for the leg.

To cut the laps, attach a custom baseplate to your router. (See the chapter "Lap Joints" for details.) It must be about 12 inches wide, wide enough to support the router as you cut the lap. You can minimize setup by clamping the four foot elements edge to edge and cutting them all at the same time. Attach a stop strip at each end of the work to control the width of the cut. (Since you are working the faces that will be glued together, you can screw the stops in place, rather than clamping them.)

Glue the foot elements together, forming the two feet. Use carpenter's glue, and clamp the feet with hand screws, C-clamps, and/or quick clamps.

After the glue has set and the clamps are off, lay out the shape of the foot, as shown in the *Foot Detail*, on each blank, then cut them on the band saw. Sand the cut edges with a belt sander.

4. Make the legs.
The legs should be 1½ inches shorter than the finished height of the router bench. If you plan to cut the bottom tenon with a hand-held router, you need to allow an extra inch or so of length when you rough out the leg.

The top tenon is ¾ inch thick, 6 inches wide, and ½ inch long. It can be formed by cutting two rabbets across the top end of the leg. Cut the rabbets ½ inch wide by ¼ inch deep. Leave the tenon the full width of the leg.

The bottom tenon is ¾ inch thick, 5 inches wide, and 3½ inches long. Since the mortise into which this tenon fits is already completed, you should make some test cuts on scraps of the working stock to ensure the tenons will fit.

Cut the tenons on the router table, if you can. (See the chapter "Mortise-and-Tenon Joints" for details on how to do this.) Use a large-diameter straight bit or hinge-mortising bit. Position the fence to control the shoulder cut—when the butt end of the leg is riding the fence, the bit is cutting the shoulder. Cut the shoulder, then slide the leg back and forth, removing the rest of the stock. The ¼-inch-deep cut is not too much to do in a single pass.

If you must do the tenon with a hand-held router, use the same custom base you did when making the feet. Use the extra leg length to support the base; that is, measure from the leg top to mark the bottom tenon shoulder. Lay out the tenon like a 3½-inch-wide lap, and leave the excess length at full thickness for the base to rest on as you sweep the router back and forth, hogging out the waste.

In either case, use a band saw to trim the tenon to its final width.

Take ½ inch from each side of the tenon, reducing it to the necessary 5-inch width.

5. Cut the leg mortises in the top.

The mortises into which the legs fit are stopped dadoes—easy to cut with a router. (See the chapter "Dadoing and Grooving" for details on cutting these.) Lay out the centerline of the mortises, and mark the ends of the cut very clearly. From the centerline, mark the position for a guide (the distance equals the radius of your router's base). Clamp the guide to the bench top, position the router, turn it on, plunge the bit, and make the cut. (With a fixed-base router, drill a hole the size of the bit at one end of the mortise; position the router with the bit in the hole, then switch it on and make the cut.)

To complete the fit, you can either round the ends of the tenon with a file, or square the ends of the mortise with a chisel. I did the latter.

6. Assemble the leg units.

Assembly of the leg units is a simple matter of gluing the leg tenon into the foot mortise. Before you spread any glue, finish sand the parts. If you want to embellish the edges, now is the time. I used a rabbetting bit to cut a shallow rabbet—about ⅛ inch deep—along the leg and foot edges.

After machining the edges and sanding the parts, glue the legs to the feet.

7. Cut the cross-brace joinery.

The cross-braces interlock in a cross-lap joint and join the top and legs in mortise-and-tenon joints. They adjoin both the top and legs at 45-degree angles. Unless you are duplicating the dimensions of my bench, you'll have to calculate the length of the braces using the Pythagorean theorem, which you learned in high school math class. (Okay, so you forgot. Check "Shop Math" at right.)

Cut 45-degree miters on each end of the braces. With a rabbeting bit, form the tenons on each end by cutting ½-inch-wide by ¼-inch-deep rabbets across each face. On the band saw, trim the width of the tenon to 1½ inches, as shown in the *Cross-Brace Tenon Detail*.

With the tenons cut, lay out and cut the mortises next. Test fit the legs and bench top; I set the legs on edge across a workbench, then "hung" the bench top on the tenons. Square the legs to the top. Label each tenon on the braces. Set one brace in position against the edges of the top and leg. Scribe along the tenon edges; then, with a square, extend the lines across the inside of the leg and the underside of the top. These lines delineate the ends of the mortises; since you want them centered on the pieces, it is easy to lay out the sides. Label each mortise for the tenon it is to take.

Repeat the process to lay out (and label) the mortises for the second brace. Set both braces in position, lining them up—as well as possible—with the marks on the edges of the legs and top. Now scribe along each brace onto the other. This is where you need to lap them together.

The mortises can be cut in the same way you did those for the legs. The laps can be cut as you did previous laps.

8. Assemble the bench.

Assuming you want to be able to disassemble the bench for storage or transport, you don't want to glue the joints

Shop Math

The Pythagorean theorem states that in a right triangle, the length of the hypotenuse (the leg that's opposite the 90-degree angle) is the square root of the sum of the squares of the two other sides. It's the old "A squared plus B squared equals C squared," where C is the hypotenuse and A and B are the triangle's other two sides.

Here's how to apply it to determine the brace length for your router bench:

Determine how far down the leg the brace will attach. Square that number. Double it. Then find the square root. That number is the length of the brace (without the required tenons). Use your calculator to find the brace length. Push the square root key, and let the calculator determine that the square root of, say, 2652.25 is 51.5.

After you've gotten the brace length, add about 1½ inches to accommodate the tenons on each end.

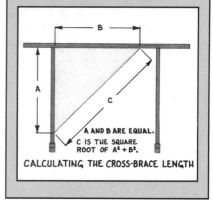

CALCULATING THE CROSS-BRACE LENGTH

together. Instead, use stove and/or carriage bolts.

With a ⁵⁄₁₆-inch twist-drill bit, bore a hole through each of the cross-brace mortise-and-tenon joints, as indicated in the *Cross-Brace Tenon Detail*. Ideally, the holes should extend through the centers of the tenons. If you use stove bolts, countersink the holes in the top and the outside of the legs. Notch the brace edges to provide a flat against which the washers and nuts can seat. I used a big V-groove bit to rout these notches.

I used 3½-inch-long bolts in these holes.

To tighten the legs in place, I drilled a hole through the top and into the leg. Then I cut a pocket into the side of the leg, intersecting the bore hole. I countersunk the hole in the top. The 4-inch-long bolt is inserted into the top; the square nut, into the pocket in the leg. Once you have the threads started in the nut, the hard part is done. Just keep the nut from turning as you tighten the fitting with a screwdriver.

9. Finish the bench. After using a bench, I decided that a small vise bolted to one end would be a practical addition to this one. The Record V175 seemed to be the right size, although it lacks a quick-release feature and a sliding dog. To compensate for the lack of a dog, Fred suggested installing wooden cauls over the vise jaws. Holes drilled into the top edge of the caul on the moveable jaw take hex-head bolts that serve as "vise dogs." A workpiece can easily be pinched between a bench dog and a vise dog.

Install the vise with four 3½-inch-long carriage bolts. Use scraps of plywood to shim the vise, so the tops of the metal jaws are about ½ inch below the bench-top surface.

To make the wooden cauls, first cut them to the size specified by the Cutting List. Set each caul in position, and scribe around the metal jaw onto the back of the caul. Rout a recess in each caul for its jaw. The recess in the back caul should be about 9⁄16

We generally think of roundovers and ogees as being the way to embellish an edge, but a shallow rabbet looks good, too. I routed the decorative rabbets on the bench's legs, feet, and cross-braces.

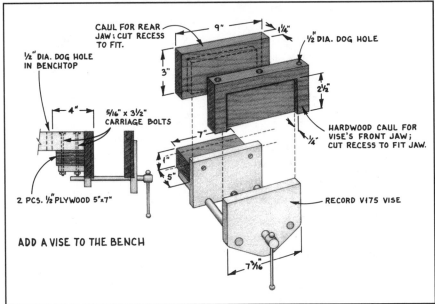

ADD A VISE TO THE BENCH

inch deep, that in the front caul only 3⁄16 inch. Attach the back cauls with 2-inch screws driven through the caul and the vise into the bench top. The front caul is attached with 1¼-inch screws driven through the vise into the caul.

Drill ½-inch-diameter dog holes next. Locate holes on 4-inch centers along the centerline of the bench top. Locate three in the top edge of

the front caul, one in the center, and one ¾ inch from each end. Use ½-inch-diameter hex-head bolts as dogs. Putting three holes in the vise provides three-point clamping for curved workpieces.

Before applying a finish, disassemble the bench. Apply your favorite finish, and after it dries, reassemble the bench.

DECORATIVE TREATMENTS

Decorative edge treatments are elementary, the most elementary router operations there are. Choose a cutter, tighten it in the collet, set the desired cutting depth, and you can run all around your project with a design-unifying, aesthetically pleasing, decorative edge. It's that simple.

Though a fair number of woodworkers never get beyond this use of the router, the natural extension is to use the router to cut design-unifying, aesthetically pleasing decorative *grooves* on the work. And to use the router to produce moldings to trim furniture, frame pictures, and finish off a room. The techniques used go beyond edge treatments. But once mastered, they apply to all sorts of other decorative and functional router operations—even cutting joinery.

PROFILE BITS

In routing decorative treatments, the tricks are less in the doing, and more in the planning and bit selection. There are a great many decorative profile bits available, and in many cases, even *most* cases, you can make a single pass with a bit to create the embellishment your project requires.

Once in a while, though, you need to make passes with two or more cutters to get the contour you want. You need to choose these cutters carefully, plan the order of cuts, and determine how you're going to support either the router or the work.

There are a few tricks here, but mostly it's straightforward routing. You simply must choose the cutters wisely.

Almost all decorative profiles can be traced to some basic molding shapes. You may have come across these mostly Latin terms, found them hard to connect to your woodworking, and so pretty much forgot them. But let's take a shot at connecting them to today's router bit catalog and

In analyzing the profile you want to cut, lay the bits themselves on the layout and line them up with the profile. This will help you determine which bits to use, how to orient the work for making the cuts, and in what order the cuts have to be made.

molding forms. I think you'll see them in the bit profiles shown and described beginning on the next page.

Scotia: A concave profile, it is greater than a quarter round. To rout a scotia, use a core-box bit to cut an arc like the one shown, or, if it is greater than 180 degrees, a radius bit.

Cavetto: This is a large, concave quarter round—a cove, in other words. So use a cove bit.

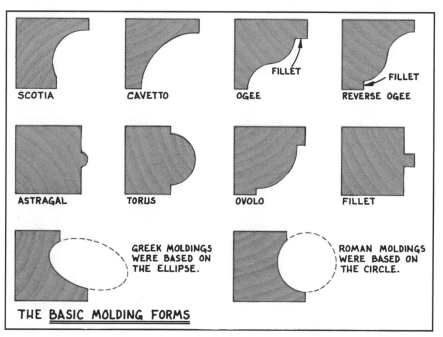

SCOTIA CAVETTO OGEE FILLET REVERSE OGEE FILLET

ASTRAGAL TORUS OVOLO FILLET

GREEK MOLDINGS WERE BASED ON THE ELLIPSE.

ROMAN MOLDINGS WERE BASED ON THE CIRCLE.

THE BASIC MOLDING FORMS

Ogee (or cyma reversa): This one we know. It's an S-shaped curve, with a convex form at the top, fairing down into a concave one. Strictly speaking, to be an ogee, the profile should have a flat, narrow step, known to architects as a listel and to the rest of us as a fillet. This fillet is at the top, ending the concave curve. You know what bit to use to form this shape.

Reverse ogee (or cyma recta): This corresponds to the Roman ogee, which is the name of the bit you'd use to cut one. It starts at the top as a concave curve, flowing down into a convex one. I'm not sure where the term *Roman,* as used in *Roman ogee,* came from. What distinguishes Roman moldings is that they were based on the circle (the Greeks based their molding forms on the ellipse). We trace the molding forms we use today back to those classical Greeks and Romans.

Astragal: A small, convex half round, the astragal corresponds to what bit makers call a full bead. In current usage, an astragal is usually a separate molding strip. To form an astragal in the strict sense requires an edge-beading bit. Making an astragal strip can be done with a bull-nose, beading, or round-over bit.

Torus: A large, convex half round, the torus is an astragal on steroids. A bull-nose bit forms a torus.

Ovolo: A convex quarter round between fillets, an ovolo is what is usually called a bead these days. Cut it with a beading bit.

Fillet: Previous definitions have already conveyed what a fillet is. It's a small, flat section used to separate other profiles. It can be a square-sectioned strip across a flat, but it's often used as a step between profiles or at the ends of a profile.

Now let's take a look at the range of decorative bits that are on the market. You'll see the connections to the basic molding forms. You may also begin to see how the multiple-form bits—like cove-and-bead bits, for example—combine the basic forms.

As you study the bits, you'll see that you can usually cut a cove-and-bead profile with a cove bit and a round-over bit, for example. The advantage of using a bit that combines both shapes on a single cutter is that you'll save setup and cutting time. The disadvantage is that these multiple-profile bits tend to blind us to our many options. If you are like me, you tend to "see" in single-bit terms. Until I worked with Fred on this chapter, I'd look for a single bit that would cut the specific profile I had in mind, rather than focusing on how I could produce it with the few fundamental bits.

I hope this chapter will serve as a jumping-off point for you—as it has for me—in developing your own special patterns, or simply in using the basic bits you have to produce more complex combinations.

I've collected the bits into two categories: edge-forming bits and groove-forming bits. This is by no means exhaustive; it leaves out quite a few decorative bits, as well as *all* those that are utilitarian. I pored over catalogs from eight bit vendors, trying to compare bits according to their forms, not the names the manufacturers gave them. Of course, there are more than eight companies making or importing and marketing router bits, but I think the eight lines are representative of what you'll find on the market. (See "Sources" on page 337 for these companies' addresses and phone numbers.)

Edge-Forming Bits

These bits shape the edges of boards, forming one of or combinations of the eight basic molding shapes.

In general, edge-forming bits are characterized by the presence of a pilot on the end of the bit. The pilot catches on the edge of the work and prevents the bit from setting out across the face of a board, forming a groove in the process. With a piloted bit, setup is pretty much limited to establishing the bit height. The width of the cut is governed by the pilot. You can switch to a different bearing size or work with a fence or edge guide to change the cut's width.

Beading: Produces a quarter round with one or two fillets. The width of one fillet is governed by the diameter of the pilot bearing, while the width of the other is governed by the depth of cut. A beading bit can be transformed into a round-over bit by changing the bearing (and vice versa). Bead radii range in steps from 1/16 inch to 1 inch; their vertical depth of cut, from 1/2 inch to 1 3/8 inches. Metric sizes are available from Byrom.

Bead-on-bead: This unusual profile is available only from Amana (as a classical molding bit) and MLCS (as a multibead bit). It seems to be a kin of the cove-and-bead, but with a two-tier quarter-round profile. Depending upon the pilot bearing used and the depth-of-cut setting, you can produce a profile with one or two fillets. Each source has two sizes listed.

Corner-beading: Three slightly different profiles can be cut using this bit, depending upon the depth of cut and the number of passes. In a single pass, you can cut a couple of different edge beads; with two passes, you can cut a full corner bead. Available with bead radii ranging in steps from $\frac{1}{16}$ inch to $\frac{3}{8}$ inch and cutter height from $\frac{1}{2}$ inch to $1\frac{3}{8}$ inches.

Leaf-edge-beading: Forms a round-edged groove near the edge of the workpiece. Making a pass in adjoining faces of the workpiece will yield an ellipsoid corner bead, hence the leaf-edge moniker. If you make a pass with a round-over bit in conjunction with the leaf-edge-beading bit, you'll get a round edge or corner bead. All of these bits have two pilot bearings, one on the shank above the cutter, one on the tip below the cutter. Bead radii range from $\frac{1}{8}$ inch to $\frac{3}{8}$ inch; their cutter heights, from $\frac{3}{8}$ inch to $\frac{7}{8}$ inch.

Edge-beading: Since this bit lacks a pilot, it has to be used in conjunction with a fence or edge guide. Although it yields a profile very similar to the corner-beading bit's, it has a roundover and a tad more extension below the bead. Working with a $1\frac{1}{2}$-inch-wide workpiece and making two passes, you could cut multiple beads along the edge of the stock. Available with bead radii of $\frac{5}{32}$ inch, $\frac{11}{16}$ inch, and $\frac{13}{16}$ inch, and cutter heights of 1 inch and $1\frac{1}{32}$ inches.

Drawing-line-beading: This bit closely resembles the edge-beading bit. Compare the profiles, however, and you'll see that this one arches away from the bead, rather than producing a pronounced fillet or flat. The depth-of-cut setting determines whether or not you get a fillet above the bead. Bead radii range in $\frac{1}{16}$-inch steps from $\frac{1}{8}$ inch to $\frac{3}{8}$ inch; cutter height, from $\frac{3}{4}$ inch to $\frac{7}{8}$ inch.

Multibead: The baseline bit in this category—available from Byrom, Amana, MLCS, and Eagle America—

cuts three $\frac{1}{8}$-inch-radius beads. Amana's bit is not piloted. MLCS also has a bit that cuts two such beads, and one (sans pilot) that cuts two $\frac{3}{16}$-inch-radius beads. Cascade sells a related bit that cuts a $\frac{3}{16}$-inch-radius bead with a matching round-over on each side; this bit has pilot bearings above and below the cutter. Bead radii range from $\frac{1}{8}$ inch to $\frac{3}{16}$ inch; cutter heights, from $\frac{7}{8}$ inch to $1\frac{1}{32}$ inches.

Variable-bead: This bit resembles the multibead bit, but each of the beads it cuts is a different radius. Byrom's bit is piloted, Amana's is not. Available bead radii are $\frac{1}{8}$ inch, $\frac{7}{64}$ inch, and $\frac{1}{16}$ inch; cutter height is $1\frac{1}{8}$ inches.

Bull-nose: A sort of big brother to the beading bits, the bull-nose bit is used to shape the full edge of a board. The "nose diameter" reflects the thickness of stock that can be nosed, i.e., given a full 180-degree roundover. Byrom refers to this bit as being "full radius." The bits have flats above and below the half round, which will create fillets on stock that's thicker than the nose diameter. In general, these bits do not have pilots. Amana and Eagle America make piloted versions of a few sizes—$\frac{17}{32}$-inch, $\frac{3}{4}$-inch, 1-inch, and $1\frac{1}{4}$-inch—that are intended for pattern work. The bearings match the smallest diameter of the cutter. In use, the bearing rides against a template clamped or tacked to the workpiece, rather than against the workpiece itself. Nose diameter ranges from $\frac{1}{8}$ inch to $1\frac{1}{2}$ inches; cutter height, from $\frac{1}{2}$ inch to 2 inches.

Fingernail: Like the bull-nose bit, this bit shapes the edges of boards. It is an unpiloted bit. It has short flats above and below the cutter arc, which will produce fillets on stock

that matches the cutter height. Unlike the bull-nose, it cuts a shallow arc—the fingernail shape—rather than a full 180-degree roundover. (The same effect can be produced on thin stock by using a large-diameter bull-nose bit.) The size of the bit is usually expressed in terms of the straight-line length of the arc, rather than the radius of it. Thus, a $\frac{3}{4}$-inch fingernail bit would round the edge of $\frac{3}{4}$-inch-thick stock, but would leave fillets on anything thicker. Available with arc lengths from $\frac{5}{16}$ inch to $1\frac{1}{2}$ inches, with bead heights from $\frac{1}{8}$ inch to $\frac{1}{4}$ inch, and with flute lengths from $\frac{9}{16}$ inch to $1\frac{3}{4}$ inches.

Chamfer: In the small sizes, this bit puts a decorative chamfer on work. In larger sizes, it can bevel dimensional stock (that is, cut a chamfer that extends through the full thickness of the stock). Every manufacturer has at least one 45-degree bit. Cutting lengths range from $\frac{3}{8}$ inch to $1\frac{1}{2}$ inches; other angles available include 7, 15, $22\frac{1}{2}$, 25, 30, 60, and 67 degrees.

Classical palace: Among the many bits labeled "classical," this style is generally used to shape the full edge of a board. Since it doesn't include a pilot, stock must be guided with a fence. It cuts a cove with a full bead. Cutting lengths range from $\frac{3}{4}$ inch to $1\frac{1}{4}$ inches; bead diameters, from $\frac{1}{4}$ inch to $\frac{7}{16}$ inch; and total relief, from $\frac{1}{4}$ inch to $\frac{1}{2}$ inch.

Cove: As its name implies, this bit cuts a cove in the edge of a board. The cove is one of the basic building blocks for many molding profiles. When used in conjunction with beads and fillets, an almost infinite variety of shapes is possible. The cove also makes up one-half of the rule joint, a special combination of profiles used to create the juncture between a drop-

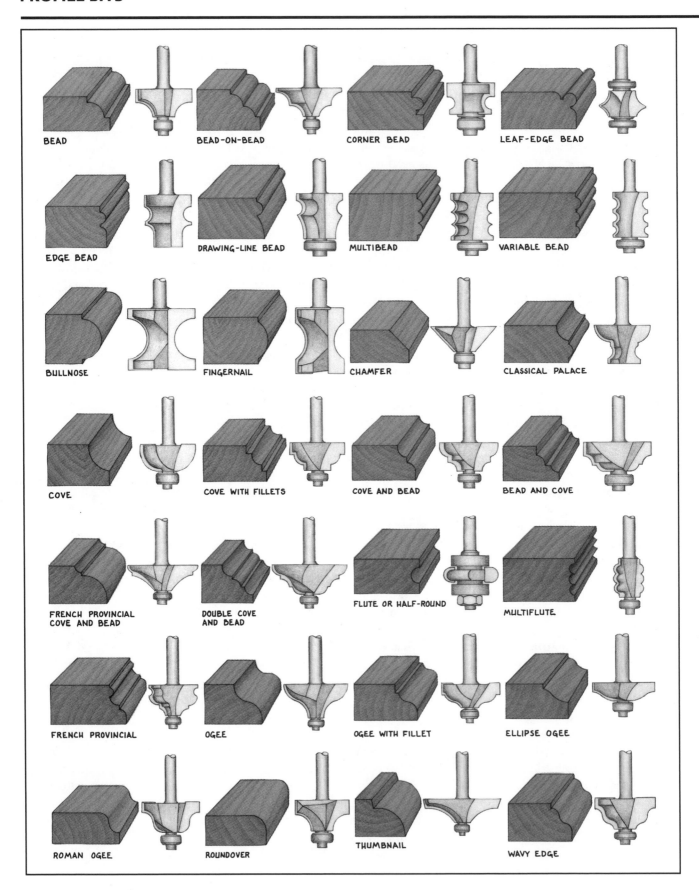

BEAD

BEAD-ON-BEAD

CORNER BEAD

LEAF-EDGE BEAD

EDGE BEAD

DRAWING-LINE BEAD

MULTIBEAD

VARIABLE BEAD

BULLNOSE

FINGERNAIL

CHAMFER

CLASSICAL PALACE

COVE

COVE WITH FILLETS

COVE AND BEAD

BEAD AND COVE

FRENCH PROVINCIAL COVE AND BEAD

DOUBLE COVE AND BEAD

FLUTE OR HALF-ROUND

MULTIFLUTE

FRENCH PROVINCIAL

OGEE

OGEE WITH FILLET

ELLIPSE OGEE

ROMAN OGEE

ROUNDOVER

THUMBNAIL

WAVY EDGE

leaf tabletop and its leaves. The other half is cut with a round-over bit. Cutting radii range from $\frac{1}{16}$ inch to 1 inch; flute lengths, from $\frac{1}{4}$ inch to $1\frac{1}{4}$ inches.

Cove-with-fillets: This bit is available with either one or two fillets. It is another of the "classical" profiles and finds use in making period moldings. Variations of the profile are possible by using different sizes of pilot bearings. Cove radii range from $\frac{3}{16}$ inch to $\frac{3}{8}$ inch; flute lengths, from $\frac{1}{2}$ inch to $\frac{5}{8}$ inch.

Cove-and-bead: A bit that goes by lots of names—classical, ogee-and-step, classical ogee, classical bold cove-and-bead, as well as cove-and-bead. (Bit marketeers just *love* that term "classical.") To me, the characteristic of all these bits is that they combine a cove and a bead separated by a fillet or step. Both cove and bead have the same radius. The bead comes off the pilot. Cutting widths range from $\frac{5}{16}$ inch to $\frac{7}{16}$ inch; flute lengths, from $\frac{1}{2}$ inch to $\frac{7}{8}$ inch.

Bead-and-cove: This profile is the reverse of the cove-and-bead, though you wouldn't be able to tell that from the bit makers' descriptions of it. (Most catalogs will identify two or three different profiles as "classical" and let you distinguish between them as you will.) As with the cove-and-bead, the bead-and-cove combines the two basic forms, separating them with a fillet. Both cove and bead have the same radius. Here the cove comes off the pilot. Cutting widths range from $1\frac{1}{4}$ inches to $1\frac{1}{2}$ inches; flute lengths, from $\frac{1}{2}$ inch to $\frac{7}{8}$ inch.

French Provincial cove-and-bead: The distinction between this bit and the regular cove-and-bead is that the bead has a markedly larger radius than the cove. It's a very graceful profile for finishing the edge of a tabletop. I found it only in the Byrom, MLCS, and Eagle America catalogs. Cutting width is $\frac{1}{2}$ inch; flute lengths range from $\frac{5}{8}$ inch to $\frac{3}{4}$ inch.

Double cove-and-bead: A Cascade exclusive is this more complex version of the cove-and-bead bit—two coves separated by a bead with fillets. The radii of the forms appear to be the same. Cutting width is $\frac{3}{4}$ inch; flute length is $\frac{3}{4}$ inch.

Flute or half-round: This bit cuts a flute—a rounded groove—at right angles to the bit axis, and it's sometimes referred to as the reverse of the bull-nose bit. It's useful for fluting a narrow edge, which wouldn't provide good footing for a router that's set up with a core-box or roundnose bit. The flute depth is controlled by the pilot bearing, the position by the router's bit-height setting. The distinction between flute and half round lies in the width of the cut. If it's $\frac{1}{4}$ inch wide or less, the cutter is a flute bit. If the cut is more than $\frac{1}{4}$ inch wide, the cutter is a half-round bit. Flute diameters range from $\frac{1}{4}$ inch to $1\frac{1}{2}$ inches; flute lengths, from $\frac{1}{8}$ inch to $1\frac{1}{2}$ inches.

Multiflute: Multiple flutes are often found on the legs of Chippendale chairs and tables. This bit cuts three closely spaced flutes in a single pass. Flute diameter is $\frac{1}{8}$ inch, and flute length is 1 inch.

French Provincial: As with some of the other bits shown here, the name the marketeers apply conveys nothing about its profile. A big chunk of steel, this $1\frac{3}{4}$-inch-diameter bit cuts a profile combining the cove and bead with a full bead. The quarter-round bead comes off the bearing, and the full bead is at the shank end of the cutter. Of the five vendors who offer such a bit—only one per vendor—only Freud lists the dimensions of its profile: $\frac{9}{32}$-inch bead radius, $\frac{13}{32}$-inch cove radius, and $\frac{1}{8}$-inch full bead radius. Available only on a $\frac{1}{2}$-inch shank.

Ogee: This S-shaped curve is convex at the top and fairs down into a concave one. What's confusing is that most bit catalogs display the profile upside down. The bit is usually portrayed in a shank-up, pilot-down attitude, and the resulting cut is an upside-down ogee. The easiest way to identify the ogee bit is to check the curve at the pilot bearing; the ogee bit has a *concave* curve there. In most designs, the radii of both the convex and the concave curves are the same. And though the ogees don't cut a fillet, you can change to a smaller-diameter pilot bearing and get one. Available cutting widths range from $\frac{5}{16}$ inch to $\frac{3}{4}$ inch; flute lengths, from $\frac{1}{2}$ inch to 1 inch.

Ogee-with-fillet: This ogee pattern has a step at the end of the concave portion of the curve. A step can be produced at the other end of the profile by switching pilot bearings. Cutting widths range from $\frac{3}{8}$ inch to $\frac{9}{16}$ inch; flute lengths, from $\frac{1}{2}$ inch to $\frac{7}{8}$ inch.

Ellipse ogee: The Roman ogee was based on the circle, but the Greeks based their ogee on the ellipse. The ellipse-based profile is found only in the Eagle America and Cascade catalogs. Cascade calls its profile a stepped ogee, and its cut, at $\frac{13}{16}$ inch by $\frac{3}{4}$ inch, is slightly wider and higher than that of the Eagle America bit.

Roman ogee: This is the reverse of the ogee; it isn't an upside-down ogee. The curve starts at the top as a concave, and fairs down into a convex curve. As with the ogee, bit catalogs can cause some confusion because they present the cut profile upside down. The easiest way to avoid the confusion is to remember that the Roman ogee bit has a *convex* curve coming off the bearing. In most bits, the radii of both the concave and convex curves are the same. Cutting widths range from ⅜ inch to ½ inch; flute lengths, from ¹⁵/₃₂ inch to ⅞ inch.

Round-over: This bit is THE basic edge-forming bit. It goes by four different names: round-over, rounding-over, corner-round, and quarter-round. Very simply, it rounds an edge to a given radius. The bit can be used to nose an edge: Make a cut, turn the board over, and make a second pass. The bit has a shoulder, so that at full extension, it will form a fillet. If a smaller pilot bearing is used, a second shoulder can be produced, in effect making the bit a beading bit. It is available from *every* bit maker in a variety of sizes. They range in ¹/₁₆-inch steps from ¹/₁₆-inch radius up to ⅜-inch radius, then in ⅛-inch steps from there to 1½-inch radius. Obviously, the diameter of the bit increases dramatically as the cutting radius increases. The 1½-inch round-over bit, at 3½ inches in diameter and 3½ inches in overall height, exceeds the size of even the biggest panel-raiser.

Thumbnail: The purpose of this bit is shaping the edges of tabletops. In most patterns, the cutter is a round-over based on an ellipse rather than a circle. Like a round-over, the cutter has a shoulder that will produce a fillet (in some cases, a slightly beveled fillet) if the bit is extended enough. A smaller pilot bearing will yield a second fillet. Freud and Eagle America have related patterns that add a bead, cove, or ogee to the profile. Cutting widths range from ⁷/₁₆ inch to 1 inch; flute lengths, from ⅜ inch to ¾ inch.

Wavy-edge: This bit produces exactly what the name says, a wavy edge. It's an undulating curve with two convex forms flanking a concave form. All the radii are equal. A shoulder on the cutter can form a fillet, depending upon the depth-of-cut setting. Cutting widths range from ⅜ inch to ⁹/₁₆ inch; flute lengths, from ¹¹/₁₆ inch to ⅞ inch.

Groove-Forming Bits

Unfettered by pilots, the groove-forming profile bits are usually more versatile and flexible in routing trims and moldings. The truth is, the pilot is often a hindrance.

For example, suppose you want to create a cove-and-bead profile of your own proportion on a board's edge. You rout the bead right along the board's edge with a beading or round-over bit. Now you are ready to nestle the cove in next to it. But the cove bit's pilot won't let you position the cove wherever you want. In this situation, the pilot is an impediment.

You need a groove-forming bit, which doesn't have a pilot. You control the bit using a fence or an edge guide or a template. The bit forms a groove with a profile.

The variety of groove-forming profile cutters is limited. Here are the main ones. (See "Sources" on page 337 for the addresses and phone numbers of the manufacturers.)

Beading: Is this a trick name? you ask. Because of their names, it is easy to confuse this groove-forming beading bit with the edge-forming bit described earlier. There are similarities beyond the names. This bit forms quarter-round profiles as it grooves, one on each side of a flat. By making repeated passes, you can form full beads. The typical beading bit makes a cut ⅜ inches wide, including two ⅛-inch-radius quarter rounds. Cascade sells several larger-diameter bits, the biggest of which forms a 1-inch-wide groove with two ¼-inch-radius quarter rounds. The scale of the beading profile distinguishes it from the groove-forming or "plunge" round-over bit, which begins where the beading bit leaves off. Used with a fence or guide, the beading bit can be used as an edge former.

Many of the almost miniature profile-grooving bits— the classical, traditional, beading, and veining—are intended for routing decorative lines. Here a flat door panel is being embellished with such a cut. A large template has been clamped to the panel and is guiding the cut.

Classical: This bit name doesn't throw any light on the nature or profile of the bit, but that's the way marketing works, isn't it? We respond to the name emotionally rather than rationally. What this is—rationally speaking—is the groove-cutting form of the cove-and-bead bit. You use it to form round-bottomed, bead-sided grooves and to embellish the inner walls of wide recesses with that cove-and-bead profile. The typical "classical bit" forms a round bottom, but a couple of bit makers have flat-bottomed versions of this bit. Bosch and Amana call the latter form a "traditional" profile. Freud and Byrom also have versions with a square step between the cove and the bead. The radii of the beads range from 3/32 inch up to 3/8 inch, with cutting widths ranging from 1/2 inch up to 1 1/2 inches.

Core-box: A primary bit for decorative work is the core-box. Every bit maker has the core-box profile, and nearly every basic bit set includes a core-box (or roundnose bit, as some forms of it are called). But it's very easy to overlook the core-box's utility in decorative work, probably because the "set bit" is only 1/4 inch or 1/2 inch in diameter—pretty small. The core-box is a cove bit without the pilot, so it can be used not only for fluting but for cove cuts as well. Quite often in decorative work, a pilot bearing gets in the way when you want to place one form right next to another. These are the situations in which you reach for the core-box. Usually, the core-box is a hemisphere-shaped cutter, but when the cutting edges are extended, the bit is known as a roundnose. The bit size is usually expressed in terms of the diameter. In section, the bit may have a 1/2-inch radius, but it'll be referred to as a 1-inch bit. Available

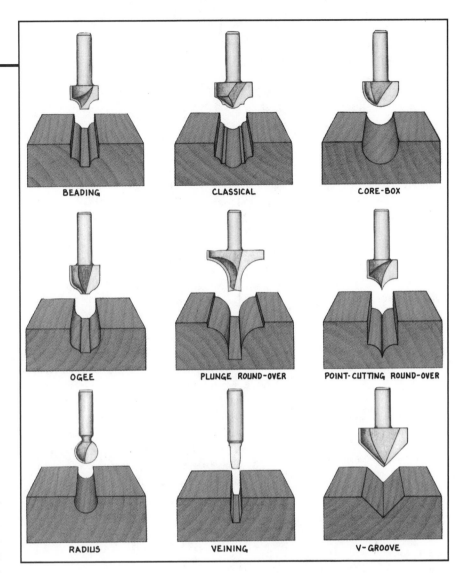

BEADING   CLASSICAL   CORE-BOX

OGEE   PLUNGE ROUND-OVER   POINT-CUTTING ROUND-OVER

RADIUS   VEINING   V-GROOVE

sizes range from 1/8 inch up to 1 1/2 inches in diameter.

Ogee: The ogee—the cyma reversa—is one of the basic molding shapes. The groove-forming versions are pretty tiny, with the radii of the profile's convex and concave sections in the range of 1/16 inch to 3/16 inch. The typical bit cuts a groove with a flat bottom, and the width of the groove ranges from 3/8 inch up to 1 3/16 inches.

Plunge round-over: This is another essential bit for decorative work. It's the groove-forming version of the familiar round-over bit. There seem to be two forms of this bit. The typical one cuts a flat between two quarter-round forms. The cutting edges of this style bit aren't

strictly quarter-round, since they have straight extensions from the radiused section. As a consequence, there's a flat between the roundover and the groove bottom. The flat varies from 1/8 inch up to 3/8 inch long, depending upon the radius of the roundover. The second style is called point-cutting by its manufacturer (Eagle America). This bit produces two quarter-round forms that converge in a V-groove rather than a flat. There's no flat spot below the roundover with this bit, which can be a valuable characteristic. The smallest of the standard plunge roundover bits cuts a 3/8-inch-wide groove with two 1/8-inch-radius beads and a 1/8-inch flat in between. The largest makes a 2-inch-wide cut, with 3/4-inch-radius

As you peruse the available profile bits, you may feel a pang of regret that you can't get the same profile assortment in the groove-forming style of bit that you can in the edge-forming style. You'd like to get a Roman ogee or a cove-and-bead shape at a spot an inch or two from the edge of a board, and there's no groove-forming bit available that'll do it.

Well, now you can buy pilot-free edge-formers. Paso Robles Carbide makes and sells a line of assembled bits featuring interchangeable cutters. You save money by buying one arbor and individual cutters. Switching from one profile to another is a matter of changing the cutter on the arbor.

In the standard Paso Robles system, the cutter fits over a spindle on the arbor, and a locknut keeps the cutter and pilot bearing in place. To prevent the cutter from spinning independent of the arbor, a hex socket in the cutter fits over a matching section on the arbor. You can eliminate the pilot bearing using a special arbor, but it still has that locknut protruding from the cutter's tip.

Paso Robles now has worked out a way to mount the cutters on a threaded shank. To eliminate any protrusion from the cutter tip, the hex socket is machined out, forming a round counterbore, and the hole for the spindle is threaded counter to the direction of bit rotation. The arbor used is a shank with a threaded section at the tip. Turn the arbor into the cutter, and the bit's ready for use.

Any Paso Robles interchangeable cutter can be customized in this way. Once it is, of course, it can't be used with the standard arbors because the hex socket is missing. And because the cutting edges don't extend all the way

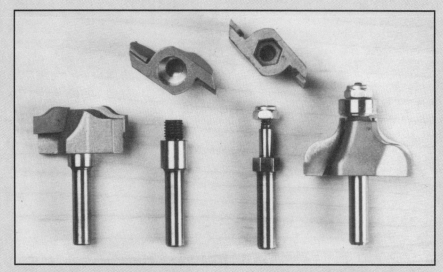

Paso Robles Carbide will turn any of its independent cutters into a groove-cutting bit. The standard cutter (top right) has a hex socket to fit over a matching section of the arbor. These cutters will fit on arbors with and without pilots (right and right center). To eliminate any projection beyond the cutter, a special threaded arbor is used (left center). The hex is machined out of the cutter body (top left) and the hole for the spindle is threaded for the arbor. The resulting bit (left) may be somewhat less convenient to use for edge treatments than one with a pilot, but it can be used easily for more operations than a comparable piloted bit.

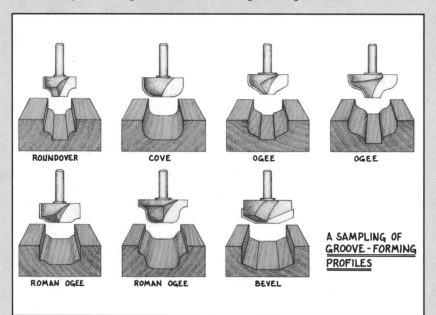

ROUNDOVER   COVE   OGEE   OGEE

ROMAN OGEE   ROMAN OGEE   BEVEL

A SAMPLING OF GROOVE-FORMING PROFILES

across the end of the cutter, it can't be plunged. You have to plow in from an edge or sweep in to start a groove. These are minor impediments.

The result is that you can cut the profile just where you want it—on an edge, fractionally in from the edge, or right smack in the middle of the board.

beads and a ½-inch-wide flat. The point-cutting style is available in radii of ³⁄₁₆ inch, ¼ inch, ⅜ inch, and ½ inch.

Radius: Looking like a ball on the flagpole, the radius bit—sometimes called an internal bull-nose—forms round grooves. In section, the groove's arc can exceed 180 degrees. While it is usually relegated to cutting drawer pulls, it can be useful for cutting coves in tight quarters, places where the core-box's shoulders yield the wrong shape. Cutter diameters start at ⅜ inch and run up to 1¼ inches.

Roundnose: See "Core-box" on page 121.

Veining: Of limited use is the veining bit. It cuts a narrow groove—⅛ to ¼ inch wide—usually with a rounded or V-shaped bottom. Typically, it's used to rout decorative veins in panels.

V-groove: This is the groove-forming equivalent of the chamfer bit. Standard V-groove bits are 90 degree, meaning the cutting edges are canted 45 degrees from the bit axis. Also available, however, are 60-degree bits. In addition, a flat-bottomed V-groove bit is made especially for routing outdoor signs; the theory is that flat-bottomed grooves will shed water better than V-grooves.

What Pilot?

The solid pilot is an integral part of the bit. It's about ³⁄₁₆ inch in diameter and extends about ¼ inch below the cutting edges. This extension rubs directly against the surface of your work to guide the cutter and control its direction. The main disadvantage to the solid pilot is that it requires a gentle, steady hand on the router to get consistent results without marring the surface where the pilot rubs.

The ball-bearing pilot is a bearing mounted on the tip of the bit. This bearing is pressed against the surface of the work and allows the cutter to spin inside it, thus protecting the surface from being marred. But the system is not foolproof. The bearings can get dirty or gummed up and seize, which makes them spin with the cutter and mar the surface. It is very important to keep these bearings clean and lubricated with a light oil (such as WD-40).

Another quirk to remember with ball-bearing pilots is that you must apply enough pressure against the work to stop the outside race of the bearing from turning. If you don't keep fairly firm contact with the work, the bearing will spin with the cutter and sometimes cause more marring than a solid pilot! This is because the bearing is four or five times the diameter of the solid pilot; its surface travels a lot faster and will burn your work sooner.

Softwoods such as cedar and redwood can be compressed by pressing too heavily. If you find this happening, try steaming the tracks a bit before you finish sand. You can use a portable clothing steamer, or simply drape a damp cloth over the compressed wood and hold a hot iron against it for a couple of seconds. The steam should soften the fibers and allow them to relax to nearly their original configuration.

Bearing interchangeability is a factor to consider when choosing cutters. There are several different configurations for mounting pilot bearings to cutters. Try to standardize your collection as much as possible so you can trade bearings from one cutter to another. This is handy if a bearing freezes up; you can grab one from another bit.

Though they appear to be slightly different sizes, the Roman ogee bits produce identical cuts, as do the two round-overs. The difference is the size of the pilot. A small-diameter pilot allows the bulk of the bit to be reduced. The smaller pilot also allows the bit to cut deeper into an inside corner.

But bearing interchangeability also makes your bits more versatile. By changing to a bearing with a different outside diameter, you change the relationship of the bit to the stock and, essentially, change the profile it cuts. You can go so far as to keep a variety of extra bearings on hand for that reason.

EDGE-ROUTING TECHNIQUES

Routing the edge of a board is pretty straightforward stuff. In most cases, you'll use a piloted bit. The pilot will control the cut width, and it will keep the router from drifting too far into the board. But this doesn't mean you can't go wrong.

Your success will be enhanced by your grasp of the fundamentals. And knowing some tricks can help you deal with unusual situations and problems.

Once you know what profile you want, you have to choose the router setup to use. The rule of thumb on this, articulated throughout this book, is that if you can manipulate the work comfortably on a table, use the router table. But if the work is too large or too heavy or too awkward, clamp it down and move the router over it.

Which way do we go? Direction of feed is critical when performing edge treatments. The key here is to be as ornery as possible. Always feed against the cutter's force. If the bit wants to drive the router in one direction, you push or pull it in the other.

This rule works both for hand-held routers and for routers mounted upside down under a router table. If in doubt, hold the router near the work and jog the switch. As the router slows to a stop, note which way the cutter was turning. Think of the cutter as a tire, and decide which way it would roll if you left it to its own devices. Then feed the opposite way.

The consequences of feeding the wrong way are usually not too dire, because the router will have a tendency to kick away from the stock without causing extensive damage.

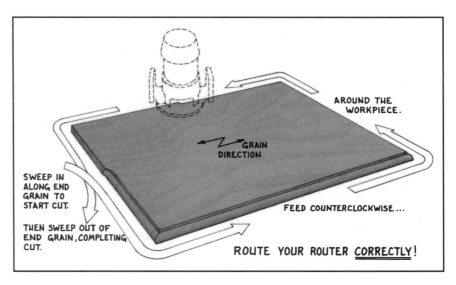

SWEEP IN ALONG END GRAIN TO START CUT.

THEN SWEEP OUT OF END GRAIN, COMPLETING CUT.

GRAIN DIRECTION

AROUND THE WORKPIECE.

FEED COUNTERCLOCKWISE...

ROUTE YOUR ROUTER **CORRECTLY**!

But even if you hold the router against the stock, you'll notice its tendency to gallop ahead and pull you along. This process, known as a climb cut, will produce a rough, inconsistent cut. Persistent climb cuts may eventually bend or break the cutter, and they can even damage the router bearings.

Where do we start? The important point is where you don't want to end. If you rout all around a piece of wood, you'll notice that you almost always get a little bit of splintering as you exit from an end-grain cut. If you then rout the splintered side, the damage is almost always removed.

The trick, then, is to avoid finishing with an end-grain exit. Start

in the middle of the end grain, then finish there. That way, you'll avoid splinters where they can spoil the finished cut.

How do we start? As always, very carefully. Actually, the best way is to sweep into the edge as opposed to starting at a corner.

If you start at a corner, there's a strong tendency for the cutter to slip around the corner and pull you and the router down the wrong side of the work, going the wrong way, with all of the attendant adverse effects. Sweeping in allows you to ease into the cut, while developing momentum in the correct direction. It also avoids the tendency to burn where you stop or start. You can

Tear-out and splintering is most likely to occur when exiting an end-grain cut, regardless of feed direction. One solution is to rout the end grain first, on the likelihood that the long-grain cuts will remove any evidence of the tear-out. But you can't count on that solution if you aren't routing completely around the workpiece. In that case, clamp a scrap against the long-grained edge, as shown here.

Problem Solver

Tip and wobble are the bugbears of edge routing. When you are routing an edge with a piloted cutter, the machine is more off the work than on. It's all too easy to put just a little too much force on the outboard handle and tip the router off the work. Often, you recover and no harm is really done. But snipes and ripples and outright gouges frequently result.

Here are a couple of tricks to help you avoid this problem.

Make and use an offset baseplate. A plan for one is in the chapter "Custom Baseplates." This simple teardrop-shaped jig changes the fulcrum point, so that much more of the overall baseplate area is resting on the work. It has an extra knob so you can exert more downward force on the work, too. This jig is especially useful on plunge routers, which tend to be even more unsteady in edge-routing situations than fixed-based machines, which generally have lower centers of gravity.

A second trick is to use double-sided carpet tape to attach a scrap of the working stock to the base-plate, as shown in the photo. When the router is resting on the work, with its bit hogging away at the work's edge, the temporary support block will keep the router flat and square. It can't tumble off the work, even if you let go of it.

sweep back out anytime you want—to change your grip, to move the cord, or just to relax.

The starting pin is an alternative available when using a table-mounted router. It is a pin or post attached to the table close to the cutter. You press your work against the pin, then swivel it against the cutter and pilot bearing. (See "Using a Starting Pin" on page 99 for more information.)

How fast do we go? Feed rate is a real trade-off issue. A high feed rate works the machine harder and can produce wide ripples in the cut surface. Moving more slowly yields a smoother finish, but the bit may burn the wood if you move too slowly.

There's no foot-per-second formula that will always work, because some woods burn more quickly and some cut more easily. Push the router fast enough that the motor has to labor, but not so fast that it obviously starts to stall. If that rate produces a rippled cut, then slow down a little to get a smoother cut. If you slow down too much, you'll notice that the wood will start to burn. If you can't get a reasonably smooth cut without burning, try working in short, sweeping strokes. That will keep the bit cooler. If that doesn't do the trick, your cutter is probably dull. Sharpen or replace it.

Special Techniques for Peculiar Problems

On all too many projects, you have areas that you can't get the router into after assembly. You've got to spot these areas during a test assembly, before glue is applied, so you can do your routing then. Ofttimes you rout inside edges before assembly and outside edges after.

Sometimes you can choose an embellishment that you can stop at convenient places, thus avoiding these problems altogether.

A piloted cutter can't always be used wherever an edge treatment is required (or just desired). Consider a beveled edge.

Piloted cutters are generally made to work on 90-degree edges. Beveled edges, where the bevel angle is acute, can be handled either by using an edge guide to control the cut instead of the pilot or by attaching an angled shim to the router's baseplate (some laminate trimmers have tiltable bases). But with obtuse-angled bevels, the pilot can get in the way. In these cases, you'll probably have to ignore the fact that the edge is an edge. Use an unpiloted cutter and guide the router along a fence clamped to the work surface.

Then there's the paneled door. Let's say you really can't rout the inside edges of the stiles and rails before they're assembled, because you want a continuous, rounded look at the joints. But you can't assemble the frames without sliding the panel in first, either. With the panel in place you have only ¼ inch of edge to work with—not enough room for any kind of a pilot.

You could do the job with an unpiloted cutter, guiding the router along a clamped-on fence. That's okay for a door or two, but if you've got six doors with two panels in each, think again. That's 48 setups to complete the job!

Put a fence directly on the router instead. Try this: Use doubled-sided carpet tape to stick a ¼-inch-thick fence to the baseplate. The router then is supported both on the rail and on the panel. Now you can follow the edges of the stiles and rails

Several years ago, Fred and our colleague Phil Gehret built an oak table for our book, Outdoor Furniture. All the exposed edges were radiused with a router and a round-over bit. During a test fitting of the table's base, they determined which edges—or sections of edges—could be rounded over before assembly, and which had to wait until after assembly. They made a practice run around the assembly with the router—yeah, it was turned off—marking starting and stopping points (top) and determining on which surfaces they'd have to rest the router to get all the spots. While it's easiest to machine individual pieces, they wanted to blend one part into another where they joined, so some edges had to be machined in an assembled state.

The legs, for example, could be radiused before assembly. The base stringer and crosspieces, however, were best worked in an assembled state, with the router riding on their top surfaces (center). Where their edges were faired into the legs, they had to be worked with the router bearing on their side surfaces (bottom).

The most important thing these photos show are the ways you have to finagle to rout the edges of a piece of furniture and to get all the edges blended together. In this project, the base stringer's shape and the router base's diameter dictated that Fred had to do part of the stringer with the leg removed, and part with the leg in place. Fred even had to block up the assembly to gain clearance when working from the side.

by adjusting an unpiloted cutter in relation to the fence. By positioning the fence on the baseplate so the cutter is at its corner, you automatically have a stop as you cut into each corner.

This type of baseplate-mounted stop/fence also works extremely well when you want to stop a pattern uniformly short of an inside corner. Cut a fence twice as long as the distance you want to leave uncut. As you attach the fence, center it on the cutter. You can then use both ends of the fence as stops.

From there, the next leap is to realize that even though you're following the edge, you don't have to cut the edge. This fence system will allow you to cut grooves parallel to the edge and up to a couple of inches away from it.

Most routers come with slots or holes to accept commercial edge guides. The edge guides come in a

The only time you really need a piloted bit for edge treatment is when you're working a contoured edge—a round tabletop, for example. For most edge work, you can use a groove-forming bit and guide the cut with an edge guide. Thus, a bit without a pilot serves well for edge work, and it can plow decorative grooves as well.

Magic on the Edge

How often do you do this? Every exposed edge on a project gets routed with a ¼-inch round-over, your most-used bit. Is this your trademark?

If it is, *give it a rest!* It's old and tired. Take another look in the bit drawer. You've got a lot of bits, but you need a kick in the seat of your creativity. Here it comes. A few less-than-ordinary edge treatments.

The appearance of a chest or book-case or bookcase or table can be altered by merely switching the orientation of the decorative edge. You can cut the main pattern into the top edge or into the bottom edge. Though these samples certainly look different, both have the same edge contour.

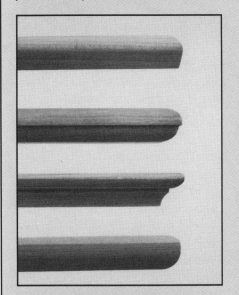

The subtly beveled shelf edge (*top*) was created using a 1-inch dovetail bit and a ⅜-inch round-over bit. On the router table, bevel the edge using the dovetail bit. Then round-over the acute angle along the top edge using the round-over bit. If you don't want a distinct crease between the profiles, a little sanding is all that's needed to blend them.

A nose with a crease is shown next. For a tabletop, it's just a little different. Use a ⅜-inch round-over to radius the upper edge, and a ⅜-inch beading bit to profile the bottom edge and introduce a fillet between the two radii.

Doing the cove-and-bead edge shown next takes three steps on the router table. Use a ⅜-inch round-over bit first. Make several passes, raising the bit slightly for each, until you have a ⁷⁄₁₆-inch-wide fillet below the quarter-round profile. Switch to a ¾-inch core-box and make a pass to create the cove profile. Leave a ⅛-inch fillet between the two forms. Finish the edge by taking a pass along the top edge with a ⅛-inch round-over. Using this approach, you can change the edge's appearance by making one form markedly bigger than the other.

The edge on the bottom is produced by one pass with a ½-inch round-over and one with a ¼-inch round-over. It's softer than the usual ¼-inch/¼-inch rounded-over edge.

The stopped coves in this door frame were routed with a core-box bit after assembly, using the baseplate-mounted stop/fence shown. The jig is planed so its thickness matches the distance from the panel surface to the frame's face. The square block is attached with a couple of drywall screws, and it's centered on the bit. Regardless of the feed direction, the block will stop the cut the same distance from the intersecting frame member.

variety of shapes and sizes, and most of them will substitute for one or more of the jigs mentioned above. But the big drawback to most of them is that they're too long and too thick to get into tight spots.

ROUTING TRIM FOR FURNITURE

Whether you are making molding to trim the interior of a house or molding to trim the exterior of a piece of furniture, the techniques are the same.

As a general rule, the moldings used on furniture tend to be smaller

in section than those used to trim a room. The upshot is that with a router, it's easier to make furniture moldings. You can either use a molding cut in one or two passes or you can build up a larger pattern using two or three such moldings. Once you see how these slender furniture moldings are routed, you'll be able to apply the same cutters and techniques to producing custom architectural moldings.

Bear in mind that you may not be able to produce the moldings you want using the router exclusively. A large-radius cove, for example, is

beyond the router. Do it on the table saw. You can easily rout a flute down the center of a 5-inch-wide board using a core-box bit, but you can't produce the reverse of that form in the same location. You'd have to rout it with a bull-nose bit, and you simply can't get the bit extension necessary to place the center of the cut 2½ inches away from the board's edge. Cut that shape with a molding head in the table saw.

Don't frustrate yourself by trying to do what's not possible. Use other tools as appropriate in making your moldings.

The most understandable way to get you started, I think, is to give some specific examples. A couple of years ago, our woodworking colleague Phil Gehret built a collection of classic furniture pieces in conjunction with Rodale's publication of the plans of the late Carlyle Lynch. Many of these projects required Phil to produce duplicates of moldings originally created using molding planes or scratch stocks. Many Phil did with a router, usually on the router table. The following moldings were selected from plans in the Lynch collection.

Cove-and-Bead Molding

This cove-and-bead molding is used around the waist and base of the linen press, a cabinet in the collection of Lynch plans. The cove-and-bead is a simple form that you know you'd cut with a round-over bit and a core-box bit. But the cove clearly is much larger than the bead.

The first job is to determine the scale of the profile. The plan has a full-sized section of the molding, and it has the thickness and width marked, but not the radii of the two

Used around the waist and base of a linen press, a cabinet in the Carlyle Lynch plans collection, this cove-and-bead is a simple form cut with a round-over bit and a core-box bit.

arcs. You can use a draftsman's circle template to determine them; just line up the different circle cutouts on the arcs until you find one that matches the arc perfectly. In this case, the cove has a ⁷⁄₁₆-inch radius, while the bead has a ¼-inch radius.

A good trick to use in assessing the size of such arcs, as well as figuring out how you'll orient the work to make the cuts, is to lay the bits themselves on the plan, and line them up with the profile. As you do this, you might have a dialogue going in your head:

"Can I stand the stock on edge and rout the bead? Nah. The bearing will be in the way. Can it be done with the stock flat? Would be a deep cut for the bit. Maybe have to cheat the shank out of the collet ¼ inch or so. But, yeah, I can do it.

"Now how about that cove? That's a ⁷⁄₁₆-inch radius. Hmmm. No ⁷⁄₁₆-inch cove bit in my collection. How about this ⅜-inch cove? Bearing's in the way again. A core-box will do it, but lemme think here . . . They're sized by diameter, so I need a ⅞-inch bit. No? I do have a ¾-inch core-box, and the difference in size won't be obvious."

Then it's time to rout. Work with a 2- to 3-inch-wide piece of

To cut the bead with a typical round-over bit, the bit has to be extended just about as far as it can be. Make several passes to work up to the final cutting depth.

The cove is cut with a core-box bit, using the fence to guide the work over the bit. Set the bit height and the fence by sighting across the bit to the workpiece.

stock. Keep it flat on the router tabletop, and cut the ¼-inch round-over on its edge first. Even though the round-over bit has a bearing, it's better to use a fence to guide the cut. The fence gives you better control of the work, and it gives you something to clamp a couple of holddowns to. Make the cuts in several passes, increasing the bit height between passes. The cut is a long reach for the typical bit, but you should be able to complete it without untoward difficulty.

The cove is next. Switch to the core-box bit, and set the height by sighting across the bit to the workpiece. You want a ¹⁄₁₆-inch-wide fillet

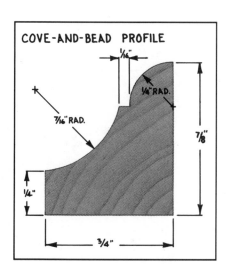

between the bead and the cove. Set the fence in pretty much the same way, sighting across the bit to the workpiece, and adjusting the fence position so the bit intersects a mark ⅝ inch from the edge. Then rout the cove.

Rip the molding from the working stock, and fit it to the linen press.

A Two-Pass Ogee and an Astragal

The moldings on the original sideboard table were most likely cut by hand with molding planes. But when Rodale photographer and woodworker Mitch Mandel made a copy, he used a table-mounted router to produce the moldings.

The ogee profile used for the large molding is formed from a cove and a quarter round. This particular ogee is larger than any available bit, so Mitch routed it using round-over and core-box bits. And though the specified radii were ⅝ inch for both cove and round-over, Mitch used ½-inch-radius bits to better blend the two separate cuts. A ⅝-inch round-over would have cut into the beginning of the cove.

To duplicate Mitch's work, start with straight, flat, defect-free stock.

It should be 1¹⁄₁₆ inches thick and 4 inches wide, so you can cut the profile on both edges and then rip the molding from it. Rout a ⅜-inch-deep by ¾-inch-wide rabbet along one edge, then roll the stock over and rabbet the second edge. Do this to all the stock, including a couple of set-up scraps.

Rout the coves with a 1-inch-diameter core-box bit. Set the stock on edge and brace it against the fence for this cut. Set the fence and the bit height, and make a test cut. Adjust as necessary, and when a test cut confirms that you've got the setting right, rout the good stock.

Now do the quarter-round form. Tighten the round-over bit in the router, then remove the pilot bearing. Adjust the bit height using the coved stock as a guide, and bring the fence into position to guide the stock. You don't want a flat between the cove and the round any more than you want a crease created by too abrupt a transition. The ogee should have a

The moldings on this sideboard table, reproduced following a plan Carlyle Lynch drew from a 200-year-old table, were cut using a table-mounted router. The large molding's ogee profile was formed using round-over and core-box bits; the astragal, using a bull-nose bit.

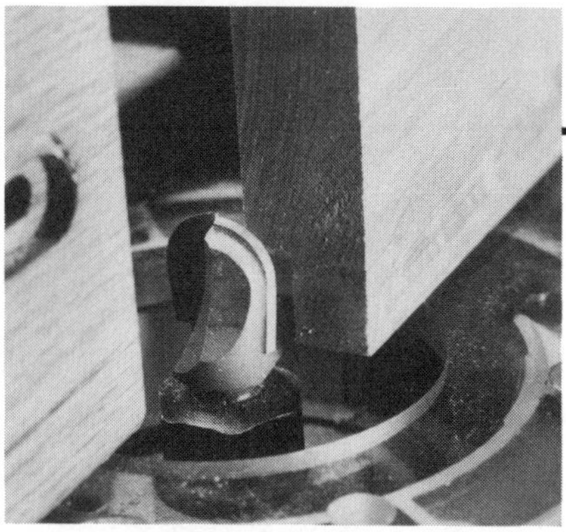

Cut the cove with a core-box bit, half-concealed by the fence. Using the split fence makes this easy to do. In adjusting the fence, set it so the bit's vertical cutting edge just grazes the bottom of the rabbet. Set the bit height to round the rabbet's inside corner.

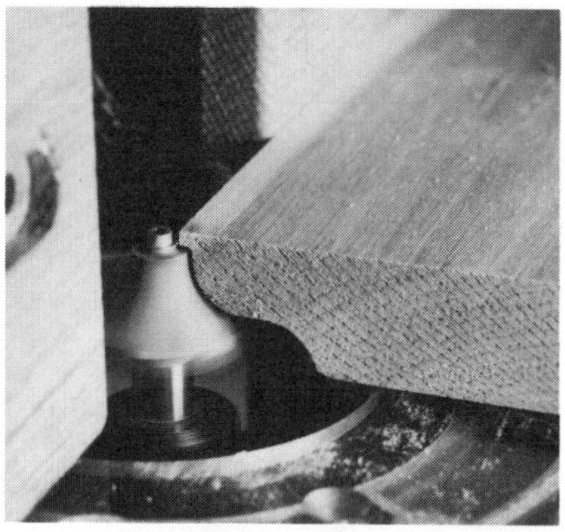

The ogee profile is completed using a round-over bit with its pilot bearing removed. As you can see, the bit must be hyperextended to make the cut. The trick is to adjust the bit to blend its cut with the previous one; the better you align the cuts, the less sanding you'll have to do. Adjust the fence in or out to establish the width of the fillet.

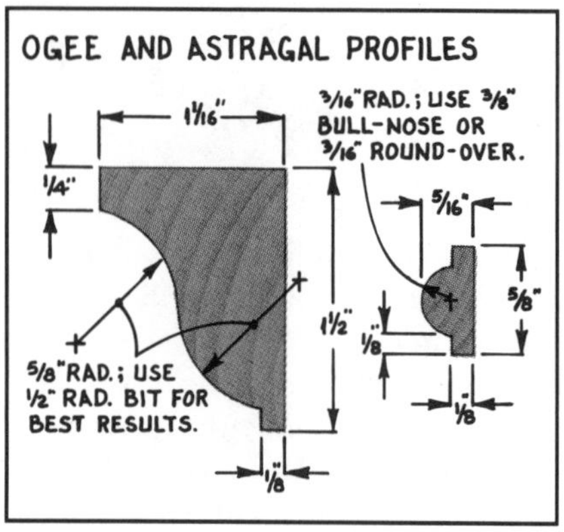

OGEE AND ASTRAGAL PROFILES
1 1/16"
3/16" RAD.; USE 3/8" BULL-NOSE OR 3/16" ROUND-OVER.
1/4"
5/16"
5/8"
1 1/2"
1/8"
5/8" RAD.; USE 1/2" RAD. BIT FOR BEST RESULTS.
1/8"
1/8"

smooth, continuous surface, with the cove blending perfectly into the quarter round. With the pilot bearing removed, you have room for lateral adjustment, because excess stock can ride over the top of the bit. The fillet this forms on the edge of the cut can be ripped off on the table saw. Make a test cut, analyze it, and make any adjustments necessary to achieve that perfect cut. When all is right, rout the good stock.

To complete this large ogee molding, rip the molded edges from the stock. Set up the stock so the molded edge falls away from the stock rather than being trapped between the fence and the blade. Sand the stock, and it's ready for application.

The smaller molding is an astragal. Rout it on the edge of 5/8-inch-thick stock, then rip off a 5/16-inch-thick strip with the profile. You can cut the form either in one pass using a 3/8-inch bull-nose bit or in two passes using a 3/16-inch-radius round-over bit.

Chest Molding

The six-board chest from the Lynch plan collection has an interesting molding around the lid and base. It combines a bull nose with an ogee on a piece of stock 7/8 inch thick by 1 9/16 inches wide.

While it's a challenge to work out the combination of bits needed to form the profile, so is working out the stock orientation. Because of the dimensions, you have to rout the profile in the face of the stock, not on the edge. After routing the ogee on a fairly wide piece, rip off the required 1 9/16-inch-wide strip and rout the bull nose. (You could actually do the ogee on both edges of a 3 1/4-inch-wide board, then rip it in half before nosing both the resulting pieces.)

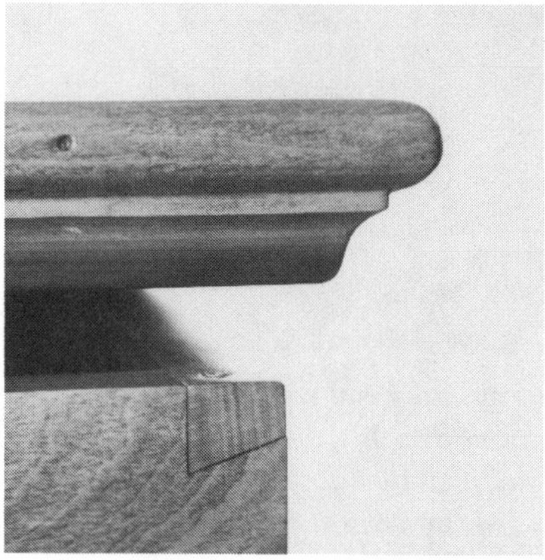

This molding is used in two places on a six-board chest that Carlyle Lynch included in his plan collection. Its use around the lid is shown here. Oriented with the cove up, the same molding is used around the bottom of the chest.

The ogee is cut using a 3/8-inch round-over bit and a 3/4-inch core-box bit. The technique for routing this ogee is the same one used to rout the ogee molding on the sideboard table above. Plow a rabbet the full length of the stock to reduce the number of passes necessary to make the ogee. Cut the cove, then the roundover.

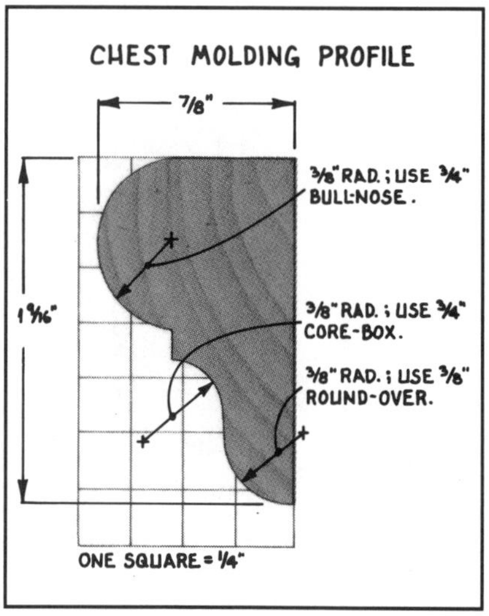

CHEST MOLDING PROFILE
7/8"
3/8" RAD.; USE 3/4" BULL-NOSE.
1 9/16"
3/8" RAD.; USE 3/4" CORE-BOX.
3/8" RAD.; USE 3/8" ROUND-OVER.
ONE SQUARE = 1/4"

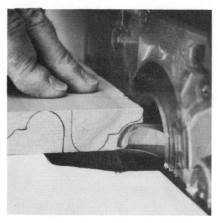

Using the horizontal router table to rout moldings is sometimes appropriate. When cutting the ogee for the six-board chest, you can keep the stock flat on the tabletop rather than balanced on edge. To help you set the bit, draw the profile on the end of a sample of the working stock, then line up the bits with the profile, as shown here.

The roundover can also be routed on the horizontal router table, as long as you remove the pilot bearing from the bit. The stem for the bearing should not interfere with the work. The advantage of working with a wide board at this stage is obvious: You don't have to worry about the stock tipping accidentally, ruining your work.

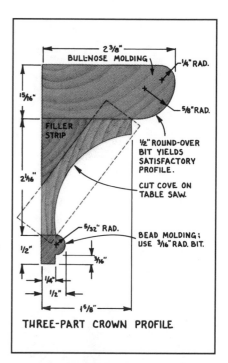

THREE-PART CROWN PROFILE

After ripping the partly completed molding to its final height, cut the nose on it with a ¾-inch bull-nose bit. Alternatively, the nose be can routed in two passes with a round-over bit, *as long as it has no pilot*

The nosing is cut on the regular router table. Rip the molding from the wider stock before making this cut. Use a featherboard to press the molding firmly against the tabletop; use a springboard to hold it tight to the fence.

protrusion to interfere with the fillet between the nosing and the ogee shape. A point-cutting round-over bit would work, as would a Paso Robles pilot-free round-over bit.

Three-Part Crown

The Salem desk and bookcase has a substantial crown molding, which is made up of three separate pieces. The top and bottom elements are easily done using the router. The central cove has a large radius, and you will have to cut this element on the table saw.

Begin with the bull-nose molding. The profile is easily cut using two round-over bits. Cut the top edge first, using a ¼-inch-radius round-over bit. Then rout the bottom edge with a ⅝-inch-radius bit. Make both cuts on the router table, and guide the stock against a fence as you make the cuts.

This substantial crown molding, found on the Salem desk and bookcase included in the Lynch plans collection, is made up of three separate pieces plus hidden blocking. The top and bottom elements are easily done using the router, but the central cove has to be cut on the table saw.

The bead molding at the bottom is cut on the router table with an edge-beading bit that forms a ³⁄₁₆-inch-radius bead. Most such bits have a shoulder on the cutter that will form the fillet below the bead

The bead for the bottom of the crown molding assembly is cut on the edge of a wide board. A 3/16-inch-radius edge-beading bit will make the profile in one pass. Rip the profile from the stock, as shown, with the profile to the outside of the saw blade.

Here's the assembly, almost ready for gluing up. The cove profile, produced on the table saw, is supported by a triangular-section filler block and set off by a large bull-nose profile (left) and the tiny bead profile (right).

on the molding. Rather than work with a flimsy strip, cut the profile on the edge of a 2- to 4-inch-wide piece of ½-inch stock. After routing the profile, rip the molding from the stock.

As noted, the central cove must be cut on the table saw. After the cove molding has been cut, sanded, and beveled as required, a triangular strip must be cut to back the cove and hold it at the proper cant. The three moldings—and the backup strip—can be glued up before the crown is installed.

It's not much of a leap from furniture moldings to picture-frame stock. Many pleasing profiles can be produced on the router table, as these one- and two-piece samples demonstrate. At left is a stock formed by cutting two coves, then insetting a bull-nosed strip of contrasting stock. The stock next to it was formed by four passes with the same round-over bit. The center stock was cut with a small panel-raising bit. The cove-and-bead profile at right center is combined with a contrasting backband at right. What makes these strips picture-frame stock, as opposed to simple trim, is the rabbet cut into the back of each.

ARCHITECTURAL MOLDINGS

Those fancy strips of wood that we tack over the cracks are really designed to accent the lines of a structure by creating parallel lines of highlight and shade. The effect is obtained by creating combinations of grooves and bevels to reflect light differently. The variety of moldings available from lumberyards attests to the fact that no one molding will suffice in all applications. But when you start to work with shapes in your own custom projects, you're bound to run into a situation where you just can't find the right shape or size in just the right wood. You gotta make your own.

If it's a question of a standard profile cut into a special wood, check your catalogs. You may be able to buy a cutter that will produce exactly what you're looking for. But if you're looking for a shape that's out of the ordinary, you'll have to go a little further.

Look for cutters that will combine to make the profile you want.

Let me warn you up front that this can be ticklish work. It's time-consuming. Make a goof on the fourth pass, and you've wasted the time it took to do the first three.

If you're a time-is-money person, sub out the molding production to a millwork shop that has a sticking machine. Pay for the custom cutters, if that's what the profiles you want require. Chances are, though, that if the shop is a busy one, its inventory of custom profiles is extensive, and you'll be able to find something suitable. Moreover, the shop will probably get a better price on the trim stock than you can. Each stick will be molded in a single pass, and you won't have the chips and frustrations to cope with.

On the other hand, if you're doing one room, then creating some one-of-a-kind moldings to trim it out is something you can reasonably do at the router table.

Specialty Bits

Nearly every bit manufacturer has a few bits specially designed for routing architectural moldings. They are worth a look, especially if your project justifies the expense of one or two of these bits. What they do is allow you to rout a profile that's about 1½ inches wide in a single setup. They aren't versatile, like round-overs and core-boxes, and because they are big bits, they tend to be pricey. But if one of them fills a need and saves you a lot of time, it's a worthwhile investment. (See "Sources" on page 337 for the addresses and phone numbers of these manufacturers.)

Astragal cutter: You'll find this bit only in the MLCS catalog, labeled simply "molding bit." It resembles the bull-nose or fingernail bit, and like those bits, it should be used with a table-mounted router. It lacks a pilot, so you need to guide the work along a fence. The two profiles cut are the stereotypical astragals. One form is a full bead, flanked on each side by a cove and fillet—three sizes of this one. The other cuts a flat, flanked on both sides by a quarter-round and fillet. These forms can be cut with round-overs and core-boxes, but if you generate and use a lot of these profiles, one of these bits might be a time-saver.

Cove molding bit: Milling cove moldings on the router table is what this specialty bit does. The bit cuts the cove and bevels the edges. To use the resulting piece as a traditional cove molding, you make two additional bevel cuts on the table saw. Depending upon your specific needs, you might use one of these bits to cut mid-sized coves for assembled moldings. The bit itself resembles the vertical panel-raiser; the largest is 1⅛ inches in diameter, with a 2¼-inch cutter height on a nearly 4-inch-long bit. Plan on using a 2-horsepower or better router, though you need not reduce the speed. The fence is essential, since the bit lacks a pilot. Cascade has four sizes, ranging from one that cuts a ½-inch-radius cove on 1-inch-wide stock, up to a cutter that makes a 1⅞-inch cove on 2-inch-wide stock. This cut exceeds that of the largest coves and core-box bits. Eagle America and MLCS stock only this large bit.

Crown molding bit: Mid-sized crown molding profiles can be routed with one of these bits. The profiles are stock ones, so you probably won't be getting a shape you can't buy from your local lumber dealer. Three different profiles are available. Cascade, Eagle America, and MLCS all have a 2-inch-high cove-and-ogee

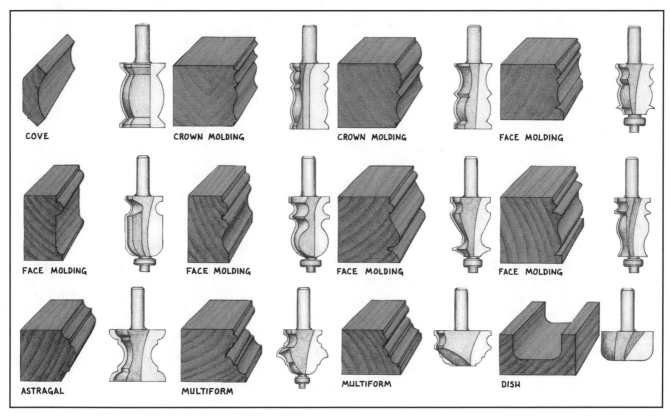

COVE   CROWN MOLDING   CROWN MOLDING   FACE MOLDING

FACE MOLDING   FACE MOLDING   FACE MOLDING   FACE MOLDING

ASTRAGAL   MULTIFORM   MULTIFORM   DISH

profile. Cascade also has bits that cut the same profile in narrower stock. In addition, Cascade has an ogee-with-fillet profile in three sizes—1¼ inches, 1⅜ inches, and 2 inches. The other two vendors have a familiar 2-inch-high cove-and-bead profile. All of these bits look basically like the cove molding cutters discussed above. The biggest of them is 1⅛ inches in diameter with a 2¼-inch-high cutter. The same caveats apply: Use a 2-horsepower router, mounted in a table, with a fence to guide the work. You are addressing a lot of stock with each pass, so take several passes to complete a cut to full depth.

Dish cutter: Surprised? This bit, marketed as a tool for hollowing coasters, trays, and bowls, is great for cutting recesses of any kind. It is a shallow bit, with radiused corners on the cutting edges. It cuts a smooth, flat-bottomed groove with a radiused transition from bottom to wall. This makes it useful for hollowing out fairly broad flats. It's also useful for cutting a relief into the back of a wide molding. (Stock moldings like baseboard and casing have a relief, which is a shallow recess, in the back surface so the molding can bridge mismatches between a wall surface and a door or window jamb.) Dish cutters are usually about 1¼ inches in diameter, with ½- to ⅝-inch-long cutting edges.

Face molding bit: These bits are designed for routing architectural moldings. Each is a combination of the basic forms—beads, coves, gentle ogees, and so forth. I don't know of any way to describe individual bits; you have to *look* at the bits and the profiles they cut, and see whether any of them meet your needs. Every bit manufacturer seems to have two to four of them in its catalog—they're the same four profiles, too—but Amana, MLCS, and Eagle America seem to have the widest assortments. In the main, these bits resemble vertical panel-raisers, in that the profile is laid out vertically on the bit (rather than horizontally, which would necessitate a propeller-like configuration). The vertical orientation allows the bit to cut beads, something it couldn't do in the horizontal orientation. Typically, the bits are an inch in diameter with a cutter height of 1½ inches. Most have pilot bearings. The bit should be used in a router table, and the stock guided along a fence with some hold-downs.

Multiform bit: With this one bit, so the hype goes, you can turn out many different molding profiles—40 to 60 of them!—by adjusting the bit height and fence settings, making multiple passes, and altering the angle of attack. While I expect this is true, I know it underplays the patience and ingenuity necessary to use this bit productively. All of the catalogs display a few of the "almost unlimited possibilities," and it always seems they're heavy, steep, and extraordinarily busy. The multiform bits are all fairly large, ranging up to 2 inches in diameter. Some versions have a pilot bearing, others don't. All should be used exclusively in router tables, with 2- (or more) horsepower routers. The larger-diameter bits should be run at reduced speed. I personally would invest the $35 to $70 each that these bits cost in some basic profile bits—round-overs, core-boxes, ogees and Roman ogees, beading, or bull-noses. By adjusting the bit height and fence settings, making multiple passes, and altering the angle of attack, you can produce a lot of different profiles with these basic bits.

Built-Up Moldings

A common practice is to stack or build up separate moldings into a wide or heavy profile. This is what we did to create the three-part crown molding shown on page 131.

To make a crown molding for a room, you might shape the edges of two boards, then assemble them into an L-shape. Next you make another strip or two that will fill in the L with complementary shapes. These strips are usually relatively narrow, so a single pass over the router generally is all that's needed.

Let's look at a couple of specific examples of built-up moldings and see how they are made and used. In each example, one or two of the elements are stock moldings.

Casing with a backband: To make this trim, we started with standard ¹¹⁄₁₆-inch by 2½-inch sanitary casing. This casing has one edge rounded-over on about a ⅛-inch radius, but it's otherwise totally unembellished. It does have the relief on the back for bridging irregularities between wall surfaces and jamb edges.

The first cut is made with a face molding bit that produces a 1½-inch-wide band with a cove and a full bead. MLCS lists this bit as item #862, but it is available from other sources as well. This bit should be used in either the regular or the horizontal router table, depending

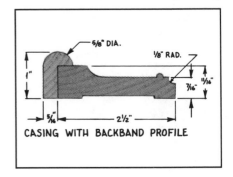

CASING WITH BACKBAND PROFILE

upon your preference. Jack up the bit so the bead is positioned about $\frac{7}{16}$ inch to a full $\frac{1}{2}$ inch from the radiused edge of the casing. (The cut will leave a ridge at the edge of the casing; this will be removed in the next step.) The full profile requires

Relatively simple to produce with a table-mounted router, this back-banded casing is a handsome step away from the casing typically stocked at home centers. Other options are to use the casing without the backband or to use the backband on a stock casing.

To cut the cove, you have to attach a shim to the router tabletop for the work to slide on; otherwise the work will be unsteady. Cut a strip to hold the work square and attach it to the tabletop with carpet tape.

a heavy cut, so you should achieve it in increments. On the regular router table, this means adjusting the fence location between passes. On the horizontal table, it means raising the router mounting board between passes.

After the main profile is cut, rout the cove on the edge. It has a $\frac{1}{8}$-inch radius. Use either a cove bit or a core-box bit. This element is now completed.

Make the backband next. Mill a length of $\frac{5}{8}$-inch by $1\frac{5}{16}$-inch stock for each piece of casing you've prepared. Rout a $\frac{5}{8}$-inch-diameter nose on each piece, using either a $\frac{5}{8}$-inch bull-nose bit or a $\frac{5}{16}$-inch-radius round-over bit. Then cut a $\frac{5}{16}$-inch by $\frac{11}{16}$-inch rabbet in each backband.

You can glue the backband to the casing, but it is just as easy to nail it in place when you install the trim.

Baseboard with cap and shoe: The baseboard used in this assemblage is a stock molding, $3\frac{1}{2}$-inch sanitary base. Like the sanitary casing used in the preceding molding project, this is $\frac{11}{16}$-inch-thick stock with one radiused edge and no other embellishment. It does have a relief area on the back. This trim is used as is.

The cap is routed from $\frac{3}{4}$-inch stock in several steps. First use the face molding bit with the profile shown in *Baseboard with Cap and Shoe.* (It's MLCS's #865, but the profile is available from other sources as well.) Rout this profile on the edge of a 3-inch-wide piece of stock. (If you need several lengths, you can rout the profile on both edges of this piece.)

Switch to a straight bit, and rout a rabbet along the top edge of the

In so many contemporary homes, the baseboard is a wimpy strip of wood. Here, a typical base has been topped with a one-of-kind cap and set off with a shoe molding along the floor.

profile, as shown in the drawing. This should remove the full bead the previous operation formed.

Switch to a $\frac{1}{2}$-inch-diameter core-box bit, and rout the cove along the top edge of the cap molding. This can be a dicey cut, since the workpiece is very thin. If the grain isn't straight, the cut may trash the edge. The best approach is to set the bit to the final height, but adjust the fence so the bit barely nicks the edge. Make about three passes, adjusting the fence for each.

Finish the cap by ripping it to width, cutting just below the fillet.

PORTION OF INITIAL PROFILE IS REMOVED IN SECOND AND THIRD STEPS.

1/4" RAD.

CAP

1½"

SANITARY BASE

3/4" 1/4" RAD.

3/4"

SHOE

3/8" RAD.

BASEBOARD WITH CAP AND SHOE

Routing architectural molding requires you to work some very long pieces. My setup for routing the cap included four fingerboards and a roller stand to support the stock on the outfeed side. To get a smooth finish, you want to keep the stock moving as steadily as possible, which is tough to do when routing a 10- or 12-foot strip by yourself. So after making a couple of passes to rough out the molding, I enlisted help to complete the final pass. You and the helper can alternate pushing and pulling to keep the stock moving.

The setup for rabbeting away the bead formed as part of the first cut demonstrates one of the reasons for routing the base cap on a fairly wide piece of wood. You'll have a flat surface to reference against the router tabletop after the initial profile cut is made. And by alternating the side on which you rout, you can get two caps from one workpiece without sacrificing the flat reference section of either face. To get the featherboard's pressure on the right spot, as here, it may be necessary to insert a spacer between the featherboard and the fence or router mounting board.

The shoe is a basic cove-and-bead cut on ¾-inch stock. Cut the cove first, using a ½-inch-diameter cove or core-box bit. Then cut the roundover using a ⅜-inch round-over bit. It goes best if you use a bit with no pilot. Again, make these cuts on a piece that's at least twice as wide as the finished shoe. You can cut two profiles on one piece, then rip it in half, separating them. If you do this, cut one profile into each face so it remains stable when you rout.

Install the baseboard, then the cap, then the shoe.

Solid, One-Piece Moldings

What if you don't want to use a bunch of strips? Your project deserves a solid molding that's all one piece with no glue line and no mismatched grain. Now you'll have to make a single molding with multiple passes over the router. This doesn't look

too difficult in theory. The tricky part comes when you realize that the shape you wanted to put in the middle would require you to extend the router bit 2 inches out of the collet. No can do. So how do you get to the middle of the board?

The trick is to stick with simple shapes out in the middle of the board. Use shapes that you can get with your unpiloted or grooving cutters. Core-box or roundnose cutters are good; dish cutters with round edges and flat bottoms are excellent. To produce beads or ribs, you'll have to make two passes with an unpiloted ogee or round-over. And you'll have to think, as you set up each cut, about how the board is to be supported during the cut.

You can accomplish molding work with a hand-held router, but you'll have a struggle. It's much easier to use the router in a router table, where you can use special runners to support the stock and keep it securely in place with featherboards. And that's critical! A tiny bit of unplanned movement can ruin a piece of molding that already has several passes complete. Or at least make you work a lot to sand out the goof.

Let's rout a hypothetical molding. This will give you a specific example of what can be accomplished that may serve to launch you in your own directions. (Hey, good luck!)

Fancy door casing: Suppose I want to trim out an entrance door in a special way. What I have in mind is fairly classical—there's that *word!* —with references to fluted columns. The casing will have two large full beads, a couple of grooves formed in routing the beads, and four flutes (see *Fancy Door Casing*).

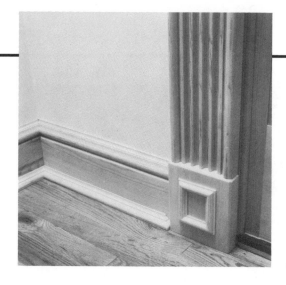

It's elaborate, to be sure, but this casing beats ranch or colonial trim for looks, to my mind. The columnlike casing rises from a plinth block and ends at a capital.

▶ **TRY THIS!**

The more pieces of molding you do, the more likely you are to lose concentration and make a miscut. And if you run longer pieces, you'll find them harder to support as you feed. Here are a few suggestions for more consistent work.

Don't try to hold a long, flexible strip down on the tabletop and firmly against the cutter while the end is swaying back and forth in space. Support the ends of your work. Auxiliary tables or even roller stands can make your life a lot easier.

You can also use all the help you can get in holding your work against the table and cutter. You can easily make a variety of hold-downs; see the chapter "Router Table Accessories" for plans. Most of these hold-downs can be used to help guide your stock for molding work. In most situations, however, you'll find that the best setup is to use two featherboards: one holding the work into the fence, and one on the fence holding down. The greatest thing about featherboards is that if you set them steep enough, they're pretty effective at stopping kickback.

The feed rate is important. If you feed the stock too fast, the cut will be rippled. And each time you stop the feed—to reposition your hands—the bit will burnish a spot on the molding. Some of these defects don't show up unless the light hits them just right (meaning the light that hits them right after you've installed the molding). With a short piece, you can usually feed the stock with one continuous movement. With a long piece, get a helper. As you reach the end of your range, the helper can begin to pull the stock, keeping it moving slowly while you reposition yourself for the next push.

I'm going to start with 1-inch-thick stock, because the total relief is going to be pretty dramatic. Plane or joint about 1/16 to 1/8 inch from a piece of 5/4 stock. Rip it to 5 inches wide. Because the ends tend to get messed up and because I need some clamping space, I'll wait to actually trim the casing until after it is shaped.

I'm going to cut the full beads first. Though I usually like to work with the stock flat on the horizontal router tabletop, I'm going to use the regular router table for these cuts. I fit the 3/4-inch bull-nose bit in the table, set the bit height of the bit and the fence, and make a test cut. I want the full bead—no flat spots—without taking off too much stock. I set up a couple of featherboards and a roller stand on the outfeed side. Then I make the cuts, one along each edge.

Cutting beads, incidentally, forms the two flat-bottomed grooves that are part of the profile.

I plow the flutes next, using a 1/2-inch core-box bit in a plunge router. I do this as a hand-held operation simply because it's easier to guide the router over the work than the work over the router table. The flutes need to be 9/16 inch deep. With the plunge router, I can use the depth turret to preset my final depth, then eyeball the depth on two or three intermediate passes.

The first cuts are the two inside flutes. One edge-guide setting will suffice for both cuts, since I reference one edge of the molding for the first flute, the other edge for the second. After cutting the first two, I reset the edge guide and rout the third and fourth flutes.

Finally, I need to plane away the

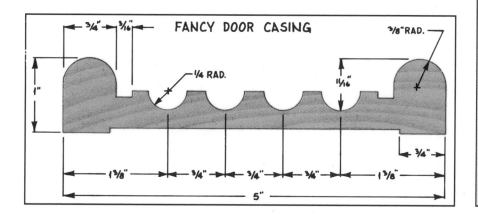

FANCY DOOR CASING

3/4" 3/16" 3/8"RAD. 1/4 RAD. 11/16" 1" 3/4" 1 3/8" 3/4" 3/4" 3/4" 1 3/8" 5"

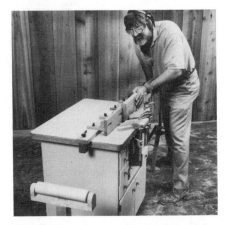

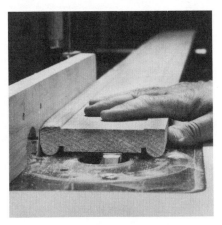

The full beads along each edge of the casing are cut with a ¾-inch bull nose bit. I set up a couple of featherboards to guide and control the stock. Because the stock is 7 to 8 feet long, the big danger is inadvertently rocking the stock—pushing down or lifting up the unsupported ends—as you feed it. Infeed and outfeed roller stands can help prevent this.

Plow the flutes with a hand-held router with an edge guide. I clamped the molding to my router bench—it's too long to be dogged. Note that both clamps are at one end. Though they are close together, they keep the stock from pivoting. I don't have to fuss with them. The piece is long enough that I can leave that section unrouted and trim it off.

The area between the beads has to be milled with a light touch. It figures, doesn't it? The most problematic cut in the process is the last one. The bit that worked the best of the several I tried is this bottom-cleaning bit from MLCS. The cutting edges run across the bottom of the bit. Note that the back of the casing has already been relieved slightly.

stock between the beads. The hazard here is tear-out along the edges of the flutes. I try several bits on a sample, and settle on a large-diameter bottom-cleaning bit. Make very shallow cuts. To mill the entire surface, I need three different fence positions. Set the fence to position the first cut

as close as possible to the bead. Make a pass with one edge against the fence, then turn the workpiece around and make a pass with the other edge against the fence. Then shift the fence and repeat. After the entire area is milled at one depth setting, raise the bit a little and repeat

the process. (At the first setting, mill a relief in the back of the molding.) I'll be judgmental about how deep I rout.

When this operation is completed, the casing merely has to be sanded, trimmed, and installed.

TEMPLATE-GUIDED WORK

▶ **A template is a quick and easy way to duplicate**

shapes like circles, squares, or even letters. That's one of its primary uses, but there are others. Many others.

The typical template is a durable wood or plastic or metal pattern. When the router, fitted either with a guide bushing or a pattern bit, is run along the edge of the template, the bit makes a cut in the exact contour of the template. So when remarkable consistency from part to part is required, a template is used to guide the cuts that produce the parts.

Commercial dovetail jigs, for example, depend on guide bushings or pattern bits to guide the cuts. Every piece has to be reproduced accurately and consistently if the dovetails are to come together successfully. The template system virtually guarantees that they will.

In a production setting, templates are used to create stacks of identical parts. You can consistently contour the edges of workpieces by clamping a template to the rough-sawn part and then guiding the router along the template. Its bit will machine the workpiece to the same contour as the template. And every part cut using the template will be identical.

Now *you* may not need to produce stacks of identical parts, but if you want to make just eight identical back legs for a set of four chairs, it's worth the trouble to make a template. In fact, you may make a template just to scribe around so you can cut them on the band saw.

Why not spend an extra half hour to make that template precise, then guide the router around it, shaping each leg to the exact contour you want. You can even cut out a window in the template so it can guide the router when you rout mortises in the legs.

Templates can be used to guide joinery cuts other than dovetails and mortises. You can rout the edges of two boards along complementary curves, so they can be edge-joined perfectly. You can use a template to guide dado and grooving cuts, to cut laps, and even to control a miter-gauge-like jig for cutting box joints on the router table.

Perfectly fitted inlay work is done with relative ease using a router and a template.

Once you try any of these techniques, you'll realize how easy and reliable template-guided work is. The potential is tremendous.

THREE SETUPS

There are three common template systems in the home shop. The first is designed to guide a round-based,

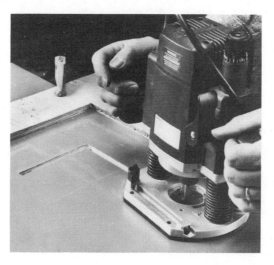

hand-held router. The second uses a guide collar or bushing attached to the base of the router. This collar guides the bit along the edge of the template. The third system uses a flush-trimming type of bit with a bearing on the shank (instead of the bit tip, as is commonplace). (A fourth system, used mostly in industrial applications, utilizes a pin guide on the side of the stock opposite the router.) There are pluses and minuses to each system.

There sometimes is confusion arising from the names given to the piece against which the bushing or bearing or pin rides. Sometimes it's called a *template,* sometimes a *pattern.* Technically, a pattern is an original part or a piece that, though different in material and thickness, is exactly the same size and contour as an original. The template, on the other hand, is simply a guide used to produce an original, and it may or may not be the same size and contour as an original. Fred and I both tend to use the term *template* more often than not, even when we mean a pattern. (I suspect that tendency will prevail throughout this chapter.)

To cut a hole in a counter for a sink, use a framelike template to guide the router base. An advantage to this approach is that the template's edge need not be perfectly smooth, since the base tends to ride over minor irregularities without telegraphing them into the cut. Moreover, because the template is beside, rather than beneath, the router, it doesn't steal any cutting depth from the tool.

Guiding the Base

The first guidance system allows the router to ride directly on the stock surface. This not only affords the best support and accuracy of depth but also allows you to cut with the full length of your bit's cutting edges, rather than having to reach past the thickness of a template.

A less obvious advantage to this system is that the template needn't be finely finished. The large radius of the router base can ride a neatly band-sawed edge without translating every little saw mark into the cut. But this also means that it smooths out details.

The need to scale the template to the size of the router's base can be a drawback, though. You can't, for example, cut an inside corner tighter than the radius of the base. The template has to be bigger or smaller, by the radius of the baseplate, than the shape you want to cut. This size difference can make it nearly impossible to clamp a template to some projects.

You can moderate the scale problem somewhat if you can use a laminate trimmer for your cut instead of a full-sized router. The trimmer usually has a baseplate diameter in the 3½-inch range, rather than the 6- to 7-inch range.

Using Guide Bushings

Let's take a look at guide bushings. This is what most woodworkers think of when template-guided work is discussed.

A guide bushing, sometimes called a template guide, is a lot like a big washer with a short tube stuck in it. The bushing fits into the bit opening in the baseplate, and the

bit projects through the tube. In use, the tube—called the collar—catches the edge of the template and rides along it. And the bit that's jutting through the collar makes a cut that, though slightly offset from the template, matches the template perfectly. You'll find that details transfer better with the collar-guided system than with the base-guided system.

While many router manufacturers provide a guide-bushing system peculiar to their routers, some have simply adopted the popular Porter-Cable system. In this design, the ring of the bushing drops into a

rabbet around the bit opening so it will be flush with the baseplate surface. A threaded flange projects into the base, and you turn a lock ring onto it to secure the bushing in place. With this design, you can change bushings without touching the bit. In fact, you may not even have to change the depth-of-cut setting. This is a handy feature when you're doing inlay work. A big plus with this universal design, to me, is that you can buy guide bushings from a variety of sources. You aren't limited to the range of sizes the router manufacturer makes.

A guide bushing is a short tube with a flange that fits into the router base. This assortment of guide bushings gives you an idea of the range of sizes available, as well as the different mounting systems. Some bushings are attached to the router base with screws (bottom right); these are usually required on plunge routers. Bosch's newest plungers have bayonet-mount bushings (top right). The most common "universal" system uses a threaded lock-ring to hold the bushing in the baseplate's rabbeted bit opening (left). Freud's set even includes an adapter ring so you can use these universal bushings in routers that have a screw-mount design.

With some other systems, you attach the guide bushings to the base or baseplate with screws. Some plunge routers have guide bushings that attach with screws to a reducer that is in turn screwed to the base. The bushing drops into place from inside the base.

Bosch has a bayonet system on their newest plunge routers. Push a button on the edge of the base to mount and release the bushing. Obviously, you have to buy bushings made specifically for that model.

With all systems, the guide collar extends ¼ inch or so below the base. You must use a template at least as thick as the collar is long to avoid having it drag on the workpiece's surface.

Some guide bushings are made for use with specific accessories the manufacturer also sells. Porter-Cable, for example, has odd-sized bushings to use with stair-mortising and hinge-mortising templates. On some of these, the collar projects 9⁄16 inch or more, which dictates that you use it with a template ⅝ inch thick or

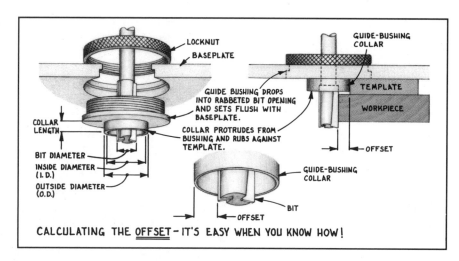

CALCULATING THE OFFSET — IT'S EASY WHEN YOU KNOW HOW!

more. Or you can, of course, grind down the collar to reduce its length.

The size of the bushing is determined not by the overall diameter, which is usually constant, but by the inside and outside diameters of the collar. You have to use a bushing with an inside diameter (I.D.) larger than the diameter of your bit. In some cases, you can manage to use a collar that's the same outside diameter (O.D.) as the cutter—if you're using a dovetail bit, for example, or if the entire body of the bit is beyond the collar and only the bit shank extends through it. But most of the time, you'll find yourself using a collar that's at least ⅛ inch bigger than the cutter.

The table below lists some common guide bushing sizes. You'll see

that there are limits to what's available.

You have to figure the offset into the size and shape of your template. The template cannot be the same size as the finished piece. Here is the formula for calculating the offset:

$$\frac{\text{Bushing diameter} - \text{bit diameter}}{2} = \frac{\text{Template}}{\text{offset}}$$

Here's an example: If you are using a ¾-inch-diameter bushing and a ⅜-inch-diameter bit, the template offset should be 3⁄16 inch. Remember, you've got to add the offset to each guiding edge of your template. In this example, to rout a 1-inch by 3-inch mortise, you'd need a template slot that measures 1⅜ inches by 3⅜ inches.

When routing with a guide bushing, the bushing rides against a template on top of the workpiece. The template must be offset by the difference between the bit and bushing diameters.

Outside Diameter (O.D.)	Inside Diameter (I.D.)	Collar Length	Manu-facturer
5⁄16"	¼"	5⁄32"	P-C, Freud
⅜"	9⁄32"	5⁄16"	P-C, Freud
7⁄16"	11⁄32"	5⁄32"	P-C, Freud
½"	13⁄32"	5⁄16"	P-C, Freud
⅝"	17⁄32"	9⁄16"	P-C, Freud
¾"	21⁄32"	9⁄16"	P-C, Freud
1"	25⁄32"	⅜"	P-C
1¼"	1⁄32"	7⁄16"	P-C
1⅜"	1⅗64"	17⁄16"	P-C

Because of the need to accommodate the offset when laying out the template, setting up for template-guided routing does take extra time. If you have only one or two pieces to shape, and the precise contours aren't all that important, it may not be worth the effort. But routers can do very precise work when guided by a template. You'll find, therefore, that when you have an especially fancy or intricate cut to make in an expensive piece of stock, it's worth spending the time to make a very precise template for only one use. It's not uncommon to spend several hours making the template, and only a couple of minutes making the actual cut.

Using Pattern Bits

This simplest form of template-guided routing is done with either a flush-trimming bit or a pattern bit. Both have pilot bearings whose diameter matches the diameter of the bit. On a flush-trimming bit, the bearing is at the bottom of the bit. On a pattern bit, the bearing is on the shank, right above the flutes. There's no offset with these bits.

Make the template (or pattern) exactly the shape you want (limited only by the bit diameter). You don't even have to make a template in many cases. Instead, make the first of the actual parts especially carefully, then use it as the template and make as many more as you want. They'll all be the same.

When routing with a flush-trimming bit, attach the template to the underside of the workpiece with double-sided carpet tape, hot-melt glue, or clamps. The bearing rides along the template, and the cutter automatically cuts the work to match. A pattern bit works the same way,

When you're pattern routing with a flush-trimming bit, the pilot bearing rides on a pattern or template attached to the workpiece. Here, a face frame trimmer— just a BIG flush-trimmer—is being used to duplicate a finished workpiece. The workpiece was carefully sawed and sanded to a curved contour, then bonded to a rough-sawn blank with carpet tape. The bearing rides on the pattern, and the cutting edges trim the duplicate workpiece to match the pattern.

When you use a pattern bit, the template is placed between the router and the workpiece (with a hand-held router, this means on top of the workpiece). For the bit's shank-mounted bearing to ride along the template edge, the bit has to be fully extended. With a fairly thick template and a short bit, you can make most cuts in two manageable passes. On the first pass, the bearing rides on the template (top). For the second pass, remove the template and adjust the bit so the bearing rides along the surface formed by the previous cut (bottom).

BIT DRAWER

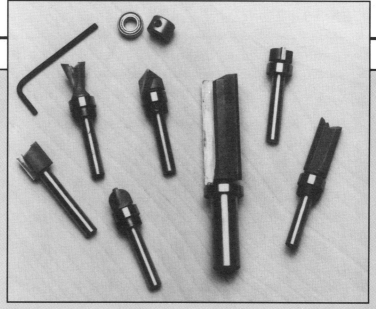

Any bit with a pilot bearing mounted on the shank is a pattern bit. The bearing rides along the edge of a pattern, while the cutting edge trims the edge of the work or plows a groove in it.

Pattern bits are available in an ever-increasing variety. And it isn't surprising. All the bit maker has to do is add a bearing to the shank. The only limitation is that the cutter diameter has to be enough larger than the shank diameter to accommodate a bearing. A ¾-inch straight bit with a ½-inch shank can be converted to a pattern bit with a bearing. A ½-inch straight on the same size shank cannot.

If you flip through a current catalog, you'll find all manner of groove-forming profile cutters with shank-mounted bearings.

Pattern bits are available in surprising variety. The bit on the far left demonstrates why. This ½-inch straight bit from MLCS has a distinct shoulder between the shank and the cutter body. Slide the ½-inch-O.D., ¼-inch-I.D. bearing at the top onto the shank, right up to that shoulder. Add the lock collar and set it with the allen wrench. You've now got a pattern bit, and a pretty useful one at that. The ½-inch cutting length is excellent. Other bits with the same sort of shoulder between shank and cutter are made into pattern bits just as easily. Others shown include (left to right) Amana's ½-inch dovetail, core-box, and V-groove bits, Byrom's 2-inch-long, ¾-inch straight, Eagle America's ¼-inch long, ½-inch dado-cleanout bit, and Amana's 1-inch-long, ½-inch straight.

but you attach the template to the top of the workpiece. In either case, you should cut the workpiece to within 1/16 inch of the final size before routing. Also, be aware of what is under the workpiece as you rout. Don't cut into your workbench by mistake.

Which System to Use?

Each system has its advantages and disadvantages. The more work you do, the more likely it is that you'll have occasion to use them all.

The base-guided approach is useful when great accuracy and detail aren't needed. You can knock out a template fairly quickly, since you don't have to worry too much about the quality of the guide edge.

Both guide bushings and pattern bits offer the ability to guide far more intricate cuts. Only the diameter of the bushing or the bearing limits the curves you can follow.

In addition, both guide bushings and pattern bits can be used with table-mounted routers. This is often an advantage with small workpieces. The template can be fitted with fences to position the blank and with a toggle clamp to secure it. Use a starting pin to help you initiate the cut. Then rout as if making a cut on a piloted bit (which is really what you are doing).

Guide bushings offer several advantages over the piloted pattern bits. Because they work in conjunction with your regular router bits, you save money: no special bits to buy. Moreover, regular bits are available in much wider variety than pattern-guided bits. Most any groove-

forming profile bit can be used in a guide bushing, so a pattern of grooves can decorate blank panels and emphasize or outline edges. Moreover, the guide-bushing system allows you to make passes around the same template with several different bits. For example, you could run a groove around a template with a ½-inch straight bit, then switch to a ¼-inch

TRY THIS!

Guide bushings can be used very productively with a table-mounted router, but you've got to make a mounting plate to accommodate them. Details on locating the centerpoint for the bit opening and for drilling and counterboring the opening are found in "Try This!" on page 50.

Because a router creates such a smooth, clean cut, it's ideal for cutting out templates. Curved segments of the overall piece can be guided by a trammel. Use a fence, as here, for routing straight runs.

straight, and cut slightly deeper, right in the center of the ½-inch groove, forming a stepped groove. Using a template enables you to position the grooves right where you want them. (See the chapter "Decorative Treatments" for a brief catalog of the groove-forming profile bits that are available.)

Depth of cut is pretty easy to deal with, too. The typical guide bushing doesn't require a template more than ¼ inch thick. You sacrifice relatively little cutting depth with the system. You can usually cheat the bit out of the collet the extra ¼ inch to ⅜ inch necessary to get the entire cutting edge engaged on the work.

Equally important, the guide is in a fixed position. Regardless of the depth-of-cut setting, the guide is next to the baseplate.

With pattern and flush-trimming bits, on the other hand, the guide changes position with every bit-height adjustment. With a flush-trimming bit, the cut has to go all the way through the workpiece on every pass, because the bearing is on the tip of the bit and the template is on the bottom of the work. With pattern bits, the guide is on top of the cutter. Unless the cutting edges are very short or the template very thick (or shimmed up somehow), you can't manage a shallow cut successfully.

MAKING TEMPLATES

The making of a template begins with a project and a design. You lay out the design on some appropriate template stock, then cut and sand it until it's just right. In other words, you make the template pretty much the way you would make the final

part if you had only one to make. Or if hardwood were cheap, and you could afford to start over on a new piece each time you goofed.

Sometimes you actually *do* make a real part in the real wood. Then that part is the pattern. But let's focus here on making a template, assuming that it will be referenced by a guide bushing. A pattern would be made the same way, except that it would be actual size, without offset.

You've got to lay out your design in full scale first. It could be as straightforward as a little rectangle for a mortise or a square inlay. Maybe it's something you draw freehand, or that you use French curves or a flexible curve to lay out. A trammel can help you draw—and even cut—arcs.

You can do this design work on paper and transfer it to the template stock. But you may also work right on the stock. Do a good job: The accuracy of the template depends on it.

There are two important considerations here in the design phase. One is the size of the guide bushing or guide bearing you'll be using. The outside dimension of the bushing's collar dictates the minimum radius of curve you can have. If you're using a ¾-inch-O.D. bushing, for example, you can't have a curve with a ¼-inch radius. The bushing just won't fit into it. With this bushing, the minimum curve radius is ⅜ inch. There are only a few situations in which it makes sense to design in sharp corners or bends so tight the guide can't get into them. A mortise is one of those few situations. If you do design in sharp turns, be prepared to do some handwork with a chisel or file.

The second important consideration is whether the template will

be an internal one (sometimes called a female template) or an external one (or male template). Your choice will impact on how inside and outside corners are translated. Check out *Choose the Right Template Style.*

• An inside corner produced by any template will be "sharp." The corner will be radiused, mind you, but the radius will be that of the cutter you're using. If you use a ⅛-inch-diameter cutter, the radius of the corner will be ¹⁄₁₆ inch, which is pretty close to sharp.

• An outside corner will translate as a bend, not a sharp change in direction. The radius of the bend will match the radius of the collar.

The real deal with the internal and external templates here is that inside corners on one template are outside corners on the other, and vice versa. If you want a corner to be just as sharp as you can get it, use the template that will make it an *inside* corner. In some instances, you may actually want to use two templates, one an internal, one an external.

After you draw the layout, you have to calculate and scribe the offset. Set a drawing compass to the offset, and use it to draw around the origi-

CHOOSE THE RIGHT TEMPLATE STYLE TO GET THE CORNERS YOU WANT

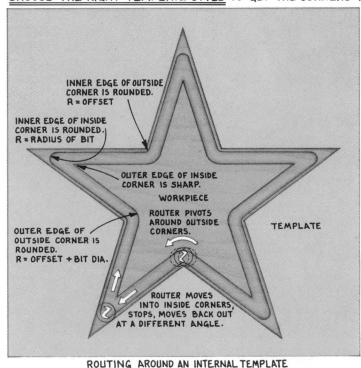

INNER EDGE OF OUTSIDE CORNER IS ROUNDED. R = OFFSET

INNER EDGE OF INSIDE CORNER IS ROUNDED. R = RADIUS OF BIT

OUTER EDGE OF INSIDE CORNER IS SHARP.

WORKPIECE

ROUTER PIVOTS AROUND OUTSIDE CORNERS.

OUTER EDGE OF OUTSIDE CORNER IS ROUNDED. R = OFFSET + BIT DIA.

TEMPLATE

ROUTER MOVES INTO INSIDE CORNERS, STOPS, MOVES BACK OUT AT A DIFFERENT ANGLE.

ROUTING AROUND AN INTERNAL TEMPLATE

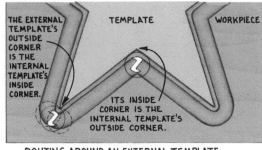

THE EXTERNAL TEMPLATE'S OUTSIDE CORNER IS THE INTERNAL TEMPLATE'S INSIDE CORNER.

TEMPLATE   WORKPIECE

ITS INSIDE CORNER IS THE INTERNAL TEMPLATE'S OUTSIDE CORNER.

ROUTING AROUND AN EXTERNAL TEMPLATE

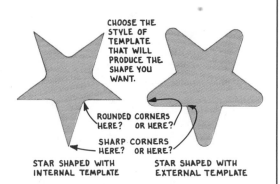

CHOOSE THE STYLE OF TEMPLATE THAT WILL PRODUCE THE SHAPE YOU WANT.

ROUNDED CORNERS HERE?   OR HERE?

SHARP CORNERS HERE?   OR HERE?

STAR SHAPED WITH INTERNAL TEMPLATE

STAR SHAPED WITH EXTERNAL TEMPLATE

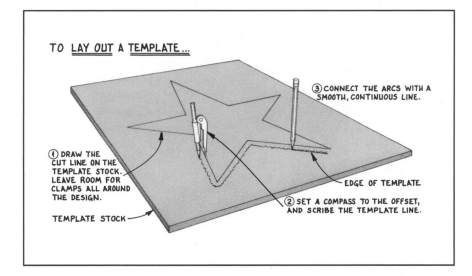

TO LAY OUT A TEMPLATE...

③ CONNECT THE ARCS WITH A SMOOTH, CONTINUOUS LINE.

① DRAW THE CUT LINE ON THE TEMPLATE STOCK. LEAVE ROOM FOR CLAMPS ALL AROUND THE DESIGN.

TEMPLATE STOCK

EDGE OF TEMPLATE

② SET A COMPASS TO THE OFFSET, AND SCRIBE THE TEMPLATE LINE.

nal line, creating a new line parallel to the original. Pivot the compass around curves as necessary to maintain parallel. If you feel you are having difficulty doing this because the line is so curvy, try scribing little arcs, then freehanding a line that hits and connects all the high points.

This new line is the one you actually cut. And if you've done the offset correctly, the router will return you to the original layout line when you cut the good stuff.

A number of different materials make good templates. Since most templates are ¼ inch thick, hardboard is a very good choice. It's relatively inexpensive, yet it gives you a good edge, has no voids, and sands well. But it is dark enough that pencil-drawn layout lines can be difficult to see. If the layout is intricate, try working on paper, then bonding the paper temporarily to the hardboard with spray adhesive (or that double-sided carpet tape stuff we're always recommending).

Quality plywood is usually okay, too. Just be careful about voids, splintered edges, and the like. If the template must be ½ inch thick, particleboard or medium density fiberboard (MDF) are good choices. Materials like acrylic and phenolic plastics make very durable templates that can be used again and again, if that's what you will be doing.

When you cut a piece of material for the template, be sure to make it big enough to support the router, and provide space for clamps that'll secure it to the workpiece without interfering with the router. Quite often, the clamping arrangements are the most challenging problem to solve.

▶ TRY THIS!

If the part to be formed or embellished is symmetrical, you may have to make a template for only *part* of the overall design.

The oval template shown was made so a design could be routed into the bottom panel of a custom door that Fred made. The template was taped to the panel, and the router was run along the various grooves. Then the template was flopped and retaped, and the grooves were routed anew. These new cuts intersected those routed on the first go-around, completing the symmetrical design.

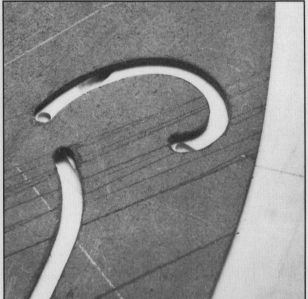

Routing an enclosed pattern with tight turns may seem impossible. But look at this design Fred produced (top). The secret is the reversible template. Although the slots in the template look like notations jotted in shorthand, they actually represent half the overall pattern. Fred uses the template to guide a laminate trimmer, which has a small footprint and is easy to maneuver. The pencil lines on the template help him position it (left). Because aligning the template is a little ticklish, and because carpet tape wouldn't let him shift the template this way and that to get it aligned, Fred instead uses packing tape to secure the template to the work. Line it up, then tape it down. It's important to clear the chips compacted into the slot after the first pass and to make a clean-up pass. Otherwise, the routed grooves can be uneven. To complete the design, lift the template after all the slots are routed and flip it over (right). The ends of the routed slots will be exposed by the pattern. This is how the tight corners are produced. After routing all the slots with the template in the second position, minor detailing with a chisel is all that's needed to finish the design.

Now it's time to cut out the template. The router ought to be your first-choice template cutter. A router bit will make a smoother cut than any saw blade, so you shouldn't have to do so much sanding. Set up fences—or a template!—to guide the router. If there are curves with consistent radii and identifiable centerpoints, you can use a router and trammel to cut them. Just be sure you don't cut too far and screw up transitions from one arc to another. Stop short and smooth these transitions by hand. You surely will want a smooth, fair line. If the template has a tight bend or two, use a bit that's the same diameter as the outside diameter of the guide you'll be using with the template. That will ensure that in (finally) making the good cut, the guide will be able to reference the entire template line.

Of course, you won't be able to use the router in every situation. The band saw and the saber saw are invaluable in cutting freehand curves. Unless the template is huge, you can quickly cut outside contours on the band saw. An easy way to cut internal shapes is with a table-mounted saber saw. You attach the saw to a mounting plate and hang it in the router table so the blade juts up through the tabletop. (See the chapter "Router Table Accessories.") Drill a starting hole in the waste area, fit the piece over the blade, then cut. You won't have problems clamping and reclamping the template as you work. You won't have to remove and remount the blade, as you would with a scroll saw. The saw doesn't obscure what you're cutting, either.

A woodworker like Fred has a steady hand and a confident manner and makes the cut right to the line, without pause or hesitation. I generally cut shy of the lines and spend time filing and sanding to refine the template.

A spindle sander is another invaluable template-making tool. So are files of various shapes. The sanding and filing can take a lot of time, but it's usually time well spent. The finer the edge on your template, the better your final work will be.

Regardless of the tool you choose, the goal is a smooth edge, remember. No wiggles, no bumps, no creases. Many little imperfections will telegraph directly into the work you rout. And depending upon the nature of the imperfection and the size of the guide, the flaw can become pretty glaring. Any guide will transfer a *convex* bump like a ridge or a pimple right into the cut. The larger the guide, the more it will magnify that bump. Conversely, a *concave* bump like a dent or dip is least likely to show up in the final cut. The smaller the guide, though, the more likely it is that the defect will transfer into the cut.

My rule of thumb—and it's only *mine*—is that you should get rid of every pimple and ridge along the template edge. Be more sanguine about saw marks and dents, however. If the guide is fairly large, don't worry too much about them. If the guide is small, sand or file them away.

Fixturing a Template

Clamping arrangements, as I pointed out a bit ago, are often the most challenging problem to solve.

A template with only one edge dedicated to guiding a cut is pretty easy to set. A couple of clamps may be all that's needed.

A template for a full perimeter cut—decorative grooves, for example—can usually be held to the work with double-sided carpet tape. To ensure a good bond, tap the template with a wood block and hammer right where the tape is, or apply clamps to it for a few seconds. You'll be surprised, probably, at how difficult it is to remove when the routing is done. Pry with a stiff putty knife or a scraper. It'll come off. (But be very careful if the template is going to be a keeper. Don't break it in prying it off the workpiece.)

But when you are making multiples, you want to expedite the posi-

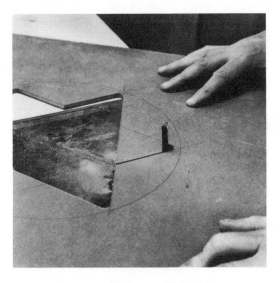

A table-mounted saber saw makes quick work of cutting out an internal template. Drill a starting hole in the waste area of the template. Fit it over the blade, and cut. The saw won't obscure what you're cutting, and you won't have to clamp and reclamp as you work.

This template is a one-piecer that is carpet-taped to a band-sawed leg. The way the template is laid out, it is used to trim the leg to shape with a flush-trimming bit, as shown. Then it'll be used in excavating mortises for a seat rail and two backrest rails. You can see the "windows" that'll be used for these joinery cuts.

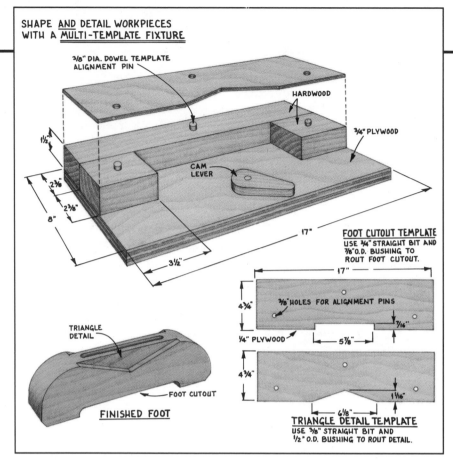

SHAPE **AND** DETAIL WORKPIECES WITH A **MULTI-TEMPLATE FIXTURE**

3/8" DIA. DOWEL TEMPLATE ALIGNMENT PIN

HARDWOOD

3/4" PLYWOOD

CAM LEVER

1½"

2⅜"

2⅜"

8"

3½"

17"

FOOT CUTOUT TEMPLATE
USE ¾" STRAIGHT BIT AND ⅞" O.D. BUSHING TO ROUT FOOT CUTOUT.

TRIANGLE DETAIL

FOOT CUTOUT

FINISHED FOOT

17"

4¾"

⅜" HOLES FOR ALIGNMENT PINS

7/16"

¼" PLYWOOD

5⅞"

4¾"

1 1/16"

6⅛"

TRIANGLE DETAIL TEMPLATE
USE ⅜" STRAIGHT BIT AND ½" O.D. BUSHING TO ROUT DETAIL.

tioning and clamping of the template as much as possible. The solutions generally involve some sort of fixture into which you place the workpiece. Either the template is an integral part of the fixture or is hinged to the fixture, or it can be quickly and accurately placed and clamped to the fixture.

Here are a few examples of such fixtures. You will be able to apply the same concepts to your own projects, I'm sure.

Ken's foot fixture. In making feet for a quilt rack, one of my woodworking editorial colleagues, Ken Burton, Jr., made a fixture to hold the foot blank and templates for routing decorative details into the blank. Each of two details had to be routed into both sides of each foot, so fast changeover was important.

The fixture is shown in the drawing. Ken made it of ¾-inch plywood and built it around one of the foot blanks to ensure that those he had roughed out would fit in it. The templates were made of ¼-inch plywood.

When both fixture and templates were done, he lined up the

two templates, one on top of the other, positioned them carefully on the fixture, and clamped them. Then he drilled through the templates and into the jig for the locating dowels. The dowels were glued into place.

To use the fixture, he dogged it to the workbench. He set a foot blank in the fixture and locked it there with the cam lever. After placing the first template over the locating pins, he routed the detail. Then he flipped the foot over and routed the same detail in the other side. Doing the

second detail required him to turn the foot blank upside down in the fixture and then use the second template.

Shelf bracket template fixture. Here's a fixture you use as a jig. It's for holding shelf bracket blanks so you can profile the exposed edges on the router table. The bracket is contoured in a symmetrical pattern, and we want to rout two full beads along the edge with a small-sized molding bit. A guide bushing will control the cut.

This fixture secures both the workpiece and the template used in embellishing the work. The holes in the template fit over dowels in the fixture to align and hold it. Ken Burton, who made this particular fixture, jotted notes on the templates, as you can see, so he'd be reminded of the bushing and bit to use with it, how to orient it, and so forth.

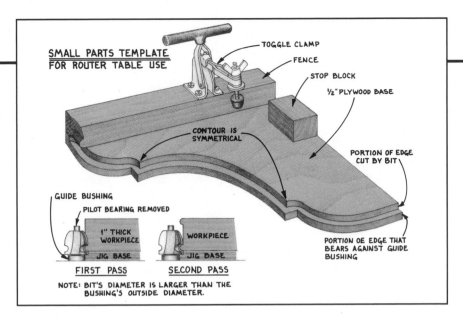

SMALL PARTS TEMPLATE
FOR ROUTER TABLE USE

TOGGLE CLAMP

FENCE

STOP BLOCK

½" PLYWOOD BASE

CONTOUR IS
SYMMETRICAL

PORTION OF EDGE
CUT BY BIT

GUIDE BUSHING

PILOT BEARING REMOVED

1" THICK
WORKPIECE

WORKPIECE

JIG BASE

JIG BASE

FIRST PASS

SECOND PASS

PORTION OE EDGE THAT
BEARS AGAINST GUIDE
BUSHING

NOTE: BIT'S DIAMETER IS LARGER THAN THE
BUSHING'S OUTSIDE DIAMETER.

The construction of the fixture is shown in *Small Parts Template*. The base of it is the template. The fence has a toggle clamp on it, which serves as both a clamp and a handle. It's quick-acting, so you can pop it open, turn the workpiece over or switch workpieces, and snap it closed in a jiffy. To position the workpiece end-to-end is a stop block, which won't trap rout-dust and throw off the position of the workpiece.

The workpieces are cut close to the final line on the band saw. The cut line has to account for bead projection, of course, but you won't get a consistently good edge if you try to hog off too much with the router bit. You should be making one pass to produce the first bead, then turning the piece over and making a second pass to rout the second bead.

This style of fixture can be used for all sorts of workpieces. Any part that has an edge that is not routed and that can be maneuvered on the router table is a candidate for this sort of fixturing.

Two-leg template fixture. Chair legs, especially the back legs, lend themselves to template-guided contouring. If you are making a dining set, you will make anywhere from four to eight chairs. You doubtless will want them to be identical, yet that's a hard order to fulfill if you rough their shape on the band saw and then sand to the final contour. Not only will they all be slightly different, but you'll spend a lot of time at the sander, blinking and choking on all the dust.

But with a template to guide your router, you can mill off that last ¹⁄₁₆ to ⅛ inch of stock in minutes, and you'll end up with identical legs.

One problem is fixturing the legs. If you use brads or small nails to attach the template, you'll not only mar the legs but also spend a lot of time pulling nails. Double-sided carpet tape won't mar the legs, but it'll be just as difficult to pry the template off the leg.

This jig solves these problems.

This jig is used on the router table in conjunction with the (relatively) small molding bit shown and a guide bushing to produce a double bead along the edges of shelf brackets. Because the bracket shape is symmetrical, it's possible to snap it in the jig, rout the edge, then free the bracket and flip it over to rout the edge a second time, producing a second bead.

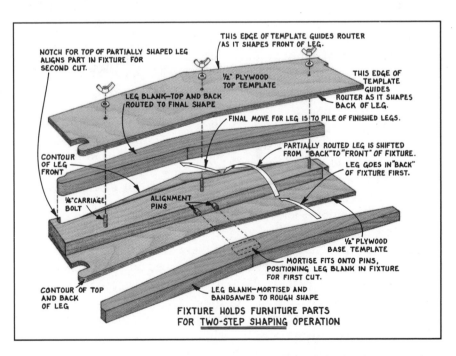

NOTCH FOR TOP OF PARTIALLY SHAPED LEG
ALIGNS PART IN FIXTURE FOR
SECOND CUT.

THIS EDGE OF TEMPLATE GUIDES ROUTER
AS IT SHAPES FRONT OF LEG.

½" PLYWOOD
TOP TEMPLATE

THIS EDGE OF
TEMPLATE
GUIDES
ROUTER AS IT SHAPES
BACK OF LEG.

LEG BLANK–TOP AND BACK
ROUTED TO FINAL SHAPE

FINAL MOVE FOR LEG IS TO PILE OF FINISHED LEGS.

CONTOUR
OF LEG
FRONT

PARTIALLY ROUTED LEG IS SHIFTED
FROM "BACK" TO "FRONT" OF FIXTURE.

LEG GOES IN "BACK"
OF FIXTURE FIRST.

¼" CARRIAGE
BOLT

ALIGNMENT
PINS

½" PLYWOOD
BASE TEMPLATE

MORTISE FITS ONTO PINS,
POSITIONING LEG BLANK IN FIXTURE
FOR FIRST CUT.

CONTOUR OF TOP
AND BACK
OF LEG

LEG BLANK–MORTISED AND
BANDSAWED TO ROUGH SHAPE

FIXTURE HOLDS FURNITURE PARTS
FOR <u>TWO-STEP SHAPING</u> OPERATION

Finding a way to position workpieces in a fixture accurately and consistently is often a challenge. Fred designed this fixture to use the apron mortise to position a chair leg so its back edge and ends can be routed. Two dowels project into the mortise and hold the leg. A second leg, which has already been partially machined, is positioned in the other half of the fixture. This leg's machined ends fit into shaped blocks, aligning it. Then the template is dropped onto the fixture and tightened down with wing nuts. After both legs have been routed, the template is removed and the workpieces shifted.

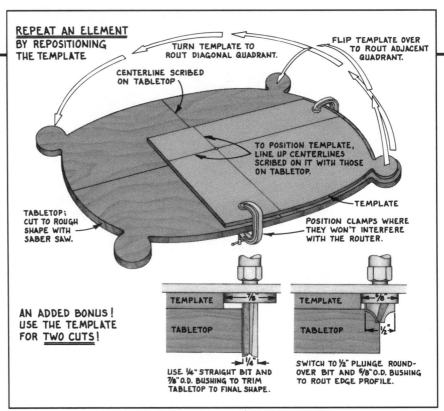

REPEAT AN ELEMENT BY REPOSITIONING THE TEMPLATE

TURN TEMPLATE TO ROUT DIAGONAL QUADRANT.

FLIP TEMPLATE OVER TO ROUT ADJACENT QUADRANT.

CENTERLINE SCRIBED ON TABLETOP

TO POSITION TEMPLATE, LINE UP CENTERLINES SCRIBED ON IT WITH THOSE ON TABLETOP.

TABLETOP; CUT TO ROUGH SHAPE WITH SABER SAW.

TEMPLATE

POSITION CLAMPS WHERE THEY WON'T INTERFERE WITH THE ROUTER.

AN ADDED BONUS! USE THE TEMPLATE FOR TWO CUTS!

TEMPLATE ⅞"
TABLETOP
USE ¼" STRAIGHT BIT AND ⅞" O.D. BUSHING TO TRIM TABLETOP TO FINAL SHAPE. ¼"

TEMPLATE ⅝"
TABLETOP ½"
SWITCH TO ½" PLUNGE ROUND-OVER BIT AND ⅝" O.D. BUSHING TO ROUT EDGE PROFILE.

It holds two legs. You rout the front edge of one leg and the back leg of the other. Then you open it up, and switch the work around.

Though you may never make chairs, the concept of this fixture may give you an idea that'll solve your particular template problem.

Tabletop template. A porringer table is a traditional form that incorporates almost outlandish circle contours at the four corners of its top. It provides an excellent example of how you can repeat an element by repositioning a template.

Instead of trying—and probably failing—to make a template with

Using the tabletop template is straightforward. The top obviously should be cut to rough shape using a saber saw or on the band saw. Use the alignment lines to position the template and clamp it outside the area of the quadrant being machined. The two different cuts can be made especially quickly if you have two routers. Set one up with the straight bit, and trim the tabletop to its final shape (left). Then, without moving the template, switch to the second router, set up with the round-over bit, and rout the decorative edge (right).

four corners exactly alike, you can make a template for one corner. Lines scribed on the template make it easy to set it accurately on the rough-sawn tabletop. Guide the router around the template, machining the tabletop to its final

contour and edging it at the same time.

Again, you may never make a porringer table. But you just may someday find a use for a template that helps you repeat a pattern several times to create a single item.

ROUTING ALONG A TEMPLATE

Position the pattern on your stock. If you are making the same inside cut in several pieces, you can attach fences to the underside of the pattern to help position it on the workpiece.

Clamp the pattern in position. Set the depth of cut, allowing for the thickness of the pattern.

If you are routing around the edge of the pattern and workpiece, just turn on the router and begin routing counterclockwise.

If you are routing inside the pattern and workpiece, such as for a mortise, you'll need to plunge the bit. With a plunge router, this is easy. Just position the router on the work and hold the guide bushing against the pattern. When you are ready, plunge the bit into the stock and guide the router clockwise around the pattern.

To rout an inside cut with a fixed-base router, you'll have to tip the tool into the cut with the motor running. If the area you're going to rout is large enough, drill a hole whose diameter is larger than the router bit diameter. Start the cut by easing the bit into the hole. Make shallow passes until you have routed to the final depth.

INLAY BASICS

Inlay is the process of cutting a shallow recess in a wood surface, then insetting a perfectly matched patch. The intent is usually decorative. You can set a square or circle of a different wood into a surface. Or instead of outlining an element with a profiled groove, you can inlay a strip of contrasting-colored wood. But you

▶ **TRY THIS!**

One of the hazards of shaping curved edges—the stuff of template-guided work—is chip-out. This occurs most frequently when moving across end grain, but it can happen anywhere.

One of the most common causes of this problem is making a cut that's wider than the radius of the cutter. The cutting edge pushes out on the wood as it exits the cut, and when the bit is more than half-housed in the cut, the cutting edge has leverage on the wood fibers along the edge. There's nothing behind those fibers to keep them in place, so they splinter out.

Here's a two-step way to moderate this problem.

First, reduce the width of the cut. Ideally, you shouldn't be removing more than 1/16 inch of material from around an edge.

Second, use the largest-diameter cutter you can. This reduces the angle between the cut edge and the exit point, thus reducing the cutting edge's leverage.

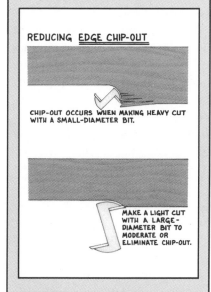

REDUCING EDGE CHIP-OUT

CHIP-OUT OCCURS WHEN MAKING HEAVY CUT WITH A SMALL-DIAMETER BIT.

MAKE A LIGHT CUT WITH A LARGE-DIAMETER BIT TO MODERATE OR ELIMINATE CHIP-OUT.

▶ Feed Direction

When doing any template-guided work, you want the bit to pull the router toward the template. When you are routing around the outside edge of the workpiece, this means you must move the router counterclockwise. If you are routing within a workpiece, such as when making a mortise, you must rout clockwise.

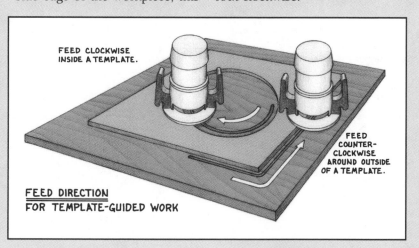

FEED CLOCKWISE INSIDE A TEMPLATE.

FEED COUNTER-CLOCKWISE AROUND OUTSIDE OF A TEMPLATE.

FEED DIRECTION FOR TEMPLATE-GUIDED WORK

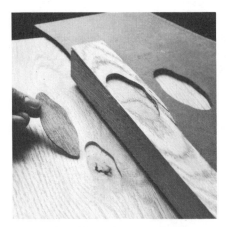

A knot that blemishes an otherwise excellent board can be excised and replaced with a carefully matched patch using inlay techniques. Guided by a template, rout an irregular recess that removes the defect. Using the same template, rout an insert with grain that matches the board as closely as possible. Can you see the already-completed patch here?

can also remove defects like knots by inlaying a patch of the same wood.

When the desire to inlay burns within you, take up your router first. The router is especially useful when the project involves multiples of the same shape. It's a template-guided operation.

With a template in the shape of your inlay and the right combination of bits and bushings (or bits and bearings), it's possible to rout both the insert and the recess for it. You cut both with the same template. Once the template is made, you can cut the same shape again and again. Best of all, the inlay is always a perfect fit. This template technique has all sorts of applications, both practical and decorative. The primary restriction is that without some handwork, the inlay can't have a radius in it smaller than that of the router bit.

The concepts used to inlay shapes

may be a little tricky to visualize at first. If Frank Rohrbach's drawings don't help, get out your router, a bit or two, and a set of guide bushings, and use them as visual aids. This technique is worth understanding.

You can use any router, plunge or fixed-base. But if you have a choice, a small router is most manageable. In most cases, inlays are fairly small, and it seems silly to cut them with a 3-horsepower plunge router. Of course, a plunge router does make it easy to begin the recessed cut, but it isn't really difficult to do with a fixed-base router. Most laminate trimmers will take guide bushings, and you may consider using one of these, if you have one.

Not all inlay work involves an enclosed shape. In some situations, you rout a shallow groove and glue a strip of material in it. You don't really need a template for this, but you can use a template rather than a fence to guide the cut. String inlay is a variation on this. Instead of a straight

groove, you rout a narrow, winding groove, then carefully bend the insert strip to the contour of the groove, insert it, and trim it flush. This is a cut to guide with a template, as we'll see presented. Let's inlay a shape first.

Offset

The critical concept in this process is *offset*. And you have to go a little further with it than is necessary for simple template-guided work. There the offset is the difference between the line of the cut and the line of the template. To calculate that offset, you just subtract the bit diameter from the bushing's outside diameter and divide the difference by 2.

Here, you work with the same offset dimension for both the recess and the insert, but you come by the measurement two different ways, depending upon whether you are calculating the offset for the recess or for the insert.

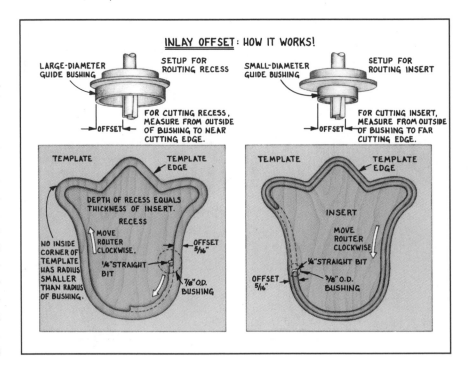

- *For the recess,* the offset is measured from the outside edge of the bushing to the *nearest* cutting edge.
- *For the insert,* the offset is measured from the outside edge of the bushing to the *farthest* cutting edge.

Bit Diameter	Bushing for Recess	Bushing for Insert	Offset
1/8"	9/16"	5/16"	5/32"
1/8"	11/16"	3/16"	9/32"
3/16"	11/16"	5/16"	1/4"
3/16"	3/4"	3/8"	9/32"
1/4"	13/16"	5/16"	9/32"
1/4"	7/8"	3/8"	5/16"

BIT DRAWER

If you want to try a small inlay project without getting caught up in the math, buy an inlay kit. The kit from CMT, which is pretty much like those from other sources, includes a 1/8-inch spiral cutter and a special brass guide bushing with a removable collar. The bushing is two sizes in one, prefigured to give the correct offset for the bit. (See "Sources" on page 337 for information on CMT.)

You use it just the way you would use two complete bushings of different sizes. To rout the recess, you use the bushing with the removable collar pressed onto the one that's integral to the bushing. Then to cut the insert, you pull off the extra collar. One bit setting takes care of both cuts. The hardest part is making the template (of course)!

The guide bushing is in the Porter-Cable style and will fit any router that accepts the Porter-Cable guides.

The offset measurements must be equal. If they are equal, and you have measured each correctly, then the insert will fit perfectly in the recess. To make it a little easier for you, here's a chart (*above*) that lists five combinations of bushings and bits that you can use for this work. As long as you use the bit size listed with the two bushing sizes listed, you won't have to do any math. These combos will work!

The offset dimension itself isn't important. What is important is that the recess offset be equal to the insert offset. It's also important that the cutter be of true dimension. A lot of bits are jjuuussst slightly undersized, and that *can* create a misfit in inlay work. The insert offset will be less than the recess offset, so the insert will be a hair too big.

Cutting the Inlay

After creating your design and determining the offset you'll use, make the template. You use the same materials and techniques for this template as you do for any other. You only make one, and you use it to cut both the recess and the insert.

Rout the recess first. Clamp, tack, or tape the template to the working stock. Remember that the actual recess will be smaller than the template, so position the template accordingly.

Set the depth-of-cut using a scrap of the template stock and the insert stock. Hold the two of them together on the router baseplate, right next to the bit. This will visually confirm that the guide bushing collar is shorter than the template is thick. Then set the router on the workbench with the two pieces under it. Lower the bit until it just touches the bench top. The just-right setting is a trifle less than the insert thickness. Assuming you are going to scrape or sand the inlaid surface before applying a finish, you need to have the insert just a bit proud of the surrounding surface. So back the bit up off the bench top by the thickness of a couple of sheets of paper.

There are two stages to routing the recess. The bit choices we've proposed are what you need to outline the shape. But if you want to excavate a 2-inch-square recess, a 3/16-inch bit will make it a daylong venture. So use a large-diameter bit, set to the just-right depth of cut, to clean out the bulk of the recess. You can probably handle this freehand, meaning you don't need to use a guide bushing. If you do this work first, you have to be very careful not to cut too close to the template. Remember that there's offset between the edge of the recess and the template. It doesn't hurt to cut the outline first, then remove the rest of the waste.

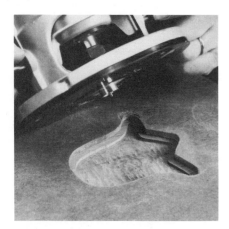

Routing the recess couldn't be more straightforward. The template is clamped to the work, the router set up with bushing and bit. Set the depth of cut, then rout out the recess.

When you cut the outside, keep the bushing firmly against the template. You don't want any little pimples along the edge. Vacuum or blow all the chips out of the recess, and run the router around the edge a couple of times. Feed clockwise, remember.

Rout the insert. This is the dicey job. First, you're cutting around an internal template, but the piece you want is the internal part. This means that the slightest drift from the template will ruin the part you want. Also, you don't want to actually cut the insert free. If you do, it will likely shift as it comes free and be gouged by the bit.

To get started on this phase of the operation, change to the smaller-diameter guide bushing. If you can do this without changing the bit setting, that's good. You want to use the same depth setting *if you routed the recess a little less than the insert thickness.* This means that when you rout out the insert, you won't actually cut completely through the stock. The insert won't shift, and it won't

get dinged. (It also means you won't rout into whatever the stock is clamped to—like your workbench.) The virtually paper-thin layer of wood holding the insert to the stock will be easy to cut through with a knife.

You do have to retract the bit to change the bushing? Don't sweat it. Just reset it. And keep it just shy of the depth necessary to cut through the insert stock.

Remove the template from the stock with the recess, and transfer it to the insert stock. Clamp everything securely. If you want, as an alternative to not completely freeing the insert with the router cut, you can bond the insert to a piece of expendable material with double-sided carpet tape. Make sure the insert area is bonded securely. Now when you cut completely through the insert stock, the insert will stay put. And the scrap will be routed instead of your bench top.

The insert can be cut from any piece of stock; it doesn't have to be thin. Rout what will be the insert in any stock of the right grain and color and size, cutting about ¼ inch deep. At the band saw, stand the stock on edge and cut a slice about ⅛ inch thick. As it clears the blade, the insert will fall into your hand.

TRY THIS!

Inlay work doesn't *have* to be done using the internal (or female) template. You can make an external (or male) template for the job. All you have to do is reverse the bushings used for the two cuts.

To cut the recess, apply the template to the stock with double-sided carpet tape. Install the *smaller* of the two guide bushings on the router, and make the perimeter cut. Keep the bushing tight against the template as you work. Pry off the template, and rout out the rest of the waste.

Then stick the template to the insert stock. Switch to the *larger* of the two bushings, and rout around the template. The resulting insert should fit the recess perfectly.

A male template, also known as an external template, is less common in inlay than in other sorts of template work, probably because it is a bit more involved. For example, to form the recess, you bond the template to the workpiece, then guide the router around it. That pass forms the perimeter. To complete the recess, you remove the template. You also remove the guide bushing from the router and reset the depth of cut.

As you make the cut, keep the guide bushing firmly against the template. You can't afford to let your attention flag for an instant, for the moment it does, the router is sure to drift into the insert and ruin it. Be especially careful on curves and at corners. These are the most likely spots for the router to drift. Feed the router around the template in a clockwise direction. This is working against the bit rotation, so it will help force the guide bushing against the template edge.

When you are done, the insert should drop right into the recess. If it is loose, your bit is probably slightly oversized. If it is too big to fit the recess, the bit is probably undersized. Assuming the insert fits correctly, glue it in place, and sand it. Perfect!

String Inlay

For centuries, craftsmen have decorated panels, tabletops, drawer fronts, and the like by carefully carving delicate grooves and patterns and filling them with inlays of contrasting wood. These inlaid lines, especially curved lines, are traditionally called "string inlay" or "stringing." You can do the same thing easily by cutting the grooves and shapes with a router guided by a template.

Design your inlay from the start so that you can cut the grooves with a router and so that the inlay wood doesn't have to be bent too much during installation. Narrow inlays have a delicate appearance and look difficult to do. But since the narrowest router bit you'll find is a 1/16-inch single-flute bit in high-speed steel (Bosch #85091, for example), Fred suggests that you design your inlay for 1/16-inch-wide lines.

A template guides the router for

The basic range of inlay work is displayed in this tulip. The stem represents string inlay; the blossom and leaves, regular template-guided inlay.

smooth, flowing curves and truly straight lines. Since it takes time to make the template, try to include repeated or mirror-image curves in your design. That way, you can use the template several times, or at least flip it over to produce a mirror image.

Bear in mind that you have to fit wood into the grooves that you rout. You can miter the inlay pieces at sharp corners and bend the wood into reasonable curves, but it's difficult to bend most 1/16-inch-thick strips any tighter than a 1/2-inch radius. Avoid the frustration of broken inlay pieces by designing the curves no tighter than you can bend the inlay wood.

Try the whole process on some scrap wood, so you develop a good feel for what the wood can do.

Templates. As you know, when it's being guided by a template, the bit cuts a groove that's offset from the template. The distance from the centerline of the groove to the edge of the template will always be half the diameter of the template guide. You'll simplify making the template if you design your inlay by drawing a line for the centerline of the groove instead of drawing two lines for the two edges of the groove.

To make the template, first trace the inlay design onto the template stock. Set a compass to half the guide bushing diameter, and strike a series of arcs on the template side of the line (not the waste side). Draw a smooth curve connecting the high points of the arcs, and saw out the template. Sand the edge to assure smooth, even curves.

To try out the template, clamp it in place on a scrap piece of wood, adjust the router to cut about 1/8 inch deep in the scrap, and cut the groove. Keep the template guide tight against the template as you cut. Clean out the grooves, and sand lightly to get rid of any whiskers raised by the cutter. Now check that the groove matches the pattern.

Cutting and fitting inlay strips. The next step is to cut inlay strips for the grooves. Choose an inlay wood with tight, straight grain, and cut several 1/16-inch by 3/16-inch strips several inches longer than the groove. If your saw leaves deep saw marks, cut the strips a bit thicker than 1/16 inch

The tulip stem requires only a modest undulation, and the template can be cut quickly on the band saw. Only a single pass is necessary to rout the string inlay groove, which is typically routed with a 1/8-inch bit.

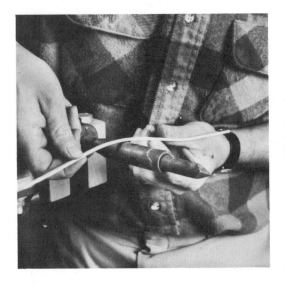

To bend the inlay strips, rest a thin strip of wood across the shaft (NOT the tip) of a hot soldering iron and press lightly to bend it. When the wood is hot enough, it will bend easily. If not hot enough, the wood will crack, and if too hot, it will scorch. You may waste a few strips before you get the hang of it.

so you can sand out the saw marks and still produce a good fit in the grooves.

If you've designed an inlay with very easy curves, you may be able to fit the strips in the grooves without prebending, but with most designs, you must prebend the strips to the shape of the design. The easiest way to bend the strips is with heat. You can bend them over the round body of an electric soldering iron. Lay a strip of wood across the hot iron and press lightly to bend the strip around it. Start at one end of the design, bending the strip to match,

and work your way from curve to curve, checking the bent strip against the design as you go. Try to be accurate with the bends. You'll be able to spring the strip a little, but the closer it is to the proper shape, the easier it will be to install. Leave the strip a bit longer than the groove.

When the strip matches the groove fairly closely, place a small amount of glue in the groove and press the strip in, starting at one end, as shown. Trim the strip to length before pressing the last end into place, then set a block of wood over the strip and tap it with a ham-

mer to seat the strip firmly into the groove.

Let the glue dry, and then sand the strip down flush with the surrounding surface. Be careful not to split the strip while you are sanding it down. A split could easily run down below the surface and show in the finished job.

And that's it—you've inlaid delicate curved lines.

JOINERY CUTS

If you think template work is strictly decorative stuff, you are misinformed. Remember that commercial dovetail jigs are all template-based units. Check out the chapter "Dovetail Joints." You'll see that the jigs require you to use either a template guide or a pattern bit.

But cutting dovetails isn't the only template-guided joinery work you can do. You can use templates to guide mortising cuts. A template stuck to a table or chair leg so you can finalize the contours with a router may also have a "window" in it to guide a mortise cut. See the chapter "Mortise-and-Tenon Joints" for more details for using templates to make these joints.

And page through the chapter "Lap Joints." A dandy variation is the mitered half-lap. Cut this one with a set of templates. Also, a dovetail half-lap is a template-guided joinery cut.

Multiple Blind Spline Joint

A template is essential to making this joint, which is a strongly reinforced miter joint.

Though it is unobtrusively attractive, the miter is weak. That's

Apply a scant bead of glue to the groove, then set the bent strip into place. Start at one end, as shown, and work toward the other, flexing the strip as necessary to fit it. Be gentle, of course. As you seat the strip, be especially careful not to break off its protruding top ridge; you want to sand this flush and not have any splits descending into the inlay.

because it's end grain to end grain. The splines used in this particular joint are small, but there are enough of them to dramatically increase the long-grain-to-long-grain gluing surface. Equally important, the splines are completely invisible. The joint looks like a miter.

Each spline is like a loose tenon. You cut a recess in both mating surfaces, and link the mating pieces together with the spline that fits into one recess and extends into the other. If the joint is to line up perfectly, the sockets for the splines have to line up. That's where the template comes in. By cutting the sockets in both pieces using the same template, you can virtually guarantee the sockets will align.

In theory, the closer together you place the splines, the more of them there will be, and thus the stronger the joint will be. But the more splines there are, the more work there will be in cutting and assembling the joint. Here's a practical compromise.

1. Make the template. Cut a 20-inch by 12-inch template from ½-inch plywood. The template has a series of slots along one edge, as shown in *Multiple Blind Spline Joint*. The size of the slots is determined by the guide bushing's outside diameter. The bushing must fit into the slot without any play. Cut the slots using a box-joint jig. (See the chapter "Box Joint" for details on making and using this jig.)

Cut a series of 1-inch-deep dadoes along one long edge of the template. The exact spacing is not critical, but making the space between the slots about twice the size of the slots achieves that practical compromise between strength and labor.

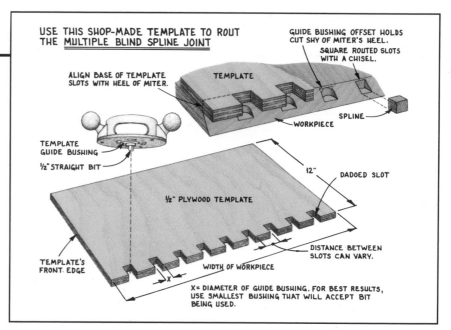

USE THIS SHOP-MADE TEMPLATE TO ROUT THE **MULTIPLE BLIND SPLINE JOINT**

GUIDE BUSHING OFFSET HOLDS CUT SHY OF MITER'S HEEL.
SQUARE ROUTED SLOTS WITH A CHISEL.
TEMPLATE
ALIGN BASE OF TEMPLATE SLOTS WITH HEEL OF MITER.
SPLINE
WORKPIECE
TEMPLATE GUIDE BUSHING
½" STRAIGHT BIT
12"
DADOED SLOT
½" PLYWOOD TEMPLATE
DISTANCE BETWEEN SLOTS CAN VARY.
TEMPLATE'S FRONT EDGE
WIDTH OF WORKPIECE
X
X= DIAMETER OF GUIDE BUSHING. FOR BEST RESULTS, USE SMALLEST BUSHING THAT WILL ACCEPT BIT BEING USED.

Routing the multiple blind spline joint is just like routing dovetails. Clamp the template to the stock, as shown, and rout the spline slots, directing the router into and out of each slot in the template.

2. Rout the spline joint. Mark one short edge of the template "Front." Always place the template with its front edge flush with the front edge of the piece to be routed. This automatically aligns the spline slots. Clamp the template to the mitered edge of the stock as shown in the photo above. The fingers extend over the miter; the base of the slots lines up with the heel of the miter.

Rout the multiple spline slots ½ inch deep. With a ½-inch chisel, square the rounded edge of the slot flush.

3. Cut splines to match the slots. Plane several lengths of wood to fit into the spline slots. Rip the required number of splines to width, and crosscut them to length.

4. Assemble the joints. Glue the splines into the spline slots in one mitered edge, then glue and clamp the mitered corner together.

Without a router, the only way to make this joint would be by hand. You'd have to lay out the sockets,

Assembling the joint is a bit laborious, since there are lots of splines, and each is a separate, tiny cube of wood. You'll have the least trouble if you glue them into the slots in one workpiece, then apply glue to the second, mate the pieces, and clamp.

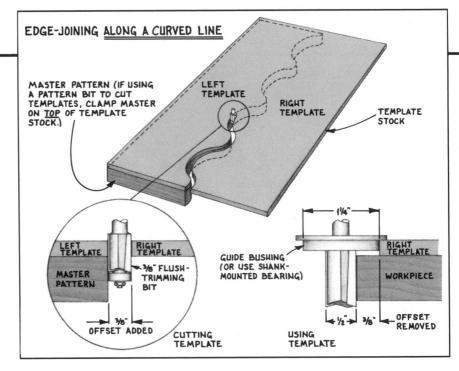

EDGE-JOINING <u>ALONG A CURVED LINE</u>

MASTER PATTERN (IF USING A PATTERN BIT TO CUT TEMPLATES, CLAMP MASTER ON <u>TOP</u> OF TEMPLATE STOCK.)

LEFT TEMPLATE

RIGHT TEMPLATE.

TEMPLATE STOCK

LEFT TEMPLATE

RIGHT TEMPLATE

MASTER PATTERN

⅜" FLUSH-TRIMMING BIT

⅜" OFFSET ADDED

CUTTING TEMPLATE

1¼"

GUIDE BUSHING (OR USE SHANK-MOUNTED BEARING)

RIGHT TEMPLATE

WORKPIECE

½" ⅜"

OFFSET REMOVED

USING TEMPLATE

then chisel them out one by one. Only your layout skill could ensure they line up from one workpiece to the next. And without a template, there's no way you could align a router-cut joint. The template guidance system makes it work.

Edge-Joining along Curved Lines

Want to join two workpieces perfectly along an irregular contour? An undulating curve, for example. Not easy, is it?

The difficulty arises from the fact that when you cut a board in two, you are removing material. This isn't a problem if it's a straight cut—ripping a board in two, for example. The two pieces should go back together perfectly.

But if the cut is curved, the two parts won't go back together perfectly. The curve's exact contour on one part will be different from the contour on the other because of the material that was removed. Think about it now. If you use a router and trammel to cut a circle, the disk removed is smaller in diameter than the hole it came from. The difference will be twice the diameter of the bit you used.

And even if you cut only a part of the circle, only an arc, the contours of the two workpieces will be different, because the radius of the convex arc will be different—by the bit diameter—from the radius of the concave arc.

The difference between the two lines is called the offset. (It's the same deal as the difference between the outside diameter of a guide bushing and the diameter of the bit.) To achieve a perfect fit, you have to eliminate the offset.

Woodworkers who do inlay work confront and overcome this problem in every project. (See "Inlay Basics" on page 151.) They do it by using combinations of template guide bushings. They introduce offset in one cut, then remove it in the complementary cut. So this process of routing boards for edge-joining is simply an extension of inlay techniques. You control the offset you introduce so that you can, in effect, back it out at the right stage of the operation. A major difference is that inlay work usually involves a single template that's used for both the recess and the insert. Here, two separate templates are used, though both are generated from the same master pattern.

Here, in a nutshell, is the procedure.

1. You make a master pattern, whose edge contour represents the joint line.

2. Use a pattern bit guided by the master pattern to cut two templates that you'll use when routing the workpieces. Let's call them the left

What's special about this box is obvious. Getting a good, tight joint along the curving lines is virtually impossible. But a router, guided by a template, can do it. We joined two long boards of contrasting color along an undulating line, then made them into a box.

TRY THIS!

If you really want to save time, use the left workpiece as the master pattern. This will allow you to eliminate a few routing procedures.

Cut the desired joint line on the workpiece with a saber saw or on the band saw. Sand it smooth. Use it as the pattern to rout the right template, and with that template as the guide, shape the mating workpiece. Glue up the two workpieces, and you are done.

and right templates, just to keep them straight. The left template will be a duplicate of the master pattern, and in fact, you can use the master pattern as the left template. The right template will be offset by the diameter of the pattern bit used.

3. When you rout the left workpiece, you use the left template (or the master pattern) to guide a pattern bit, making a duplicate.

4. When you rout the right workpiece, you use the right template to guide a homemade pattern bit or a bit and guide bushing. The bearing (or bushing) must be larger in diameter than the cutting diameter of the bit. The difference between the diameters must equal twice the offset.

(Before going into detail on this template-guided approach, I do want to mention that you *can* satisfactorily edge-join two boards along a gently curved line if you joint them using a fence referenced by the router baseplate. The details of this procedure are in the chapter "Edge Joints.")

Deal with the offset. The trick here is to introduce an offset that you can remove, without getting into bizarre combinations of bit and guide bushing or bit and bearing. Stick

with the system you are most comfortable with: home-brewed pattern bits or guide bushings.

Make your initial cut with the smallest-diameter bit you can. This reduces the offset. A ⅜-inch bit (on a ¼-inch shank) is the smallest-diameter pattern bit I know of. (It's available from Woodhaven; see "Sources" on page 337.) To back this offset out requires a 1-inch-diameter bearing (or bushing) with a ¼-inch bit. This is manageable.

To back out the offset if you use a ½-inch bit for the initial cut, you'll need a combination like a 1¼-inch-diameter bearing or bushing with a ¼-inch bit, or a 1½-inch-diameter bearing (or bushing, if you can find one that big) with a ½-inch cutter. Clearly, any offset in excess of ½ inch requires an unwieldy (and unlikely) combination of bearing or bushing and bit. Bear in mind that your options are not endless. You'll find the range of bushing sizes is limited, as is the range of available ball bearings.

All right now. Are you flummoxed by this business with the bearings? I know you won't find in any catalog a bit that has a bearing on its shank that's larger than the cutting diameter. You have to make

up these bits yourself. It really isn't difficult. It is, after all, what the bit manufacturers are doing to create pattern bits.

You can buy the bearings from a number of bit vendors, including Woodhaven, CMT, Amana, and Eagle America. (See "Sources.") What you want is a ball bearing with an inside diameter that matches the shank diameter, and an outside diameter that creates the offset you need. Theoretically, you shouldn't have to do anything to keep the bearing in place. It's trapped between the cutter and the collet. If it does ride up the shank, you can add a stop collar, which you can buy from a number of bit manufacturers, including Woodhaven and CMT. The loose knot here is that ¼-inch bit, which won't have a shoulder between the cutter and the shank. You need to use a couple of stop collars on this bit. Some woodworkers use a fluid called Locktite—you can buy it at an auto-parts place—to "glue" these bearings in place. With a stop collar, you can remove the bearing. I'm not sure if you can after you've locked it tight with Locktite.

If you don't want to get into "making" your own pattern bits, use those guide bushings.

The bearing must be larger than the cutting diameter. That's essential in an offset pattern bit, but so is having a shoulder between the cutter and the shank to catch the bearing. Slide the bearing onto the shank and trap it between that shoulder and a collar.

Pin Routing

The pin is a guide device used in router table woodworking. It is positioned in the same axis as the bit, either above or below it. The key is that the guide pin is located on the opposite side of the work from the router. It rubs against a template attached to the work (occasionally, the pin rubs against the work itself), controlling where the bit cuts.

Pin routing can be done with the router above or below the work. That means that you're going to need a sturdy overarm to hold either the router or the pin above the worktable. Mounting the router in an overarm is a lot more challenging than mounting the pin that way. The router itself is the focal point of all the stresses, so an overarm supporting the router has to be incredibly strong and rigid. The pin, on the other hand, is tiny and bears only modest side pressure. Its position has to be held precisely, but that's relatively easy to do. So in the typical home shop configuration, an overarm pin is a router table accessory. (And in fact, we've got a plan for one in the chapter "Router Table Accessories.")

A big advantage of pin routing is the fact that you can move the workpiece around. The template is screwed or stapled to the back of the work. This leaves the routed face untouched, which is good. You don't have to worry about balancing the router on the work, and you don't have the router obstructing your view of what you're doing. Of course, you can't see the bit, but surprising as it may seem, that's seldom a problem. You can see the pin, and it is centered precisely above the bit.

Another advantage is that there's no offset to account for. You match the diameter of the pin to the diameter of the bit. You can introduce offset, of course, and there

What's most obvious here is that you can't see what's going on. Mr. Hands has a board on the router table, and it's got a template nailed to it. But the bit is hidden from view, as is the work it is doing.

are occasions when you do that. But for the most part, you make and use a *pattern* with a pin router setup. You also have a lot more options in terms of bits you can use, since you're not working through the template and a guide bushing.

You'll need to be able to raise and lower the overarm, not only to accommodate different thicknesses of stock but also to get into an enclosed template.

To start a cut, you can either drill a starting hole or plunge the work over the bit. In either approach, you position the work on the bit with the router switched off. Then set the arm. Until you get the hang of it, thus gaining confidence, take light cuts—⅛ inch to 3/16 inch at a pass. Follow the outline of the template, then methodically clear the rest of the waste.

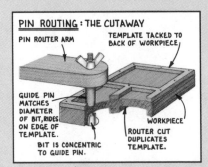

PIN ROUTING: THE CUTAWAY

PIN ROUTER ARM

TEMPLATE TACKED TO BACK OF WORKPIECE

GUIDE PIN MATCHES DIAMETER OF BIT, RIDES ON EDGE OF TEMPLATE.

WORKPIECE

ROUTER CUT DUPLICATES TEMPLATE.

BIT IS CONCENTRIC TO GUIDE PIN.

Rout the templates. The first step here is to lay out and cut the master pattern. This is making a template, nothing more or less. Keep the edge smooth. No nicks or gouges, pimples or ripples. No curve should exceed the diameter of the largest bearing or bushing you'll use, anywhere along the line. That's the only restriction on the contour.

The second and final step in this phase of the work is to rout the working templates. Clamp the master to another piece of template material, positioning it so the working templates will have space for clamps where they won't interfere with the router. Use a pattern bit to cut the working templates. Don't goof, or you'll have to start again

TRY THIS!

You can cut both halves of your curved joint—and simplify setup in the bargain—if you take half the total offset from each of the workpieces when you rout them to shape. This means your joint line will not *perfectly* match the master pattern contour, but I doubt that it will be obvious.

Using the master pattern, cut the two templates using a ½-inch pattern bit. The offset is ½ inch.

When using the templates to cut the workpieces, use a ¼-inch bit in a ¾-inch guide bushing for both cuts. You'll back out ¼ inch of the offset from each piece. Thus, in the two cuts, you'll remove the full ½ inch of offset. (Yes, of course, you can use a different bit-bushing combination, so long as it produces a ¼-inch offset.)

That will save you the time it takes to switch from the "flush" pattern bit to the "offset" pattern bit.

See Also . . .

Page 327 for a jig for cutting box joints that's trapped on a template guide bushing.

Page 293 for templates for cutting dovetail laps and mitered half-laps.

Page 305 for commercial dovetail jigs that use fixed and adjustable templates.

with a fresh piece of template material. Before you start, check the bit's bearing and the edge of the master for dirt.

Use an offset baseplate (see the chapter "Custom Baseplates" for details) or a support block that's the thickness of the master under the baseplate. Better yet, use both! You don't want to risk a bobble that will ruin the cut. And *concentrate* during the cut! Don't let the router drift away from the master edge. The router will probably try to pull away from the master as you negotiate the curves. Use the offset baseplate's outboard knob to pull the router firmly against the master.

If the the working template is ¼ or ⅜ inch thick, you should be able to power through it in a single pass. Thicker material will necessitate two or three passes. Unfortunately, this increases the opportunity for a goof.

When the working templates are done, mark them clearly. On each, note the bit and bearing or bushing that must be used with it.

Rout the workpieces. This is standard template-guided work. With the left template, you cut with a pattern bit. The diameter of the bit doesn't matter. Usually, you'll get a smoother cut with a large-diameter bit. Just keep in mind that the left template guides a flush cut.

The cut guided by the right template is the one that makes up the offset.

Probably the most important advice I can give here is the reminder to concentrate on keeping the router against the template as you make these cuts. The template has to be clean, as does the bearing.

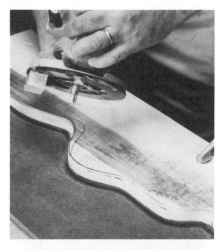

Cutting the templates is the critical operation. If the templates have the slightest mismatch, the joint won't be right. To minimize the chance for goofs, make the cut in one pass. Use a short-flute, small-diameter bit, and stick a support block to the baseplate to keep the router from wobbling. Lay the template stock—hardboard is the material here—atop an expendable surface, set the master pattern on it, and clamp them very firmly to the workbench.

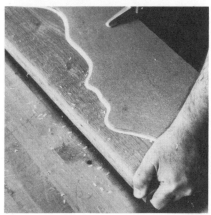

The penultimate operation: fitting the just-routed edges together to test the fit. If they do, you glue them. If they don't, you can back the template away from the edge and try another pass. And if they still don't fit? Cut a new set of templates.

The workpieces are cut roughly to the designed contour on the band saw, then routed. To prevent damage to the bench top, the work and template are raised with a spacer. Use plenty of clamps, and position them as close to the edge being cut as you can without interfering with the router's movement. Here I'm using a 1-inch-diameter bit with a Delrin-rimmed 1½-inch bearing. Thus, half the offset comes out of this workpiece and half out of its mate.

ROUTING CURVES AND CIRCLES

Working in circles is considered a waste

of time, but you'd be surprised how often you really need to. In fact, there's been a lot of time wasted by people who couldn't figure out how to cut a good, clean circle (or arc) when they needed one.

To cut a circle with the router, the basic need is to get the router to move smoothly around a given point. You'll find that there are numerous ways to accomplish that and that each of the ways has advantages in certain applications. Almost always, you'll use a trammel of one sort or another. Occasionally, a template will guide the router.

But what about curves that aren't circles? Ovals. Arcs. Combinations of arcs. Here again, the router will do the work. To cut ovals, you use a special trammel. For those arcs and combinations of arcs, you are often best served by a template.

the same thing with a lot more flexibility by attaching a hardwood arm to the base and setting the pivot point in a sliding block on that arm. Infinite adjustment—almost.

Cutting circles is the natural turf of the plunge router. The plunger makes it easy to get the bit into the work and to deepen the cut after each lap. But plunge routers tend to be pretty beefy, too much so for a lot of trammel work, in my estimation. Don't get me wrong. I have routed a lot of circles with plunge routers. But I'm inclined to use a small machine rather than the 3-horse behemoths.

What I really like to use is a laminate trimmer, which you can hold in one hand. The hitch, of course, is that with the lam trimmer, as with any fixed-base router, you stand a good chance of gouging the work trying to tip the bit into it. So you *do* have to practice. But it can be done. Manageability is a big plus in this kind of operation. With one hand on the pivot and the other on the router, you can make the cut quickly and accurately.

And if you are worried about a

lam trimmer being down on power, just remember: It doesn't take 3 horses to spin a ¼-inch bit.

Of course, this whole discussion may be academic for you. You may be in the same boat as one of my colleagues, Jeff Day, who says, "I only have one router, so it doesn't take a lot of thought which one I'm going to use."

In any case, with a trammel, you drive a pivot nail into the workpiece. Better yet, drill a pilot for the nail. A drilled pilot will ensure that the pivot is perdendicular. And by boring clean through the stock, you can use the same centerpoint on either side. I *would* recommend working both sides. That is, use the router and trammel to groove one side, cutting about halfway through the stock. Then flip the piece over and make a cut. Then keep going until you are through. You get a better finish on all the edges, and you don't have to cut so deeply.

Trimmer Trammel

The trimmer trammel is a simple cutout. It can be cut from acrylic, hardboard, or thin plywood. The

CIRCLE TRAMMELS

The most common way to cut circles or arcs with the router is to use a trammel. Your router may have one among its accessories. Usually, the trammel will be a part of the edge guide attachment.

If you don't have one, it's easy to cut out an oversized plywood baseplate, mounting the router on one end and driving a nail for a pivot at the other. You can accomplish

Routing out the wheels for a wooden 18-wheeler is a good job for a laminate trimmer equipped with the trimmer trammel. Wheels are usually pretty small, and it is easier to see what you are doing—as well as to do it—with a trimmer than with a full-sized router.

trammel in *Trimmer Trammel* was made for a Ryobi tilt-base trimmer.

To make such a trammel for your laminate trimmer, remove the baseplate. Trace the plate on cardboard, then draw an extension for the pivot

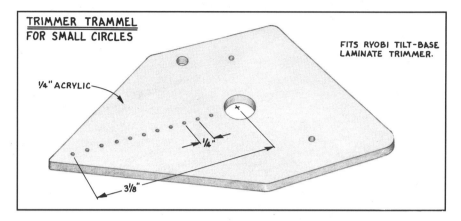

TRIMMER TRAMMEL FOR SMALL CIRCLES

FITS RYOBI TILT-BASE LAMINATE TRIMMER.

¼" ACRYLIC

¼"

3⅛"

holes. Cut out the pattern and attach it to your stock with double-sided carpet tape, then cut it to shape and drill the necessary holes.

This is the perfect device for making wheels for wooden toys. Oh, I know you can buy wheels cheap, but using them is like assembling a model. If I'm making a toy, I like to make the whole toy.

When making toy wheels, by the way, experiment with groove-forming bits. You can scoop out the wheel disk with a round-nose bit, then chamfer the edge with a V-groover, then complete the wheel by cutting it free with a straight bit. (Just don't use too big a bit in the trimmer; its low-horsepower motor may be overtaxed and succumb.) And you don't have to limit yourself to wheels for toys. How about wheeled furniture—the sort of stuff you'd have on a deck or patio?

Large Trammel

For those large arcs and circles—tabletops come immediately to mind—you do need a bigger trammel. The plywood teardrop shown below is more than 3 feet long overall, so with it you can rout a 3-foot-radius arc (that's a 6-foot-diameter circle). With its reinforced edges, this trammel also doubles as jig for rabbeting assembled cases. (See the chapter "Rabbeting.")

Here's the quick and dirty approach to making this jig. Cut a rectangle of ¼-inch plywood as wide as your router's base and about 6 inches longer than the radius of the arc or circle you want to cut. Use your router's baseplate to lay out the trammel's head with mounting-screw holes and a bit hole. Measure, mark, and drill the pivot hole you need. Attach the base to the router, and you're in business.

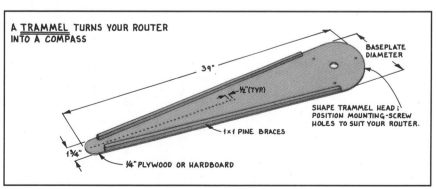

A **TRAMMEL** TURNS YOUR ROUTER INTO A COMPASS

BASEPLATE DIAMETER

39"

½" (TYP.)

SHAPE TRAMMEL HEAD; POSITION MOUNTING-SCREW HOLES TO SUIT YOUR ROUTER.

1×1 PINE BRACES

1¾"

¼" PLYWOOD OR HARDBOARD

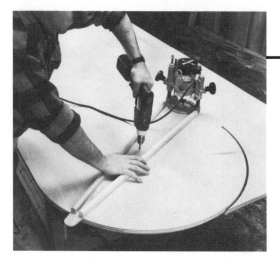

With a large trammel making a wide arc, the most secure pivot is a screw driven into the work. You can use both hands to operate the router without worrying that the trammel will jump off the pivot, allowing the router to forge its own route through the workpiece.

What is shown in the photo above is the result of the quick but tidy approach. The task begins the same—cutting the plywood blank and laying out the head from the router baseplate. But then the trammel is cut to an elongated teardrop shape on the band saw or with a saber saw. And a series of pivot holes are drilled. After being bull-nosed, 1 x 1 braces are glued to the edges. Finally, a finish is applied.

Adjustable Trammel

What you will probably discover if you use the trammel often enough is that the fixed size is sometimes a nuisance. So the next step is to make a trammel with interchangeable arms for different ranges of arc size. This way you don't have to deal with 5 feet of arm sticking out the back when you're cutting a 10-inch radius. Two-foot, 4-foot, and 6-foot arms will cover most of your needs nicely, and it's no problem to make longer ones if you need them.

But what about shorter ones? With your pivot point on a sliding block, the smallest radius you can cut is limited by the size of the base, right? Not really. Fred's trammel design demonstrates that it's a simple matter to make a pivot block that reaches a couple of inches under the router base, enough that you

can get the pivot point within an inch of the cutter. I can't think of many reasons to want to trammel-cut an arc smaller than that.

This design is indeed clever. Fred's shop colleague Phil Gehret made two prototypes: one that accommodates a laminate trimmer; the other, a 1½-horsepower Porter-Cable router. (Both the fixed base and the 6931 plunge case will fit the trammel baseplate shown.) Naturally, you can easily modify the shape of the trammel baseplates to suit other brands and models of routers.

The key to adjustability is the pivot base. It has a clamp that pinches the arm between its jaw and the pivot base. A couple of turns of the plastic knob will loosen the clamp so you can slide the pivot back and forth on the arm. Remove the two

machine screws that attach the arm to the router baseplate and you can switch to a different arm.

To make the bigger trammel, you need a few scraps of good-quality ¼-inch plywood, several strips of straight-grained, defect-free hardwood (Phil used oak), and a handful of hardware.

1. Cut the parts to the sizes indicated on the Cutting List. Remember that the hardwood needs to be straight-grained and defect-free so it won't warp.

2. Remove the factory baseplate from your router, set it on the plywood baseplate blank, and trace around it. Mark the mounting-screw holes and the bit opening. Lay the arm in place on the edge of the plywood baseplate and mark it to ensure you leave a big enough tab for it. Mark the locations of the two mounting-screw holes on both the baseplate and the arm. Mark off the quadrant that will be cut away.

3. Cut the baseplate on the band saw or with a saber saw. Drill and countersink the mounting-screw holes. In the arm, drill holes large enough to accommodate the T-nuts.

Setting the adjustable trammel is a matter of measuring from bit to pivot. (With a tape, it's usually more accurate to avoid using the inch with the hook.) Slide the pivot base as necessary to get the correct setting, then tighten the lock knob.

PLASTIC KNOB WITH ¼" BLIND THREADED HOLE

10-32 x 1" THUMBSCREW WITH TIP GROUND TO POINT

10-32 T-NUTS

10-32 WING NUT

BIT OPENING

CLAMP JAW

ARM

¾"

3"

2"

2"

⅜"

¼" PLYWOOD PIVOT BASE

¼" PLYWOOD ROUTER BASEPLATE

6½"

CLAMP BASE

PIVOT STRIP

2"

2¼"

3¼"

ROUTER MOUNTING-SCREW HOLE

5¾"

10-32 x 1" MACHINE SCREW

¼" x 1½" CARRIAGE BOLT; HEAD IN COUNTERBORE BENEATH PIVOT BASE

5"

10-32 T-NUT

LAMINATE TRIMMER VERSION

INDICATES GRAIN DIRECTION

The adjustable trammel's pivot can't be driven securely into the work, so it's a good idea to keep a hand on it as you rout. Use both hands to plunge the bit, then hold the pivot with one while pushing or pulling the router with the other.

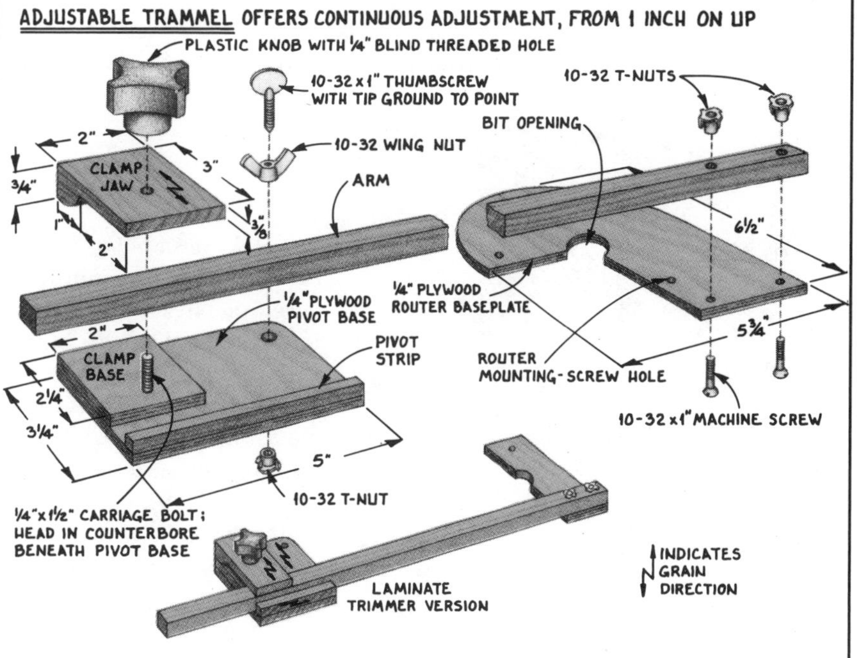

CUTTING LIST

Piece	Number	Thickness	Width	Length	Material
Arm	1	½"	¾"	24"	Oak
Clamp jaw	1	¾"	2"	3"	Oak
Pivot strip	1	¼"	¼"	5"	Oak
Pivot base	1	¼"	3¼"	5"	Plywood
Clamp base	1	¼"	2"	2¼"	Plywood
Router baseplate	1	¼"	5¾"	6½"	Plywood

Hardware

1 pc. ¼ × 1½" carriage bolt

1 pc. ¼"-20 plastic knob, with blind hole. Available from Reid Tool Supply Co., 2265 Black Creek Road, Muskegon, MI 49444 (800-253-0421). Part #DK-59.

3 pcs. 10-32 T-nuts

1 pc. 10-32 wing nut

1 pc. 10-32 × 1" thumbscrew

2 pcs. 10-32 × 1" flathead machine screws

4. Glue the hardwood strip and the plywood clamp base to the pivot base, as shown in *Adjustable Trammel*.

5. Cut the clamp on the band saw, then drill the hole for the carriage bolt.

6. With a ¾-inch Forstner bit, drill the counterbores for the carriage bolt head and for the flange of the last T-nut. The T-nut must be flush with the bottom of the pivot base, but because the plywood is thin, you must be careful not to bore too deep. Drill the hole for the body of the T-nut and for the carriage bolt.

7. Glue the T-nut in the hole with epoxy. After the glue dries, file away the portion of the T-nut that sticks above the pivot base, and round off the corner of the pivot base to the edge of the T-nut. Before turning the thumbscrew into the T-nut, grind or file its tip to a sharp point, and grind away the ends of the thumb pad so the screw can be turned down between the wings of the wing nut. Turn the wing nut onto the thumbscrew, then turn the thumbscrew into the T-nut. Finally, drive the carriage bolt into the pivot base, set the clamp in place, and turn the knob on the bolt. Slide the arm into the channel under the clamp and cinch it down.

TRY THIS!

If the circle you want to cut is smaller than the diameter of your router base, don't bother with the trammel. Drill a pivot hole in the factory baseplate. Then the baseplate is the trammel. Fit the router over the pin in the work, and turn it. Not flashy, but it works.

To get the pivot point "inside" the router base, as shown here, you have to remove the thumbscrew. Slide the pivot base into position, then reinsert the thumbscrew. Adjust the trammel to the radius of the circle to be routed. If the pivot point must actually be under the base itself, grind a point on the tip of a flathead screw and substitute it for the thumbscrew.

Arcs and circles larger than wheels for toys can be routed with a laminate trimmer, but something larger than the trimmer trammel will probably be needed. The adjustable trammel is just the ticket.

The procedure for making the smaller trammel is basically the same. The parts are smaller, and all of them are cut from hardwood. When you glue the parts of the pivot together, be sure you cross the grain in the two layers. The grain direction of each part of Phil's prototype is shown in *Adjustable Trammel*.

No-Mar Trammel

What if, you ask now, I don't *want* to have a pilot hole? What if, you propose, a pilot hole is going to mar my tabletop?

The solution is a trammel that uses my favorite shop tape—the so-

called double-stick stuff—carpet tape. Actually, there are two models. One is designed for use with routers that use two rods for the edge guide. The other, designed for those routers that can't use the double-rod model, incorporates a baseplate on which you mount the router.

In both models the critical part is the acrylic plastic pivot plate, which you stick to the work—temporarily—with carpet tape. The square plate has a hole at dead center. The pivot bolt in the trammel block projects just enough to catch in this pivot hole, but not enough to bottom in that hole and scratch the workpiece.

The plastic plate is durable and

bonds well to the tape. I tried using hardboard initially, but the pivot hole got deformed pretty quickly, and the tape didn't stick to it very reliably. With the plastic plate, the tape sticks almost too well—I have to work a putty knife under a corner to pry the plate off the work.

One negative to this trammel is that you can work from only one side of the blank. You *do* have a deep cut to make.

With the double-rod trammel, you adjust the radius of the circle at the router or at the trammel block. With the wooden-bar trammel, you adjust the radius at the trammel block only.

To make the double-rod trammel:

1. Fit the trammel rods into the holes for them in the router base, then measure the distance between them (labeled "D" on *Double-Bar No-Mar Trammel*). Measure the length of the

This pivot plate is the key to the no-mar trammel's no-mar operation. Apply carpet tape to the plate, then stick the plate to the work. If the centerpoint is critical, mark the point with extended crosshairs, then align the corners of the plate with those lines. That's why it's a square—so you can do that.

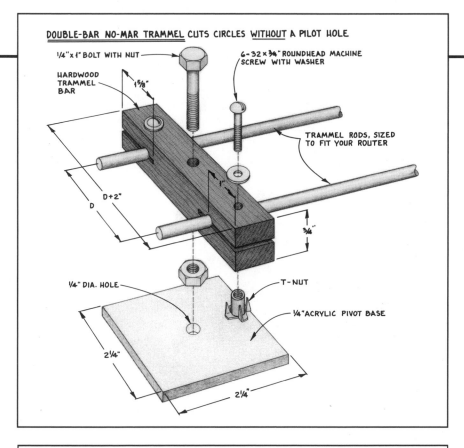

DOUBLE-BAR NO-MAR TRAMMEL CUTS CIRCLES <u>WITHOUT</u> A PILOT HOLE

1/4"x1" BOLT WITH NUT

6-32 x 3/4" ROUNDHEAD MACHINE SCREW WITH WASHER

HARDWOOD TRAMMEL BAR

1 5/8"

TRAMMEL RODS, SIZED TO FIT YOUR ROUTER

D+2"

D

3/4"

1"

1/4" DIA. HOLE

T-NUT

1/4" ACRYLIC PIVOT BASE

2 1/4"

2 1/4"

CUTTING LIST

Piece	Number	Thickness	Width	Length	Material
Trammel bar	1	3/4"	3/4"	D + 2"*	Hardwood
Pivot base	1	1/4"	2 1/4"	2 1/4"	Acrylic

Hardware

1 pc. 1/4" × 1" bolt with nut
2 pcs. 6-32 × 3/4" roundhead machine screws with washers
2 pcs. 6-32 T-nuts
2 steel rods of a size to fit your router

*See Step 1 to determine "D."

Don't want to leave a pivot hole in your work? Use this no-mar trammel! The trammel pivots on a small square of plastic attached to the work with carpet tape. To adjust the radius of the circle, loosen the screws on the trammel bar and reposition it on the trammel rods. Adjustments can also be made at the router.

edge guide's rods. If you need longer rods, buy them. (One hitch we discovered in this regard is that not all router makers use standard-diameter rods. The Elu—made in Switzerland—uses 1/4-inch rods. The Porter-Cable—made in the U.S.A.—seems to use metric rods. Quarter-inch rods were too small, 5/16-inch were too big, and getting 9/32-inch rods at the corner hardware store—I don't think so. I ended up using the 1/4-inch rods on the Porter-Cable and just cinching the setscrews as tight as I could. I fretted about it at first, but the trammel has worked fine.)

2. Cut the trammel block to length, which is 2 inches longer than your distance D.

3. The trammel rods slide through holes in the trammel block and are pinched to hold them. The pinches are provided by machine screws turned into T-nuts, the pinchable leeway by kerfs extending from the block's ends to the trammel-rod holes.

Drill holes for the rods and for the screws, then counterbore the latter holes for the T-nuts. Drill the pivot hole equidistant from both ends of the bar; counterbore the bottom so the nut will be partially recessed.

4. Kerf the ends of the bar, as shown. To do this on the table saw, crank up the blade to make a cut at least 1 5/8 inches deep. (The kerf should extend at least 1/2 inch beyond the hole for the pinch to be secure.) Set the fence so the cut will pass through the center of the hole. Stand the trammel block on end to make the cut, and use a scrap block to back it up.

5. Assemble the trammel. Insert the bolt through the pivot hole and turn the nut onto it. The nut should protrude just a bit so that the whole trammel block doesn't rub on the pivot plate. Drive the T-nuts in place, and turn the machine screws into them. Insert the trammel rods and tighten the screws, pinching the rods.

6. Cut the pivot plate from a scrap of acrylic plastic. It must be square. Scribe diagonals to locate the center point, then drill a ¼-inch pivot hole there.

To make the wooden-bar trammel:

1. The size of the clear acrylic baseplate blank may need to be adjusted to accommodate your router. Cut it to the appropriate size, then attach your router's factory baseplate to it with carpet tape. Drill and countersink the mounting-screw holes. Then trim one end of the new baseplate to match the factory baseplate, using a router and a flush-trimming bit. After separating the two baseplates, drill and countersink the mounting-screw holes for the transition block.

2. Chuck a plunge-cutting straight bit in your router. Mount the new baseplate on the router. Plug it in, switch it on, and advance the bit that's cutting the bit opening in the baseplate.

3. Cut the pivot block, the trammel arm, and the transition block. Shape the transition block, as shown in *Wooden-Bar No-Mar Trammel*, and attach it to the baseplate.

4. On the router table, cut the dovetail slot in the pivot block. Use the same dovetail bit to bevel the ends of the trammel arm, trimming the arm to fit the slot in the pivot block. Switch to a ¼-inch straight bit and rout the slot in the trammel arm.

If your router doesn't have the double-rod setup for an edge guide, or if the rods are too big, try this model of the no-mar trammel. The trammel bar is attached to a plywood baseplate that you fit to your router.

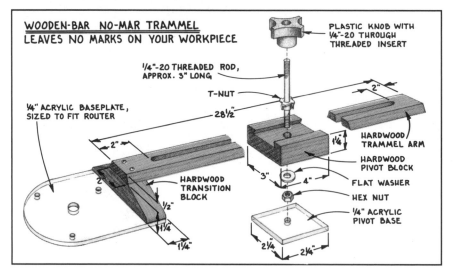

WOODEN-BAR NO-MAR TRAMMEL LEAVES NO MARKS ON YOUR WORKPIECE

PLASTIC KNOB WITH ¼"-20 THROUGH THREADED INSERT

¼"-20 THREADED ROD, APPROX. 3" LONG

T-NUT

¼" ACRYLIC BASEPLATE, SIZED TO FIT ROUTER

28½"

2"

2"

HARDWOOD TRAMMEL ARM

¼"

HARDWOOD PIVOT BLOCK

3"

4"

FLAT WASHER

HARDWOOD TRANSITION BLOCK

HEX NUT

½"

¼" ACRYLIC PIVOT BASE

2"

1¼"

¼"

2¼"

2¼"

CUTTING LIST

Piece	Number	Thickness	Width	Length	Material
Trammel arm	1	½"	2"	28½"	Hardwood
Transition block	1	1¼"	1¼"	base dia.	Hardwood
Pivot block	1	1¼"	3"	4"	Hardwood
Pivot base	1	¼"	2¼"	2¼"	Acrylic
Baseplate	1	¼"	sized to fit router		Acrylic

Hardware

1 pc. ¼" threaded rod, approx. 3" long

1 pc. ¼" plastic knob, with through threaded insert. Available from Reid Tool Supply Co., 2265 Black Creek Road, Muskegon, MI 49444 (800-253-0421). Part #DK-54.

1 pc. ¼" I.D. flat washer

1 pc. ¼" hex nut

2 pcs. #6 × 1" roundhead wood screws

Problem Solver

Trammels imply circles, but sometimes you need only a piece of the circle—an arc. The trammels we've shown so far will help you lay out and cut arcs. But when you need one with a really radical radius, those trammels aren't big enough.

Here's the solution.

Cut a trammel bar as long as the radius you need. Hinge it to a shop wall at one end, and position your workbench so the router, attached to the other end of the trammel bar, is supported. The hinge provides a secure pivot. Your trammel bar can be a strip of 1/4-inch plywood. You need not be limited by the 8-foot length of a plywood sheet. Scab strips together to extend them. You need only be limited by the size of your shop. (And if *that's* too small for you, do the job outside!)

I made my own hinge using a couple of screw eyes turned into the wall. I round off the end of the trammel strip, as shown in *Radical-Radius Arc-Cutting Trammel*, and drill a hole in it. Slip the strip

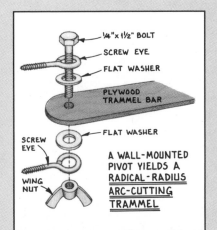

between the two screw eyes, drop a bolt through the holes, and the pivot is ready for use.

Now you can put a pencil in the other end of the trammel to scribe the arc, then cut it with a saber saw or on the band saw. But I use this most often to make templates, and swinging the router on the trammel assures me of a much smoother arc than I would get by sawing it freehand. Then I use the template with a template guide or a pattern bit to actually shape the workpiece. (See the chapter "Template-Guided Work" for more on this technique.)

A router table affords a whole new range of possibilities. Obviously, the big difference is that you turn the workpiece instead of the router. Just place a nail, screw, or dowel in the tabletop as a pivot. Then set the stock on the pivot, and turn it to cut your circles or arcs.

In most cases, of course, you're not going to want to mess up your nice, smooth top. Instead of putting a hole in the tabletop itself, use a piece of scrap plywood or hardboard and either tape it or clamp it to the tabletop. Run the bit up through it, and install any kind of pivot you desire in this auxiliary top.

With the bit retracted, you slip the blank on the pivot. Hold the blank, switch on the router, and turn the micro-adjusting knob to raise the bit enough to engage the work. Turn the blank one full rotation; then, still holding the blank and with the router still running, reach under

If you are uncomfortable about the proximity of your fingers to the bit when routing out disks on the router table, use a pusher to move the workpiece. This commercial pusher has a dense foam rubber sole that grips the work and won't let it slip. Here, the last corner is being trimmed off the workpiece.

5. Drill and counterbore the pivot hole in the pivot block. The counterbore for the washer and nut on the bottom of the block shouldn't be too deep. The nut should be just a bit proud of the block's bottom surface, so it—and not the block—bears on the pivot plate.

6. To assemble the trammel, fit the T-nut into the pivot block. Slide the arm into the dovetail slot, and stick the threaded rod through the slot in the arm and into the T-nut. Turn it through the hole and tighten it in

place with the nut. The end of the rod should project enough to catch in the pivot-plate hole, but not so much that it will bottom in that hole and thus mar the workpiece. (That would defeat the whole purpose of this trammel!) Turn the plastic knob onto the free end of the rod. Drill pilot holes, and screw the trammel arm to the transition block.

7. Cut the pivot plate from a scrap of acrylic. It must be square. Scribe diagonals to locate the centerpoint, then drill a 1/4-inch pivot hole there.

Overarm Pivot

One kind of pivot point that doesn't harm the table's surface is the overarm. Instead of being under the work, the pivot is on top of it.

A job-specific overarm pivot can be made using a strip of ½-inch plywood and a scrap of the working stock. Drive the pivot point through the plywood, then tack or screw the plywood to the scrap. The distance from the pivot to the scrap has to be long enough to accommodate the workpiece, of course.

The big advantage to this system is that it also provides a positive hold-down for the work. If you set one clamp well back from the work, you can usually spring the arm enough to get the work under it. Then set a closer clamp to secure the setup. The work won't jump off the pivot.

Having an adjustable overarm pivot on hand can save you some time. Phil Gehret made us a simple but effective jig that has an overarm joined to a base block in a sliding dovetail. You slide the base along the arm, setting it to suit the job. Then clamp it to the tabletop. The clamp not only holds the jig on the tabletop but also secures the arm-to-base setting. The pivot is a thumbscrew with a point ground on the end.

Set the overarm jig on the tabletop, measuring from bit to pivot point to align it. Set two clamps on it to keep it from swiveling out of position. Then slip the workpiece under the arm, and turn the pivot down into it.

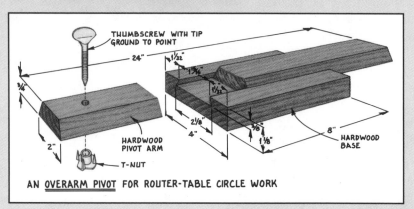

THUMBSCREW WITH TIP GROUND TO POINT

24"

1/32"

1½"

1½"

¾"

2⅛"

4"

⅜"

1⅛"

8"

HARDWOOD PIVOT ARM

T-NUT

2"

HARDWOOD BASE

AN OVERARM PIVOT FOR ROUTER-TABLE CIRCLE WORK

the router table and raise the bit a little more. Turn the blank again. Eventually, following this sequence, the bit comes through.

This works well with a plunge router, because the micro-adjusting knob raises the bit straight up into the work. Moreover, it raises the bit with a mere turn of the knob; you can raise the bit with one hand while holding the work with the other.

Fixed-base routers present two problems in this regard. One is that you need two hands to adjust the cutting depth, so you can't make the adjustment with the machine running. The other is that fixed-base routers generally have sideplay when you loosen the clamp to raise the bit. The motor—and thus the bit—can jiggle from side to side. The bit thus can gouge the work.

Few real limits exist on the circle work you can do on the router table, though there definitely are some practical ones.

Too small a circle puts your fingers in jeopardy. All I can advise is that you try manipulating little disks next to a stationary bit and develop your own sense for this. Some of my colleagues wouldn't cut anything smaller than about a foot in diameter; I've done 6-inch disks without qualms. I do 2- to 3-inch wheels with the trimmer trammel. These are *your* fingers, and even with a bit guard, you can get them into the bit if you let your concentration lapse even for a moment.

Another practical limit is at the other end of the size scale. Too big a circle ranges beyond the capacity of the tabletop. Measure from the bit to the far corner of your router table. That's the maximum radius you can cut without resorting to some sort of supplementary tabletop.

OVAL CUTTING

An oval (or ellipse) is a two-dimensional geometric shape, an enclosed curve with a continuously changing radius. It's a wonderfully plastic shape. A circle is always a circle; only the size changes. But an oval can be all-but-a-circle, or it can be extremely elongate. One of my colleagues here at Rodale, Bob Moran, refers to ovals as "squashed circles."

Bob's the one who got us started making squashed circles. He talked about a jig he had made back in his professional woodworking days, which he used to cut oval tabletops, oval frames, and the like. The cutting tool he used was the router.

Most woodworkers know how to draw ovals using two tacks and some string. But those same woodworkers probably think that to actually cut out an elliptical form, you have to draw the ellipse, make a template, trace it out on your workpiece, band-saw the rough shape, and flush-trim to your template. With this jig, you can rout a geometrically correct ellipse, directly. All you need to know is its length and width.

Oval-Cutting Trammel

Moran came across this idea when he was thumbing through an old book on carpentry. Back in the eighteenth century, Benjamin Asher was telling carpenters how to build a jig for *drawing* ovals. When Bob saw it, he adapted it for the router.

That's what he *says*, anyway. To the rest of us, the jig bears a striking resemblance to the old "BS grinder" or do-nothing machine. It's got two keys that travel back and forth in perpendicular slots. They're con-

nected by an arm. What's interesting, and surely something you never realized when grinding a load of BS, is that the arm traces out an oval.

The adaptation for the router is a blessing when you want to make oval tabletops or oval frames. That's not BS.

The particular jig shown here is one Fred made. You can rout dovetail slots in medium-density fiberboard (MDF) or particleboard or even real wood, but Fred cut strips of cherry for the tracks and nailed them to a plywood base. The use of thumbscrews and T-nuts enhances the easy adjustability of the jig. The thumb-

screws go through holes drilled in the trammel bar so the keys can pivot freely.

Let me explain how to set it up. (I'd explain how it works if I could; what I can explain is how to set it up. I think you'll get the picture from that.)

An oval has two measurements of particular importance in setting up the jig. One is the longest dimension, more properly called the major axis, and the other is the shortest dimension, called the minor axis. Draw two centerlines on the stock, one the long way and one the short way. You position the two tracks

The structure of the oval-cutting trammel is pretty clearly exposed here: the dovetail-slotted tracks formed of separate strips, the plywood base, the router mounting, the trammel bar, and the sliding keys. Note the bushing on the long thumbscrew; it reduces wear on the wooden parts, while freeing the mechanical action of the trammel.

Routing an oval doesn't demand more of the operator than routing a circle. You turn on the router, plunge the bit, and move the router in the right feed direction. The action of the trammel, however, is considerably different. And as the slides move back and forth in their tracks, barely missing each other at the crossing, the router follows a far different path.

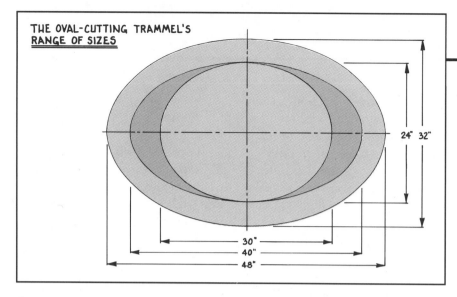

24" 32"

30"
40"
48"

Now move the router to one end of the minor axis. Insert the second sliding key in its track, line it up at the track junction, and run a thumbscrew through the trammel bar into it. This setup establishes the *proportion* of the oval, which is to say, the difference between the major and minor axes. You adjust the *size* of the oval by moving the router on the trammel rods.

The range of the jig is determined by the size of the trammel's base, the length of the tracks and the sliding keys, and the distance between the holes in the trammel bar. It is not infinitely variable. Rather, it is a relatively modest range of proportions, a wider range of sizes. Let me explain.

directly over the two centerlines. Then you fasten it there. If the area to which the jig is attached is waste, you can just nail the tracks to the stock. For tabletops, you can fasten it with double-sided carpet tape.

To set up the jig, mark the ends of the major and minor axes on the

appropriate centerlines. Park the router at one end of the major axis first. Insert a sliding key in the track that's perpendicular to the major axis. Line it up at the junction of the tracks, under the trammel bar. Then run a thumbscrew through the arm into the key.

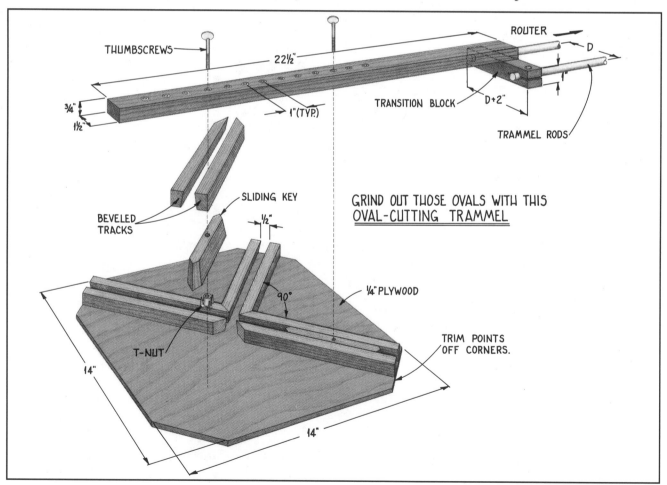

ROUTER

THUMBSCREWS

22½"

D

3/4"
1½"

1"(TYP.)

TRANSITION BLOCK

D+2"

TRAMMEL RODS

BEVELED TRACKS

SLIDING KEY

½"

GRIND OUT THOSE OVALS WITH THIS OVAL-CUTTING TRAMMEL

90°

¼" PLYWOOD

T-NUT

TRIM POINTS OFF CORNERS.

14"

14"

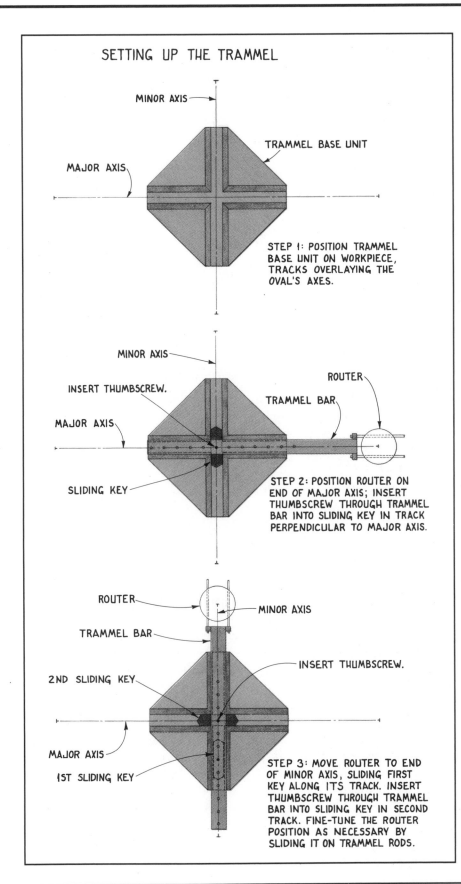

SETTING UP THE TRAMMEL

MINOR AXIS

TRAMMEL BASE UNIT

MAJOR AXIS

STEP 1: POSITION TRAMMEL BASE UNIT ON WORKPIECE, TRACKS OVERLAYING THE OVAL'S AXES.

MINOR AXIS

INSERT THUMBSCREW.

ROUTER

TRAMMEL BAR

MAJOR AXIS

SLIDING KEY

STEP 2: POSITION ROUTER ON END OF MAJOR AXIS; INSERT THUMBSCREW THROUGH TRAMMEL BAR INTO SLIDING KEY IN TRACK PERPENDICULAR TO MAJOR AXIS.

ROUTER

MINOR AXIS

TRAMMEL BAR

INSERT THUMBSCREW.

2ND SLIDING KEY

MAJOR AXIS

1ST SLIDING KEY

STEP 3: MOVE ROUTER TO END OF MINOR AXIS, SLIDING FIRST KEY ALONG ITS TRACK. INSERT THUMBSCREW THROUGH TRAMMEL BAR INTO SLIDING KEY IN SECOND TRACK. FINE-TUNE THE ROUTER POSITION AS NECESSARY BY SLIDING IT ON TRAMMEL RODS.

The shortest minor axis you can cut is established by positioning the router as close to the base as you can get it. Depending upon the router you use, you can't get the bit closer to the base than about 3 to 3½ inches away. The diagonals for the base—and thus the tracks—are roughly 17 inches long. This adds up to 23 or 24 inches as the shortest minor axis this jig will produce.

Given that minor axis measurement, the shortest major axis you can get is 30 inches long. The determining factor? The length of the sliding keys. If you position their pivots closer together than 3 inches, they collide at the crossing. Trimming the keys from a 3-inch length to a 2-inch length would get you a closer setting. The disparity in radii doubles, obviously, when you talk about diameters (in this case axes), so the major axis ends up being 6 inches longer than the minor one.

Let's not leave that last factor unexplored. When you shift the pivots, you must move in 1-inch increments. The holes in the trammel bar are spaced that far apart. The 1-inch increment doubles when viewed in terms of axis length. The adjustability of the jig is therefore in 2-inch increments.

Given that 6 inches is the smallest difference between axes you can achieve, what's the greatest? Sixteen inches. The track length sets this figure. If you position the keys more than 8 inches apart, one will be out of its track.

Speaking in terms of oval proportions, then, this jig will range in 2-inch increments from 24 inches by 30 inches up to 34 inches by 48 inches.

You can rout larger ovals with the jig. The router can be moved out the trammel rods far enough to cut an oval with a maximum axis of 86 inches. The trammel rods are about 22 inches long, providing enough room to shift the bit position about 18 inches, so at any proportion setting, you have a 36-inch range in axis length. If you wanted to rout an oval frame, you would set the proportion and size to rout the outside edge, then slide the router in on the rods to cut the inner edge.

To make the trammel:

1. Cut the 14-inch square base from thin plywood.

2. Make the tracks and sliding keys. Use a hardwood, like maple or cherry, beginning with straight-grained, defect-free stock about ¾ inch thick and 2½ inches wide. Mark the top surface of the stock. Set the table saw to cut a 7-degree bevel, then rip a ¾-inch-wide strip from the working stock. Turn the stock around, keeping the top up, and repeat the cut. The strips cut are the tracks; the "waste" will yield the two sliding keys. Joint the cut edges lightly to remove any saw marks.

3. Assemble the tracks and the base. Clamp a single strip of the waste to the base, positioning it diagonally. Miter the tracks as necessary to form the joints at the base's center. With a single sheet of paper between the waste and the rails to create sliding clearance, butt the rails to the waste and nail them in place. When the first set of tracks is set, reposition the waste across the other diagonal and repeat the process to install the second set of tracks. Cut off the corners of the base assembly, as shown in *Oval-Cutting Trammel.*

4. Cut two keys, each about 3 inches long. Drill a hole for a thumbscrew

through each, equidistant from the ends. Drive a T-nut into the bottom of the hole.

5. Make the transition block. Start by determining how big it needs to be. Fit the trammel rods into the holes for them in the router base, then measure the distance between them (labeled "D" on the drawing). Cut the trammel block 2 inches longer than your distance D.

The trammel rods slide through holes in the transition block that are kerfed, so the rods can be "clamped" in place. Drill holes for the rods and for the screws, then counterbore the latter holes for T-nuts. Kerf the ends of the bar. To do this on the table saw, crank up the blade to make a cut at least 1⅝ inches deep. (The kerf should extend at least ½ inch beyond the hole for the pinch to be secure.) Set the fence so the cut will pass through the center of the hole. Stand the trammel block on end to make the cut, and use a scrap block to back it up.

6. Cut the trammel bar and drill 13 holes, 1 inch apart, for the thumbscrews to pass through. Glue and screw the trammel bar to the transition block.

Ellis 'n' Fred's Oval-Cutting Rig

Bigger, more flexible, and even more mysterious is this oval-cutting rig developed by Fred Matlack and Ellis Walentine. You know Fred. Ellis is an editor of *American Woodworker,* a custom cabinetmaker and furniture maker. Inspired by the basic oval-cutting trammel, Ellis and Fred worked to overcome its shortcomings and particularly to expand its range.

What they came up with will

cut the largest oval possible from a sheet of plywood, as well as one smaller than the minimum size the previous trammel would. What a range! Unlike that trammel, which produced 1-inch-sized steps in proportion, this rig is infinitely variable. It allows you to rout ovals in a continuous range of sizes and shapes, from ½ inch by 4½ inches to at least 48 inches by 96 inches.

The most overt change is that with this rig, the router is fixed and the work moves. Simply adjust the jig for the shape of the ellipse, place your stock on the platform, set up the router, and rotate the platform. The stationary router creates the ellipse on the moving stock. You can cut an oval, rabbet it for glass, even rout elliptical inlay grooves, all as easily as routing a circle.

The contraption consists of a base, a platform, and a separate fixture to hold the router over the platform. When you turn the platform, hardwood tracks attached to its underside slide back and forth on two dovetail keys screwed to the base. The platform therefore moves in an elliptical path. By changing the spacing of the dovetail keys, you can change the *shape* of the ellipse. The *size* of the ellipse is determined by where you place the router.

To make it easier to change the shape of the oval, Fred and Ellis attached one of the dovetail keys to a strip that slides in and out of the base in a sliding dovetail. (The second key is fixed.) Pull the adjustment slide outward, and you move the first key farther from the second, thus changing the length of the oval's major axis in proportion to the minor axis.

And to capture any setting, they installed a lock strip, which is so

Remember your old hi-fi's turntable with its tone arm? The oval-cutting rig is an eccentric turntable, with the router set up as the tone arm. The workpiece is set on the platform, and the router is set on the workpiece. With the router switched on and the bit plunged into the work, the operator turns the platform, and thus the work. Instead of revolving on a steady axis, however, the rig's platform revolves on a shifting axis. Instead of a circle, it makes an oval. Instead of following a groove, the router's tone arm makes a groove.

simple that I'll have to explain how it works in detail a little later.

Two prototypes were built. The first has T-slot tracks, a fir plywood platform, and a plastic-laminate-covered base. The second has dovetail tracks, a birch plywood platform, and a melamine-covered particleboard base. The following construction sequence (and Cutting List on page 176) represents a melding of the two versions, as does *Ellis 'n' Fred's Oval-Cutting Rig*. The photos show the T-slotted version.

To make the rig:

1. Make the platform first, using ¾-inch plywood. Cut your platform to an exact 36-inch by 48-inch rectangle, and carefully lay out perpendicular centerlines on one face. You'll center your tracks on these lines later. Continue your centerlines up the edges and across the top face of the platform.

2. Make the tracks next. Fred and Ellis used oak for the first-generation prototype, cherry for the second-generation rendition. Any strong, straight-grained, defect-free hardwood will do. It's important for the tracks to be perfectly straight, so rip them slightly oversized, then joint them and rip them to their finished dimensions.

Before routing the dovetail grooves in the tracks, remove as much waste as possible by cutting a ⅝-inch-wide by ⁷⁄₁₆-inch-deep dado down the center of each blank. Then rout the required slots with a 1-inch dovetail bit in a table-mounted router. If you don't have a 1-inch bit, you can make two passes with a ½-inch bit, referencing from the same edge to keep the width of the groove constant. The rake of the dovetail isn't critical as long as you cut the sliding dovetail keys to a matching angle.

3. Make the dovetail keys next. These should slide in the tracks with no sideplay. Taper the leading edges slightly with a file so they won't catch as they slide back and forth across the intersection of the assembled two tracks. (To help you align the tracks during their installation, you may want to rout an extra—and extra-long—strip of the key stock now.)

4. The tracks are screwed to the bottom of the base next. Miter one end of each track. These points formed by the miters should be exactly 90 degrees and centered perfectly on the dovetail grooves so opposite tracks will line up. After cutting the miters, fine-tune them on a stationary disc sander.

Attach the tracks with 1¼-inch drywall screws, making certain the dovetail grooves are exactly perpendicular and centered on the platform's centerlines. That extra strip of dovetail slide stock can help you line up the tracks, but Fred likes the eyeball method.

The tracks are attached to the bottom of the platform with drywall screws. To get all the pieces forming one slot parallel, and to ensure that the slot is the proper width, use a strip of the slide stock, as shown here.

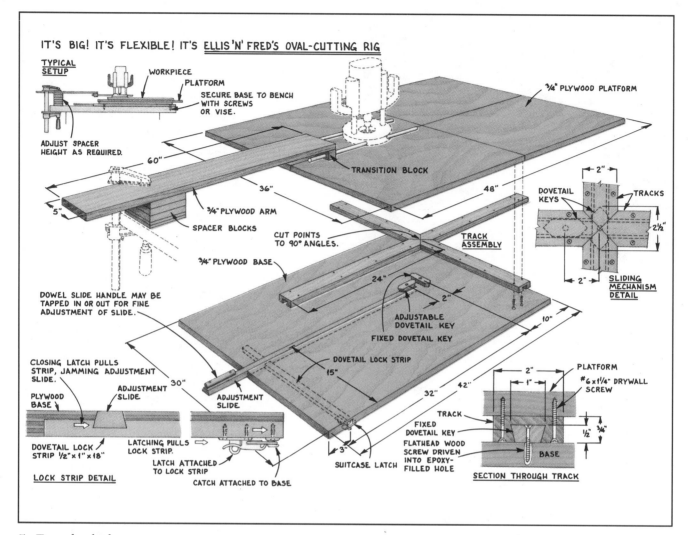

IT'S BIG! IT'S FLEXIBLE! IT'S ELLIS 'N' FRED'S OVAL-CUTTING RIG

TYPICAL SETUP

WORKPIECE

PLATFORM

SECURE BASE TO BENCH WITH SCREWS OR VISE.

ADJUST SPACER HEIGHT AS REQUIRED.

¾" PLYWOOD PLATFORM

60"

5"

36"

¾" PLYWOOD ARM

SPACER BLOCKS

TRANSITION BLOCK

48"

DOVETAIL KEYS

2"

TRACKS

2½"

CUT POINTS TO 90° ANGLES.

¾" PLYWOOD BASE

TRACK ASSEMBLY

2"

SLIDING MECHANISM DETAIL

DOWEL SLIDE HANDLE MAY BE TAPPED IN OR OUT FOR FINE ADJUSTMENT OF SLIDE.

24"

ADJUSTABLE DOVETAIL KEY

FIXED DOVETAIL KEY

2"

10"

CLOSING LATCH PULLS STRIP, JAMMING ADJUSTMENT SLIDE.

ADJUSTMENT SLIDE

30"

DOVETAIL LOCK STRIP

15"

PLATFORM

#6 x 1¼" DRYWALL SCREW

2"

PLYWOOD BASE

ADJUSTMENT SLIDE

DOVETAIL LOCK STRIP ½" x 1" x 18"

LATCHING PULLS LOCK STRIP.

LATCH ATTACHED TO LOCK STRIP

CATCH ATTACHED TO BASE

32"

42"

3"

SUITCASE LATCH

TRACK

FIXED DOVETAIL KEY

FLATHEAD WOOD SCREW DRIVEN INTO EPOXY-FILLED HOLE

1"

BASE

½"

¾"

LOCK STRIP DETAIL

SECTION THROUGH TRACK

5. To make the base, use a rectangular piece of plywood or other ¾-inch-thick sheet stock. The first-generation rig has a plastic-laminate-covered plywood base, while Ellis's second-generation unit has a melamine-coated particleboard (MCP) base. Both provide a low-friction surface for smooth operation. Cut the base to size, and apply the plastic laminate to one side and backer to the other. (See the chapter "Router Table Design" for more about backer.)

6. Mark the locations of the fixed dovetail block and the dovetail grooves for the adjustment slide and the lock strip, as shown in *Ellis 'n' Fred's Oval-Cutting Rig.* The adjust-

CUTTING LIST

Piece	Number	Thickness	Width	Length	Material
Platform	1	¾"	36"	48"	Plywood
Base	1	¾"	30"	42"	Plywood
Tracks	4	¾"	2"	24"	Hardwood
Dovetail keys	2	¾"	1"	2½"	Hardwood
Adjustment slide	1	½"	1"	40"	Hardwood
Slide handle	1	1"-dia.		8"	Dowel
Lock strip	1	½"	1"	18"	Hardwood

Hardware

1 pc. 30" × 42" plastic laminate
1 pc. 30" × 42" laminate backer
32 pcs. 1¼" drywall screws
2 pcs. #8 × 1¼" flathead wood screws
1 suitcase latch
epoxy

ment slide's dovetail groove is on the base centerline, and it is cut into the top surface. The lock strip's dovetail groove is cut into the underside, about 3 inches from the edge; it intersects the adjustment slide groove and extends about 3 inches beyond it.

Rout the groove for the lock strip first, cutting it ½ inch deep by 1 inch wide. Make a hardwood slide for the groove—the lock strip. It should be flush with the bottom surface of the base. Slide this lock strip all the way into the groove, and clamp it.

Now turn the base faceup, and rout the groove for the slide bar, cutting it ½ inch deep by 1 inch wide, too. You'll cut through the lock strip when you do. Make the adjustment slide several inches longer than this groove. The length isn't critical, but the slide's fit should be just barely snug, not too tight.

7. Install a lock-strip latch. Here's how the strip works. When you insert the adjustment slide, it passes through the lock strip. If you could pull on the end of the lock strip, it would pull the adjustment slide to one side, tight against the wall of its groove. Then the slide would be immobilized. Locked in place!

The way you "pull on the end of the lock strip" is with a suitcase latch, which you should be able to pick up for a buck at the local hardware store. The catch portion spans the lock strip itself and is screwed to the base. The latch is screwed to the strip. Be sure the cam action of the latch clamps the lock strip firmly against the slide bar and prevents it from moving. Any slippage in use will spoil your ellipse.

8. To attach the dovetail keys to the base and slide bar, first drill and

countersink the keys for #8 by 1¼-inch flathead wood screws. To keep the screws from working loose, Fred seated their threads in epoxy. The epoxy "glues" them into the plywood base, yet the bond can be broken if you end up needing to remove the screws.

Before drilling pilots for the screws, push the adjustment slide all the way in; then mark the hole locations, one in the base and one in the slide, exactly 2 inches apart. Any closer and the blocks will not clear each other when they rotate. Drill the pilots, then dribble a gob of epoxy into each. Rub all surfaces of the dovetail blocks with paraffin, then screw them down, snug to the base and slide.

9. The final step in preparing the base is to calibrate the adjustment slide. With the slide pushed all the way in, you should have exactly 2 inches between the centers of the fixed and adjustable blocks. Disc sand the nose of the slide bar if you need to reduce the spacing, or pull out the slide bar slightly to increase it to 2 inches.

Now, use a try square to scribe a line across the face of the slide bar at

the exact point the slide bar leaves the base, and label it "4." Mark off ½-inch increments from this mark toward the dovetail block. Since the space between the two dovetail blocks equals *half the difference* between the major and minor axes of a given ellipse, each mark corresponds to a 1-inch difference.

10. Assemble the platform and base. With the adjustment slide removed, carefully line up one track opening at the nose of the fixed dovetail key. Slide the platform onto the key, stopping when the platform is centered on the base. Complete the assembly by inserting the slide in its groove and pushing the adjustable dovetail key into the other track.

11. The last part to make is the router fixture. The simple fixture Fred and Ellis came up with holds your router above the workpiece. The double-rod system, a common mounting for edge guides, lets you lock the router in position quickly.

To make the head, epoxy two rods (of a size that fits your router) into a 1½-inch by 2-inch by 5-inch block, then screw the block to a ¾-inch by 5-inch by 60-inch plywood arm.

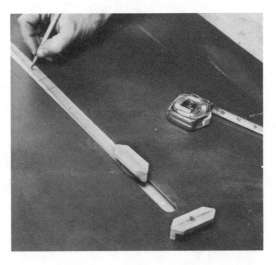

Markings on the adjustment slide make it easy to reset the proportion of the ellipse. Since each half-inch movement of the slide translates into a full inch of difference between the oval's axes, you must mark the slide accordingly. Make marks at ½-inch intervals on the slide, and write the appropriate numbers on the slide.

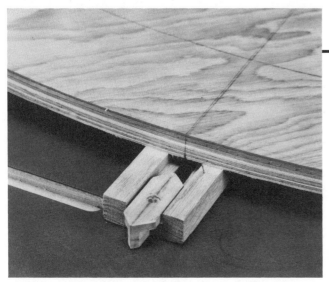

Set up the rig by first dogging the base to the workbench. Then install the platform. Do this by positioning the track at the nose of the fixed dovetail key (left) and pushing (or pulling) the platform so the key slides in the track. Next, align the cross-track with the slot for the adjustment slide. Start the slide into the slot, get its dovetail key nosed into the cross-track, and push the slide into place (right).

A 5-inch-high spacer block elevates the router fixture above the jig, so the platform—with workpiece in place—can rotate freely under the fixture. For routing thick stock, you simply add spacers to raise the fixture as necessary.

To use the rig, you first must dog (or screw) the base of the assembled jig to the workbench, making sure the lock-strip latch remains accessible.

Lightly scribe a centerline on your workpiece, which will coincide with the major axis. Position the work on the platform, aligning its centerline with that on the platform. Attach the work with screws, double-sided carpet tape, or hot-melt glue. Set the adjustment slide for the desired difference between the major and minor axes. To avoid undue strain on the dovetail keys, always center the long axis of the platform above the slide before making adjustments. Then unlatch the lock strip, move the adjustment slide to the desired difference on the scale, and relatch the lock strip.

Before shifting the platform—the major axis should still be aligned with the slide—mark one end of the desired oval's major axis on the workpiece. Line up your router bit on the waste side of that mark.

Here's an example: If you want to rout an oval that's 18 inches by 24 inches, set the adjustment slide at 6 inches (the difference between the major and minor axes), and mark a point 12 inches from the center on the major axis.

Be sure you clamp the router fixture firmly to the bench. Start the router, plunge the bit about ¼ inch into the work, and rotate the platform slowly and evenly in a clockwise direction. To prolong the life of your platform, don't plunge too much beyond the thickness of the work. It's a good idea to cut a little outside your line and follow up with a final trim pass once you've plunged all the way through.

For cutting out ellipses, a ⅜- or ½-inch straight bit will work fine. If you'd like to chamfer or round-over the edge of your ellipse, use a hand-held router and a piloted bit after you've cut out the elliptical shape.

If the ovals don't turn out quite as tidy as you had hoped, troubleshooting is straightforward. If the groove doesn't pass through the start-

The centerline of the platform must be centered over the adjustment slide when positioning the bit at the end of the ellipse's major axis. Otherwise the oval will be skewed. The router fixture can be positioned at any angle. Remember that the proportion of the oval is adjusted with the slide. The size of the oval is adjusted by repositioning the router, as shown here.

Penciling In the Profile

This jig's real advantage, to Ellis Walentine, is that you don't have to hassle with templates or inexact drawing methods. You can make a full-sized or scale drawing of your project right on the platform of the jig.

All you need to generate drawings of ovals is Fred's easy-to-make pencil holder. It's nothing more than a scrap of wood with a pencil stuck through it, screwed to a long strip of ¼-inch plywood.

Drill a hole big enough for a pencil through the center of a 2-inch-square scrap of ¾-inch stock. To lock the pencil in the hole, rip a 1½-inch-long kerf from one end through the pencil hole. (Use the band saw or a coping saw for this.) Drill a hole though the scrap, as shown in *Pencil Holder,* and insert a bolt with a wing nut. (With a pencil in the hole, tighten the wing nut to close the kerf, locking the pencil in the hole.) Attach the scrap to the plywood strip with a couple of ¾-inch screws.

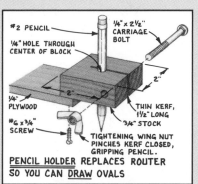

PENCIL HOLDER REPLACES ROUTER SO YOU CAN **DRAW** OVALS

To draw ellipses, tape your paper to the platform and lightly trace the platform's centerlines on it. The intersection of the lines will always be the exact center of your ellipse. Mark one end of the major axis on the paper. With the long centerline of the platform aligned with the adjustment slide, clamp the pencil holder fixture to the bench, with the point of the pencil on your mark. You don't want too much pressure on the pencil point, so adjust the pencil as necessary. Draw the ellipse by turning the platform in either direction.

The perfect way to establish the size and proportion of the oval you are about to rout is to draw one first. In fact, you can draw dozens of them, all different, to settle on which one you like. This pencil holder, which is set up exactly as the router is set up, makes it easy. A hand on the pencil holder will keep it on the paper as you rotate the platform.

ing point after one revolution of the platform, chances are that something has slipped slightly. Be sure the jig's base is screwed down properly, that the router fixture is securely clamped, and that the adjustment slide hasn't moved.

If your ellipses appear slightly skewed, either your tracks aren't centered properly on the platform or you didn't have the platform centerline directly over the center of the slide when you set the router on the major axis.

Finally, any wobble in the dovetail keys could translate into a slight wandering of the cut. Try tightening the screws slightly to take out the slop. Or consider upgrading the fasteners. In a model of this jig that Ellis made for his own shop, he used ¼-inch bolts to secure the dovetail keys.

If you need to cut ellipses with a larger axis difference than the 48 inches possible here, you can add extension channels or make a larger jig.

TEMPLATE-GUIDED CUTS

For small arcs—including small circles—you're often better off to use a template. A template guides the cut by controlling the path of the router. With the template, you use either a pattern bit, which has a pilot bearing mounted on the shank, or a guide bushing, which is a flange surrounding the bit. The bushing's flange or the bit's bearing rides along the edge of the template, preventing the router from wandering outside of the template's confines.

Templates are usually made of hardboard, plywood, or MDF. You temporarily attach the template to

Problem Solver

All too often, as an enclosed curved cut is completed and the outer ring separates from the center, the two pieces actually shift. Because the bit is still in the divide and still spinning, one of the pieces—usually the outer ring—gets gouged. (The disk seldom takes the hit, because with a trammel the router is moored to it, and with a router-table setup, the disk is moored to the pivot.)

If the outside portion is scrap, this shifting and gouging isn't a problem. But if that's the piece you want, then you need to hold it in position in relation to the center. Here are some ways to do that.

One is to use sandpaper. You can usually do this when routing with a trammel. Fold a sheet in half, abrasive out, and bond it with double-sided carpet tape. Slide three or four pieces of this stuff between the workpiece and the work surface. Be sure it is positioned where it can keep both inside and outside areas from shifting.

Another is carpet tape. If you simply stick your workpiece to a piece of scrap, you can cut through your work and leave the scrap to hold the pieces together. As a rule of thumb, this procedure will work well as long as the smallest piece is at least twice as wide as it is thick. The taller and thinner a piece is, the more likely it is to be torn loose from the tape and become a projectile.

On jobs where the piece being cut out is bigger than the router base, you can often get by very nicely by working carefully on a gripping surface such as one of the dense foams. Obviously, you don't want to cut into these surfaces, so cut halfway through and flip the work. A word of caution, here. Many of the foams are not dense enough to retain two pieces in the same plane. You may find that as you cut the pieces apart, they tilt toward each other.

On very large pieces, you can hold parts in the proper relationship by taking partial cuts and stopping periodically to tape a ripping or a straightedge across the cut. Fred uses 3M plastic packing tape. It is strong and sticks well to wood, yet it pulls off cleanly when the time comes.

Fred spent a lot of time routing this circular frame and certainly doesn't want it spoiled when it is finally cut free of the inner disk that's anchoring the trammel's pivot. As you can see, the final cut—breaking through!—is completed only partway around the frame. Here Fred's applying long strips of packing tape across the back. The tape will keep the frame from shifting just as the cut is completed.

the workpiece—use clamps, double-sided carpet tape, hot-melt glue—then move the router over it. You can make through cuts with straight bits, or decorative cuts with groove-forming profile bits.

There are several good reasons for using templates in routing curves and circles.

• Multiples. You need to duplicate a curve or circle again and again. A trammel will do it, but it's often faster and easier to position a template than to work with a trammel.
• Holes. Here you confront the difficulty of holding a centerpoint if you're cutting out the area where the point is. Once it is set, the template doesn't need the center point.
• Complex curves. A trammel is great for a constant arc, but what about undulating lines? You need multiple centerpoints, different radii. A lot of setup time, and if you're cutting good stock, you don't have a margin for error. But you can fiddle with a template, trimming and sanding that curve until it is just what you want. Then you can duplicate it *perfectly* with your router.

More details on making and using templates are found in the chapter "Template-Guided Work." Suffice it to say here that you can use your various trammels and router-table pivots to produce the template, then use the template to guide the cut on the good stock.

Circle-Cutting Templates

Before leaving the topic, however, here's a simple-to-make pair of templates that can demonstrate concretely how versatile and useful templates can be in routing curves and circles.

Each template has several holes cut in it, three in one, four in the other, and each corner is rounded at a different radius (eight in all). To rout a matching hole, you simply clamp the template to the work, fit a pattern bit in your router, and let the template guide the router through the cut.

But wait! There's more!

Each template hole can be used to rout at least five different sizes of hole. Use guide bushings to offset the bit from the template edge, and you'll reduce the diameter of the hole that's routed. If you use a ¼-inch bit with a guide bushing whose outside diameter is ¾ inch, you'll reduce the diameter of the template hole by ½ inch.

The sizing chart on page 182 lays it all out for you. Two different guide bushing sizes are used, in combination with three different bit sizes. If you have a broader selection of either bushings or bits, or both, you may be able to come up with some additional sizes. Just as an example, a ¼-inch bit used in a ⁷⁄₁₆-inch O.D. bushing reduces the hole ³⁄₁₆ inch.

Safety First!

Whether you are routing a circle using a trammel or on the router table, feed the work or the tool in a counterclockwise direction. This will keep you out of trouble. With either setup, a clockwise feed yields a climb cut.

When you are using a trammel (or, on a router table, a fixed pivot) to rout a circle *as a groove-forming operation,* feed direction doesn't make a whole lot of difference. The rotation of the bit probably won't help you or hurt you, so long as your pivot is secure. With a clockwise feed—the climb cut— the rotation is pulling on the pivot. With a counterclockwise feed, the rotation is pushing against the pivot.

But if the bit ever emerges from the groove to form an edge, or when the entire cut is *an edge-forming operation,* feed direction becomes a real issue. I'm talking about cutting a circle from a square, when the circle's diameter and the square's width are the same. In this situation, the bit is cutting a groove as it rounds off the corners of the square, but it's forming the edge elsewhere around the circumference. I'm also talking about routing an edge on a disk you've roughed out on the band saw.

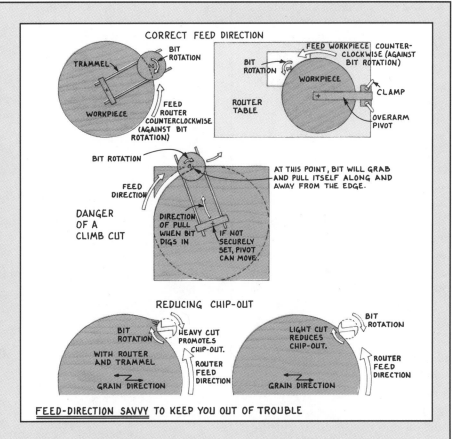

FEED-DIRECTION SAVVY TO KEEP YOU OUT OF TROUBLE

This is a safety issue primarily, because climb cuts are such grabby, galloping cuts. The bit can dig in and jerk the router or the disk out of your control. But when routing a disk from a square, the grab that comes when the bit comes out of the groove can give you a start. If the pivot isn't set securely, it can be jerked out of position.

Feed direction becomes a quality issue because of chip-out. Chip-

out occurs as the cutting edge of the bit sweeps off the wood, taking chips out of the edge. There's often a temptation to make a climb cut to avoid chip-out. In a climb cut, the cutting edge is sweeping into the wood, forcing the wood fibers in, so there are no chips lifting out. A safer approach is to make a light finish cut in the proper (counterclockwise) feed direction, to clean up the edge.

Though each template hole is labeled with the size of hole it'll produce if used with a pattern bit, its range is expanded through the use of guide bushings, as shown here. The bushing's offset reduces the diameter of the hole produced.

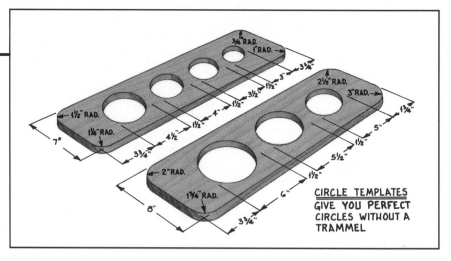

CIRCLE TEMPLATES GIVE YOU PERFECT CIRCLES WITHOUT A TRAMMEL

The 3-inch template hole would then yield a 2¹³⁄₁₆-inch routed hole.

But wait! *There's still more!*

Remember those rounded corners on the templates? Clamp the template at a corner, and you can round the corner using your router and pattern bit. No saw marks to sand away, no ripples or flat spots. Use the same template at each corner of the tabletop, for example, and you can round the corners smoothly and consistently.

The templates give you corner-round guides starting at a ¾-inch radius and jumping in ¼-inch increments to 3 inches.

Making the templates is a simple matter. You can use a fly cutter chucked in a drill press to cut the holes, but Phil Gehret, who made the templates shown, used a small trammel. He laid out the corners using drafting templates, then rounded them off on a stationary sander. Template layouts are shown in the drawing. You *can* make individual templates—one for each size of hole—but ganging them gives you space-efficient clamping area.

Template Diameter	Guide Bushing	Bit Diameter	Hole Diameter
3" hole	¾" O.D.	¼"	2½"
	⅝" O.D.	¼"	2⅝"
	⅝" O.D.	⅜"	2¾"
	⅝" O.D.	½"	2⅞"
	none	pattern bit	3"
3½" hole	¾" O.D.	¼"	3"
	⅝" O.D.	¼"	3⅛"
	⅝" O.D.	⅜"	3¼"
	⅝" O.D.	½"	3⅜"
	none	pattern bit	3½"
4" hole	¾" O.D.	¼"	3½"
	⅝" O.D.	¼"	3⅝"
	⅝" O.D.	⅜"	3¾"
	⅝" O.D.	½"	3⅞"
	none	pattern bit	4"
4½" hole	¾" O.D.	¼"	4"
	⅝" O.D.	¼"	4⅛"
	⅝" O.D.	⅜"	4¼"
	⅝" O.D.	½"	4⅜"
	none	pattern bit	4½"
5" hole	¾" O.D.	¼"	4½"
	⅝" O.D.	¼"	4⅝"
	⅝" O.D.	⅜"	4¾"
	⅝" O.D.	½"	4⅞"
	none	pattern bit	5"
5½" hole	¾" O.D.	¼"	5"
	⅝" O.D.	¼"	5⅛"
	⅝" O.D.	⅜"	5¼"
	⅝" O.D.	½"	5⅜"
	none	pattern bit	5½"
6" hole	¾" O.D.	¼"	5½"
	⅝" O.D.	¼"	5⅝"
	⅝" O.D.	⅜"	5¾"
	⅝" O.D.	½"	5⅞"
	none	pattern bit	6"

SURFACING WITH THE ROUTER

The tools of choice for preparing rough-sawn lumber

are the jointer, thickness planer, and table saw. Nevertheless, there are occasions when the router can do a lumber surfacing job that the three massive, expensive shop tools can't.

- Maybe you're on a remote job site, stuck without the shop tools.
- Or you need to joint a batch of plywood panels, too big to balance on edge on the jointer, and with glues too hard on the jointer knives.
- Or you have a butcher-block slab to trim. It's too heavy to maneuver on the table saw, and it's too wide for the radial arm. And your circular saw will leave an unsuitably ragged cut.
- Perhaps you have a board to be planed that has an impossibly difficult grain, which neither the jointer nor the planer can satisfactorily machine.

- How about hollowing out a thick board? Or planing and smoothing a convex surface? The router can do these jobs. Can the jointer or planer?

If you have the time, the router—set up with the appropriate jig or fixture—can do all of these jobs. Some better than others, but all adequately.

FLUSH TRIMMING

True or false: Flush trimming is an operation used only when working with plastic laminates. Flush trimming is an operation done only with a flush-trimming bit.

Both false, thanks to the "only" in both statements.

Flush trimming *is* an operation used when working with plastic laminates. But it also is done in order to machine edge banding, trim plugs and keys, and level all manner of lumps and projections in otherwise flat surfaces. And, set up with the proper jigs and baseplates, you can do the job with straight bits, mortising bits, pattern bits, and bottom-cleaning bits, as well as flush-trimming bits.

Plugs covering screws that are close to an edge can easily be trimmed with a flush-trimming bit. The off-set-base laminate trimmer is great for this sort of application.

Using a Flush-Trimming Bit

The least complicated flush-trimming setup is a laminate trimmer and a flush-trimming bit. As explained in the chapter "Working Laminates," the laminate trimmer is a compact router, devoid of knobs or handles, designed to fit in one hand. Despite its name, it's good for chores other than trimming plastic laminates. It has enough power to trim edge banding and the like. And it's as perfect a package as the industry has come up with for balancing on a narrow edge.

The flush-trimming bit, though usually listed amongst bits for laminate work, is also useful for jobs beyond that realm. Not only is it useful for trimming wooden edge banding, screw plugs, and keys, it is often used as a pattern bit. (See the chapter "Template-Guided Work.") The bit has two and sometimes three cutting edges and a pilot bearing on the tip. To accomplish its job, it would seem that the cutting diameter should exactly match that of the bearing, but in fact, the cutting diameter is several thousandths of an inch smaller than the bearing. This is so the cutting edge won't slice into the surface that the pilot references. Given the thinness of the color layer in plastic laminates, this is a capital idea.

To trim that edge banding, set the bit height so the cutting edge not only pares the edge banding but also cleans away any glue that's squeezed out of the joint.

The biggest concern may be the potential for bearing tracks. These can range from outright scratches through burn marks to a burnished

TRY THIS!

One of the vexing aspects of using a flush-trimming bit is trying to keep the router—even a little laminate trimmer—square on a narrow edge. If the router wiggles one way, you get a hump, which, of course, you can remove with another pass. But wiggle the other way and you get a snipe out of the material you're trying to trim flush. And that you can't fix up with another pass.

This simple brace that Fred made provides bearing for a laminate trimmer on the face of the workpiece. Hold the trimmer horizontally against the edge being trimmed. Then bear down on the brace to help keep the trimmer square to the edge. (Some router manufacturers make an extra-cost trimming guide that's a lot like this one.)

The brace is easy to make from a scrap of ¾-inch plywood and

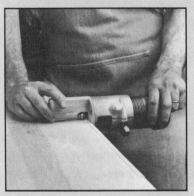

The flush-trimming brace is a simple outrigger that helps you keep the laminate trimmer square to the edge when trimming edge banding. Keep pressure on the brace, as shown. You particularly want to prevent the trimmer from tipping down, which will gouge the edge.

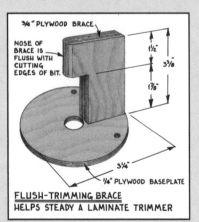

¾" PLYWOOD BRACE

NOSE OF BRACE IS FLUSH WITH CUTTING EDGES OF BIT.

1½"
3⅛"
1⅛"

3¼"

¼" PLYWOOD BASEPLATE

FLUSH-TRIMMING BRACE HELPS STEADY A LAMINATE TRIMMER

another of ¼-inch plywood. To bring the brace's bearing surface flush with the bit's pilot bearing, mount the baseplate on the trimmer, and fit the bit in the collet. Set a square on the baseplate, and use it to carry the plane of the bearing to the edge of the brace. Sand the nose of the brace until it's flush and square with the bearing.

If you don't have a laminate trimmer, this same concept can easily be adapted to a small router. Or attach a wooden facing to the router's edge guide and use it as a brace.

Flush-Trimming Jig

Edge banding can be trimmed with a straight bit if you use this jig. The model shown in the following two photos attaches to a laminate trimmer, but you should be able to adapt the design (and size) to fit any lightweight router.

Just remember that because of the router's position, the balance of the jig can be really hurt by a heavy machine. That's why a lam trimmer is nice.

As you can see, the jig consists of a baseplate attached to a shoe. The side of the shoe is rabbeted and has a hole into which the bit projects. By pivoting the baseplate up and down, you adjust the position of the bit, determining how much or little it will remove from the work. At its highest setting, the bit may not even touch the work, while at its lowest setting, it'll probably cut a rabbet (a fact that might be useful to remember if you have a rabbet to cut).

Bear down on the jig's front end with one hand and push it along the work with the other. You can see how a heavy router would throw the jig way out of balance and increase the work for you.

band that's only visible when the light strikes it at a certain angle. Before you begin, be sure the bearing is clean and that it turns freely. If it has a spur or grit on it, it can scratch. If it's frozen, it will burn the wood. When you work, be sure you don't press the bearing against the work too hard. This can lead to a burnished track. More often, though, burnishing is caused by *too little* pressure, which allows the bearing to spin with the cutter and buff the wood's surface.

To use the jig, you rest the shoe's sole on the work; the rabbet fits over the edge band to be trimmed. Turn on the router and slide the jig along the workpiece, almost as though you were hand planing it. A feed direction note: Because of the orientation of the router, the proper feed direction is right to left. The jig, as shown, is set up to facilitate that.

The hand-planing comparison is pertinent, too, to how you set up the jig. Turn the jig over and sight along the sole as you adjust the baseplate setting. Watch the bit's cutting edge, just as you watch the plane iron when setting it.

The jig is simple to make. The shoe is a piece of poplar 1¼ inches by 3 inches by 12 inches. One edge is rabbeted; the cut is ½ inch wide by ⅛ inch deep. Drill a hole for the

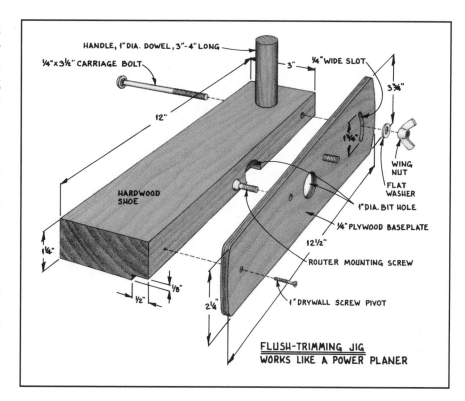

FLUSH-TRIMMING JIG
WORKS LIKE A POWER PLANER

To adjust the bit in the flush-trimming jig, you swing the baseplate on its pivot to raise or lower the router in relation to the shoe. Sight along the sole as you move the baseplate, and watch the bit's cutting edge, just as you watch a hand plane iron when setting it. The cutting edge should be just flush with the sole.

bit into the side that will get the baseplate. Since the hole is offset and is not completely housed, we used a 1-inch-diameter Forstner bit to bore it. Drill a shallow hole for the 1-inch-diameter dowel handle, and glue the dowel in place. Finally, bore a ¼-inch-diameter hole for the baseplate adjustment bolt.

The baseplate is cut from a piece of ¼-inch plywood. The pattern shown will accommodate a Porter-Cable laminate trimmer, and probably most other brands of laminate trimmers, too. For a regular router of light weight, you'll have to enlarge the baseplate.

Cut the shape of the baseplate, and drill the bit hole and mounting-screw holes. Cut the short slot for the adjustment bolt. Then clamp the baseplate to the side of the shoe and drive a 1-inch drywall screw pivot through the plate into the shoe. Install the washer and wing nut, hang the router on it, and you are ready to go.

Edge Band-Trimming Baseplate

So far, I've given you baseplates and jigs that'll work with laminate trimmers, and *maybe* with lightweight routers. But what do woodworkers with regular-sized horse-and-a-half Porter-Cables, Boschs, and the like do? For trimming edge banding, this jig is the answer. It perches the router atop the edge banding and uses a mortising or bottom-cleaning bit to do the trimming.

It has a fair amount in common with the offset baseplate and the homemade edge guide, found in the chapters "Custom Baseplates" and "Dadoing and Grooving," respectively. What makes it different is the recess routed across the bottom at the bit hole. The recess functions exactly the way the rabbet in the flush-trimming jig does, capturing the unit over excess edge banding. The fence bolted to the underside of the baseplate references the edge of the work to guide the router, but it also adjusts to narrow the bit exposure.

The offset of the baseplate helps you steady the unit and keep it flat on the work. The operational bugbear, as with most of these gizmos, is the wobble or tilt, which produces a gouge in the area being trimmed. The hefty knob gives you something to grasp and press firmly upon.

To use the baseplate, replace your router's standard baseplate with it. Fit a ¾-inch bottom-cleaning bit in the collet, and adjust it to just clear a flat surface the baseplate rests on. Adjust the fence to cover the part of the bit that isn't necessary to trim the banding, and cinch it tight.

All set! Place the router on the edge of the work, with the bit perched atop the edge banding and the fence against the work's edge. Tip the router

If you don't have a laminate trimmer, this baseplate allows you to use a regular router and a bottoming-cleaning bit for flush trimming edge banding. Rather than addressing the edge from a horizontal position, the router is upright. And the baseplate has an offset that gives the operator extra leverage to keep the router square to the surface.

so the bit is just free of the work, switch on the machine, and lower the bit.

Ordinarily, left to right is the proper feed direction for this sort of edge-guided operation. But we've found that you reduce the risk of tear-out if you make a climb cut,

which is to say, move the router right to left.

To make the baseplate, begin with a 7¾-inch by 10½-inch rectangle of ½-inch plywood (the baseplate) and a 2½-inch by 7¾-inch strip of ¾-inch hardwood (the fence).

1. Remove your router's factory baseplate, and set it on the plywood. The jig shown is for a router with a 6-inch-diameter baseplate; if yours is larger, increase the width of the plywood accordingly. Since the router is deliberately offset a little toward the pivot edge, there's room for the adjusting slot without increasing the plywood's width. When the finished baseplate is attached to the router, you'll doubtless want the handles aligned either parallel to the fence or perpendicular to it. Position the baseplate mounting holes now so you'll have the router oriented as you prefer it later. Drill and countersink the holes.

2. Fit the bit you're going to use in the router, then mount the plywood on the router. With the router turned on, advance the bit into the plywood, cutting the bit hole. Remove the plywood from the router.

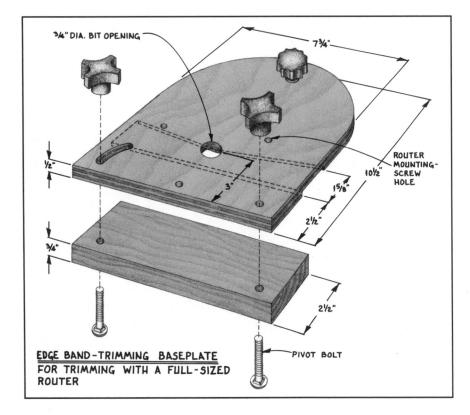

¾" DIA. BIT OPENING

7¾"

ROUTER MOUNTING-SCREW HOLE

½"

10½"

15⅛"

3"

2½"

¾"

2½"

PIVOT BOLT

EDGE BAND-TRIMMING BASEPLATE FOR TRIMMING WITH A FULL-SIZED ROUTER

Muskegon, MI 49444; 800-253-0421; part #DK-330; but a hand-turned knob may be more attractive.

Attach the baseplate to your router and you're ready to trim some edge banding.

Flush-Trimming Baseplate

One last flush-trimming approach, then I'll move on to something else. This baseplate is the one to use where the area to be trimmed is distant from an edge or too wide for other approaches. This is the baseplate I used, for example, to trim the edge banding on the router bench and around the bit cutout on the horizontal router table. For plugs concealing screws, this is ideal.

Flush-Trimming Baseplates shows

The work is done underneath. The recess allows the baseplate to fit over the untrimmed edge banding and sit flat on the countertop. For maneuvering the jig around a corner, the angle of the recess away from the bit needs to be quite steep.

3. Clamp the fence to the bottom of the plywood. The inner edge should be about ⅛ inch shy of the bit hole. Scribe a line along this edge.

Now drill the pivot-bolt hole and the adjusting-bolt hole through the fence and base. Insert the pivot bolt in its hole, and loosen the clamps. Swing the fence on the pivot bolt until it just covers the bit hole. Scribe along the fence to lay out one edge of the recess. Then, using the existing adjusting bolt hole in the fence as a guide, drill through the base a second time. The two holes mark the beginning and end of the adjusting slot. Finally, pull the pivot bolt and insert the adjusting bolt, positioning the fence to lay out the last edge of the recess.

4. Rout the adjusting slot on the router table. Use an overarm pivot inserted in the baseplate's pivot hole to locate the slot's arc from hole to hole.

5. Rout the recess in the baseplate next. Make it about ⅛ inch deep. For the most tidy results, use a fence to position the shoulder cuts, and rout out any remaining waste freehand. It isn't essential that the edges be perfectly straight, of course, so you could do the entire job freehand.

6. To finish up, lay out the shape of the baseplate and cut it on a band saw or with a saber saw. Sand the edges and apply a finish. Bolt the fence in place, and install the knob. We used a plastic knob from Reid Tool Supply, 2265 Black Creek Road,

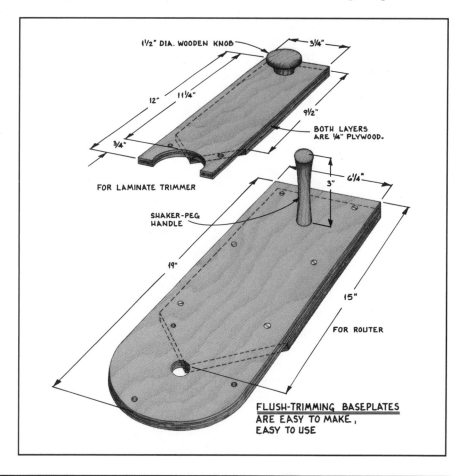

Problem Solver

A saber-saw cut that's not square. A circular-saw cut that's too rough to the touch. A slab that's almost too beefy to move. The problem—getting a smooth, straight, *true* edge—has a lot of forms, but the solution is always the same: Use your router to trim and true the cut.

Minimize setup by using a self-positioning fence, such as the self-positioning dado guide shown in the chapter "Dadoing and Grooving." When you make the cut with a saber saw or circular saw, leave the line; in other words, deliberately cut well to the waste side of the line, so the cut line itself remains visible on the board. Then set your router guide *on* the line and make a pass with a straight bit. The bit will trim right to the line and leave a smooth, square edge.

Of course, if the work is thick and your bit is short, the base of the self-positioning fence may rob you of essential depth of cut. Go to a T-square and position it with a locating jig. (Both of these are also described in the chapter "Dadoing and Grooving.")

To prevent tear-out at the end of the cut, clamp scrap wood to the edges of the work.

If all you are doing is truing the edge, routing away about 1/16 inch of stock, then a single pass that addresses the full thickness of the stock should do the trick. Use the

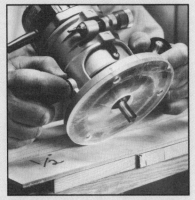

A saber saw blade seldom makes a truly square cut. Because the blade is thin and fixed at only one end, it tends to flex as it cuts, giving you a cut edge that wavers between about 85 degrees and 95 degrees. The solution, of course, is to trim the edge with your router and straight bit, which gives you a clean edge.

largest-diameter straight you have to get the smoothest finish. The bit should be long enough to extend about 1/4 inch below the bottom of the stock.

If you are actually making the cut with your router, do it in a series of passes. Make the cut 1/4 inch deeper with each pass. If the stock is thick—say 8/4 oak or 10/4 maple—try cutting about halfway through, then turning the slab over to rout from the other side. When you are through, after the waste has fallen away, shift your fence 1/32 inch or so and make a last full-depth pass to really clean that edge.

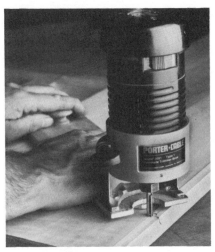

To avoid gouging the work, the router must be held upright by pressing down firmly at the end of the long baseplate extension with one hand. Grasp the baseplate near the router with your other hand, and oscillate the machine in small circles, nibbling at the waste.

JOINTING WITH A ROUTER

There's a certain chicken-or-egg quality to this operation. Maybe you picked up on it. Why, you ask, would anyone joint with a router? Well, you tell yourself, because he (or she) doesn't have a jointer. He (or she) has to joint boards for edge-gluing, and the router can make a square, clean cut along the edge of a board. An essential, of course, is a straight, true fence to guide either the router or the work. And how do you get that? Why, you joint . . . it . . . .

Ahhh . . . The sigh of recognition.

Well, recognize, first of all, that your router can do a darn good job substituting for a jointer. If you don't have a jointer, if you want to joint glue-laden materials like plywood or medium-density fiberboard (MDF), if you want to joint a board or panel

two different sizes of baseplate. One is for the laminate trimmer, the other for a regular router.

In both versions, the idea is to raise the router 1/4 to 1/2 inch above the surface so it can clear protrusions. You set the bit so it's just clear of the surface. Advance the bit right up to the protrusion, be it a plug concealing a screw or a strip of edge band-

ing, and begin nibbling at its edges. As you work, the baseplate can slide onto the newly trimmed surface, as you extend the trimmed area even further.

To make either baseplate, cut the upper layer to size, fit the router to one end, then glue the bottom layer to it. Add a knob of some sort, and you are ready to trim.

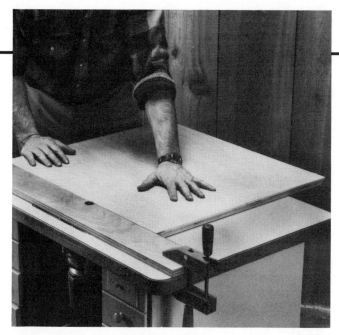

Before edge-banding a plywood panel, you want to joint it. Standing this broad panel on edge to run it across the jointer would be venturesome, to say the least. But you can slide it across the router table's broad surface confidently, jointing it with a carbide-tipped straight bit.

that's too big to maneuver, think seriously about using the router. You can do the job on the router table with an easily made jointing fence, or using a hand-held router guided by a straight edge.

And how do you get that straight edge without a jointer? Plywood, of course. The factory edge is going to be straight and true. Make your fence using that edge as the guide.

But remember, too, that even though you have—or have access to—a jointer, you still might want to do selected jointing with your router. *One example:* Jointing man-made panels on the jointer will dull its cutters pretty quickly. A carbide-tipped straight bit will joint miles of MDF or plywood without losing its edge. *Others:* jointing the freshly cross-cut edge of a butcher-block panel that's much too heavy to maneuver on the jointer. Or jointing a bowed board that simply can't be held against the jointer fence, though it can be clamped flat to joint with a hand-held router.

Using a Hand-Held Router

One of the best ways to joint a board is with a hand-held router. All you really need is an absolutely straight and true guide that's about half a foot longer than the board that needs to be jointed. Plywood, particleboard, or MDF fit the bill, certainly. The factory edge on any of these should be straight and true, and so long as you don't leave it in the rain, it should remain so. Cut a 4-inch-wide strip from a new sheet, mark the factory edge, and use that edge as the guide. A strip cut across the sheet will do boards up to 3½ feet long, while an 8-foot strip cut from the long dimension of the sheet will serve for boards up to about 7½ feet long.

You can reference the router base against this fence, but you can also reference the pilot bearing of a flush-trimming bit (or a pattern bit) against the fence. It depends upon where you position the fence vis-à-vis the edge to be jointed.

As you set the fence, bear in mind that you should trim no more than 1/16 inch from the edge.

Because any bit you use must address the full thickness of the board at once, it has to be a stout one. Use the largest-diameter ½-inch-shank bit in your collection. Its cutting edges should be ¼ to ½ inch longer than the board's thickness.

• If you're using a pattern bit, the fence can be set atop the workpiece and clamped to the work with just the amount of stock that's to be removed exposed.

• Using a flush-trimming bit means the fence must be clamped to the underside of the work, again, with just the amount of stock that's to be removed standing proud of the fence edge. Because the fence is beneath the work, getting it set can be troublesome.

• If you're guiding the router base against the fence, setup is easy. Use a locator like the T-square locating jig. A big brother to the self-positioning dado guide is even easier to set up. (Both of these gizmos are described in the chapter "Dadoing and Grooving.")

In any case, the fence has to be protected from bumps and dings if you intend to maintain it as your jointing fence. Any dip or dent will be telegraphed into the workpiece edge. (The fence-rider baseplate shown in the chapter "Custom Baseplates"—or a baseplate with a similar straight edge—will skim over dips and dents without telegraphing them into the cut, though it will magnify ridges, bumps, or any other *projection* on the fence edge.)

Working on the Router Table

To joint on a router table, you need a jointing fence. But it's a different sort of fence than the one used with a hand-held router. Like the jointer's infeed and outfeed tables, the router table's jointing fence needs infeed and outfeed sections, adjusted to support the work both before the bit trims away stock and after.

The most simple jointing fence is a strip of ¾-inch plywood with a bit notch and a strip of plastic laminate glued to it, left of the bit, as shown in *Jointing Fence*. You can bond the laminate to the fence with contact cement, or you can use double-sided carpet tape. The fence doesn't need to be as high as the stock being jointed, though of course the bit does.

If you've equipped your router table with a split fence, as presented in the chapter "Router Table Accessories," you don't need a jointing fence. All you have to do is adjust the two fence sections separately, to serve as infeed and outfeed supports.

The least vexing way to do this, according to Fred, who knows this stuff, is to line up the two sections using a straightedge. Then set the fence to remove the amount of stock you have in mind, say, ¹⁄₁₆ inch. Feed a test board along the infeed half of the fence, across the bit, and about a foot beyond. Stop, and turn off the

BIT DRAWER

If you want to use a flush-trimming bit to joint boards and you are really serious about it, get yourself the mother-of-all-really-serious-flush-trimmers, made by Paso Robles Carbide. It's called a face-frame trimmer.

The bit is ideal for squaring up large, thick, *heavy* panels. Butcher-block sort of stuff. Crosscut the work with a circular saw, then plane and true the end-grain edge with this trimmer in a hand-held router. And even though the bit is a flush-trimmer, it can be used in a router table with a jointing fence setup.

On a ½-inch, heat-treated shank, Paso Robles mounts a 1⅛-inch-diameter, 2½-inch-long spiral power-plane cutter. The pilot can be mounted above or below the cutter. And because it is soft-rimmed, the pilot can be resized when the cutter is sharpened. This is a BIG bit, and you need BIG power to run it—a minimum, says Paso Robles, of 2½ horsepower. I've used it in a 2-horsepower Milwaukee router with good results.

The relatively large diameter of the cutter helps minimize chip-out. The spiral contour of the cutting edges allows the bit to slice the wood rather than chop it, yielding a particularly smooth surface.

The price is pretty big, too: The face frame trimmer lists for over $100. See, I said you had to be serious. (If the size and price trouble you, consider the half-height version, also shown in the photo.)

To set up the router table jointing fence, hold a straightedge against the outfeed side of the fence. Align the cutting edge of the bit flush with the straightedge.

The split fence is easy to set up for jointing, and it allows you to vary the cut depth much more easily than the jointing fence. To set the fence, mark the amount of material you want to remove on the workpiece (top). Use that mark to set the fence. Cut about 10 inches of the workpiece (center), then stop. Note the gap between the workpiece and the outfeed fence. With the workpiece held firmly against the infeed fence (bottom), loosen the outfeed fence. Push it up to the workpiece, then retighten it. Now you can complete this first cut and make subsequent cuts with the work fully supported on both infeed and outfeed sides of the bit.

┐ **BIT DRAWER**

The biggest constraint in using the router for jointing is the bit's cutting-edge length. The typical straight bit has a 1-inch cutting capacity, with longer ones extending that to 1½ inches. With the longer bits, you can barely handle a 6/4 board.

Freud has a ½-inch straight—catalog number 12-130—with a 2½-inch cutting length. (See "Sources" on page 337.) This is the longest straight bit I've seen. Cutting judiciously, you should be able to joint up to 10/4 stock with this bit. And you can use it for many other straight-bit jobs.

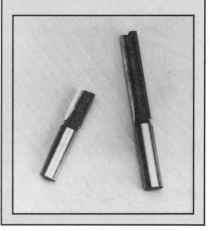

router. The board should be free of the outfeed fence. Clamp the board tightly against the infeed fence, and adjust the outfeed fence so it supports the routed edge. Remove the clamp and resume routing the test board. It should be supported through the remainder of the cut by both the infeed and outfeed fences. If this is the case, you are set up to joint your good stock.

The ideal bit, in all these cases, is a fairly heavy but well-balanced straight bit. Always use a ½-inch-shank bit if possible.

Just as you can taper legs on a jointer, you can do it on the router table. And you'll probably feel safer doing it with the router, too. Mark the extremity of the cutting edge on the tabletop, and mark where you want the taper to begin on the leg blank. Line up the two marks and "joint" from that point to the end of the leg. Keep repeating this operation until you've achieved the degree of taper you want.

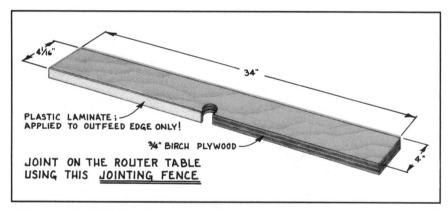

4 1/16"

34"

PLASTIC LAMINATE;
APPLIED TO OUTFEED EDGE ONLY!

3/4" BIRCH PLYWOOD

4"

JOINT ON THE ROUTER TABLE
USING THIS <u>JOINTING FENCE</u>

The horizontal router table can easily function as a jointer. Use carpet tape to stick a strip of plastic laminate to the tabletop—forming the outfeed surface and establishing the amount of stock to be removed per pass. Set the bit's cutting edge flush with this surface.

THICKNESSING

Now we're getting to the gut of this chapter—surfacing rough stock. Yes, you can dress stock using a router.

But make no mistake here. You'd be nuts to habitually prepare lumber using the router. You can't beat the jointer-planer–table saw ensemble to dress rough-sawn boards, making the faces smooth, flat, and parallel and the edges smooth, square, and parallel. The job can be done quickly and accurately by any beginner. And even if you don't have the dough for a jointer and a planer, you usually can buy the service economically from your lumber dealer.

BUT every once in a while, there's a special project where router thicknessing is appropriate. Maybe it is centered around a curly maple board—beautiful but difficult to surface without tear-out. Or you've acquired a small log of some native exotic, a log you can saw into boards on your band saw. Perhaps you need a small amount of thin stock for a box or for a drawer or two. There are a lot of reasons to do it. Someday, you may have a problem, and router thicknessing will be your solution.

Here are the basics of how to do it.

What you need is a sturdy router, a large-diameter bottom-cleaning kind of bit, and a fixture that suspends the router above the stock, allowing it to move side to side and back and forth in a level plane.

We've got a surfacing platform here that's pretty flexible. It'll accommodate stock a few inches wide by a few inches long, up to a 3-foot-long plank that's 2 1/4 inches thick and 11 inches wide. You can build it and, when you have a board to thickness that's in its range, pull it off the shelf. Obviously, you can change the dimensions to revise the range. Or you can keep the concept in mind and make a job-specific fixture when the need arises.

The Surfacing Platform

The concept of the platform is this: The workpiece rests between two level tracks. A double-rail carriage that supports the router spans the tracks. The carriage is designed so the router can slide from one track to the other. And the carriage can slide from one end of the tracks to the other.

To plane a board, you set it between the tracks, with the router in its carriage at one corner. Then you slide the carriage along the tracks, routing a strip as wide as the bit from one end of the board to the other. Move the router in its carriage an increment, and slide the carriage back, widening the machined strip. Just keep moving the router and sliding the carriage. It's a methodical, even tedious, operation, but it gets the job done.

The platform consists of a base with two sides—the tracks. One side is fixed (though it is easily removed). The second side adjusts, as *Surfacing Platform and Carriage* makes clear. The base must be flat—plywood, particleboard, and MDF are good materials for it. The sides must be straight and true. A straight-grained hardwood makes durable, as well as smooth-sliding, tracks. The carriage consists of two rails and two guides, cut from the same stock as the sides.

The real key to getting flat stock with parallel faces from the platform is accuracy in the platform itself. Each side must be straight with par-

The surfacing platform has two parts: a base with tracks and a carriage for the router. You set the material to be surfaced on the base between the tracks, and you set the router that's to do the surfacing in the carriage. Work your way across the stock in a series of back-and-forth passes, smoothing and flattening it. The setup is useful for surfacing badly twisted boards, end grain (as here), and material with particularly gnarled grain.

CUTTING LIST

Piece	Number	Thickness	Width	Length	Material
Base	1	¾"	19½"	42"	Plywood
Sides	2	1¼"	2½"	42"	Hardwood
Carriage rails	2	1¼"	2"	20"	Hardwood
Carriage guides	2	1¼"	2"	10¾"	Hardwood
Spacers*	2	¾"	12"	42"	Plywood
Spacers*	2	¼"	12"	42"	Plywood
Spacers*	2	½"	12"	42"	Plywood

Hardware

6 pcs. ⁵⁄₁₆" × 3" flathead stove bolts
6 pcs. ⁵⁄₁₆" T-nuts
4 pcs. ¼" × 3" carriage bolts
4 pcs. ¼" flat washers
4 pcs. ¼" wing nuts

*Optional

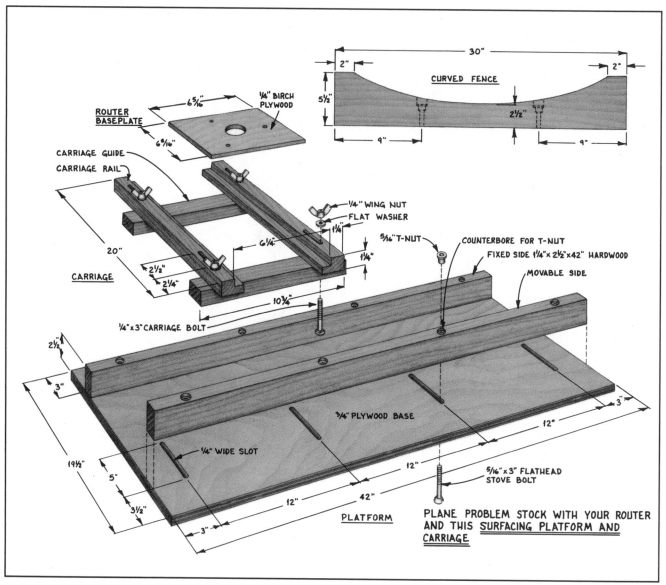

ROUTER BASEPLATE

¼" BIRCH PLYWOOD

CURVED FENCE

CARRIAGE GUIDE
CARRIAGE RAIL

¼" WING NUT
FLAT WASHER

⁵⁄₁₆" T-NUT

COUNTERBORE FOR T-NUT
FIXED SIDE 1¼"× 2½"×42" HARDWOOD

MOVABLE SIDE

CARRIAGE

¼"×3" CARRIAGE BOLT

¾" PLYWOOD BASE

¼" WIDE SLOT

⁵⁄₁₆"×3" FLATHEAD STOVE BOLT

PLATFORM

PLANE PROBLEM STOCK WITH YOUR ROUTER
AND THIS SURFACING PLATFORM AND
CARRIAGE

allel edges, and the sides must be of identical height. If one side is even ¹⁄₆₄ inch higher than the other, whatever you machine in the platform will have a slight taper across its faces. This important caveat aside, the platform is easy to make.

1. Cut the parts to the sizes specified by the Cutting List. You don't *have* to cut the spacers, but depending on the stock you are starting with and its final thickness, it may be handy to have several spacers to boost it up in the platform.

2. Position the sides 3 inches from the edges of the base and clamp them. Drill the mounting-screw holes through them. (For the adjustable side, these holes will serve as the starting points for the slots.) Countersink the holes for the fixed side. With a Forstner bit, slightly counterbore the holes on the sides, so the T-nuts will be slightly recessed. Drive the T-nuts into place.

3. Use a router and straight bit to extend 5-inch-long slots from the mounting holes for the adjustable

side. I used a T-square to guide the router, and I eyeballed the length of the cut, which isn't *that* critical. After the slots are cut through, use a V-groove bit to "countersink" each slot.

4. Bolt the sides to the base, and make sure the bolt ends don't extend above the sides' top edges (they shouldn't even be flush). They've got to be *below* the surface for the carriage to slide easily.

5. With the platform done, turn to the carriage. Cut a ¾-inch by ¾-inch rabbet into each rail. Mark and rout the 2½-inch-long slots for the adjusting bolts that secure the guides to the rails. These are easiest to cut on a router table.

6. Assemble the carriage, bolting the guides to the rails.

BIT DRAWER

The best bit to use for surfacing is designed chiefly for hollowing out compartments in a tray. It's called a dish cutter. The one shown is from CMT.

What makes the dish cutter ideal for surfacing? The cutting edges are radiused at the bottom of the bit. This gives you a nice radius inside a recess, but it also means you don't have a hard edge between adjacent passes.

CMT offers the dish cutter in several sizes, in both ¼-inch- and ½-inch-shank configurations. The one in the photo has a cutting diameter of 1¼ inches, which means you cut a broader swath than with a ½-inch or ¾-inch straight bit. Because of the radiused edges, you do have to overlap passes a bit more than if you were using a 1¼-inch bottom-cleaning bit. But the latter bit tends to leave ridges between sweeps.

The CMT bit is also available with a bearing on the shank, which allows you to use it with a template.

An optional part of the rig is a square baseplate. Some routers, plungers particularly, have a flat edge or two on their bases. But most are round, and the round ones, we've found, tend to rock on the carriage. The solution is a square or rectangular baseplate. I've found surfacing is a job where a good view of the bit and the workpiece is important. Clear acrylic or polycarbonate thus might be your best choice.

Using the platform and carriage is not difficult. The workpiece has to be about 4 to 6 inches shorter than the platform, of course, so the bit can move off the edge of the work without the carriage tumbling off the ends of the tracks. (You may even want to tack stops to the ends of the tracks to prevent this from happening accidentally.)

Trapping the stock may be the hardest part. To avoid gouging the sides, you should set them so there's about a half-inch of space between each side and the workpiece. Center the workpiece, then tap wedges between stock and sides to keep it from shifting.

Four-quarter stock will probably have to be elevated so the bit can reach it, and anything thinner than

that surely will need a lift into the router bit's range. You should be able to mix and match the different spacers listed in the Cutting List to put even the thinnest stock where you need it. Keep your roll of double-sided carpet tape handy if you are concerned that either the workpiece or the spacers will shift.

The most troublesome stock to position for machining is warped stuff. Yet this is stock that's best reserved for router thicknessing. If it's warped enough, it can be the devil to joint flat so you can feed it through the planer. And if you plane it without flattening one face, you'll get a smooth but still warped board—smooth because the planer's feed rollers will press it flat while it's in the machine, warped because it'll be warped when the pressure of the rollers is off. So if you can plant the board and use the router to plane one face flat, you can plane the second face in the planer *or* in the router thicknessing rig.

What you need to do is set the warped stock in your platform, and shim the corners as necessary so it doesn't rock, like shimming cabinets to level them during installation. Try to set the board so you can get a

Warped and oddly shaped material, such as this disk cut from the base of a cypress trunk, is a challenge to set in the platform, but the effort can save it from the woodstove. At those spots where the stock curls up off the base, slide shims under it. The goal is to steady the stock. Then drive wedges between the stock and the sides, as here, to keep it from shifting.

Because the cutter isn't addressing the entire width of the material in a single pass, it's natural to have some indications of overlap. In the job shown—surfacing cypress end grain—the quality of the initial pass is affected also by the extremely soft, punky character of the wood. The feed rate also has an impact; rough tracks suggest that the router was moved too quickly.

flat surface with minimal stock removal. When the board is set, tap those wedges in place, so it doesn't shift. Then you're ready to set up the router.

Set the carriage in place and adjust the guides. Chuck the bit, set the depth of cut to remove no more than 1/8 to 3/16 inch from the high spots, and place the router in the carriage. Then rout.

The conventional wisdom seems to be that you must make your sweeps in the direction that the grain runs. In our experience, that doesn't seem to be the case. Sweeping back and forth across the board doesn't yield a lesser finish than coursing from end to end. As Fred points out, the router bit's cutting edges don't sweep the surface in the same way that planer and jointer cutters do. Cut across the grain or against the grain on one of these machines, and you will have a choppy finish. But with the router, however you move the router itself, the bit is addressing the wood with the same motion. It is just this difference in cutting action that enables the router to plane curly maple and other twisted-grain woods.

Be methodical, however. Wheth-

er you work back and forth or end to end, be an automaton. Sweep on one axis, then click over a notch in the other. Sweep, then click over. Sweep, then click over.

After a first pass over the entire surface, make as many additional passes as necessary to flatten the board. Then make a final skim cut to make the surface as smooth as you can get it with the router. Scraping and sanding will then remove any remaining tracks or swirl marks.

Job-Specific Setups

The surfacing platform is my style, the job-specific setup is Fred's. He'll make some ugly fixture that works for the job at hand, and not worry about whether it'll adapt to another job. If he ever does another job requiring that fixture, he'll just make the needed fixture then. And the one he makes then may be considerably different from the one he's making now. "Why make more of the setup than you need to?" seems to be his attitude. Very practical.

A while back, Fred made a wide plywood baseplate for one of the Rodale shop's routers and fitted it with two handle grips. (See *Fred's Surfacing Baseplate;* how to duplicate it should be evident.) It doesn't have stops, and it can be used to do wide lap joints and a lot of other work, as you'll see. But he's used it for thicknessing, too. To do that, all Fred does is set up tracks on both sides of the board. He might screw them to a base, but more likely he'll plant a track on both sides of the board, then trap the works between the vise and a bench dog, or set it all up on a couple of bar clamps. The surfacing baseplate is the carriage he uses.

The completed work won't be pristine. But it will be flat and sufficiently smooth that a lick or two with a belt sander or a cabinet scraper can finish it. Compare the rough disk with the routed and belt-sanded one on top of it.

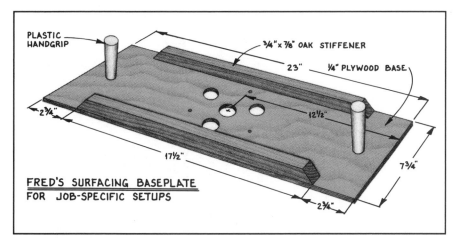

FRED'S SURFACING BASEPLATE
FOR JOB-SPECIFIC SETUPS

PLASTIC HANDGRIP

¾" x ⅞" OAK STIFFENER

23"

¼" PLYWOOD BASE

2¾"

12½"

17½"

7¾"

2¾"

Everything he does is the same as what I do, except that Fred's tracks get chewed up and tossed out when the job's done, and mine see use another day. (And mine take up space in the shop until that day, Fred points out.)

SHAPING SURFACES

Beyond thicknessing, the router can surface stock in ways that a planer or jointer cannot. It can excavate a recess. It can taper. It can hollow out a concave depression, or cut away the edges, forming a hump. A determined and creative woodworker can probably produce an undulating surface with it.

Excavating Recesses

It's a small step from thicknessing a board to routing a recess in it. Use the surfacing platform and carriage, but plunge the bit into the stock, rather than sweeping in from an edge. This is easiest to do if you use a plunge router.

Work out a system of stops to confine the area that the router bit can address, so that you surface only the area to be relieved. You don't want to accidentally move outside the recess area. A drywall screw driven partway into the track or rail is all you need for a stop.

A job-specific approach would be to make a template and attach it to the work. Then, with a guide bushing mounted in Fred's surfacing base-

plate, do the job as a template-guided one. See the chapter ''Template-Guided Work'' for more on this.

If you have a large area to excavate—to make a pie-crust tabletop, for example—the platform and carriage simply have to be reconfigured to accommodate the workpiece.

Tapered Surfaces

Tapering is accomplished two ways. You can use tapered tracks with the surfacing rig. Or you can use tracks of different heights. Which approach you use depends upon the stock and what you are trying to achieve. Tapering a board from edge to edge? Use tracks of different heights. Tapering table legs? Use tapered tracks.

Make the appropriate tracks for the surfacing platform. Drill and counterbore the mounting holes, and insert the T-nuts. Depending upon your approach, remove one or both of the standard tracks, and install the tapering tracks.

Setting the stock is the same as for thicknessing, and the router operation itself is the same. Just the result is different.

Rout a recess, forming a small tray, with a roundnose pattern bit. Here, the bit is in a router mounted on Fred's surfacing baseplate. The workpiece has a template clamped to it. The baseplate spans the template, and the bit, since it's a pattern bit, has a bearing on the shank that keeps it from cutting into the template.

To taper blanks for hand mirrors, Fred traps the blank between tracks of different heights. When his surfacing baseplate is rested on the tracks, it's tilted. The simplicity of the setup is evident.

Forming Convex and Concave Surfaces

If this is all a logical progression, then the next step is to machine rises and depressions, using the same basic technique. If the tracks are cut to a concave or convex curve, the router carriage will rise and fall (or fall and rise, as the case may be) as it is advanced along them. The bit will penetrate deeper at one point than at another.

If you like cabinets or other furniture pieces with curved surfaces, this is a great way to produce those surfaces.

The surfacing platform can be adapted to this work easily. Just change the tracks. The stock carriage should work fine. (You don't have to keep the fences when the job's done. Unless you are going to use them again and again, just toss them.)

Work out your curve, laying it out directly on a piece of the track stock or laying it out on a template. A good way to find a fair curve requires a relatively thin strip of wood, plywood, acrylic, plastic laminate, or even metal as a guide. Flex it so it

The only real difference between flattening a board with the surfacing platform and scooping out a hollow with it is the contour of the tracks. With these curved tracks, it's easy to hollow a plank, something you can't do on a jointer or with a planer.

bows. Have a helper trace along the strip to record the curve. You can mark starting and ending spots, as well as the deepest (or highest) part of the curve, and develop an even curve that connects them. (Check through the previous chapter, "Routing Curves and Circles," for ideas on using your router to create the arcs you need.)

However you do it, lay out and then cut the curve for the tracks. Make the curve as smooth and even as you can. If you can get one good track, use a your router and a flush-trimming bit to produce a duplicate.

Drill the mounting holes, install the T-nuts, and mount the tracks on your surfacing platform.

To get the curve aligned properly on the workpiece, you have to position it carefully between the tracks. Scribe centerlines across both the tracks and the workpiece. When you fit the work between the tracks, line up its centerline with those on the tracks. Fit scraps against the ends of the work and clamp them to the platform. This will prevent the work from shifting out of alignment. Then use the wedges to secure the work so it doesn't shift from side to side.

Set the carriage in place and drop the router into it. If you are using a plunge router—it will make it easier to get to the finished depth if you do—slide the carriage to position the bit at the beginning of the cut. Lower the bit until it just touches the wood, then set the depth stop so that this is the deepest the bit will be able to cut.

To begin routing, raise the bit so you'll be taking off between ⅛ inch and ¼ inch at the point of deepest penetration. Start with the carriage at one end of the track and the router positioned at one side. Slide the car-

Laying out a smooth, even curve calls for a flexible strip of thin wood, metal, or, as here, acrylic, and a couple of hand screws. Stand the strip on edge and clamp one end to the workpiece. Flex the free end until you have a curve that appeals to you. Clamp the free end, then trace the strip's shape onto the work.

TRY THIS!

Customize your surfacing platform so you can use it to hollow seats for stools. All it takes is a lazy-Susan bearing and a couple of plywood squares to make a swivel base.

To use the swivel, you mount a blank on it, then position it between the concave fences. Chuck the appropriate bit in the router, set the cutting depth, then lock the router in the center of its carriage. As you make a pass with the router, hold the blank. (The swivel spins easily, and you'll quickly discover that the bit can make it really whirl.) When the bit is free of the work, turn the blank ever so slightly. Make another pass. Turn the blank again, and make another pass. Just keep at it until the entire blank is hollowed.

Making the swivel is easy. You need a 6-inch lazy-Susan bearing. The base is an 11-inch-square piece of ¼-inch plywood. Scribe centerlines on it, dividing it into quarters, then scribe diagonals. Set the bearing on it and mark where you will drive screws that will mount one of the bearing's flanges to the base; these points should be on the diagonals. On the centerlines, mark

the centers of the access holes. Cut the access holes, including one at the center of the base. Now screw the bearing to the base.

Lay out and cut the turntable next. Its diameter should equal the diagonal dimension of the bearing. Drill a pilot hole at the turntable's center. Then mount the turntable on the bearing. Be sure it is centered.

To mount a blank on the turntable, drive a screw through the centerpoint of the turntable into the blank's centerpoint. One screw is all it takes to secure the work.

Scoop out a stool seat on your surfacing platform! With seat blank mounted on the turntable and the router pinned in the middle of the carriage, simply feed it back and forth on the curved tracks. To keep the turntable from moving when you make a pass, stick a strip of scrap between the track and the turntable. Just use a strip that's long enough to keep your hand clear of the router.

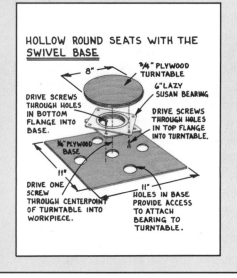

HOLLOW ROUND SEATS WITH THE SWIVEL BASE

8"

¾" PLYWOOD TURNTABLE

6" LAZY SUSAN BEARING

DRIVE SCREWS THROUGH HOLES IN BOTTOM FLANGE INTO BASE.

DRIVE SCREWS THROUGH HOLES IN TOP FLANGE INTO TURNTABLE.

¼" PLYWOOD BASE

11"

DRIVE ONE SCREW THROUGH CENTERPOINT OF TURNTABLE INTO WORKPIECE.

11"

HOLES IN BASE PROVIDE ACCESS TO ATTACH BEARING TO TURNTABLE.

riage to the other end of the tracks, shift the router slightly, and return. Shift the router and make another pass. Work methodically in this fashion until you have completed a first pass over the entire workpiece. Plunge a little deeper and repeat the process.

Make as many additional passes as necessary to achieve the curve you've laid out. Make the final pass a skimming cut to leave the surface as smooth as you can get it with the router. Scraping and sanding will then remove any remaining tracks, swirl marks, or unevenness.

FRAME-AND-PANEL CONSTRUCTION

The early woodworker dealt with wood's instability

using frame-and-panel construction. The rails and stiles forming the frame are relatively narrow, and the dimensional changes in it that accompany humidity changes are correspondingly modest. While the panel is much wider than the stiles, it's set into a groove or rabbet in such a way that dimensional changes are "absorbed" without damaging the structure, even cosmetically. So the frame contributes dimensional stability, and the panel (usually) contributes good looks.

The most commonplace examples of frame-and-panel construction are doors and windows. It's used in elaborate architectural paneling and in custom cabinetry and furniture. In these uses, frame-and-panel construction is styled to be attractive as well as functional. But inside casework, it can be functional, and appearance is of little consequence.

The router can be a pivotal tool in profiling and joining the frame members and in shaping the panels. In a well-equipped production shop, the shaper is the tool used. But the router can do the job, regardless of the joinery selected.

MAKING FRAMES

The minimal frame consists of two stiles and two rails. When the frame is displayed vertically, as in a cabi-

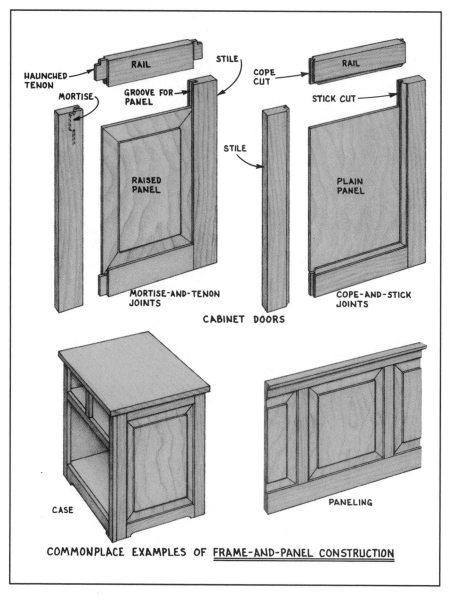

COMMONPLACE EXAMPLES OF FRAME-AND-PANEL CONSTRUCTION

net door, the stiles are the vertical elements and the rails the horizontal elements. The rails invariably fit between the stiles. The edges are unembellished.

In more elaborate constructions, the frame can have three or more rails, as well as intermediate vertical members called mullions or muntins. The edges are embellished with quarter rounds, ogees, coves, or combinations of these shapes.

A number of different joints can be used to assemble the frame: miters, laps, dowels, biscuits, and—the strongest, the most traditional—mortise-and-tenon.

One of the big challenges in frame-and-panel construction is finding practical, economical ways to meld strength and utility with beauty. The joinery has to be strong, especially if the unit is to be a door. A mortise-and-tenon is the traditional framing joint, since it resists all four forms of stress (tension, compression, shear, and racking). But it can be time-consuming to make, especially if you are assembling a couple dozen cabinet doors. And attractive appearance is often as important as the joinery. Adding a series of operations to embellish a workpiece adds to the project's cost.

In relatively recent years, more and more of these frames—for cabinet doors in particular—have been assembled with what's known as the cope-and-stick joint (sometimes it's called a cope-and-pattern joint). It's a form of the mortise and stub tenon that's cut on the shaper or router table. At the same time that the joinery is cut, the piece is embellished. The woodworker's productivity is increased!

The router bit used has two cutters on the shank. One forms a decorative profile on the edge of the frame member while at the same time the other cuts the groove for the panel. The bit is reconfigured (by repositioning these cutters), then it's used to cut the ends of the rails, forming a tongue and a reverse of the decorative profile. When the cuts are properly aligned on the workpieces, the tongue fits into the groove and the rail end conforms perfectly to the profile. Bonded with a modern glue, it is a strong joint.

The terms *cope* and *stick* are carryovers from hand-tool woodworking. Cope is the more familiar term, since it is the name of the technique carpenters still use to fit one piece of architectural trim to another at inside corners. The pertinent dictionary definition of *cope* is "to shape one structural member to conform to the shape of another member."

Stick, as it's used here, isn't in the dictionary. In the old days, a woodworker would clamp—or "stick"—a board to his workbench, then use a profile plane to form a decorative shape on an edge. Then he'd rip the shaped edge from the wider board. The process was called sticking.

One focus of this chapter is setting up and making cope-and-stick frames. We won't go into mortise-and-tenon joinery here, because it merits its own complete chapter. Nor will we get into routing decorative edges on frame members, because it is covered thoroughly in the chapter "Decorative Treatments." Suffice it to say that cope-and-stick joinery is just one of several frame construction options available to the router woodworker.

Preparing the Stock

Cope-and-stick bits, by industry convention, are designed to work with ¾-inch stock. This is a standard stock thickness in most areas of the United States and Canada. If you buy dressed stock, you should have no problems.

There is some leeway in the bit design, comfortably about 1/16 inch either way, but as much as ⅛ inch either way if you really stretch it. The typical sticking bit is designed to produce a ⅜-inch cut and leave a tongue ⅛ inch wide as the groove's panel-retaining wall. If your stock's

thickness dictates it, you can shift the position of the cut slightly to either reduce the profile width and increase the groove wall's thickness or vice versa. That's the leeway.

If you find yourself with stock that's a 16th light or heavy, you'll still be okay. With 11/16-inch stock, you'll be able to finesse the bit height to produce a panel-retaining wall that's 3/32 to ⅛ inch thick without noticeably affecting the profile. And if your stock is thicker, say, 13/16 inch, you can hold the width of the profile while increasing the groove-wall thickness (which might be considered a plus).

The usual wood specs apply: Use defect-free, straight-grained lumber.

We usually take such provisos with a grain of salt, and you can get away with using slightly bowed or twisted stock for a frame-and-panel unit *so long as it isn't a door.* If the wood in a frame-and-panel unit is warped, the unit will be warped. If the unit is a structural part of case, it will be anchored to other elements that will pull it into line and hold it there. But if it is a door, it won't hang flat, and you won't be able to conceal that.

For doors, the stock *must* be flat, straight, and true.

Dress the chosen stock to whatever thickness you've settled on. Rip it to width, and crosscut it to rough lengths for rails and stiles. You can trim the rails to final length after making the sticking cut. Trim the stiles after assembly. Make several extra pieces to use for testing the setups (and to replace the good piece that gets screwed up along the way). Finally, set aside one length of the working stock so you can make a coped backer for the sled you use when making the cope cuts.

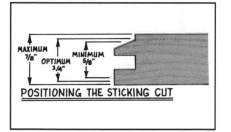

POSITIONING THE STICKING CUT

MAXIMUM 7/8" · OPTIMUM 3/4" · MINIMUM 5/8"

There are three styles of cope-and-stick cutters on the market: the two-bit set, the assembly, and the stacked bit.

All these styles are marketed in an assortment of profiles: bead, quarter-round, ogee, cove-and-bead (sometimes called classical), and bevel (sometimes called traditional or straight). All, however, cut a groove ¼ inch wide and ⅜ inch deep.

A 1½-horsepower router has enough power to drive one of these bits, and it can be run at full speed. While some bit makers offer these sets or assemblies on ¼-inch shanks, it's a much better proposition to buy them on ½-inch shanks.

Solid two-bit sets. With two-bit sets, one of the bits makes the stick cut and the other makes the cope cut. The Freud set is typical.

The profile cutter is an integral part of the shank, while the bearing and the slot cutter are separate parts, secured on an arbor projecting from the bit. The sticking cutter has a bearing mounted on the tip, so it can be used to make curved cuts, as is required to make arched rails. The cope bit has the bearing mounted between the profile cutter and the groover.

One difference between the Freud bits and most of the other two-bit sets is their bulk. The chip-limiting design of the Freud bits requires a larger body. (See "Bit Drawer" on page 29 for more about these bits.)

Cascade markets a slightly different style of two-bit set. The profile and slot cutters are integral parts of Cascade's SY-brand bits. There's a bearing mounted on the tip of both the sticking and cope

bits, but it is positioned to work against a template, not the work itself. For straight cuts, the bit *must* be used with a fence. The plus of this design is that you can work stock up to 1 inch thick. The minus is that you must use a template to make curved sticking cuts.

The overall advantage of the two-bit set is that you don't have to break down the bit to switch from one cut to the other. For those who do lots of frame-and-panel work, this means that two

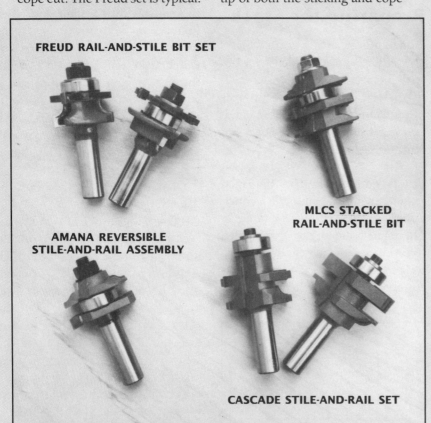

FREUD RAIL-AND-STILE BIT SET

MLCS STACKED RAIL-AND-STILE BIT

AMANA REVERSIBLE STILE-AND-RAIL ASSEMBLY

CASCADE STILE-AND-RAIL SET

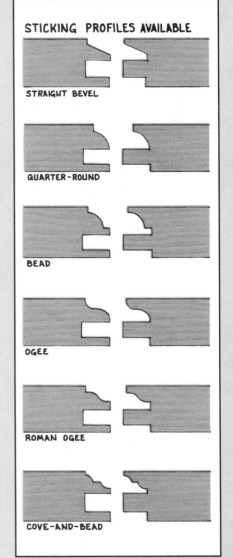

STICKING PROFILES AVAILABLE

STRAIGHT BEVEL

QUARTER-ROUND

BEAD

OGEE

ROMAN OGEE

COVE-AND-BEAD

routers can be set up, one for each bit. This makes the switch from sticking to coping even easier.

Reversible assembly. Typical of the assemblies is the one from Amana. It consists of an arbor with an integral shank, two removable cutters—one for the profile, the other the slotter—and a bearing. When setting up the assembly for sticking cuts, you mount the slotter directly against the profile cutter, and position the bearing at the tip. Just like the set's sticking bit. To set up the assembly for the cope cut, you turn the profile cutter over, and separate it from the slotter with the bearing. Again, just like the set's cope bit.

Amana's assembly is a more compact bit, and it is supplied with a selection of brass shims you use to adjust the fit of the joint. The shims usually aren't needed until after the cutters have been resharpened a time or two.

The advantage of the assembly—the cost difference aside—is the perfectly matched cuts. Since you are using the same cutters to produce both the cope and the sticking cuts, they're guaranteed to match. The disadvantage, of course, is that you have to dismantle the bit when switching from one cut to the other.

Stacked bit. A third, seldom-seen, style of bit is the stacked bit. The one I've seen is like an assembled bit with an extended arbor and a second profile cutter. Stacked on the arbor are a profile cutter, a slot cutter, the bearing, and another profile cutter. To cut sticking, you raise the bit to its maximum height; the upper profile cutter is above the work. To switch to a cope cut, you lower the bit, so the lower profile cutter is below the router table mounting plate.

Cutting the Joinery

Use a table-mounted router to cut the joinery. Although you are making a one-pass cut, you don't need a big-horsepower router. And though the cope and sticking bits are hefty, they aren't large-diameter, so you don't really need to reduce the router's speed. What you do need are two or three hold-downs to hold the stock both flat against the tabletop and tight against the fence.

Rout the sticking on each stile and rail first. Tighten the sticking bit in the router collet, and adjust the bit's height to cut the desired profile. As previously noted, the objective in setting the bit height is to position the profile for its best appearance without getting the groove too close to the back. So long as you are working with stock between $^{11}/_{16}$ and $^{7}/_{8}$ inch thick, this shouldn't be too difficult. Make test cuts as necessary to establish the optimum bit height.

For a safe operation, set up the wooden fence so the bit is mostly buried in the fence and the guiding edge of the fence is even with the edge of the bit's bearing. The more closely matched the fence opening

▶ **TRY THIS!**

Cut the stiles about 2 inches longer than they'll be in the finished frame. After assembly, trim off the excess.

You'll find it easier to assemble the frame if you aren't trying to get the ends of the stiles perfectly flush with the edges of the rails. Scribe pencil lines across the face of stiles where the rails are to align. After the glue dries, you can trim these "horns" and have perfectly flush top and bottom edges.

is to the bit contour, the better the fence will back up the cut and minimize—if not completely eliminate—chipping ahead of the cutter. Using the split fence makes this easy to accomplish. You simply shift the two fence elements toward the bit until they nearly touch it, then lock them down.

Set the hold-downs next. Use a couple of featherboards or the springboard to keep the work tight to the fence. Fred's plesiosaur hold-down

The split fence allows you to set the fence around the bit, providing backing for the work. Before making the sticking cuts, set up hold-downs to control the movement of the work past the cutter. A good arrangement has two featherboards clamped to the fence, one on each side of the cutter, holding the work against the tabletop. The featherboards prevent the stock from being kicked back.

Exceptions to woodworking's many general rules abound, and here's one of them. When you are working a curved rail, it's better to cut the cope before the stick. Stick a scrap to mate with the cope (top left), and trim the end as necessary to blend into the curved edge. Then when you cut the sticking (bottom left), you've got solid material backing up the wood at the fragile end of the cut, as well as stock to maintain contact with the pilot bearing and carry the workpiece safely past the cutter. Since you can't use a fence for this operation, use a starting pin to help start the cut (the rounded edge of the dust pickup served as the starting pin here) and guide the workpiece against the pilot bearing.

the cut, the fence has to be perfectly parallel to the tabletop edge.

But it isn't necessary to fuss that much. Just make a practice cut using the sled but not the fence. (Of course, you have to establish a coarse bit-height setting to do this, but it doesn't have to be perfect for this setup task. Just do it by eye.) With the router switched off, use the cut piece to set the fence. Position the sled at the bit, and slide the piece along the sled's backstop so its leading corner is against the bearing. Then bring the vertical edge of the fence into position against the back corner and clamp it to the tabletop.

(With the SY-style bit—see "Bit Drawer" on page 202—the work-

To set the fence as a stop for cope cuts, Fred cradles a square-cut scrap in the sled. Hunkering down at tabletop level, he sights across the end of the scrap, lining it up with the bearing on the bit. After the toggle clamp is snapped onto the scrap, he'll bring the fence—with the outfeed section removed—up to the scrap. The fence must be parallel with the front edge of the table, or the setup won't be accurate; so he'll slide the sled back and forth, lining up the fence with the end of the scrap. Only then will he lock it down.

is ideal for pressing the work against the tabletop. (See the chapter "Router Table Accessories" for plans for these safety devices.) You can position both of them right at the bit, where you need the pressure.

When everything seems to be set up properly, cut the profile and groove in the inside edges of the stiles *and* rails. If the frame has an intermediate middle rail or rails, or if it has one or more mullions, these parts must be routed on both edges. One pass should be sufficient to complete each cut.

Cope the ends of the rails. There are a number of setup tasks to perform before you actually make the cuts.

First you have to replace the sticking cutter with the cope cutter. If you are using a set, you replace one bit with the other. If you're using an assembly, you must loosen the locking nut and switch the cutter and bearing positions on the arbor.

Reset the fence, positioning it as before, *but remove the half of the fence that's to the left of the bit.* The reason for this is simple. The bit's pilot bearing controls the cut, a sled guides the workpiece, and the fence serves only to position the workpiece in the sled. (See "Sled" on page 90 for the sled plan.) The sled rides against the tabletop's front edge. If the work is against the fence for the full distance you move it in making

Cutting across end grain is perilous because the cutter usually tears splinters out as it exits the stock. The sled's fence backs up the rail—preventing the tear-out—when the rail's square edge is tucked against it, but that's only half of the cuts. For the others, insert a coped piece of scrap into the stick cut before clamping the rail in the sled, as shown here. For the rail to be properly aligned in the sled, make sure the scrap is at least as long as the sled's fence.

A quick and pretty reliable way to set the height of the cope bit is to match it against a piece of the sticked stock. Set the stock beside the bit, as shown, and adjust the bit to align with it. Check the setting with a test cut, but if you're careful, it should be right on.

Always have the rail firmly clamped to the sled when making a cope cut. With the sled tight against the tabletop edge, slide the rail up to the fence and lock the toggle clamp. Feed the sled past the bit, making the cut. When the cut is done, you can simply ease the sled away from the edge of the tabletop and thus the work from the bit. You don't have to pull the work back across the cutter.

▶ **TRY THIS!**

Make your frames a little oversized. In the long run, it can save you extra worry and work. Fred does it all the time.

If you are making a door, for example, crosscut the rails and stiles so the assembled frame will be 1/16 to 1/8 inch longer and wider than your specs call for. The final step is to trim the door, *not to the specified dimensions,* but to *fit.* If a door opening is slightly large or slightly out-of-square, you've given yourself a margin for error. You have some room to trim the door to fit.

Making the frames slightly oversized can free you from some of the cares of woodworking, too. No more fumbling with cauls to protect the frame edges from clamp jaws. So what if you get a crease or two! The damage gets trimmed off.

piece may not touch the bearing because it's above the cut. Instead of butting the test cut against the bearing, you butt it against the deepest recess of the cutting edge. It's particularly important for you to get the fence set carefully with this style of bit—and to lock the workpiece in the sled with a toggle clamp. Otherwise, you shorten the rails as you make the cope cuts.)

Now to fit a workpiece in the sled, you merely have to slide it along the backstop until it butts against the fence. Flip the toggle to lock it down, and you're ready to cut. But not yet.

You first need to refine your coarse bit-height setting through test cuts. The cope cutter is designed to cut a profile that locks into the sticking cut. Fit your test cut to one of the stiles. Keep adjusting the bit height until the stile and rail surfaces are flush when assembled. (If the coped piece is proud of the sticked piece, lower the cutter. If the sticked piece is higher, raise the bit.)

When the proper bit height is set, rout a cope *along the edge* of that backer strip I suggested you set aside. The sled's backstop serves to prevent the cutter from blowing out chips as it exits the good stock. But because the backstop has a square edge, it can only do this when the flat edge of the rail is against it. For half your cope cuts, you'll have the sticked edge against the backstop. So use this coped-edge strip as an auxiliary backstop.

Finally, you have to trim the rails to finished length before coping their ends. The width of the profile is what you must account for. For example, if you are making an 18-inch-wide door and using 1¾-inch-wide stiles, the distance between the stiles is 14½ inches. But the rails must be long enough to overlap the sticking profile. If that's ⅜ inch wide (which seems to be the standard), then you need to add ¾ inch to the length of the rails (⅜ inch for each stile, or twice the width of the profile). The easy way to measure the profile is to stick a rule into the groove and see how deep it is; the depth of the groove will match the width of the profile.

One critical issue is whether or not the coping cut actually shortens the rail. If the cut is controlled by a bearing on the bit, you shouldn't be concerned about this issue. The cut won't shorten the rail. If the bearing on the bit is strictly for template-guided cuts, you'd better check. The best way to determine is with test cuts, followed by close measurement.

With your setup tested and the rails trimmed to length, you should be ready to cut. One final caveat: The sled we use has a big toggle clamp. The clamp is important. The cutters have a tendency to pull the workpiece as the last corner clears the bearing. It's the same effect you experience when routing an edge with a hand-held router. As you get to the corner, you have to be very careful that you clear the corner without slipping around it. If you are using your fingers to hold the work on the sled, you may not be able to prevent this kind of self-feeding. The clamp *can*. So use it, and save yourself extra work.

As with the sticking cuts, the cope cuts should be completed in one pass. Repeating a pass *can* enlarge the cut and create a loose fit. Fred argues that a second pass can enlarge the cut only if there's some movement in your setup. In that case, you'll find some (not all, but *some*) of the joints coming out less than flush when clamped tight.

MAKING PANELS

The panel used in frame-and-panel construction ordinarily is a wood that matches the frame, but it can be a contrasting wood. The most simple panel would be a hardwood plywood matching the frame. Most familiar, however, may be the so-called raised panel, a natural wood panel with a beveled or shouldered band around its edge.

Whatever panel you choose can be set flush with either the front or back surface of the frame, or elevated so that it projects beyond the frame. (Of course, to fit flush with either the front or the back frame surface, the panel has to be rabbeted.)

If you are using a natural wood for the panel, it's not unlikely that you'll have to glue up narrow boards to form the wider panels that are necessary. Even if you do have boards wide enough, it may be advantageous to rip the boards into narrow strips, then glue them back together. This is a good way to minimize cupping. See the chapter "Edge Joints" for a variety of router techniques that can improve the strength and quality of your edge joints.

The router is the best tool in your shop to use for raising panels, unless you have a shaper. A lot of woodworkers use the table saw or radial arm saw to raise panels in a straight bevel, but there are some distinct shortcomings to this.

First, you can get the straight bevel only at some angle dictated by the width of the cut area and the thickness of the stock. Also, the saw blade will probably leave fairly prominent marks that take a lot of time, elbow grease, and sandpaper to eradicate. Finally, you can't get the ¼-inch-thick by ⅜-inch-long tongue around the panel that's necessary to properly fit it into the frame's groove.

All panel-raising router bits (and shaper cutters, too) are designed to produce a tongue of the appropriate width. They'll leave a far smoother finish to the cut. You'll have to sand it, of course, but not nearly as much. And finally, you have a pretty interesting assortment of profiles from which to choose. (See "Bit Drawer" on page 210).

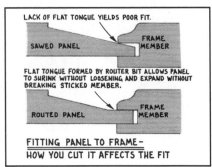

LACK OF FLAT TONGUE YIELDS POOR FIT.

SAWED PANEL — FRAME MEMBER

FLAT TONGUE FORMED BY ROUTER BIT ALLOWS PANEL TO SHRINK WITHOUT LOOSENING AND EXPAND WITHOUT BREAKING STICKED MEMBER.

ROUTED PANEL — FRAME MEMBER

FITTING PANEL TO FRAME—HOW YOU CUT IT AFFECTS THE FIT

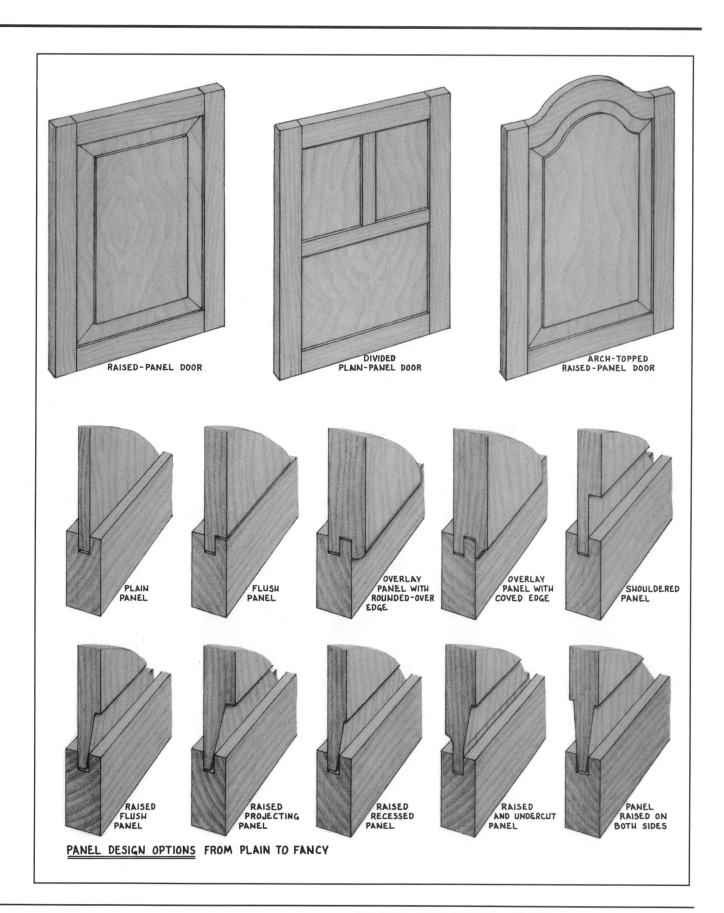

RAISED-PANEL DOOR

DIVIDED PLAIN-PANEL DOOR

ARCH-TOPPED RAISED-PANEL DOOR

PLAIN PANEL

FLUSH PANEL

OVERLAY PANEL WITH ROUNDED-OVER EDGE

OVERLAY PANEL WITH COVED EDGE

SHOULDERED PANEL

RAISED FLUSH PANEL

RAISED PROJECTING PANEL

RAISED RECESSED PANEL

RAISED AND UNDERCUT PANEL

PANEL RAISED ON BOTH SIDES

PANEL DESIGN OPTIONS FROM PLAIN TO FANCY

Preparing the Panel Stock

The first step in preparing stock for raised panels is to evaluate your design in terms of the cope-and-stick joinery on the frame members, as well as the proportions of the typical panel-raising bit.

The industry convention is to use ⅝-inch-thick stock for the panels. Neverthless, you can satisfactorily use ¾-inch stock, and even ½-inch stock. Let's look at the reasons.

As noted elsewhere, the cope-and-stick cutters produce a groove for the panel that's ¼ inch wide and ⅜ inch deep. If the frame stock is ¾ inch thick—the industry convention—then the groove is positioned with its centerline between ¼ inch and 5⁄16 inch from the frame member's back edge (depending upon how deep you cut the profile).

Panel-raising bits are proportioned to produce the optimum relief—not too shallow, not too deep— and the proper tongue thickness—¼ inch—on ⅝-inch-thick stock. If you use ¾-inch stock for the panel, you'll have to cut deeper than the optimum relief to get the ¼-inch tongue. Or you'll have to "undercut" the back of the panel that's been raised to the optimum. The undercut—a sort of rabbet—produces a relief in the back of the panel so the tongue is ¼ inch thick.

There's another choice here, too. Will the panel be flush or projecting? If you raise a ⅝-inch panel the optimum and fit it into a frame sticked to the industry standard, then the panel's field will be flush with the surface of the frame. That's a flush panel. If you do the same with a ¾-inch panel, the field will be ⅛ inch proud of the frame surfaces.

That's a projecting panel. With the projecting panel, the relief may not look quite right because it is too deep.

By undercutting the ¾-inch panel, you can reduce the relief, yet also pull it back in the frame and make it a flush panel.

Decisions, decisions.

When you've made yours, plane the stock to the chosen thickness. If necessary, glue up the wood to produce the widths needed, and crosscut the rough panels to finished length.

Remember that the straightness and flatness of the panel are as important to the overall straightness and flatness of the structure as those of the frame. In most circumstances, if the panel is warped, it will twist the frame. So chose the panel stock accordingly. (There are circumstances, Fred points out, in which burled, unstable wood is used for panels. The trick is to keep this stock thin enough that it doesn't have the strength to overpower the frame and warp it.)

Sizing the panels has to be done before you raise them. In doing this, you have to account for the relative moisture content of the wood. The length of the panel won't change over the course of time, but the width will come and go with the seasons.

You want an easy slip fit during assembly. If the panel material (and the frame stock, too) were perfectly stable, you could measure from the bottom of one groove to the bottom of the opposite one and cut the panel to that dimension minus about 1⁄16 inch for assembly clearance. But of course, none of the stock is really stable. When cutting the panel to

Depending upon the panel stock thickness and whether or not you undercut the panel as well as raise it, you can produce (top to bottom) recessed, flush, or projecting panels.

Problem Solver

You have to select the mounting based on the panel. A wooden panel, of course, is installed permanently in a groove cut in the edges of the rails and stiles.

But glass is another story. Since it is breakable, the frame is usually rabbeted for glass so it can be replaced without damaging the frame. Knowing that you just might like to put glass in a cope-and-stick-jointed frame, bit manufacturers offer window-sash cutters. Like cope-and-stick bits, these bits form a decorative profile at the same time they form a recess to receive the glass. But instead of a groove, the recess is a rabbet.

The panel doesn't have to be wood or plain glass, though. Leaded glass could be used. Or expanded metal sheets or punched tin sheets. Or caning. Use your imagination.

In most of these situations, the "panel" should be mounted in a rabbeted recess. All of these materials are too thin to fit the sticked groove. For a finished appearance, cut retainer strips with the same profile as the sticking. Miter the ends of the strips and install them with brads.

length, you need only allow that $\frac{1}{16}$ inch assembly clearance, since wood doesn't get longer when it expands. Ripping the panel to width is a little trickier.

In the dead of a cold winter, when the relative humidity is generally low and the furnace's heat is drying the shop air even more, the panel stock is as shrunken as it will ever be. The cabinetmaker's rule of thumb is to allow about $\frac{1}{8}$ inch per foot of width for expansion. And don't forget the assembly clearance.

In the slough of a sultry summer, on the other hand, the stock is as swollen with moisture as it will get. Cut it to fit pretty tightly in the frame; make it about $\frac{1}{16}$ inch less than the groove-to-groove dimension.

Raising Panels

Panel raising is a router table operation. In a nutshell, to work a rectilinear panel, you set the fence and bit, clamp a couple of featherboards in place, and rout. Outside of the nutshell, there's a little more to it.

Deal with the bit first. As far as I am concerned, the bit you use dictates which router table you use. With the horizontal bit, you use the regular router table. With the vertical bit, you use the horizontal table. These dictates have to do with the angle of attack. They allow you to keep the work flat on the tabletop.

With a small workpiece, this may not seem too critical. But consider some typical work. My kitchen has 42-inch wall cabinets with 38-inch-high panels in the doors. I have a pantry cabinet with a pair of 60-inch-high doors with 56-inch-high panels. Just think about holding those panels against a router table fence, even if it's a foot high. Yoiks! Panels

that big are the reason you want to keep the work flat on the tabletop.

To reiterate: If you have a horizontal bit, use the regular router table, and if you have a vertical bit, use the horizontal table.

If you plan to use a horizontal bit, make sure your router will accommodate it. You need high horsepower and speed control, as we've noted several times. But the router's structure has to accommodate it, too. The mounting plate's bit opening will undoubtedly have to be bored out to accept a $3\frac{1}{2}$-inch-diameter bit. But check the router, too. All the big plunge routers except the Porter-Cables have some restriction to the bit opening. Usually it is tabs for mounting a template-guide adapter. A big panel-raiser will hit these tabs, and you don't want to be there for the collision.

Here's trouble. The opening in the base of this table-mounted router simply isn't big enough to really accommodate this large panel-raiser. You can see a portion of the guide bushing mounting flange under the bit. This integral part of the base casting clearly intrudes into the space the bit needs. Recognize the potential for metal-to-metal conflict here, and avoid that at all costs.

BIT DRAWER

A panel-raising bit is serious business. It is as big a cutter as you will buy, and it represents as big a cut as the router can make. It's a big investment. It can be a dangerous investment.

Panel-raisers are available in two configurations: horizontal and vertical. The horizontal bits are more widely available than the vertical bits, and they are made in a much greater variety of sizes and profiles.

Horizontal panel-raising bits. If what you are used to is standard straight, round-over, and cove bits, the *size* is the first thing you notice about a horizontal panel-raiser. As bits go, it is huge. The CMT horizontal panel-raiser shown in the photo is just under 3½ inches in diameter and weighs 11 ounces. That's a lot of metal to spin.

The size of these bits is their drawback, of course. A high-horsepower router is required to drive them. A 3½-inch bit spinning at 22,000 rpm is moving about 230 mph at the cutter tips. When you bend the path of that whizzing cutter around a 3-inch circle, you begin to develop centrifugal forces that put some pretty serious strain on the materials holding it together. Just think about a carbide tip pulling loose and you'll understand why most manufacturers recommend limiting the larger cutters to 10,000 rpm. To do this, obviously, you must use a variable-speed router (or a speed control).

In addition to urging you to operate the biggest of the horizontal panel-raisers at a reduced speed, several manufacturers, Freud and CMT among them, configure their bits to limit the size of the chip that can be taken. By restricting the bite, the designs

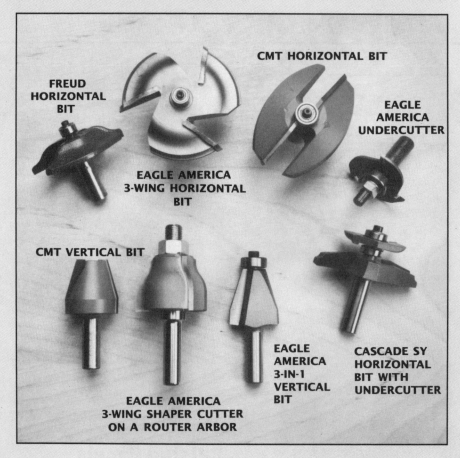

FREUD HORIZONTAL BIT

CMT HORIZONTAL BIT

EAGLE AMERICA UNDERCUTTER

EAGLE AMERICA 3-WING HORIZONTAL BIT

CMT VERTICAL BIT

EAGLE AMERICA 3-IN-1 VERTICAL BIT

CASCADE SY HORIZONTAL BIT WITH UNDERCUTTER

EAGLE AMERICA 3-WING SHAPER CUTTER ON A ROUTER ARBOR

reduce the chance for kickback. Eagle America enhances the chip-limiting feature by making its largest cutters in a three-wing design. The extra cutting edge helps smooth the cut made when the bit is spun at 10,000 rpm.

The reason these bits are so big is, of course, the demand for a wide reveal. If you want a 1½-inch-wide reveal—it's pretty standard in the cabinet industry, where shapers are used to raise panels—you need a bit that's just about 3½ inches in diameter. A smaller bit will suffice if you are willing to accept a narrower reveal—1¼ inch, for example, or 1 inch, or 13/16 inch.

The widest assortment of profiles is Eagle America's, with 20 variations of ogee, bevel, and cove profiles in three different reveal widths. Most other manufacturers list three to six profiles in a couple of sizes. The point here is that you need not feel limited to a

beveled reveal; you can have an ogee, a cove, or any of these shapes with a bead around the panel's field.

Vertical panel-raising bits. You don't *need* a high-horsepower, variable-speed router to raise panels. With a vertical panel-raiser, a 1½-horsepower, fixed-speed router is all you need.

That's because the vertical panel-raiser, while still pretty massive, is small in comparison to an equivalent horizontal one. Although, at a cutter height of 1½ inches, it's taller than the horizontal bit, it's usually no more than 1½ inches in diameter. And that reduced diameter is the whole point. Driven at 22,000 rpm, the tip speed of the vertical bit is just under 100 mph (compared to 230 mph for the horizontal bit).

The bit shares the operating concept of those architectural molding cutters. The cut's "width" is dictated by the bit height rather

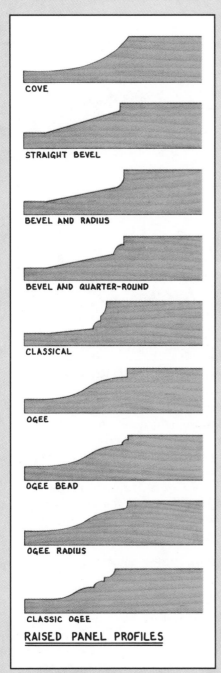

COVE

STRAIGHT BEVEL

BEVEL AND RADIUS

BEVEL AND QUARTER-ROUND

CLASSICAL

OGEE

OGEE BEAD

OGEE RADIUS

CLASSIC OGEE

RAISED PANEL PROFILES

than by its diameter. The bit designer is simply changing the angle of attack. The vertical panel-raisers currently on the market will cut a standard 1½-inch reveal (but nothing less). Available patterns include ogees, coves, and standard bevels.

The typical vertical bit has two flutes. Because it has no pilot, it has to be used in conjunction with a fence, and it cannot be used to raise the edges of curved panels.

At this writing, only Byrom and CMT have vertical bits in their catalogs.

An interesting twist on the vertical concept is offered by Eagle America. It is a "3 in 1 Moulding Cutter Kit" that comes with three different bearings. The bit will produce 18-degree chamfers, as well as forming chamfered moldings and raised panels. The pilot would seem to be pointless for panel raising, however, since it's about 1½ inches above the tabletop.

Undercutters. A subset of the horizontal panel-raisers are those with undercutters. The undercutter is a bit that produces a recess much like a rabbet on the back of the panel. This allows you to use ¾-inch-thick stock for panels without having to cut excessively deep with the panel-raising cutter. The undercut panel ends up being flush with both the face and back of the frame.

A few bit vendors—Cascade, for one—mate an undercutter with a horizontal panel-raiser, putting both cutters on the same shank. Some woodworkers believe this bit's configuration, which places the work between two cutters, is hazardous. Fred figures that with the proper hold-downs, you shouldn't have problems. It's worth noting that with this bit, you creep up on the final cut depth not by adjusting the bit height but by shifting the fence position. (As an alternative, Fred suggests removing the undercutter for the first two or three passes. Reinstall it for the final pass only.)

An undercutter can be purchased as a separate bit from Eagle America. You use it after raising the panels to the degree that suits your aesthetics, and relieve that panel back as necessary to size the tongue.

This doesn't mean you can't use these routers for the job. It does mean that the mounting plate's thickness is a big part of your margin of bit-height adjustment. Even with the bit set as low as you can get it, you may still be cutting the full 1½-inch width of the reveal on the first pass. So making a shallow pass may require you to overcenter the fence on the bit, so you're addressing less than the full reveal width. For the second pass, move the fence back, and for the third, begin raising the bit.

Not all router bases have these obstructions, of course. The base of the big Porter-Cable production router we use in our main router table would accommodate an even bigger bit (if someone were foolhardy enough to make it and we were foolhardy enough to use it).

Set the bit to a height appropriate for the first pass. Depending upon the router, set the bit either as low

TRY THIS!

If you want to raise a panel with a vertical bit on a regular router table, try using a trap fence in conjunction with the standard fence.

Set the regular fence for the cut, and adjust the bit setting. Set a sample of the working stock against the fence, and set a board ¾ inch thick or more against it. The board should be as long as the fence. Clamp it to the tabletop. Now you have a chute just wide enough for the panel.

As you start the cut, put a little pressure on the stock, pressing it to the regular fence. The trap fence will keep the bottom of the panel from skidding away from the regular fence. (See page 104 for a photo of a trap fence in use.)

Raising Panels with a Straight Bit

You don't have to spend 50 to 100 bucks for a panel-raising bit. You can cut a straight bevel on a panel with a ½-inch straight bit. And you don't need a router table to do it, either.

All it takes is this nifty jig that Fred designed and built, along with a router, a ½-straight bit with a 1-inch cutting length on a ¼-inch shank, and a ⅜-inch rabbeting bit.

Here's how the operation works.

To form the tongue around the panel, you cut a rabbet along each edge. To form a crisp edge around the field, either kerf the panel on the table saw or—better for a routerhead—groove the panel with a roundnose bit.

Set up the router and jig next. Chuck the straight bit in the router. Remove the router's baseplate, and attach the jig in its place. Set the bit height so the cutting flutes will be above the tongue as the board is fed through the jig. You don't want to bevel that. Clamp the jig across a couple of sawhorses.

Switch on the router, and feed the panel through the jig, passing it against the cutter rotation. When the panel is between you and the cutter, the feed direction would be left to right. Do the two end-grain cuts and then the two long-grain cuts.

That's all it takes!

The tricks in building the jig are to cant the trap fences to match the angle of bevel you want, and to position the router laterally so the bit makes just the right cut. The design technique Fred used to establish this is one that's useful for designing and dimensioning all sorts of jigs and fixtures.

First, draw the cut you are trying to achieve in actual size. Then stretch in the bit at the cut. Then add the fences that will guide the cut. When you are done, you have a cross section of the jig.

To make the jig:

1. Cut the parts to the sizes specified by the Cutting List. Bevel the edges of the trap fences, as indicated in *Fred's Panel-Raising Jig,* and cut the contour of the braces.

2. Lay out the position of the panel channel on the hardboard, as well as the hole for the bit. Use the router's factory baseplate to position the holes for the router-mounting screws. Drill

This is a poor man's panel-raising setup, and it gives much better results than the well-known table-saw/radial-arm-saw approach. A relatively low-horsepower router, a commonplace (and versatile) straight bit, and this homemade jig are all that's needed. After rabbeting and scoring the panel, you slip it between the jig's fences and feed it past the bit.

the mounting-screw holes and the 1-inch-diameter bit hole. Glue the base blocks in place.

3. Glue and screw the plywood bases to the trap fences. Glue the braces in place, and drive a screw through the plywood base into each brace. With a 1½-inch-diameter Forstner bit, drill through the plywood and into the bottom of the trap fence that will par-

as you can, or low enough for the first pass. One-eighth inch is probably enough for a first bite. It's better to be conservative on the first pass. If you are confident that you can increase the bite significantly after a first full cut, then go ahead. On the horizontal router table, you can set the bit height on the router for the final setting and adjust the depth of cut between passes by raising the router mounting board.

With a big horizontal bit, don't forget to dial back the router speed. Set the router to run as slowly as possible.

Setting the fence and hold-downs. Even if the bit has a pilot, use a fence to guide straight cuts. (Obviously, you can't use the fence for making curved cuts, though you can use two starting pins.) A fence gives you much better control of the work than does the bit's pilot.

tially house the bit. This will create the opening in the fence for the bit, as well as an exit point for chips.

4. Glue the fence assemblies to the hardboard base. Drive screws through the bases into the base blocks, and extend the mounting-screw holes through the plywood layer.

After mounting the router and making a test cut or two, you may need to shift the router position slightly to get the correct cut. This is easiest to do if you are using longer screws than those supplied with the router. Ream out the mounting holes so you can shift the router position, then retighten the screws. Do this as necessary to get the correct cut.

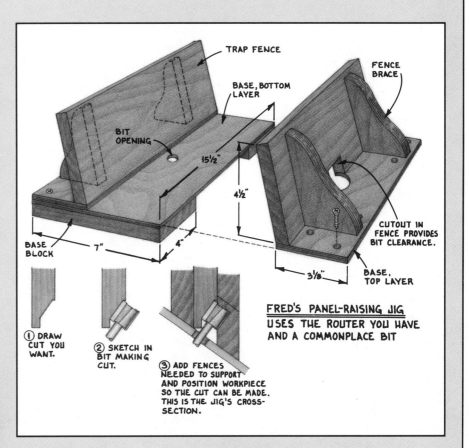

FRED'S PANEL-RAISING JIG
USES THE ROUTER YOU HAVE
AND A COMMONPLACE BIT

The finished panel has a tongue around the edge that fits perfectly into the frame's groove. The bevel is smooth, needing only a lick or two with fine-grit sandpaper, if that.

CUTTING LIST

Piece	Number	Thickness	Width	Length	Material
Base, top layers	2	¼"	3"	15½"	Plywood
Base, bottom layer	1	⅛"	7"	15½"	Hardboard
Base blocks	2	¾"	4"	7"	Hardwood
Trap fences	2	¾"	5"	15½"	Hardwood
Fence braces	4	¾"	2"	4"	Plywood

Hardware
12 pcs. #6 × 1" drywall screws

Moreover, use a high fence, since this provides a place to clamp holddowns like featherboards. A basic, one-board fence will guide the work, but you really need the featherboards to control it and prevent the work from lifting from the tabletop. So use a fence with a 3- or 4-inch-high back, and clamp two featherboards to it, one on each side of the bit.

If you can't really lower the bit below the tabletop, set the fence closer to you for the first pass or two, then back it away so the fence is flush with the edge of the pilot for subsequent passes.

A curved cut can be done only in the regular router table. Use a starting pin to help you control the cut. Obviously, you can't use featherboards, but a hold-down like Fred's plesiosaur can help hold the work firmly to the tabletop. (See the

(continued on page 217)

Making Architectural Doors and Windows

Doors and windows for a building—your house, for example—are built using the same frame-and-panel construction as we've presented in this chapter. Usually the stock is heftier—ranging in thickness from a full inch up to 1¾ inches—but the same bits and techniques used for cabinetry will work for this architectural work.

Cope-and-stick joinery is probably satisfactory for interior doors and for fixed and double-hung windows. It provides enough glue surface for contemporary glues to provide a strong, long-lasting bond, even on a door. What makes it less than adequate for exterior doors and for awning or casement windows is exposure to weather. After a few years of baking in the sun and soaking in the rain and freezing in the snow, the wood's expansion and contraction will probably knock cope-and-stick joinery apart. Here you need full mortise-and-tenon joinery.

Making an interior door. The parts and dimensions of a fairly typical interior door are shown in *Architectural Door*. To make the door, you would cut the frame parts to size, then rout the sticking on the appropriate edges and cope the ends of the rails. You can use standard cope-and-stick bits to work heavy stock if you make two passes. Make the first pass with the workpiece facedown, the second pass

An architectural door typically has thicker rails and stiles than a cabinet door and is styled the same on both sides. You can use a regular cope-and-stick bit set or assembly to rout these frame pieces. When making the stick cut, adjust the bit height so the groove is centered, then make two passes (top right) to get the profile on both edges of the stock. Similarly, the cope cuts are made in two passes. But you must remove the slotting cutter from the cope bit (bottom right).

with it faceup. Obviously, you have to adjust the bit height so the groove (or tenon) will be centered across the stock. Depending on the stock thickness and the sticking pattern, you may want to make the groove (and consequently the tongue) wider than ¼ inch. When you raise the panels, do it on both faces, but don't make the tongue less thick than the sticking groove is wide.

Making an exterior door. An exterior door would be made in pretty much the same way. But after sticking all the frame parts and coping the rails, cut mortises in both stiles and rails for long, loose tenons. Obviously, you have to trim the stub tenons from the rails. Use the longest ½-inch bit you can to rout the mortises. Freud sells a ½-inch straight with 2½-inch-long cutting edges and a 4⅜-inch overall length. With it, you should be able to cut mortises about 3 inches deep in the stiles and 2⅜ inches deep in the rails (the coping on the rail ends limits the bit's reach). The tenons should be cut from solid wood. Use waterproof glue to assemble the door.

An exterior door should have its cope-and-stick joinery reinforced with mortises and loose tenons. Cut the mortises on the horizontal table, as shown. Use a spiral bit the same size as the stub produced by the cope cut, and line it up even with that stub. When you cut the mortise, the operation will remove a section of the stub.

THE CONSTRUCTION OF AN <u>ARCHITECTURAL DOOR</u>

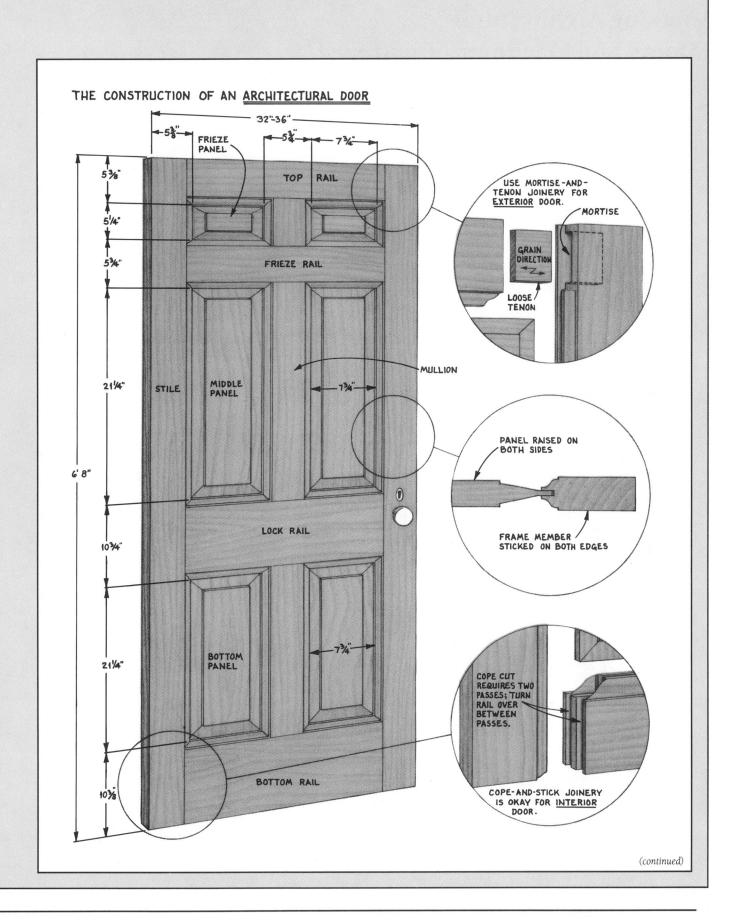

FRIEZE PANEL

TOP RAIL

FRIEZE RAIL

STILE

MIDDLE PANEL

MULLION

LOCK RAIL

BOTTOM PANEL

BOTTOM RAIL

32"-36"

5⅜"

5¾"

7¾"

5⅜"

5¼"

5¾"

21¼"

6' 8"

10¾"

21¼"

10⅜"

7¾"

7¾"

USE MORTISE-AND-TENON JOINERY FOR <u>EXTERIOR</u> DOOR.

GRAIN DIRECTION

MORTISE

LOOSE TENON

PANEL RAISED ON BOTH SIDES

FRAME MEMBER STICKED ON BOTH EDGES

COPE CUT REQUIRES TWO PASSES; TURN RAIL OVER BETWEEN PASSES.

COPE-AND-STICK JOINERY IS OKAY FOR <u>INTERIOR</u> DOOR.

(continued)

Making Architectural
Doors and Windows—*Continued*

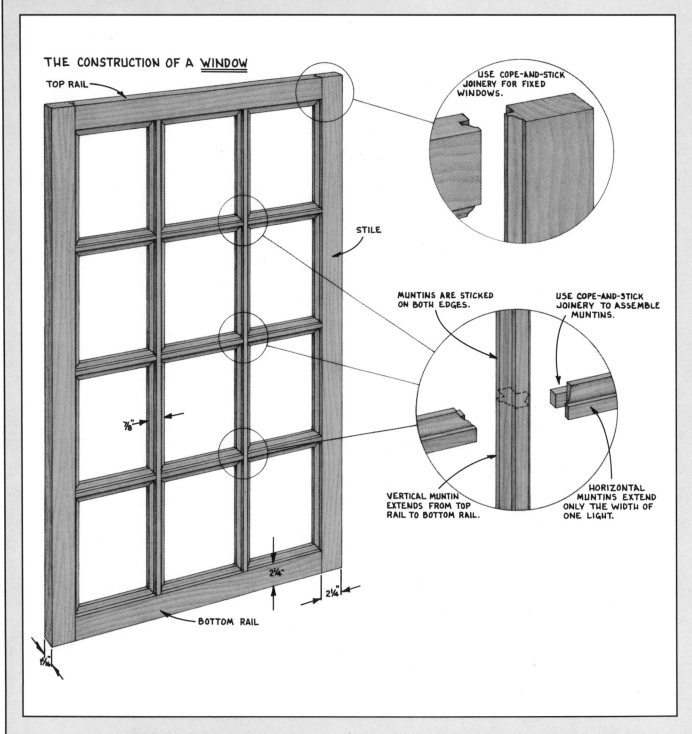

THE CONSTRUCTION OF A <u>WINDOW</u>

TOP RAIL

STILE

USE COPE-AND-STICK JOINERY FOR FIXED WINDOWS.

MUNTINS ARE STICKED ON BOTH EDGES.

USE COPE-AND-STICK JOINERY TO ASSEMBLE MUNTINS.

⅞"

2¼"

2¼"

VERTICAL MUNTIN EXTENDS FROM TOP RAIL TO BOTTOM RAIL.

HORIZONTAL MUNTINS EXTEND ONLY THE WIDTH OF ONE LIGHT.

BOTTOM RAIL

1¹¹⁄₁₆"

Making windows. The difference between making doors and making windows is the bit. A window sash bit (or bit set) will rout sticking with a profile and a rabbet for glass. The setups and steps are the same as with cope-and-stick bits: Do the sticking cuts, then cope the ends of the rails.

The drawing shows a 12-light storm window Fred made using a sash cutter.

Two different window sash bit configurations are available. Cascade's SY window sash bit set (top) has separate bits for the stick and cope cuts. Eagle America sells a single bit for both cuts (bottom). To configure this bit for the cope cut, you remove the rabbet cutter and replace it with a bushing.

A sash bit (or set) makes window construction relatively easy. In addition to shaping the rails and stiles that frame the window, you can shape the narrow muntins that partition it. Here, short horizontal muntins are joined to a tall vertical one.

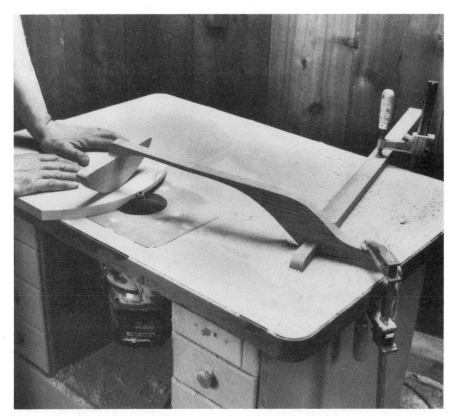

For curved work, Fred's plesiosaur is the ideal hold-down. Since you can't use the fence with curved work, you can't use the usual hold-down, which clamps to the fence. Position the plesiosaur to bridge the bit itself, with the hammerhead bearing on the work, as shown. The strip butted against the side of the hold-down keeps it from twisting out of position.

A light first pass can be set up by adjusting the fence position well ahead of the pilot bearing, as shown here, rather than by lowering the bit. This may be the only approach possible where the bit can't be lowered into the router's base area.

chapter "Router Table Accessories" for details on making the plesiosaur.)

On the horizontal router table, you won't need the fence, of course, but you will need the featherboards. Clamp them to the mounting board, just as you would to a fence. Remember that you will be feeding the work left to right on this table, and position the featherboards accordingly.

Making the cuts. With everything set up, start making the cuts. Cut the end grain first. This cut is most likely to cause tear-out, but any tear-out will almost surely be routed away when you make the long-grain cuts.

See Also . . .

A number of joints other than the cope-and-stick can be used in frame-and-panel construction.

The big advantage of the cope-and-stick is the appearance of the decorative profile routed on the inside edge of the frame. Were you to assemble a frame and *then* rout the decorative profile, the profile would lack the crisp corners. Instead of being sharp and square, the transitions from rail to stile would be rounded. And any approach in which you make a stopped cut will also yield those rounded corners. The cope-and-stick seemingly is the only joinery that gives you those crisp corners. *Seemingly.*

See the joint described in the chapter "Splined Miter Joint." The miter is weak, but the splines reinforce it. And before cutting the miters, you can rout a decorative profile on the inner edges. Because of the nature of the miter, the profile cuts will meet in crisp, square corners.

See "Routing Mitered Half-Laps" on page 289. The mitered half-lap is inherently stronger than the miter joint, even one reinforced with splines. But you still can embellish the edges with a routed profile and have the profiles meet clean and square at the corners.

The strongest joint, especially for doors, is the mortise-and-tenon. See the chapter "Mortise-and-Tenon Joints" for an explanation of how to use your router in making these joints. To incorporate the mortise-and-tenon into a cope-and-stick joint, use the loose-tenon variant. Cut a mortise into both the sticked piece and the coped piece. The loose tenon is a strip of wood that extends into both mortises. The thickness of the tenon should match the groove width. There's a photo of a mortise cut into a coped rail on page 214.

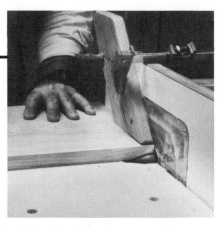

Raising panels on both the regular (left) and the horizontal router table (right) is remarkably similar. Set the bit, a horizontal raiser in the regular table, a vertical one in the horizontal table. Clamp a featherboard or two in place to hold the panel flat on the table and to prevent kickback. Then feed the work across the table.

Make your first cut on every workpiece, then adjust the setup to increase the cut. Depending upon how you've set things up, that may involve moving the fence or merely raising the bit. Make a second pass on every piece, adjust the setup, and so forth.

When you are all finished, you probably will need to sand the cuts lightly. Especially when cutting across the grain, the bit tends to lay the end grain down a little. The wood will feel smooth to the touch when you stroke one direction but rough when you stroke the other direction. A couple of light passes with a pad sander should take care of this.

▶ TRY THIS!

Raising panels requires a heavy cut. You need to make several passes to complete the job, usually between three and five. To cut down on router wear and tear and to speed up the process, you can bevel the edges of the panel on the table saw to remove most of the waste. Then use the router to clean up the cut.

There's no faster way to produce a lip around your assembled cabinet doors than with a door-lip bit. The bit in use here simultaneously cuts a roundover and a rabbet on the edge of the frame. The rabbet's shoulder has a bevel, so it doesn't strike the cabinet face frame when the door is opened and closed.

◀ BIT DRAWER

If you are serious about making cabinet doors but you don't have the bits required, an economical way to get them may be in a set. Several bit makers collect the four or five essential bits in a set. Freud's includes a pair of cope-and-stick bits, a panel-raiser, a door-lip bit, and a glue-joint bit. You choose the cope-and-stick and panel profiles.

WORKING LAMINATES

Here's the reason for those one-hand-sized routers, called laminate trimmers. Never was a tool so well suited for a job. The router's high-speed cutter is about the only way to cut laminate accurately without chipping it.

In a nutshell, the procedure for working with laminates is: Cut a piece of plastic laminate to a size just a few fractions of an inch larger than the plywood, particleboard, or other substrate it is to cover. Bond it to the substrate; contact cement is the most popular glue for this. You position the laminate so its edges overhang those of the substrate just a little. With your router or laminate trimmer and a flush-trimming bit, zip around the edges, trimming away the excess laminate and making it flush with the substrate's edges. Perfect!

There's a little more to working with plastic laminates than that, but the router is the key tool used throughout the process. In addition to trimming the edges to finish a laminate project, you can also use the router to cut the pieces you need from the laminate sheets to start the project.

THE MATERIAL

Plastic laminate is made by impregnating several layers of kraft paper with phenolic plastic resin. The color and pattern is in a separate sheet of paper, impregnated with melamine plastic resin, which covers the core. The surface can be embossed with a design or texture. The paper layers and the plastics are bonded together under high heat and pressure. The resulting material is hard and durable—easily cleaned and scratch- and wear-resistant. For all this, it isn't expensive.

The material is used to cover anything that needs a wear-resistant, easily cleaned surface. Countertops. Cabinets, inside and out. Tables. Even walls. If a stable, flat surface is needed, the laminate should be applied to both sides of the core to prevent warping. In some instances, it's appropriate to apply laminate to both surfaces, but where one surface will be hidden from view, money can be saved by using what's called backer on the hidden side. Backer is laminate without the color layer.

Plastic laminate is sold in several grades, the most commonly used being the horizontal grade, which is about 1/16 inch thick. Many sheet sizes are available, ranging in width from 30 inches up to 60 inches, and in length from 8 to 12 feet. Most lumberyards sell several different brands and will have an incredible assortment of 1-inch by 2-inch samples to choose from. Order the color and finish you want, select the sheet size, and in a few days—most likely—your plastic laminate will be ready for you to pick up, tied up in a 2- to 3-foot-diameter roll.

CUTTING LAMINATE

The table saw is a great tool for cutting plastic laminate . . . almost. The basic sheet is so large, and sooooo limp, it's darn near impossible for a lone woodworker to make a decent cut. Adding to this disadvantage is the fact that any saw will chip the cut edge badly.

Although the laminate is only 1/16 inch thick, it's hard enough to make this a pretty heavy cut. So use your regular router, rather than a laminate trimmer. The fence under the laminate guides the flush-trimming bit's pilot, ensuring that the cut will be perfectly straight.

Enter the router. It allows you to lay out the sheet of laminate, then slide a tool across it that won't chip the edge as it cuts. A sheet of plywood set on a couple of sawhorses makes a good worktable. Pencil your cut line on the laminate, then slide a fairly wide, straight fence *under* the laminate, line it up right under the cut line, and clamp the laminate to the fence. Use wooden hand screws or cauls with metal-jawed clamps to avoid breaking the laminate. And position them so they won't interfere with the router as it makes the cut. Use a ¼-inch flush-trimming bit. The pilot bearing rides along the fence and guides the cut. It should be straight and chip-free.

This technique will allow a lone woodworker to reduce the largest of sheets to whatever sizes the project calls for.

TRIMMING LAMINATE

Laminate can be trimmed either flush or to one of several bevel angles, depending upon the purpose of the edge. For example, if you are applying laminate to plywood panels that will be joined together into a cabinet, you will trim the laminate flush with the plywood's edges. However, if the laminate is the top surface of a counter, you will probably bevel it.

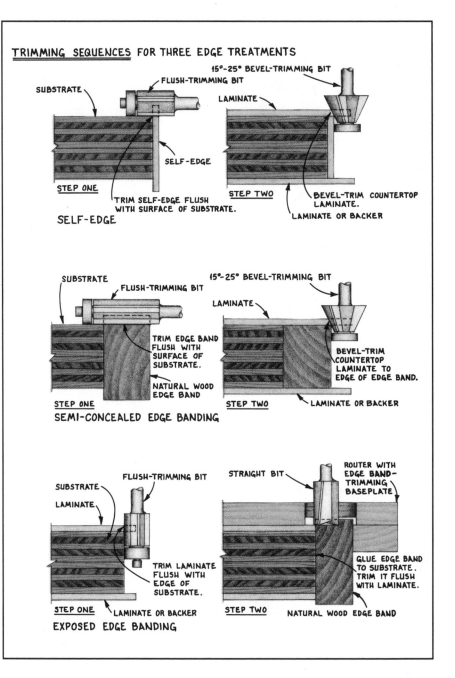

TRIMMING SEQUENCES FOR THREE EDGE TREATMENTS

SELF-EDGE

SUBSTRATE — FLUSH-TRIMMING BIT — SELF-EDGE
STEP ONE — TRIM SELF-EDGE FLUSH WITH SURFACE OF SUBSTRATE.

15°-25° BEVEL-TRIMMING BIT — LAMINATE
STEP TWO — BEVEL-TRIM COUNTERTOP LAMINATE. LAMINATE OR BACKER

SEMI-CONCEALED EDGE BANDING

SUBSTRATE — FLUSH-TRIMMING BIT — TRIM EDGE BAND FLUSH WITH SURFACE OF SUBSTRATE. NATURAL WOOD EDGE BAND
STEP ONE

15°-25° BEVEL-TRIMMING BIT — LAMINATE — BEVEL-TRIM COUNTERTOP LAMINATE TO EDGE OF EDGE BAND. LAMINATE OR BACKER
STEP TWO

EXPOSED EDGE BANDING

SUBSTRATE — LAMINATE — FLUSH-TRIMMING BIT — TRIM LAMINATE FLUSH WITH EDGE OF SUBSTRATE. LAMINATE OR BACKER
STEP ONE

STRAIGHT BIT — ROUTER WITH EDGE BAND-TRIMMING BASEPLATE — GLUE EDGE BAND TO SUBSTRATE. TRIM IT FLUSH WITH LAMINATE. NATURAL WOOD EDGE BAND
STEP TWO

The difficulties you have in making these cuts is influenced by the work location. If you are constructing laminate-covered cabinets in your shop, you'll have an easier time than if you are building them at the installation site. The same is true of laminating a countertop: It's easier to do in the shop.

The work sequence and the trim cuts you make will, of course, be affected by the edge treatment you've selected. The *self-edge* has laminate applied to it, and that laminate is applied and trimmed before the faces of the panel or counter are covered. *Edge banding* of natural wood can be applied either before or after the laminate, yielding two different appearances.

BIT DRAWER

Laminate work doesn't *require* special bits, although they are available. Any carbide or carbide-tipped bit will cut through laminate just fine. The several laminate-covered router tabletops presented in this book were actually trimmed with a standard 45-degree chamfer bit.

The typical flush-trimming bit—the one you get in a bit set—has two cutting edges about 1 inch long and a ½-inch cutting diameter. For trimming laminate, this bit has a couple of shortcomings.

• You don't use more of the cutting edges than the ⅛ inch closest to the pilot. The risk in extending the bit too much is that it will scuff the face of the laminate, especially if the router is bobbled momentarily.

• The two cutting edges won't give you the finest possible finish.

If you do a lot of laminate work, you may want to buy a real laminate trimming bit.

Bit manufacturers with a base of commercial and industrial customers usually make an assortment of laminate-trimming bits. Most of these bits have ¼-inch shanks, for use in laminate trimmers. The cutting-edge length is 7⁄16 inch or less (remember the overall caveat to always use the

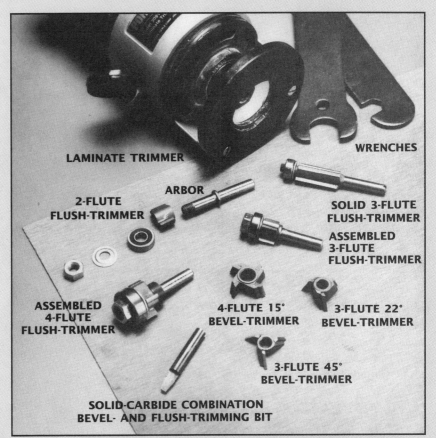

LAMINATE TRIMMER
WRENCHES
2-FLUTE FLUSH-TRIMMER
ARBOR
SOLID 3-FLUTE FLUSH-TRIMMER
ASSEMBLED 3-FLUTE FLUSH-TRIMMER
ASSEMBLED 4-FLUTE FLUSH-TRIMMER
4-FLUTE 15° BEVEL-TRIMMER
3-FLUTE 22° BEVEL-TRIMMER
3-FLUTE 45° BEVEL-TRIMMER
SOLID-CARBIDE COMBINATION BEVEL- AND FLUSH-TRIMMING BIT

shortest cutting edge that will do the job). The most economical are the double-flute style. For better finishes, they also make bits with three and even four flutes. A range of bevel angles are available, including flush, 7 degrees, 15 degrees, 25 degrees, and occasionally 45 degrees.

In some cases, the bits are assemblies, and the cutters can be interchanged. The advantage here is that you need buy only a single arbor, even though you get several cutters. It isn't likely you'll be using more than one cutter at a time.

To eliminate marring of the laminate's finish, a few manufacturers are now making Delrin-rimmed pilot bearings available. Delrin is a synthetic material similar to nylon and will leave no marks on the material being cut.

Applying the Laminate

Before you can trim the laminate, you've got to apply it to a substrate (sometimes called an underlayment). The best substrates are sheet goods—plywood, particleboard, medium-density fiberboard (MDF)—because they're generally more flat and stable than natural wood panels.

Contact cement is what bonds the laminate to the substrate. It's a sophisticated rubber cement that you spread on the mating pieces and leave to dry. When you touch the dried cement on the laminate to the dried cement on the substrate, they stick. Immediately. On contact.

To avoid alignment problems that can easily arise, the standard approach is to cut the laminate about ½ to ¾ inches larger in length and width than the substrate. The laminate merely has to be positioned so it overhangs on all four sides, and you're okay. The overhang doesn't have to be even, though any pattern should probably be aligned parallel with the substrate's edges to look right.

A typical application approach is to lay spacers, such as dowel rods or sticker strips, across the substrate and to set the laminate on them. Beginning either in the middle or at one end, you pull the spacers one at a time and press the laminate to the substrate. For a large panel, use a laminate roller to press the laminate firmly to the substrate, so you get a good, uniform bond between the two. On a small panel, you can achieve the same end by sliding a wood block methodically around the panel, rapping it with a hammer.

That's all there is to it. The laminate is immediately ready for trimming.

Work Sequences

Depending upon the edge treatment, your application and trimming sequences vary. If you are doing a self-edge, you apply and flush-trim the edge strips one at a time. When the edges are done, then you apply laminate to the faces and bevel-trim those pieces.

If you are applying laminate to an edge-banded substrate, you must be sure to flush-trim the wooden edge banding so the entire surface is flat and smooth. Apply the laminate to the faces, and bevel-trim them.

The third option is to apply and flush-trim the laminate, then glue edge banding to the panel. To complete the treatment, flush-trim the wooden edging. If desired, you can then rout a decorative edge on the wood.

Before you flush-trim laminate applied to the face of the substrate, you must check the panel's edges to make sure the pilot bearing will have a smooth, clean surface to reference. Plywood—fir plywood especially— sometimes has voids in the inner plies, and they can be exposed on the edges. If the pilot rolls into one, the bit will take a nice bite out of the laminate. Check the edges, and if necessary, fill voids with wood putty or the like, and sand them smooth.

A test cut on scrap is also in order before you trim the work. After the bit is adjusted, cut a piece of

To set the depth of cut, set the router or trimmer on the work and lower the bit so the cutting edge extends no more than 1/16 inch below the bottom of the layer to be trimmed. If it extends beyond that, you risk cutting into the surface that the bearing references, which in many cases is a laminated surface.

The strips forming a self-edge are applied and trimmed one at a time. Holding a full-sized router steady against a counter edge is not easy, which is why folks who do this work regularly have and use laminate trimmers. If you can minimize the overhang, you reduce the trimmer's work and speed the cut.

laminate-covered scrap. Lay a straightedge across the trimmed edge, and look for a whisker of light under the straightedge. Usually the cutting diameter of the bit is a mini-micron less than the diameter of the bearing. As long as the mini-micron really is small, you can shave the laminate absolutely flush with a lick or two of a file. If, however, the bit cuts perfectly flush or scuffs the substrate, you should try a second test. But this time, apply a strip or two of masking tape where the bearing will ride on it. This should pull the cutting edges away from the substrate edge and solve the problem.

Although the flush-trimmer generally leaves a satisfactory edge, sometimes you want a fit that's a little bit better than that. When you're going to lap the strips of a self-edge at an

outside corner, it's extremely important to get the first strip trimmed perfectly flush. Fred never trusts the cut made by the router in this case. It's too easy for it to leave just one little bump that will hold the next sheet up just a little bit. So he always uses a file to be sure. Hold the file flat on the second surface, and push it along the edge you just routed. Any little imperfections left by the router will be quickly wiped away.

As I mentioned, you seldom flush-trim every edge. Believe it or not, laminates can be sharp enough to give you a nasty cut. To make the exposed edges look and feel just a little softer, you bevel them. What Fred likes to do is to cut all of his edges with the flush-cutter, then clean up any glue balls before making a final pass with the bevel-trimming

Problem Solver

The contact cement you use to bond that laminate to its substrate usually turns into sticky wads of rubber when you try to cut through it. It sticks to the bit's pilot bearing and prevents it from following the edge of the stock exactly. If you don't catch it in time, it can even gum up the bearing so it spins with the cutter and burns the edge of the work.

Many companies coat their laminate bits with some form of repellent, but Fred says he's yet to discover one that's 100 percent effective. There are also numerous bearing lubes on the market that are supposed to prevent the bearings from jamming. But the best remedy, says Fred, is to keep a can of aerosol oil such as WD-40 or CRC with your laminate tools. All it takes is a small psssst of the oil every few cuts to keep the bearings running smoothly. The amazing part is that something in the oil makes the contact cement pull up and come loose from the cutters and bearings. Double good!

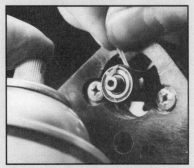

Contact cement is rubbery, stretchy stuff that gums up a bit and its pilot pretty quickly. A squirt of WD-40 or the like makes it easy to pull cleanly from the bit.

At an outside corner, you flush-trim the first strip across the counter edge. Be sure it is really flush, using a file if necessary. The second strip must be long enough to overhang the corner. Trim it flush, then make a finish pass with the bevel-trimming bit to soften the edge.

After the edges are trimmed, apply the laminate to the top. Your impulse may be to switch to a bevel-trimming bit and rout away the overhang. But you'll get better results if you first flush-trim the edge, then clean up any strings and gobs of contact cement. After that's done, make a finish pass with the bevel-trimming bit.

Bevel-trim the edges of a surface that was edge-banded and then covered with laminate. On this particular job, we used a regular router and a 45-degree chamfer bit.

bit. In areas of regular human contact, he takes a quick swipe over the very corner of the cut with a file just to be sure it's not sharp.

In many projects, there are tight corners that are inaccessible to a router, even a compact laminate trimmer. You're trimming a self-edge with an inside corner, for example, or an edge that meets a wall. Now you can't trim the last couple of inches on either side of the corner or next to the wall because the base of the router hits the adjoining edge or the wall.

Here's what to do: Nibble off the excess laminate with a pair of diagonal cutters—the kind of wire cutters electricians use—then carefully flush the ragged edges with a fine file.

Another sticky situation is where you have to trim an edge or an outside corner that is not 90 degrees. The problem is that your pilot bearing runs a little below the corner, and with an off-square corner you'll end up either leaving some overhang or gouging into the intended corner. To prevent this you can go back to the nibble-and-file technique. Or you can cut a tapered shim to stick to your router's baseplate with double-sided carpet tape. Cut the shim to the angle necessary to keep the bit shank parallel to the surface it's following.

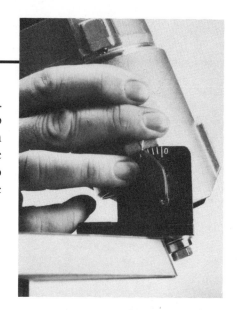

Here's an edge the tilt-base lam trimmer was made for. You tilt the motor and thus the bit to match the angle of the edge.

Offset-Base Laminate Trimmer

If you find yourself doing a lot of counter installations, and you get tired of hand trimming the few inches on either side of an inside corner or at the wall, you can buy an offset-base trimmer.

This little gem is the only router with the collet not mounted directly on the motor. In this instance, the arbor and collet are out on a corner of the router base. What this does is allow you to rout well within an inch of most obstructions, which really cuts down on the nibble-and-file work.

But you'll quickly discover some other nifty tricks it can do for you to expedite counterwork. One of the best is trimming to a wall. If you want a counter to fit against a wall, with or without a backsplash, you usually have to set the counter in place near but not against the wall. Then you use a compass to scribe along the wall and transfer its contour to the laminate. Cutting or sanding to the line is ticklish handwork. Good results are achieved only through practice.

With the offset-base trimmer, you leave the compass in your toolbox. Instead, you guide the edge of the trimmer along the wall and trim the laminate to a perfect fit.

The offset-base trimmer is also great for normal edge work because now the whole weight of the router is sitting securely on the counter instead of being halfway off the edge. No more tipping.

Getting a counter to fit seamlessly to a wall is tough. The edge must be scribed, and making the cut is usually handwork. With the offset-base trimmer, however, you block the workpiece so that the back edge of the laminate is about ¾ inch from the wall. Then run the trimmer between the wall and the backsplash, feeding from left to right. The nose of the baseplate transfers every hump and hollow in the wall to the laminate.

Before the countertop and backsplash are set and screwed in place, you can run the trimmer along the top edge of the backsplash and trim the front edge (top). The baseplate shape and bit location even allow you to get into inside corners (bottom). Only a snap with diagonal cutters and a couple of licks with a file will be needed to square it completely.

DADOING AND GROOVING

Dadoes and grooves are fundamental joinery cuts,

and they can be decorative as well. Making these cuts is one of the operations every woodworker tackles quite early in the learning process. You tire of butt joints after a couple of beginning projects, and the dado joint and its variants (dado-and-rabbet, tongue-and-groove, sliding dovetail, and so forth) are among the first improvements you try. A router makes them easy to cut.

As router-produced joinery cuts, both dadoes and grooves are essentially the same thing: a flat-bottomed channel cut into the wood. (Done with hand tools, and even with some power tools like the circular saw, the cutters and techniques may differ from dado to groove. With the router, however, the distinction is pretty much moot.) I think of the dado as a cut across the grain, and a groove as a cut with the grain. The distinction gets a little confusing when you talk about plywood and its layers with alternating grain directions. In the end, it's a semantical distinction, since the cutters, accessories, and basic methods are the same for both a dado and a groove.

Moreover, the term "groove" embraces curved and decorative cuts, along with the straight joinery cuts. The principal difference here between a joinery cut and a decorative cut is the cutter used. While I'll stick with straight bits in the following few pages, bear in mind that a groove-forming cutter of any profile usually can be substituted.

HAND-GUIDED THROUGH CUTS

The router, perhaps obviously, is an excellent tool for cutting dadoes and grooves. A saw-mounted dado cutter hogs away dadoes and joinery grooves more quickly, but the router has a lot of pluses that compensate for its lower cutting speed.

One of the pluses is that the dado can be precisely sized—the diameter of the cutter determines the width of the dado. Not all saw-mounted dado cutters are so precise: They require trial-and-error adjustments to achieve a specific cutting width. Another plus is that the cut is invariably clean and square—no raggedy bottom to the cut. Also, routers are particularly good for making dadoes and grooves in plywood. Plywood splinters easily, but the router leaves a smooth cut, even in plywood.

Another plus for the router is the ability to cut stopped grooves, curved grooves, or any combination of these. Circular-saw dado sets cannot cut curves, and any time you stop a cut, you're left with a "scoop" that matches the curve of the blade.

The primary reason I like the router for dadoing and grooving is its maneuverability. It's so much easier to maneuver a compact 5-pound router along a fence than it is to guide a hefty, unwieldy board across a dado cutter. If the workpiece is bigger than a bread-box side, I don't want to dado it on my table saw. I'd rather have at it with a router. Usually a hand-held router.

For some reason, I think of dadoing and grooving as hand-held router operations. Clamp a fence to the work, and rout. Of course, when I *stop* and think about it, I recall lots of dadoing and grooving operations done on the router table. I do smallish work like drawer sides on the router table, for example. But I mainly think of dadoing as an operation in which I clamp a fence to the work and guide the router along it, making the cut.

Dadoing is the quintessential fence-guided router operation. But beware! Because the router follows a fence so well, you have to be careful that your fence is *straight* if you want a straight cut. You can easily make a curved groove by using a curved fence. Just don't inadvertently make that curved cut when you are expecting a straight one.

Everyone has a favorite fence setup. Some are clean, simple, and practical. Fred, for example, is inclined to use whatever straight-and-true scrap is at hand as a fence. Others try some pretty complicated approaches. Intoxicated by grand visions, I've made a couple of dadoing gizmos that have gathered a ton of dust since they were last used. They were simply too involved to use.

The jigs and fixtures that follow are the survivors.

T-Square

Probably the first step past the scrap-board fence every router woodworker makes is to the T-square. He (or she) glues and screws two straight-and-true scraps together in a T-shape. One piece, called the crossbar or the head, butts against the edge of the workpiece; the other, called the fence or the guide or the blade, extends at a right angle across the workpiece surface.

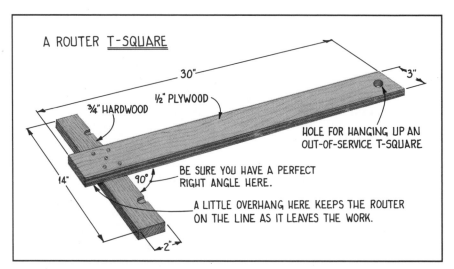

T-squares are easy to make, so make yourself several different sizes. Use a little one for relatively small work, a big one for long cuts.

The big advantage of the T-square is that it saves setup time. Instead of having to mark the full length of the dado, usually a single tick-mark is sufficient. So long as the fence is perpendicular to the crossbar, you can be assured that the dado will be square to the edge.

In addition, the crossbar acts as a brace, allowing you to secure the typical T-square with a single clamp. If you were to guide a router along an unadorned board fence secured with a single clamp, that clamp would become a pivot. With the crossbar butted firmly against the workpiece edge, that pivoting can't happen.

The typical T-square has a fence between 30 and 36 inches long and a crossbar between 12 and 18 inches long. (See *T-Square*.) For narrow work, a smaller guide is more manageable. If you do a lot of cabinet work, make a really big T-square, and cut both case sides at one time.

A lot of woodworkers make their T-squares like capital *T*'s, which is to say without extensions. My T-squares are like lower-case *t*'s. I

make the fence extend 4 to 6 inches beyond the crossbar to steady the router as it exits a cut. This is particularly useful with big routers and those with straight-edged or oversized baseplates.

You can make a T-square from straight, defect-free hardwood scrap, but I always use plywood for the fence, if not for the crossbar. Plywood is strong and stable. Half-inch material is satisfactory for the typical fence, in my experience, but by all means use ¾-inch material if you are concerned about deflection. The crossbar should be ¾-inch stock. When you cut the fence and the crossbar, be sure the edges are perfectly parallel.

Glue and clamp the pieces together, and check to be sure they are exactly square. An out-of-square T isn't a jig, it's scrap. When the glue dries, drill pilot holes and drive a few screws of the appropriate length to reinforce the glue joint.

Every T-square I've seen has notches routed in the crossbar. There seem to be two schools of thought here.

For those of the first school, the notches have the purpose of posi-

tioning the T-square. After assembling a T-square, you carefully rout a dado across the crossbar on each side of the fence, using the bit that will be used with the T-square. The jig can then be positioned simply by aligning the crossbar dado with the layout marks on the work. This is a useful approach, especially if you do a *lot* of dadoes of one particular width. But for some of us, it means having a different T-square for every router-and-straight-bit combination possible in our shops.

I'm frankly of the other school. To those of my ilk, the notches aren't purposeful, they are simply consequences of routing through dadoes. I use a different technique for lining up the guide, the so-called T-square Locating Jig.

T-Square Locating Jig. A scrap of thin plywood or hardboard or even plastic is all you need to make this jig. The idea is to trim a 6- to 12-inch-long strip of material to match the distance between a bit's cutting edge and the router's baseplate edge. With this jig, you can speedily and accurately position a T-square, using a mark for the dado's edge as a starting point.

Rather than drive nails into our maple bench top, I positioned an old painted shelf-board along the edge, then clamped it and the T-square to the bench. I tacked an odd-shaped scrap of Masonite in place, one edge tight against the square, the other overhanging the shelf-board. Then I pulled the router along the square and trimmed off the excess Masonite.

To make the jig, clamp a fence near the edge of a workbench. Butt the jig stock to the fence and tack it down with a couple of brads. Guide the router along the fence, cutting through the jig stock. Pry up the jig and remove the brads. You now have a jig to position your T-square when using that router-and-bit combination.

Mark the jig indelibly with the bit and router used. I like to drill a "hanging hole" in the jig, too.

To use the jig, measure and mark one edge of each dado. You don't have to square a line across the workpiece. You don't have to mark both edges. Just a single tick-mark per dado is all you need.

Align one edge of the locating jig with the mark, and butt the T-square against the other edge. The T-square's crossbar will ensure that the fence is square to the edge. The locating jig ensures that the fence is the proper distance from the dado location.

Quick, simple, and direct.

If you feel like being picky, make sure you have a different jig for each dado-cutting bit in your collection. This doesn't mean simply one for each *size* of bit you have, but one for every *individual* straight. Your ½-inch-shank ¾-inch straight may actually be slightly different in cutting diameter than your ¼-inch-shank bit of the same size. And it should go without saying—but I'll say it anyway—that you can't use a jig cut with one router to set the T-square for use with a different router.

Self-Positioning Dado Guide

A logical extension of the fence and locating jig "co-operative" is this all-in-one jig. The locating jig is glued to the underside of the fence, and the router rides on it. In the version shown in the photo on page 228, you mark—two tick-marks per dado are all you need—one edge of the dado to be cut, align the edge of the guide with the marks, then clamp it.

Although I've never done it, it would be easy to incorporate a crossbar, so you could align and square the guide on a single mark.

The guide is quick and easy to make, so you can cobble up a short one for narrow work and a long one for dadoing both of those base cabinet sides at one time.

To make the guide, glue the fence to a strip of hardboard or thin

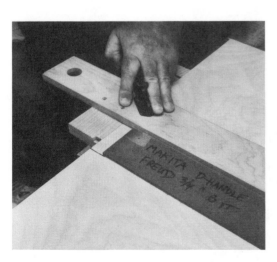

Using the locating jig is as simple as aligning one of its edges with the layout mark and then butting the T-square against the other edge. The T-square's crossbar will ensure that the fence is square to the edge.

> ## ► TRY THIS!
>
> Making cabinets? Try dadoing both sides of a cabinet at one time by lining them up side by side. It's a trick that saves time, since you only have to set up the guide fence once.
>
> Just as important, it ensures that the dadoes will line up and that the cabinet and its shelves will be square when it's assembled.

The self-positioning dado guide has two edges, so it can be used to guide cuts made with two different bits. Align the guide's edge right on the cut. The guide's "out-of-service" side is the perfect place for clamping.

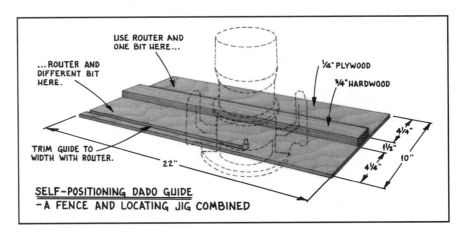

USE ROUTER AND ONE BIT HERE...

...ROUTER AND DIFFERENT BIT HERE.

TRIM GUIDE TO WIDTH WITH ROUTER.

¼" PLYWOOD

¾" HARDWOOD

4¼"

1½"

10"

4¼"

22"

SELF-POSITIONING DADO GUIDE
—A FENCE AND LOCATING JIG COMBINED

plywood. Chuck the bit that you'll use with the guide in your router, and run it along the fence, trimming off the excess plywood or hardboard. Each guide will accommodate two different bits, so mark clearly and indelibly along each edge which bit to use.

Double-Bar Dadoing Guide

Maybe the best quality of the double-bar guide is that it traps the router. Regardless of the feed direction, the router can't veer off course. A corollary is that since the router is trapped, you can give it room to play side to side, thus producing a cut—a controlled cut—that's wider than the bit being used.

I made this particular version of the double-bar guide after talking to my fellow woodworking writer/editor David Schiff. He described a jig used by a carpenter friend. The carpenter wanted to pare down the array of tools and equipment he had to haul

from job site to job site—*without* sacrificing versatility. Versatility encompassed being able to cut dadoes for 5/4 stock. A version of this jig enabled him to cut a range of dado and groove widths, including the 1¹⁄₁₆-inch-wide ones for the 5/4 stock, with a single bit—a ½-inch straight.

As you can see in the following photos and drawings, the guide consists of two crossbars glued and screwed to a fixed fence. The crossbars are perfectly perpendicular to the fixed fence. When either crossbar is tight against an edge of the workpiece, the fence will be at a right angle to that edge.

The second fence is attached in a way that allows it to move. The distance between the fences deter-

mines the width of the dado. When they are as close together as they can be, the router baseplate will just fit between them. And when they are as far apart as they can be, the baseplate will have about 1¼ inches of play. So, with a ½-inch bit, you can use this jig to cut dadoes between ½ inch and 1¾ inches wide. The challenge is to adjust this movable fence so it is both the correct distance from the fixed fence *and* parallel to it. (You can adjust this fence to help you cut a tapered dado. While you might never want a tapered dado, you might want a tapered dovetail slot. See the chapter "Sliding Dovetail Joints.")

To expedite the setting of the fences, I make plywood or hardboard

This double-bar dadoing guide traps the router between two fences, so you don't have to worry about it veering away from the fence. Giving the guide versatility is the movable fence, which allows you to cut dadoes two to three times wider than the bit.

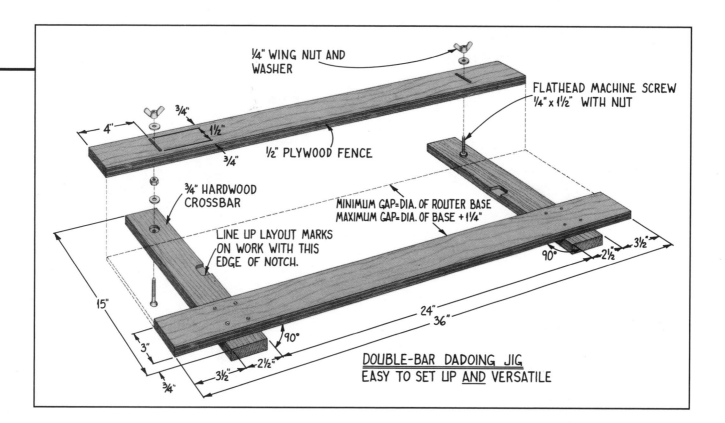

¼" WING NUT AND
WASHER

FLATHEAD MACHINE SCREW
¼" x 1½" WITH NUT

4"   ¾"

1½"

¾"

½" PLYWOOD FENCE

¾" HARDWOOD
CROSSBAR

MINIMUM GAP=DIA. OF ROUTER BASE
MAXIMUM GAP=DIA. OF BASE + 1¼"

LINE UP LAYOUT MARKS
ON WORK WITH THIS
EDGE OF NOTCH.

90°   2½"   3½"

15"

3"

90°

24"

36"

3½"   2½"

¾"

DOUBLE-BAR DADOING JIG
EASY TO SET UP <u>AND</u> VERSATILE

Problem Solver

Here's a familiar problem. You want to make a series of ⅜-inch-deep dadoes in some cabinet sides.

As every routerhead knows, the machine is a trimmer, and you shouldn't really cut deeper than about ¼ inch per pass. Your router is a fixed-base machine, so for each dado, you set the depth of cut to ¼ inch and make a pass, then advance the setting to ⅜ inch and make a second pass.

When you are done, you assess the process. Adjusting the router twice for each dado took a lot of time. *And* it didn't give you consistent results: Some dadoes are ⅜ inch deep, but a few are shy of that, and several others are deeper. Moreover, the play in the adjusting mechanism throws some dadoes off, leaving the dado too wide at the surface, with a ridge along one wall near the bottom. (See *Ridged Dadoes*.)

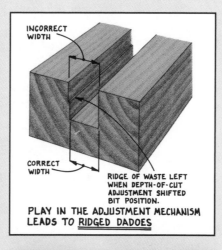

INCORRECT
WIDTH

CORRECT
WIDTH

RIDGE OF WASTE LEFT
WHEN DEPTH-OF-CUT
ADJUSTMENT SHIFTED
BIT POSITION.

PLAY IN THE ADJUSTMENT MECHANISM
LEADS TO <u>RIDGED DADOES</u>

The double-bar dadoing guide offers a single solution to all these woes. *Slot the spacer to give it an extra dimension.*

After you trim the spacer to the proper width, rout a slot the same way you would a dado. When using the guide, set your fixed-base router for the final depth, but make the first pass with the spacer in place. You can cut up to about ½ inch deep in two passes that way.

You have only a single adjustment to make, so you save time. All your dadoes will be of a consistent depth, and play in the mechanism won't displace parts of dadoes.

A hardboard or plywood spacer makes it easy to set the movable fence for a particular width of cut. Make a set for cuts of common widths, and prominently mark each. If you rout a slot in the spacer, it can help you make your cuts in two steps, without having to adjust the router's depth of cut.

Fractionating Baseplate

This baseplate *looks* like a square, but it's a trickster developed by Nick Engler, one of my favorite woodworking writers. The measurement from the axis of the bit to each of the four baseplate edges is different. With this baseplate, you expand the cutting width of any straight bit in your collection, and you give yourself the ability to produce a greater incremental range of cuts.

Cutting a 9/16-inch-wide dado, or a 5/8-inch-wide dado, or an 11/16-inch-wide dado is as simple as turning the router to reference a different edge against the guide fence. Use a 1/2-inch straight bit and make a pass with the "zero" side against the fence. Turn the router so the "+1/8" side is against the fence, and make a second pass. The additional 1/8 inch between the bit and the fence adds 1/8 inch to the width of the cut.

Using a 3/4-inch bit with this base gives you dado widths of 3/4 inch, 13/16 inch, 7/8 inch, and 15/16 inch. A 1/4-inch bit yields widths of 1/4 inch, 5/16 inch, 3/8 inch, and 7/16 inch.

If you are *really* clever, you'll see that Nick's idea is an inexpensive solution to undersized plywood. One of the shortcomings of plywood, especially hardwood stuff, is that it's often (usually?) a 64th or a 32nd undersized. Three-quarter ply is more likely 23/32 inch or 47/64 inch. So it rattles in the dado you cut for it with your 3/4-inch straight. Maddening.

One solution is to buy special dadoing bits that *are* 23/32 inch. But a less costly solution is to make a version of this fractionating baseplate that'll allow you to make those off-sized dadoes in two passes with a 1/2-inch or 5/8-inch bit.

To make the baseplate, cut a square of plywood or acrylic. Drill mounting holes using the factory baseplate as a template. Screw the plate to the router, and bore a 1/4-inch bit hole by switching on the router and advancing the bit into the baseplate. *Now* remove the baseplate from the router. Measure from the bit hole to the edges

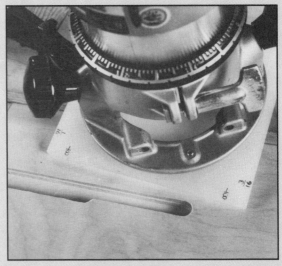

Make a pass with the "zero" edge of the fractionating baseplate against the fence; the cut will match the bit's diameter. Turn the router so a different edge rides the fence, and make a second pass. The bit is repositioned farther from the fence, widening the cut.

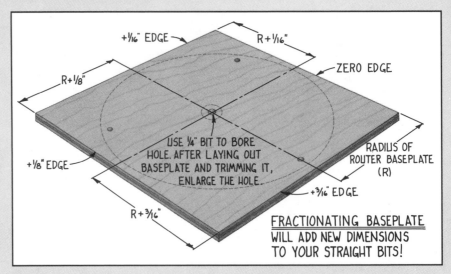

+1/16" EDGE   R+1/16"

R+1/8"   ZERO EDGE

+1/8" EDGE

USE 1/4" BIT TO BORE HOLE. AFTER LAYING OUT BASEPLATE AND TRIMMING IT, ENLARGE THE HOLE.

RADIUS OF ROUTER BASEPLATE (R)

+3/16" EDGE

R+3/16"

FRACTIONATING BASEPLATE
WILL ADD NEW DIMENSIONS TO YOUR STRAIGHT BITS!

spacers. Each spacer is a strip that's the length of the fences. I drop it between the fences, snug the movable fence against the spacer and in turn the spacer against the fixed fence, then lock down the movable fence.

To use the guide, measure and mark just the top of each dado. This is easy to do with a square to extend lines across the work: All you need is a little tick-mark.

The trick here is the notch routed in the crossbar. Because only one router and bit is ever used with the guide, that notch tells you how close to the fixed fence one edge of the cut

To position the guide, use the notch made in the crossbar. Align the edge of the notch that's closest to the fixed fence with the edge of the dado you want to rout.

of the baseplate, as indicated in *Fractionating Baseplate*. Trim the baseplate to produce the desired result. Remount the baseplate and you're ready to cut some odd-sized dadoes.

Cam Baseplate

Taking Nick's idea one step further, Fred made a baseplate whose circumference is a curve of steadily increasing radius. The baseplate is thus a cam that displaces the bit by ¼ inch when you rotate the router three-quarters of a turn.

The theory is: If you cut and mount the baseplate accurately, you should have no trouble cutting a dado or groove of the oddest width to an exact fit. When you make the first pass, set the base's zero point against the fence. You'll get a cut the width of the bit. Then you just "dial in" the amount by which you want to increase the width of the groove, by rotating the router and making a second pass with the appropriate spot against the fence.

To make the baseplate, begin with a 10- to 12-inch square of ¼-inch baseplate material. Fred used a piece of white acrylic plastic, but you can use plywood, polycarb, phenolic, or whatever you have that's appropriate. Using the router's factory baseplate as a pattern, drill mounting-screw holes (only) and mount the blank on the router. Using a ¼-inch-diameter straight bit, bore a bit opening through the blank.

A string compass is used to scribe

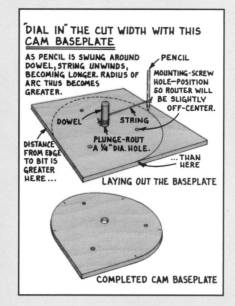

"DIAL IN" THE CUT WIDTH WITH THIS CAM BASEPLATE

AS PENCIL IS SWUNG AROUND DOWEL, STRING UNWINDS, BECOMING LONGER. RADIUS OF ARC THUS BECOMES GREATER.

PENCIL

MOUNTING-SCREW HOLE—POSITION SO ROUTER WILL BE SLIGHTLY OFF-CENTER.

DOWEL — STRING

PLUNGE-ROUT A ¼" DIA. HOLE.

DISTANCE FROM EDGE TO BIT IS GREATER HERE...

...THAN HERE

LAYING OUT THE BASEPLATE

COMPLETED CAM BASEPLATE

This teardrop-shaped baseplate is a cam. The radius of its edge's arc is steadily changing, so you can alter the bit's position in relation to the fence by turning the router. Once you calibrate the baseplate, you can widen a dado or groove by any fractional amount between zero and ¼ inch simply by twisting the machine and referencing a different spot against the fence during a second pass.

the circumference of the baseplate. (You can do this with the blank still mounted on the router, though you do have to remove it to cut it.) Tape the end of the string to a ¼-inch dowel or router-bit shank. Insert this swing point—you don't actually *pivot* the dowel or bit—in the bit opening. Wrap the string around the dowel or bit several times, then tie the free end around a pencil or marker. Set the marker on the blank and swing an arc of about 270 degrees (three-quarters of the way around the blank). As the arc is made, the string unwinds from the dowel and becomes longer. (Don't let the dowel turn as you scribe.) Instead of having a fixed radius, the curve you scribe has a steadily changing radius.

On the table saw, cut down the blank so you have one 90-degree corner forming tangents to the ends of the

arc, as shown in *Fractionating Baseplate*. Use a saber saw or band saw to carefully cut to the curved line. Sand the sawed edge smooth.

Remount the baseplate on the router, and use a larger-diameter bit to enlarge the bit opening. Then make a series of test cuts to calibrate your baseplate. The zero point should be with one flat side against the fence, the maximum offset with the other flat side against the fence. Maybe you want to mark the plus ¹⁄₁₆-, plus ⅛-, and plus ³⁄₁₆-inch spots. Plus ⁵⁄₃₂ inch will lie roughly midway between the ⅛ and ³⁄₁₆ marks.

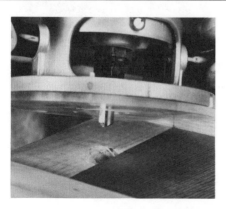

will be. Align the notch's edge with your tick-mark. If you're going to make a cut wider than ½ inch, the extra width is going to be toward the

If you don't have a plunge router, the double-bar guide helps you make do with your fixed-base router. Instead of tipping the bit into the work, start with it in the crossbar notch.

movable fence. (Unless you have a different T-square for each bit, you can't reliably use a T-square's crossbar notch to line up the work like this.)

Now clamp the jig in place on the work. Set the movable fence, and you're ready to go. Make a pass from left to right, cutting a ½-inch dado; then return from right to left, widening the dado from ½ inch to your final width.

CUTTING LIST					
Piece	Number	Thickness	Width	Length	Material
Fences	2	½"	3"	36"	Birch plywood
Crossbars	2	¾"	2½"	15"	Hardwood
Spacer	1	¼"	variable	36"	Lauan plywood

Hardware

8 pcs. #8 × 1" flathead wood screws
2 pcs. ¼" × 1½" flathead machine screws with washers and nuts
2 pcs. ¼" wing nuts

To make the jig:

1. Glue and screw the fixed fence to the crossbars. A right angle between the fence and crossbars is *essential*.

2. Rout the slots in the movable fence.

3. Cut a ¼-inch by 36-inch plywood strip. Rip it to the width that exactly matches the diameter of the router baseplate. The edges of the plywood spacer must be parallel.

4. Butt the spacer against the fixed fence, then butt the movable fence to the spacer. Trace the slots onto the crossbars. Mark the center point for the fence's machine screw "stud" at the end of the slot that's farthest from the fixed fence. Then drill a ¾-inch-diameter counterbore about ⁵⁄₁₆ inch deep. Bore a ¼-inch hole for the stud. Countersink the bottom of the crossbar.

(NOTE: The spacer's utility goes beyond its use in making the guide. The guide's basic cut is the ½-inch dado, and though you won't need the spacer to set the fences for that cut, you may want to use it as a spacer in making two-pass cuts. See "Problem Solver" on page 229.)

5. Drive a machine screw into each hole, fit washers on the screws, and tighten the nuts down into the counterbores.

6. Drop the movable fence over the studs, add the washers, and cinch the assembly in place with wing nuts.

To make a spacer:

1. Clamp the jig to a scrap workpiece.

2. Determine the width of the dado. Because you will always use a ½-inch straight bit with this guide, that's the width of cut you get when the distance between the fences equals the diameter of the router's baseplate. To get a cut wider than ½ inch, subtract ½ inch from the width, then add the difference to the router baseplate's diameter. The sum is the width of the spacer.

Example: To make a spacer for a ⅞-inch dado, subtract ½ inch from ⅞ inch. The difference is ⅜ inch. Add ⅜ inch to the diameter of the router baseplate. If it is 6 inches, then the spacer must be 6⅜ inches wide.

3. Cut the spacer and use it to set the movable fence. Remove the spacer from the jig. Make a test cut in a scrap piece. Measure the dado's width. If it is too wide, trim the spacer and repeat the test procedure. If it is too narrow, cut a new spacer, making the second wider than the first. Repeat the test procedure. If it is right on, return the spacer to the guide and rout the slot.

Fred's Dadoing Baseplate

The T-square is great for a dado that's perpendicular to an edge, and the edge guide is great where a groove runs parallel to an edge. But neither will help you cut a dado or groove that skews across the work.

With this jig that Fred cooked up, you line up a strip of hardboard or ¼-inch plywood right on the edge of the cut. This is the fence.

Attach the auxiliary baseplate to the router's baseplate next. Use double-sided carpet tape. As you position the auxiliary baseplate, make sure its straight edge is tangent to

Using the dadoing baseplate is a lot like using a pattern bit and template, but without the router tippiness. Line up the fence directly on the edge of the dado. The bit will cut right along the fence's edge. This setup is especially good where, as here, the cut skews across the workpiece, rather than being square or parallel to an edge.

BIT DRAWER

A truism of woodworking is that the material seldom is the advertised dimension. One-by isn't. It's ¾. Two-by isn't either; it's 1½. Depending on the weather.

Even sheet goods often deviate. Hardwood plywood, for example, is manufactured to a given thickness, but then finish sanded. It ends up being a 64th or a 32nd undersized. Similarly, sheet goods with a melamine or laminate face are often "fat" by the same fractions.

The upshot for the router woodworker is that dadoes cut for these materials using "full-dimension" bits aren't right. The dado's exactly ¾ inch wide, but the material either rattles or won't fit. A solution is available—"¾-inch" straight and dado bits that are ⅓₂ inch either over- or undersized.

• Woodhaven stocks a ²³⁄₃₂-inch downshear dado bit.

• Eagle America has a ²³⁄₃₂-inch straight bit (as well as a ³¹⁄₆₄-inch straight bit for that not-quite-half-inch plywood).

PASO ROBLES' ⁴⁹⁄₆₄" DADO BIT

PASO ROBLES' ²⁵⁄₃₂" DADO BIT

EAGLE AMERICA'S ²³⁄₃₂" STRAIGHT BIT

WOODHAVEN'S ²³⁄₃₂" STRAIGHT BIT

A dado cut with a ¾-inch bit (right) is too wide for the typical hardwood plywood. But the plywood fits a ²³⁄₆₄-inch-wide dado perfectly (left).

• Paso Robles Carbide makes downshear dado bits in ³³⁄₆₄-inch and ¹⁷⁄₃₂-inch diameters (½ plus a 64th and ½ plus a 32nd), in ⁴¹⁄₆₄-inch and ²¹⁄₃₂-inch diameters (⅝ plus), and in ⁴⁹⁄₆₄-inch and ²⁵⁄₃₂-inch diameters (¾ plus).

By the time you read this, other manufacturers may have jumped on the bandwagon, making these sizes even more available. Woodhaven, Paso Robles, and Eagle America are listed in "Sources" on page 337.

---

the bit's cutting edge. Then burnish it down.

To make the cut, slide the auxiliary baseplate's straight edge against the hardboard fence's edge, and the cut will be just where you want it. You don't have to fret about the router tipping, because the base is fully supported—partly by the auxiliary baseplate and partly by the fence.

The baseplate is made in a jiffy. Bore a hole through a scrap of Masonite with a 1-inch Forstner bit. The hole should be partially off the edge, as shown in *Fred's Dadoing Baseplate*.

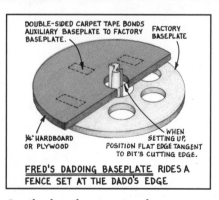

DOUBLE-SIDED CARPET TAPE BONDS AUXILIARY BASEPLATE TO FACTORY BASEPLATE.

FACTORY BASEPLATE

¼" HARDBOARD OR PLYWOOD

WHEN SETTING UP, POSITION FLAT EDGE TANGENT TO BIT'S CUTTING EDGE.

FRED'S DADOING BASEPLATE RIDES A FENCE SET AT THE DADO'S EDGE

On the band saw, trim the scrap to roughly the shape of the router baseplate. It's done! Rip that fence, get out the carpet tape, and you're ready to rout.

GROOVING WITH AN EDGE GUIDE

The edge guide is a basic router accessory that's particularly useful for cutting grooves. Some manufacturers include an edge guide with the router, others charge extra for it. Some routers have good edge guides, others have lousy ones.

In the typical configuration, the edge guide is a metal and/or plastic outrigger. This shoe, suspended out from the router on one or two metal rods, bears on the edge of the work-

TRY THIS!

A major limitation of the edge guide is its need to reference an edge.

So try this: Make a shoe that'll slide in a previously cut dado or

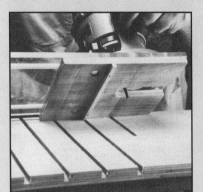

groove, and reference that cut. This is a practical way to knock out evenly spaced dadoes for shelves in bookcase sides, or slots in a tape or CD storage box.

The drawing here shows one way of making the slide and mounting it on the edge guide rods.

To cut a series of closely and evenly spaced dadoes, modify the homemade edge guide with a strip to slide in a just-cut dado. That way, you can position each new dado in relation to the previous one. It's a lot faster than setting a T-square for each cut.

Elu makes an excellent edge guide for its plunge routers. The shoe has an easy-sliding plastic facing. The locking knobs are easy on the fingers, and they seem vibration-proof—they don't work loose unexpectedly. Mr. Hands has his thumb and finger on the adjusting knob you use to fine-tune the guide's position.

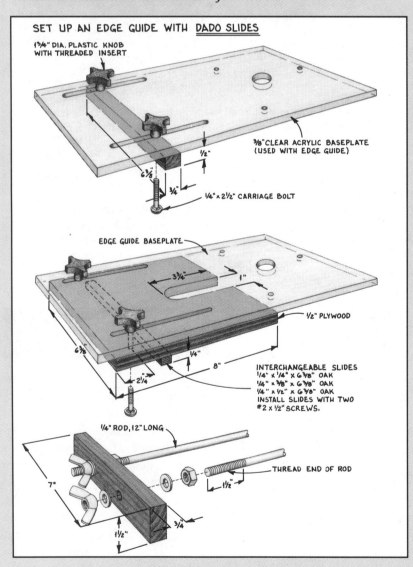

SET UP AN EDGE GUIDE WITH DADO SLIDES

1¾" DIA. PLASTIC KNOB WITH THREADED INSERT

⅜" CLEAR ACRYLIC BASEPLATE (USED WITH EDGE GUIDE)

½"

6⅜"

¾"

¼" × 2½" CARRIAGE BOLT

EDGE GUIDE BASEPLATE

3¾"

1"

½" PLYWOOD

6⅜"

¼"

8"

2¼"

INTERCHANGEABLE SLIDES
¼" × ¼" × 6⅜" OAK
¼" × ⅜" × 6⅜" OAK
¼" × ½" × 6⅜" OAK
INSTALL SLIDES WITH TWO
#2 × ½" SCREWS.

¼" ROD, 12" LONG

THREAD END OF ROD

7"

1½"

1½"

¾"

piece, guiding the router in a path parallel to that edge.

The best edge-guide designs allow you to install two guides on those rods, one on either side of the bit. They have knobs rather than thumbscrews, and those knobs set the guide securely. The router's vibrations won't shake them loose. They have provisions for you to add auxiliary faces to the guide(s).

Crummy edge guides are one of my pet peeves. The rods are too thin and limber, so the shoe tends to grab and chatter along the edge. The setscrews are either slotted screws or thumbscrews. Thumbscrews, in my vocabulary, are medieval torture instruments, and, true to their heritage, these modern versions torture your fingers. The slotted screws, on the other hand, get tortured and deformed by whatever screwdriver

A Homemade Edge Guide

This edge guide is sturdy, flexible, and reliable. You can adjust it from a position tangent to the bit out to one about 10 inches away. Thus, you can use it to make a straight bit cut a rabbet or cut a groove—it all depends upon where you lock the guide.

A significant part of the guide's utility is the kind of setscrews you use. We used plastic knobs that don't torture your fingers; they're big enough to turn easily. With a washer as an interface, the plastic knobs and plastic baseplate get a bite that even a big router can't vibrate loose.

It's easy to make, too. It's a BIG baseplate with a wooden fence hung beneath it. Study the drawing, then get to work.

This edge guide features a wooden shoe attached with two carriage bolts to an elongated acrylic baseplate. The plastic knobs are easy to grip and turn, so you can set the guide securely without trouble.

1. Dress the hardwood (we used maple), sand it smooth, and glue the parts together.

2. Cut the acrylic, rounding off the sharp corners. Sand and polish the edges if desired. Cut the slots with a ¼-inch straight bit. This is easiest to do on the router table.

3. Using the factory baseplate as a template, lay out the router location, the bit hole, and the mounting-screw holes. Give some thought to the orientation of the router handles in relation to the plane of the guide. Cut the bit hole, and drill and countersink the screw holes.

4. Set the maple edge guide under the baseplate, and mark the locations of the carriage-bolt holes. Drill and counterbore the holes.

5. Insert the carriage bolts into the guide, and tap them home with a hammer. Insert the projecting studs through the baseplate slots, drop washers onto them, and turn the plastic knobs onto them. Mount the unit on your router in place of the factory baseplate.

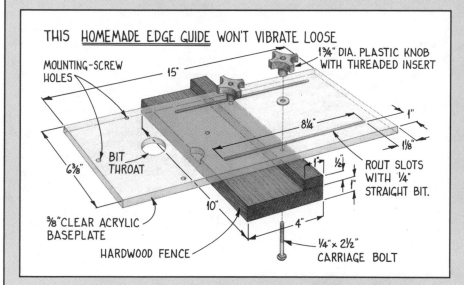

THIS <u>HOMEMADE EDGE GUIDE</u> WON'T VIBRATE LOOSE

MOUNTING-SCREW HOLES

15"

1¾" DIA. PLASTIC KNOB WITH THREADED INSERT

BIT THROAT

6⅜"

8¼"

1"

1⅛"

1" ½" 1"

ROUT SLOTS WITH ¼" STRAIGHT BIT.

⅜" CLEAR ACRYLIC BASEPLATE

10"

HARDWOOD FENCE

4"

¼" x 2½" CARRIAGE BOLT

CUTTING LIST

Piece	Number	Thickness	Width	Length	Material
Fence	1	1"	4"	10"	Hardwood
Spacer	1	½"	1"	10"	Hardwood
Baseplate	1	⅜"	6⅜"	15"	Clear acrylic

Hardware

2 pcs. ¼" × 2½" carriage bolts
2 pcs. ¼" I.D. flat washers
2 pcs. 1¾" dia. plastic knobs, with ¼" threaded through insert. Available from Reid Tool Supply Co., 2265 Black Creek Road, Muskegon, MI 49444 (800-253-0421). Part #DK-54.

Cutting Denticulated Strips

Making dentil molding is as simple as dadoing a board and then ripping it into strips. The challenge lies in cutting crisp, evenly spaced dadoes. The router produces the crisp cuts, and this simple-to-make baseplate generates the even spacing.

The trick is the little strip on the baseplate. When you make the first cut, the strip slides along the end of the workpiece, positioning the cut. When you make the second cut, the strip slides in the first. The second dado thus is the same distance from the first as the first is from the edge. Each new cut is referenced from the previous one.

To make the baseplate, cut a scrap of ½-inch plywood, drill a bit hole and mounting-screw holes, then mount it on the router base. Cut a sample dado

The denticulating baseplate need not be limited to flat-bottomed cuts. The baseplate on the router has a strip made by ripping a dowel. Used in conjunction with a core-box bit, the baseplate creates a different sort of dentil molding.

in scrap, and cut and plane a strip to fit it. Wax the strip well so that it will slide in the dado without binding. Then attach it to the plywood baseplate with a single screw at one end. Adjust the position of the strip, then drive a second screw through the other end, fixing it in place.

A more versatile unit can be made by marking position increments on the baseplate. Then you can alter the space between dadoes without remeasuring; just pull the screw, swing the strip, and reset the screw.

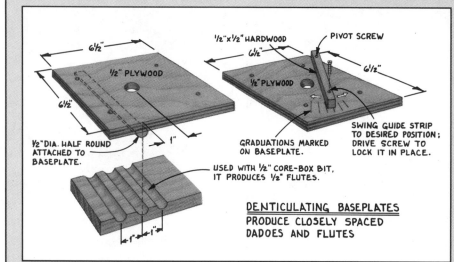

½" PLYWOOD

6½"

6½"

½"DIA. HALF ROUND ATTACHED TO BASEPLATE.

1"

½"x½" HARDWOOD

6½"

½" PLYWOOD

PIVOT SCREW

6½"

SWING GUIDE STRIP TO DESIRED POSITION; DRIVE SCREW TO LOCK IT IN PLACE.

GRADUATIONS MARKED ON BASEPLATE.

USED WITH ½" CORE-BOX BIT, IT PRODUCES ½" FLUTES.

1" 1"

DENTICULATING BASEPLATES PRODUCE CLOSELY SPACED DADOES AND FLUTES

you use to set them. And of course, no matter how hard you try to *set* either of these setscrews, the router's vibrations inevitably shake them loose. The guide slides away from the position you set. Naturally, you don't catch it in time, and your work's ruined.

If the router that you have is "equipped" with one of these buggers, or if you don't have a manufactured edge guide, make your own.

As I mentioned, the edge guide bears against the workpiece edge to guide your cut. Obviously, there's a limit to how far you can work from the edge.

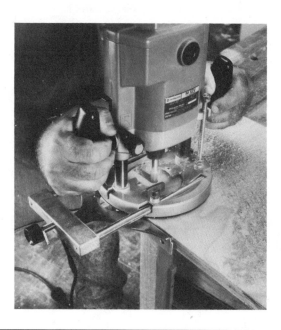

Feed direction is important when routing with an edge guide. Moving in the correct direction enlists the bit's help in pulling the guide against the reference edge as you cut.

Problem Solver

You cut a dado, guiding the router along a fence. But when you are done, the dado isn't absolutely straight!

Is there something wrong with the fence? Not necessarily. There may be something wrong with the router's baseplate. It may not be concentric to the bit.

Contrary to what you might think, a round router subbase isn't always perfectly round, and it isn't always perfectly aligned on the router base. This misalignment can be exacerbated if you remove the subbase for any reason. A consequence of this misalignment is that the position of your dado or groove can be shifted by 1/32 inch (or more) depending upon the spot that bears against your guide fence.

So if, as you slide the router along the fence, you also turn it, you may be moving the bit away from the fence. You probably will end up with a wandering dado.

Here's a simple solution: Paint a spot on your router's base. The spot will remind you to keep the same part of the router against the fence during the entire cut.

GROOVING THE WORK'S EDGE

When we talk about cutting dadoes and grooves, the first cuts that come to mind are those made into the face of the work. But there are times when you need to groove the narrow edge of the work. T-squares and double-bar guides are useless for this.

Four approaches come to my mind:

• Use two edge guides to steady your router on the work's edge. Set tight against both faces of the work, the guides prevent tipping as you make the cut with the appropriate straight bit.

• Use a slot-cutter of the appropriate size. (See the chapter "Edge Joints.")

• Make the cut on a router table.

• Clamp the board to the edge of a work surface, like our router bench, with the edge to be worked flush with the work surface. This gives broader support to the router, since roughly half of it can bear on the work surface. Use the appropriate straight bit, and guide the cut with an edge guide.

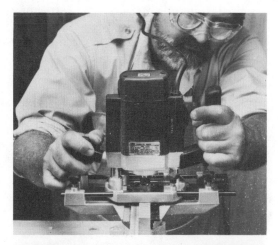

Grooving the edge of a board can be a hand-held router operation if you have two edge guides. Attach a 3- to 4-inch-wide scrap-wood face to one guide (it's on the left here). Then set up the guides, as shown, to capture the board between them. The wood face will broaden the bearing surface and keep the router perpendicular to the workpiece's edge.

The difficulty in grooving the edge of a board is the lack of support for the router. The edge is too narrow, and the router wobbles and tips from side to side. One solution to this problem is to clamp the board in such a way that additional support is offered to the router. The narrowness of the router bench I built (see the chapter "Router Bench") allows me to clamp work to its edge. Here, I am using the edge of the bench as the bearing for the edge guide, as I rout a groove in the edge of my work.

ROUTER TABLE THROUGH CUTS

Cutting grooves and dadoes on a router table has a lot in common with doing it on a table saw with a dado cutter. In both approaches, you have to set the fence, then slide the work across the table, keeping it squarely in contact with the fence as you do.

The biggest difference is the speed: Unless it is a shallow cut—½ inch or less—the dado cutter is going to be faster. For large workpieces—cabinet sides, for example—the setup of your table saw may favor the dado cutter also. If you work with plywood a lot, you may have long fence rails and a table extension to the right of the blade, as well as a big outfeed table. These accessories facilitate dadoing large panels as much as they do cutting large panels. *But . . .* it's unlikely that your router table is set up this way.

As I've said before, I'd opt to use

BIT DRAWER

If you like the speed of the power-saw-mounted dado cutter, but the clean cut of the router and straight bit, here's a compromise. It's the dado-cleanout bit from Eagle America.

With a shank-mounted bearing and cutting edges that are only ¼ inch long, the bit is designed to tidy up after your power saw. The design theory is that the bearing follows the dado's side, while the cutting edges clean the uneven dado bottom. And it does work, so long as your dado is at least ⅜ inch deep. Deeper is better, of course, since that will put the bearing in contact with more of the dado side.

The bit can also be used as a pattern bit, and as such, it can be used with a fence to cut shallow dadoes.

Three diameters—½, ⅜, and ¾ inch—are available, all with ¼-inch-long cutting edges, all in ¼-inch shank. Look for Eagle America in "Sources" on page 337.

► TRY THIS!

A shop-made sled can help you do a better job of dadoing pieces like drawer sides. The sled "adds" some length to the workpiece so you can slide it along the fence smoothly. It backs up the work to minimize tear-out as the bit exits the cut. And it helps you hold the work in a spot well clear of the bit.

Make one from a piece of plywood. To help you manipulate and maneuver it, add a knob or handle. A length of dowel jammed in a hole in the plywood can serve as a handle. Use your imagination, but remember that use chews up such sleds. Make the handle either expendable or easy to move to a new piece of plywood.

You can use any scrap to back up a dado cut, but by adding a peglike handle, you make the scrap easier to control. When the end of the sled gets too chopped up to prevent tear-out, trim it off. When the sled gets too short, move the handle to a new one.

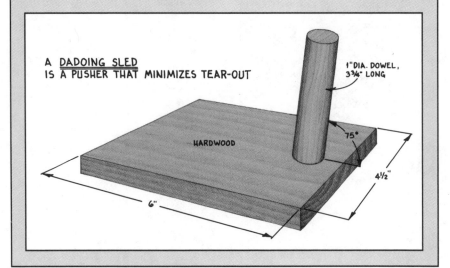

A DADOING SLED IS A PUSHER THAT MINIMIZES TEAR-OUT

1" DIA. DOWEL, 3¾" LONG

HARDWOOD

75°

4½"

6"

a hand-guided router for large or unwieldy workpieces. I'd just rather maneuver a compact router than a large panel. But small parts—drawer sides and fronts, for example—I'd dado or groove on the router table.

The technique is self-evident, I think. Select the bit, chuck it in the router, and set the depth of cut. Adjust the fence to properly locate the cut. Make the cut. If necessary, raise the bit and make a second pass to deepen the cut.

STOPPED CUTS

When a dado or groove doesn't extend completely from one edge of a board to the other, it's referred to as a stopped cut or a blind cut. It can begin at one edge and end before it reaches the other (half-blind), or it can begin and end shy of both edges (full-blind).

As I mentioned before, the router is unparalleled in its the ability to cut stopped grooves. It can get into and out of the cut with relative ease. Think how you'd have to do it with a saw-mounted dado cutter.

Using a Hand-Held Router

Fully stopped cuts are the stuff of plunge routers and plunge cutters. You lay out the dado, indicating the cut's ends. You set your fence. Position the router, plunge the cutter, rout until the end-of-cut mark aligns with the bit, and retract the bit, ending the cut.

But not all of us have plunge routers. What other options are there?

Obviously, ending a stopped cut is easy, even with a fixed-base router. Turn off the router and lift it, carefully, straight up from the work. The real

---

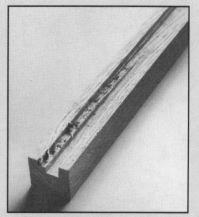

Safety First!

Cutting a groove wider than the bit can create feed-direction surprises.

Most router table operations—including plowing a groove the full width of the cutter—feed from right to left across the cutter. Widening an existing groove is where you have to *think*. Here's an example:

Needing a ¾-inch-wide groove in 1½-inch-square oak edge banding, I decided to use a ½-inch straight and to set the fence to center the groove across the oak's width. The first pass went fine. I turned the strip around and started the second pass. The cutter snatched the strip right out of my hand and shot it a good 10 feet across the shop. What gives here!!?

Fred explained what gives. Here, in brief, is what *you* need to take from it:

• If the bit is widening the groove by cutting on your side (away from the fence), feed right to left.

• If the bit is cutting on the fence side of a groove, you must feed from left to right.

The latter situation is tricky, even when you are feeding the stock in the correct direction. This is because the rotation of the cut-

Here's a literal climb cut. In making a second pass to widen the groove, I fed this stock in the wrong direction. The cutter snatched the strip from me, shot it across the shop, and in the process, butchered the end of the cut.

ter will be trying to pull the stock away from the fence as you feed. If you must do the cut this way for some reason, set up featherboards to hold the stock against the fence, both before it contacts the cutter and after. (See "Problem Solver" on page 89 for information on making featherboards.) But the best approach is to set up the cut in the first place so that the bit will be widening the groove by cutting on *your* side of the groove. See "Feed Direction" on page 151 for a fuller explanation.

---

trick is *starting* a stopped cut with a fixed-base router.

One option is to tip in or drag in the bit. If it is a bit designed for plunging, meaning that its cutting edges extend across its bottom, you can tip it in. Align the cutter with the start mark. Rear the router back so its baseplate, though not flat on the work, nevertheless *is* in contact with both the fence and the work.

Turn on the router and carefully, slowly, lower the spinning bit into the work. Practice. You want the axis of the bit aligned with the dado so you don't create a bulb where the bit enters the work.

If the bit is not a plunging type, you can get it into the work by moving the router along the fence as you lower it into the work. The bit will cut a ramp from the surface down to

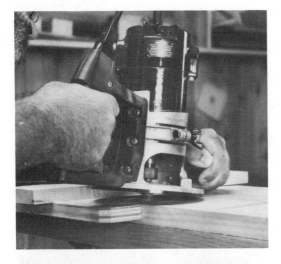

Tipping in the bit to begin a stopped dado isn't difficult. Just have one spot on the baseplate in contact with the work, and another against the fence. With the bit clear of the work, switch on the router and carefully lower the spinning bit into the work.

Using a Forstner bit of the same diameter as the router bit, bore beginning and end holes for each stopped cut. With the router bit in the starting hole, switch on the router and advance it to the end hole. A router with a trigger switch makes this easy to control.

full depth, and once the bit's in the work, you can carefully feed the router back along the fence to rout this ramp out to full depth.

Remember, while neither method is foolproof, either can be done. Practice! Just practice.

You may find that a double-fence guide, where the base is firmly captured between two fences, helps you keep the cut straight.

A second, more foolproof, approach is to *drill* a starting hole for the bit. Obviously, the hole has to match the diameter of the bit. It should be the same depth as the intended depth of the dado. Set the bit in the hole, turn on the router, and cut.

The Router-Table Approach

Stopped grooves are easily cut on the router table. Easily cut, that is, if the workpiece is of a manageable size. To make such cuts, you must lower the work onto the spinning bit, move it to make the cut, then lift it free of the bit. Obviously, if the workpiece is too big or unwieldy, you are going to have trouble maneuvering it.

To know where to begin and end a stopped cut, mark the outer edges of the bit on a piece of tape stuck on the fence or the mounting plate. (Use art tape rather than masking tape; you'll find it easier

to remove.) With the body of a try square flat against the fence, butt the blade gingerly against the cutting edge of the bit. Scribe along the blade onto the tape. Then switch the try square to the other side of the bit and repeat.

The correct feed direction for this sort of cut is right to left. So line up the mark for the beginning of the groove with the mark on the fence that's to the left of the bit. Now drop

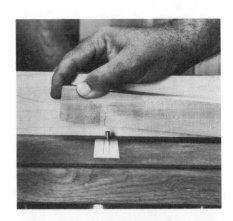

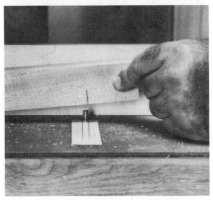

Marks on masking tape help you begin and end a stopped groove in the right spots. With the cutting edges parallel to the fence, mark tangents on the tape, as shown. To start the cut (top), align the mark on the workpiece with the tape marking that will place the bit **inside** *the groove. Then feed the work until the end mark on it aligns with the other tape mark. Tip the work up off the bit (bottom).*

the stock onto the bit, beginning the cut, and feed the work to the left. As the end-of-cut mark on the stock comes up to the mark on the fence to the right of the bit, carefully lift the end of the workpiece off the bit. Shut off the router.

Using Stop Blocks

How about stops, you ask.

Stop blocks are good when precisely set. They're real time-savers in doing repetitive cuts, where they supplant layout markings. But a lot of times, especially for one-of-a-kind cuts, stop blocks are just extra setup work. Fred, I know, is inclined to eyeball the cut, mark to mark.

Nevertheless, here are a few stop block tips.

Tip One. The easiest way to set stop blocks, I've learned from Fred, is to make an initial cut mark-to-mark, *without stop blocks*. With the cut done, use *it* to set blocks for the subsequent cuts. Position the router (or the work, with a router table setup) at the beginning of the cut and attach a stop to the fence. Move the machine (or the work) to the end, and set the second block. This way, you can skip the math and the ruler work, the test cuts, and the resetting.

Tip Two. Small hand screws make good stops to use on the router table. You can use any sort of clamp to secure little scraps to the fence, but hand screws are pretty direct. The clamp *is* the block. When you tighten them on the fence, set them just a little above the tabletop so rout-dust can blow under them. Then it won't collect against the stop, throwing off the accuracy of it.

Tip Three. You can make rudimentary (but reusable) stops by lam-

To cut several matching stopped dadoes, cut the first from mark to mark, then use it to position stops on the T-square. Use scraps and just nail them to the T-square. Move the square to guide the next cut, and the stops will control its length.

inating two scraps of plywood to form an end lap. Set the stops against a router T-square, and drive brads or screws through the stop into the square. It may not be pretty, but it works.

Tip Four. If you prefer pretty, make more finished stops. Laminate two pieces of birch plywood, forming an end lap as in Tip Three. Cut them to a handsome profile. Drill a hole for a mounting screw through the part of the stop that'll overlap the fence. Slot the T-square (or other) fence for stop-mounting machine screws. Countersink the underside so the screw heads will be recessed.

Tip Five. "Try This" on page 87 shows stop blocks you can make to use with a router table fence.

BIT CHOICES

When you cut an ogee edge on a board, there really are only a couple of bits that will do—an ogee (of the appropriate size) in either a piloted or an unpiloted configuration. But cutting joinery dadoes and grooves is an entirely different situation. A lot of different bits lend themselves to the job.

How do you decide what to use?

On a pragmatic level, most of us will use whatever straight bit we have that's the right diameter for the cut we want to make. Maybe you bought a set, and it included ¼-, ½-, and ¾-inch straight bits. You use those three bits for all your grooving and dadoing, because those are the bits you have.

On a more idealistic level, here's some background to help you decide

See Also . . .

Grooves aren't always straight. Page through the chapter "Routing Curves and Circles" for ideas on routing curved grooves using trammels, templates, and other devices.

Though this chapter has focused on fence-guided cuts, you can rout dadoes and grooves guided by a template. You reference the template with either a template guide bushing or the shank-mounted bearing of a pattern bit. See the chapter "Template-Guided Work" for more information on making and using templates.

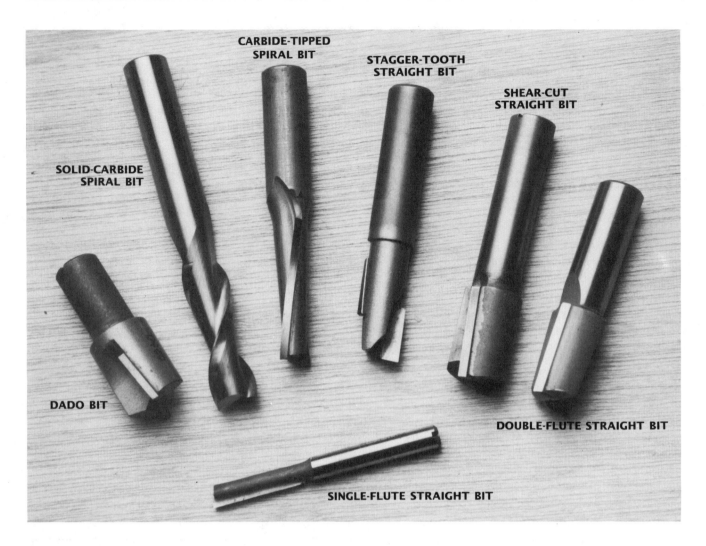

what bits to buy when expanding your inventory.

Double-flute straight bits are THE basic router bits. Each bit has two vertical cutting edges, and thus it makes two cuts per revolution. Use a double-flute straight when the finish is primary and the feed rate is secondary.

An enormous variety of sizes is available. Some manufacturers list 50 or more different double-flute straight bits. Cutting diameters from ¹⁄₁₆ inch to 2 inches, with flute lengths from ¼ inch to 2½ inches. Even metric sizes are available (from Byrom; see "Sources" on page 337). The typical catalog may list ½-inch-

diameter bits with flute lengths of ¾, 1, 1¼, 1½, 2, and 2½ inches.

So how do you choose which to buy (or use)?

Take the shortest length for work to be done. For dadoes, choose the one with the ¾-inch-long flutes. That's plenty long for cuts that will seldom exceed a ½-inch depth.

If you have a plunge router, make sure you are getting bits that have plunge-cutting ends. Most do these days, but check before you buy.

Finally, remember that bits at the extremes of the size range are generally not guaranteed by their manufacturers, simply because they take the tooling to the outer limits.

Shear-cut straight bits are variants of the double-flute straights. A bit of this design is called shear-cut because the cutting edges are at a slight angle (usually about 3 degrees) to the bit's axis. In a broad sense, the shear-cut bit shaves the work, rather than chopping it. A shear-cut bit is often recommended when the finish from a standard bit would be inadequate or when the bit will be used in a relatively low-horsepower router.

Single-flute straight bits should be used where the cutting speed is more important than the cut finish. These bits cut once per revolution, allowing faster feed rates but yielding rougher cuts. Because there's only a single flute, there's extra chip clearance. The tip is generally designed for fast plunge cutting.

Available cutting diameters range from $\frac{1}{16}$ inch to $\frac{5}{8}$ inch; flute lengths range from $\frac{3}{4}$ inch to $1\frac{1}{2}$ inches. Byrom markets a 14-millimeter-diameter single-flute bit.

The single flute is easy to sharpen by hand, by the way.

Stagger-tooth straight bits are so called because they have two cutting edges spaced 180 degrees apart, each half the length of its flute. One extends from the tip to the middle of the flute, the other from the middle to the end. The benefit of the design? It combines the cutting speed and chip clearance of a single-flute bit with the finish of a double-flute bit. Stagger-tooth bits are intended for cutting dense or abrasive man-made materials and panel goods.

Available sizes range from $\frac{1}{4}$-inch to $\frac{3}{4}$-inch cutting diameters with $\frac{3}{4}$-inch to $1\frac{1}{2}$-inch flute lengths.

Paso Robles makes its stagger-tooth straights with downshear and upshear on alternate edges. This way, the shear angles on a through cut are toward the center of the stock. This is great for veneered stock (like plywood). An upshear tends to lift the veneer at the edge of the cut, leaving a raggedy, fuzzy edge. A downshear pushes the veneer down, slicing it cleanly. The Paso Robles stagger-tooth shears down on both surfaces at the same time. Dynamite!

Spiral bits are shaped very much like twist-drill bits. Spiral-flute straights combine a shearing action in cutting with an augering action in chip clearance. The shearing action yields an especially clean, accurate cut, while the augering action clears the chips up (or down) and out of the cut. A trade-off is a reduced cutting rate.

Spirals are available in upshear and downshear designs. In a dado-cutting operation, the upshear spiral will lift the chips out of the cut. But it will also lift the wood fibers along the edges of the cut—it's paring from the bottom of the cut toward the surface, after all. The downshear spiral is a response to the latter problem. Its cutting action is from the surface down, so it leaves a smooth edge at the surface. But it is also augering the chips toward the bottom of the cut.

There is a subsidiary dynamic stemming from the shear direction. The upshear action pulls the work against the router, while the down-shear action pushes the work away from the router.

To get the twist, manufacturers make the *entire* bit from either carbide or high-speed steel (HSS). (Paso Robles spirals are carbide-tipped, but they don't have the degree of twist that other brands do. They seem more like shear-cut straights than spirals.) The HSS spiral is sharper to begin with, but it dulls relatively quickly. The carbide spiral holds its edge a long time, but it is brittle. It is also pricey: A carbide spiral generally costs about two-and-a-half times what a comparable HSS spiral does.

Spirals are available in cutting diameters of $\frac{1}{8}$ inch through $\frac{3}{4}$ inch, with flute lengths varying from $\frac{3}{4}$ inch to $1\frac{1}{2}$ inches.

Dado bits, curiously enough, are listed by only two sources, Paso Robles and Woodhaven. (And I suspect that Woodhaven gets its dado bits from Paso Robles.) Chunky straights are what they are, being an inch or more shorter than comparable straights. Their advantage over common straight bits is reduced vibration—a result of the short, thick body—coupled with downshear cutting. The cutting edges are short, too—$\frac{5}{8}$ inch. The cutting diameters range from $\frac{1}{2}$ inch to $\frac{13}{16}$ inch.

RABBETING

A rabbet is one of the joinery cuts the router does best.

Essentially an edge treatment, it is done with a piloted bit.

Select the rabbeting bit with the correct cutting width, chuck it in the router, set the depth of cut, and rout. That's all there is to it . . .

Until you sit down and think about rabbets and rabbeting, that is. Then you realize there's more to the repertoire of rabbet cuts than can be executed with a rabbeting bit. There are extra-deep and extra-wide rabbets. Rabbets in curved shapes, rabbets in narrow edges.

RABBETING WITH A PILOTED BIT

The first choice for the average rabbeting operation is the rabbeting bit, which has a pilot. It minimizes setup: The only adjustments you can make are the depth of cut and the angle of attack. The measurement between the bit's cutting edge and its pilot governs what I call the width of the rabbet. (A lot of bit manufacturers call this the depth of the rabbet.) You insert the bit, adjust the depth setting, and rout. It is simple, but because it is, it doesn't allow much variation.

Freud offers two rabbeting bits in its basic catalog. The difference between them is the shank size: One is ¼ inch, the other is ½ inch. Both cut a ⅜-inch-wide rabbet up to ½

inch deep. With either bit, one of the rabbet's dimensions is going to be ⅜ inch; the other can vary only up to ½ inch. Bosch and Amana take this a step further by adding bits that cut ½-inch-wide rabbets to the basic ⅜-incher. If you scrutinize the listings of Byrom and Cascade, which seem to be longer, you'll find the variation is in the length of the carbide flute, not in the space between cutting edge and pilot.

To alter the width of the rabbet with such bits, you can do two things. One is that you can change your angle of attack, as shown in *Angle of Attack*. This can be a useful approach, since it can change the dimension over which *you* have control, while preserving the simplicity of setup and operation that pilot bits provide.

The other thing you can do is to change the pilot bearing. Several bit manufacturers sell bearing "kits" that

will give you four different widths of cut from one bit. (See "Bit Drawer" on page 249.)

(There is a third thing you can do, and that is to circumvent the pilot somehow—using an edge guide or a fence. You can only narrow the cut using this approach, but it's valid, it works. If you take this approach, though, you probably should question why you are using a rabbeting bit and not a straight bit.)

The piloted bit can be used in both hand-held and table-mounted routers, of course. Because the bit is piloted, you don't *have* to use the router-table fence. (You *should* use a starting pin if you don't use the fence.) If you do use the fence, set it so it lines up with the pilot. Hold a straight edge against the fence so it bridges the bit gap, and adjust the fence until the straight edge just touches the pilot bearing.

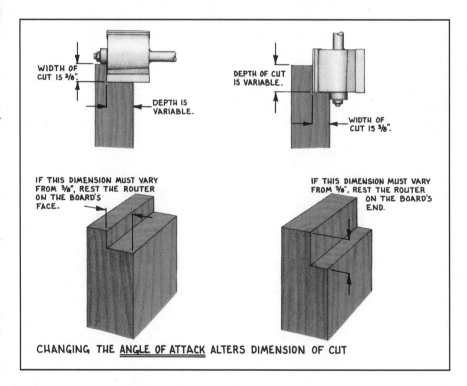

WIDTH OF CUT IS ⅜".
DEPTH IS VARIABLE.

IF THIS DIMENSION MUST VARY FROM ⅜", REST THE ROUTER ON THE BOARD'S FACE.

DEPTH OF CUT IS VARIABLE.
WIDTH OF CUT IS ⅜".

IF THIS DIMENSION MUST VARY FROM ⅜", REST THE ROUTER ON THE BOARD'S END.

CHANGING THE ANGLE OF ATTACK ALTERS DIMENSION OF CUT

RABBETING WITH A STRAIGHT BIT

A straight bit is a very flexible rabbet-cutter. If there is a drawback, it is only that the setup can take a bit more time, especially with a hand-held router. This is because you need a fence (or edge guide) to control the cut.

On the router table, you tighten the bit in the collet, then set the fence to expose only enough of the bit to make the desired rabbet. If your router table is like ours, then it's like the table saw—the fence is always in place, and adjusting its setting before making a cut is second nature.

With a hand-held router, you can either clamp a straightedge to the work, or you can break out the edge guide. Some commercial edge guides are pretty shoddy, so you might try making a custom baseplate for rabbeting. (See "Custom Rabbeting Baseplate" on page 250.)

STOPPED RABBETS

A stopped rabbet, of course, is one that does not extend the full length of an edge. It can be stopped at one or both ends.

Here's a list of techniques for beginning and ending stopped rabbets using a hand-held router:

• Mark the beginning and ending points on the work. Make the cut between the two marks, visually aligning the bit with the starting mark to begin, and stopping the cut when the ending mark is reached. The accuracy of this approach depends upon the clarity of your vision and the

steadiness of your hand. (It can be easier to do this if your marks reference the outer edge of the base rather than the bit, since this relieves you of the need to sight through the baseplate's bit opening and the operation's chip storm.)

• Clamp stops to the work. The position of the stops would correspond to the marks that reference the base. You butt the router against the stop at the starting point and rout until it hits the stop at the end point. Clamping stops to the work can more easily be said than done in many cases. You might want to try using a dadoing jig with adjustable stops. (See the chapter "Dadoing and Grooving" for plans.)

Doing the same cuts on the router table can be a little easier. Visually align beginning and ending marks by penciling marks on the router-table fence that correspond to the edges of the bit (put a little masking tape on the fence if you don't want to mark directly on it). Obviously, your view of these marks won't be obscured.

To make the cut, you simply align the work beside the bit, push it against the fence (and thus onto the bit), make the cut, and pull the work away from the fence.

Almost easier still is to use stops. You can apply small hand screws to the router table fence as stops. The hard part is calculating the positions.

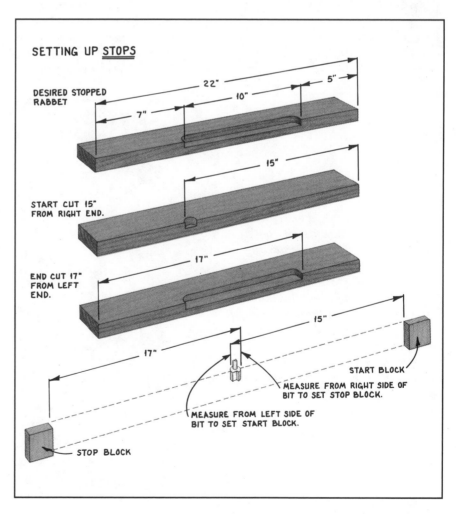

SETTING UP STOPS

DESIRED STOPPED RABBET

22"
10"
7"
5"

START CUT 15" FROM RIGHT END.

15"

END CUT 17" FROM LEFT END.

17"

15"

17"

START BLOCK

MEASURE FROM RIGHT SIDE OF BIT TO SET STOP BLOCK.

MEASURE FROM LEFT SIDE OF BIT TO SET START BLOCK.

STOP BLOCK

In an ideal situation, the router woodworker can mark starting and stopping points on the workpiece itself and track the bit's progress visually. Setup is thus minimized, since you don't have to extrapolate from end points to stop-block positions.

A hand screw can serve double duty when you are making a stopped rabbet. Properly positioned, the hand screw can both secure the work to the router bench and be the stop.

Cutting a stopped rabbet on the router table is easy. Lay the work on the table. Brace the right end of it against the fence, and keep the left end free of the bit. Align the starting point mark on the work with the mark on the fence to the left of the bit. Push the work flat against the fence, thus beginning the cut. Feed the work to the left, making the cut. Stop when the end point on the work aligns with the mark on the fence to the right of the bit. Pull the end of the work away from the fence, ending the cut.

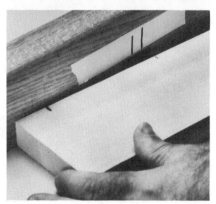

The stop for the starting point will be to the right, the one for the ending point will be to the left. *To set the starting block:* Measure from the end of the work to the beginning of the cut. That's the distance the block must be from the left side of the bit. *To set the ending block:* Measure from the beginning of the work to the end of the cut. That's the distance the block must be from the right side of the bit. *Example:* The workpiece is 22 inches long and the rabbet is 10 inches long. The rabbet starts 7 inches from one end, and it ends 5 inches from the other. The starting block will be on the right, 15 inches from the left side of the bit. The ending block will be on the left, 17 inches from the right side of the bit.

Obviously, the length of your fence can pretty easily be outstripped. When this happens, either you can attach a temporary facing that's long enough for the task at hand, or you can revert to the visual alignment of pencil marks.

WIDE RABBETS

For purposes of this discussion, a wide rabbet is one that's more than ½ inch wide, since that's the maximum width possible using a piloted cutter. To cut such a rabbit, you need to use a straight bit. With a hand-held router, use an edge guide or fence to control the cut. Obviously, on the router table, you'll use the fence.

Most router woodworkers have a ¾-inch straight bit. Larger straights *are* available, though not that many of us have 2-inch, 1½-inch, or even 1-inch bits. Do you have a large-diameter mortising, planer, or bottom-cleaning bit? Any of these will do a

Dealing with Chip-Out and Tear-Out

It's a hazard of routing rabbets. As the bit cuts, it tends to tear wood strands (tear-out) and lift chips (chip-out) along the edges of the cut. Tear-out seems to happen most along the shoulder of the cut, while chip-out occurs along the bottom edge. The explanation is depicted in the drawing.

When you are feeding the router in the proper direction, chip-out occurs as the cutting edge of the bit sweeps off the wood. Because the cutting edge is almost perpendicular to the work's edge, it's cutting end grain as it exits. With nothing backing them up, the outer wood fibers tend to be forced out from the cut, and they break and split. Often the splitting extends below the base of the case, taking chips out of the cut's bottom edge.

In a climb cut, the cutting edge is sweeping into the wood, forcing the wood fibers in so there are no chips lifting out. But you are feeding with the bit's rotation, and the router wants to gallop ahead, even if it has to pull you along.

Tear-out is influenced by grain direction rather than feed direction. If the grain is straight and your cut is paralleling it, the cutting edge sweeps easily and cleanly. But if the grain bows and shifts and curls, the cutter tends to bring up shavings that don't get sliced off but instead curl up along the edge of the wood. It's the same problem you have planing wood with shifting, changing grain directions.

Most experienced router woodworkers have settled on some approach that—if only in their minds—minimizes these tendencies. The most common approach is to rout the full rabbet in two or more passes, and to make one of those passes a climb cut—cutting *with* the rotation of the bit, rather than against it. There are two schools of thought here. One says you make the first pass a shallow climb cut—this is often called a scoring cut. The other says you make the second pass the climb-cut.

In theory, neither pass needs to be a climb cut. The drawing shows how a shallow first pass will alter the angle between the cutting edge and the work's edge at the exit point. Chip-out is minimized if the cutting edge is skimming the edge, slicing along the grain rather than chopping across it. The second pass should be the deep one.

Hold on to the router if you do make a climb cut. The bit will grab and jerk the tool along the cut, and it can startle you if you aren't expecting it. The caveat to hold on applies doubly when doing this on the router table. If the bit grabs the work, it can jerk it out of your grasp, not inconceivably resulting in injury (and a botched workpiece).

great job. Use the largest-diameter bit you have—however big it is—to produce those wide rabbets.

As the cut gets wider—wide to the point that you have to make three or four passes to complete it—avoiding wobbles and dips is the challenge. On the router table, you have to keep the uncut surface of the piece tight against the table. And if the ultimate cut is wider than the remaining uncut surface, then the last pass or two can be dicey. Pressure on the wrong area of the work can cause it to tip, gouging it. Doing the cut with a hand-held router isn't likely to be any easier.

One solution is to treat the rabbet as a wide dado or groove. Cut the work with some excess width or length (whichever is appropriate).

By supplanting the pilot with a fence, you can greatly increase the width of the rabbet you can cut with the router. Here, the rabbet matches the diameter of the bit. But by adjusting the fence away from the bit, the rabbet could be made even wider.

Leave a ridge of unrouted stock at the outer edge of the cut. This will support the router or the work. After the router cut is done, you trim the ridge of waste away on the table saw, reducing the work to its final width and simultaneously turning the dado into a rabbet.

An alternative is to use double-sided carpet tape to stick a couple of shims to the router table at the fence after making the first pass. The shims will support the workpiece as you make subsequent passes.

Another approach is to deal with the rabbet as a deep cut. Address the depth of the rabbet with the fence or edge-guide setting, and

TRICKS FOR
CUTTING WIDE RABBETS

TO CUT A WIDE RABBET, CUT THE WORKPIECE OVERSIZED.

WITH A HAND-HELD ROUTER

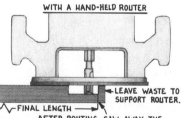

← LEAVE WASTE TO SUPPORT ROUTER.

←| FINAL LENGTH |→

AFTER ROUTING, SAW AWAY THE EXCESS STOCK, BRINGING THE WORKPIECE TO ITS FINAL LENGTH.

FENCE

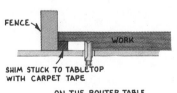

WORK

SHIM STUCK TO TABLETOP WITH CARPET TAPE

ON THE ROUTER TABLE

Rabbeting an Assembled Box

Need to rabbet an assembled case for a back? Or a box for a lipped lid?

The problem in such operations is the narrow bearing surface. It is very difficult to prevent the router from wobbling as you move it along a surface ¾ inch wide. The solution is a custom baseplate.

A long trammel is ideal. The entire piece is 2 or 3 feet long, with the router at one end. In use, the router is perched on the edge of one side of the case, while the free end of the baseplate is resting on the other side. The machine is thus held square to the case. As you work around the case, always keep the baseplate resting on adjacent or opposite sides.

A very narrow bearing surface can make rabbeting an assembled box or case pretty vexing. If you use a baseplate that's wide enough to bridge the gap from side to side, however, you can keep the router bolt upright and allow the pilot bearing to guide the cut.

address the width with the router's depth-of-cut setting. On the router table, you'll set the work on edge and feed it past the bit.

DEEP RABBETS

What's a *deep* rabbet? Depending upon the perspective, a deep rabbet could be seen as a wide rabbet. And cut like one, too. But let's look at it as a rabbet that exceeds the capacities of the standard piloted rabbeting bit and, for whatever reason, needs to be attacked as a deep cut.

Before you abandon the rabbeting bit, however, see what you can do to extend its reach. You can sometimes cheat the shank out of the collet a few fractions of an inch. Make a couple of passes to max out the bit's cutting depth, then back the bit out of the collet for another pass or two. You want to keep at least 1 inch of the shank in the collet. And it's better to be using a ½-inch-shank bit for this than a ¼-inch-shank one.

Another alternative is to make the first passes to the full cutting depth of the rabbeting bit, then extend the cut even deeper using a straight pattern bit. This bit has a pilot bearing on its shank. The bearing rides along the shoulder of the rabbet to guide the cut.

Finally, you can use a straight bit. With a hand-held router, use a

Interchangeable bearings and interchangeable cutters are two approaches to rabbeting bit versatility. A number of manufacturers, Eagle America among them, offer bearing sets to complement their rabbeting bits (*left*). Eagle America's set consists of three bearings (two of them with Delrin rims) plus an allen wrench. Depending upon the bearing used, their ½-inch rabbeting bit will also give you ⅜-inch, ⁷⁄₁₆-inch, and ⁹⁄₁₆-inch cuts. Their ⅜-inch rabbeting bit will make cuts of ¼ inch, ⁵⁄₁₆ inch, and ⁷⁄₁₆ inch in addition to the "stock" ⅜-inch cut. That's six different cut widths from two bits.

Paso Robles Carbide takes a different tack. You *can* change bearings, but more important, you can change cutters (*right*). The cutter for a ⅜-inch rabbet will fit either the ¼-inch-shank arbor or the ½-inch size. Want to make a ⅛-inch rabbet? Pull the ⅜-inch cutter off the arbor and pop the ⅛-inch cutter in place. You don't even need to take the arbor out of the router collet. Want a ³⁄₁₆-inch rabbet? Switch to a different bearing.

Addresses and telephone numbers for both Eagle America and Paso Robles Carbide are in "Sources" on page 337.

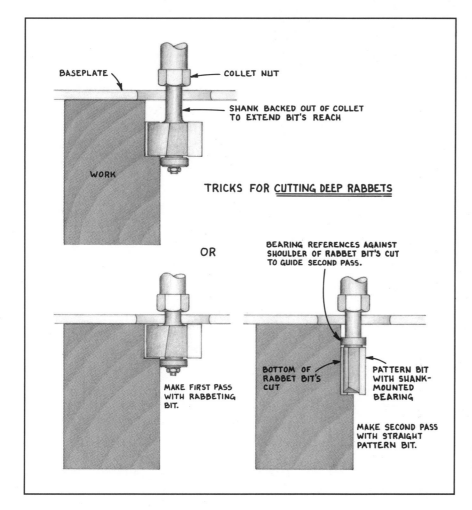

BASEPLATE

COLLET NUT

SHANK BACKED OUT OF COLLET TO EXTEND BIT'S REACH

WORK

TRICKS FOR CUTTING DEEP RABBETS

OR

MAKE FIRST PASS WITH RABBETING BIT.

BEARING REFERENCES AGAINST SHOULDER OF RABBET BIT'S CUT TO GUIDE SECOND PASS.

BOTTOM OF RABBET BIT'S CUT

PATTERN BIT WITH SHANK-MOUNTED BEARING

MAKE SECOND PASS WITH STRAIGHT PATTERN BIT.

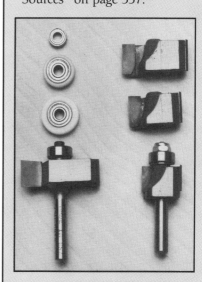

Custom Rabbeting Baseplate

You *can* use a hand-held router to cut rabbets without using a piloted rabbeting bit. Use your router's edge guide. Or make a custom baseplate, like this one.

To cut a rabbet, use a straight bit. Adjust the guide bar to establish the rabbet's width. As you can see, the guide bar pivots, which makes adjustment easy. Loosen the wing nut and swing the bar. Use a short steel rule to measure your setting. (The technique roughly parallels that of cutting a rabbet on the router table. As you know, to fine-tune the router table fence setting, you cinch down one end of the fence and, ruler at the bit, move the other end back and forth.)

The advantages of this approach?

• You don't need to buy rabbeting bits. The straight bits you have can do the job.

• You can cut the width of rabbet you need, rather than the width(s) that piloted rabbeting bits cut.

• You can exceed the ⅜-inch maximum depth of cut that most piloted rabbeting bits have. If you need a rabbet a full inch deep, you can produce it with a straight bit of the requisite length.

• The base serves double-duty! You can use it to rout grooves parallel to—and within a couple of inches of—the edge of the workpiece.

To make the rabbeting baseplate, cut a rectangle of some appropriate baseplate material. (See the chapter "Custom Baseplates" for more information on this.) I used ½-inch birch plywood. Make the rectangle about 9

Save yourself the cost of rabbet bits by making this rabbeting baseplate from scrap-bin materials. With it, you can cut rabbets of infinitely variable width using straight bits.

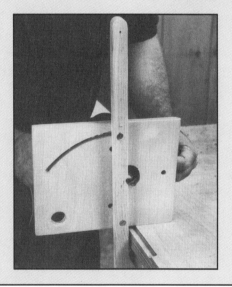

The baseplate is made of plywood, with a straight-grained hardwood guide strip. The long guide virtually eliminates wiggling at the beginning and end of cuts, where a pilot tends to duck around the corner of the workpiece.

fence or edge guide. Using the latter, remember that its facing has to extend below the bit at its deepest setting so it can bear on the work. You'll probably have to attach an auxiliary facing to a commercial edge guide, which is easy enough to do. If you use a shop-made guide, such as the rabbeting baseplate shown above, you'll need to use a deep guide bar.

With a router table, you may need to add an auxiliary facing to the fence, one extending well above the bit, to support the stock.

If you have stuck with us this far, the operation should be pretty evident. Set the fence (or guide) and make the cut. Make several passes, working down to the final depth.

RABBETING CURVED WORK

The most obvious examples of curved workpieces that need to be rabbeted are frames. In many cases, the technique of choice is to use a piloted rabbeting bit. The pilot bears on the edge of the work, regardless of the contour.

A rabbet that deviates from the dimensions that piloted bits cut, however, calls for a different technique. This is a situation in which to use the router table's pin routing accessory. (Construction details for this device are found in "Pin Router Arm" on page 91.) Fixed directly above the router bit, the pin serves as a pilot and controls how wide the cut can be.

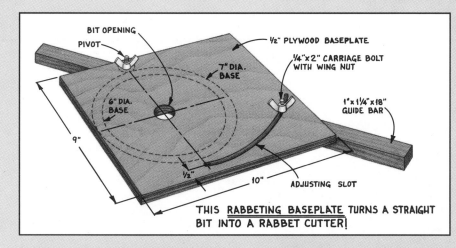

BIT OPENING
PIVOT
7" DIA. BASE
6" DIA. BASE
½" PLYWOOD BASEPLATE
¼"x2" CARRIAGE BOLT WITH WING NUT
1"x1¼"x18" GUIDE BAR
9"
½"
10"
ADJUSTING SLOT

THIS RABBETING BASEPLATE TURNS A STRAIGHT BIT INTO A RABBET CUTTER!

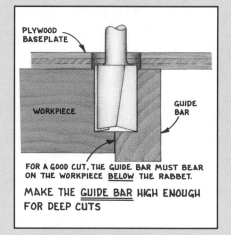

PLYWOOD BASEPLATE
WORKPIECE
GUIDE BAR

FOR A GOOD CUT, THE GUIDE BAR MUST BEAR ON THE WORKPIECE BELOW THE RABBET.

MAKE THE GUIDE BAR HIGH ENOUGH FOR DEEP CUTS

inches by 10 inches, or bigger if your router's base is more than 7 inches in diameter. (You need turning clearance for the guide-bar wing nut; if the base crowds it too much, you won't be able to adjust the guide bar easily. I discovered this the hard way!)

As shown in *Rabbeting Baseplate,* the router is offset. Position the router's baseplate, and transfer the bit-clearance hole and the mounting-screw locations. Next, mark the pivot-hole location and the end of the adjustment slot closest to the router base. Drill holes of the appropriate size for the mounting screws, and drill ¼-inch-diameter holes for the pivot and the start of the slot. (You can also bore a 1-inch-diameter hole in the off corner, as I did, so you can hang the "out-of-service" base on a nail.)

You can cut the slot with a router mounted on a trammel base, or on a router table. (See the chapter "Routing Circles and Curves.") The bored hole serves as a starting hole. If you capture the router's bit in the hole, it helps you set up the trammel (or a pivot fixture on the router table).

Cut a guide bar. Bear in mind that the guide bar has to extend below the bit, so that it will ride on the work. If the bit extends below the bar, then the bar will contact the work only in front of the bit, not below the cut and behind the bit. You need contact all around to keep the router—and the cut—steady and bobble-free.

A good basic size is ¾ inch to 1 inch square by 18 inches. This will serve for the usual ¼-inch-deep, ⅜-inch-wide rabbets. If you need DEEP rabbets, you also need a DEEP guide bar—say, 1½ inches square for rabbets up to 1 inch deep. Lay out, bore, and countersink holes to match the

pivot hole and slot in the baseplate. Use a stove bolt, washer, and lock nut to mount the bar to the base at the pivot. Use a stove bolt, washer, and wing nut at the adjusting slot.

To cut the bit opening in the new base, mount it on your router, and fit the router with the biggest-diameter straight bit you have. With the guide bar swung out of the way, turn on the router, and slowly advance the depth of cut until you have bored through the base. Very carefully, swing the guide bar against the bit as it turns, notching the bar.

If a finished appearance is important to you, disassemble the new base, sand it to smooth it and soften the edges, then apply a coat or two of your favorite finish. Or do as I did: Apply several successive coats of paste wax. Reassemble the base, and it's ready for use.

The width of cut made by a particular bit is determined by halving the difference between the diameter of the pin and the diameter of the bit. For example, a ¾-inch straight bit used with a ¼-inch pin will yield a ¼-inch-wide rabbet:

$$(¾ - ¼) \div 2 = ¼$$

By altering the diameter of the bit as well as the diameter of the pin, you can vary the width of the rabbet. The longer the cutting flutes of the bit, the deeper the rabbet can be cut.

Cutting a deep rabbet in a curved frame is easy with a pin routing accessory. An arm extending over the router table holds a pin directly above the bit. Like a pilot, the pin controls how far into the work the bit can penetrate, thus establishing the width of cut. Any irregular shape can be guided along the pin.

EDGE JOINTS

If you intend to glue up stock

to make large, flat panels, you will use some variation of the edge joint. In many, many instances, the edge joint is a simple butting together of two boards. A lot of woodworkers, however, prefer to work the edges a bit, to produce a means to simultaneously help align the two boards during glue-up and increase the joint's strength by interlocking the boards and expanding the glue area.

At the very least, the edges of the mating boards require surfacing to remove saw marks, dings, and chips. Traditionally, this surfacing, called jointing, was done with a long-soled jointer plane. These days, it's ordinarily done on a jointer.

The router lends itself to the jointing operation, as well as to edge treatments that yield some stronger edge joints.

• Beyond mere jointing is routing an edge joint. It is almost imperceptible, it works with gently curving edges as well as straight edges, and you can only make it with a router.
• A common approach is to use splines: Plow a stopped groove in the edges of the boards and insert a spline of hardwood or plywood in it. The router is the ideal tool to make the groove.
• Biscuit joinery has become popular in recent years. A special power tool, called a biscuit joiner, saws a slot into which a thin, elliptical wooden spline just fits. Thus, instead of a continuous spline reinforcing

Thoughtfully applied, the router edge-jointing technique can give you eye-catching results. When it's used to prepare boards for gluing up, it can produce nearly invisible seams. But you can do that on the jointer. What you can't do on the jointer is prepare boards for joining along a sinuous seam, as here. Contrasting boards edge-jointed this way can be a smashing element in a small box, a big blanket chest, or a tabletop.

the butt joint, short splines are spaced along the joint. Save yourself the cost of a biscuit joiner; you can cut the slots with your router.
• Similar effects can be achieved by cutting rabbets or tongues and grooves along the edges of the boards. Yeah, the router does it.
• Specialty router bits cut a variety of edge shapes that provide a mechanical interlocking of the boards, while at the same time expanding the glue area.

So when tackling edge joinery, don't overlook the help your router can offer.

ROUTING AN EDGE JOINT

The first step in preparing any edge joint is to joint the edges of the mating boards. Suffice it to say here

that this is an operation you can do easily with the router. Details are found in "Jointing with a Router" on page 188. But you can joint most boards more quickly and accurately on the jointer, and there's no reason why you shouldn't use the jointer if you can.

But a router can help you do a special job of the fundamental woodworking task of edge-joining two or more boards to make a wide panel. A well-conceived and well-executed routed edge joint will virtually disappear—if that's what you want—because you can rout the mating edges to follow the direction of the grain, even though it meanders sinuously from one end of a board to the other. If you want the joint to stand out, you can make it do that in a special way, too.

I first ran across this technique about 15 years ago in a magazine article, and I've run across explanations of it in several places since. The concept is to rout the mating edges as positive-negative images. Making the edges positive-negative images will allow them to join much better than simply trying to give them both perfect, smooth, straight edges. And making one edge the negative image of the other is what allows you to join them along a gentle curve as well as a straight line.

In brief, the technique is this: You clamp a fence atop the first workpiece and, guiding the router base against the fence, trim about ¹⁄₁₆ inch from the workpiece. Then you secure the second workpiece directly opposite the first. By guiding the router along the same fence—you haven't moved it—you trim the second workpiece and produce an edge that's a negative image of the first.

To execute the technique, you should have an edge-routing platform and matching fence, which you can easily make from a third of a sheet of good-quality ¾-inch plywood. I have one that's 4 feet long, sufficient for the work I've done using this technique. But you are limited only by plywood's sheet sizes.

You can use whatever router you have, though a fairly powerful fixed-base machine is probably the ideal. A horse-and-a-half is probably minimum.

By all means, use a ½-inch-shank bit, which will withstand side stresses better than a ¼-inch-shank bit. Naturally, the bit's cutting edges must be longer than the workpiece is thick. A large-diameter cutter, ¾-inch or more, will probably be less prone to vibrate under load than a ½-inch-diameter (or smaller) bit. Because the tip speed is higher, the large-diameter bit will give a smoother

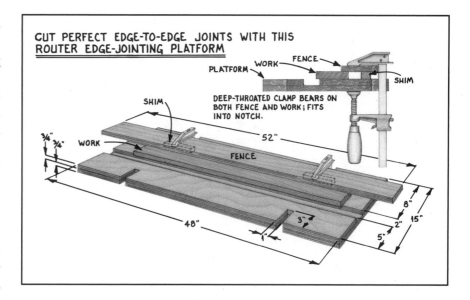

CUT PERFECT EDGE-TO-EDGE JOINTS WITH THIS ROUTER EDGE-JOINTING PLATFORM

cut, too. And, of course, a shear-cut bit would be even smoother.

To make the platform, cut three 4-foot-long strips of ¾-inch plywood. Cut one about 15 inches wide, the second one about 8 inches wide, and the last one about 5 inches wide. Glue the two narrower pieces atop the widest, as shown in *Router Edge-Jointing Platform*. The 2-inch-wide channel thus formed allows the bit to cut below the wood without marring the platform. It also gives all the chips and dust generated by the operation a place to go.

Cut a fence about 6 inches wide and about 4 inches longer than any stock you anticipate edge-joining with the router. (Although the platform shown here is only 4 feet long, you can use it to position longer boards for router edge-joining. But regardless of the length of the platform, the fence must be longer than the workpieces.)

To use the platform, you have to rest it across sawhorses or some other support(s) that permit you to clamp the work to both sides. A regular workbench will probably be too wide for this. I trap the platform between

the dogs on my router bench, which works fine.

To router edge-join two boards, set one of the two on the wider half of the platform. Set the fence on it, and adjust its position vis-à-vis the board's edge so you'll be routing away no more than ¹⁄₁₆ inch of stock. Clamp the fence and the work to the platform. (If the work is narrow, you may need to shim the fence; just be sure both the work and the fence are clamped so neither will move.)

Stand with the fence in front of you. Rout from right to left, pulling the router against the fence as you go. Check the edge. If it is less than smooth, square, and clean, shift the fence a tad and make a second pass.

When the first board is done, leave it right where it is. You don't move it or the fence. You simply position the second board along the opposite side of the platform, parallel with the first piece. You need a gap between the two boards that's ¹⁄₁₆ inch less than the diameter of the bit you are using. Got the gap set? Clamp down the second board.

Now the router will rest on both

The router is an excellent tool for preparing boards for edge joining. Using this simple rig, you can produce an almost seamless joint. Set the first board on the platform and clamp the fence to it. Trim the edge with a router

(left). Then clamp the second board opposite the first. Guiding the router in the reverse direction along the fence, trim the second board (right). The two should mate perfectly.

boards, but the bit shouldn't fit between them (if it does, check that gap again!).

To rout the second board, stand in the same place as before. But this time, you have to feed the router left to right. Pull it against the fence as you move it. Make the cut in a single, continuous pass. If you interrupt the cut for any reason, it's likely to be botched. You can rescue the work, of course, simply by finishing the cut, then shifting the second board slightly and making another attempt.

When the second board is machined, unclamp it—NOT the first piece or the fence—and pull it against the first piece. The two should mate perfectly. You may have to juke the second piece back and forth fractionally to get the two in sync, since there's only one correct alignment. A bump on the first piece should fit into a corresponding hollow in the second piece. That's because any

imperfections in the fence are telegraphed into the two workpieces differently—in effect, in positive form to one, in negative form to the other. When the two are in sync, they'll virtually merge together.

To help you line them up for gluing, slash a pencil line or two across the seam.

Of course, if the two pieces *don't* mate perfectly, it may be that you've failed to rout deeply enough. I'd try another pass on the second board, and if that didn't cure the mismate, I'd go back to the beginning and repeat the process.

To mate two boards in a curved joint, you must first roughly cut the

The amount of wood that's removed in a pass is very modest, and though the bit appears to be cutting two boards at once, it's not. On this pass, it is cutting only the board on the left. To limit the cut, the boards have to be set very carefully. You'll easily spend more time doing that than actually routing.

line on the workpieces as well as on the fence. The prime caveat is that the technique will not work with tight curves, because the bit is actually creating a different curve on each piece. The contour of one curve is offset from the contour of the other by the bit's diameter. When you rout along a gentle curve, however, the two pieces should be sufficiently close to fit together nicely, forming a clean joint. Using a small-diameter bit minimizes the offset.

Just be forewarned: The more curve you use, the less perfect the fit. For a good glue-up, you probably should deviate no more than about 5 degrees off a straight line. Use your platform as a guide. Its channel is only 2 inches wide, so your curve can't range much more than ¾ of an inch off a baseline. (See "Edge-Joining along Curved Lines" on page 158 for a technique that allows you to join two boards perfectly along almost any curve.)

Lay out your curve, transferring it to the first workpiece and the fence. After cutting these two pieces with a saber saw or on the band saw, use one to trace the curve onto the second workpiece. Remember that this second piece must be the reverse of the first, not a duplicate.

Set up the first workpiece and the fence on the platform, much as if it were a straight joint. Rout the piece. Then position and rout the second workpiece.

SPLINED EDGE JOINERY

One of the best edge-joint reinforcement techniques is perfectly suited to the router. It's the spline. You cut grooves (or call them slots, if you prefer) in the adjoining edges, extending them nearly the length of the boards. Fit a strip of plywood or hardboard into the joint as you glue it up.

The spline strengthens the joint by expanding the glue area and by providing a mechanical lock. It also makes the boards a little easier to align and clamp during glue-up. If done properly, the spline will bring even slightly bowed boards into flush alignment.

The table saw might seem to be the fastest cutter of the necessary slots, and it probably is. But spline slots are usually stopped for the sake of appearance—who wants to see the spline at the edge of a tabletop, for example. A sawed slot that's stopped will have a 4- or 5-inch section at each end that won't accommodate the spline, because the slot isn't full-depth.

So do the job with a slot cutter and hand-held router, or a straight bit on the router table.

Slotting for Splines

If you want—or need—to do the job with a hand-held router, use a slot cutter. You can rest the router on the face of the workpiece, and even use an offset baseplate to help avoid bobbles and tips. The job can be done in a single pass, as opposed to having to make two or three passes to get it to depth.

Moreover, those slightly bowed boards can be forced flat and held that way with a few clamps. The router will have a flat surface to slide across, and the cutter will make that kerf a consistent distance from the surface.

Rather than get too worked up about trying to center the slot, just mark a reference face of each board. Always keep that face up—through all machining and assembly stages. The slots will all be the same dis-

To rout the first curved edge, the fence has to be positioned on the workpiece with its undulations in sync with those cut into the workpiece. Then the second piece has to be positioned in sync with its mate-to-be. Here, the walnut edging for the panel shown on page 252 is being trimmed. Because of the narrowness of the piece, the cut has to be started and stopped three times so the clamps can be shifted out of the router's path. The challenge is to shift them without jostling the workpiece in the least.

A slot cutter is usually an assembly, consisting of an arbor, a cutter, and a pilot bearing. The arbor includes a nut that secures both cutter and bearing on the threaded end of the arbor. Often, the arbor will include a slinger or two, and several spacers.

The cutters themselves are available in two-, three-, and four-wing designs. With only two carbide cutting edges, the two-wing model is least costly, but the plate holding the carbide is smaller and thus less stiff. The cutter won't cut quite as fast as those with three or four cutting edges.

The size specified for a cutter is the width of the kerf it makes. The standard cutting depth, regardless of the cutter size, is ½ inch.

In the manner typical of piloted bits, you can change pilot bearings to alter the cutting depth.

Using the spacers supplied by some vendors allows you to alter the position of the cutter on the arbor. This enables you to extend the range of your router's bit-adjustment mechanism. Remember that changing the router's bit-height setting adjusts not the cut's depth but the cut's position.

These assemblies also allow you to put the pilot bearing either above or below the cutter, according to the job. You can even use two bearings on some long arbors, one above and one below.

Because you are dealing with an assembly, you can save by buying a single arbor, a single set of bearings, and a *selection* of cutters. Buying a single assembly as separate components never saves you money, though.

To give an example, a ⅟₁₆-inch three-wing assembly costs $26.14 from one supplier. The cutter, arbor, and standard-diameter bearing purchased separately cost $30.72. For one cutter, the assembly is cheaper, clearly. But if you buy five different-sized cutters (⅟₁₆-, ⅛-, ⁵⁄₃₂-, ³⁄₁₆-, and ¼-inch) as assemblies, the cost totals $131.60. Buy an arbor, a bearing, and just the cutters for those sizes, and the total is $104.18. If the convenience of having a separate arbor and bearing for each cutter is worth more than $25.00 to you, you know what to do.

Byrom makes an extensive selection of slot cutters. Shown below are the three- and four-wing cutters on ¼-inch and ½-inch shanks. All the cutters can be used on either shank size. The two-wing cutter from MLCS is less costly, but the cutter is fixed on the shank.

An interesting addition to any bit drawer is this adjustable slotting assembly, sold by Amana as the Quadraset (above). It's a slot cutter stack set—conceptually like a table-saw dado set—that includes ⅛-inch, ³⁄₃₂-inch, ³⁄₁₆-inch, and ¼-inch two-wing cutters, a ½-inch-shank arbor with a pilot bearing, and a handful of spacers, washers, and shims. You can use the cutters individually on the arbor, or you can combine two, three, or all of the cutters on the arbor. Thus you can cut slots that range in ⅟₃₂-inch increments from ⅛ inch wide up to ²³⁄₃₂ inch wide.

TRY THIS!

A pilot bearing isn't the only means of governing a slot cutter's depth of cut. If you need to cut a shallow slot, a quick and cheap guide block made from a scrap of ¾-inch stock can be attached to the baseplate with double-sided carpet tape. On the band saw or with a saber saw, make a cutout for the slot cutter, as shown. When you stick the block to the baseplate, set it so the cutter can only cut the depth you want.

The slot cutter is an unusual bit, in that it cuts at right angles to the bit axis. It's great for cutting slots for splines, since the router can rest squarely on the broad part of the workpiece, yet be cutting into the narrow edge (top left). A hand-held router can keep a slot positioned even in mildly bowed stock, since it has a relatively small contact patch that can follow the board's contour. On the router table (bottom left), the work must be very flat, or the slot position can shift.

tance from that face, so when the splines are inserted and the boards joined, their reference faces will be flush.

The slot cutter can also be used on the router table. The advantage of the slot cutter over a regular straight bit is that you can lay the workpiece flat on the tabletop. Save yourself the time it takes to position and clamp hold-ups and hold-ins, not to mention hold-downs. Fit the cutter in the router, adjust the height, set the starting pin, and rout. Be consistent about whether you have the reference face up or down when you cut, and you'll get a good fit.

Are one or two of the boards slightly warped? Just force them flat with a few clamps. Bowed boards are the province of the hand-held router.

A final note on the slot cutter. It's a dirt generator. If you have a dust collector accessory, by all means use it.

Grooving for Splines

There are other approaches to use if you have a straight bit but not a slot cutter. The best of them involve the router table or the horizontal router table. In a pinch, you can do the job with a hand-held router.

If your working stock is good and flat, cutting the grooves for the splines is the same as cutting any stopped groove on the router table. Mark your starting and stopping points on the table and the workpiece. Guide the cut with the fence.

Using the horizontal router table gives you the advantage of having

the workpiece flat on the tabletop. If the boards are broad and fairly long, this is a plus that should not be discounted.

The singular disadvantage in both approaches is that you have to make two passes to get to a reasonable depth, or you have to settle for a very narrow spline. To save time, make a first pass in all the boards before resetting the bit height and doing the second cut.

If your working stock includes a board or two with some bow to them, you may need to replace the fence. It may be too difficult to press the bowed boards flat against the fence (or the horizontal table's top). The groove for the spline may end up an inconsistent distance from the reference face, a woodworking disaster.

Instead of the fence, use a pivot

Here's how to cut stopped spline grooves on the horizontal router table. The board is flat on the table-top, held there by the featherboard. Sight down on the bit to align it with the start mark on the workpiece. Push the board onto the bit to start the cut. Feed left to right.

block to support the stock. As shown in *Pivot Block*, you make the pivot by gluing and screwing a support into a groove plowed down the center of a base board. The support projects beyond the base by a couple of inches at one end. Line up this end of the support just shy of the bit. The distance between the bit and the pivot, of course, is the distance the groove will be from the

working stock's face. Clamp the pivot to the tabletop. Then set a board at right angles to the pivot, bracing it so that pressure in the proper feed direction won't force the pivot to swing out of position. Clamp the brace to the tabletop.

The use of this pivot is self-evident. Keep the board tight against the end of the pivot. At any time during the operation, it's irrelevant where the *ends* of the workpiece are, so long as its reference face is tight against the pivot. But you must keep the work perpendicular to the line between the bit and the pivot. Don't swivel the work, or the groove will wander.

If for any reason the job must be done using a hand-held router and a straight bit, you've still got an option or two.

Balancing the router on the work-piece's edge is pretty dicey, but you can trap the workpiece between two edge guides. That'll keep the router pretty much centered and upright. Another approach is to clamp the workpiece to the edge of the router bench—or a similar work surface—with its edge flush with the bench top. Use an edge guide to locate the

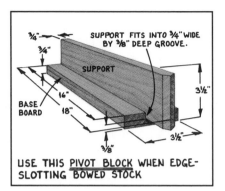

USE THIS <u>PIVOT BLOCK</u> WHEN EDGE-SLOTTING <u>BOWED STOCK</u>

groove, and enjoy the extra router support the bench top affords. See the chapter "Dadoing and Grooving" for more details on both of these approaches.

However you produce the slots for the splines, completing each joint is a matter of cutting strips of spline stock and gluing it into a slot in one board. Then bring the mating board into alignment, fit it over the spline, and clamp the joint closed.

BISCUIT JOINERY WITH A ROUTER

Want to try biscuit joinery? Use your router to cut the biscuit slots. We've come up with a baseplate that makes it quick and easy.

The best thing about biscuit joiners is their simplicity. You mark the center of each biscuit slot, then you cut the slot with a quick in-and-out movement of the tool. If you had round biscuits, you could do exactly the same with a slot cutter in a router.

But biscuits aren't round, they're elliptical. To cut a slot long enough for a biscuit, you have to move the router from side to side. The question is, how far?

The answer is, from one side of the bit hole to the other.

Set the router on the work, and line up the pencil mark you made

A pivot block, much like you would use to support stock during resawing on the band saw, also supports bowed stock for splining on the router table. And if you need to groove a workpiece that's curved by design, this is the way to do it. The brace clamped to the table beside the pivot block keeps it from twisting out of position. And note the featherboard hold-ing the workpiece against the pivot block's nose.

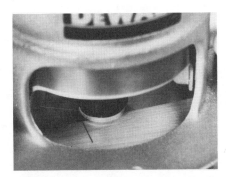
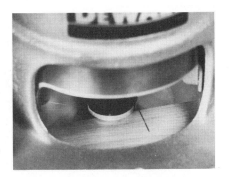

Problem Solver

Trying to adjust your router so that the slot cutter addresses the exact center of the workpiece can make you prematurely bald.

Hey! Don't pull out your hair over something this pointless. Just mark a reference face on each of the pieces to be joined. Lay out the pieces as they'll be assembled. Mark the face that's up. Now rest the router on the marked face when you cut the biscuit slots. It doesn't matter if the slot is centered. It'll be the same distance from the marked face on each piece, so the slots will line up with one another during assembly. Perfect.

With the right baseplate, you can rout biscuit slots as quickly as you can saw them with a $250 biscuit joiner. Align one side of the bit hole with your center mark and push the cutter into the work (top left). Then feed the router until the other side of the bit hole hits the mark (top right). The slot is done and the biscuit fits it perfectly (left). Except for the unusually small bit hole, the biscuit-joining baseplate doesn't look out of the ordinary. But this plastic disk is all you need to do biscuit joinery with your router. No templates or fences required.

on the work with right side of the bit hole. Then push, plunging the cutter into the work's edge. Feed the router to the right, until the other edge of the bit hole lines up with the pencil mark. Done!

You've cut a slot long enough to accommodate a #20 biscuit. And you've done it as simply as you would have with a biscuit joiner.

To make the baseplate, you need a square of clear acrylic and a 5/32-inch slot cutter. The 5/32-inch slot is the right width for a #20 biscuit. What you need to determine is how far you must move the router to produce the length of slot you need, given the diameter of the slot cutter you have. For the typical #20 biscuit, you need a 2½-inch-long slot. Subtract the diameter of the cutter from 2½ inches. The difference is the diameter of the bit hole you drill in the baseplate.

Example: A 1⅜-inch-diameter slot cutter calls for a ⅞-inch diameter

hole: 2½ inches − 1⅜ inches = ⅞ inch.

With the hole size determined, get to work on the baseplate. Use double-sided carpet tape to attach your router's baseplate to the acrylic. Drill and countersink the mounting

holes. With a saber saw or on the band saw, trim the acrylic fairly close to the factory baseplate. Then use a flush-trimming bit to trim the acrylic baseplate to match the factory one.

Next, fit a V-groove bit in your router, then mount the acrylic on

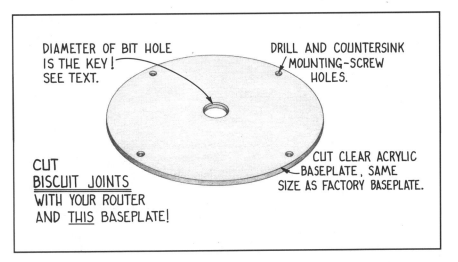

DIAMETER OF BIT HOLE IS THE KEY! SEE TEXT.

DRILL AND COUNTERSINK MOUNTING-SCREW HOLES.

CUT BISCUIT JOINTS WITH YOUR ROUTER AND <u>THIS</u> BASEPLATE!

CUT CLEAR ACRYLIC BASEPLATE, SAME SIZE AS FACTORY BASEPLATE.

The Less Elegant Solutions

I really like the biscuit-joining baseplate Fred and I came up with. It's *so* simple. There are no templates or stops to clamp to the work. When you are cutting the slot, the bit hole is right there by the edge of the work, readily visible, easily referenced regardless of the router's orientation—handles parallel to the work's edge, cocked, or at complete right angles to it.

It works so well, I'm reluctant to suggest any alternatives. But just as there's more than one way to offend a politically correct person, there's more than one way to cut biscuit slots with a router.

The first alternative is the first-generation biscuit baseplate. If there's a shortcoming to the elegant second-generation design, it is that the bit hole is pretty small. It's smaller than the collet nuts on every router we have in our shop except an old Stanley. Depending upon the shank length of your slot cutter, as well as the location of the slot, the collet nut could contact the baseplate.

The solution? Reference *lines* across a baseplate with a standard-sized bit hole. The lined baseplate is easy to use. You just have to make sure the router is oriented so the lines are perpendicular to the work's edge, and you have to extend the biscuit slot's centerline enough that you can line it up with the baseplate lines. But otherwise, the procedure is: Line up the right-hand baseplate line with the workpiece mark, push the router cutter into the work, slide the machine to the right, and pull the router when the second baseplate line reaches the workpiece mark.

To make this alternative baseplate, you need a square of clear acrylic and your ⁵⁄₃₂-inch slot cutter. Do the math and determine the distance between the baseplate lines.

With the line space determined, get to work on the baseplate. Use double-sided tape to attach your router's baseplate to the acrylic, and drill the mounting holes. Take some time with alignment. If you're like me, you'll

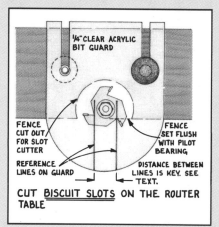

Less elegant, but just as effective, are these router biscuit-joining alternatives. One is a baseplate that has lines routed into it. The other is a fence-mounted bit guard to use on the router table, which has a line scribed on it, too. With either jig, you rout from one line to the other to cut the biscuit slot.

want the router's handles aligned with the edge of the work. You need to drill the mounting holes so one edge of the acrylic will parallel the handles.

Mount the acrylic on the router next, and dimple the plastic with the V-groove bit to establish the center of the bit hole. With a scratch awl and a ruler, or with a V-groover in a table-mounted router, scribe the two lines across the baseplate, as shown in *Lined Biscuit-Slotting Baseplate*. The gap between them, of course, is the distance you have to move the router.

You can leave the baseplate square, or you can round off all but the reference edge.

The router table alternative involves the use of a fence with a bit cutout large enough to accommodate your slot cutter and with a bit guard inscribed with the reference lines.

Operation is basically the same, though you must accommodate feed direction to the router table. Line up the biscuit slot centerline with the right-hand reference line, plunge the work into the cutter, feed it to the left, then pull the workpiece off the cutter when the centerline reaches the left-hand reference line.

To slot the butt ends of workpieces, you should use a backup sled to stabilize the movement of the work along the fence.

the router. Switch on the motor and advance the bit just enough to dimple the plastic. This establishes the center of the bit hole. Remove the baseplate from the router and drill the hole, making it exactly the diameter that your math established it should be.

Remount the baseplate on the router, fit the slot cutter in the collet, and you are ready for some biscuit joining.

TONGUE-AND-GROOVE JOINTS

The tongue-and-groove joint is the older brother of the splined edge joint. Instead of a separate spline, you have a solid spline that's an integral part of the board.

Like the splined edge joint, the tongue-and-groove joint is used where surface loading might be considerable—in tabletops and the like. It's also a traditional joint used in breadboard constructions. The most familiar uses these days may be in the carpentry realm—tongue-and-groove siding, paneling, and flooring. Here the joint provides a mechanical lock between boards that are fastened to another surface or a frame, rather than to each other. It also provides a rudimentary aesthetic—the wood can shrink without opening the joint enough to expose whatever is behind it.

You probably think of the tongue-and-groove as a through joint, but if cut with a router, it can easily be stopped so the interlock doesn't show on exposed edges. In addition to stopping the grooving cut, you have to trim back the tongue so the joint will close.

Typically, on ¾-inch stock, you have a ¼-inch-wide by ¼-inch-deep

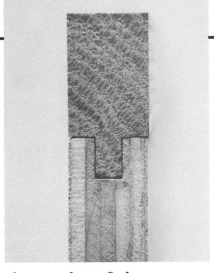

The tongue has to fit the groove properly to get the most out of the tongue-and-groove joint. If the tongue is too long, it bottoms in the groove and prevents the joint from closing. Too short a tongue, on the other hand, weakens the joint. If the tongue's too thick, it can spread— and possibly break—the groove, giving you an uneven surface. But this perfect fit is strong and attractive.

groove, centered across the edge. The tongue thickness matches, but its width is usually ³⁄₁₆ inch. The ¹⁄₁₆-inch difference is there to accommodate wood movement and glue. Thicker stock calls for a thicker, longer tongue. If the joint will be exposed, or if it isn't to be a glued joint (as in a breadboard end application), the disparity between tongue width and groove depth can be narrowed.

The joint should be a firm press fit: If you have to knock the pieces together, then struggle to pull them apart, the joint's too tight. But you don't want it to rattle either.

Cutting the tongue-and-groove, the way I do it, involves the horizontal router table and a hand-held router, a straight bit, and a rabbeting bit. On the horizontal table, I use the straight to plow the groove. Then I cut the rabbets, forming the tongue, with the other router and bit. Doing it this way allows me to maintain both setups until the job is completely done. I don't know that I *need* to preserve them, but I'm more comfortable psychologically if I do. That should count for something.

All the stock has to be the same thickness, and you need a couple of scraps to test the setups.

On the butt end of a scrap, mark the proportions of the joint. Only mark the groove. With the scrap on the far side of the bit, set the depth of cut and the height of the bit above the table to match the layout. As a practical matter, don't try too hard to get the cut centered on the stock.

Make one pass with the scrap, then flip it over and make a second pass with the other face on the table.

To set the bit to form the tongue, use a grooved scrap. Hold the scrap on the router table with the grooved edge against the cutting edge of the slot cutter or rabbeting bit. Adjust the bit height to exactly match the distance to the groove.

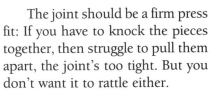

If you have a lot of tongues and grooves to cut, a special tongue-and-groove assembly may be a worthwhile investment.

The typical assembly—Amana's is shown here—consists of an arbor with an integral shank, two identical, removable cutters, and a couple of bearings. The bit is intended for use in a table-mounted router, and its configuration guarantees that you'll be able to keep the stock flat on the tabletop as you rout it. The bit will work on stock between ½ and ¾ inch thick.

When setting up the assembly for cutting the tongues, you sandwich one bearing between the two cutters. Line up a piece of the stock next to the cutter, and adjust the cutter height to center the tongue on the stock's edge. Make a few test cuts and monkey with the setting a bit until you are happy with it. Then set up a couple of featherboards or other hold-downs, and rout the tongues.

To set up for cutting slots, you mount one of the cutters between

the two bearings. Don't remove the shank from the router; it's easier to do this when it's still held by the collet. Use a piece of the stock with the tongue to set the cutter height. Simply line the cutter up even with the tongue. If the tongue is slightly offset, then the groove will be equally offset. Make a test cut, and fit it on the tongue to confirm that your eye is good. Happy with the setup? Make sure the featherboards are still in the right places, then rout the grooves.

Amana's assembly is a compact bit, and it is supplied with a selection of brass shims you use to adjust the fit of the joint. According to the manufacturer, the shims usually aren't needed until after the cutters have been resharpened a time or two.

The advantage of the assembly is the perfectly matched cuts that are possible. Since you are using the same cutters to produce both the tongues and the grooves, they're guaranteed to match. And

Amana's tongue-and-groove bit assembly is a worthwhile investment if you'll be doing a lot of tongue-and-groove work. It's configured here to cut the tongue, which it can do in a single pass. And if the groove should be cut off-center, as in the sample, you can easily make the tongue off-center too.

because you cut both shoulders of the tongue in one pass, you can make the tongue offset to match an offset groove (and vice versa). The disadvantage, of course, is that you have to dismantle the bit when switching from one cut to the other.

This centers the groove. It may be a tad wider than ¼ inch, but as a practical matter, that's irrelevant. Besides, many bits are a trifle undersized.

Now use the scrap to set the height of the rabbeting bit in the other router. Cut the tongue on a second scrap, then test the fit, adjusting the rabbeting bit setting if necessary. When the settings are right on, cut the good stuff.

You can do the job in other ways, of course, depending upon your equipment, your bits, and your work predilections.

On the horizontal table only, set up for the groove as I've already described. Cut all the grooves necessary. Remember to make the two passes for each groove so it is

The same horizontal table setting serves for both rabbeting cuts necessary to form the tongue. Make the cut on the tabletop side of the stock. Feeding the bulk of the stock between the tabletop and cutter is risky business, with lots of kickback potential.

centered on the edge. Then change the setup to do the tongues. Keep the same bit; use a sample of the grooved stock to reset the bit projection and the bit height so you can cut the rabbets that form the tongue. Cut a sample, and test its fit in the grooved material. Make a pass with one face down to cut the first rabbet, then flip the board over and make a second pass to complete the tongue. Adjust your settings if necessary. Then rout the job.

On the router table, the routine is pretty much the same as for the horizontal table. While you can use a straight bit to cut both the groove and the rabbets that form the tongue, Fred uses a ¼-inch slot cutter.

Set the cutter height for the

To slot the edge of a large panel, rest it on the back of the router table. Note that the fence is positioned to keep the workpiece off the slot cutter's pilot, so the depth of the cut will be reduced. Note also that the fence is blocked up so that the bit guard will clear the arbor nut.

grooves, getting as close as you can to centering the slot on the stock. Typically, slot cutters make a ½-inch-deep cut, so you need to set the fence to limit the cut depth to ¼ inch. To center the grooves, make a pass with one face against the tabletop, then flip the stock over to make a second. Groove all the stock in this two-pass fashion.

For the cuts that form the tongue, use a rabbeting bit. Change bits, and use a piece of the grooved stock to set the height. Always make the cuts on the tabletop side of the stock; otherwise you could trap the work between the bit and the tabletop. Adjust the fence as necessary so that the tongue won't be as long as the groove is deep. Cut a test piece and check the fit. Adjust the bit height or fence if necessary. Then rout the tongues on all the stock.

With a hand-held router only, use the slot cutter–rabbeting bit combination. This way, you can keep the router on the face of the work for both the grooving and tongue-forming cuts.

Setting up for the cuts follows the routine described for setting up the router table. Instead of a fence, use an edge guide to control the slot cutter's depth of cut.

SHIPLAP JOINTS

The shiplap is formed by overlapping rabbets cut into opposite faces of adjoining boards. I'd call it a carpentry kind of thing, used in siding and natural-wood paneling.

For example, in our shop here at Rodale, Fred cladded several walls with ship-lapped cedar. (The cedar is photogenic, and it's easy to hang things on—just drive a nail anywhere.) Rather than just butt the 1 by 12 boards edge to edge, he rabbeted the edges so each board could overlap its neighbor. Once in the warm, dry shop for a few weeks, the cedar dried further, and naturally it shrank pretty dramatically. The shiplaps prevented the real guts of the walls from being exposed.

And that's the whole point of shiplaps. The rabbets are quickly cut—precision is irrelevant—yet they serve a valid purpose. A piloted rabbet bit and a router are all you need to make them. Lay the board across sawhorses and run the router along one edge, cutting the rabbet half the thickness (or a little more) of the stock. Roll the board onto its back and repeat.

The utility of the shiplap as a precision-fitted joint? Not much.

SPECIAL JOINERY BITS

Woodworkers are constantly seeking the perfect edge joint.

As we've seen in this chapter so far, there are plain edge-to-edge butt joints, which are only as strong as your glue on a narrow surface can be. The tough part is getting the adjacent boards flush along their entire lengths during glue-up. So woodworkers have come up with joints that provide some mechanical interlock and an expansion of the glue surface—splined edge joints, biscuit joints, tongue-and-groove joints.

Bit manufacturers have come up with a variety of special bits for edge joinery. All the bits require but a single setup. The edge configurations they produce offer some mechanical interlock, expanded glue surfaces, and fast glue-up.

Glue-joint bit. The simplest of these bits produces a sort of tongue-and-rabbet profile. It's a solid bit without a pilot, made only on a ½-inch shank. It's clearly intended for router table use.

The Amana bit shown on the next page (*top*) can be used with stock from ⅝ inch to 1 inch thick.

A glue-joint bit is designed to shape the edges of mating boards so they interlock. One setting services all: One board is routed with its face up, the other with its face down. This Amana bit is intended for router table use, and since it has no pilot, a fence must be used to guide the work. It will handle stock between ⅝ inch and 1 inch thick.

The idea is to mark the faces of the stock to be edge-joined. One board in a joint is routed faceup, the other facedown. If the height of the bit is just right, the two boards will fall together with their faces flush. Because of the interlock, the boards can't shift up or down.

Some details must be attended to in using the bit. The stock has to be flat, and it has to be held firmly to both the tabletop and the fence. If the tongue isn't parallel to the edges, either the joint won't close or the surfaces won't be flush along their entire lengths. Stout hold-downs are essential.

There's no pilot, so you must use a fence, housing the bit to the maximum degree possible. Use a straightedge to set the fence flush with the deepest part of the cutting edge to mimimize the amount of stock removed. You really want to make the full cut in one pass; the more passes you make, the greater the chance that you'll flub up, with an edge either drifting from the fence or lifting off the tabletop.

To set the bit height, the most important adjustment, you have to make test cuts on two pieces and fit them together. If the joint is off by ¼ inch, raise or lower the bit only ⅛

inch. This will move the cut that ⅛ inch on both boards in the joint, amounting to a full ¼-inch change.

Lock-miter bit. The primary purpose of this bit is cutting an interlocking profile on pieces to be joined in an edge miter. The treatment makes it easier to assemble the joint—a plain-edged miter is òrnery at glue-up—and increases the glue area.

The trick is that one setup suffices for cuts on both pieces to be joined. When the bit height is just right, you feed one panel flat on the tabletop, the other on edge against a tall fence. Obviously, if the panels are for something on the order of a

kitchen cabinet, the fence especially must be very tall and securely braced. Hold-ins are essential, too.

An interesting trick you can do with this bit—and the reason I've included it here in the edge joint chapter—is to edge-join flat panels. As with the glue-joint bit, you rout one board with its face down, the other faceup. The two should go together perfectly. All the caveats about working with flat stock and using strong hold-downs apply here.

Amana's lock-miter bit is an impressive chunk of metal. It's close to 3 inches in diameter, so a high-horsepower router with speed control is essential. Run the bit at a reduced speed.

Finger-joint assembly. If you like dado cutters, you'll love this assembly. If you like intricate joints that are a breeze to produce, you'll love this assembly.

The finger joint is a positive-negative interlock, in which tapered projections (the fingers) on one piece fit into tapered grooves in the other. The profile expands the glue area threefold. It's the sort of joint used to assemble scraps end to end to

Though you may think of the lock miter as a joint for casework, it makes a splendid edge joint for gluing up flat panels as well. The bit—Amana's version of it is shown—forms a shape that provides a mechanical lock at the same time it vastly expands the glue surface in the joint.

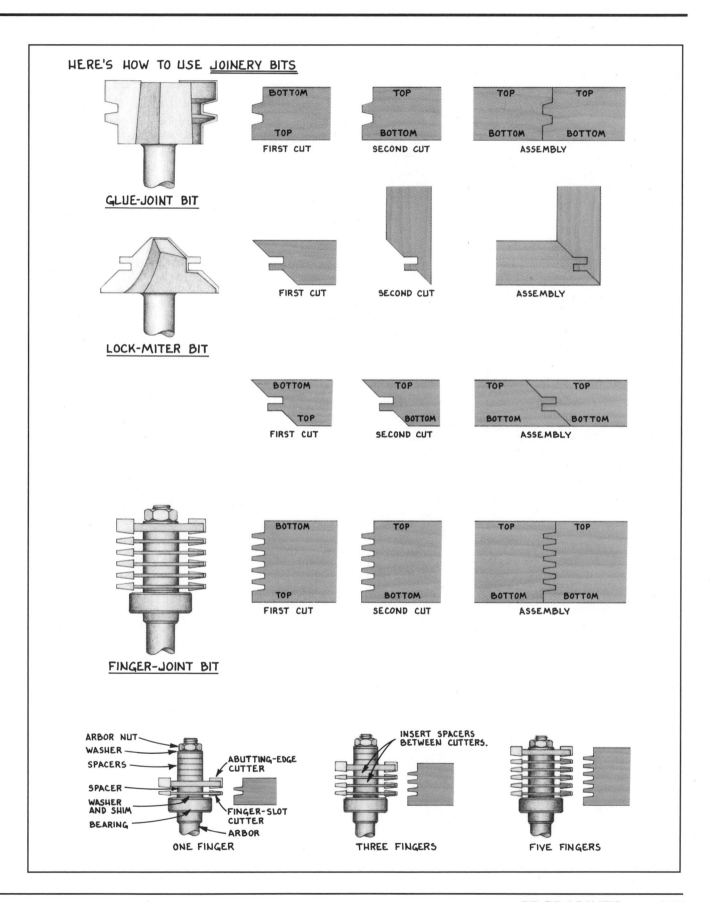

HERE'S HOW TO USE JOINERY BITS

GLUE-JOINT BIT

FIRST CUT
BOTTOM
TOP

SECOND CUT
TOP
BOTTOM

ASSEMBLY
TOP TOP
BOTTOM BOTTOM

LOCK-MITER BIT

FIRST CUT

SECOND CUT

ASSEMBLY

FIRST CUT
BOTTOM
TOP

SECOND CUT
TOP
BOTTOM

ASSEMBLY
TOP TOP
BOTTOM BOTTOM

FINGER-JOINT BIT

FIRST CUT
BOTTOM
TOP

SECOND CUT
TOP
BOTTOM

ASSEMBLY
TOP TOP
BOTTOM BOTTOM

ARBOR NUT
WASHER
SPACERS
SPACER
WASHER AND SHIM
BEARING
ABUTTING-EDGE CUTTER
FINGER-SLOT CUTTER
ARBOR

ONE FINGER

INSERT SPACERS BETWEEN CUTTERS.

THREE FINGERS

FIVE FINGERS

make paint-grade trim. You can use it to join boards edge to edge and, with some trepidation, end to end.

The assembly used to cut the joint is not cheap, and when you see it, you can understand why. The Amana assembly shown in the photo at right includes five individual finger cutters, one straight cutter, a ball-bearing guide, a ½-inch-shank arbor, shims, spacers, and washers. Amana's cutters all feature the European chip-limiting design, which restricts the size of the chip removed per pass. This puts a governor on the feed rate and thus makes for a safer cut. The full assembly is *impressive,* though it isn't particularly large. At 1½ inches in diameter, Amana's bit can be run at full speed in a 1½-horsepower router—either hand-held or table-mounted.

To set up the bit, you remove the spindle nut and stack cutters and spacers on the spindle. As with a dado cutter, it's best if you stagger the positions of the cutting teeth from one layer to the next. The bearing is always positioned at the bottom of the stack, next to the shank. The paper-thin brass shims are used between the cutters and spacers to tighten a joint. You probably won't need to use the shims until after the cutters have been resharpened. Even then, a test cut should demonstrate

This is the bit you use to violate one of the basic rules of woodworking, joining boards end to end. You can't glue end grain to end grain, but this bit forms many tapered fingers that present long grain to one another as they interdigitate. The end-to-end joint is surprisingly strong, and as an edge-to-edge joint, it's even better.

that they're necessary before you add them to the stack. Setup is easiest to do with the arbor chucked in a router that's either standing on its head or suspended in a router table.

The particular configuration you use depends upon the thickness of the stock being routed.

- For stock 7/16 inch to 5/8 inch thick, use one finger cutter.
- For stock 5/8 inch to 13/16 inch thick, use two finger cutters.
- For stock 13/16 inch to 1 inch thick, use three finger cutters.
- For stock 1 inch to 1 3/16 inches thick, use four finger cutters.
- For stock 1 3/16 inches to 1 3/8 inches thick, use all five finger cutters.

The cutters should be positioned next to the bearing, and the gap

between the last cutter and the nut should be occupied by the spacers. The straight slot cutter (or abutting-edge cutter, as it is sometimes called) is always used and is always on the top of the stack. This cutter, by the way, is actually a micromicron smaller in diameter than the finger cutters. The grooves that the finger cutters form thus are deeper than the shoulder formed by the straight cutter. This provides space for surplus glue at the tip of each finger.

The cutting sequence is the same as with the previously described specialty bits. You rout one workpiece's edge with the stock faceup and the other piece with the stock facedown. When the bit height is correct, the two pieces should slide together with their faces perfectly flush.

MORTISE-AND-TENON JOINTS

From post-and-beam to furniture, the essential frame joint

is the mortise-and-tenon. Examples of the joint that date back 5,000 years exist in museums. Even today, it's widely used in everything with a wooden frame. Yet it is a joint that many woodworkers avoid, because it seems too involved and time-consuming to make and fit properly.

One of the most common applications of the mortise-and-tenon joint is in the leg-and-rail construction used in tables and chairs. It's used in all sorts of frame-and-panel construction, particularly frames for doors.

Mortise-and-tenon joints take many different forms. The basic elements are the mortise, which is a hole—round, square, or rectangular—and the tenon, which is a tongue cut on the end of the joining member to fit the mortise. Once assembled with glue or pegs, the mortise-and-tenon joint resists all four types of stress—tension, compression, shear, and racking. And it does it better than any other type of joint. The joint's strength stems from the way it interlocks. The shoulders on both sides of the tenon prevent twisting.

Principal among the types of mortise-and-tenon joints are:

- Open mortise-and-tenon
- Through mortise-and-tenon
- Blind mortise-and-tenon
- Haunched mortise-and-tenon
- Stub mortise-and-tenon
- Round mortise-and-tenon
- Mortise and loose tenon

The router is an excellent tool for making any of these, so long as the mortise isn't too narrow and deep.

The traditional way to make the mortise is to chop it out with a mallet and chisel. The tenon is sawed out with a backsaw. It's slow work, and doing it well demands the kind of skill that comes with repetition. To speed the job, most woodworkers rough out the mortise on the drill press, then clean the walls with the chisel. (A woodworker who does a lot of mortising may invest in a hollow-chisel mortising attachment for the drill press, which actually bores a *square* hole.) Most woodworkers cut the tenons on a table saw. But the router can do both jobs just as quickly.

The main advantages of the router for mortising include the smoothness of its finished cuts and the accuracy of placement and siz-

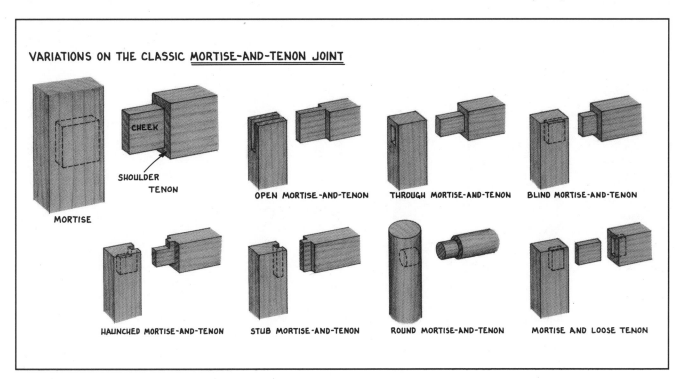

VARIATIONS ON THE CLASSIC MORTISE-AND-TENON JOINT

CHEEK

SHOULDER
TENON

MORTISE

OPEN MORTISE-AND-TENON

THROUGH MORTISE-AND-TENON

BLIND MORTISE-AND-TENON

HAUNCHED MORTISE-AND-TENON

STUB MORTISE-AND-TENON

ROUND MORTISE-AND-TENON

MORTISE AND LOOSE TENON

An open mortise is a slot through the end of the workpiece. To cut one, use the tenoning sled on the horizontal router table. Set the bit for the final depth of cut, and keep the sled tight against the tabletop edge for each pass. But for the first pass, hold the work back from the mounting board so the bit only cuts about ¼ inch deep. After each pass, advance the work toward the router, cutting deeper and deeper.

THE BASIC PROCESS

Cutting mortises and tenons with a router has a lot in common with cutting dovetails or box joints. The basic process is to cut a cavity in one piece of wood that will accept a projection that you've cut on another piece. Joining the pieces is the primary motivation. The big difference is that in mortise-and-tenon joinery, most of the joint is invisible. That means that as long as the joint is structurally sound, you don't have to worry too much about cosmetic fit. In fact, with many of today's glues, you're better off to "leave room for the glue." In other words, don't make your joints too tight.

Obviously, that doesn't mean you should be careless. The big requirement of mortise-and-tenon joinery is structural integrity, but a very close second is location during assembly. If your joints are properly cut, you should be able to assemble the unit without glue and have everything fit. You don't want to have to overcome ill-placed parts when you're gluing and clamping. That means that your mortises and tenons not only have to be in the right places but they also have to be cut perpendicular to the same faces.

That's where the router really shines. Given a jig or template to place the cut, the router will make clean, true cuts perpendicular to the surface you're working from. So we'll talk about some of the jigs that will let you make joints accurately.

Most mortising jigs are set up to guide the cutting of mortises. You can cut the tenons on the router table, regular or horizontal. The thing is that they'll have square corners, while any mortise you cut with a

ing that's possible. The handwork can be minimized—you don't need to clean out the mortises with a chisel, as you do with those roughly formed with a drill bit. And you don't need specialized, single-purpose accessories—like a hollow-chisel mortising attachment—that are so involved to mount and remove. A plunge router, a spiral bit, and an edge guide (or two) will handle most of the mortising you'll ever want to do.

The only disadvantage that comes to mind is the limited reach of the router bit. A narrow, deep mortise—¼ inch wide by 1¾ inches or more deep, for example, or ⅜ inch wide by 2½ inches deep—is problematic for a router but relatively easy for a hollow-chisel mortiser. With savvy project design, you can get around this limitation.

Once you try doing some mortise-and-tenon joinery using the router, you'll realize how easy it is. And your joinery universe will explode!

This cutaway shows the difference in finish between a routed mortise (left) and a chiseled one (right). The differences are immaterial cosmetically, since the insides of the mortises are hidden. But a smooth surface yields a superior glue joint.

To make router-cut tenons fit into router-cut mortises, you can round-over the tenon edges with a file or rasp. Especially on a ¼- to ⅜-inch-thick tenon, the job takes only a swipe or two on each of the tenon's four edges.

router is going to have rounded corners. That leaves three options. You can trim the tenons round with a chisel or rasp, you can trim the mortises square with a chisel, or you can cut the mortises a little bigger than the tenons so the square corners clear the round ends.

HAND-ROUTED MORTISES

Basically, a mortise is a deep stopped groove. If it weren't for the depth, the mortise would be really easy to do. But the job takes a straight bit to its outer limits in many cases.

Consider the width of mortise you'd be most likely to cut in ¾-inch-thick stock: ¼ inch. Check out the cutting length of ¼-inch straight bits in your bit catalogs. The longest I've found is 1 inch. Now if that bit has a ½-inch shank, you are going to be limited to its 1-inch length because of the transition from cutter body to shank. If the bit has a ¼-inch shank, and it's long, you will be able to cut deeper than the length of the cutting edges. That means you could rout a mortise 1⅜ or 1½ inches deep, maybe even 1¾ inches deep if you really press your luck.

The cut, expecially that initial plunge, puts a lot of stress on a slender shank. You have to make incremental cuts, which puts the job in the province of the plunge

router. Don't take bites that are too big, or you'll snap the cutter from the shank.

Can you do the work with a fixed-base router? Of course, but it would involve a lot of fiddling around. If you have more than one mortise to rout—and what project would involve only one?—you will have to adjust the depth of cut between passes. With a lot of routers, that can result in fairly inconsistent mortises—different depths, uneven walls, slightly different widths. The alternative is to make a first pass on each mortise before adjusting the bit height, then make a second pass on each, then a third, and so on. An incredible amount of clamping and unclamping.

If you don't have a plunge router, do the job on the horizontal router table.

Mortising Setup

Here are the typical challenges in cutting a projectful of mortises with a hand-held router:

- Positioning the router consistently from mortise to mortise
- Providing adequate bearing surface, so no cut is compromised by a router tip or wobble
- Minimizing the workpiece handling

How well you meet these challenges will dictate how well your mortises will turn out.

Positioning the router. The easiest way to position the router is using an edge guide. This common router accessory slides along an edge of the work and positions the bit in reference to that edge. (You don't have to reference the work edge, of course. You could fit the work into some sort of holder and reference an edge of it.)

To set up the edge guide, you first have to lay out one mortise with a square and pencil. Then you need to transfer the extremities of the mortise to each of the other workpieces. The edge-guide setting will position the mortise laterally, but the markings will allow you to begin and end each mortise at the correct places. Just set the workpieces together and square the lines across the lot of them.

Chuck the bit in the router. Set the depth of cut, then set the router on the marked-up workpiece. Position the bit over the mortise layout; you probably will want to plunge the bit down to the stock, so you can be sure it is aligned within the layout lines. Set the edge guide, and

Designing the Joint

The main goal in designing a mortise-and-tenon is to maximize the glue area, especially the long-grain-to-long-grain glue surface. Choose the joint and its proportions according to the job it must do.

Here are rules of thumb for establishing the width and length of your tenons. The size of the mortise follows, obviously, from the size of the tenon. (It's much easier to match the tenon to the mortise, so when making the joint, you nearly always make the mortise first.)

The bigger the tenon, the stronger it will be, but at the possible expense of the piece with the mortise in it. You don't want the mortise walls to be too thin.

You have to keep in mind what will be required of the pieces involved. For example, aprons mortised into table legs will be under tension-compression stress, so the tenons need as much height and length as you can provide. While the tenons won't get much shear or torque stress, the legs will be heavily leveraged, so you don't want to weaken them. The upshot: Make the tenons fairly thin.

In frame-and-panel work, where the pieces are likely to be the same thickness and will be experiencing similar stresses, your tenon should be somewhere between one-third and one-half the total stock thickness. In door construction, where a panel is set in a groove inside the frame, it's common to use the haunched tenon and to

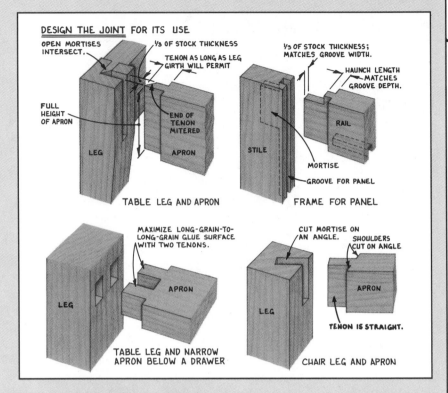

DESIGN THE JOINT FOR ITS USE

OPEN MORTISES INTERSECT. 1/3 OF STOCK THICKNESS TENON AS LONG AS LEG GIRTH WILL PERMIT FULL HEIGHT OF APRON END OF TENON MITERED LEG APRON

TABLE LEG AND APRON

1/3 OF STOCK THICKNESS; MATCHES GROOVE WIDTH. HAUNCH LENGTH MATCHES GROOVE DEPTH. RAIL STILE MORTISE GROOVE FOR PANEL

FRAME FOR PANEL

MAXIMIZE LONG-GRAIN-TO-LONG-GRAIN GLUE SURFACE WITH TWO TENONS. LEG APRON

TABLE LEG AND NARROW APRON BELOW A DRAWER

CUT MORTISE ON AN ANGLE. SHOULDERS CUT ON ANGLE LEG APRON TENON IS STRAIGHT.

CHAIR LEG AND APRON

make the tenon thickness match the width of the groove. The haunch on the tenon fits in the groove, and it enhances the joint's resistance to twisting—an important consideration in door construction.

When the tenon piece is narrow, there's sometimes a temptation to run the tenon across the grain. An example is the apron above or below a drawer in an occasional table. The tenon has long grain, but the mortise in the table leg will be all end grain; the result is a weak gluing situation. It's better to make two short, narrow tenons.

Occasionally, you'll need to make

an angled mortise-and-tenon joint. A good example is a chair, where the seat tapers from front to back; the side rails meet the legs at an angle. The mortise can be cut square to the leg's surface and the tenon on an angle. But sometimes the resulting tenon is weakened because it doesn't have enough long grain extending from its end all the way into the rail. Better choices would be to cut the mortise on an angle and the tenon straight, or to use loose tenons. Loose tenons are a particularly good choice for router-cut joinery because both the mortises can be easily referenced perpendicular to the mating surfaces.

cinch down its setscrews. Now you are ready to rout.

Plunge-cut the ends of the mortise first. Doing this ensures that the ends of the mortise will be vertical. Then rout out the waste between the ends in a series of passes. Plunge a little deeper for each pass.

When you cut, be sure you feed the router in the right direction, the one that uses the force of the bit

rotation to pull the guide against the work. This will ensure that the mortise is straight.

You can position the router even more positively using *two* edge guides. With one against each side of the work, the router can't drift. Not every commercial edge-guide system will allow you to do this. The router may accommodate one, but not two. You can make your own, of course, as

shown in the plan for the double edge guide in the chapter "Sliding Dovetail Joint."

The double edge-guide setup is particularly useful for routing mortises that have a width greater than the bit diameter. The guides can't both be smack against the sides of the workpiece, of course. To set them, position the router on the work, with the bit plunged to the work surface

Depending upon the setup you use, you may only need to transfer the extremities of the mortises from one fully laid-out part to all the others. Stack the parts, ends flush, and use a square to do this.

When the mortise width exceeds the bit diameter, use the double edge-guide baseplate. To set the guides, align the bit over the laid-out mortise. With it aligned at one side, set the far guide, as shown. Then shift the router to the opposite side of the mortise and set the second guide.

> ### ▶ TRY THIS!
> A common routine is to plunge the bit and then push or pull the machine to actually rout the waste. Then you return the machine to its original position and plunge a little deeper. The risk in this is that the bit will grab on the return, gouging the mortise wall. To avoid this risk, you should make the cutting pass, then retract the bit clear of the work before drawing the router back and replunging the bit for another pass.

and aligned over the laid-out mortise. With the bit aligned at one side, set the far guide. Then shift the router to the opposite side of the mortise and set the second guide.

As you make the cut, remember to feed the router so the bit rotation pulls the far guide against the workpiece. You still plunge both ends of the mortise to full depth; you just have to plunge at least twice at each end to accomplish this. Then waste the intervening stock in a series of incrementally deeper passes.

Providing adequate bearing surface. This is one of the perpetual bugbears of router woodworking. It's like balancing a #10 soup can atop a board fence, when the soup inside is being stirred 22,000 times a minute.

The typical plunge router is a top-heavy 12-pounder with a base 7 inches in diameter. If it's centered on a workpiece 1½ inches wide, you won't have support directly under the plunge rods. Should there be the slightest drag on one rod or the other as you plunge, the router's going to tip.

You *need* adequate support for the machine. How do you get it?

One good way is to clamp several workpieces together. For example, if you are mortising table legs, you can clamp three legs side by side in a bench vise. (Any more than three would be cumbersome to flush up and, later, to shift around.) Collectively, they'll provide a flat surface for the router base. If you mortise the middle leg, you'll have equal support for the router's entire base.

After mortising this first leg, simply reposition the legs, with a new one in the middle position. Keep shuffling the legs until all have been mortised.

The approach minimizes setup time and provides excellent support for the operation. It doesn't work as well, however, when you're mortising ¾-inch stock, since three such members don't add up to enough support. You might better sandwich such pieces between straight, flat lengths of beefier stock.

Fred's had good luck holding work in a vise. He blocks it up on

When mortising table legs, you can support the router by clamping three of them in a bench vise. Your first setup should have the leg with the fully laid-out mortise in the middle. Set the router's edge guide to reference one of the outside legs.

the vise rods until the top is flush with the jaws, then routs. If you need a fence to guide the router, you can use double-sided tape to stick a tall wooden facing to one of the jaws. With it projecting above the work, it can serve as your fence.

Minimizing the workpiece handling is most important when you have a tall stack of parts to mortise—stiles for six or eight cabinet doors or legs for a set of chairs. I'm willing to shuffle three-leg bundles in and out of a bench vise when four legs is the total. If the extent of the job is beyond that, I want a jig into which I can quickly clamp the workpieces.

The Excellent Mortising Platform

Here it is, and it *is* most excellent. Pivotal to its ease of use is the pair of DeStaCo toggle clamps (model TC-605 push-pull type). Once the movable fence is adjusted for the thickness of stock being mortised, securing a workpiece is a matter of slipping it between the fences and pushing the two toggle clamps simultaneously to clamp it. When the mortise has been routed, pull the two toggles simultaneously to release the workpiece. Lift it out and drop another in its place. The movable fence is attached to the toggle clamps, so it won't get bumped out of alignment or tumble off the workbench. No loose clamps either. And no extra blocking.

The platform can be clamped or dogged to a workbench or the router bench. I orient the platform so the fixed fence is at the workbench edge, so I can have the router's edge guide referencing my side of the jig. It's easy to reach across to the toggle clamps.

This jig holds a workpiece between two wide fences that provide good support for the router as well as a reference surface for the edge guide. Stops can be added to eliminate the need to lay out the workpieces. And the jig can be adjusted to accommodate work varying in thickness and height, too. Altogether, it's most excellent!

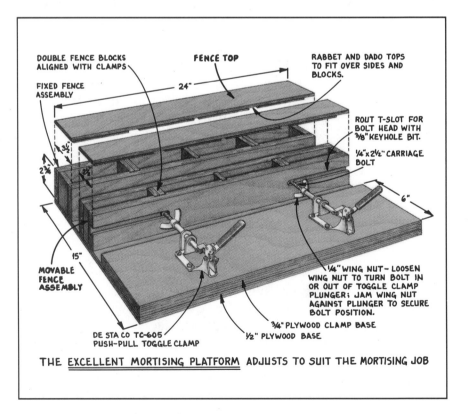

THE <u>EXCELLENT MORTISING PLATFORM</u> ADJUSTS TO SUIT THE MORTISING JOB

CUTTING LIST

Piece	Number	Thickness	Width	Length	Material
Base	1	½"	15"	24"	Birch plywood
Clamp base	1	¾"	6"	24"	Birch plywood
Fixed fence top	1	½"	3½"	24"	Birch plywood
Fixed fence sides	2	½"	2¾"	24"	Birch plywood
Fixed fence blocks	7	½"	2¾"	3"	Birch plywood
Movable fence top	1	½"	2½"	24"	Birch plywood
Movable fence sides	2	½"	2¾"	24"	Birch plywood
Movable fence blocks	7	½"	2¾"	2"	Birch plywood

Hardware

2 DeStaCo TC-605 push-pull toggle clamps. Available from Reid Tool
   Supply Co., 2265 Black Creek Road, Muskegon, MI 49444
   (800-253-0421).
2 pcs. ¼"-18 × 2½" carriage bolts
3 pcs. #6 × 1¼" drywall screws

To make the mortising platform:

1. Cut the base and the clamping base to size, and glue the two together.

2. Make the fences next. Start by cutting the fence parts to size. Glue the doubled fence blocks together; you need three such blocks for each fence. Cut the dadoes in the fence sides, as shown in *Excellent Mortising Platform*. Rabbet the sides, top, and end blocks. Assemble the fences.

3. Using a ⅜-inch keyhole bit, rout two slots in the movable fence for the heads of the carriage bolts that attach the fence to the toggle clamps. You may need to widen the slots to accommodate the bolt heads; rout the slots to fit.

4. Glue the fixed fence to the base. Align it flush with the edge opposite the clamp base. Drive drywall screws through the base into the fence.

5. Mount the toggle clamps on the base. To position them, turn the carriage bolts into the toggle clamp plungers as far as they will go. Roughly position the clamps, then fit the mov-able fence over the bolt heads. Align the fence; adjust the clamps so they are perpendicular to the fence and equidistant from the edge of the base. Fasten them in place with screws.

To use the mortising platform, you must first set the fence to secure the workpiece you are routing.

The gap between the fences is adjusted by turning the carriage bolts in and out of the toggle clamp plungers. The plunger is tapped 1 inch deep, so to vary the gap more than about ½ inch, you need to switch bolts.

To set the fence, install bolts of the proper length for the coarse setting. When they are seated in the plungers, you should be able to push and lock the clamps and have the fence against (or almost against) the workpiece. To tighten the fence so it will in fact secure the workpiece, push and lock the clamps. Turn the bolts as tight as you can, seating the fence against the workpiece. Then pull the clamps, and give the bolts an additional fraction of a turn—about one-eighth turn.

Test the setting by pushing the clamps and locking the fence. If you can move the workpiece, you need to tighten the setting further. If you can't push the clamps completely closed, you need to loosen the setting.

Lay out the mortise on the workpiece. Chuck the bit you are using in the router, and set the plunge depth. Set the router on the work, and plunge the bit, aligning it over the mortise layout. Set the edge guide, and cinch down its setscrews. Now you are ready to rout.

The guide is set for all similar mortises. If you are doing 50 mortises, all in the same place on each workpiece, you don't have to mark each piece. Instead, mark the fixed fence. Make an alignment mark on the fence top to use in positioning the workpiece. Then mark the ends of the mortises on the fence top. Use a different color for this, if that'll help you keep the different marks straight in your mind. The router's edge guide will establish the mortise position laterally, and you can eyeball the beginnings and ends of the cuts from the marks on the fence. (When you're done, erase—or sand, if necessary—the marks from the fence.)

Better yet, if you have a rectilinear baseplate on your plunge router, attach stops to the fixed fence. Use a piece of double-sided tape to stick a thin stop block to the inner wall of the fence; butt the workpiece against this stop when setting it in place. Trap your already-mortised workpiece in the jig, plunge the router bit, and set it—with the router switched off, of course—in the mortise. Set a stop against the router base and stick it to the fence top. Move the router to the other end of the mortise, and set a second stop. As long as you don't smack the router against these stops, you can set them

Problem Solver

Mortising is a good job for a plunge router with electronic speed control. You can slow down the bit to compensate for the low feed rates that mortising generally entails. And that will prolong the life of the bit you use.

Mortising can be really hard on bits. Wood is a surprisingly good insulator. The heat generated as the bit cuts a mortise isn't dissipated through the material; it's retained in that confined pocket. The danger here isn't burning of the wood so much as dulling of the cutter. Burn marks are going to be concealed inside the joint, but a dull cutter hampers your ability to even make the joint.

Mortises aren't very long, but they usually are deep. It is hard to both plunge the bit and move it back and forth quickly. Heat builds up.

The alternative is to slow the bit down. Try running the router at about 15,000 rpm. It won't really affect the practical cutting rate, but it'll be easier on your bit.

Attach temporary shims and a positioning stop to the fixed fence using carpet tape. The shim lifts the work so it is flush with the top of the jig. Set the work in place, and flip the toggles to wedge the second fence against it.

with that carpet tape. (You know. Pretend you're parking your new car, and you don't want to ding the shiny chrome.)

The usual routing technique, as noted before, is to plunge-cut the ends of the mortise and then rout out the waste between these holes with a series of incrementally deeper passes. Remember to feed the router in the direction that will pull the guide against the work.

Trough-Style Mortising Fixture

A useful, practical, and easy-to-make mortising fixture is this miter-box-like construction that clamps in a bench vise. The router is supported by the sides of the fixture, and its edge guide references the outer face of one side. (You *could* use two guides with this fixture, to trap the router in position.) Stops screwed to the side control the length of the mortise by limiting the travel of the edge guide.

To use the fixture, you clamp it in a vise. Remember to make a workpiece alignment mark on the fixture. Position the workpiece in the trough, clamping it to the main side. (You

may need to use a scrap block under the workpiece to bring it up to the top edges of the trough.) As with other setups, you position the bit over the laid-out mortise and set the edge guide to establish the lateral alignment. If you want to use stops, just drive a couple of screws through each into the side.

With a simple modification, this fixture is ideal for routing angled mortises, such as those you'd want in chair legs. All you have to do is bevel one of the sides, reducing its height in the process. When the router is set on the fixture, the bit will be cocked off-plumb.

A dandy way to mortise legs is in this troughlike fixture. The fixture is held in a vise, and it in turn holds the leg. A stop clamped at the end of the trough helps you position each leg without a lot of to-do. The router's edge guide locates the mortise. And stops screwed to the back keep you from inadvertently routing too long a mortise.

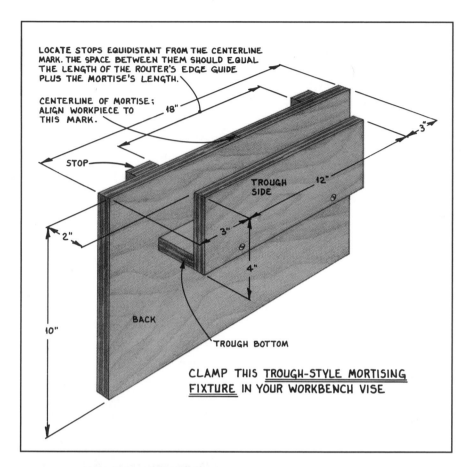

LOCATE STOPS EQUIDISTANT FROM THE CENTERLINE MARK. THE SPACE BETWEEN THEM SHOULD EQUAL THE LENGTH OF THE ROUTER'S EDGE GUIDE PLUS THE MORTISE'S LENGTH.

CENTERLINE OF MORTISE; ALIGN WORKPIECE TO THIS MARK.

18"

STOP

3"

TROUGH SIDE

12"

2"

3"

4"

10"

BACK

TROUGH BOTTOM

CLAMP THIS <u>TROUGH-STYLE MORTISING FIXTURE</u> IN YOUR WORKBENCH VISE

Simply by staggering the height of the fixture's sides, you can tilt the router without sacrificing its stability, so you can rout angled mortises. The edge guide references the taller side to position the mortise, but also to keep the router from skidding off the jig.

The construction of the fixture should be evident from looking at *Trough-Style Mortising Fixture*. It's a good idea to assemble it with screws—no glue—so you can replace one of the sides for cutting angled mortises.

Template Systems

Using a template to guide and control a mortising operation has several advantages. It isn't the ideal approach for every mortise, but there are occasions when it is absolutely the best.

The major disadvantage is that the template thickness steals depth from the mortise. If the maximum depth you can achieve with a particular bit is 1½ inches, then using a ½-inch-thick template reduces the achievable depth to 1 inch. Obvi-

ously, you'll want to use the thinnest template material you can for this application.

So what are the advantages? You can cut mortises of a consistent length and width, without fiddling with edge guides. If you are mortising narrow stock, the template itself can provide support for the router, and it can serve as a clamping base for the workpiece. With a template, you can rout mortises that are wider than the bit diameter. You can rout aesthetically pleasing through mortises of the sort you'd use in a plank bench.

The chapter "Template-Guided Work" has all the details on the best materials to use for templates, on scaling them to use with guide bushings, and so on. For mortising, given that you want to conserve as much of the depth capacity as possible, use ¼-inch hardboard or plywood for the template. If the guide bushing's collar is less than ⅛ inch high, you can get by with ⅛-inch material for the template if you apply strips of ¾-inch stock around the edges to reinforce it. In any case, cut the tem-

A through mortise can be template-guided. Use the crossing centerlines on the template to align it with similar lines on the workpiece. After the router work is completed, square the mortise corners with a chisel.

If the mortise isn't too deep and the workpieces aren't too big and heavy, you can make an oversized template from ½-inch plywood. Screw a locating cleat to the underside of the template, and clamp the template to the router bench, as shown. Clamp the work against the cleat, and rout. Here, a positioning block is clamped to the cleat and a Vise-Grip C-clamp is used to clamp the walnut workpiece in place.

plate blank so it's three or four times longer and wider than the mortise.

Work out the dimensions of the mortise you want, then bump it up to the size of the template opening that's necessary, given the bit and guide bushing you'll be using. In mortising operations, it's a good idea to use a large-diameter bushing so that the chips augered out of the mortise can escape through the gap between bit and bushing. To bump up the mortise size to template size, subtract the diameter of the bit from the outside diameter of the bushing and add the difference to both the length and width of the mortise.

Lay out the template opening on the template blank. As you lay out the opening, scribe indelible centerlines through the length and width of the opening, extending them well beyond the opening. These will later help you align the template for a mortising cut. Routing is probably the cleanest way to make the opening. You can use a T-square with stops to control this cut.

To use the template, you simply clamp it to the work. Use a plunge router, the appropriate guide bushing, and, of course, an upcut spiral bit to make the cut.

How you position and clamp the template depends a lot on the nature of the workpiece. If you are mortising narrow frame members, glue and screw a cleat to the underside of the template to both position the template and provide clamping surface. If you are mortising a bench seat, you can align the centerlines of the template with matching centerlines scribed on the workpiece, and simply clamp the template to the work. In most situations, double-sided carpet tape will do a good job of holding the template in place.

TABLE-ROUTED MORTISES

The horizontal router table is my choice for mortising all but the biggest work. I've made two mortising sleds that securely hold the work, control the mortise's end-to-end size, and let me plunge the work onto the bit in stages.

You can sort of freehand mortises on the machine, marking bit tangents on a snatch of tape and eyeballing the cut from mark to mark. That's a good way to get the first

mortise, which you use to set up the sled. But the sled allows you to plunge-cut the ends of each mortise, then nibble out the intervening waste in stages. Doing that is a lot easier on a frail solid carbide bit, and it eliminates the need to monkey with the bit's depth setting during a session. And doing it with the work clamped in a sled like this one makes it easier to manipulate and control the workpiece.

I used T-handled toggle clamps on the sleds. While the cost of them does mount up—especially when you use three on one little sled!—they are very versatile. (You can back out the mounting screws and use them on a different jig for the next job.) The clamps make quick work of swapping workpieces, and they double as handles for the sled. I used three on the stile-mortising sled so I can use one to secure a positioning stop and two to hold the workpiece.

There are two sleds because loose-tenon joinery requires you to mortise rail ends, which in more traditional approaches have the tenons cut on them. The sled for stiles isn't suitable for mortising rails.

To make the stile-mortising sled:

1. Cut the parts to the sizes specified by the Cutting List. I made the base from birch plywood, and the fence and guides from scraps of hardwood.

2. Lay out and rout the slots for the guide bolts. Use a plunge router and an edge guide to do this. Keeping the same edge-guide setting, switch to a V-groover and countersink the slots.

3. Glue and screw the fence to the base, using drywall screws. Screw the toggle clamps to the fence.

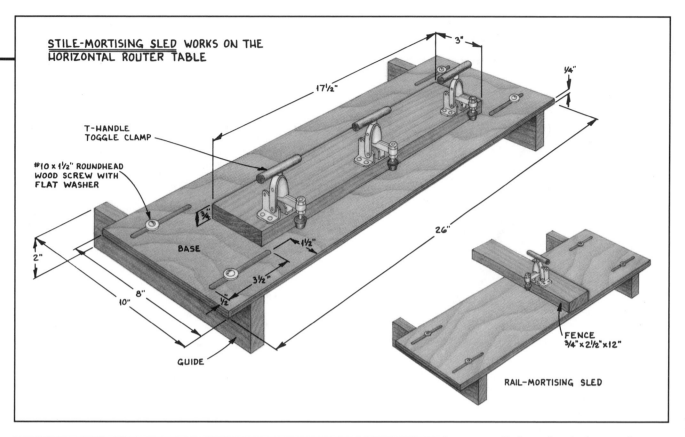

STILE-MORTISING SLED WORKS ON THE HORIZONTAL ROUTER TABLE

3"

17½"

T-HANDLE TOGGLE CLAMP

#10 x 1½" ROUNDHEAD WOOD SCREW WITH FLAT WASHER

¼"

BASE

¾"

1½"

26"

2"

3½"

½"

8"

10"

GUIDE

FENCE
¾" x 2½" x 12"

RAIL-MORTISING SLED

CUTTING LIST

Piece	Number	Thickness	Width	Length	Material
Base	1	¼"	8"	26"	Birch plywood
Fence	1	¾"	3"	17½"	Hardwood
Edge guides	2	¾"	2"	10"	Hardwood

Hardware

3 DeStaCo TC-202-TU vertical-type toggle clamps. Available from Reid Tool Supply Co., 2265 Black Creek Road, Muskegon, MI 49444 (800-253-0421).

4 pcs. #10 × 1½" roundhead wood screws

5 pcs. #6 × 1¼" drywall screws

The mortising sled gives you a comfortable grip on the work, so you can maneuver it confidently, with your hands well clear of the bit. When you have a lot of pieces to mortise, you can use one of the toggle clamps to fix a positioning block, as shown here. There are still two clamps left to secure the workpiece. Switching workpieces is fast and sure.

4. Drill the pilot holes in the two edge guide strips. Use roundhead wood screws to attach them to the sled.

To use the stile-mortising sled, you first need to adjust the guides to govern the length of the mortise. The easiest way is to set one guide somewhat arbitrarily, then adjust the second to allow just the amount of movement necessary to produce the mortise.

But you also have to adjust the extension of the bit and its height above the tabletop. The thickness of the jig's base, of course, must be accommodated.

I have a centerline on my jig's base. I like to have the middle of the mortise roughly on that line. So I line up the centerline under the bit, then shift the jig about half the length of the mortise to one side. I push the base against the table's router mounting board, bring the guide flat against the edge of the tabletop, and tighten the guide-mounting screws. The first guide is now set, square to the jig's

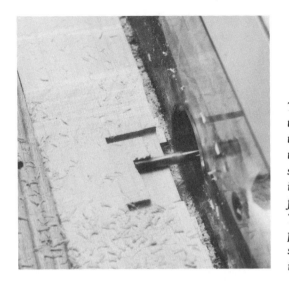

To rout a mortise, you plunge the work onto the bit, cutting to full depth at each end of the mortise. Then back a series of shallow cuts, moving the work back and forth from one end to the other. This special cutaway of a partially routed mortise shows what the bit is doing inside the stile.

base and parallel to the bit. I move the jig the other direction only the amount I have to move it to rout the mortise. Again, I keep the base against the router mounting board and tighten the guide screws. The guides are now set.

The amount you have to move the jig is equal to the length of the mortise minus the diameter of the bit.

To quickly position each workpiece, I use one of the toggle clamps to lock a stop to the jig. Butt the end of the workpiece against the stop and lock the other two clamps.

With the jig set up, I then adjust the bit's extension and its height above the jig. A test cut confirms the correctness of the setup (or demonstrates the need for fine-tuning).

A fast way to set up the works is to rout a sample mortise freehand, then use it to set the jig's guides as well as the bit settings.

You're now ready to go.

My routing routine is this: Clamp a workpiece in the jig. Turn on the router—a foot switch makes this easy. With the jig shifted to one side as far as possible, plunge the work onto the bit, cutting one end of the mortise to the full depth. Back the work

off the bit, shift the jig to the opposite stop, and plunge the work again, boring the other end of the mortise. Back the work off the bit again.

Now remove the waste between these two holes. You can do it by sliding the jig back and forth, incrementally routing out the waste. Or you can do it as if you were drilling out the waste, by plunging and replunging. When most of the waste is removed, clean the mortise walls

by plunging to full depth and sliding the jig from side to side.

As you back off the bit to swap workpieces, lift your foot from the switch and cut the power to the router. Don't get back on the pedal again until you're ready to plunge the new workpiece onto the bit.

And be sure you switch workpieces after routing a mortise. Don't flip the piece and rout a mortise in the other end. You should have one face of each workpiece marked as the reference face and that face should always be consistently oriented— either always up or always down. When you've got a mortise done in

> **TRY THIS!**

If you need to do a mortise in a part that is shaped some way in the finished project, cut the mortise before you shape the part. A tapered leg, for example, will be easier to mortise while its faces are all still parallel.

> **TRY THIS!**

Instead of routing a mortise freehand on the horizontal router table, try clamping two fences to the tabletop. The fences will keep you from making the mortise wider than you want, which is one of the risks in working completely freehand. Use wood scraps wide enough that you can clamp them at the edges of the tabletop, as shown. Set the bit to the correct extension and height above the table. Then slide the stock confidently along the fence to plunge it onto and withdraw it from the bit.

Problem Solver

Trying to adjust your router setup so the mortise is exactly positioned on the workpiece is difficult and often frustrating. A better focus for your attention is marking each workpiece so the mortises will be *consistently* positioned.

Example: You rout mortises in the stiles of a frame-and-panel cabinet door. The mortises aren't quite centered on the stile edges. The tenons are centered, so when assembled, the faces of the rails and stiles aren't flush. A typical solution is to sand the assembled frame to bring the faces flush.

But because you referenced the back face for one mortise and the front face for the other, the faces of the assembly aren't parallel. One end of the rail is proud of the stile's back face, and the other end is proud of the front face. See *Twisted Frames.* Moreover, the panel will have to be twisted slightly to fit into the groove for it. The assembly is more likely to warp,

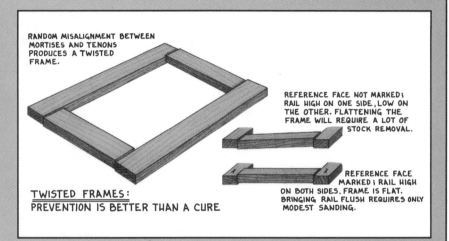

RANDOM MISALIGNMENT BETWEEN MORTISES AND TENONS PRODUCES A TWISTED FRAME.

REFERENCE FACE NOT MARKED; RAIL HIGH ON ONE SIDE, LOW ON THE OTHER. FLATTENING THE FRAME WILL REQUIRE A LOT OF STOCK REMOVAL.

REFERENCE FACE MARKED; RAIL HIGH ON BOTH SIDES. FRAME IS FLAT. BRINGING RAIL FLUSH REQUIRES ONLY MODEST SANDING.

TWISTED FRAMES: PREVENTION IS BETTER THAN A CURE

and though sanding will improve its appearance, it just won't be totally satisfactory.

If the mortises are consistently closer to one face or the other, the misalignment is a whole lot easier to cure with a little planing or sanding. The planes of the rails and stile will be parallel, so the panel will be flat.

So mark a reference face on each of the pieces to be mortised. Lay out the pieces as they'll be assembled. Mark the face that's

up. When you rout the mortises, always have the reference face oriented the same way. The mortises may not be perfectly positioned, but all of them will be the same.

Doing this will require two slightly different setups for a full frame-and-panel job. For example, if you rout the mortises on the horizontal router table, you have to shift the location of the workpiece positioning stop. Rout one mortise on each stile, then move the stop and do the other mortise.

each piece, move the locating stop so you can do the second mortise in each and still keep that reference face properly oriented.

The rail-mortising sled is a mutation of the stile-mortising sled. The fence is parallel to the bit axis rather than perpendicular to it. Its construction is virtually the same as the other sled. Align the fence as shown in *Stile-Mortising Sled.*

Setup and use of this jig also mimics the other sled. Set the guides to govern the side-to-side movement but also to position the mortise in the workpiece. A good way to set up

To keep the reference face up, you need to relocate the positioning block for the second mortise on each stile. Do this only after all the stiles have one mortise cut in them.

BIT DRAWER

The bit of choice for excavating mortises is the upcut spiral bit. This is the router bit that looks a lot like a twist-drill bit.

There are several reasons you want to use this bit. First of all, it's a true plunge-cutting bit. It's designed to bore straight down into the work, cutting a clean hole. In addition, it has an augering action that *moves* the chips sliced from the workpiece; the upcut configuration moves them up and out of the mortise. Finally, a spiral bit has both high hook and shear angles, so it doesn't take a lot of horses to power one. Nevertheless, it slices smoothly through wood and cuts aggressively.

A second-choice bit for mortising would be an upshear straight bit. This won't auger the chips from the cut so efficiently as a spiral, but the upshear flutes still slice the wood rather than scraping it. The cut is still smooth without requiring major horsepower.

The last choice—the one used more often than not, unfortunately—is the common plunge-cutting straight. It does the job, and if that's what you have, don't be deterred from mortising. It won't clear the chips, and consequently, it'll run hotter.

In selecting a bit for mortising, look for the longest one you can find. The cutting length is less important than the overall length. You'll be trimming about ¼ inch at a time as you plunge deeper and deeper into the mortise, so the cutting is being done at the tip of the bit. A long cutting edge isn't particularly useful. A long shank, however, is essential to reach into that deep mortise.

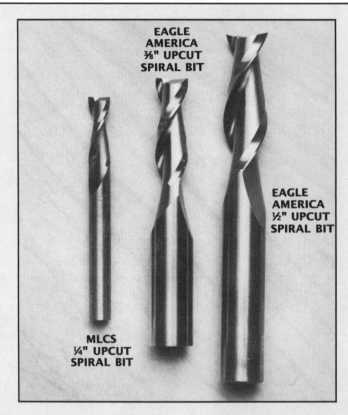

EAGLE AMERICA ⅜" UPCUT SPIRAL BIT

EAGLE AMERICA ½" UPCUT SPIRAL BIT

MLCS ¼" UPCUT SPIRAL BIT

Usually we advise you to use the ½-inch-shank version of any bit. This is the exception. For mortising, try to match the shank diameter to the cutting diameter. A ¼-inch cutter should be on a ¼-inch shank. A ⅜-inch cutter should be on a ⅜-inch shank (assuming you have either a ⅜-inch collet or a reducer for your router). The reason is that deep reach.

A ¼-inch cutter on a ½-inch shank has a transition—often an abrupt one—from the cutting diameter to the shank diameter. Usually the transition is right at the end of the cutting edges. When it contacts the work, the transition will chamfer the edges of the cut just a little and burn the wood quite a lot. You just can't get the bit to cut deeper than its cutting length.

The bit I like to use for ¼-inch-wide mortises is this 2½-inch-long upcut spiral from MLCS. The cutting length is 1 inch, but its ¼-inch shank will reach nicely into the cut, so I can, with care, plunge about 1½ inches into a mortise with it—and still have at least ¾ inch of the shank in the collet. This is a solid carbide bit, so you can't be too aggressive. It will break.

For mortises ⅜ inch wide, I use Eagle America's ⅜-inch solid-carbide upcut spiral. The cutting length is 1¼ inch, and it's on a ½-inch shank, so the cutting length represents the maximum cutting depth.

Once you get to the ½-inch diameter, there are a lot of long-shank bits available. Eagle America has a 4-inch-long spiral, and even though the cutting edges end at 1½ inches, the shank will get those edges 2½ inches or more into a mortise.

Setting up the rail-mortising sled should be done with a marked workpiece clamped to it. Raise and extend the bit. Align the bit with layout marks made on the face of the workpiece. Move the edge guide against the table-top edge and tighten the setscrews.

Chair-making frequently involves cutting angled mortises. It's easy with the rail-mortising sled. Cut a wedge or spacer and stick it to the sled base beside the fence. Then the rail is clamped in place for mortising.

the jig is to lay out the ends of the mortise on the *face* of a workpiece. Clamp it in the jig; with the mounting board set high (so the bit is above the work), align the bit with the marks, then set the guides.

To cut a mortise, plunge-cut the ends to the full depth, then nibble away at the waste in between, either with additional plunge cuts or by working the sled side to side, cutting a bit deeper with each pass.

ROUTING TENONS

Once you've routed the mortises, doing the tenons is relatively easy. The operation has a great deal in common with routing end-lap joints.

The difference between cutting laps and cutting tenons—and it is

an important difference—is that with a tenon, you cut into both faces (and sometimes the edges). The challenge is to get the shoulders lined up all around the piece.

Because the tenons are usually cut *after* the mortises, you need to adjust the thickness of the tenons to fit the mortises. Cut a test tenon, see how it fits the mortise. Ideally, you'll make the tenon a bit too thick on the first pass, and subsequent bit-height adjustments will thin it to the perfect fit. Remember to trim both cheeks each time you adjust the bit, so the tenon remains centered on the work (unless your project design requires it to be off-center, of course).

Loose tenons are the most easily made of all. Rip lengths of straight, defect-free stock to the width and thickness required. Round-over the

edges with a bull-nose bit or a round-over bit. Then crosscut the tenon stock to the lengths required.

Use natural wood for these tenons. Some woodworkers advocate using hardboard, but it's got no strength. You can snap a strip of it in half with your hands. It will line up the joint for you, but you'll have little more than an end-grain-to-long-grain glue joint. The natural wood will provide the same long-grain reinforcement across the joint that an integral tenon does, and it gives the joint a lot of long-grain-to-long-grain glue surface, to boot.

HAND-ROUTED TENONS

Read through the chapter "Lap Joints." There you'll see several lap-cutting approaches that apply equally well to cutting tenons with a hand-held router. You can clamp several rails together and run the cutter across all at the same time, for example.

One useful tenoning jig is designed to help you keep the shoulders square. The fixture is a T-square fastened to a base. It has a stop fence that corresponds to the T-square's crossbar, against which you butt the work. A second fence—a router guide—extends across the face of the work and serves both to clamp the work in the fixture and to guide the router. A homemade toggle speeds up the shifting and switching of workpieces. The guide fence is long enough that you can clamp two or three rails at a time under it, but you may find that it's just as fast and less hassle to cut the tenons one at a time.

To use the fixture, you dog it to the workbench, then clamp the work in it. The stop fence has a dado

To expedite things, clamp a positioning stop to the stop fence or jig base, as shown. With the pressure off the guide fence, the workpiece should be easy to slide into place, right up against the stop. Push down the home-made toggle to lock the work under the fence.

Routing a tenon is much like routing a dado with a T-square. Guide the router along the fence and cut into the work, feeding through into the stop fence (the stop fence prevents tear-out). Make as many sweeps as necessary to complete the cut.

routed in it, and so long as you always use the same router and bit with the fixture, you can use this dado to line up the work. The edge of the dado, of course, corresponds to the shoulder of the tenon. Guide the router along the fence, and feed toward the stop fence. It will back up the work, preventing tear-out when the bit exits the cut. If the tenon is longer than you can cut in a single pass, make two or three, always feeding toward the stop fence.

Tenoning on the Router Table

Tenoning is a snap on either the router table or the horizontal router table. You need the right bit—a different one for each table—and an easy-to-make tenoning sled. Then you're ready to go.

The scheme is this: You want to cradle the work in the sled and push it over the bit, making the necessary cut in a pass or two.

On the horizontal router table, this means you adjust the bit extension to control the length of the tenon, and move the mounting board up or down to establish how deep the cut is. One pass should complete the cut into each face.

For example, if you need a ¼-inch-thick by 1¼-inch-long tenon on ¾-inch stock, you adjust the router's depth control to extend the bit 1¼ inches, then adjust the mounting board so the bit makes a ¼-inch-deep cut. Set the workpiece in the sled, butt its end against the mounting board, and clamp it. Switch on the router and advance the sled, making the cut. Pull the sled back, release the workpiece, and turn it over. Reclamp and make another pass. The tenon is done.

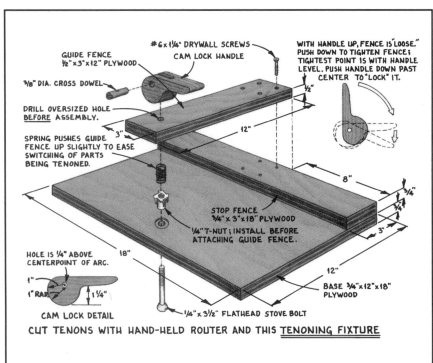

GUIDE FENCE ½" x 3" x 12" PLYWOOD

#6 x 1¼" DRYWALL SCREWS
CAM LOCK HANDLE

WITH HANDLE UP, FENCE IS "LOOSE." PUSH DOWN TO TIGHTEN FENCE; TIGHTEST POINT IS WITH HANDLE LEVEL. PUSH HANDLE DOWN PAST CENTER TO "LOCK" IT.

⅜" DIA. CROSS DOWEL

DRILL OVERSIZED HOLE BEFORE ASSEMBLY.

SPRING PUSHES GUIDE FENCE UP SLIGHTLY TO EASE SWITCHING OF PARTS BEING TENONED.

STOP FENCE ¾" x 3" x 18" PLYWOOD

¼" T-NUT; INSTALL BEFORE ATTACHING GUIDE FENCE.

HOLE IS ¼" ABOVE CENTERPOINT OF ARC.

1"
1" RAD.
1¼"
CAM LOCK DETAIL

¼" x 3½" FLATHEAD STOVE BOLT

BASE ¾" x 12" x 18" PLYWOOD

CUT TENONS WITH HAND-HELD ROUTER AND THIS <u>TENONING FIXTURE</u>

The horizontal router table is ideal for tenoning, and the sled is an essential part of the operation. The sled's fence backs up the cut to prevent tear-out and, as well, provides a mounting for the toggle clamp to anchor the workpiece. Smooth, square tenons can be cut with one pass on each face.

The tenoning sled for the regular router table has a fence that extends well beyond the bit so you can clamp a positioning block to it. The large toggle clamp has the range to accommodate both wide and thick workpieces. Set the workpiece in the sled, butt it against the stop, and clamp it. Then make the cut. Subsequent cuts are made by unclamping the work and backing it away from the bit. More support for the sled and workpiece are gained by making the sled to reference the table's back edge (rather than its front edge).

BIT DRAWER

CMT 1¼" MORTISING BIT

MLCS 1½" BOTTOM-CLEANING BIT

AMANA 2"-LONG ½" STRAIGHT BIT

PASO ROBLES ⅜" CARBIDE-TIPPED UPCUT SPIRAL BIT

EAGLE AMERICA ⅜" SOLID-CARBIDE UPCUT SPIRAL BIT

Here are the bits of choice for cutting tenons. None of them is limited to tenoning; all are useful for other routing operations. Don't feel you need a special-purpose bit for tenoning. You don't.

With the horizontal router table: Use a spiral bit if at all possible. The configuration—upcut or downcut—is immaterial in tenoning. You aren't using the spiral for its ability to move the chips away from the cut. You are using it for its smooth cut in all sorts of wood.

A ½-inch cutting and shank diameter is best (while we're talking about ideal setups). For this operation, unlike for cutting mortises, the entire cutting length will be addressing the work on each pass. You do need a cutting length that matches the length of the tenon.

Though a spiral cuts aggressively, doesn't require a lot of power to drive, and yields that smooth finish, the bit I use most frequently, especially for long tenons, is Amana's 2-inch-long ½-inch straight cutter. What it has going for it is length: It cuts tenons a full 2 inches long.

With the regular router table: Any large-diameter straight bit will do, as will mortising bits. But my favorite is what's sometimes called a bottom-cleaning bit, other times a planer. It's got very short cutting flutes, so it can't cut too deeply in one pass. But in a large diameter, say, 1½ inches, it can mill a wide swath. The finish, as you might expect from something called a planer bit, is smooooooth.

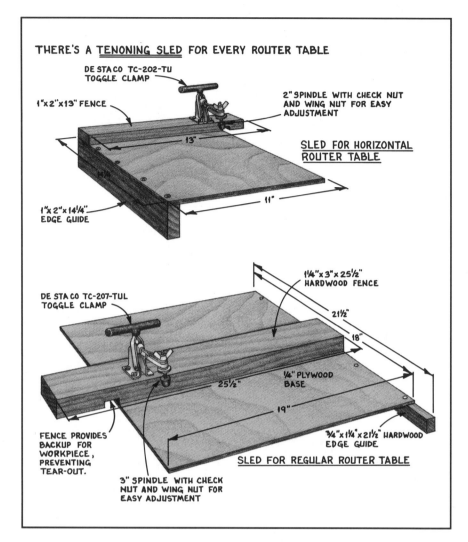

THERE'S A <u>TENONING SLED</u> FOR EVERY ROUTER TABLE

DE STA CO TC-202-TU TOGGLE CLAMP

2" SPINDLE WITH CHECK NUT AND WING NUT FOR EASY ADJUSTMENT

1"x 2"x 13" FENCE

13"

SLED FOR HORIZONTAL ROUTER TABLE

11"

1"x 2"x 14¼" EDGE GUIDE

DE STA CO TC-207-TUL TOGGLE CLAMP

1¼"x 3"x 25½" HARDWOOD FENCE

21½"

18"

¼" PLYWOOD BASE

25½"

19"

FENCE PROVIDES BACKUP FOR WORKPIECE, PREVENTING TEAR-OUT.

¾"x 1¼"x 21½" HARDWOOD EDGE GUIDE

SLED FOR REGULAR ROUTER TABLE

3" SPINDLE WITH CHECK NUT AND WING NUT FOR EASY ADJUSTMENT

Cutting Round Tenons

Tenons can be milled on dowels and spindles on either router table using a straight bit and, to hold the work, a V-block fixture.

The V-block is common fixture, used to hold rounds for drilling and the like. What makes this fixture a little different is that it has a plywood base so you can clamp it to the tabletop, and a hold-down to keep the round in the groove while you turn it. It also has an integral stop to control the length of the tenon.

To use the fixture, position it on the router tabletop with the bit protruding through the hole between the V-block and the stop. Measure from the V-block side of the bit to the stop. The distance from bit to stop must equal the tenon length you want, so shift the jig back and forth as necessary. When you've got

To rout round tenons, feed the spindle into the bit, all the while turning it. The cutter will reduce the diameter of the spindle. The larger the bit diameter, the smoother the tenon will be. Here a dish cutter is being used, since a square shoulder isn't required on the chair rung being worked.

On the regular table, adjusting the router's depth of cut takes care of the cut depth, and positioning the work in relation to the bit controls the tenon length. Depending upon the bit diameter, you may have to make two or three passes on each face to cut a long tenon.

Make the initial pass with the workpiece positioned in the sled so the cut will establish the tenon's shoulder. Then pull the workpiece away from the bit for subsequent passes, which will clean off the remaining waste. Your first thought may be to use the router table's fence as a stop, to establish that shoulder

cut (as you would with a table saw). But you can only use the fence for this if you position it *parallel to the front edge of the tabletop*. It's easier to clamp a stop block to the sled's fence for this purpose. The fence on the sled shown is extralong specifically to allow this.

To make the tenoning sled, cut the base, guide, and fence to size. Glue and screw the fence and guide to the base. The fence must be perpendicular to the guide, which references the front edge of the tabletop. Screw the toggle clamp in place. Our sled has a DeStaCo TC-202-TU clamp.

the setting, clamp the jig to the tabletop.

Loosen the hold-down, and insert a scrap of the round stock to be tenoned. Use the scrap to adjust both the hold-down and the bit height.

The idea of the hold-down is to free both your hands for turning the round and sliding it back and forth. The toggle on one side allows you to loosen the hold-down quickly to switch workpieces. The compression springs ensure you won't have to lift the hold-down to get the work under it. To set the hold-down, lay the test workpiece in the groove and slide it under the hold-down. Lock the toggle, then adjust the wing nut so the work

is held firmly enough in the groove that it won't bounce up and down, but not so firmly that you can't turn it.

In adjusting the bit height, start with a very shallow cut, and work up to the proper fit.

To make a cut, you pull the round back in the V-groove so that it is fully clear of the bit. Switch on the router, and slide the round forward in the groove; as it engages the bit, rotate the stock, while at the same time continuing to slide it forward in the groove. Eventually, the end will hit the stop.

See Also . . .

page 287 for ideas on cutting tenons that resemble end-laps.

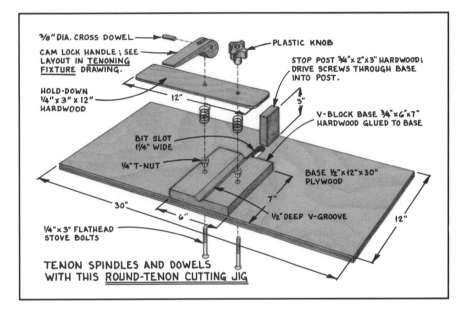

TENON SPINDLES AND DOWELS WITH THIS ROUND-TENON CUTTING JIG

LAP JOINTS

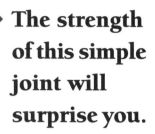

The strength of this simple joint will surprise you.

Used for small or simple frames, like picture frames, face frames, cabinet door frames, and simple chairs, the lap joint is usually considered to be of intermediate strength—that is, stronger than a butt, weaker than a mortise-and-tenon. The truth is, a well fitted and glued lap joint will be stronger than a comparable mortise-and-tenon. (The reason is that in a lap joint, each member retains more of its original girth. Usually, the joint doesn't fail, the wood does. In a lap joint, there's more wood, so it is stronger.)

In a lap joint, one member is notched to accept the other member. These joints—the variations abound—are a simple way of joining two pieces that cross or meet, forming an X, L, or T. Essentially, the joint consists of dadoes or rabbets cut in one or both pieces. The pieces are thus interlocked with their faces flush.

In a full lap joint, only one piece is notched; the other's full dimension is set into the notch.

In any of the half-lap joints, both members are notched, usually with half the total material to be removed coming from each piece. The British call these "halved joints," which is sensible and thus somewhat surprising.

Within these broad categories, there are many variations. In the end-lap joint, both members are lapped at their ends. In a cross-lap joint, the laps are somewhere other than the ends; the members can cross at any angle. In a T-lap joint, one member is lapped in the middle, the other at an end. Other variations include the mitered half-lap and the dovetail half-lap.

In an edge cross-lap joint, the members are notched rather than dadoed so that the lapping is edge-to-edge, rather than face-to-face.

ROUTING LAPS

Conceptually, cutting laps is a lot like cutting rabbets and dadoes. Don't reach for the rabbeting bit, though. Laps are usually much wider than cuts we typically think of as dadoes and rabbets. In some cases, a *lot* wider, and therein lies whatever rub there is. But I'll get to that.

Because of their similarity to dadoes and rabbets, the techniques for routing laps mimic those for cutting dadoes and rabbets. You use some variety of straight bit—straight, shear-cut, spiral, what have you. And you use a guide—a fence, a T-square, a straight template.

The depth of cut necessary makes the plunge router the first choice for this job. The correct depth setting—exactly half the thickness of the stock—can be elusive. To have to monkey around with intermediate depths compounds the frustration. And if you have to repeat the operation to lap both ends of each piece, it can send you over the top. Now if the total depth isn't more than 3/8 inch, you can probably do it in one pass; the first cut is unavoidably heavy, but as you work back and forth, widening the cut, you can nibble. But the plunge router is the real solution here. You can set the final depth right at the start, but use two or three intermediate settings before that ultimate depth.

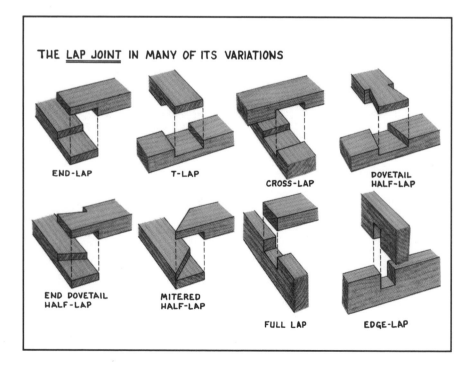

THE LAP JOINT IN MANY OF ITS VARIATIONS

END-LAP

T-LAP

CROSS-LAP

DOVETAIL HALF-LAP

END DOVETAIL HALF-LAP

MITERED HALF-LAP

FULL LAP

EDGE-LAP

Routing End- and Cross-Laps

The usual technique for laying out end- and cross-laps is to use the work itself. Lay one workpiece on top of the other, right where they are supposed to be lapped. Scribe along the edges of the top piece, marking the bottom piece. Turn the two over and repeat.

Now clamp a guide of some sort to the work, set up the router, and cut. If you are cutting several pieces—end-laps on four sides to a frame, for example—save time by aligning all the pieces, clamping them together, and cutting them all at once.

If you are cutting end-laps, you can use a T-square—along with a T-square locating jig (see "T-Square" on page 225) to position it—as the router's guide. The end-lap has only one shoulder, so you need only one guide. But you can also use the self-positioning dado guide or, in conjunction with a template guide bushing or a pattern bit, a straight template. (See the chapter "Template-Guided Work.")

The rumple in the operation is router tippiness. Usually, you make the first pass with the router riding the fence, to establish the shoulder of the lap. Then you make passes back and forth, working out to the end. For most of the operation, there's support for the router on both sides of the bit. But as you make that last pass, you're removing vital support. The router's going to tilt, and the bit's going to gouge the work.

Several possibilities present themselves.

• Lay out and cut the end-laps as cross-laps, thus leaving a ridge of waste to support the router. Trim the waste away after the laps are

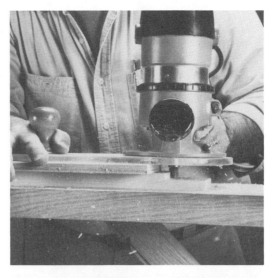

An offset base can help you cut end-laps with a pattern bit. Push down firmly on the outboard knob to keep the base flat on the work, ensuring that the lap is a consistent depth. The pattern bit's bearing rides the template, ensuring that you get a crisp, square shoulder cut.

Two T-squares can be used to guide your router in cutting a cross-lap. Use a locating jig to position them from the layout lines. Alternate the crossbars so they don't conflict.

TRY THIS!

Before cutting good wood, test your depth-of-cut setting on scrap. Since a lap cut removes half the thickness of the stock, you need to make pairs of test cuts. Do the initial setting with a ruler. Snick the corner of your scrap, flip the scrap over, and snick a second corner so the two cuts just intersect, as shown. If the depth of cut is too shallow, the two cuts won't connect. If it is too deep, you'll see that. Keep adjusting and testing until the two cuts just merge.

CUT TOO SHALLOW   CUT TOO DEEP   CUT JUST RIGHT

The trick in cutting end-laps with a hand-held router is supporting the tool squarely. If you cut the workpieces overlong and leave a band of full-thickness waste, the laps are in effect cross-laps. Here a T-square is clamped to all four workpieces. The first pass is made with a spacer between the router and the T-square (left). With the spacer removed, the shoulder cut can be made with the router against the T-square, then any intervening waste routed away (right).

TRY THIS!

One way to support the router while cutting end-laps is to leave a band of waste, which you trim off after the laps are completed. But how can you be sure you're cutting them long enough?

Use a spacer cut to the width of the lap between the fence and the router base.

Set up the work, clamping together all the parts to be machined, with scrap pieces on the outsides. Clamp your fence to the work to guide the router and position the shoulder cut. Cut your spacer.

Set up the plunge router, and make the shoulder cut first, making as many passes as necessary

to cut to the full depth. Then fit the spacer in place—you'll probably need to clamp it, too—and make the end cut, again cutting to the full depth (*left*). This should

leave a band of stock at the butt ends of the workpieces. Remove the spacer, and rout the waste material from between the first two cuts (*right*).

---

routed. You can only do this, of course, if you leave the workpieces overlong to begin with.

• Clamp expendable rails on each side of the lap. Rout into them, but not through them.

• Start the cuts at the very end of the piece, and work toward the shoulder. This way you'll have the router half-supported throughout the cut.

• Use an offset router baseplate. (See, for example, "Offset Baseplate" on page 54.) This will work if you use a straight template that guides a pattern bit or a template guide bushing.

• Use carpet tape—you know, the stuff that's sticky on both sides—to temporarily attach a small scrap of the working stock to the router baseplate.

If you are cutting a cross-lap, you need two fences to guide the cuts as well as to limit their total width. You don't need to worry about tipping unless the lap's width is more than half of the baseplate's diameter. (If your router's baseplate is 6 inches

in diameter, you can cut a 3-inch-wide lap with a ¾-inch bit and have the baseplate bearing on both sides of the cut at all times.) If the lap is to be wider than that, skim ahead to "Cutting *Wide* Laps" on page 292.

T-squares will work as fences, as will self-positioning dado guides and straight templates.

Routing Pocket Laps

A stopped lap, a lap that doesn't cut all the way across the face of the workpiece, is known as a pocket lap. You might use pocket laps in a face frame where you didn't want end grain showing on the sides. The lap joint between rail and stile would be hidden on the inside of the cabinet.

The easiest way to cut pocket laps is with a U-shaped jig made out of a square of ¼-inch plywood (or hardboard) for the base and several strips of one-by stock for the fences.

To make the jig, do some measuring and easy calculating first.

• Determine the width of the lap.
• Measure the diameter of the router baseplate.
• Decide which bit you'll use to make the cut.
• Add the width of the cut to the diameter of the baseplate.
• Subtract the diameter of the bit.

The result is the distance between the jig's parallel fences. Add the combined widths of two pieces of the one-by stock, and you have the width of the jig.

Here's an example. The lap width is 2½ inches. Our Bosch D-handle has a 6¼-inch-diameter baseplate. We'll use a ¾-inch bit to make the cut:

$$6¼ + 2½ - ¾ = 8$$

So the distance between the fences must be 8 inches to get the cut we want with the bit we're using. Add another 3 inches—the combined widths of two pieces of 1 × 2—and we know we need an 11-inch-square piece of ¼-inch plywood for the jig's base.

Cut the base. Make sure the sides are parallel and that they are perfectly square to the end. Likewise, make sure the one-by stock is straight and square, with parallel edges. Cut one strip 11 inches long and two strips 9½ inches long.

With 18-gauge nails or brads, nail the long strip along the base's end. Then add the shorter strips along the sides. Drive the nails through the base into the fences.

Secure the bit in the collet. Clamp the jig to a scrap. Rout the cutout into the jig's base. Push the router into the jig along the left fence. When it hits the back fence, advance the router to the right, then pull it back toward you when it contacts the right fence.

The resulting cutout in the jig base should match the width of the pocket lap you want to make.

The design of the pocket-lap jig allows you to position its cutout directly on the layout lines. The fences should be wide enough to provide clamping space without interfering with the router handles, as shown here. Note that the corners of the pocket match the radius of the bit used to cut the pocket.

To use the jig, first lay out the pocket lap on the workpiece. Line up the jig with the cutout on the layout lines. Clamp it to the work. Cut the lap the same way you routed the cutout in the jig.

After the pocket is routed, you will need to square the corners with a chisel.

The jig can also be used to cut through laps. Just align it across the workpiece, with the back of the cutout clear of the work's edge.

The caveat about lap width—if the lap's width is more than half the diameter of the router's baseplate, use an oversized baseplate—applies here, just as it did with end- and cross-laps.

Routing Mitered Half-Laps

The mitered half-lap combines the structure of the half-lap with the appearance of the miter. You can't just miter two pieces that have already been half-lapped, of course. One part of the joint could be done this way, since on the rails, the shoulder cut is square while the butt end is mitered. But on the stiles, the shoulder cut is mitered while the butt end is square.

What you need is a set of three guides or templates. Ideally, you

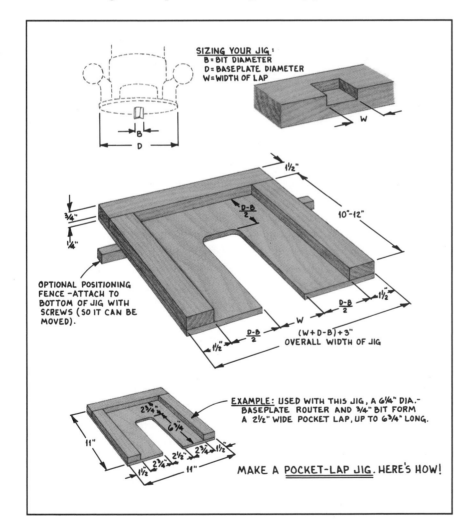

SIZING YOUR JIG:
B = BIT DIAMETER
D = BASEPLATE DIAMETER
W = WIDTH OF LAP

OPTIONAL POSITIONING FENCE –ATTACH TO BOTTOM OF JIG WITH SCREWS (SO IT CAN BE MOVED).

$\frac{D-B}{2}$

$(W+D-B)+3$" OVERALL WIDTH OF JIG

10"-12"

EXAMPLE: USED WITH THIS JIG, A 6¼" DIA.-BASEPLATE ROUTER AND ¾" BIT FORM A 2½" WIDE POCKET LAP, UP TO 6¾" LONG.

MAKE A <u>POCKET-LAP JIG</u>. HERE'S HOW!

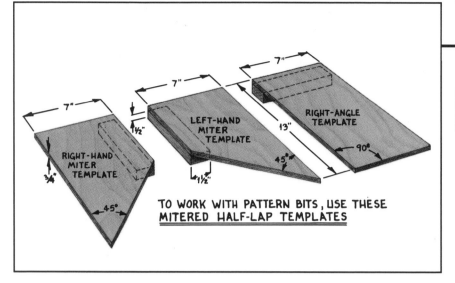

RIGHT-HAND MITER TEMPLATE

7"

1½"

¾"

45°

LEFT-HAND MITER TEMPLATE

7"

13"

1½"

RIGHT-ANGLE TEMPLATE

7"

90°

45°

TO WORK WITH PATTERN BITS, USE THESE
MITERED HALF-LAP TEMPLATES

If you like the look of pro-filed molding that meets in a crisp miter, you'll love assembling frames with mitered half-laps. The joint is strong yet easy to rout, and it allows you to unerringly rout a profile on the inside edge before assembly. After assembly, the profile will meet, fair and square, at the miter (right). A joint that must be edge-routed after assembly yields a rounded corner (left).

would make these templates to use with a pattern bit, but you can add a router fence to them if you don't have a pattern bit and don't want to get one. One template is a right-angled guide. The others are right-hand and left-hand miter guides. All are made using birch plywood and strips of hardwood. They are sized to allow you to lap stock up to 5½ inches wide.

To make the templates, cut three pieces of ¾-inch birch plywood to 7 inches by 13 inches. These are the bases. Be sure they are absolutely square. (The ¾-inch thickness ensures that the pattern bit's bearing will have a reference surface without having to cut too deeply in the work. If your bit's cutting length is 1 inch, a common one, you'll be cut-

ting ⅜ inch into the work with the bearing just barely in contact with the template.)

For fences, cut three pieces of ½-inch hardwood to 1½ inches by 7 inches. The hardwood should be straight-grained and defect-free.

The right-angle template has the fence attached along one 7-inch edge, as shown in *Mitered Half-Lap Templates.* Use glue and three or four 1-inch screws. For the template to be accurate, the fence has to be perfectly parallel to each base's short dimension and square to its long dimension.

The miter templates have the fences attached along one of the long edges, also as shown. Cut a 45-degree miter across each template. Be sure you locate the fences and cut the

miters to create right and left templates; the templates are NOT duplicates. As with the right-angle template, accuracy is essential if the frames you make with them are to be square.

Guides with fences are made pretty much the way the templates are. The biggest change is the addition of fences to guide the router. To provide guidance throughout the same range as the templates, you need to make the bases for the miter guides wider.

The router fences can be made of the same material as the other fences. The goal is to have the cutting edge of the bit grazing the guide's edge. To achieve this, position the fences so the bit will trim the base edge on the first pass. You can cut back on the thickness of the base material, of course. Quarter-inch plywood or hardboard is fine.

Again, because accuracy is so important, take special pains to ensure that the fences are placed at accurate angles.

Both the templates and guides are used in the same way. Begin by machining the workpieces, cutting

Here's how to use the right-angle guide. Put both rails together and align the guide exactly on the shoulder. One clamp should anchor both rails and the guide. Use carpet tape to affix a support block to the baseplate. Here, the block is made up of a scrap of the working stock and a scrap of ¼-inch plywood (the stuff used for the guide's base). To avoid chip-out and tear-out, feed the cutter into the work from all sides.

a groove or rabbet for a panel, if there is to be one, then routing in that profile—a bead, an ogee, whatever. Now trim the pieces to final length. In doing so, miter the ends of two pieces and square-cut the other two. Usually the rails are mitered, the stiles square-cut.

The rails are lapped across their backs. To ensure they're identical, lap both at the same time, using the right-angle guide. Butt them edge to edge, faces down, and clamp them together. Set the guide in place, its reference edge right on the shoulder-cut line. Clamp it; one clamp should do. Set the router's depth of cut, and have at it. If you are using a pattern bit, an offset baseplate can help eliminate tippiness, which could cause you to gouge the work. With a regular straight bit, a support block attached to the baseplate with double-

When routing the stiles, you can orient them as shown, so the guides or templates together support the router.

sided carpet tape is probably the best solution to router tippiness.

With the rails done, turn to the stiles. The stiles are lapped across their faces. Clamp the appropriate guide to each piece and, with the router setting unchanged, rout each lap. Repeat until all are cut.

Router tippiness can be a problem in lapping the stiles, too, but a different solution presents itself here. Try positioning two stiles at right angles to each other, their ends almost touching, each with a guide clamped to it. The router can straddle the guides for sure support *and* cut both laps at the same time.

Dovetail Half-Lap

A mechanical lock is offered by the dovetail half-lap. The end-lap can't just slip out of the cross-lap, it's got to be lifted. So it is a stronger joint than the standard half-lap. It has that dovetail look, to boot, so it imparts a touch of class to your frame.

To get these benefits, you have to do a little extra work.

If you have only a couple of these joints to craft, use a saw to cut the tails out of routed end-laps. Then use the tail to lay out the socket for it on the mating workpiece. Clamp a self-positioning guide or template on each line, and rout the socket.

However, if *production* is what you have in mind, a couple of templates can be made to expedite your work. The templates shown require the use of a pattern bit. It's possible to resize them to use with a guide bushing, if that's your preference. (If you switch to wider stock, you'll have to scale up the layouts and make new templates. You can probably make these work on narrower stock, though I won't guarantee it.)

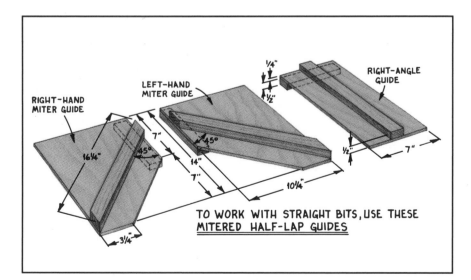

TO WORK WITH STRAIGHT BITS, USE THESE
MITERED HALF-LAP GUIDES

Finding the right balance between template thickness and your pattern bit's range is critical in cutting joinery with templates. Routing the dovetail shape into a half-lap may take a couple of passes if you use a very short pattern bit with a thick template. The first pass is made with the template clamped to the work and the bit cheated out of the collet (left). The bearing rides on the template, while the cutter addresses the workpiece. To complete the cut, remove the template and reset the bit. The bearing then rides on the surface of the previous cut (right).

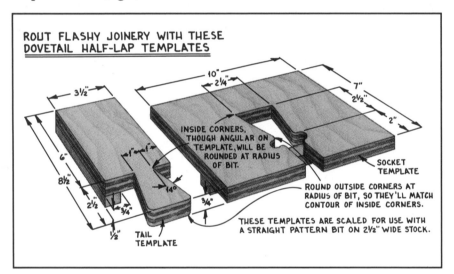

ROUT FLASHY JOINERY WITH THESE DOVETAIL HALF-LAP TEMPLATES

INSIDE CORNERS, THOUGH ANGULAR ON TEMPLATE, WILL BE ROUNDED AT RADIUS OF BIT.

SOCKET TEMPLATE

ROUND OUTSIDE CORNERS AT RADIUS OF BIT, SO THEY'LL MATCH CONTOUR OF INSIDE CORNERS.

TAIL TEMPLATE

THESE TEMPLATES ARE SCALED FOR USE WITH A STRAIGHT PATTERN BIT ON 2½" WIDE STOCK.

the latter were substantial cuts, and Phil, in the interest of speed, made almost all of them with a radial arm saw equipped with a dado cutter. As you can imagine, the cuts all had the corrugated bottoms characteristic of the dado cutter.

Consider these cuts in terms of the router. With a 6-inch-diameter router base and a ¾-inch bit, a 3-inch-wide lap is about as wide as I'd want to cut. Beyond that, the router will lose its support on one side of the cut. To cut these laps, you need a custom baseplate to bridge the recess you and your router are creating.

For that 5½-inch-wide lap, I'd make a rectangular baseplate a minimum of 12¼ inches long, with the router bit at dead center. With a ¾-inch bit doing the cutting, I'd have at least 1 inch of bearing on both sides, even at the shoulders of the cut. *Determining Baseplate Length* gives you my formula for determining how long to make the baseplate. Use it to tailor your baseplate to your lap.

Make the bases out of plywood and the fences from a straight-grained hardwood. Cut the bases, but "tune" them before adding the fences.

To tune the templates, you should use them to cut test joints. If the tail won't go into the socket, do a little trimming on whichever template seems appropriate. If the tail is loose, well, start over. When the templates are tuned, add the positioning fences to the socket template.

To use the templates, cut an end-lap on the piece that's to have the tail. Clamp the tail template to the stock, and use your pattern bit

to trim the edges of the lap. Then clamp the socket template in position and, again, use the pattern bit to cut the socket.

Cutting *Wide* Laps

In designing and building projects for our book *Outdoor Furniture*, Fred and our colleague Phil Gehret used lap joints for many of the chairs and loungers. In some applications, the pieces being lapped were 1 inch thick and 2½ inches wide, while in others they were as much as 1½ inches thick or 5½ inches wide. Obviously,

Because the router creates rounded inside corners on the tail, you have to make your dovetail socket template so it produces outside corners of a matching radius. That's the reason for the goiterlike cutouts on the neck of this template.

In many applications, the half-lap is hidden on the back of the finished assembly. But the dovetail half-lap needs to be exposed. The joint is pretty and strong, and when routed with complementary templates, it's tight yet easy to assemble.

To eliminate any possibility that a heavy router could cause this broad baseplate to sag, I'd make it out of ½-inch plywood.

Using a baseplate this wide means the fences have to be backed away from the cut. Cutting the hypothetical 5½-inch-wide lap with my new 12¼-inch-long baseplate means I have to position my fences a very real 23¾ inches apart.

TRY THIS!

Cutting a 5½-inch-wide half-lap in ¾-inch-thick stock with a router can be time-consuming. And dirty.

Even though you end up with a clean cut.

Think about it. If you use a ¾-inch bit, you need eight passes. Eight passes at each of two depth settings. And every half-lap involves two pieces of wood, so you're cutting a combined recess 5½ inches wide and 11 inches long. That's a lot of chips in *your* lap, as well as a chunk of time out of your work session.

Do yourself a favor. If you have a stack of really wide boards to lap, rough out those cuts with a dado cutter or on the band saw, then bring them to final depth and pristine smoothness with your router. You won't need as much time, and you won't get quite so much dirt in your lap.

And do this work on the router table. Work from the side or back, so the workpiece is well supported, and use the fence as a stop.

The real trick in bottom-cleaning a wide lap is preserving the shoulder. If you can mount a bearing on the shank of your bottom-cleaning bit, turning it into a pattern bit, do it. If you can't, tape Fred's dadoing baseplate to the router (see the chapter "Dadoing and Grooving"), and clamp a matching fence across the lap's shoulder, as shown here. This will stop the router at the shoulder.

At this point, I think I'd turn to the template guide bushing. Using the guide bushing would allow me to position my fences just ¹⁄₁₆ inch from the shoulder lines. But because the baseplate is so wide, the fences also would have to be wide—8 inches or so—so that the clamps wouldn't interfere with the baseplate.

EDGE-LAPS

The edge-lap is formed by notching two boards halfway across their faces, then slipping them together. It's the joint used to create egg-crate-like drawer dividers, for example. Depending upon the girth of the stock, this can be dealt with using a router.

On the router table, the edge-lap notch can be cut as though it were a box-joint notch. (See the chapter "Box Joint.") In this approach you use a bit that matches the stock thickness. Set the bit height to half that of the stock being notched. Stand

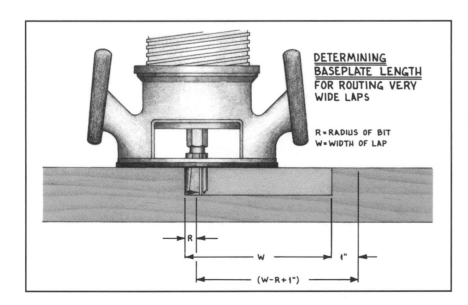

DETERMINING BASEPLATE LENGTH FOR ROUTING VERY WIDE LAPS

R = RADIUS OF BIT
W = WIDTH OF LAP

R
W
1"
(W-R+1")

the stock on edge and, using a sled, guide the stock into the bit.

Obviously, you are limited in what you can edge-lap in this fashion on the router table. The typical straight bit has a cutting length of about ¾ to 1 inch, though you can find straights with up to 2½ inches of cutting length (but that extreme only in the ½-inch diameter). Nonetheless, where the parameters of the job permit this approach, it works well, yielding a clean, precisely sized notch. No additional handwork is required.

If you can remove the key from a box-jointing jig, you can use it to guide the cut. If not, make a sledlike jig, patterned after the box-jointing jig. Here's how:

Cut a base from ¼-inch plywood or hardboard, and cut a handle, support, and back from ¾-inch stock (plywood is great). Dimensions are suggested in *Edge-Lapping Sled*.

Glue the support flat to the base, then add the back, driving screws through the base into the back and through the back into the support. Add the handle to ensure that the back and base are at right angles to one another.

Put the bit selected for the job in the router. Set the sled on the router table and trap it between two fences made of the same thickness of hardboard or plywood used for the base. Switch on the router and feed the sled into the bit, cutting a notch through the base and into the back. (In subsequent uses, you can position the sled and set the fences using the notch.)

To cut the work, lay out the required notches (or at least one edge of each). Stand the workpiece on edge in the sled, and line up the marks with the edges of the slot in the base. Make the cut.

With a hand-held router, you cut the notches as if they were deep, stopped dadoes. (See the chapter "Dadoing and Grooving" for details.) The advantage to this approach is that you can deal with long cuts.

Lay out the position and length of the notch, set a fence with a stop, and make the cut with a straight bit. Because you are cutting completely through the workpiece, either you need to position it on an expendable work surface or you need to cantilever it off the edge of the router bench. A plunge router facilitates making the total cut in bites of manageable depth. Unlike the router table approach, there's a final bit of handwork to do. The end of the cut is rounded, and you need to square the corners.

Making drawer dividers—for a kitchen cabinet's utensil drawers, for example—is a duck-soup operation on the router table. Taping identical parts together keeps them from getting mixed up, but it also aligns them for edge-lapping. The edge-lapping sled, trapped between two fences, guides the cut. Position the work in the sled by the eyeball method.

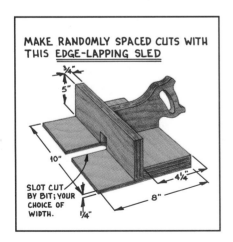

MAKE RANDOMLY SPACED CUTS WITH THIS EDGE-LAPPING SLED

¾"
5"
10"
4¼"
8"
SLOT CUT BY BIT; YOUR CHOICE OF WIDTH.
¼"

You can expedite the work if you stand all the pieces to be lapped on edge, gang them together, and clamp them with scraps on the outsides. Cut through the lot of them in one swipe. Here, a T-square guides the cut.

DOVETAIL JOINTS

Dovetails. The very word elicits a sense of wonder.

Any piece of woodwork that contains them is somehow special. In a way, we've come to worship this particular joint, and with good reason. But it wasn't always so. In fact, up until a relatively few years ago, dovetails were hidden when used in fine furniture.

The dovetail joint was developed (before reliable glues and cheap fasteners were available) as a very utilitarian means of holding pieces of wood together. In this it has some major advantages. The dovetail allows expansion and contraction of the wood without losing any of its structural integrity. This is extremely desirable when joining large pieces of wood, such as cabinet cases or chest sides. The joint's strength is not dependent on glue or mechanical fasteners, so it can be used to good advantage in "natural wood" projects.

The big disadvantage in the dovetail joint has always been that it requires not only a lot of time but a lot of skill to make. Of course, that's a large part of the reason it has become so popular. In order to be considered a real woodworker, you have to cut dovetails.

Enter the router. The router doesn't eliminate the need for skill or time in cutting dovetails. But it does change the focus of skill and time you invest. Set up your router carefully, and you can cut hundreds of dovetails quickly and accurately. Just like a factory.

Wanna see how? You have to use jigs.

HALF-BLIND DOVETAIL JIGS

The least expensive to buy and the easiest to set up are the many half-blind dovetail jigs. No matter how wide or thick the wood is, you clamp it into the jig, run the router through both pieces at once, and get equal-width pins and tails that are rounded to fit into each other at the back. This is the very institutional-looking joint that is often used to assemble drawers for kitchen or other production cabinets. The trickiest part of this one is to get the two parts offset just half a pin in the jig so they come out flush when you assemble them.

The worst part about this jig is the very fact that it is so foolproof and has been around long enough that macho woodworkers look down on it. Its perfectly even spacing is easy to recognize and everyone knows that even though your dovetails fit well and perform well, you didn't work your butt off to get them that way.

All of these jigs consist of a metal base with a clamping system to hold the mating workpieces and a comb-like template to guide the router in cutting both pieces at once. The biggest difference from one brand to another, from one model to another, is the quality of the materials and hardware and the precision with which it's made and assembled. The cheapest ones have stamped parts that tend to flex and buckle, threads that strip quite easily, wing nuts that chew at your fingers. The expensive versions have basic parts that are extruded rather than stamped or die-cast, big plastic knobs instead of wing nuts, and a measure of adjust-

SOCKET PIECE — SOCKET — PIN — TAIL PIECE — SHOULDER — TAIL

THROUGH DOVETAILS

HALF-BLIND DOVETAILS

THE NOMENCLATURE OF THE DOVETAIL JOINT

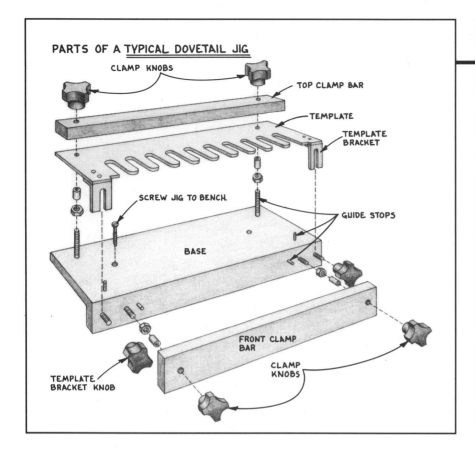

PARTS OF A TYPICAL DOVETAIL JIG

CLAMP KNOBS

TOP CLAMP BAR

TEMPLATE

TEMPLATE BRACKET

SCREW JIG TO BENCH.

GUIDE STOPS

BASE

FRONT CLAMP BAR

TEMPLATE BRACKET KNOB

CLAMP KNOBS

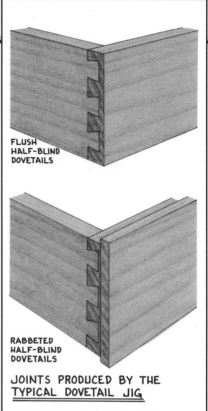

FLUSH HALF-BLIND DOVETAILS

RABBETED HALF-BLIND DOVETAILS

JOINTS PRODUCED BY THE TYPICAL DOVETAIL JIG

The typical dovetail jig with a one-piece template will enable you to rout flush and rabbeted half-blind dovetails. Some models also produce box joints.

The typical dovetail jig makes half-blind dovetails, cutting both pins and tails at the same time with the same bit. Although this elderly Stanley model is no longer manufactured, it is nonetheless representative of the better grade of dovetail jigs. It has a rigid extruded aluminum base and durable phenolic template. Its large clamp-knobs are easier on the hands during extended dovetailing sessions than the wing nuts found on less-costly jigs of this type.

ability. Some even have additional templates that let you cut ¼-inch half-blind dovetails in addition to the standard ½-inch variety, and ¼-inch and ½-inch box joints as well.

You have to look 'em over and decide if you want to spend 40 bucks or three times that for a jig that basically produces a single joint. (You can make similar jigs yourself, but be prepared to spend *a lot of time* fine-tuning the templates to get the precision required to repeatedly produce the desired results.)

In addition to the jig, you need a router, a dovetail bit (usually the ½-inch, 14-degree variety), and a guide bushing (usually one with a ⁷⁄₁₆-inch outside diameter, which limits you to a ¼-inch-shank bit). The best router to use is a 1- or 1½-horsepower fixed-base model. The ability to plunge is

For the sake of appearance (it won't affect the strength of the joint), you want to begin and end with a half-pin. But machine-cut half-blind dovetails are inflexible. You can't alter their size to distribute them evenly across the width of board you're working with. What you have to do is alter the width of the board.

The ½-inch dovetail lays out on ⅞-inch centers. That is, the distance from the center of one pin to the center of the next is ⅞ inch. So, as the drawing shows, you should try to adjust the width of the work to achieve the even spacing.

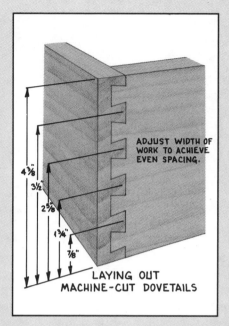

ADJUST WIDTH OF WORK TO ACHIEVE EVEN SPACING.

4⅜"
3½"
2⅝"
1¾"
⅞"

LAYING OUT
MACHINE-CUT DOVETAILS

With your router and the typical dovetail jig, you can cut dovetails in different thicknesses of stock. It's not unusual, for example, to make drawers with ¾-inch-thick fronts and ½-inch-thick sides and backs. This doesn't present any difficulty. Even in plywood, the router cuts excellent dovetails without a hitch. From top to bottom, these dovetails join a ½-inch front and side, ¾-inch front and ½-inch plywood side, ¾-inch front and ½-inch solid-wood side, and ¾-inch front and side.

irrelevant in this operation, and brute power doesn't contribute much, if anything.

Here's what is involved in setting up and using one of these jigs.

Setting Up

The first thing you want to do is get some wood for test cuts. It ought to be the same stock you are using for the drawers or boxes you are making. Just rough out an extra front and side. If you have to make more than

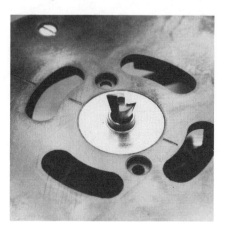

one complete test cutting, simply crosscut the dovetails off each test piece and try again.

Set up the router. Install the ⅞₆-inch guide bushing in the baseplate. Then adjust the router so the collet is relatively close to the bushing and carefully insert the ¼-inch-shank bit. Tighten the collet nut.

Adjust the depth of cut next. The usual setting is ½ inch, though your jig's instructions may specify some other figure.

The last step in router setup is to check that the bit is centered in the bushing. Rotate the bit by hand—be sure the machine is unplugged, not merely switched off—to ensure that the bit doesn't contact the bushing anywhere and that it is centered. If it isn't centered, try to shift either the bushing or the entire baseplate to correct the problem.

Set up the jig itself. Most jigs need to be attached to a ¾-inch plywood base, which can then be clamped to a workbench. Obviously, the jig has to be positioned at the edge of the bench, so the drawer or box side can be clamped in the jig.

The workpieces have to be clamped in the jig in a particular way. The socket piece, which has the pins—it's the drawer front—is clamped to the top of the jig. The

The first thing you'll notice when inserting your ½-inch dovetail bit through a ⅞₆-inch guide bushing and into the router collet is that the largest part of the bit doesn't fit through the bushing. So when you set the depth of cut, turn the bit slowly by hand to absolutely ensure that the bit doesn't contact the bushing. Most guide bushings are steel, which will damage the bit's carbide if the two come into contact.

tail piece—it's the drawer side—is clamped to the front of the jig. The socket piece must be butted against the face of the tail piece. The end of the tail piece must be flush with the top surface of the socket piece.

Here's the easiest way to do it. Roughly position the tail piece in the jig, with its top end well above the jig. Slip the socket piece in the jig, and butt it tightly against the tail piece. Clamp it firmly. Now loosen the clamps holding the tail piece and lower it until its end is flush with the other workpiece. Clamp it firmly.

Both pieces need to be against the alignment pins or stops. These stops align the two workpieces so that they are offset exactly $\frac{7}{16}$ inch. This is the amount they must be offset so the edges of the assembled joint will be flush. Every jig has these stops—they're adjustable if your jig takes more than one template—and it has a pair on the right and on the left. Use the pair on the left for now.

Fit the template in place next. If you have a choice, adjust it so it will yield a flush dovetail. The template needs to be flat on the workpieces, and the holdfast must be cinched tightly.

Now you are ready for your first test cut. Set the router on the template, its bit free of the work. Switch on the router and make a quick, shallow scoring cut across the tail piece, feeding from right to left (yes, this is a climb cut). This will help prevent the bit from pulling chips out along the tail piece's shoulder as it exits each cut.

Rout the dovetails, slot by slot, beginning on the left and working to the right. You may want to zip back through them when you are done, just to be sure you didn't pull out of

Before setting the template in place, be sure the workpieces are properly clamped in the jig. Both should be snug against the alignment stops and snug against each other. The top end of the tail piece, which is clamped to the jig's front, should be flush with the top surface of the socket piece, which is clamped to the jig's top. Typically, the template is screwed to a couple of L-shaped brackets. A slot in each bracket fits over a stud projecting from the jig base. A stop nut on the stud serves both to adjust the fore-and-aft position of the template and as a stop against which the lock-down nut or knob jams.

Actually machining the dovetails takes only a few seconds. To ensure yourself of a clean shoulder on the tail piece, make a very light climb cut along the edge. Then work along the template, feeding the router as far into each template slot as it will go. The router cuts both sockets and tails at the same time.

a slot too soon, leaving the work only partially cut.

Don't just *lift* the router from the template. The bit will ruin both the cut and the template. Instead, cut the power and pull the router toward you, getting it well clear of

the jig before lifting it. Take a good look at the work and be sure you haven't missed a spot. (If you have, rout it now, before moving anything.) Only then should you remove the template, unclamp the work, and test assemble the joint.

Fine-Tuning the Setup

Chances are, your setup needs a little fine-tuning. You slip the two test pieces together, and something's not quite right. Perhaps the fit is too loose. Or too tight. Or the sockets aren't deep enough. Or the parts are a little offset. All of these ills are cured with some fine-tuning.

Fit too tight? The bit's cutting too deep. *Reduce* the depth of cut slightly.

Fit too loose? The bit's not cutting deep enough. *Increase* the depth of cut slightly.

Are the sockets too shallow or too deep? The template is misaligned. To reduce the socket depth, move the template very slightly toward you. To increase the socket depth, move the template away from you. Your jig's instruction sheet should explain exactly how to accomplish these adjustments on your jig. Just remember that as you alter the depth of the sockets, you are also altering the thickness of the tails.

Are the two parts slightly misaligned when assembled? The top and bottom edges should be flush. If they aren't, you may not have had the workpieces snug against the alignment pins. Or the pins may be slightly misadjusted.

Any other problems you have will stem from misalignment of the workpieces in the jig. Make sure the top surface of the socket piece is flush with the top end of the tail piece, that they are at right angles to each other, that the template is square to the workpieces, and so forth.

When you've successfully fine-tuned the setup using the alignment pins on the left, cut a test joint using the right end of the jig. Do any additional tuning needed there.

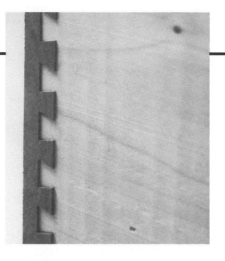

When adjusting the socket depth, you theoretically want the surfaces to come flush when the joint is assembled. But as a practical matter, it's better to have the socket piece just proud of the tail piece. That way a pass with the belt sander will bring the joint flush, without requiring you to sand the entire side.

Cutting the Good Stuff

Before starting on the good wood, make sure you're organized for complete success. It doesn't matter if you are dovetailing one drawer or fifty drawers, it's all too easy to get mixed up and cut the dovetails in the wrong places. So label your workpieces.

Bear in mind that you must clamp the work in the jig in an orientation that seems *calculated* to befuddle. You probably noticed this when you assembled the test pieces. When the workpieces are clamped in the jig, it's the assembly's *inside* faces that are exposed. What's exposed in the construction is hidden in the assembly. What's hidden during fabrication is exposed in the finished product. Confused now?

Do this. Label the parts on what will be their inside faces. If you can read the labels when the parts are in the jig, you've got the orientation correct. If you are doing drawers, the sides *always* go on front,

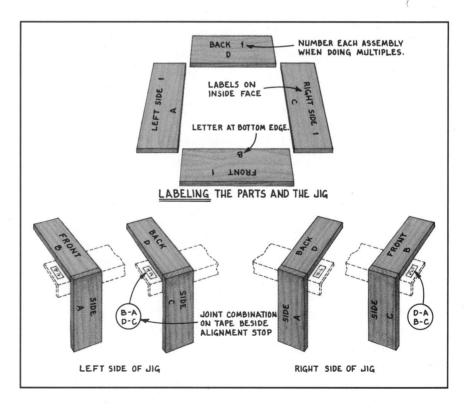

LABELING THE PARTS AND THE JIG

LEFT SIDE OF JIG

RIGHT SIDE OF JIG

and the fronts and backs *always* go on the top.

And you need to label more than part names. Consider that each drawer or box has four joints. When you are doing machine-cut dovetails, two of the four joints must be cut on the left side of the jig and two on the right side. You don't want to get them mixed up.

The most simple organizational labeling system I've come across is shown in *Labeling*. There are few labels, but where you put them is as important as what they are. The labels indicate which is the inner face, and thus which face is up in the jig. The letters are always associated with a particular part. Each letter is placed at the bottom edge of the piece, to indicate which edge goes against the jig's alignment stops. On the jig itself, you mark two two-letter combinations beside each pair of alignment stops, as indicated in the drawing. As you clamp the parts into the jig, orient the letters toward the stops, and check the combination. If it isn't on your list of two, you are at the wrong end of the jig.

A more commonplace approach is to label each piece with its part name, to mark the bottom edge, and to number the joints in sequence around the assembly. The trick is remembering which joints get cut on which end of the jig.

Dovetailing a Lipped Drawer

More often than not, the half-blind dovetail jig is used in dovetailing drawers. Being limited to the flush version of this joint is a pretty severe design restriction, though. Very often you want to make lipped drawers, in which the drawer front has a rabbet cut around the inner face.

A few of the standard dovetail jigs have a template adjustment that makes it possible to cut this joint, and their instruction manuals lay out the procedure fairly lucidly.

But you can dovetail lipped drawers with any half-blind dovetail jig. The trick is to cut the fronts separately from the sides. What the template adjustment does, in those jigs that allow you to cut the so-called rabbeted half-blind dovetail, is to shift the template position ⅜ inch away from the operator, so the sockets can be extended that ⅜ inch. (This assumes, of course, that the rabbet around the drawer front will be ⅜ inch wide.) What you do is set up the jig, clamp the boards in place, and cut the pins and tails. Then you shift the template and make a second pass, extending the sockets.

You can accomplish the same thing by positioning the drawer front farther forward than its usual position and then routing the sockets in one pass. And you can accommodate most any width of rabbet. Here's how.

Rough out the drawer parts, and rabbet the fronts. At the same time, cut some scraps of the drawer-front stock to use to back up the sides when routing the tails in them. And cut one scrap of the drawer-side stock to use in positioning the fronts in the jig. This scrap needs a rabbet across one end. The depth of the rabbet must be the same as the width of the drawer-front rabbet. For example, if your drawer-front rabbet is the standard ⅜-inch width, then the depth of the rabbet is ⅜ inch. And if the drawer-front rabbet is wider than the drawer-side stock is thick, you need to substitute a thicker scrap so that you can cut a rabbet to the necessary depth and still have a tab

To rout dovetails into a rabbeted piece, like a lipped drawer front, you have to rout the tails and sockets in separate operations. This is because the socket piece has to be brought forward from its usual position. A rabbeted positioning jig is clamped in the tail piece position, as shown, and the end of the rabbeted socket piece is butted against the side of the jig's rabbet. Once the socket piece is secured, you can remove the jig, place the template, and rout the sockets.

left against which to butt the drawer front (as you'll see in a minute).

Finally, if the rabbet extends across the top of the drawer front as well as along its sides, you need a spacer. The spacer offsets the drawer front from the alignment stop so the first socket is a half-pin from the shoulder of the rabbet. To determine how thick the spacer must be, subtract the width of the drawer-front rabbet from ⅞ inch, which is the center-to-center spacing of ½-inch dovetails. That ⅜-inch rabbet calls for a ½-inch spacer.

Rout the sockets in the drawer fronts first. Clamp the positioning scrap in the jig in place of a drawer side. Set the spacer against the alignment stop, then set the drawer front in the jig, as shown in *Rabbeted Dovetails*. Butt the end against the tab of the positioning scrap, the bottom edge against the spacer. Clamp the front, then rout the sockets.

Problem Solver

Machine-dovetailing a drawer whose sides are less wide (high) than its front need not stump you. It takes an extra setup step, but it can be done quite easily.

What you want to avoid is routing one socket too many in the drawer front. You know how it is. Routing along the fingers of the dovetail template tends to sap your attention. The router base is covering a lot of the work, and you can see there's still some uncut wood, so you kind of lose track. Then, OUCH! You've cut sockets right up to the end of the front. Just one too many!

You need to clamp a stop to arrest the router at the last template slot you intend to rout. You finish that slot and the router can't move any farther.

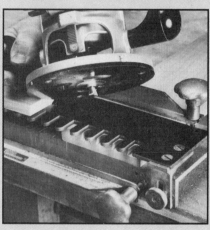

A drawer with sides that are lower than the front can be dovetailed confidently if you clamp a stop to the template.

With the router bit positioned in the last slot to be routed, butt a scrap against the base and clamp it to the template. The stop is the piece of light wood under Mr. Hands, and the last template slot the router can access is the fourth from the right. (The side has already been removed here, but be assured that you can rout both side and front at the same time.)

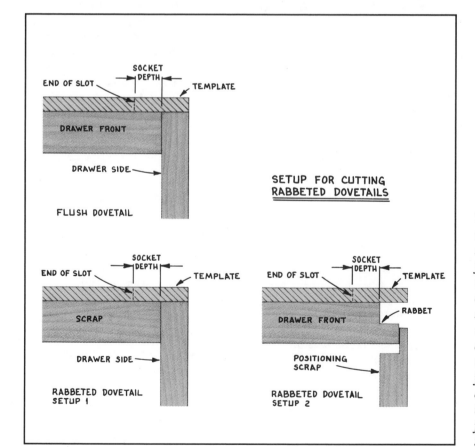

SETUP FOR CUTTING RABBETED DOVETAILS

The logic in the setup for cutting rabbeted dovetails is evident in these section views. In the setup for cutting flush dovetails, the template overlays the front and side more or less equally. The tail thickness will match socket depth. When you rout tails on the sides in making the rabbeted dovetail—Setup 1—the position of the template duplicates that in the flush dovetail setup. To get a socket deep enough to accommodate the tails, the socket piece must be shifted forward the width of the rabbet—Setup 2.

Here's an assembled rabbeted dovetail joint. The rabbet in the drawer front can conceal a drawer slide or overlay the casework or the cabinet's face frame.

Naturally, you have to switch to the other end of the jig to rout the sockets in the other end of the drawer front.

After the sockets are routed, fit the drawer sides in place, one by one, and rout the tails. To help you position each side, and to prevent tear-out, clamp one of those scraps of drawer-front stock in place of the drawer front.

KELLER TEMPLATES

A big step up the sophistication ladder you'll find fixed-template jigs like the Keller. The Keller dovetail templates produce through dovetails with an absolute minimum of setup fiddling. Compared to those cut by most other jigs, the dovetails produced by Keller's midsized model are relatively large, which makes this jig a good choice for carcase joinery. The unit cuts ⅝-inch-wide pins spaced 1¾ inches on center. While it's easiest to cut evenly spaced pins and tails, you can vary both the size and spacing by repositioning the jig.

The jig is simplicity itself. No knobs, no adjustments, no moving parts at all. What you get are two ½-inch-thick machined aluminum templates, one to cut the pins, the other for the tails. The templates come with a dovetail bit and a straight bit, both with shank-mounted guide bearings. No need for a guide bushing.

Before you can use the templates, they must be screwed to a wooden backing block. The block both positions the template on the workpiece and prevents tear-out when the bit exits the cut. During this initial setup, you need to adjust the fit of the dovetails. The fit is adjusted *only* by altering the pin template location. Once it is set, it is set; you won't need to fiddle with it on every job. Just adjust the depth of cut to suit your stock thickness, and you're set.

To cut dovetails, you hold the tail board vertically in a vise, clamp the dovetail template over the end of the board with a couple of clamps, and rout the tails using the dovetail bit. Because you position the template relative to the board's center,

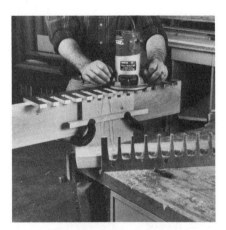

The Keller dovetail templates help you rout through dovetails. You mount the templates on backing blocks, which both position the templates and prevent tear-out during routing. The work is held in a vise, and the template is clamped to it. Shank-mounted bearings ride on the templates and guide the cuts.

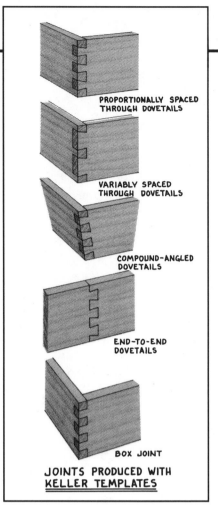

PROPORTIONALLY SPACED THROUGH DOVETAILS

VARIABLY SPACED THROUGH DOVETAILS

COMPOUND-ANGLED DOVETAILS

END-TO-END DOVETAILS

BOX JOINT

JOINTS PRODUCED WITH KELLER TEMPLATES

Using the appropriate bits guided by Keller templates, you can cut proportionally spaced through dovetails, variably spaced through dovetails, compound-angled dovetails, end-to-end dovetails, and box joints.

the tails are evenly spaced on either side of center. Next, you transfer one or two tail locations to the pin board, just as you would with hand-cut dovetails. With variably spaced dovetails, you do need to scribe every pin. Line up the second template with these marks, switch to the straight bit, and rout the pins. When cutting dovetails on several identical pieces, it saves a lot of time to clamp stops to the backing blocks.

There's no limit on the width of board that can be accommodated. Simply reposition the template if your work is wider than your template is long.

THE LEIGH JIG

At the upper end of the flexibility-complexity group you'll find the Leigh jig, which has loose fingers that you can adjust. The fingers slide across the jig and back on two steel rods. The fingers can be arranged in an almost infinite number of patterns and spacings.

This actually is a template system, though glorified somewhat by the fact that each set of fingers has a side for guiding the cutting of pins and one for guiding the cutting of tails. You can set the jig to produce wide tails, narrow tails, or oddly spaced tails. It will automatically be set to produce perfectly matched pins. You want four, maybe five pins on a 16⅗₆-inch-wide board? Variable pin spacing? No problem! You can set the pins as closely as 1 inch on center and cut pins as small as ⅜ inch wide.

What the Leigh jig does best is cut through dovetails. First you clamp the tail board vertically and

Individually adjustable fingers are the reason for the versatility of the Leigh jig. With the workpiece clamped in place, you align the fingers to establish the size and spacing of the pins and tails, then tighten the setscrews.

arrange the movable fingers over the end of the board to determine the spacing. Then you flip the finger assembly and rout the tails with a dovetail bit. To rout the pins, you switch to a straight bit, flip the finger assembly again, cut a sample joint or two to get the right fit between tails and pins, then clamp the board vertically and rout the pins.

In addition to through and half-blind dovetails, the Leigh jig will help you cut box joints and, with

additional accessories, multiple mortises and tenons. To make these joints, you *must* use cutters that match the jig, you have to set the depth of cut just right, and a few other items have to be adjusted according to the over-100-page manual that comes with the jig. Because you have to adjust and tighten down as many as 12 separate elements, the Leigh jig is time-consuming to set up.

Obviously, this unit is for the serious woodworker who intends to cut a lot of dovetails and doesn't want to be stuck with only a couple of configurations. It'll cost you $300 plus, and you'll have to invest a considerable amount of time to get your competence up to the potential of the jig. But that done, by golly, you can cut some slick dovetails!

With the large Leigh model, you can cut through dovetails in stock up to 1¼ inches thick and 24 inches wide, and half-blind dovetails in stock as thick as 1½ inches. The small model handles only 12-inch-wide stock. A 1½-horsepower router is adequate for this work, though Leigh recommends it have both ¼-inch and ½-inch collets. A couple of different straight and dovetail bits are supplied with the jig. (Most bit makers sell bits specially designed for use with the Leigh jig, and getting a selection can run up the cost of routing with the Leigh jig.) Needed, but not supplied, are two guide bushings—one ⅗₆-inch-diameter and one ⁷⁄₁₆-inch-diameter.

With the Leigh jig and the appropriate accessories and bits, you can cut flush and rabbeted half-blind dovetails, variably spaced through dovetails, compound-angled dovetails, sliding dovetails, and box joints.

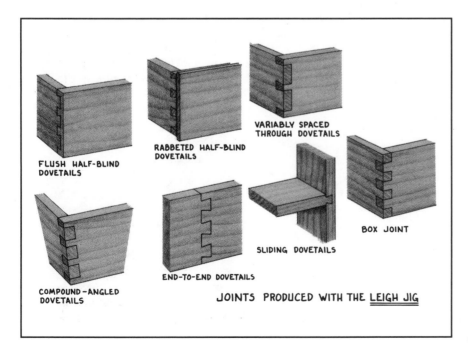

FLUSH HALF-BLIND DOVETAILS

RABBETED HALF-BLIND DOVETAILS

VARIABLY SPACED THROUGH DOVETAILS

COMPOUND-ANGLED DOVETAILS

END-TO-END DOVETAILS

SLIDING DOVETAILS

BOX JOINT

JOINTS PRODUCED WITH THE <u>LEIGH JIG</u>

Precision Positioning Systems

Though not specifically dovetailing jigs, the Incra and Jointech jigs can help you rout dovetails because of their incremental accuracy and repeatability. Though they will cut half-blind and sliding dovetails, equally or variably spaced, dovetails are only a part of their repertoire. Vigorously marketed as precision, incremental positioning devices, they're tough to pigeonhole because there's nothing else quite like them.

Attached to a router table, either jig is an incremental fence positioner. You can move the fence in increments of exactly 1/32 inch, without measuring and with a claimed accuracy of plus or minus 1/1000 inch. This is machine-shop precision.

Here's how the Incra jig works: Each half of the jig has a pair of acrylic, sawtooth positioning racks with a tooth-to-tooth spacing of 1/32 inch. Put the two halves of the jig together and the racks interlock, meshing perfectly anywhere along their length. You can extend or retract the end of the jig notch by notch. Each notch moves the end of the jig (and the fence attached to it) exactly 1/32 inch.

Central to the Jointech jig is a 3/4-inch, hardened chrome-steel lead screw with 32 threads to the inch. It has two adjustment controls. A push button disengages the indexer from the lead screw, allowing free in-and-out movement of the jig-mounted fence. This is the control you use for 99 percent of your adjustments. For micro-adjustments, a vernier thumbwheel rotates

the lead screw, signalling with a click each movement of 2/1000 inch.

An essential element of the marketing of these devices is the catalog of "templates" each manufacturer supplies with the device. The template is a tape strip with colored markings to tell you where to align the fence for each cut. You want to cut a "1/2-inch double dovetail"? Slide the template into a holder on the jig and follow the markings on the template. Align the pointer with the first red line, and make a cut. Shift the pointer to the next red line, and make a cut. Do all the red-line cuts, then switch workpieces and do all the black-line cuts. Then switch workpieces again and do all the dotted-red-line cuts. You just

Adjusting the Jointech fence is a matter of loosening the lock-down knob, depressing a button, and moving the arm while you line up the pointer with either the 1/32-inch graduations on the tape or the markings on one of the interchangeable templates.

keep adjusting the fence and making cuts as directed. Eventually, you end up with a "double-dovetail joint."

What *is* a double-dovetail? It's a garish three-piece joint in which a contrasting wood outlines the seam between the two principals to the joint. It's strictly for show, because it certainly doesn't fortify the joint. (If anything, it weakens it.) But for the makers of the Incra and Jointech jigs, it dramatically demonstrates the precision of their gizmo. The only place I've actually seen this joint is in their ads.

Don't let this showmanship put you off. Both the Incra and Jointech jigs do what their makers say they do, and you can cut strong, practical joints with them.

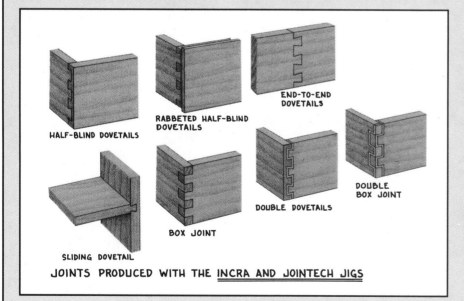

HALF-BLIND DOVETAILS

RABBETED HALF-BLIND DOVETAILS

END-TO-END DOVETAILS

SLIDING DOVETAIL

BOX JOINT

DOUBLE DOVETAILS

DOUBLE BOX JOINT

JOINTS PRODUCED WITH THE <u>INCRA AND JOINTECH JIGS</u>

With the precision positioning jigs like the Incra and Jointech, you can cut flush and rabbeted half-blind dovetails, hand-cut-style half-blind dovetails, flush and rabbeted box joints, sliding dovetails, and showy joints like double half-blind dovetails.

PORTER-CABLE'S OMNIJIG

If I were *doing* woodworking for a living instead of writing about woodworking, the dovetail jig I'd buy is the Porter-Cable Omnijig. (I *think* I'd buy it, anyway. My wry colleague Bob Moran, who *did* do woodworking for a living, says the Omnijig is a tool that no one working wood for a living can afford to buy.) It's certainly designed and built for sustained use. Everything about it is heavy-duty. And it certainly is flexible.

The base is a thick aluminum casting. It has broad clamping surfaces on top and in front, so that aligning stock for dovetailing can be done quickly. Holes through the base's end flanges and its 60-pound weight indicate that the Omnijig isn't a unit that gets stashed on a shelf when not in active use. Rather, it gets bolted to a table and is a workstation.

A feature that anyone who's routed dovetails in 40 or 50 drawers will appreciate is the lightning-fast, lever-operated clamping system. You hold the workpiece in position with one hand and yank the clamp lever with the other. An eccentrically

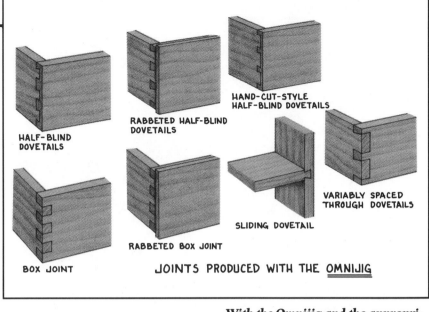

HALF-BLIND DOVETAILS

RABBETED HALF-BLIND DOVETAILS

HAND-CUT-STYLE HALF-BLIND DOVETAILS

BOX JOINT

RABBETED BOX JOINT

SLIDING DOVETAIL

VARIABLY SPACED THROUGH DOVETAILS

JOINTS PRODUCED WITH THE OMNIJIG

mounted 1¼-inch-diameter steel bar rotates against the full width of the board. There's enough force behind it to flatten cupped boards. No more sore hands and aching wrists.

All the templates—and there are a lot of them available—are machined from ¼-inch-thick aluminum stock. The assortment includes ¼- and ½-inch flush or rabbeted half-blind dovetails, ½-inch flush or rabbeted box joints, ½-inch hand-cut-style dovetails, and ¼- and ½-inch tapered sliding dovetails. A template for ½-and ¾-inch through dovetails has adjustable fingers, à la Leigh, so you can vary the sizes of the pins and tails. The half-blind dovetails and box joints

The Omnijig is industrial-strength. Instead of a lightweight stamping, the base is a heavy casting. Instead of plastic, the templates are machined aluminum plates. Lever-operated clamping rods supplant the typical wing nut–secured bars. And a range of dovetail and box joints can be machined without endless guide adjustments. Setup and operation are fast.

With the Omnijig and the appropriate templates and bits, you can cut flush and rabbeted half-blind dovetails, hand-cut-style half-blind dovetails, flush and rabbeted box joints, sliding dovetails, and variably spaced through dovetails.

are cut on both socket and tail pieces at the same time, using the same bit. The so-called hand dovetails and the sliding dovetail require two templates, two passes, but only one bit. And, of course, the through dovetails require straight and dovetail bits.

The templates are used with a ⅝-inch guide bushing, which allows you to use ½-inch-shank bits.

The larger of the two models accommodates stock from ½ inch to 1 inch thick and up to 24 inches wide.

ROUTED TAILS, HAND-CUT PINS

In the Rodale shop, Fred and Phil Gehret often start dovetails with the router, then finish them by hand. Most of the projects they do are one-of, special, even oddball ones that don't lend themselves well to mass-production-type jigs. They'll start by cutting either the pins or the

The basic dovetail bit, the one that's in the sets of basic bits, the one that's used with the basic dovetail jigs, is the 14-degree, ½-inch-diameter, ½-inch-cutting-length variety.

Now, the traditional cabinet-maker's wisdom is that the optimum slope for a dovetail in softwoods is 1 in 6, and in hardwoods 1 in 8. (The difference in slope stems from the fact that softwood cells compress more easily, and so require a steeper slope.) Let's convert those traditional slope ratios to the bit maker's angles: 1 in 8 is 7 degrees, and 1 in 6 is 9 degrees. The standard 14-degree bit works out to a 1 in 4 slope. Pretty steep.

The 14-degree angle is one of the reasons machine-cut dovetails look different than hand-cut ones. If you have a fixed-template dovetail jig, it's likely to *require* the use of a 14-degree bit. (An 8-degree dovetail bit used with the jig, even one of the same cutting diameter and used with the same guide bushing, won't cut dovetails that will assemble.)

MLCS 1" 14° BIT

MLCS 13/16" 8° BIT

PORTER-CABLE ½" 14° BIT

PORTER-CABLE ¾" 14° BIT

CMT ½" 14° BIT

MLCS ¾" 14° BIT

PORTER-CABLE ½" 14° BIT

MLCS ½" 8° BIT

By the traditional wisdom, the 14-degree bit should produce an unsatisfactory dovetail. Too steep a slope is supposed to yield a dovetail with weak short grain at the corners. That doesn't appear to be a problem in practice. Fred points out that in the context of adjusting a router bit, the 14-degree dovetail isn't as demanding to fit.

tails with the router. Sometimes they'll use a simple T-square type of guide, other times a box-joint jig. (See the chapter "Box Joint.") They've even been known to work freehand. With one element of a joint cut, they'll trace it onto the mating piece and cut the second element to fit with saw and chisel, the old-fashioned way. For a single, oddball job, that's usually quicker than setting up a jig.

See Also . . .

"Dovetail Splice" on page 328 for jigs for cutting dovetail and box joints on the router table.

A dovetail-splice jig can aid you in cutting tails, preparatory to hand cutting the pins. If you use the key with it, you can evenly space the tails. But you can also lay out oddly spaced or sized tails and, as here, use the jig only to hold and guide the workpiece while you eyeball the positions of the cuts.

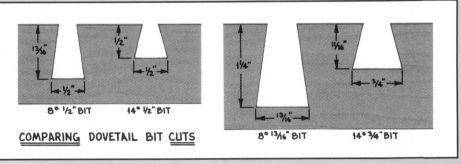

COMPARING DOVETAIL BIT CUTS

A 7-degree dovetail that's a 32nd off will be a lot poorer fit than a 14-degree dovetail that's off the same fraction.

As it works out, you can buy bits with 7-degree tapers, as well as with 7½-, 8-, and 9-degree tapers. The reason these are available, it seems, is because of the Leigh and Incra jigs. To give their dovetails more of a hand-cut look, the jigs' designers had bits custom-made in the 7- to 9-degree tapers they wanted. An increasing number of bit manufacturers now include 7- to 9-degree dovetail bits in their catalogs.

A benefit of the more gentle taper is that it allows a deeper cut. Check out the comparative bit dimensions in the drawing. A ½-inch-diameter bit with a 14-degree taper can cut only ½ inch deep because, at that point, the bit has tapered to a ¼-inch diameter. The girth at the same spot on an 8-degree bit is about ¹¹⁄₃₂ inch. If the bit can safely taper down to a ¼-inch diameter, then the 8-degree bit can cut ¹³⁄₁₆ inch deep. This is enough to make a through dovetail in dressed 4/4 stock.

Regardless of what's available, using a commercial dovetail jig means you need whatever size and taper dovetail bit the jig is designed around. If, however, you are using your router to reduce the work in hand-cutting dovetails, you can use a variety of bit sizes and angles to your design advantage.

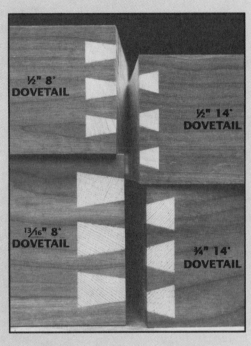

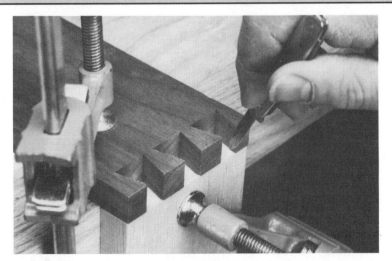

After the tails are cut, use the tail board to lay out the pins. Clamp the tail board at the edge of the bench, and position and clamp the pin board, as shown. Scribe along the edges of the tails with a knife to lay out all the pins. Mark each piece with the joint number so you don't get them mixed up.

The moment of truth comes when you try assembling the joint for the first time. You should get to this point a lot quicker, thanks to the router. Yet the handwork you've done should enhance the appearance of the joint and make the achievement of a good fit more satisfying to you.

SLIDING DOVETAIL JOINT

It's a hybrid of the dado and the dovetail.

In the sliding dovetail joint, one of the mating pieces has a groove plowed in it, the other has a tongue formed on it; the tongue fits in the groove. Because both the groove walls and the tongue sides are angled like dovetail slots or tails, the joint has to be assembled by sliding the tongue into the groove.

The advantage of the joint is its mechanical strength. Even without glue, the mating pieces will stay linked together. Only if the wood breaks will the two pieces separate. One wonderful consequence of this is simplified assembly routines. The parts won't fall away from one another while you're fumbling with clamps or fasteners. Slightly bowed panels will be pulled into line without elaborate clamping configurations. A mere two hands will usually be sufficient.

Another advantage is that the joint allows the parts to move without coming apart. A good example of this is a tabletop's breadboard end. Here you apply a narrow strip of wood across the end of a glued-up panel to conceal its end-grain and to keep it straight. The joint allows the tabletop to expand and shrink across its width even though the end strip isn't elongating and shrinking.

This characteristic of the joint, taken a little further, makes it an excellent one for moving joints. It's used for all sorts of sliding connections—drawer slides, table extension slides, and the like. We've used it in a number of our router jigs.

A variant of the joint is the woodworking equivalent of speaking softly while brandishing a big stick. The tapered sliding dovetail—if cut with precision—allows especially easy assembly, but closes extremely tight. The narrow end of the tail enters the wide end of the groove and slides effortlessly through the groove. But as the groove closes down on the tail, the joint gets tighter, and you

often have to whack the work smartly to force everything into line and seat the joint. Cutting the tapered sliding dovetail requires finesse, but final assembly calls for brute force.

CUTTING THE JOINT

How you cut the sliding dovetail depends on the router setups at your disposal, as well as the location of the cuts. For example, the tails are almost always easiest to cut on a horizontal router table, most difficult with a hand-held router. Slots in casework usually are best done with a hand-held router, while those in a workpiece edge are easiest to cut on a router table.

The joint's disadvantage is that fitting the two pieces is a trial-and-error process that can get tedious. And the working stock can snooker you in the bargain.

Ideally, the sliding dovetail is a precision-fitted joint. You want the fit tight, but not so tight that friction stalls the tail as it slides into the slot. On the other hand, you don't want the fit to be too sloppy, however easy that makes the joint to assemble. The usual fitting technique is to plow the slot, then creep up on a tail dimension that fits that slot.

There's a danger in that. Because of the dovetail shape, a mismatch of the tail and slot anywhere along their lengths can prevent assembly. This is where variances in stock thickness and flatness can give you a migraine. A tail that has a thick spot, stemming from a bow in the stock or a subtle taper in its thickness, is a tail that may bind in the slot. Of

Routing a sliding dovetail slot is as straightforward as routing a dado. The same guides used in dadoing— here, a T-square—can be used to guide dovetail slotting.

course, it'll seize about halfway in, just after you've applied a little glue to the extremities of tail and slot. And as the wavy lines course before your eyes, signaling the onset of that migraine, the parts wedge so firmly that you can't whack them completely together *or* apart. Then your head *really* hurts.

To get the groove as right as possible, Fred suggests making two passes through it, making a special effort to keep the work (or the router)

Problem Solver

We all know the router is a trimmer, that the full depth of every cut has to be achieved by making a series of trimming passes. Try cutting a sliding dovetail slot in three passes! Doesn't work too well, does it? It looks like a dado with a fat lip.

Okay, okay. As a practical matter, most sliding dovetails aren't all that deep. Just ¼ inch or so. But what about those ⅜-inch-deep cuts? Those ½-inch-deep cuts? Especially in dense hardwoods. Especially in situations where you're limited to a ¼-inch-shank bit. What then?

Make a pass or two with a straight bit. This will clean out the bulk of the material, leaving only the walls of the cut to be formed by the dovetail bit. Use a straight whose diameter matches (or is slightly smaller than) that of the dovetail bit's waist, which is usually about three-quarters of the bit's stated diameter. Set the bit to cut just shy of the groove's bottom, so when you do make the dovetail cut, you'll get a good bottom finish.

against the fence on both passes. If you do get a bump on the first pass, you may trim off the high spot on the second. And what Fred does to check the tail is to cut the groove in a small piece of wood, then make sure it'll slide all the way across the end of the piece before trying to assemble the joint.

I don't, however, have a *foolproof* approach that'll guarantee you won't have an assembly glitch. I don't think there is one, though quite a number of woodworkers have presented one method or another as the perfect solution. The usual clichés apply, as far as I'm concerned: Work with stock that's been carefully milled, that's flat and true and as free of defects as possible. They are clichés, yes, but they're true clichés (which are a lot like true facts).

Working with a Hand-Held Router

Of the two operations involved in making the sliding dovetail joint, only one—cutting the slot—can really be done well with a hand-held router. This operation is done quickly, easily, and accurately. But cutting the tails on something other than a broad panel involves what to me is a lot of busywork: You clamp and unclamp each workpiece two or three times. Nevertheless, it *can* be done.

Cutting the slots is a lot like cutting dadoes. Clamp a straightedge to the work to guide the router, and make the cut. Depending on your setup, the straightedge can guide the router base, a template guide, or a pattern bit's bearing. The approach will work regardless of the width of the workpiece and regardless of the positioning of the cut on the piece.

TRY THIS!

A shallow sliding dovetail—cut only ⅛ inch deep—is plenty for joining casework. The slot taper is enough to confer the dovetail's mechanical blessings. The depth is sufficient to withstand the shear stresses applied to a cabinet and its parts. Yet the cut is easy for any router to make in a single pass.

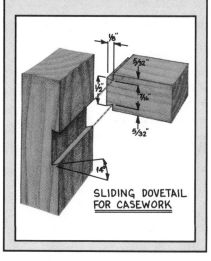

SLIDING DOVETAIL FOR CASEWORK

The difficult part of the setup? Positioning the fence. Because of the dovetail shape, you need to reference the centerline of the cut when setting your fence. But to make a rough-out cut with a straight bit, then a finish cut with the dovetail bit, either you have to switch bits for each cut—way too much hassle—or you have to be able to return the fence to its position. Can't do it if you rely exclusively on the centerline. So here's the routine.

If you like to guide the router base against the fence, then use a locator to position the fence. Rip a scrap of plywood or Masonite to match the radius of the router base. Line up one edge of the locator right on the centerline, then butt your T-square or other straightedge against

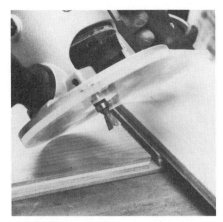

Here's a dovetail slot routed using a dovetail pattern bit. You have to set your guide carefully. The bearing is concentric to the cutter's largest diameter, so the guide needs to align with the widest part of the cut, not the edge at the surface. This quirk makes it tricky to rough out the cut with a straight bit before finishing it with the dovetail bit.

the other edge and clamp it. Now scribe a line along the fence and mark it as the fence position. Make your pass with the straight bit, and move the fence to the next spot.

After all the straight-bit cuts are completed, change bits and return the fence to the marked positions to make the dovetail-bit cuts.

If a template is your preferred guidance system, offset the straight template from the diameter by the radius of either your pattern bit's bearing or your template guide. Again, mark the template's position so you can come back to it for the dovetail-bit cut.

Cutting the tails with the hand-held router requires you to use some sort of router support. The support can be clamped to the workpiece, or it can be mounted on the router itself. In either case, the smaller the router the better (although I don't think I'd use a laminate trim-

mer for this). A bulky, heavy router isn't as manageable as a lightweight one, and 1 horsepower is surely sufficient power for the cut.

Right-angle routing platform. The platform shown in *Right-Angle Routing Platform* provides a way to rout a tail across the end of a board by providing a wide, solid base for the router. It helps you avoid tipping the router as you work.

Obviously, this platform serves you in working relatively narrow stock. Once your workpiece exceeds a foot in width, the platform required becomes awkwardly wide. If you are working with a deep cabinet or a wide tabletop, consider some form of the double edge-guide approach, explained below.

To make a platform, use a stable hardwood, such as maple or poplar.

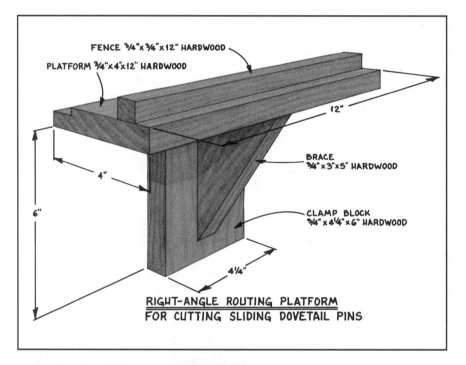

FENCE ¾"x ¾"x 12" HARDWOOD

PLATFORM ¾"x 4"x 12" HARDWOOD

12"

BRACE ¾" x 3"x 5" HARDWOOD

CLAMP BLOCK ¾"x 4¼"x 6" HARDWOOD

4"

6"

4¼"

RIGHT-ANGLE ROUTING PLATFORM FOR CUTTING SLIDING DOVETAIL PINS

The right-angle routing platform is useful for routing dovetail pins on the ends of relatively narrow stock. The platform supports the hand-held router, and its adjustable fence positions the cut, thus controlling the thickness of the tail.

A couple of tricks can make platform fence adjustments just a little easier to make.

To square the fence, cinch down one screw. Set a try square against the end of the platform top, its blade at the fence. Pivot the fence against the blade and tighten the second screw.

To alter the fence position, position the square at the fence, but insert a spacer of some sort between the blade and the fence. The spacer will establish how much the fence will move. Clamp the square to the platform. Remove the spacer, loosen the setscrews, and move the fence tight to the square. Tighten it.

Putting the square on the inner side deepens the cut (narrowing the tail). Putting it on the outer side reduces the cut (widening the tail).

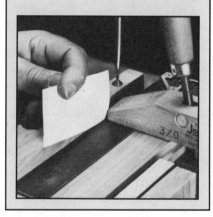

Cut the parts and fasten them together with 1¼-inch-long drywall screws, as shown in the drawing. The fence has ¼-inch-diameter mounting holes, which provide a little play for adjustment purposes. To adjust the fence, loosen the screws, shift the fence, then retighten the screws.

Set up the cut on a scrap of the working stock. Clamp the platform to the scrap, then clamp it in a bench vise. Guide the router against the fence to rout one side of the tail.

Shift the platform to the other side of the board to rout the other side of the tail.

Test fit the resulting dovetail in one of the dovetail grooves. If you need to adjust the size of the tail, loosen the fence screws and move the fence. Move the fence toward to the board if the tail is too wide, away from the board if the tail is too narrow. Always keep the fence parallel to the shelf. When the fit is right, rout the tails on the workpieces.

Modified double edge guide. This approach eliminates a lot of the clamping and unclamping. With two edge guides fitted to the router, you can run it across the end of a board. The two guides trap the board, keeping the bit in the same relative position on each pass. If you attach a deep facing to one of the guides, it will keep the router perfectly upright on its perch.

If your router has an edge guide that mounts on twin rods, and the rods can be adjusted to project from the base on both sides, you can make this work simply by purchasing a second edge guide. Cut a 4-inch-wide strip of hardwood stock and screw it to one of the edge guides.

You can make your own double edge jig, of course. It's akin to the homemade edge guide, described in the chapter "Dadoing and Grooving," using the same hardwood guides. But with this fixture, you use two guides bolted to a baseplate that extends equally on two sides of the router. With the fixture screwed to the router, set the router on the workpiece and establish the bit's proper position. Slide the guides against the workpiece's sides and cinch them tight. The fixture can be used for edge-grooving, mortising, and other operations, as well as cutting sliding dovetails.

The facing screwed to the guide, as shown in *Double Edge-Guide Baseplate*, is an add-on, of course.

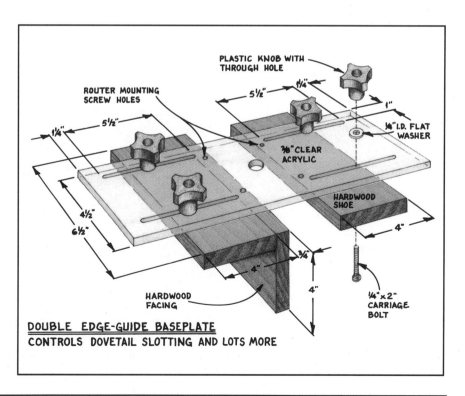

DOUBLE EDGE-GUIDE BASEPLATE
CONTROLS DOVETAIL SLOTTING AND LOTS MORE

The Half-Dovetail Rabbet

As an alternative to more familiar case corner joints such as rabbets and lock miters, Pat Warner, a router wizard from California, developed this router-cut corner joint. Simple to make with a router, the joint comes together neatly and squarely. It is more resistant to racking than a conventional rabbet joint.

Warner prefers to work with hand-held routers, and his technique for cutting the joint reflects his preference. I think it's easier to do the cuts on the router table or the horizontal router table.

To make the half-dovetail cut on the case sides, Warner fits a 1⅛-inch outside diameter (O.D.) pilot bearing on the shank of a 1-inch dovetail bit, then clamps a fence to the work for the bearing to ride against. You can achieve much the same effect by positioning the fence so the router base rides against it.

Next, Warner cuts the dovetail rabbet on the horizontal pieces. He uses a right-angle platform, much like the one we made for routing tails, but Warner references the platform edge with an edge guide to control the cut. He secures the workpiece in a vise, then clamps the platform to it and sets the router's edge guide. The router's depth of cut should be the same as before. Then he makes the second cut.

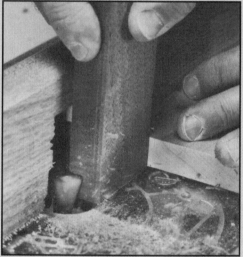

Cutting a half-dovetail rabbet is a two-pass operation. Both use the same bit with one height and fence setting. The first pass is made with the workpiece flat on the router tabletop, as shown on top right. To make the second cut for the joint (bottom right), stand the mating workpiece on end and brace it against the fence. For both cuts, back up the work, especially if it is narrow like these pieces, to keep it square and to prevent the bit from blowing out the edge.

You'll find that you can use this to great advantage where the workpiece is clamped flat on the bench top. Hold the router horizontally, and fit it onto the work. The weight of the router will press the facing against the bottom of the work, and the facing will keep the machine level.

For cutting the sliding tail, the bit must be largely housed in one of the guides, so it makes only a shallow cut in the work. Make one pass, cutting one face of the board, then turn the router around and make a second pass to cut the other face, completing the tail. Test the tail in a slot, and adjust the guides as necessary to get the fit you prefer.

With two edge guides on it, the router can literally be hung on the edge of the work (right). That enables you to use a hand-held router to cut dovetail pins on the edges of case parts. By adjusting the guides, you control the bit's position in relation to the work, and thus alter the thickness of the dovetail pin. Since few commercial edge guides are designed to be doubled up on the router, you probably will have to make a double edge-guide baseplate like that shown. Once you have it, you'll discover other uses for it—like mortising and slotting.

The half-dovetail rabbet is a "designer" joint: It looks just a little different, just a little more stylish than the rabbet joint you're used to. And that Z-shaped inter-lock enables a well-fitted one to resist some stresses a little better than the standard rabbet joint.

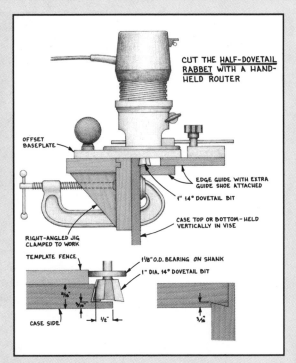

CUT THE <u>HALF-DOVETAIL</u> <u>RABBET</u> WITH A HAND-HELD ROUTER

OFFSET BASEPLATE

EDGE GUIDE WITH EXTRA GUIDE SHOE ATTACHED

1" 14° DOVETAIL BIT

CASE TOP OR BOTTOM-HELD VERTICALLY IN VISE

RIGHT-ANGLED JIG CLAMPED TO WORK

TEMPLATE FENCE

1⅛" O.D. BEARING ON SHANK

1" DIA. 14° DOVETAIL BIT

CASE SIDE

½"

⅜"

To adjust the fence, you should "read" your test cuts. The samples at left indicate that the setting is right on. The samples in the center indicate that you need to move the fence to expose more of the bit. The samples at right indicate that you need to house more of the bit.

As I said before, I think it's a lot easier to make this joint on either the regular router table or the horizontal one. When you set the fence properly, it becomes a halving process. Both halves of the joint are cut with the same setup. The difference is in the angle of attack: One piece is laid flat on the table and pushed across the bit, while the other is held upright against the fence. But the fence position is the same for both cuts. What could be more simple?

To cut this joint on ¾-inch stock, you need at least a ¾-inch dovetail bit. The ½-inch bit, which is the most common size, won't give you a satisfactory joint because it is just a little too small. The angle of the bit is irrelevant, since you use the same bit for both cuts. Use the bit you have. The bit height for this operation is up to you. It's irrelevant to the fit of the joint, so set a height that looks right. The fence setting is what makes it come together perfectly. Take the time to cut tests on scraps of the working stock.

Here's how to make the double edge guide:

1. Dress the hardwood for the guides, sand it smooth, and glue the parts together. After the glue has dried, screw—but don't glue—the facing to one of the guides (for some operations, you may need to remove it).

2. Cut the acrylic, rounding off the sharp corners. Sand and polish the edges if desired. Cut the slots with a ¼-inch straight bit. This is easiest to do on the router table.

3. Using the factory baseplate as a template, lay out the router location, the bit hole, and the mounting-screw holes. Give some thought to the orientation of the router handles in relation to the plane of the guide. Cut the bit hole, and drill and countersink the screw holes.

4. Set the edge guides under the baseplate and mark the locations of the carriage-bolt holes. Drill and counterbore the holes.

5. Insert the carriage bolts into the guide and tap them home with a hammer. Insert the projecting studs through the baseplate slots, drop washers onto them, and turn plastic knobs onto them. Mount the unit on your router in place of the factory baseplate.

Sliding the Dovetail on the Router Table

The advantage of the router table is that you move the work over the bit. Unless the workpiece is inordinately large, this is a plus in forming tails. And in cutting a dovetail slot in the edge of a workpiece, this is a distinct plus. But if you are doing something like routing dovetail slots in bookcase sides, do it with a hand-held router. There just isn't a good way to locate the slots on the router table.

To rout a slot in an edge, set the tail height and the fence position. You'll probably want the slot centered across the edge. While that's a

Drawers with a Different Dovetail

The dovetail joint is traditionally used in drawers because it has mechanical strength. Think about how you jerk drawers open and slam them shut. Use a namby-pamby joint, and one day you'll yank that drawer and its front'll pull off.

That's not likely to happen with a dovetailed drawer. Its tapered interlocks will hold the joint together, even if the glue fails.

But real dovetails are time-consuming to make, even if you use a dovetailing jig and your router. The sliding dovetail gives you the mechanical strength of the dovetail without demanding a lot of your shop time in return. It requires one basic router table setup, with a fence shift about halfway through. No parts to clamp and unclamp, clamp and unclamp, as with a dovetailing jig.

Here's how to do it.

Each slot in the drawer front has to be inset about a half-inch so its shoulder has enough meat to resist splitting out. In most cases, you need to provide space for drawer slides, and this overhang will conceal them. If you use the same offset in cutting the slots in the sides for the back, you extend the use of the first setup, thus saving time.

Fit a ½-inch dovetail bit in the table-mounted router. This bit will work whether the drawer sides are ¾-inch stock or ½-inch stock. It's the most

The assembled drawer is clean and functional. The sliding dovetail joint is a natural for this application, since its shape mechanically resists the tendency of the front to separate from the sides. And assembly is quick—no fasteners or clamps required.

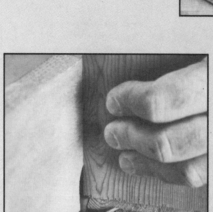

To conceal the end of the dovetail slot in the drawer front, the tail routed on the end of the side must be trimmed slightly. The easiest way to do it is to snick off the end, as shown, at the same time you cut the tail.

common size of dovetail bit, too, being the size any router bit set includes. Adjust the cutting depth to ¼ inch. Set the fence so the slot's centerline will be ¾ inch from the end of the drawer front. Test it by slotting some scraps of the working stock.

To cut the slots, butt the workpiece end against the fence, back it up with a plywood sled, and feed the work from left to right, cutting the slot.

pretty difficult setup to achieve, you can always center the slot by making two passes, one with each of the two faces against the fence. Though the slot is wider than the bit diameter, this shouldn't be a problem, since you will next cut the tail to fit whatever size slot you have.

To cut the tail, you must reset the fence, but don't monkey with the bit height. Leave it right where it was when you cut the slot. In setting the fence, don't ever position it so that the work is trapped between it and the bit. Always bury the bulk of

Routing the dovetail slot in two passes centers it across the edge, but you have to pay attention to the position of the cut to avoid feed direction problems when you do. The first pass is never a problem. But be sure the bit is cutting the slot wall farthest away from the fence on the second pass—as shown here—so the pass can be made right to left, as usual.

You may want to stop the dovetail slots shy of the front's top edge. If so, clamp a stop block to the fence. The problem is that feeding left to right, as is proper, you can make only one slot in the drawer front. To cut the second slot, you have to feed the work in the opposite direction. Yes, it's the *wrong* direction. Because it is the wrong direction, you need to be especially watchful that the bit doesn't force the workpiece away from the fence.

If the stopped slot is what you want, set the fence and stop, and make one slot in each drawer front. Then shift the stop to the left side of the bit and make a second slot in each drawer front.

The slots in the sides will surely be through slots, which you can cut before or after the fronts.

With all the slots cut, including a few in scraps, you must shift the fence to cut the tails. Don't change the bit height; the height for the slots also works for the tails. Move the fence so the bit is all but concealed. Make test cuts on your scraps and test how the resulting tails fit the slots.

Now the fit you want is such that

One stopped dovetail slot in each drawer front must be routed using a climb cut (feeding left to right). In my experience, this sounds dicier than it turns out to be. The stop clamped to the fence limits the length of the cut, preventing you from inadvertently routing a through slot.

the parts will assemble easily, without serious persuading. The assembly process probably will take just enough time that the wood will absorb a little moisture from the glue, causing it to swell. The slot will be a little narrower, the tail a little fatter. If a dry fit is tight, a damp fit will be impossible. Fit the tails accordingly. Make fence adjustments as necessary, then cut the tails.

If you cut stopped slots, you need to trim the tails on the sides with a chisel.

With the sliding dovetails cut, change

your setup to cut slots for the drawer bottom.

To assemble the drawer, apply a bit of glue to the leading edges of the tails and slide them into their slots. The glue will be spread along the tail and slot as the two slide against one another. After front, sides, and back are joined, slide the bottom into its grooves and drive a couple of brads through it into the back. The bottom should square the drawer. Unless the fit of the sliding dovetails is unusually sloppy, you shouldn't need to clamp the drawer.

the bit in the fence, letting the cut be made by the small section that protrudes. Set the fence, then form the tail by making two passes. This will center the tail on the stock.

The most common approach here? Make a fat tail, and in a series of adjustments, work to thin it down just enough to fit the slot. Remember as you adjust the fence after the first cutting that you'll be doubling whatever amount you move it, because you make two passes to form the tail. And since moving only one end of the fence halves the change

at the bit, you should move one end of the fence the amount you want to change the cut. Confusing, huh? Here's an example: If the tail is $\frac{1}{16}$ inch too wide, move one end of the fence $\frac{1}{16}$ inch. This changes the cut by $\frac{1}{32}$ inch at the bit. Taking $\frac{1}{32}$ inch off each side of the tail will reduce its width $\frac{1}{16}$ inch.

When you cut the work, it's a good idea to use featherboards to jam the work against the fence. If the work does drift off the fence—and because the actual cut is so shallow, it doesn't have to drift far to

have impact—it can leave a section of the tail too thick to fit the slot. The uneven thickness probably won't be obvious, and that's a disaster just awaiting assembly. Prevention is the best cure. Though it's an extra setup step, the featherboards can save several extra assembly steps. For good measure, zip the stock past the bit twice on each side.

As good as the router table is, the horizontal router table is even better. Consider that you can rest the work flat on the table to cut the tails or to slot an edge.

Breadboard Ends

The sliding dovetail is ideal for joining a breadboard end to a glued-up panel, like a tabletop or chest lid.

The breadboard end, which is simply a narrow strip of wood, is a traditional method for preventing wide, glued-up panels from cupping. It is attached across the panel's end, concealing the end grain. The breadboard end prevents the cupping, but because its grain direction is perpendicular to that of the panel, it introduces a new problem: It has to be attached in a way that allows the panel to expand and contract, as wood is wont to do.

The sliding dovetail does this. You plow a dovetail groove in the breadboard and cut a tail across the end of the panel. Slide the breadboard end onto the tail, and drive a nail or dowel through the assembly, roughly at the center, locking the two pieces together. The breadboard end can't pop off the tail, but the panel can expand and contract.

The tough part is achieving the appropriate fit. Glue can tighten a loose sliding dovetail in a lot of situations, but not this one. If you glue the parts together, you'll defeat the purpose of the joint. Be as precise as you can in the fit, and before assembly, rub some paste wax on the tail.

Dovetail pins are easy to rout on the horizontal router table because the work can rest flat on the table. A featherboard keeps the workpiece firmly on the table.

The process doesn't change significantly. The bit-height adjustment has the same effect on either router table. But on the horizontal router table, you adjust the router height rather than adjust the fence. Again, for safety's sake, the cut should be made between the work and the tabletop, so you don't trap the work between the bit and the table.

A couple of featherboards clamped to the router mounting board help keep the work flat on the tabletop, in consistent contact with the cutter. These hold-downs can even straighten out minor bowing.

SPLINED MITER JOINT

The miter represents the best and worst in joinery.

Tightly crafted, it is almost totally hidden: There's a barely discernible seam, and *right there,* the figure of the wood changes direction sharply. You don't see any end grain. That's the best of it.

The worst is that the simple miter joint is—structurally—a terrible joint. It's sissy weak. If you glue it, you're trying to glue end grain to end grain, a hopeless cause. Run some fasteners into it, and you're running them into end grain, where they won't hold very well. Moreover (when things go bad, they go *really* bad), the joint is vexing to assemble. Because of the angles involved, a mitered corner always wants to slide out of line when you apply clamping pressure to it.

The *solution* to all the problems, a solution that doesn't affect the pure, pristine appearance of the miter in any way, is a spline.

A spline is a separate piece of wood, often plywood, that reinforces a joint. Usually, the spline is set into slots in the mating surfaces in such a way that the grain of the spline will run across the main joint to resist splitting along that joint. This placement just happens to be ideal for holding the pieces in place for gluing, too.

The question is how to cut the slots in the right places. There are several answers, and all involve the router as the cutting tool. The main reason that there are several answers, which are spread out on these pages, is that there's fair variety among miters. How many can you list? Here are three main groups:

• Flat miters, in which the angled cuts run across the faces of the pieces
• Edge miters, in which the pieces to be jointed are actually beveled rather than mitered
• Compound miters, in which the pieces are cut with combination miter and bevel cuts

Each kind of miter joint requires a slightly different approach to cutting the grooves for the splines—a different router table fence, perhaps, or a different router fixture. Within each group, it's possible to isolate variations that require a change of approach.

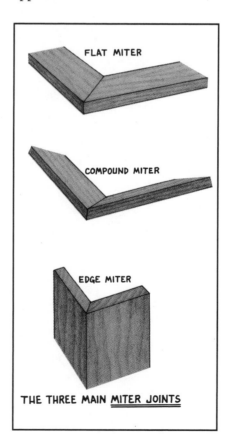

FLAT MITER

COMPOUND MITER

EDGE MITER

THE THREE MAIN <u>MITER JOINTS</u>

FLAT MITERS

Cutting slots for splines in a flat miter joint can be done with a hand-held router or on a router table. Use common sense in matching the router and bit and setup to the particulars of the job. Assuming the workpieces aren't totally unwieldy, I think these slots are cut most easily and safely on the router table.

As a hand-held operation, cutting these slots, especially stopped ones, is problematic. To cut a through slot, a laminate trimmer (preferably an offset-base model) and a slotting cutter work swell. The router rides on the broadest face of the stock; the slot cutter makes a clean, consistent groove. But stopped grooves are another matter. When you make a stopped groove with the slot cutter, it has a somewhat oval section—a lot like a biscuit-joiner cut. This is okay if you are using biscuits (see "Biscuit Joinery with a Router" on page 258), but it creates extra work if you are making splines from wood or plywood scraps.

Hand-held routing of stopped grooves is really a job for a plunge router with a straight bit. But moving that tool over the area to be worked is touchy. A flat mitered surface is typically narrow and short, making a precarious perch for a plunge router. You can fit the machine with two edge guides to create a kind of chute for the workpiece (see "Grooving the Work's Edge" on page 237) or you can double up the workpieces to expand the support surface. But all this demands a lot of jockeying with the router and edge guides, the vise, and clamps.

Save yourself some time. Do it on the router table.

For cutting through grooves in the ends of relatively narrow stock, a small, easy-to-maneuver router, like this offset-base laminate trimmer, is ideal. Fitted with a slotting cutter, you can plow from edge to edge.

To set up the router table, close down the baseplate's throat as much as possible, and use a tall fence. You'll be standing your work on end and sliding it over the bit, so you must be sure the work surface is as free of snags as possible and that the

work is well supported as it slides over the bit.

To set up the work, cut the miters as accurately as possible, of course. But mark a reference face on each piece, too. By *always* placing the reference face against the fence as you cut, you can ensure that the joints will line up properly at assembly time.

Through groove. If you don't mind having the spline be a visible part of the joint, cut through slots. This is a "zzzppp zzzppp" operation. (Because, as Fred says, you just take the router and, zzzppp zzzppp, the job's done.)

Set the depth of cut, set the fence. Holding the marked face of the workpiece against the fence, feed it from right to left, cutting through the piece from edge to edge.

If tear-out is a problem when cutting through grooves in flat miters, use a pusher made from scrap, mitered so it fits tightly against the trailing edges of the workpiece. To back up the cut on the other end of the workpiece, turn the scrap over. It should fit perfectly into the acute angle between the work and the tabletop.

Stopped groove. Use the same basic setup to cut a stopped groove that you use to cut a through groove. What you need to add are a couple of erasable markings on the router

TRY THIS!

It's possible to accurately slot work for splines without laying out each slot on each piece. You can save a bit of layout time, especially if there's a need to slot a lot of pieces.

Because the alignment of the slot will undoubtedly be different in one end of each piece than the other, you actually have to do two setups. Do the setup for the left end, then cut all the slots in the left ends of the workpieces. Then redo the setup for the right end, and cut all those slots.

To set up your router table, lay out the slots on both ends of a test workpiece. Cut the two slots. Now, with the router switched off, slip one end of the slotted piece over the bit, and on the tabletop, mark the position of the workpiece's leading edge at the start of the cut. Move the piece to

the end-of-cut position, and mark where the trailing edge is.

To cut duplicate slots in that end of the other pieces, you now need only align the leading edge with the starting mark on the tabletop. Plunge the work onto

the bit, and feed it right to left. Stop the cut when the trailing end of the work aligns with the appropriate mark.

After all the lefts are cut, redo the setup in the same way for the rights. Then cut all of them.

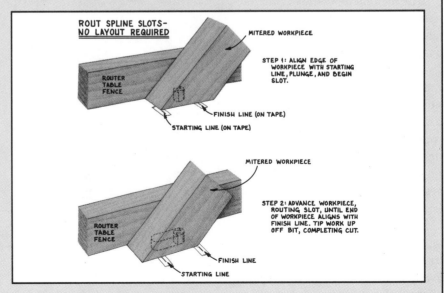

ROUT SPLINE SLOTS—
NO LAYOUT REQUIRED

MITERED WORKPIECE

ROUTER TABLE FENCE

STEP 1: ALIGN EDGE OF WORKPIECE WITH STARTING LINE, PLUNGE, AND BEGIN SLOT.

FINISH LINE (ON TAPE)

STARTING LINE (ON TAPE)

MITERED WORKPIECE

ROUTER TABLE FENCE

STEP 2: ADVANCE WORKPIECE, ROUTING SLOT, UNTIL END OF WORKPIECE ALIGNS WITH FINISH LINE. TIP WORK UP OFF BIT, COMPLETING CUT.

FINISH LINE

STARTING LINE

Safety First!

A throat opening that's substantially larger than the bit can be a hazard when feeding the narrow end of a board across the router table. The leading and trailing points can dip into the throat and hang up, startling you, trashing your work, and maybe even leading to an injury.

To close down the throat and provide secure bearing for the work, lay an auxiliary top on your router table. Using double-sided carpet tape, secure a sheet of thin plywood or hardboard to the router table. Cover the baseplate and its throat. Now chuck the bit you plan to use in the collet, turn on the machine, and advance the depth of cut until the bit penetrates the auxiliary top.

You can't get a tighter, safer fit.

When your operation is done, strip off the auxiliary top and set it aside for the next time you use that bit. (Next time you want to use it, align it over the protruding bit, square up the corners, then tape it down.)

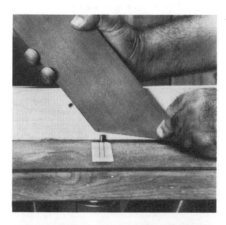

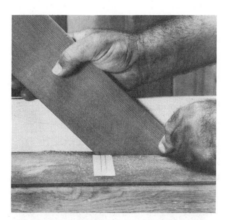

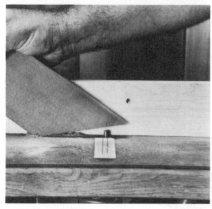

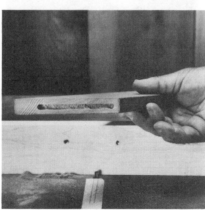

The sequence for cutting a stopped slot in a flat miter is straightforward. With the workpiece tipped up so it clears the bit (top left), align the mark on the work with the appropriate mark by the bit. Lower the work onto the bit and advance it right to left (top right). As the end-of-cut mark comes into alignment with the mark by the bit, tip the work up off the bit (bottom left). The cut is clean and straight, with its ends rounded on the same radius as the bit (bottom right).

table (or on masking tape applied to the router table) indicating the diameter of the bit. (Set a square against the fence and slide its blade against the bit; scribe along the blade on the tabletop. Move the square to the other side of the bit and repeat.) On the face of the workpiece that will be visible as you rout, mark the ends of the desired slot.

When you cut the slot, always move the work from right to left. And always keep the reference face against the fence. Brace it against the fence and slide it to the bit. Tip the leading edge up and over the bit, aligning the starting mark on the workpiece with the left bit mark on the table. When the marks line up, plunge the work onto the bit and feed the work to the left. When the end mark on the workpiece aligns with the right bit mark on the table, tip the trailing edge up off the bit, thus ending the cut.

Quick and simple.

Each piece can be cut in the same way, regardless of the angle of the miter, regardless of whether it leans to the right or to the left. Just mark the ends of each slot.

EDGE MITERS

Edge miters lend themselves to a greater range of applications than do flat miters. You might find them in casework as well as framework. The scale of casework—the size of the individual parts—makes it worthwhile to find some practical ways of cutting spline slots with a hand-held router. Muscling a cabinet side along an angled router table fence may not be as easy as sliding a lightweight router and jig along the cabinet side. So, here are several options, beginning with the router table.

Router Table Fence

To cut spline slots in edge miters on the router table, you need a fence that's canted at the same angle as the edge miter. This allows you to keep the reference face of the workpiece flat against the fence and have the cut surface flat on the router table.

There are two directions, of course, in which the fence can be angled. In one direction, the fence forms an acute angle with the tabletop. In the other, it forms an obtuse angle. Fred likes the acute-angle fence, simply because it traps the work, ensuring that the groove will be where he wants it. I see possibilities in both, largely because I can envision workpieces that would be difficult to maneuver along almost any acutely angled fence. Let's take a look.

The acute-angle fence: Make a fence canted to 45 degrees from a straight, flat 2 × 4, and you'll have the fence that you'll use 90 percent of the time. Tilt your table saw to 45 degrees, and with the broad face flat on the saw table, rip one edge off the

2 × 4. (Obviously, if you are splining edge miters of some angle other than 45 degrees—the sides of a hexagonal or octagonal case, for example—your fence needs to be beveled at that angle.) On the band saw, cut the ends to form clamping ears on the ends of the fence, as shown in *Acute-Angle Fence.* Set up and clamp this fence as you would a conventional one.

Cutting through slots with this setup is as simple as trapping the work in the crotch formed by the fence and the tabletop, then feeding it into the bit. As with the flat miters, an expendable push stick can help prevent tear-out that often comes when the bit exits the work, so long as it fits tightly against the edge of the work.

To cut stopped slots, mimic the flat miter slotting operation. That is, mark parallel tangents to the bit on the tabletop. Mark the ends of the desired slot on the work. Hold the work against the fence, tip the leading edge over the bit, align the mark on the work with the appropriate mark on the tabletop, and plunge the work onto the bit. Feed the work from right to left, cutting the slot. When the cut is done, tip the work up off the bit. The routine is easier to do than to describe.

Use the workpiece—or a beveled scrap of the working stock—to set the acute-angle fence. Adjust the bit to the desired height first. With one end of the fence clamped and the setup scrap trapped behind the bit, you can sight along the tabletop and fence and see exactly where the bit is going to cut. Position the fence so the slot will be where you want it.

Use the same setup scrap to mark the bit size on tape applied to the mounting plate. You can butt the wood against the cutting edge without damaging it, then scribe along the edge of the scrap on the tape.

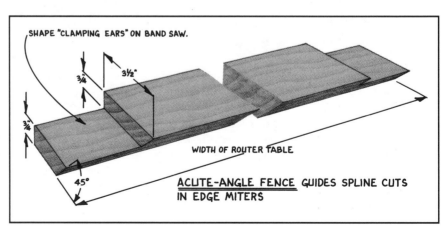

SHAPE "CLAMPING EARS" ON BAND SAW.

3/4"

3 1/2"

3/4"

45°

WIDTH OF ROUTER TABLE

ACUTE-ANGLE FENCE GUIDES SPLINE CUTS IN EDGE MITERS

To make the cut, push one end of the work into the V formed by the fence and tabletop, and hold the work firmly against the fence. Line up the marks and tip the work onto the bit. Feed the work to the end of the cut, and tip it off the bit. The key is keeping the work up against the fence.

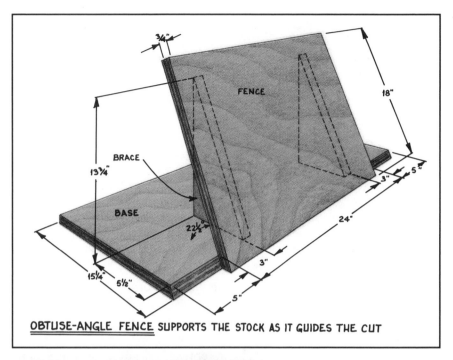

OBTUSE-ANGLE FENCE SUPPORTS THE STOCK AS IT GUIDES THE CUT

The stopped slot looks weird because of the way the bit enters and exits the workpiece. As long as the bit doesn't penetrate the work completely, you're okay. The joint will be secure.

The obtuse-angle fence will support the workpiece for you, but you've got to clamp a trap fence opposite it (and parallel to it) to prevent the work from skidding down the fence, across the tabletop, and onto the floor. A catch block clamped to the workpiece to ride along the top edge of the fence is a nice idea, but doesn't work terribly well. Hence the trap fence.

The obtuse-angle fence: Once in a while you have a workpiece that's a little too unwieldy for the acute-angle fence. That fence traps the bevel well enough, but you have to support the stock as well as feed along the fence. Here's one that helps you with your burden.

Make it from ¾-inch plywood. *Obtuse-Angle Fence* gives the dimensions of the fence shown in the photo, but you can modify them to suit your router table and the job you have to do.

Cut the fence to size and rip a bevel along one edge. The bevel, naturally, matches that of the work you are going to spline; a 22½-degree angle is shown. That angle is half of a 45, so the braces are easily made by cutting on a diagonal any rectangular piece that's twice as long as it is wide. The base has to be long enough that it can be clamped—at the back or side of the tabletop.

Assemble the pieces with drywall screws.

To use this fence, position it so the slot will be where you want it in the edge of the workpiece. Clamp it to the table. To keep the work in place, use a trap fence, as shown. All you have to do is lean the workpiece on

If you have a small router, you might try grooving casework miters for splines with a modified slotting cutter. There are two tricks involved in this approach, and the cutter modification is one of them. The other is how you clamp the work.

To prepare the cutter, switch the positions of the cutter and the pilot bearing. (And while you are at it, change to a slightly larger bearing so the cut depth is reduced from the standard ½ inch.) You simply have to remove the locking screw or nut, switch the cutter and bearing, then reinstall the fastener. (You can't do this on *all* slot cutters.)

To prepare the stock, you lay two pieces together, face to face, and line up the miters, as shown in the photo. Clamp them securely. The router rides on one mitered suface while the cutter grooves the other. Your bearing surface will be a tad wider than ¾ inch, and the piloted bit will give the tool bearing on a second edge. A lightweight router enhances your control.

As you can see, by switching the bearing and cutter, the pilot has sure contact with the miter edge, while the cutting edge is in the meaty part of the miter.

the fence and let it drop. The catch fence will keep it from skidding across the tabletop and onto the floor. Slide the piece across the fence. A stopped slot is created through the typical tip-rout-and-tip sequence.

Edge-Miter Slotting Fixture

Though simple, this fixture for slotting an edge miter is quite versatile. To work large pieces like the side of a cabinet, attach it to the router as an auxiliary base, and run the unit over the clamped-down work. With smaller work, you can clamp the router and fixture to a bench to make it convenient to pass the stock through it. You can even make a custom version to clamp to a router table.

The fixture consists of a plywood base and two fences, canted to 45 degrees. The model shown was made from scraps of ¾-inch plywood. (The thickness of the base

does limit the depth of cut somewhat, but you're not going much deeper than ⅜ inch in edge-mitered ¾-inch stock.) If you foresee a need to clamp down the fixture to feed work through it, or if you want a router-table version, adjust the dimensions of the base accordingly.

Construction is simple.

1. Glue and screw the main fence and its braces to the base.

2. Position the catch fence to fit the thickness of the mitered stock you want to spline. Attach this fence to the base with screws only, so you can reposition it to accommodate stock of a different thickness.

3. Bore a 1-inch hole where the cutter will pass through the base. You'll be cutting a groove in a captured piece of stock, and you need lots of space for the chips to escape if you don't want them to jam up in the cut.

4. Mount the router to the base. With the bit you'll be using to cut the spline slots in the collet, set the

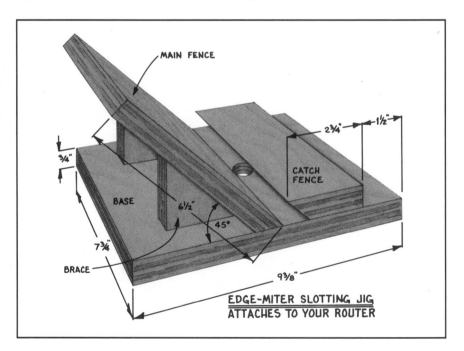

EDGE-MITER SLOTTING JIG
ATTACHES TO YOUR ROUTER

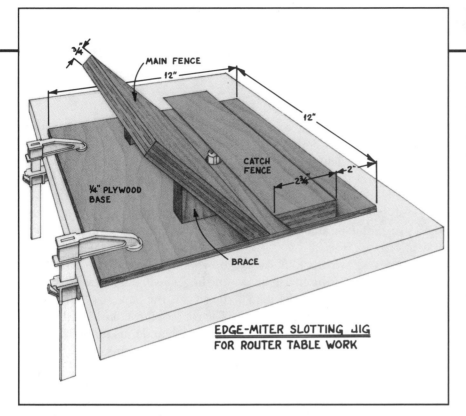

MAIN FENCE

CATCH FENCE

¼" PLYWOOD BASE

BRACE

12"

12"

2¾"

2"

¾"

EDGE-MITER SLOTTING JIG FOR ROUTER TABLE WORK

The edge-miter slotting jig allows you to use a standard straight bit in a hand-held router to slot mitered edges. The jig traps the work between two fences. You just slip the router and jig onto the workpiece as shown and rout. The router can't slip off the edge, and the slot will be perfectly positioned.

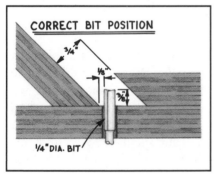

CORRECT BIT POSITION

¾"

⅛"

⅜"

¼" DIA. BIT

router on the fixture. Adjust its position, setting the bit well into the stock area. Be sure the cutter doesn't come too close to the catch fence; you don't want to weaken the stock you are splining. With the position set, scribe around the router base and, if possible, tick-mark both the baseplate and the fixture.

Remove the router from the fixture, and unfasten its baseplate. Return the baseplate to the fixture, aligning the tick-marks. Now mark the locations of the mounting-screw

holes. With a long bit, drill the holes, penetrating the fences as well as the base. Turn the fixture over and drill counterbores so you can get the mounting screws into the holes to mount the fixture on the router.

5. Screw the fixture to the router.

Catch the edge of the clamped-down stock in the chute formed by the two fences. The main fence should be beneath the work. Switch on the router and feed it over the stock from left to right. The rotation of the cutter will tend to push the stock against the catch fence and keep it accurately placed. If you must feed the opposite way, you'll need to exert plenty of pressure to be sure that the cutter doesn't push away from the stock. If that happens, the groove will be shallow and in the wrong place.

For this operation, you may want to use an upshear or spiral bit, which

will tend to eject the chips. Depending on the job, you'll want a ⅛- to ¼-inch cutter.

It is possible to plunge, stop, and exit with this jig by simply attaching it to a plunge router. But if you want to do stopped splines, you may be ahead of the game by making the next jig, one that clamps to the workpiece.

▶ **TRY THIS!**

If your router base has a pronounced flange, you may be able to drill three or four holes completely through it. Then you can quickly attach wooden fixtures, such as the edge-miter splining fixture. Set the router on the fixture and get it aligned. Drive a panhead or roundhead wood screw through each hole into the fixture.

BOX JOINT

> **Think of this as a square-cut through dovetail.**

The box joint is used in the same situations as the dovetail—assembling boxes, assembling drawers, and casework. (I used it on my bit case—see the chapter "Bits.") It has pretty fair mechanical strength, but what it does is generate long-grain-to-long-grain glue area (the sort of glue area that yields the strongest bonding).

The box joint is a machine-cut one (as opposed to something like a dovetail, which, although it is easily machine-cut, is nonetheless regarded generally as a hand-cut joint).

A lot of woodworkers think the only way to cut the slots is on a table saw with a dado cutter. Make a little jig to attach to the miter gauge, and go to town. Well, I'm here to tell you the table-mounted router does a cleaner job in the same amount of time. You make a little sledlike jig,

but once that's done, it is strictly repetitive cutting.

The router bit yields a cut that's not only square but also flat-bottomed and clean all around. The cuts are fast, too. If your router has enough moxie, you should be able to cut the full depth in one pass.

(You may know this joint as a finger joint. We're using that name for an interlocking edge-to-edge joint that's cut with a special bit. See "Special Joinery Bits" on page 263 for a rundown on the finger-joint bit.)

THE BOX-JOINTING JIG

The box-jointing jig is simply an adaptation of the one you'd make and attach to your table saw's miter gauge. It's a specialized miter gauge for your router table, one that's guided by a couple of fences rather than a slot in the table. (It would be easy enough to build it like the sled—see the chapter "Router Table Accessories"—so it would be guided by the edge of the table. But that would eliminate the very fine adjustment that's possible

A dado cutter cuts slots quickly but tends to leave an uneven, ridged bottom. The router-cut slot, on the other hand, is square and clean all around. Which would you prefer for your box joints?

when you use two fences to position and guide the jig, as you'll see.)

The critical element of any box-jointing jig is the key and its position relative to the bit. The jig itself can be any old scrappy thing, so long as the key is properly sized and positioned.

Before making the jig, decide how wide and deep the slots between the fingers will be. The slots and the fingers are the same size, by the way. The router bit establishes the width of the slot, and thus the width of the fingers. The depth should be governed by the thickness of the working stock. If you are joining ¾-inch-thick parts, the slots and fingers need to be ¾ inch deep. If it's ½-inch stock, then the depth is ½ inch.

My advice is to make a separate jig for each different size of finger you make. While you probably can get acceptable results cutting ½-inch-deep slots on a jig set up for a ¾-inch depth of cut, splintering or "blowout" is likely to occur as the bit exits a cut. The backing has been cut away.

To make the jig, select suitable materials from your scrap pile. I used plywood because it's stable, and because we've always got odd scraps around. The one part that's hardwood is the key. It is subjected to a lot of wear, and if it is too soft, it will wear and throw off the accuracy of your cuts. The joints won't join, in other words. The key should be replaced if it gets worn, dented, or deformed.

1. Cut the parts to the sizes specified by the Cutting List. The handle is reduced in size as it is shaped, but you'll need the extra size to cut the shape.

2. The back ultimately has two slots cut in it, one for the cutter, the other for the key. Cut *only* the key slot at this time.

Chuck the straight bit you'll be using in the table-mounted router, and set it for the desired cutting height. Set the fence to position the notch, as shown in *Box-Jointing Jig*. Cut the notch. Stand the back on edge, and back it up with a sled or scrap of two-by stock. Guide both the scrap and its backup along the fence.

3. Next, fashion the key from the hardwood, making it the same width and thickness as the desired slot. Test fit the key stock in the key slot; it should fit snugly. If it rattles or has any play, rip a new key, making it a little fatter. If it's too thick, plane it until it fits properly. Finally, cross-cut the key stock into two pieces, each about 5 inches long.

4. Assemble the base, support, and back. Glue the support to the base, then glue the back in place. Drill pilot holes and drive two drywall screws through the base into the back. Be sure you position the screws toward the outer edges, so the bₗ won't hit them.

5. Make the handle. On the handle blank, scribe two lines, each 1 inch in from an edge and parallel to it, as shown in *Box-Jointing Jig*. The lines should be along adjacent sides so that they cross, forming a 1-inch square. Drill a ⅛-inch-diameter hole in the center of that square. This is the pivot hole for routing the arc profile.

Cobble an overarm pivot. (See "Overarm Pivot" on page 170.) I nailed a scrap of ½-inch plywood atop a scrap of ¾-inch plywood so that the top piece would overlap the

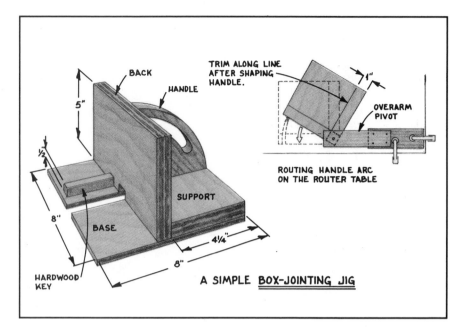

A SIMPLE BOX-JOINTING JIG

CUTTING LIST

Piece	Number	Thickness	Width	Length	Material
Base	1	¼"	8"	8"	Plywood
Support	1	¾"	8"	4¼"	Plywood
Back	1	¾"	8"	5"	Plywood
Handle*	1	¾"	6"	6"	Plywood
Key	1	½"	¾"	10"	Hardwood

Hardware

4 pcs. #6 × 1⅝" drywall screws

*Start with a piece this size; cutting the profile reduces its size.

The typical box-jointing jig is fairly job-specific. The jig at right cuts ½-inch slots in ¾-inch stock. Using a smaller bit requires a different jig. The one at left cuts dovetails that join boards end to end.

TRY THIS!

Minimize "blowout" and at the same time extend the utility of your box-jointing jig with interchangeable cutting slot backers.

The box-jointing jig provides backing, but if the existing cutting slot in the back is higher than the one you're cutting in a workpiece, you risk blowout. So change the backing each time you use the jig for a new project.

Before gluing the back in place, rout a dovetail slot in it, as shown in *Interchangeable Backer*. Then cut backers to fit tightly in the slot. They can be hardwood or hardboard. Make a handful of them at one time so you'll have several on hand. Assemble the jig, then slide a backer into the dovetail slot. (A hole drilled in the backer makes it easier to remove, and you can hang your spares on a screw driven into the jig's back.)

Each time you cut a different height of slot, change the backer.

HARDBOARD BACKER; SIZED TO FIT SLOT.

5"

ROUT DOVETAIL SLOT IN BACK.

14°   1/4"

3 1/4"   1 1/2"   3 1/4"

BOX-JOINT JIG WITH INTERCHANGEABLE BACKER

Building one box-jointing jig with interchangeable backers allows you to make different-sized joints. Attach the key with small screws so you can easily reposition it. And for each new bit, slide a new hardboard backer into place.

workpiece. I drilled a hole in the 1/2-inch plywood and turned a 6-32 machine screw through it into the pivot hole in the workpiece. Clamp the overarm to the tabletop so the pivot is 4 3/4 inches from the edge (not the center) of the bit.

To cut the arc, raise the bit about 1/4 inch. Switch on the router, and swing the workpiece on the pivot, feeding it into the bit. After sweeping forward and back, raise another 1/4 inch or so, and make another sweep. Repeat the process until the bit cuts through the workpiece.

While you could use the same general procedure to rout a hand hole, I drilled a series of overlapping holes with a 1-inch Forstner bit. Then I routed the curved handle edge, as well as the hand-hole edges, with a 1/4-inch round-over bit.

Finally, cut along the two lines you marked first on the handle blank, reducing it to its final size.

6. Attach the handle to the jig with glue and a couple of drywall screws. Be sure to position the screws where they won't be hit by the bit.

7. To rout the cutting slot, insert the key in its slot in the back. Set the second piece of key stock next to it. For this step, both keys should be long enough to extend beyond the base's front edge.

Now set the jig on the router table, with the keys between the bit and the fence. The idea is to use the loose key as a spacer to establish the thickness of the finger that will be left between the cutting slot and the already-cut key slot. Bring the fence against the edge of the jig, and slowly turn the bit by hand to ensure you are accurately positioning the jig and fence. Clamp the fence.

Use the key to set the height of

A jig doesn't have to be attractive to work, but if you are a woodworker who likes to make attractive things, why not make it good-looking?

Use those scraps of walnut and cherry. They *are* scraps, aren't they?

Invest a little time in fairing the shape, in routing a decorative edge. If this adds 10 minutes to a one-hour job, so what!

Make a big, comfortable handle, one that's easy to grip. Use a hand saw as a pattern. Trace the saw handle on a scrap of cardboard, cut it out, then transfer it to the handle stock. Cut the jig handle outline on the band saw, then drill and cut the hand hole. Round-over the edges on the router table and glue and screw the handle to the jig.

Template Guide–Centered Jig

You don't have to use a fence to cut box joints with this jig, so long as you modify it to fit over a template guide bushing.

As you know, the guide bushing is a metal fitting that mounts in the router baseplate. It has a low collar that surrounds the bit. If you widen the slot in the jig's base, it will drop over the collar. The jig is trapped! It can slide back and forth as far as the slot will allow. It'll pivot around the collar. But unless you lift the jig, it is in the control of that collar.

One of the biggest advantages is that it saves some setup time. Drop the jig over the template guide, set the bit height, and start cutting those box joints. No fence to set.

If this is an appealing way to guide your box-jointing jig, it's easy to modify it to accommodate the guide. When you cut the jig parts, make the base about 3 or 4 inches longer than specified by the Cutting List. Match the thickness of the plywood to the height of the guide bushing collet. Make the parts and assemble them as specified, but when routing the cutting slot, plunge-cut into the base, beginning about 2 inches in from the front edge.

When the jig has been completed and tested, widen the cutting slot in the base. Set it up, complete with fence, for routing box-joint slots, but use a bit whose diameter matches that of the outside diameter of the template guide's collar. Adjust the bit height to ¼ inch—just enough to cut through the base, not into the support. Plunge-cut, widening the slot. Don't break through the front edge of the base; you need a stopped slot.

Dovetail Splice

Dovetails joining two boards end to end are pretty glitzy, but it turns out they're also pretty easy to make.

A version of the box-jointing jig is the router aid that produces these dovetail splices. The dovetail-splice jig is built just like the box-jointing jig, except that you use a dovetail bit to rout the cutting slot.

When making this jig, the first thing to do is cut a couple of dovetail slots with your dovetail bit in scrap stock. Because of the nature of the joint, the thickness of the stock has no particular bearing on the length of the tails (or depth of the slots). But remember that to function with the jig, the bit will have to be set ¼ inch higher than you set the bit for these test cuts (¼ inch is the thickness of the jig's base). If you can come up with a way to get a piece of the base material under your scrap for the test cut, then you'll see exactly what you'll get.

Use the test cuts to size the key, as well as the slot you'll cut for the key. The narrowest part of the dovetail cut is the width of the key, and thus the width of the key slot. Use a straight bit—bit diameter to match key width—to cut this slot; that will ensure that the key won't wiggle.

Cut your key slot, make the key, then make and assemble the jig. To correctly position the cutting slot, you have to carefully, accurately measure the widest part of the dovetail slot. To close the splice, remember that the tails and the slots have to be the same size. Set the fence to position the cutting slot just that far from the key slot.

Adjust the bit height to align with the top of the key, then rout the cutting slot. Finally, to prove the accu-

The dovetail-splice jig looks a lot like the box-jointing jig, and you make cuts in the same fashion. But the cuts only allow you to joint workpieces end to end, as the samples show.

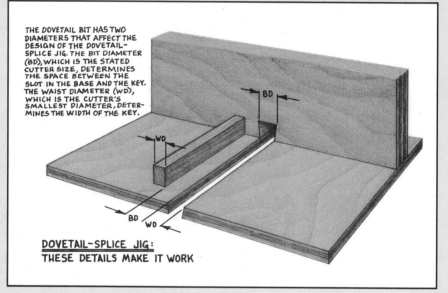

THE DOVETAIL BIT HAS TWO DIAMETERS THAT AFFECT THE DESIGN OF THE DOVETAIL-SPLICE JIG. THE BIT DIAMETER (BD), WHICH IS THE STATED CUTTER SIZE, DETERMINES THE SPACE BETWEEN THE SLOT IN THE BASE AND THE KEY. THE WAIST DIAMETER (WD), WHICH IS THE CUTTER'S SMALLEST DIAMETER, DETERMINES THE WIDTH OF THE KEY.

WD   BD   BD   WD

<u>DOVETAIL-SPLICE JIG:</u>
THESE DETAILS MAKE IT WORK

racy of your work, make test cuts on two pieces of scrap stock, and see if you can close the joint.

Using the dovetail-splice jig is like using the box-jointing jig. You make the first cut in the first piece with the edge against the key. Then

lift the stock to fit the slot over the key, and cut the next slot.

The second piece begins with a slot, so you must align the edge of the stock with the edge of the cutting slot. Then just step and cut your way across the wood.

---

the bit. The height of the cut must match the height of the key.

Now remove the loose key, and rout the cutting slot through the base and into the jig's back. With the slot routed, you can trim the key so it doesn't extend beyond the base. And you probably should drive a small screw through the base into the key to keep it from working loose.

Your jig *should* be ready to use. To be sure, cut fingers on a couple of scraps of the working stock and see whether you can assemble the joint. If it turns out that you *can't* get the joint closed or if it is too loose, you've got the spacing wrong—the fingers are either too wide or too narrow.

All is not lost. You can easily

fine-tune the fit. To loosen a tight fit, shift the jig so the bit is a hair closer to the key. To tighten a loose fit, shift the jig so the bit is a hair farther away from the key. Cut additional test pieces to check the new setup.

To make subsequent setups easier, write notes right on the jig. For example, mark one edge of the slot in the base, and note "Bit tight to this edge." You can even note the bit used, especially if you have more than one in a particular size.

USING THE JIG

To use the jig, you need to use a fence no higher (thicker) than the jig's base. This is so the workpieces can extend beyond the jig's edge. Use a strip of plywood or hardboard.

Stand the workpiece in the jig, its edge snug against the key. Cut a slot. Move the workpiece, fitting the slot over the key. Cut another slot. Repeat the process until all the fingers are formed.

The mating workpiece must begin with a slot, rather than a finger. For the first cut, position this piece so it just covers the slot in the jig. (You can also drop a loose piece of the key between the fixed key and the cutting slot. Butt the edge of the work against this loose key for the first cut.) Otherwise the process is the same.

Getting the depth of cut just right can be pretty tricky. If the slot is too shallow (bottom), you'll have to either replane the stock or recut the slots. If the slot is too deep (next up), you'll have a lot of extra sanding to do. The better alternative is to knowingly cut the slot a tad too deep (third from bottom), and plan to sand the projecting fingers (top).

▶ Swinging Fingers

Turning the box joint into a hinge is surprisingly easy. Before cutting the slots for the joint, round-over the ends of the workpieces. Because you won't have a square edge for a pilot bearing to reference after the first pass, you need to do this on the router table. The radius of the roundover must equal half the thickness of the working stock. (A bull-nose bit will do the job in a single pass; its cutting diameter must equal the stock's thickness.)

Before you actually round-over the edges, use a square and a pencil to lay out the centerpoint for the hinge pin.

Chuck the bit and adjust its height. Set the fence so the bit is buried; if the bit has a pilot bearing, the face of the fence should be flush with it. After a test cut to confirm that the bit setting is correct, radius the good stuff.

Change over the router table, and cut the box joint. Assemble it, and bore the hole for a hinge pin. Insert the pin, and test the hinge's action.

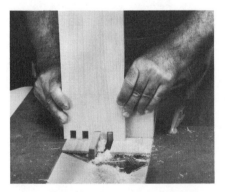

To use the box-jointing jig, simply trap it between two Masonite or ¼-inch-plywood fences. This way you can be sure it won't drift to one side while you're concentrating on holding the workpiece and watching your fingers and the bit. If need be, you can work from front to back on the router table, as here, rather than side to side.

Box joints can be turned into wooden hinges. Round-over the ends of the workpiece before cutting the slots, and drive a nail into each end of the assembly to act as a hinge pin.

SPLINE AND DOVETAIL KEYS

What we're looking at here is a paradox

of woodworking. Fitting spline keys or dovetail keys is an operation that gussies up one of woodworking's really elegant joints, the miter joint. Why would we want to do this?

The miter joint, after all, is the one you use when you *don't want the end grain to show*. We go to a lot of trouble to conceal the end grain, then we rout grooves in the corner and glue keys in them so their end grain shows. Looks like dovetails, you know?

Why we do this is not entirely a mystery. The miter is a lousy joint structurally. The keys are just another way to spline the joint for added strength. The router is the tool to use to cut the spline slots. You need to make a jig. Here's how.

MAKING THE JIG

The jig is in effect a V-block that helps you to cut easily and consistently through a corner of a box. The jig's supports embrace the box's sides, and the base provides a firm work surface that perfectly bisects the planes of the corner.

For smallish work, you use the jig on a router table. The box to be worked rests in the jig. For casework or any other box that's too big to maneuver back and forth on the router table, you clamp the jig to the corner of the work. In either situation, the bit projects through a slot in the jig's base, and when you move the

jig or the router, the appropriate cut is made.

A key in the jig helps you position the slots consistently. For the first cut, the work is butted against the key. But for the second and subsequent cuts, the previous cut is indexed over the key.

1. Cut the plywood parts, which means everything but the key. The base is simply a rectangle. The supports are beveled at 45 degrees along one edge, as are the braces.

2. Glue and screw the supports to the base, as shown in the drawing.

This can be a vexing task. I had a lot of trouble making the first jig, but the second one took maybe 20 minutes. Try this: Use the two braces to trap the supports, so they don't slide out of alignment as you try to drill pilots and drive the screws.

Scribe a line across the middle of the base with a try square. Clamp a brace flat against the base along the line. The brace's miter should form an acute angle with the base.

A small box can be set in the key jig and worked on the router table. Using thin trap fences to position the jig allows the assembly being slotted to protrude from the jig without interference.

The secret behind the uniformly spaced slots is the strip of wood visible beside the bit. A slot fits over that key, positioning the work for the next slot to be cut by the bit. The key can be switched to the unoccupied slot beyond the bit to produce a different spacing.

Stand one of the supports on its mitered edge and push it under the brace's miter. Lay the second brace on the base and slide it in behind the support, trapping it. Clamp the second brace. You should now be able to extract the support, apply glue to it, and return it to its position. Drill pilot holes, and drive two 1-inch screws through the base and into the support. Unclamp the braces.

Now clamp a brace to the face of the support you just installed. With one of its square edges down, this brace forms an acute angle with the base, allowing you to trap the second support in place. Complete the trap with the second brace, and glue and screw the second support to the base. Unclamp the braces.

(It is entirely likely that the points of the screws will now be jutting through the faces of the supports. File these points off after the braces are installed.)

3. Install the braces next. To ensure that the two supports form a right angle, rest a square (or a square scrap of wood) in the V. Apply glue to the brace edges and slip one into position. Push it farther under the support until you see that the V forms a right angle. Hold the brace in place while you drill pilot holes and drive two 1⅝-inch screws through the support into the brace.

Repeat the process to position the second brace.

When both braces are glued and screwed to their supports, turn the jig over, drill pilots, and drive the remaining screws through the base into the braces.

4. What remains is to cut the slots in the jig and to fit the key to one of them. The first slot is what I would call the cutting slot, since it's the

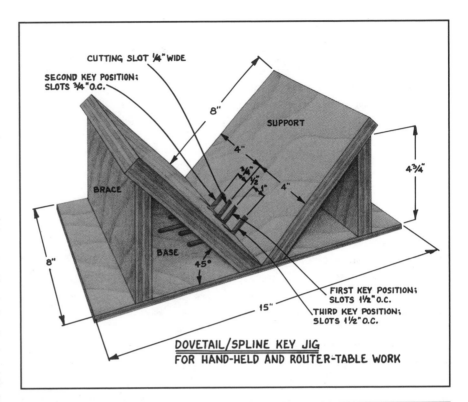

DOVETAIL/SPLINE KEY JIG
FOR HAND-HELD AND ROUTER-TABLE WORK

CUTTING LIST

Piece	Number	Thickness	Width	Length	Material
Base	1	¼"	8"	15"	Plywood
Supports	2	¾"	8"	8"	Plywood
Braces	2	¾"	8"	4¾"	Plywood
Key	1	⅜"	⅝"	4"	Hardwood

Hardware
8 pcs. #6 × 1" drywall screws
4 pcs. #6 × 1⅝" drywall screws

one the cutter is in when the jig is being used. It should be equidistant from both sides.

Set the fence on the router table 4 inches from the center of the bit (whatever bit you're using). With the jig tight against the fence, rear it back and plunge it over the spinning bit so that it punches a hole in the base between the forward brace and support. Slide the jig forward, cutting a slot clear through both supports. Lift the back end of the jig up off the bit and switch off the router.

5. Determine next what spacing you want between the slots. Following the same procedure as in the previous step, set the fence and cut a slot to one side (or the other) of the cutting slot. Then make a key from a hardwood—maple, cherry, or what have you—and plane it to a tight press-fit in the key slot.

Now you are ready to put the jig to work.

It's worth noting that you can add a second (and possibly a third and a fourth) key slot to your jig. If you have a second spacing that you plan to use with *the same bit*, mark off its key slot on the other side of the cutting slot from the first. Work additional slots out on paper before trying to cut them. It may be that if the increment is large enough, you can set up your jig for third or four alternative spacings for a particular bit.

You need to resist the temptation to use different bits with one jig. I took a jig already slotted by a big cutter, and tried using it with a small bit. As I suspected it would, the bit blew splinters out of the work when exiting the cut. There was nothing backing up the cut, so it was bound to happen.

So if you want to do dovetails *and* splines, you should have two jigs. If you want to do ¼-inch splines *and* ½-inch splines, you should have two jigs. If you want the two sizes of splines, plus two sizes of dovetails, that's four jigs.

SLOTTING ON THE TABLE

Because it's likely that your work will extend beyond the periphery of the jig, you can't use your standard router table fence. Use a strip of hardboard or plywood that's the same thickness as the jig's base. That way the jig can make positive contact with the guide, while the work can overhang it.

To set the fence, you first need to get the jig set up over the bit. Chuck the correct bit in the router. Set the jig over it, and position it so the bit is in the center of the V. Adjust the height of the cutter, and turn it so the cutting edges are aligned across the jig. To establish the correct position of the jig on the tabletop,

TRY THIS!

Keep a work sample with each jig. It can help you size work, decide which slot spacing to use, and so forth. The slotting jigs I've made all have two spacings. I use a short scrap as a sample. I cut one spacing on one end, the second spacing on the other. I keep the slotted sample on the shelf with its respective jig.

When my woodworking plans call for dovetail (or spline) keys, I get out the samples and use them while I sketch my project plan. The samples help me determine what slot spacing is going to look best, given the width of the box or drawer I'll be working. It may even prompt me to adjust a dimension or two to get a better appearance.

To rout key slots in casework, you must clamp the jig to the case firmly enough that the cutting action doesn't force it out of position. A scrap stuck through the jig and clamped as shown works well. Note that the router is fitted with a guide bushing. This fits into the jig's cutting slot to control the cut. The alternative is to attach fences to the jig's base.

Swinging on a Template Guide

Worried about your slotting jig drifting off the fence while you're cutting slots? A momentary lapse in concentration, a slightly errant push can produce a skewed slot. A botched job.

Here's a way to eliminate the problem: Modify the jig to work in conjunction with a template guide bushing. Then you can eliminate the fence entirely. The jig will swivel around the guide's collar but will always be in the correct alignment with the cutter.

Moreover, this approach eliminates the need to add fences to the base when you use the jig for hand-held router work.

Build the jig following the directions in "Making the Jig" on page 330. After cutting both the cutting and key slots, line up the fence so the cut resides in the cutting slot. Set the jig aside, and change bits in the router. Pick the template guide you'll use with the jig, and measure the outside diameter of its collar. The bit you need to use now is a straight that matches that measurement. Chuck that bit in the router and set the depth of cut to equal the height of the collar.

Now enlarge the cutting slot only. Butt the jig against the fence, tip it back, and start the router. Plunge the jig, feed it through the cut, then lift the back end of the jig off the cutter. Switch off the router.

The new slot should accommodate the guide collar without interfering with the cutting of slots for your chosen keys.

To use this jig, install the template guide in the mounting plate. Chuck the correct bit in the router. Set the jig over the template, and adjust the height of the cutter. Cuts are made just as if you were using the fence.

You'll notice, however, that the template guide provides positive stops at the extremes of a cutting stroke. You never have to wonder whether the cutter is housed in the work, or whether it's free of the work and you're extending the slot in the base. Pull the jig toward you until it stops. Push it away from you until it stops. No doubts.

With the slotting jig's movement regulated by the template guide, you need never worry about the jig—and the work it carries—drifting away from a fence and boogering both the jig and the work. The template guide allows the jig to swivel—giving you freedom of motion—without compromising the cut placement.

To slot the box or drawer, set it in the jig and butt it against the key. Push and pull the jig, cutting the first slot. Lift the box to slip this first slot over the jig's key. Push and pull again, cutting the second slot. Keep going until the corner is done. Switch corners and keep at it until the box is done.

slide the jig so the cutter is housed in one of the supports. Slide the fence against the edge of the jig's base and clamp it. The jig should slide back and forth along the fence without catching on the bit as it passes through the slots in the supports.

To cut the slots, you rest the assembled box in the jig, with one edge butted against the key. With the router switched on, push and pull the jig, cutting the first slot. Lift the work slightly, shift it toward the key, and lower it again into the jig,

dropping the cut over the key. Make another cut, lift and shift the work, and make a third cut.

You just repeat this process over and over until the job is done.

In the ideal situation, one of your preestablished spacings will suit the work at hand. But you may need to make the first cut without the key in place, so you can alter the space from the work's edge to the first key. If this is the case, you can use carpet tape to stick a temporary stop in the jig for the first cut. I'd suggest making that first cut on all four corners

of the box before pulling out the temporary stop and reinserting the key to finish out the job.

HAND-ROUTED SLOTS

Where the work is too unwieldy to maneuver on the router table, you must rest the jig on the work and cut the slots with a hand-held router. This is unlikely to be as quick and easy as doing the job on the router table.

Splining a Frame

The miter joint is very commonly used in light frames—picture frames, face frames. A spline key in each corner strengthens the joint, and it adds a subtle embellishment, too.

While you might be able to clamp temporary support blocks in the key jig to hold a frame over the cutting slot, you can make a jig just for frames almost as easily. It works on a router table two ways. You can slide it along the L-shaped fence to cut the slot with a straight bit. And you can lay it flat on the tabletop, sliding it along a low fence, and cut the slot with a slot cutter.

The construction is evident from the drawing. Miter the ends of the two frame supports, then glue and screw them to the plywood back. The supports must be at a 45-degree angle to the baseline and at right angles to each other. Having done this, you have the jig to use with the slot cutter.

You *can* use the same jig upright, braced against the L-shaped fence, too. But you'll have better support if you make a fence hook, consisting of a spacer that's about 1/32 inch thicker than the fence stock and a plywood flange. If you simply clamp this accessory to the jig when you need it, then the jig can serve you both ways. If you glue it on, you're stuck using it always with the fence and straight cutter.

Obviously, to use the jig, you set the frame in the V formed by the supports. Snap a spring clamp on each side of the jig to hold the frame. Hit the switch and push the jig and frame through the cutter.

With the frame-splining jig riding the router table fence, you can use a straight bit to cut the spline slots. To keep the frame from tipping away from the fence, clamp a catch fence to the jig, as shown. If you always use the jig this way, attach the catch fence permanently.

If you rest the frame-splining jig over the tabletop, you need to use a slot cutter, as shown. Use the fence to control the depth of the slot you cut.

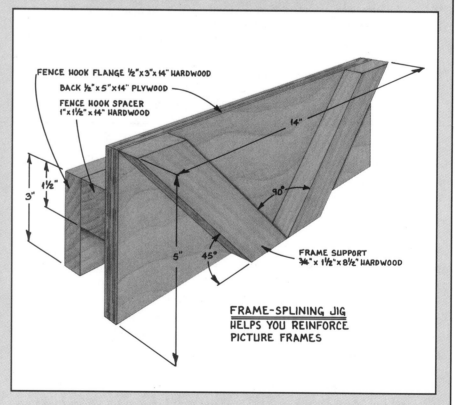

FENCE HOOK FLANGE 1/2" x 3" x 14" HARDWOOD
BACK 1/2" x 5" x 14" PLYWOOD
FENCE HOOK SPACER 1" x 1 1/2" x 14" HARDWOOD

14"
1 1/2"
3"
90°
5"
45°

FRAME SUPPORT 3/4" x 1 1/2" x 8 1/2" HARDWOOD

FRAME-SPLINING JIG
HELPS YOU REINFORCE
PICTURE FRAMES

For this work, the first thing you should do is add a fence (or better, two fences) to the base of the jig. The fence will guide the router through each cut. Two fences trap the router.

In most cases, the jig will have to be clamped in place. If the work is a cabinet, one of the jig's supports will be vertical, the other horizontal. And the base upon which the router rests and slides will be at a 45-degree angle. Obviously, this needs to be held securely in place. If you've got a helper available, maybe he or she can hold the jig while you concentrate on operating the router. Perhaps the work can be tipped and secured, so the base of the jig is horizontal.

But if none of these options seems workable, build a jig just for this use. Make one of the supports about 16 inches wide, so it extends about 4 inches beyond the base on each side. Use a bar or pipe clamps on these "ears" to clamp the jig to the cabinet. It'll be secure enough to work comfortably at the 45-degree angle.

The problem, of course, is that the jig and router are two separate pieces. Linked together—using fences that are rabbeted to overlap the router base, for example—the two pieces might be manageable with two hands only. Otherwise, the operation requires a lot of clamping and unclamping.

The process is in all other ways like that performed on the router table. Rest the jig on the corner of the work with the key tight against the edge to make the first pass. Then lift the jig and shift it to the side so the key drops into the just-completed cut. Make the next pass. Repeat and repeat.

TRY THIS!

If your router is relatively small, or has a good handle for one-handed operation like this D-handled Bosch model, try trapping the router on the jig for those jobs that can't be done on the router table. We machined L-shaped fences and screwed them to the jig's base. When you pick up the router, the jig comes along. The router can be operated with one hand—the other holds the jig to the work—yet it's powerful enough to make the cut.

Lift the router and the jig comes along. To position the cuts and keep the jig from being moved by the cutting action, clamp a stop to the case. We've found it easier to push the router down the jig when cutting.

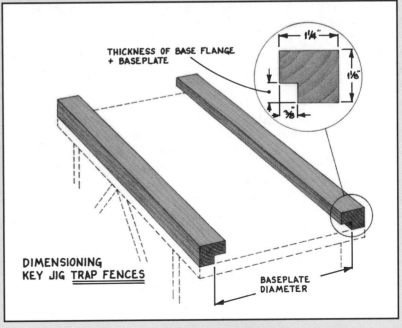

THICKNESS OF BASE FLANGE + BASEPLATE

1¼"

1⅛"

⅜"

DIMENSIONING KEY JIG <u>TRAP FENCES</u>

BASEPLATE DIAMETER

FITTING THE KEYS

Once the slots are cut, the keys must be made.

Cutting splines (keys for slots cut with a straight bit) is a table-saw task. Rip strips of stock to the appropriate thickness, and if necessary, plane them to fit. Crosscut the strips into bits, and glue a bit into each slot. The project will look pretty ratty until the glue dries and you can trim the keys.

Cutting dovetail keys is a router-table chore. Use the same bit that cut the slots. First, cut a sample slot in a short piece of scrap. Then cut a dovetail pin along the edge of a board. In a process of trial and error, start with an oversized pin and methodically trim it to fit the slot in the scrap. When you've got a good fit,

Cut the key strips parallel to the grain of the stock. Always work with the dovetail bit housed in the router table fence, as here. Trapping the work between the fence and the bit can be dangerous.

rip the pin from the board. Then cut another pin and rip it from the board. Repeat the process until you have enough key stock. Next, cut the stock into short keys, and glue a key into each slot.

After the glue is dry, the keys must be trimmed flush. The usual technique is to saw off the keys as

close to the surface of the workpiece as possible without scuffing it. Then trim the remaining stubs flush with a chisel—work from the corner in, so you don't tear out splinters of the keys—or sand the stubs flush with a belt sander. Or use coarse sandpaper wrapped around a block of wood. A file also works well.

TRY THIS!

Use your router to trim the keys. A laminate trimmer or other *small* router, fitted with a flush-trimming baseplate, will make quick work of this job. The baseplate holds the router about ¼ inch above the working surface, so it can clear the material to be trimmed away. The bit is set flush with the work surface.

To use this technique, trim the keys as short as possible with a saw. Trim the remaining projec-

tions with the lam trimmer and the special baseplate, as shown in the photo.

Plans for the baseplate are in "Flush-Trimming Jig" on page 184.

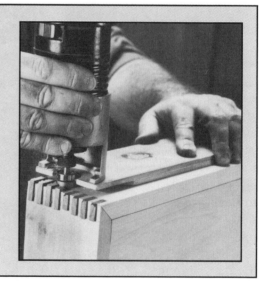

A good complement to the flush-trimming baseplate is the dado-cleanout bit being used here. The bit has cutting edges designed to smooth the bottom of the cut as much as the sides.

SOURCES

Here are addresses of selected router and bit manufacturers. This is our way of acknowledging the help of these businesses in developing this book. Without the routers and bits they graciously provided, we would have been hard-pressed to develop as wide-ranging a guide to router techniques as we did.

And while we weren't *testing* the tools, just using them pretty much the way you would, we can honestly say that we didn't find a dog among them.

As a general rule, router manufacturers sell through dealers, including direct-mail retailers that advertise in woodworking magazines. Several of the bit manufacturers and importers listed below sell only through dealers, though many of them sell directly to retail customers. A toll-free (800) telephone number usually is a tip-off that the firm will sell directly to you.

If you can't find a dealer for a particular brand of router or bits in your area, call the manufacturer or importer.

Amana Tool Corp.
120 Carolyn Boulevard
Farmingdale, NY 11735
(800) 445-0077
Amana makes bits.

Black & Decker
10 North Park Drive
P.O. Box 798
Hunt Valley, MD 21030
(301) 683-7000
Black & Decker makes Black & Decker, DeWalt, and Elu fixed-base and plunge routers and accessories.

Robert Bosch Power Tool Corporation
100 Bosch Boulevard
New Bern, NC 28562
(919) 636-4200
Bosch makes fixed-base and plunge routers, accessories, and bits.

Cascade Tools, Inc.
Box 3110
Bellingham, WA 98227
(800) 235-0272
Cascade imports and sells router accessories and bits.

CMT Tools
5425 Beaumont Center Boulevard
Suite 900
Tampa, FL 33634
(800) 531-5559
CMT makes and sells bits.

Eagle America Corp.
124 Parker Court
P.O. Box 1099
Chardon, OH 44024
(800) 872-2511
Eagle America makes and sells router accessories and bits.

Freud
P.O. Box 7187
High Point, NC 27264
(919) 434-3171
FAX (919) 434-5468
Freud makes plunge routers, accessories, and bits.

Hitachi Power Tools USA Ltd.
3950 Steve Reynolds Boulevard
Norcross, GA 30093
(404) 925-1774
Hitachi makes plunge routers.

The Irwin Co.
92 Grant Street
Wilmington, OH 45177
(513) 382-3811
Irwin makes Byrom-brand bits.

Makita U.S.A., Inc.
14930-C Northam Street
La Mirada, CA 90638
(714) 522-8088
Makita makes fixed-base and plunge routers.

Milwaukee Electric Tool Company
13135 West Lisbon Road
Brookfield, WI 53005
(414) 781-3600
Milwaukee makes fixed-base routers.

MLCS Ltd.
P.O. Box 4053 C-12
Rydal, PA 19046
(800) 533-9298
MLCS imports and sells router accessories and bits.

Paso Robles Carbide Co.
731-C Paso Robles Street
Paso Robles, CA 93446
(805) 238-6144
Paso Robles makes Ocemco-brand bits.

Porter-Cable Corporation
P.O. Box 2468
4825 Highway 45 North
Jackson, TN 38302-2468
(901) 668-8600
Porter-Cable makes fixed-base and plunge routers, accessories, and bits.

Ryobi America Corp.
1501 Pearman Dairy Road
Anderson, SC 29625
(800) 323-4615
Ryobi makes fixed-base and plunge routers.

Woodhaven
5323 West Kimberly
Davenport, IA 52806
(800) 344-6657
Woodhaven makes and sells router accessories and bits.

INDEX

Note: Page references in *italic* indicate illustrations, photographs, and captions. **Boldface** references indicate tables and project cutting lists.

A

Acrylic
   as baseplate material, 48–49
   bending, 51, *51*
   cutting, 50
   joined with solvent, 54, *54*
   for mounting plate, 63
Acrylic bit guards. *See* Bit guards, stand-alone
Acute-angle fence for edge miters, 320, *320, 321*
Adhesives. *See also* Cement
   holding workpiece, 36, *37*
   joining plastic, 52–55, **52**
Amperage ratings, 2, 3–4
Angles
   bevel, 21
   hook (rake), 21–22
Anti-kickback bit design, 29, *29*
Arbors, 19, 24, *24*
Architectural doors and windows, 214, *214–16*, 217, *217*
Architectural moldings. *See* Moldings, architectural
Arcing, heat buildup from, 4
Arcs. *See also* Circle trammels
   template-guided cuts, 179–82
Assembled bits, 18
Astragal, *115,* 116
   cutter, 133, *133*
   two-pass ogee and, 129–30, *129, 130*

B

Ball bearings. *See* Bearings
Baseboard with cap and shoe, 135–36, *135, 136*
Base of router, 1, 8–10, 15. *See also* Fixed-base routers; Plunge routers
   depth-setting gauges, *11*
   four-pin double helix, *10*
   helical spiral, *9*
   lever-controlled plunge lock, *11*
   loss of depth setting and, 34–35
   rack-and-pinion mechanism, *10*
   ring and spiral, *9*
   squareness to motor of, 35, *35*
   types, 8
Baseplates, 1, 10–12, *11–12*
   attached to router with carpet tape, 49
   for biscuit joinery, 259–61, *259, 260*
   custom, 47–55
      for dadoing, 230-31, *230, 231, 232–33, 232*
   for dadoing, misaligned baseplate, 237, *237*
   for denticulated strips, 236, *236*
   double-edge guided, for mortise-and-tenon joints, *271*
   double edge-guides, for sliding dovetails, 311–13, *311, 312*
   edge band–trimming, 185–87, *186, 187*
   fence-rider, 53, *53*

flush-trimming, 187–88, *187, 188,* 336, *336*
   maintenance, *44*
   materials, 47–49, *47*
   offset, 54, *54,* 125
   plastic work, 49–55, *50, 51,* **52,** *53, 54*
   for rabbeting, 250–51, *250, 251*
   template guide bushings and, 50
   throat of
      clearing, 52, *52*
      size of, 52, *52*
   as trammels, 165
   upgrading mounting screws, 48, *48*
   for wide laps, 292–93, *293*
Bead-and-cove bits, *118,* 119
Beading bits
   edge-forming, 116, 127
   groove-forming, 120, *121*
Bead-on-bead bits, 116
Bearing-piloted bits, 26–27, *26, 27*
Bearings
   ball-bearing pilots, 123, *123*
   cleanliness, 26, *26,* 32
   interchangeable, 123
      for rabbeting, 249, *249*
   maintenance, 44
   work burned by, 102
Bell-mouthing, 45, *45*
Bench. *See* Router bench
Bevel angle, 21
Bevel bits, groove-forming, *122*
Beveled edges, 125, 127, *127*
Biscuit joinery with router, 258–59
   baseplates, 259–61, *259, 260*
   centering cuts, 259
Bit guards
   on fence, 102
   for horizontal router table, 79, *79*
   for safety, 81
   stand-alone, 80
      adjustable acrylic, 81–82, *81*
      bent acrylic, 80–81, *81*
      clamp-on acrylic, 83, *83*
      three-in-one guard, 84, **84,** *84*
Bits, 17–32. *See also specific types*
   for architectural moldings, 133–34, *133*
   carbide-free, 19
   carbide-tipped, 17, 18, 19
   care, 30–32
   changing, 15, *15*
      with router table, 94, *94, 95, 95*
   chucking, 33–34, *33*
   cutting-edge length of, for jointing, 191, *191*
   for dadoes
      choices, 241–43, *242*
      dado-cleanup bit, 238, *238*
      over- and undersized, 233, *233*
   dimensions, *20*
   for dovetail joints, 306–7, *306–7*
   edge-forming, 116–17, *118,* 119–20
   for edge joinery, 263–64, *264, 265, 266, 266*
   extension adjustment with horizontal router table, 78

feed rate, 28
flush-trimming, 142, *142,* 144, 183–84, *183, 184*
   fence-frame trimmer, 190, *190*
geometry, *23*
groove-forming, 120–23, *120, 121, 122*
height setting
   with horizontal router table, 78
   with router table, 94–96, *95, 96*
interchangeable cutter systems, 24, *24*
for laminate work, 219, 221, *221, 223*
manufacturers, 337
matching to bit opening, 97, *97*
materials and quality, 17–18, *18,* 19, *19,* 21
for mortise-and-tenon joints, 280, *280*
for panel raising, 209, 210–11, *210, 211, 218*
pattern (*see* Pattern bits)
pilots, 26–27
profile (*see* Profile bits for decorative treatments)
for rabbeting, 244–45, *244,* 249
resharpening, 32
router speed and, 28–29
safety, 29, *29*
selection, 17–18
   for beginners, 23–26
   for specific job, 26, *26*
shank, 20–21
   collet and, 6–7, *7,* 25, 27–28, *27, 33*
   diameter, 21
   O-rings on, *95*
   sizes, 25, *25*
   undersized, 34, *35*
   slippage in collet, 34, *34, 35,* 45
   solid vs. assembled, 18, *20*
   storage case design, 30–31, *30–31,* 62, *62*
   for tenoning, 283, *283*
   terminology, 18–23
Blind cuts. *See* Stopped cuts
Bonding plastic, 52–54, **52**
Bottom-cleaning bits, for tenoning, 283, *283*
Box joints, 324–29
   applications and advantages, 324
   box-jointing jig, 324, *325, 327*
      construction, 324–26, **325,** 328
      depth of cut, 329, *329*
      interchangeable cutting slot backers, 326, *326*
      preparing to use, 328–29
      using, 329, *329*
   with dado cutter vs. router, *314,* 324
   dovetail-splice jig, 328, *328*
   template guide–centered jig, 327, *327*
   turned into wooden hinges, 329, *329*
Breadboard ends, 316
Buffing plastic edges, 55
Bull-nose bits, 117, *118*
   for chest molding, 131
   for two-pass ogee and astragal, 130

C

Cabinet router tables. *See* Router tables, cabinet
Cabinets, dadoes for, 227

INDEX